D1777849

REFERENCE

WAYNE PUBLIC LIBRARY

SEP 2 0 2007

MASTERPLOTS II
CHRISTIAN LITERATURE

MASTERPLOTS II

CHRISTIAN LITERATURE

4

Ser–Z
Indexes

Edited by
JOHN K. ROTH
Claremont McKenna College

SALEM PRESS
Pasadena, California   Hackensack, New Jersey

Editor in Chief: Dawn P. Dawson
Editorial Director: Christina J. Moose
Acquisitions Editor: Mark Rehn
Research Supervisor: Jeffry Jensen
Research Assistant: Keli Trousdale

Manuscript Editor: Rowena Wildin Dehanke
Production Editor: Andrea E. Miller
Graphics and Design: James Hutson
Photo Editor: Cynthia Breslin Beres
Editorial Assistant: Dana Garey

Cover photo: Joan of Arc, 15th c. manuscript illumination
(The Granger Collection, New York)

Copyright © 2008, by SALEM PRESS, INC.
All rights in this book are reserved. No part of this work may be used or reproduced in any manner whatsoever or transmitted in any form or by any means, electronic or mechanical, including photocopy, recording, or any information storage and retrieval system, without written permission from the copyright owner except in the case of brief quotations embodied in critical articles and reviews or in the copying of images deemed to be freely licensed or in the public domain. For information address the publisher, Salem Press, Inc., P.O. Box 50062, Pasadena, California 91115.

∞ The paper used in these volumes conforms to the American National Standard for Permanence of Paper for Printed Library Materials, Z39.48-1992 (R1997).

Library of Congress Cataloging-in-Publication Data
Masterplots II. Christian literature / edited by John K. Roth.
    p.   cm.
    Includes bibliographical references and index.
    ISBN 978-1-58765-379-7 (set : alk. paper) — ISBN 978-1-58765-380-3 (vol. 1 : alk. paper) — ISBN 978-1-58765-381-0 (vol. 2 : alk. paper) — ISBN 978-1-58765-382-7 (vol. 3 : alk. paper) — ISBN 978-1-58765-383-4 (vol. 4 : alk. paper)
    1. Christian literature—History and criticism. 2. Christian literature—Stories, plots, etc. I. Roth, John K. II. Title: Masterplots 2. III. Title: Masterplots two.

BR117.M15 2007
230—dc22

2007024245

First Printing

PRINTED IN THE UNITED STATES OF AMERICA

LIST OF TITLES IN VOLUME

	page
Complete List of Titles in All Volumes	lxxxix
A Serious Call to a Devout and Holy Life — *William Law*	1581
The Sermons and Treatises — *Johannes Eckhart*	1586
The Seven Storey Mountain — *Thomas Merton*	1591
The Seventh Seal — *Ingmar Bergman*	1595
She Who Is — *Elizabeth A. Johnson*	1598
The Shepherd of the Hills — *Harold Bell Wright*	1602
The Shoes of the Fisherman — *Morris West*	1605
Showings — *Julian of Norwich*	1609
The Shunning — *Beverly Lewis*	1612
Silence — *Shūsaku Endō*	1616
The Silver Chalice — *Thomas B. Costain*	1620
Simply Christian — *N. T. Wright*	1624
The Singer Trilogy — *Calvin Miller*	1627
Sinners Welcome — *Mary Karr*	1631
Sir Gawain and the Green Knight — *Pearl-Poet*	1635
The Social Teaching of the Christian Churches — *Ernst Troeltsch*	1639
The Song of Albion Trilogy — *Stephen R. Lawhead*	1643
Song of the Sparrow — *Murray Bodo*	1648
Songbird — *Lisa Samson*	1651
Songs of Innocence and of Experience — *William Blake*	1655
Soon — *Jerry B. Jenkins*	1660
The Soul of Christianity — *Huston Smith*	1664
The Souls of Black Folk — *W. E. B. Du Bois*	1668
The Source of Human Good — *Henry Nelson Wieman*	1672
The Sparrow — *Mary Doria Russell*	1676
The Spiritual Exercises — *Saint Ignatius of Loyola*	1680
"Station Island" — *Seamus Heaney*	1685
The Stream and the Sapphire — *Denise Levertov*	1689
Strength to Love — *Martin Luther King, Jr.*	1693
The Subversion of Christianity — *Jacques Ellul*	1698
Suffering — *Dorothee Sölle*	1702
Summa Theologica — *Saint Thomas Aquinas*	1706
The Supplicating Voice — *Samuel Johnson*	1710
Sutter's Cross — *W. Dale Cramer*	1714
Synoptic Gospels — *Matthew, Mark,* and *Luke*	1717

MASTERPLOTS II

	page
The Tasks of Philosophy — *Alasdair MacIntyre*	1722
The Temple — *George Herbert*	1726
Their Eyes Were Watching God — *Zora Neale Hurston*	1730
Theodicy — *Gottfried Wilhelm Leibniz*	1734
A Theology for the Social Gospel — *Walter Rauschenbusch*	1738
A Theology of Liberation — *Gustavo Gutiérrez*	1742
A Theology of the Jewish Christian Reality — *Paul M. Van Buren*	1746
The Theory of Moral Sentiments — *Adam Smith*	1749
"They Are All Gone into the World of Light!" — *Henry Vaughan*	1753
The Third Spiritual Alphabet — *Francisco de Osuna*	1756
This Present Darkness — *Frank E. Peretti*	1760
The Thorn Birds — *Colleen McCullough*	1764
Thr3e — *Ted Dekker*	1768
Three Essays — *Albrecht Ritschl*	1772
The Three Hardest Words in the World to Get Right — *Leonard Sweet*	1776
"Three Versions of Judas" — *Jorge Luis Borges*	1779
Tiger in the Shadows — *Debbie Wilson*	1782
Time Lottery — *Nancy Moser*	1786
To Kill a Mockingbird — *Harper Lee*	1790
To Scorch or Freeze — *Donald Davie*	1794
Transgression — *Randall Scott Ingermanson*	1798
Traveling Mercies — *Anne Lamott*	1802
A Treatise Concerning Religious Affections — *Jonathan Edwards*	1806
Treatise on Divine Predestination — *John Scotus Erigena*	1812
The Trip to Bountiful — *Horton Foote*	1816
The Triumph of Love — *Geoffrey Hill*	1820
True Honor — *Dee Henderson*	1823
The Truth Teller — *Angela Elwell Hunt*	1827
The Twilight of Courage — *Bodie Thoene and Brock Thoene*	1830
Two from Galilee — *Marjorie Holmes*	1834
Unattainable Earth — *Czesław Miłosz*	1837
Uncle Tom's Cabin — *Harriet Beecher Stowe*	1841
The Uneasy Conscience of Modern Fundamentalism — *Carl F. H. Henry*	1845
Unspeakable — *Os Guinness*	1849
The Unutterable Beauty — *G. A. Studdert Kennedy*	1853
The Varieties of Religious Experience — *William James*	1856
Velma Still Cooks in Leeway — *Vinita Hampton Wright*	1862
Veritatis Splendor — *John Paul II*	1866

LIST OF TITLES IN VOLUME

	page
The Vicar of Wakefield — *Oliver Goldsmith*	1870
A View of the Evidences of Christianity — *William Paley*	1875
Violence and the Sacred — *René Girard*	1879
Virgin Time — *Patricia Hampl*	1883
The Vocation of Man — *Johann Gottlieb Fichte*	1887
Waiting for God — *Simone Weil*	1891
Waiting for Godot — *Samuel Beckett*	1897
Walking by Faith — *Angelina Emily Grimké*	1901
War in Heaven — *Charles Williams*	1905
Warranted Christian Belief — *Alvin Plantinga*	1909
The Way of All Flesh — *Samuel Butler*	1913
The Way to Christ — *Jakob Böhme*	1917
We Hold These Truths — *John Courtney Murray, S.J.*	1923
What Are People For? — *Wendell Berry*	1927
What I Think I Did — *Larry Woiwode*	1931
What Jesus Meant — *Garry Wills*	1934
When Jesus Came to Harvard — *Harvey Cox*	1937
While Mortals Sleep — *Jack Cavanaugh*	1941
The Wind in the Wheat — *Reed Arvin*	1945
"The Windhover" — *Gerard Manley Hopkins*	1949
The Winter Garden — *Johanna Verweerd*	1953
Wise Blood — *Flannery O'Connor*	1957
With Head and Heart — *Howard Thurman*	1961
With the Grain of the Universe — *Stanley Hauerwas*	1965
The Woman of the Pharisees — *François Mauriac*	1968
Wonderful Words of Life — *Richard J. Mouw and Mark A. Noll*	1972
"A Word made Flesh is seldom" — *Emily Dickinson*	1976
Bibliography	1979
Electronic Resources	1986
Chronological List of Titles	1994
Core Issues Index	2007
Genre Index	2058
Geographical Index	2082
Title Index	III
Author Index	XIII

COMPLETE LIST OF TITLES IN ALL VOLUMES

Volume 1

	page
Publisher's Note	ix
Contributing Reviewers	xiii
Editor's Introduction	1
The Bible in History	10
Abortion and Divorce in Western Law — *Mary Ann Glendon*	23
Acts of the Apostles — *Unknown*	27
(Ado)ration — *Diane Glancy*	31
"Advice to a Prophet" — *Richard Wilbur*	35
African Heritage and Contemporary Christianity — *J. N. K. Mugambi*	38
After the Lost War — *Andrew Hudgins*	41
Against Heresies — *Saint Irenaeus*	44
Agape and Eros — *Anders Nygren*	47
The Age of Anxiety — *W. H. Auden*	50
Aids to Reflection — *Samuel Taylor Coleridge*	54
Aké — *Wole Soyinka*	58
All New People — *Anne Lamott*	62
Amazing Grace — *Kathleen Norris*	65
"Amazing Peace" — *Maya Angelou*	69
And I Alone Have Escaped to Tell You — *Ralph McInerny*	73
The Angel of History — *Carolyn Forché*	77
Apocalypse — *Ernesto Cardenal*	80
Apocrypha — *Eric Pankey*	84
Apologia pro vita sua — *John Henry Newman*	88
Apology — *Tertullian*	92
Arena — *Karen Hancock*	96
Argument Against Abolishing Christianity — *Jonathan Swift*	99
The Arrival of the Future — *B. H. Fairchild*	103
Ascent of Mount Carmel *and* Dark Night of the Soul — *Saint John of the Cross*	107
The Augsburg Confession of Faith — *Philipp Melanchthon*	112
Awakening Mercy — *Angela Benson*	116
Baptismal Instruction — *Saint John Chrysostom*	120
Barabbas — *Pär Lagerkvist*	123

MASTERPLOTS II

	page
Basic Christianity — *John R. W. Stott*	127
The Beasts of Bethlehem — *X. J. Kennedy*	130
Belief or Nonbelief? — *Umberto Eco and Carlo Maria Martini*	133
Ben-Hur — *Lew Wallace*	136
Beowulf — *Unknown*	140
Beyond God the Father — *Mary Daly*	144
Bible and Theology in African Christianity — *John Samuel Mbiti*	147
Billy Budd, Foretopman — *Herman Melville*	150
Bioethics — *Gilbert Meilaender*	154
The Bishop in the Old Neighborhood — *Andrew M. Greeley*	157
The Bishop's Mantle — *Agnes Sligh Turnbull*	161
A Black Theology of Liberation — *James H. Cone*	165
Black Zodiac — *Charles Wright*	169
Blood Ties — *Sigmund Brouwer*	173
The Bloudy Tenent of Persecution for Cause of Conscience — *Roger Williams*	176
Blue Like Jazz — *Donald Miller*	180
Book of Common Prayer — *Thomas Cranmer*	184
Book of Divine Works — *Hildegard von Bingen*	188
The Book of God — *Walter Wangerin, Jr.*	192
The Book of Mormon — *Joseph Smith*	196
Book of Revelation — *John*	202
Books of the Prophets — *Isaiah, Jeremiah, Amos, and Micah*	206
Bread and Wine — *Ignazio Silone*	211
Bread for the Journey — *Henri J. M. Nouwen*	215
Brideshead Revisited — *Evelyn Waugh*	218
A Brightness That Made My Soul Tremble — *Stella Ann Nesanovich*	222
Broken Lance — *Michele Sorensen*	226
The Brothers Karamazov — *Fyodor Dostoevski*	229
The Burning Fields — *David Middleton*	233
Called to Question — *Joan D. Chittister, O.S.B.*	237
The Canterbury Tales — *Geoffrey Chaucer*	240
A Canticle for Leibowitz — *Walter M. Miller, Jr.*	245
A Capital Offense — *Gary E. Parker*	248
Care of the Soul — *Thomas Moore*	251
Casti Connubii — *Pius XI*	254
Catechism of the Catholic Church — *Council of Trent*	257
Catholics — *Brian Moore*	261
Centesimus Annus — *John Paul II*	265
The Cherubinic Wanderer — *Angelus Silesius*	268

COMPLETE LIST OF TITLES IN ALL VOLUMES

	page
Christ — *Jack Miles*	272
Christ Clone Trilogy — *James BeauSeigneur*	275
Christ in a Pluralistic Age — *John B. Cobb, Jr.*	280
Christ the Lord — *Anne Rice*	284
The Christian Faith — *Friedrich Schleiermacher*	288
The Christian Tradition — *Joseph Mitsuo Kitagawa*	292
Christianity and Democracy — *Jacques Maritain*	296
"A Christmas Carol" — *Charles Dickens*	299
Christy — *Catherine Marshall*	303
The Chronicles of Narnia — *C. S. Lewis*	307
The Church — *Jan Hus*	312
Church Folk — *Michele Andrea Bowen*	316
The Circle Trilogy — *Ted Dekker*	320
The City of God — *Saint Augustine*	325
The Cloud of Unknowing — *Unknown*	329
The Color of Faith — *Fumitaka Matsuoka*	334
The Color Purple — *Alice Walker*	338
Come Sweet Death — *Bunyan Davie Napier*	342
The Coming of the Cosmic Christ — *Matthew Fox*	346
A Complicated Kindness — *Miriam Toews*	350
Conferences — *John Cassian*	354
Confessio Amantis — *John Gower*	357
"Confession" *and* "The New Birth" — *Menno Simons*	361
Confessions — *Saint Augustine*	365
The Confessions of Nat Turner — *William Styron*	370
Constantine's Sword — *James Carroll*	374
The Country Parson — *George Herbert*	378
The Courage to Be — *Paul Tillich*	382
Crawl with God, Dance in the Spirit — *Jong Chun Park*	386
The Creation — *Bruce Beasley*	390
Credo — *William Sloane Coffin*	393
The Crucified God — *Jürgen Moltmann*	397
Cur Deus Homo — *Saint Anselm*	401
Cure for the Common Life — *Max Lucado*	405
The Da Vinci Code — *Dan Brown*	408
A Dangerous Silence — *Catherine Palmer*	412
The Dawning of Deliverance — *Judith Pella*	416
Dear and Glorious Physician — *Taylor Caldwell*	420
Death Comes for the Archbishop — *Willa Cather*	423
A Death in the Family — *James Agee*	427
The Death of Ivan Ilyich — *Leo Tolstoy*	431

MASTERPLOTS II

	page
Death on a Friday Afternoon — *Richard John Neuhaus*	435
A Declaration of the Sentiments of Arminius — *Jacobus Arminius*	439
The Destiny of Man — *Nicolai Berdyaev*	443
Devotions upon Emergent Occasions — *John Donne*	447
The Dialogue — *Saint Catherine of Siena*	453
"A Dialogue of Self and Soul" — *William Butler Yeats*	458
The Diary of a Country Priest — *Georges Bernanos*	462
Directed Verdict — *Randy Singer*	465
Divine and Human — *Leo Tolstoy*	469
The Divine Comedy — *Dante*	473
The Divine Conspiracy — *Dallas Willard*	477
The Divine Milieu — *Pierre Teilhard de Chardin*	480
The Divine Relativity — *Charles Hartshorne*	485
Divini Redemptoris — *Pius XI*	488
The Divinity School Address — *Ralph Waldo Emerson*	491
Doctor Faustus — *Christopher Marlowe*	496
Don't Throw Away Tomorrow — *Robert H. Schuller*	500
The Double Search — *Rufus M. Jones*	503
The Drama of Atheist Humanism — *Henri de Lubac*	508
"The Dream of the Rood" — *Unknown*	512
The Dream Songs — *John Berryman*	515

Volume 2

Drummer in the Dark — *T. Davis Bunn*	519
Early Christian Doctrines — *J. N. D. Kelly*	523
Early Theological Writings — *Georg Wilhelm Friedrich Hegel*	527
Economy of Grace — *Kathryn Tanner*	531
Edge of Honor — *Gilbert Morris*	534
Elmer Gantry — *Sinclair Lewis*	538
The Enneads — *Plotinus*	542
"An Epistle Containing the Strange Medical Experience of Karshish, the Arab Physician" — *Robert Browning*	545
The Epistle to the Romans — *Karl Barth*	549
Essays and Addresses on the Philosophy of Religion — *Baron Friedrich von Hügel*	553
The Essence of Christianity — *Ludwig Feuerbach*	557
Ethics — *Dietrich Bonhoeffer*	561
Ethics After Babel — *Jeffrey Stout*	565

COMPLETE LIST OF TITLES IN ALL VOLUMES

	page
Evangelium Vitae — *John Paul II*	568
Even in Quiet Places — *William Stafford*	571
Everyman — *Unknown*	574
Eve's Striptease — *Julia Kasdorf*	578
Evil and the God of Love — *John Hick*	582
Exclusion and Embrace — *Miroslav Volf*	586
An Existentialist Theology — *John Macquarrie*	590
Ezekiel's Shadow — *David Ryan Long*	594
The Face of the Deep — *Christina Rossetti*	597
The Faerie Queene — *Edmund Spenser*	601
"The Fall" — *Joseph Bottum*	606
Faust — *Johann Wolfgang von Goethe*	610
"Feet of Jesus" — *Langston Hughes*	614
Fifteen Sermons Preached at the Rolls Chapel — *Joseph Butler*	618
Figuring the Sacred — *Paul Ricœur*	621
Final Witness — *James Scott Bell*	625
Fire by Night — *Lynn N. Austin*	629
The First and Second Apologies — *Saint Justin Martyr*	633
The First Coming — *Thomas Sheehan*	636
Flabbergasted — *Ray Blackston*	640
Fools and Crows — *Terri Witek*	644
For the Time Being — *Annie Dillard*	647
"For the Union Dead" — *Robert Lowell*	650
Foundations of Christian Faith — *Karl Rahner*	654
Four Books of Sentences — *Peter Lombard*	657
Four Quartets — *T. S. Eliot*	660
The Freedom of a Christian — *Martin Luther*	664
The Friendly Persuasion — *Jessamyn West*	669
Gaudium et Spes — *Vatican Council II*	672
Ghost Pain — *Sydney Lea*	676
Gift from the Sea — *Anne Morrow Lindbergh*	680
Gilead — *Marilynne Robinson*	683
Go Tell It on the Mountain — *James Baldwin*	687
God and Philosophy — *Étienne Gilson*	691
God Has a Dream — *Desmond Tutu*	694
God Was in Christ — *D. M. Baillie*	698
The God Who Commands — *Richard J. Mouw*	704
Godric — *Frederick Buechner*	708
God's Silence — *Franz Wright*	712
God's Trombones — *James Weldon Johnson*	716

	page
The Good Book — *Peter J. Gomes*	720
The Gospel According to Jesus Christ — *José Saramago*	724
The Gospel of Christian Atheism — *Thomas J. J. Altizer*	728
Gospel of John — *Saint John*	731
The Gospel of Mary of Magdala — *Karen L. King*	735
The Great Divorce — *C. S. Lewis*	739
The Great Exemplar — *Jeremy Taylor*	743
The Great Mysteries — *Andrew M. Greeley*	746
The Great Wheel — *Paul Mariani*	749
The Greatest Story Ever Told — *Fulton Oursler*	752
Hebrew Bible — *Unknown*	756
"Here Follows Some Verses upon the Burning of Our House July 10th, 1666" — *Anne Bradstreet*	768
Here I Stand — *John Shelby Spong*	772
The Hiding Place — *Corrie ten Boom*	775
Hinds' Feet on High Places — *Hannah Hurnard*	779
His Watchful Eye — *Jack Cavanaugh*	783
A History of Christianity — *Paul Johnson*	787
A History of God — *Karen Armstrong*	791
Holocaust Politics — *John K. Roth*	795
"Holy Sonnets" — *John Donne*	799
Home to Harmony — *Philip Gulley*	802
How Should We Then Live? — *Francis A. Schaeffer*	806
Humanae Vitae — *Paul VI*	811
Humani Generis Redemptionem — *Benedict XV*	815
Hymns — *John Greenleaf Whittier*	818
Hymns and Spiritual Songs — *Isaac Watts*	822
The Idea of a Christian Society — *T. S. Eliot*	826
The Idea of the Holy — *Rudolf Otto*	830
The Imitation of Christ — *Thomas à Kempis*	834
"In Distrust of Merits" — *Marianne Moore*	839
In His Steps — *Charles Monroe Sheldon*	843
In Memoriam — *Alfred, Lord Tennyson*	847
In Memory of Her — *Elizabeth Schüssler Fiorenza*	851
In the Beauty of the Lilies — *John Updike*	855
"In the Holy Nativity of Our Lord God" — *Richard Crashaw*	859
In This House of Brede — *Rumer Godden*	863
The Infidel — *Joe Musser*	866
Inscribing the Text — *Walter Brueggemann*	870
Insight — *Bernard J. F. Lonergan*	873

COMPLETE LIST OF TITLES IN ALL VOLUMES

	page
Institutes of the Christian Religion — *John Calvin*	877
The Instructor *and* Miscellanies — *Clement of Alexandria*	881
Interior Castle — *Saint Teresa of Ávila*	887
Interrogations at Noon — *Dana Gioia*	891
Introduction to Christianity — *Joseph Ratzinger*	895
Isaiah — *Daniel Berrigan*	898
J. B. — *Archibald MacLeish*	902
The Jefferson Bible — *Thomas Jefferson*	906
Jesus Christ and Mythology — *Rudolf Bultmann*	909
Jesus Christ Superstar — *Tim Rice and Andrew Lloyd Webber*	913
The Jesus I Never Knew — *Philip Yancey*	917
Jesus in History — *Howard Clark Kee*	921
Jesus Through the Centuries — *Jaroslav Pelikan*	925
Journal of a Soul — *John XXIII*	928
The Journal of George Fox — *George Fox*	931
The Journal of John Woolman — *John Woolman*	936
The Journey — *Billy Graham*	941
The Keys of the Kingdom — *A. J. Cronin*	945
The Kingdom of God Is Within You — *Leo Tolstoy*	948
King's Ransom — *Jan Beazely and Thom Lemmons*	952
Knowledge and Faith — *Edith Stein*	956
Kristin Lavransdatter — *Sigrid Undset*	960
The Labyrinth of the World and the Paradise of the Heart — *John Amos Comenius*	964
The Ladder of Divine Ascent — *John Climacus*	968
Lake Wobegon Days — *Garrison Keillor*	973
The Last Days of Pompeii — *Edward Bulwer-Lytton*	977
The Last Puritan — *George Santayana*	981
The Last Temptation of Christ — *Nikos Kazantzakis*	985
The Late Great Planet Earth — *Hal Lindsey*	989
Learning Human — *Les A. Murray*	993
Leaves of Grass — *Walt Whitman*	997
Lectures on Revivals of Religion — *Charles Grandison Finney*	1001
Left Behind series — *Tim LaHaye and Jerry B. Jenkins*	1005
Left to Tell — *Immaculée Ilibagiza*	1010
"Letter from Birmingham Jail" — *Martin Luther King, Jr.*	1014
Letters and Papers from Prison — *Dietrich Bonhoeffer*	1018
Letters from the Earth — *Mark Twain*	1021
The Letters of Saint Jerome — *Saint Jerome*	1024

MASTERPLOTS II

	page
Letters to a Young Catholic — *George Weigel*	1029
Life Abundant — *Sallie McFague*	1033
Life Is Worth Living — *Fulton J. Sheen*	1037
A Life of Jesus — *Shūsaku Endō*	1040

Volume 3

The Life of Jesus — *Ernest Renan*	1043
The Life of Jesus Critically Examined — *David Friedrich Strauss*	1046
The Lilies of the Field — *William E. Barrett*	1050
The List — *Robert Whitlow*	1054
The Little Flowers of St. Francis — *Unknown*	1058
Loaves and Fishes — *Dorothy Day*	1062
The Long Trail Home — *Stephen A. Bly*	1066
The Lord — *Romano Guardini*	1070
The Lord of the Rings — *J. R. R. Tolkien*	1073
The Lord's Prayer and the Beatitudes — *Saint Gregory of Nyssa*	1078
Love Comes Softly series — *Janette Oke*	1082
Magnificent Obsession — *Lloyd C. Douglas*	1087
A Man for All Seasons — *Robert Bolt*	1090
The Man Nobody Knows — *Bruce Barton*	1094
The Man Who Died — *D. H. Lawrence*	1098
The Marriage of Heaven and Hell — *William Blake*	1102
Mary Magdalene — *Ellen Gunderson Traylor*	1106
The Master and Margarita — *Mikhail Bulgakov*	1110
Mater et Magistra — *John XXIII*	1114
The Meaning of Persons — *Paul Tournier*	1118
The Meaning of Prayer — *Harry Emerson Fosdick*	1121
Meeting Jesus Again for the First Time — *Marcus J. Borg*	1125
Memoirs of Pontius Pilate — *James R. Mills*	1128
Memories, Dreams, Reflections — *Carl Gustav Jung*	1131
The Merchant of Venice — *William Shakespeare*	1135
Mercy's Face — *David Craig*	1139
Mere Christianity — *C. S. Lewis*	1143
The Metaphysical Demonstration of the Existence of God — *Francisco Suárez*	1147
Midquest — *Fred Chappell*	1151
The Mind of the Maker — *Dorothy L. Sayers*	1155
The Mind's Road to God — *Saint Bonaventure*	1159

COMPLETE LIST OF TITLES IN ALL VOLUMES

	page
The Miracle of the Bells — *Russell Janney*	1164
Misquoting Jesus — *Bart D. Ehrman*	1168
Mit brennender Sorge — *Pius XI*	1172
Moments of Grace — *Elizabeth Jennings*	1176
Morte d'Urban — *J. F. Powers*	1180
Music to Die For — *Radine Trees Nehring*	1184
My God and I — *Lewis B. Smedes*	1188
The Mystical Element of Religion — *Baron Friedrich von Hügel*	1191
Mystical Theology — *Pseudo-Dionysius the Areopagite*	1197
Mysticism — *Evelyn Underhill*	1200
The Name of the Rose — *Umberto Eco*	1204
The Nature and Destiny of Man — *Reinhold Niebuhr*	1207
A New Kind of Christian — *Brian D. McLaren*	1211
A New Song — *Jan Karon*	1215
New Testament Letters — *Saint Paul*	1219
Newpointe 911 — *Terri Blackstock*	1223
No Greater Love — *Mother Teresa*	1227
North of Hope — *Jon Hassler*	1230
The Nun's Story — *Kathryn C. Hulme*	1234
Octogesima Adveniens — *Paul VI*	1238
"Ode: Intimations of Immortality" — *William Wordsworth*	1241
Of Learned Ignorance — *Nicholas of Cusa*	1245
On Being a Christian — *Hans Küng*	1249
On Christian Theology — *Rowan Williams*	1252
On Divine Love — *John Duns Scotus*	1255
On First Principles — *Origen*	1259
On Listening to Another — *Douglas V. Steere*	1263
On Loving God — *Saint Bernard of Clairvaux*	1268
On Providence — *Ulrich Zwingli*	1272
On the Freedom of the Will — *Desiderius Erasmus*	1276
On the Incarnation of the Word of God — *Saint Athanasius of Alexandria*	1280
On the Truth of Holy Scripture — *John Wyclif*	1284
One Tuesday Morning — *Karen Kingsbury*	1288
The Orthodox Church — *Timothy Ware*	1291
Orthodoxy — *G. K. Chesterton*	1295
Out of My Life and Thought — *Albert Schweitzer*	1299
Out of the Red Shadow — *Anne de Graaf*	1303
Oxygen — *Randall Scott Ingermanson and John B. Olson*	1307

MASTERPLOTS II

	page
Pacem in Terris — *John XXIII*	1311
Paradise Lost — *John Milton*	1315
Paradise Regained — *John Milton*	1319
Passing by Samaria — *Sharon Ewell Foster*	1323
Paul — *Walter Wangerin, Jr.*	1327
Pearl — *Mary Gordon*	1331
Pearl — *Pearl-Poet*	1335
The Penitent Magdalene — *David Brendan Hopes*	1339
Pensées — *Blaise Pascal*	1342
Phantastes — *George MacDonald*	1346
Philokalia — *Scott Cairns*	1350
Philosophy of Existence — *Karl Jaspers*	1354
The Philosophy of Existentialism — *Gabriel Marcel*	1358
Piers Plowman — *William Langland*	1362
The Pilgrim's Progress — *John Bunyan*	1366
A Place Called Wiregrass — *Michael Morris*	1371
The Place of the Lion — *Charles Williams*	1375
A Plain Account of Christian Perfection — *John Wesley*	1378
The Poisonwood Bible — *Barbara Kingsolver*	1384
The Politics of Jesus — *John H. Yoder*	1389
Pontius Pilate — *Roger Caillois*	1393
Populorum Progressio — *Paul VI*	1397
The Power and the Glory — *Graham Greene*	1401
The Power of Positive Thinking — *Norman Vincent Peale*	1405
A Prayer for Owen Meany — *John Irving*	1408
Praying God's Word — *Beth Moore*	1412
The Presence of the Word — *Walter J. Ong*	1415
Prison Meditations of Father Alfred Delp — *Alfred Delp*	1419
Prison Meditations on Psalms 51 and 31 — *Girolamo Savonarola*	1423
The Problem of Christianity — *Josiah Royce*	1426
The Prodigal Girl — *Grace Livingston Hill*	1430
Prophesy Deliverance! — *Cornel West*	1434
The Protestant Ethic and the Spirit of Capitalism — *Max Weber*	1438
Psalms — *David*	1442
Purity of Heart Is to Will One Thing — *Søren Kierkegaard*	1446
The Purpose Driven Life — *Rick Warren*	1452
Quadragesimo Anno — *Pius XI*	1455
Questions for Ecclesiastes — *Mark Jarman*	1459
Quo Vadis — *Henryk Sienkiewicz*	1462

COMPLETE LIST OF TITLES IN ALL VOLUMES

	page
The Reasonableness of Christianity as Delivered in the Scriptures — *John Locke*	1466
Reconciliation — *John W. de Gruchy*	1470
The Red and the Black — *Stendhal*	1474
Redeeming Love — *Francine Rivers*	1478
Religio Medici — *Sir Thomas Browne*	1482
Religion — *Leszek Kołakowski*	1486
Religion in the Making — *Alfred North Whitehead*	1490
Religion Within the Bounds of Mere Reason — *Immanuel Kant*	1494
Rerum Novarum — *Leo XIII*	1498
Resting in the Bosom of the Lamb — *Augusta Trobaugh*	1502
The Resurrection of God Incarnate — *Richard Swinburne*	1506
Revelation and Reason — *Emil Brunner*	1510
The Rime of the Ancient Mariner — *Samuel Taylor Coleridge*	1514
A River Runs Through It — *Norman Maclean*	1518
The Robe — *Lloyd C. Douglas*	1522
Rose — *Li-Young Lee*	1525
Rule of St. Benedict — *Benedict of Nursia*	1529
Saint Joan — *George Bernard Shaw*	1533
Saint Manuel Bueno, Martyr — *Miguel de Unamuno y Jugo*	1537
Saint Maybe — *Anne Tyler*	1541
Sapphics and Uncertainties — *Timothy Steele*	1545
The Scarlet Letter — *Nathaniel Hawthorne*	1549
Scenes of Clerical Life — *George Eliot*	1553
Science and Health with Key to the Scriptures — *Mary Baker Eddy*	1557
The Screwtape Letters — *C. S. Lewis*	1560
The Seal of Gaia — *Marlin Maddoux*	1564
The Second Coming — *Walker Percy*	1568
Secrets in the Dark — *Frederick Buechner*	1571
The Secrets of Barneveld Calvary — *James C. Schaap*	1574
The Sense of the Presence of God — *John Baillie*	1578

Volume 4

A Serious Call to a Devout and Holy Life — *William Law*	1581
The Sermons and Treatises — *Johannes Eckhart*	1586
The Seven Storey Mountain — *Thomas Merton*	1591
The Seventh Seal — *Ingmar Bergman*	1595
She Who Is — *Elizabeth A. Johnson*	1598

MASTERPLOTS II

	page
The Shepherd of the Hills — *Harold Bell Wright*	1602
The Shoes of the Fisherman — *Morris West*	1605
Showings — *Julian of Norwich*	1609
The Shunning — *Beverly Lewis*	1612
Silence — *Shūsaku Endō*	1616
The Silver Chalice — *Thomas B. Costain*	1620
Simply Christian — *N. T. Wright*	1624
The Singer Trilogy — *Calvin Miller*	1627
Sinners Welcome — *Mary Karr*	1631
Sir Gawain and the Green Knight — *Pearl-Poet*	1635
The Social Teaching of the Christian Churches — *Ernst Troeltsch*	1639
The Song of Albion Trilogy — *Stephen R. Lawhead*	1643
Song of the Sparrow — *Murray Bodo*	1648
Songbird — *Lisa Samson*	1651
Songs of Innocence and of Experience — *William Blake*	1655
Soon — *Jerry B. Jenkins*	1660
The Soul of Christianity — *Huston Smith*	1664
The Souls of Black Folk — *W. E. B. Du Bois*	1668
The Source of Human Good — *Henry Nelson Wieman*	1672
The Sparrow — *Mary Doria Russell*	1676
The Spiritual Exercises — *Saint Ignatius of Loyola*	1680
"Station Island" — *Seamus Heaney*	1685
The Stream and the Sapphire — *Denise Levertov*	1689
Strength to Love — *Martin Luther King, Jr.*	1693
The Subversion of Christianity — *Jacques Ellul*	1698
Suffering — *Dorothee Sölle*	1702
Summa Theologica — *Saint Thomas Aquinas*	1706
The Supplicating Voice — *Samuel Johnson*	1710
Sutter's Cross — *W. Dale Cramer*	1714
Synoptic Gospels — *Matthew, Mark,* and *Luke*	1717
The Tasks of Philosophy — *Alasdair MacIntyre*	1722
The Temple — *George Herbert*	1726
Their Eyes Were Watching God — *Zora Neale Hurston*	1730
Theodicy — *Gottfried Wilhelm Leibniz*	1734
A Theology for the Social Gospel — *Walter Rauschenbusch*	1738
A Theology of Liberation — *Gustavo Gutiérrez*	1742
A Theology of the Jewish Christian Reality — *Paul M. Van Buren*	1746
The Theory of Moral Sentiments — *Adam Smith*	1749
"They Are All Gone into the World of Light!" — *Henry Vaughan*	1753
The Third Spiritual Alphabet — *Francisco de Osuna*	1756
This Present Darkness — *Frank E. Peretti*	1760

COMPLETE LIST OF TITLES IN ALL VOLUMES

	page
The Thorn Birds — *Colleen McCullough*	1764
Thr3e — *Ted Dekker*	1768
Three Essays — *Albrecht Ritschl*	1772
The Three Hardest Words in the World to Get Right — *Leonard Sweet*	1776
"Three Versions of Judas" — *Jorge Luis Borges*	1779
Tiger in the Shadows — *Debbie Wilson*	1782
Time Lottery — *Nancy Moser*	1786
To Kill a Mockingbird — *Harper Lee*	1790
To Scorch or Freeze — *Donald Davie*	1794
Transgression — *Randall Scott Ingermanson*	1798
Traveling Mercies — *Anne Lamott*	1802
A Treatise Concerning Religious Affections — *Jonathan Edwards*	1806
Treatise on Divine Predestination — *John Scotus Erigena*	1812
The Trip to Bountiful — *Horton Foote*	1816
The Triumph of Love — *Geoffrey Hill*	1820
True Honor — *Dee Henderson*	1823
The Truth Teller — *Angela Elwell Hunt*	1827
The Twilight of Courage — *Bodie Thoene and Brock Thoene*	1830
Two from Galilee — *Marjorie Holmes*	1834
Unattainable Earth — *Czesław Miłosz*	1837
Uncle Tom's Cabin — *Harriet Beecher Stowe*	1841
The Uneasy Conscience of Modern Fundamentalism — *Carl F. H. Henry*	1845
Unspeakable — *Os Guinness*	1849
The Unutterable Beauty — *G. A. Studdert Kennedy*	1853
The Varieties of Religious Experience — *William James*	1856
Velma Still Cooks in Leeway — *Vinita Hampton Wright*	1862
Veritatis Splendor — *John Paul II*	1866
The Vicar of Wakefield — *Oliver Goldsmith*	1870
A View of the Evidences of Christianity — *William Paley*	1875
Violence and the Sacred — *René Girard*	1879
Virgin Time — *Patricia Hampl*	1883
The Vocation of Man — *Johann Gottlieb Fichte*	1887
Waiting for God — *Simone Weil*	1891
Waiting for Godot — *Samuel Beckett*	1897
Walking by Faith — *Angelina Emily Grimké*	1901
War in Heaven — *Charles Williams*	1905
Warranted Christian Belief — *Alvin Plantinga*	1909

MASTERPLOTS II

	page
The Way of All Flesh — *Samuel Butler*	1913
The Way to Christ — *Jakob Böhme*	1917
We Hold These Truths — *John Courtney Murray, S.J.*	1923
What Are People For? — *Wendell Berry*	1927
What I Think I Did — *Larry Woiwode*	1931
What Jesus Meant — *Garry Wills*	1934
When Jesus Came to Harvard — *Harvey Cox*	1937
While Mortals Sleep — *Jack Cavanaugh*	1941
The Wind in the Wheat — *Reed Arvin*	1945
"The Windhover" — *Gerard Manley Hopkins*	1949
The Winter Garden — *Johanna Verweerd*	1953
Wise Blood — *Flannery O'Connor*	1957
With Head and Heart — *Howard Thurman*	1961
With the Grain of the Universe — *Stanley Hauerwas*	1965
The Woman of the Pharisees — *François Mauriac*	1968
Wonderful Words of Life — *Richard J. Mouw and Mark A. Noll*	1972
"A Word made Flesh is seldom" — *Emily Dickinson*	1976
Bibliography	1979
Electronic Resources	1986
Chronological List of Titles	1994
Core Issues Index	2007
Genre Index	2058
Geographical Index	2082
Title Index	III
Author Index	XIII

A SERIOUS CALL TO A DEVOUT AND HOLY LIFE
Adapted to the State and Condition of All Orders of Christians

Author: William Law (1686-1761)
First published: 1728
Edition used: A Serious Call to a Devout and Holy Life, with an introduction by G. W. Bromiley. Grand Rapids, Mich.: Wm. B. Eerdmans, 1966
Genre: Nonfiction
Subgenres: Didactic treatise; instructional manual; spiritual treatise
Core issues: Daily living; devotional life; discipline; God; guidance; morality; poverty; prayer; Protestants and Protestantism; resignation; responsibility; salvation; self-control; service; virtue; works and deeds

Refusing to pledge allegiance to the House of Hanover in 1714, Law lost his fellowship at Cambridge and retired to King's Cliffe. There he lived "the devout and holy life" to which he exhorted others in the classic bearing his name. This book, a rational defense of a program of spiritual discipline, inspired the Holy Club at Oxford through which John and Charles Wesley laid out the main lines for their evangelical revival in England.

Overview

Responding to the challenge that the Age of Reason posed for Christian faith and practice, William Law crafted a tight, rational argument for "a devout and holy life." Devotion, as he defined it, should involve all of life—living according to God's will and not for one's own selfish desires. If religion covers all of life, then it follows that Christians must observe rules that govern all their actions and not merely times of worship. Scripture does not contain a single instruction regarding worship, but almost every verse gives something on the ordinary actions of life. If we do not practice humility, self-denial, renunciation of the world, poverty of spirit, and heavenly affection, therefore, we do not live as Christians.

Sad to say, many who call themselves Christians do not incorporate these traits into daily living. What is the difference, he asks, between Leo, who shows little regard for religion per se but lives a respectable life, and Eusebius, who has a huge appetite for religious things and cannot stop talking about religion but does not differ from Leo as regards his everyday life?

Why do we Christians fail to live devout lives? Law asks. We can plead neither ignorance nor inability, for we have the same knowledge and the same Spirit early Christians did. What prevents us, rather, is a lack of intention. Failure of intention puts us in real spiritual danger. Although we have ample assurance of God's mercy when we sin unavoidably, we cannot count on that mercy when we sin through a lack of intention, as many Scriptures prove. Scriptures show that "our salvation depends upon the sincerity and perfection of our endeavours to obtain it." Law's main contention is that we can please God only by intending and devoting all of life to God's glory and honor. God takes no more delight in one station or position than another. His concern, rather, is that we offer reasonable service in whatever place we occupy in singleness of heart and thus live lives of reason and piety.

A person of leisure himself after his retirement from Cambridge, Law believed such persons held a special responsibility to devote themselves to God in a higher degree. The freer one is from pursuit of necessities, the more one should "imitate the higher perfections of angels." Law continues:

> As we have always the same natures, and are everywhere the servants of the same God, as every place is equally full of his presence, and everything is equally his gift, so we must always act according to the reason of our nature; we must do everything as the servants of God; we must live in every place as in his presence; we must use everything as that ought to be used which belongs to God.

Law applied the same rationale to use of estates and fortunes, expending his own for care of others. The humble, meek, devout, just, or faithful person is not one who has done acts of humility, meekness, devotion, justice, or fidelity now and then, but one who "lives in the habitual exercise of these virtues." In the matter of estátes or fortunes, it is not enough to deny oneself needless expenses or be moderate and frugal sometimes so as to aid the needy; we must do so at all times. Unwise use of one's estate corrupts both mind and heart. Law posits two "maiden sisters," Flavia and Miranda, to illustrate his point. As Flavia, a perfect example of the self-centered rich person, illustrates, the religion of such a person exists only in the head; it has no place in the heart. Although Law will not go so far as to say that such a person as Flavia cannot be saved, he judges that "she has no grounds from Scripture to think she is in the way of salvation," since her whole life conflicts with the "tempers and practices which the Gospel has made necessary to salvation." On the opposite side, wise and pious use of an estate leads to perfection in all the virtues attendant on the Christian life. As Miranda, a perfect example of the other-directed person, shows, right stewardship of money and time will benefit both ourselves and other persons.

From the beginning, Law writes, there have been two orders of Christians: those who feared and served God in secular vocations and those who devoted themselves to voluntary poverty, virginity, devotion, and withdrawal so they might live wholly for God. Nevertheless, all orders of Christians are obliged to devote themselves to God in all things; to do otherwise is contrary to Christian nature and rebellion against God. Rebellion in any form is equally odious to God. To forsake prayer is no worse than forsaking other responsibilities, for prayer is only a small part of devotion. Unless our lives match our prayers, the latter are at best only "lip labour" and at worst pure hypocrisy.

The end products of the devout and holy life, Law argued, will be peace and happiness. Peace and happiness become possible as we reduce desires to what nature and reason require, control passions by the rule of religion, and remove ourselves "from that infinity of wants and vexations which torment every heart that is left to itself." Persons who do not regulate their lives by strict piety resort to all sorts of poor contrivances to secure happiness, but they cannot succeed since they do what is contrary to nature. Even the most regular kind of life suffers miseries, wants, and emptiness when it lacks piety. On this the whole world is a book of instruction.

In the second part of *A Serious Call to a Devout and Holy Life* (chapters 19-24), Law deals with times and hours of prayer. The reason he relegated prayer to the second place should be self-evident in the light of his understanding of devotion as living out our commitment to God in all of life and prayer as only "the smallest part" of devotion. No one should deduce from that statement, however, that Law took prayer lightly. "Prayer," he insisted, "is the nearest approach to God, and the highest enjoyments of Him that we are capable of in this life." We therefore must pursue it with all the energy we can muster.

True to his Anglican heritage, Law drew his understanding and proposals for the practice of prayer from the early Church. In imitation of early Christian custom he urged prayer five times daily with a specific focus for each: praise and thanksgiving on arising, humility at the third hour (9:00 A.M.), universal love with intercessions at the sixth (12:00 noon), resignation at the ninth (3:00 P.M.), and particular confession of sins and self-examination in the evening. Throughout he stressed discipline. Christians should not sleep too much, for instance, "because it gives a softness and idleness to your soul" and conflicts with the spirit of true devotion. They should begin with forms of prayer at all the regular times. If in praying they "break forth into new and higher strains of devotion," then they should abandon the forms. It is good to have both fixed and free elements. In later years Law emphasized mystical elements much more than he did here.

Law did not dwell at length on the mechanics of prayer, but he suggested a few simple matters that he deemed important: (1) Shut the eyes and, in a brief period of silence, "let the soul place itself in the presence of God." (2) Always pray in the same place. (3) At the beginning recall God's attributes with various expressions so as to remind yourself of God's greatness and power. (4) Combine fixed elements for each time of prayer with spontaneous petitions.

For the early-morning praise and thanksgiving in which we try to develop "right apprehension and right affections toward God," the whole aim of devotion, Law urged chanting and singing of Psalms, for nothing "so clears a way for your prayers, . . . disperses dulness of heart, . . . purifies the soul from poor and little passions, . . . opens heaven, or carries your heart so near it" as the Psalms. Reading or merely reciting Psalms will not suffice to lift up the praises a heart that serves God will feel. Singing is the natural way to express joy. Use of imagination will put one in the proper frame of mind for singing.

Like the medieval saints, Law too perceived humility as a precondition for communion with God and proposed that prayer at 9:00 A.M. focus on it. A prayer for humility may loosen the bonds of sin, reform the heart, and draw down divine grace upon us. We should not think any day safe without putting ourselves in this posture and calling on God to assist us in maintaining it. Humility does not consist in excessive self-deprecation but "in a true and just sense of our weakness, misery, and sin." It is not easy, however, to live in a spirit of humility, for it means we are dead to the world and alive to Christ in us. Being Christian requires nothing less than "absolute conformity to that spirit which Christ showed in the mysterious sacrifice of Himself upon the cross." We must not think of Christ as acting as substitute for us but as "our representative acting in our name" and enabling us to join with him as persons acceptable to God. Education also makes it difficult sometimes to practice humility. Therefore, Christians must make an effort to secure the kind of education that fosters humility.

For noontime prayer Law recommended concentration on universal love with intercession as a primary act of it. No "principle of the heart" is more acceptable to God than "a fervent universal love of all mankind, wishing and praying for their happiness," for none is more like God. We must not play favorites when it comes to compassion. All orders of persons must intercede, for nothing makes us love others so much as praying for them. It is not only "the best arbitrator of all differences, the best promoter of true friendship, the best cure and preservative against all unkind tempers, all angry and haughty passions," but also it enables us to discover "the true state of our own hearts."

For the ninth hour Law recommended resignation and conformity to the will of God. Resignation entails "a cheerful approbation and thankful acceptance of everything that comes from God." Such approbation should cover both God's general providence over the world and his particular providence over us.

Finally, in the evening prayer, Law advised, we should take inventory of all we have done from the beginning of the day. We must not gloss over our sins if we wish to be cleansed and renewed. The more exact the confession, the greater the compunction and sorrow of heart. At bedtime it is good to pray again regarding death.

Christian Themes

For Law, Christian devotion entails the dedication of the whole, and not just a part, of one's life to God. Most Christians, Law believed, fall short of true devotion because they do not intend to please God in all they do. Although God is merciful to those who sin out of ignorance, we cannot expect him to be so tolerant of those who lack the intention to avoid sinning, as Scriptures amply attest. All Christians, therefore, are obligated to order their everyday lives in such a way as to turn them into continual service of God. Persons who have leisure time have a special obligation to devote themselves to God to a higher degree, living for God "at all times" and "in all places"; this duty includes proper religious use of estates and fortunes as well as time. Religious exercises, such as prayers, represent only a small part of devotion to God, and unless common life matches prayers, they are nothing but "lip labour" or, worse still, hypocrisy. True devotion will bring peace and happiness, for it reduces desires to such things as nature and reason require and thus removes those that torment an uncontrolled heart. Christians ought to be disciplined in their life of prayer, and if apprehensions and perceptions of God are right, they will do so readily.

Sources for Further Study

Brown, R. LaMon. *Growing Spiritually with the Saints: Catherine of Genoa and William Law*. Macon, Ga.: Peake Road, 1996. Brown, a theology professor, here studies the spiritual lives of Catherine and Law, focusing on the notion of sacrificial service. He emphasizes confession, service, prayer, simplicity, and Holy Communion.

Clarkson, George E. *The Mysticism of William Law*. New York: P. Lang, 1992. Law later became attracted to the German mystics, particularly the thought of Jakob Böhme. Includes an eight-page bibliography and an index.

Overton, J. H. *William Law: Non-juror and Mystic*. London: Longmans, Green, 1881. An old but still useful biography.

Rudolph, Erwin Paul. *William Law*. Boston: Twayne, 1980. A comprehensive yet accessible biography in Twayne's English Authors series. Includes a bibliography and index.

Walker, A. Keith. *William Law: His Life and Thought*. London: Society for Promoting Christian Knowledge, 1973. An excellent critical biography.

E. Glenn Hinson

THE SERMONS AND TREATISES

Author: Johannes Eckhart (c. 1260-1327/1328)
First transcribed: c. 1300-1327 (English translation, 1941)
Edition used: Meister Eckhart: A Modern Translation, translated by Raymond B. Blakney. New York: Harper & Brothers, 1941
Genre: Nonfiction
Subgenres: Meditation and contemplation; mysticism; sermons; spiritual treatise
Core issues: Asceticism; attachment and detachment; silence; soul; suffering; union with God

In this collection of sermons and treatises, Eckhart speculates on the nature of the human soul, God, and how one may attain unity with the Godhead.

Overview

Born in Thuringia of noble parents, Johannes Eckhart entered the Dominican order in Erfurt. He moved up in the order after attaining his master's degree (hence receiving the title "Meister") in Paris. Concerning himself mainly with union with the Godhead, which already is within the person, he became a popular and famous preacher at Strassburg and Cologne. His preaching finally led him to be tried as a heretic, and after his death some of his teachings were declared heretical. However, in 1980 the Dominican order formally requested that all censures be lifted.

Eckhart is concerned in his preaching, as are his followers Henry Suso (1295-1366) and John Tauler (c. 1300-1361), to emphasize the unfathomable depth and greatness of God, which can be "known" experientially but not rationally, and to encourage his listeners to seek this experiential knowledge. Another primary concern is "the birth of God in the soul." This occurs through detachment from all creatures (this detachment aided by the usual ascetic practices) and is the union of the soul with God, both soul and God sharing the same ground. Eckhart is speculative and dualistic, even in his sermons, and frequently weaves his speculations into his preaching. His Neoplatonism is evident throughout his works. Here, rather than "proof text" from a number of sermons, we will examine a few of his sermons that illustrate major themes and finish with a brief look at one of his treatises, "About Disinterest."

In a Christmas sermon Eckhart emphasizes the importance of the eternal birth of Christ in the soul. Christ was indeed born in Bethlehem, but Meister Eckhart asks, "Yet if it does not occur in me, how could it help me? Everything depends on that." This birth can occur only in a pure soul, pure because God is pure, and in the soul because only the soul is, at its core, like God; that is, without thought or action.

The senses serve the soul, providing it with information and possibility, but the core of the soul is without information about itself, since, being like God, it cannot be apprehended by the senses. Because the soul is free of senses and ideas, because it simply is, God can unite with it. Like unites with like. Thus God begets God's Son in the soul because it is there that Creator and creature (soul) are already one. Thus it is an event in and of itself, rather than an idea or knowledge of an event. The soul may receive God when it ceases to rely on its agents (the senses), hoping to receive some idea about God.

In silence and withdrawal, in forgetting the ideas and concepts gained through thought and perceptions, the soul receives not the right idea of God, but God himself. The birth of the Son in the person is at the same time the birth of the person in God. Eckhart tends to interpret Scripture in an extremely dualistic manner. He interprets, for example, Christ's admonition to forsake self and even father and mother to mean, "'Whosoever will not depart from the externality of creatures cannot be born or received in this divine birth.' By robbing yourself of all externalities you are admitted to the truth."

In another Christmas sermon, Eckhart again points out that the birth of Christ occurs in the essence of the soul, "For creatures are only God's footprints, but by nature, the soul is patterned after God." Thus the soul alone is designed to receive the birth of God, which brings all joy and peace. In the cores of their beings sinners and saints are alike, but the birth of God in the soul brings "new light," which radiates out through the believer. To receive the birth of God in the soul, then, one must rid it of ideas and the effects of creatures. If the agents of the soul (the senses) are not to clutter the person's being, then they must be recollected by the soul and used for the soul's purposes.

Eckhart claims that the sinful person's core is filled with darkness and thus cannot comprehend the new light, and yet it is to this very core that the person must go if one is to find light and truth in the first place. On one hand we are to remain uncluttered by our faculties, and on the other we are to "focus all our faculties on the contemplation, the knowing of the unique . . . eternal truth." Typical of contemplative mystics, Eckhart advises the seeker to forget all ideas and remain in un-self-consciousness, in stillness and silence. "Our blessedness does not depend on the deeds we do, but rather on our passiveness to God." Elsewhere, however, he also says that even if one is caught up in contemplation, it is better to go help the needy person.

Even in a sermon on Luke 2:49 ("I must be about my father's business"), Eckhart finds occasion to preach about the eternal birth, for "To know this birth at the core of the soul it is necessary above all that one should be about his Father's business." In this sermon Eckhart's anthropology comes out: "Man has an active intellect, a passive intellect, and a potential intellect." Active intellect is the thinking mind, passive intellect is the mind that remains inactive and lets God work in it, and potential intellect is the mind that has "a prevision of what is to be done."

If one is to be detached from temporal things, is one to give up acts of love as well? Hardly, for contemplation and the acts of love that flow from it are one in God. Even Paul's admonition to Timothy to "preach the word!" is spiritualized; Eckhart states expressly that this refers not to the spoken word but to the "inborn, secret word that lies hidden in the soul. This is what he preached, so that it might instruct the faculties of people and nourish them."

This must occur in stillness and in solitude, for in silence God does for the contemplative what the active intellect does for the natural person. The stilled mind is God's workshop, as it were, because it can experience God "the bedrock": "The object and existence of the mind are essential and not contingent. The mind has a pure, unadulterated being of its own." Again Eckhart sets up an apparently contradictory situation. We are to be still, yet "There is Truth at the core of the soul but it is covered up and hidden from the mind," and thus the mind cannot come to rest.

Nonetheless, we are urged to stillness. "Above all, claim nothing for yourself. Relax and let God operate you and do what he will with you." At the same time we are urged to "external acts of virtue": praying, reading, singing, watching, fasting, doing penance—all meant to keep us from ungodly things. These are contingent, however, and may be boldly dropped when one has a "true spiritual experience." Vows and practices that are no longer necessary or that turn out to be hindrances rather than helps are to be dropped, for unity with God takes precedence over everything.

In a sermon on Matthew 15:4, "Honor thy Father," Eckhart covers several areas integral to his thought. First he points out that while no one is so simple that he or she cannot find help in Scripture and no one is so clever as to discover all the mysteries of Scripture, there is always "a second or hidden meaning, for [the literal] reading of the Scriptures differs from what they really intend."

Second, he speculates on the meaning of the birth of God's Son as "the idea of [God's] own nature." God cannot be demonstrated by analogy, but must be encountered within the core of the soul, for God remains withdrawn within the core of God's own being. Thus as "each takes what it can identify in itself," so our soul can receive God because "the idea of the soul and the idea of God are identical."

This leads to a third important element, ascetic practices. Because our sense perceptions, and our dependence upon them, cloud the soul, and because it is the unclouded soul that receives God, nature's "symbols" must be destroyed and its essence, where God dwells, must be sought. Here a key sentence for Eckhart is, "If you want the kernel, you must break the shell."

Suffering, fourthly, plays a key role, for "when a man suffers and knows discomfort, he is nearest to the light." In the darkness in which we know nothing the light of God will shine. Eckhart then hastens to warn against attaching ourselves to this darkness, lest we miss the light.

In the treatise "About Disinterest" (translated elsewhere as "On Detachment") Eckhart begins by interpreting "the one thing necessary" (Luke 10:42) as disinterest. Disinterest is that state of being in which one is again similar to God as the soul and God were one before creation. Eckhart even argues with Saint Paul (1 Corinthians 13), putting disinterest higher than love. Since "Everything likes its own habitat best," and God dwells in purity and unity (which are due to disinterest), the disinterested heart naturally draws God to itself. This identification of God and the person, then, means salvation for the person. Second, Eckhart puts disinterest ahead of love because love compels one to suffer for others or for God and suffering causes one to be at least aware of the source of suffering, whereas disinterest (which draws God) is aware of nothing and is therefore sensitive only to God. Experience must be of something, but disinterest "comes so close to zero [nothingness] that nothing but God is rarefied enough to get into it." He also puts disinterest above humility, for humility requires self-denial while disinterest goes beyond that (and thus can attract God). As one abases oneself before creatures in humility, one at least is aware of them, and awareness, of course, precludes the disinterest necessary to draw God. Disinterest is also superior to mercy, for mercy is a response to human need and troubles the heart.

What, then, is disinterest? A disinterested mind is "unmoved by any contingent affection or sorrow, or honor, or slander, or vice.... Unmoveable disinterest brings man into his closest resemblance to God." Here Eckhart is speaking of God in God's essence. The incarnation, according to Eckhart, made not the slightest ripple in the disinterest of God. Thus disinterest does not preclude activity, per se, but it does preclude any sort of investment in the activity, or outer person. Eckhart uses the example of a door—the swinging door is the outer person while the hinge is the inner person, unmoved and unchanged despite the movement of the door it supports. "Pure disinterest is empty nothingness."

If God is to do God's will, God must find a disinterested heart and can enter and work only "according to the preparation and sensitivity he finds in each." In fact, a disinterested person has no prayer but one, that he or she may be uniform with God.

At its height, disinterest is not even aware of its knowledge, or loves its own love, and is even "in the dark about its own light." Eckhart even interprets the sending of the Holy Spirit in this manner; it is as if Christ was saying, "You take too much pleasure in my visible form and therefore the perfect pleasure of the Holy Spirit cannot be yours." Thus disinterest brings God and, therefore, life. Eckhart's basic dualistic understanding of the world is clearly reflected in his statement, "There is no physical or fleshly pleasure without some spiritual harm, for the desires of the flesh are contrary to those of the spirit and the desires of the spirit are contrary to those of the flesh." Eckhart goes so far as to say that "the pleasure we take in the physical form of Christ diminishes our sensitivity to the Holy Spirit."

Thus we must flee all contact with things temporal—ideas, people, creatures, and preconceptions—and remain empty and still so that God, who is beyond creatureliness and is void, may be united with the void of our soul. Any experience of God will only be temporary, and our loss of it will bring great pain, but we are immediately to set about inwardness of contemplation.

Christian Themes

Meister Eckhart's *Sermons and Treatises* above all emphasizes that the ground of God and the ground of the soul are the same ground; therefore, it behooves the person to enter his or her soul through ascetic practices in order to facilitate union with God. Union with God, or "the birth of God in the soul," requires utter disinterest, or detachment from things temporal. Thus, the highest goal of humanity is total stillness and silence, for God is utterly still and silent, and like attracts like. The way to utter disinterest through stillness and silence is the ascetic way: an embrace of suffering, such as keeping vigils and fasting. However, these practices must always be seen as helps to detachment and never as ends in themselves, lest they become mere "externals" that interfere with the quest for detachment as much as the very things they are intended to help the seeker overcome. Those seeking union with God must bear in mind that beneath literal statements Scripture is a hidden message, which is to be interpreted in the light of the superiority of spirit over matter and the interior life over the exterior life. Finally, the experience of God cannot last and must be sought again and again until one is united eternally with God in the hereafter.

Sources for Further Study

Clark, James M. *The Great German Mystics*. 1949. Reprint. New York: Russell & Russell, 1970. A basic introduction to the lives and thought of Eckhart, Tauler, and Suso.

Eckhart, Meister. *The Essential Sermons, Commentaries, Treatises, and Defense.* Translated with an introduction by Edmund Colledge, O.S.A., and Bernard McGinn. New York: Paulist Press, 1981. An excellent, if brief, collection and translation of a wide variety of Eckhart's Latin and German works, with a very good introduction.

McGinn, Bernard. *The Harvest of Mysticism in Medieval Germany, 1300-1500*. New York: Crossroad, 2005. This overview of medieval German mysticism includes a chapter on Eckhart, "Meister Eckhart: Mystical Teacher and Preacher." Bibliography, index.

Woods, Richard. *Mysticism and Prophecy: The Dominican Tradition*. Maryknoll, N.Y.: Orbis Books, 1998. Includes the chapter "Meister Eckhart's Wayless Way and the Nothingness of God." Bibliography.

Zagano, Phyllis, and Thomas C. McGonigle. *The Dominican Tradition*. Collegeville, Minn.: Liturgical Press, 2006. Part of the publisher's Spirituality in History series; includes a chapter on Meister Eckhart. Bibliography.

Gary R. Sattler

THE SEVEN STOREY MOUNTAIN

Author: Thomas Merton (1915-1968)
First published: 1948
Edition used: The Seven Storey Mountain. 50th anniversary ed. Introduction by Robert Giroux. New York: Harcourt, Brace, 1998
Genre: Nonfiction
Subgenre: Autobiography
Core issues: Conversion; faith; God; grace; monasticism; self-abandonment

Merton, who lost his parents at an early age, grew from a nonreligious background to what he later came to view as a godless life of careless and sinful living. Through reading, discussions, and prayer, he came to faith, eventually converting to Catholicism. His ever-increasing love for God and prayer led him to become a Cistercian monk.

Overview

Like Saint Augustine of Hippo of the fourth century, the twentieth century Thomas Merton experienced a remarkable conversion in his young adulthood and became an influential Catholic writer and mystic. Merton's autobiography describes his life from childhood through his adult conversion to Roman Catholicism and entrance into a monastery.

The title and format of the autobiography was inspired by Dante's *La divina commedia* (c. 1320, 3 vols.; *The Divine Comedy*, 1802). Like *The Divine Comedy*, Merton's biography is divided into three parts: The first describes his life without God ("Hell"); the second, the beginning of his search for God ("Purgatory"); and the third, his baptism and entrance into a monastic order ("Paradise"). In retrospect, Merton's life and that of the narrator of *The Divine Comedy* followed a similar pattern. That narrator begins the poem in the middle of his life, and Merton wrote *The Seven Storey Mountain* in the middle of his life; he died at the untimely age of fifty-three.

Merton relates that he was born at the beginning of World War I in France to artist parents. He spent his early childhood in the United States. He lost his mother at the age of six and his father while he was in high school. Several people around him, including a French farming family, exemplified good living and happiness, but Merton had no real conception of God or rightful living. He was educated in secular schools in France and England. One of his teachers equated the Christian idea of charity to the concept of gentlemanliness.

Merton recalls that he spent most of his time at Cambridge University in debauchery; perhaps the only good thing that happened that year was that he was introduced to *The Divine Comedy*. His reputation ruined, he left England for Columbia University in New York.

It seems to me that I was armored and locked in within my . . . self by seven layers of imperviousness, the capital sins of which only the fires of Purgatory or of Divine Love . . . can burn away.

At Columbia, Merton continued his carefree ways but found them increasingly unsatisfying. Recognizing that modern society promoted materialism, selfishness, and irresponsibility, he briefly supported sit-ins against war and capitalism. He also made his first true friends and found a mentor, Professor Mark Van Doren. Aldous Huxley's *Ends and Means* (1937) convinced Merton of the importance of spirituality, and he explored the mysticism of the East. The works of William Blake, which he had decided to use as the basis for his master's thesis, convinced him of the importance of faith. Finally, a Hindu monk advised him to read medieval and contemporary Catholic philosophy.

Merton describes a pivotal moment when, as a graduate student in 1938, he decided to attend a Catholic mass. He states that an inner voice told him to go. He was impressed by the piety of everyday people and the solemnity and ritual of the services. The sermon, concerning the divinity of Christ, the importance of grace, and the history of the Catholic Church, was the grace that inspired Merton to seek God further. He was awakening spiritually for the first time in his life.

A few weeks later, Merton sought guidance from a local priest. His faith developed through meditation, contemplation, and reading of spiritual authors. However, he recalls that he was just beginning his spiritual quest, beginning the purification he characterized as climbing the "seven storey mountain" of Dante's Purgatory. The mountain is a powerful biblical image of faith and covenant: Noah's ark landed on a mountain, Moses received the Ten Commandments on a mountain, and Jesus was seen with Moses and Elijah on a mountain.

Baptism was an initial step toward God, but not a sufficient one, Merton says. At first, he became convinced of his weakness and helplessness without God's grace. However, he did not seek out more grace by asking for spiritual advice or by attending Mass and communion daily, so he slid into everyday indifference and lived as he had before baptism. He thought that an intellectual conversion was enough to ensure spirituality. He developed understanding of the life of Jesus; Mary, Mother of God; and many saints, such as Francis of Assisi and Therese of Lisieux. He began to think that he was called to the priesthood.

Merton recalls that he continued writing and teaching but prayed more earnestly and immersed himself in the spiritual and grace-filled life of the Catholic Church. Rebuffed by the Franciscan order, he nonetheless began reciting the daily prayers the Catholic Church required of all priests. The oncoming horror of World War II haunted him. He worked briefly with Catherine de Hueck, who had organized Christian service work in New York's Harlem. Finally, in 1941, he was admitted to the Cistercian (Trappist) monastery as a postulant; the Cisterian Order is a cloistered order of monks totally devoted to prayer, contemplation, and manual labor. "I was free. I had recovered my liberty. I belonged to God, not to myself, and to belong to Him is to be free." In giving all to God, he says, he had climbed the many-layered mountain and found paradise.

Christian Themes

Merton's religious themes are centered in pre-Vatican II Roman Catholic spirituality and theology, but much of his writing concerns universal Christian ideas. A chief theme is the importance of grace. Life is empty without God and offers only empty pleasures and inescapable woes. Modern society enslaves its members with distractions and material goods; self-sacrifice can help people distance themselves from the false promises of the world. According to Merton, only through the sanctifying grace of God, which is the full participation in God's life that supports us to good actions, can peace and happiness be found. Natural goodness is transformed by grace to bring us and others closer to God. Grace thus saves us and allows us to become our best selves.

As Merton experienced it, conversion was preceded by grace-filled moments provided by good people, reading and contemplation, and the inspiration of an "inner voice" that directed him to carry out his thoughts. However, even baptism was not sufficient for true conversion. After his baptism, Merton continued acting as he had previously. Only after a while did he realize that conversion means conversion of every moment of each day, of turning toward God in thought and action constantly. Conversion means disregarding the concerns of the world, even denying pleasures to one's self. Conversion means abandoning the self to the will of God; understanding this led Merton to decide to join a monastery and become a priest.

Inherent in Merton's choice is the traditional Christian choice between contemplative prayer and good works. The parable of Martha and Mary from the New Testament exemplifies the issue. Merton did social service work in Harlem and anticipated doing more social service if he did not join a monastery, but he believed that prayer and contemplation were the necessary underpinnings to any fruitful actions in the world. The sacrifices of the contemplative monks were the basis for much of the good in the world. Contemplation, rather than action, was clearly the better choice. Later in his life, Merton, while still in the cloister, would campaign against social injustice and war, stating that there is no true division between contemplation and social action.

True happiness and true freedom come from giving all to God. The giving is easy and the rewards are great, says Merton. While this involves a kind of loss of self, in the end it allows for growth of the real self in God.

Sources for Further Study

Cunningham, Lawrence. *Thomas Merton and the Monastic Vision*. Grand Rapids, Mich.: Wm. B. Eerdmans, 1999. Merton's life and thought after he entered the monastery, including his development during the civil and spiritual changes of the 1960's.

Elie, Paul. *The Life You Save May Be Your Own: An American Pilgrimage*. New York: Farrar, Straus and Giroux, 2003. Discusses connections between Catholic authors Merton, Dorothy Day, Flannery O'Connor, and Walker Percy, three of whom were converts.

Pennington, M. Basil, ed. *I Have Seen What I Was Looking For*. Hyde Park, N.Y.: New City Press, 2005. Merton wrote more than seventy works; this book presents excerpts from his writings organized by major themes.

Shannon, William H. *Thomas Merton: An Introduction*. Rev. ed. Cincinnati, Ohio: St. Anthony Messenger Press, 2005. An excellent introduction to Merton's life and works, with a fairly detailed discussion of *The Seven Storey Mountain*.

Shannon, William H., Christine M. Bochen, and Patrick F. O'Connell, eds. *The Thomas Merton Encyclopedia*. Maryknoll, N.Y.: Orbis Books, 2002. Useful for both the scholar and the serious reader of Merton.

Zuercher, Suzanne. *Merton: An Enneagram Profile*. Notre Dame, Ind.: Ave Maria Press, 2001. A study that links Merton's biography, personality, and spirituality as a search for one's true self in connection with God.

Mary Moore Vandendorpe

THE SEVENTH SEAL

Author: Ingmar Bergman (1918-2007)
First published: Det Sjunde inseglet, 1956 (English translation, 1960)
Edition used: The Seventh Seal, in *Four Screenplays of Ingmar Bergman*, translated by Lars Malmström and David Kushner. New York: Simon and Schuster, 1960
Genre: Drama
Subgenres: Historical fiction (fourteenth century); screenplay
Core issues: Death; doubt; faith; fear; God; holiness

In his film set during the bubonic plague, Bergman explores different human responses to death. The son of a Lutheran minister, he attributed much of his own fear of death to the religious concepts with which he grew up. In a 1990 work on his films, Bergman noted that eventually he found satisfaction and a sense of liberation in believing there is nothing beyond this world. The depiction in The Seventh Seal *of Death as a white clown with no secrets, he said, was his first step against his unbearable fear of death, and he attributed the film's success to its ability to connect with the doubts and torment of others.*

> Principal characters
> *Antonius Block*, a knight
> *Jöns*, the knight's squire
> *Death*
> *Jof*, an actor
> *Mia*, Jof's wife and fellow actor
> *Raval*, the man who had inspired Block to join a crusade

Overview

Antonius Block, a knight newly returned from a crusade, turns around from his morning prayers to encounter Death. Block challenges Death to a game of chess, asking to live while the game is in progress and to be released if he wins. Death agrees, and they begin to play. The images of a knight playing chess with Death and of Death leading a communal dance (in the film's last sequence) are two images that Ingmar Bergman saw as a boy in churches. They suggest the inevitability of death, no matter the strategies we employ: All must eventually dance with him.

Jöns, the knight's skeptical, irreverent squire, wakens, and he and Block resume their journey to the knight's castle, passing a wagon in which sleep a troupe of actors.

Jof, one of the actors, tells his wife, Mia, of a vision he has had of the Virgin Mary and her child. Sometimes he makes up stories, he admits, but he asserts this vision was real. The names Jof and Mia are meant to make us think of the Holy Family. Jof and Mia's infant son, Mikael, can be considered a type of Christ, for the apocalyptic vision that ends the book of Daniel mentions the coming of Michael, a great prince, just as the Christian book of Revelation refers to the coming of Christ at the end of time.

The knight and Jöns enter a church, and Jöns converses with an artist painting a fresco of The Dance of Death. He describes to Jöns the horror of death by plague and mentions the mobs of people who believe it is God's punishment and so travel the country flagellating themselves. Meanwhile, the knight approaches a confessional and talks to the figure there. Block confesses he is not content with faith and wants God to reveal himself. His life has been a futile pursuit, and he wants to perform one meaningful deed. He reveals his strategy only to learn he has been talking to Death.

Outside, Jof and Mia's performance of a farce is brought to a halt by a dismaying procession of monks and flagellants. Patrons in an inn discuss the plague, omens, and the judgment day. A farmer suggests that if the rumors are true, one should try to enjoy life as long as one can, and a woman mentions people who have died purging themselves with fire to atone for sins. Also in the inn is Raval, the man who ten years earlier had convinced Block to join the crusade. Jöns recently came upon him menacing a girl who had found Raval robbing the dead. After disarming him, Jöns invited the girl to travel with him. Now, entering the inn, Jöns finds Raval and a smith tormenting Jof (the smith's wife had run off with Skat, the director of the acting troupe). Jöns slashes Raval's face, while Jof escapes.

Jof rejoins Mia, who comforts him and introduces him to the knight, with whom she has been chatting. Block talks about the faith that torments him, comparing it to loving someone in the dark who never appears. However, in the company of this peaceful and loving family, such thoughts seem unimportant to him, and he says he will treasure his memory of the time.

When Block and Jöns resume their journey, the blacksmith and Jof's family join them. In the forest, they come upon a girl they had seen earlier, who is accused of having had carnal intercourse with the devil. Now she is about to be burned to death. Block asks her about the devil, saying surely she knows about God, but when he looks into her eyes, he sees only fear and gives her a potion to ease her pain. Jöns tells him there is no God or devil to look after her, but only emptiness. As the journey continues, the blacksmith's wife rejoins him, and Skat pretends to commit suicide. After the group travels on, Skat climbs a tree in which to sleep and is sawed down by Death.

When the travelers stop, Raval appears, begs for water, and then dies of the plague. Jof sees the knight playing chess with Death and tells Mia they must escape. The knight distracts Death by knocking over the pieces, while Jof, Mia, and Mikael get away unnoticed. Death tells Block that when they meet again, he will take the knight and those with him. Block asks if he will then divulge his secrets, and Death replies that he has no secrets.

When the knight and his companions arrive at his castle, his wife invites them in to eat while she reads from the book of Revelation about the breaking of the seventh seal. Death enters, and the knight and his guests respond to him in different ways.

The film ends with Jof describing to Mia his vision of the knight and others dancing with Death. (It may or may not be significant that he mentions Raval and Skat, who were not at the knight's castle, but he does not mention the knight's wife and the girl traveling with Jöns, who were.) Mia chides him about his visions and dreams.

Christian Themes

The Seventh Seal raises the related issues of the existence of God and of reality and meaning beyond this world. The film's protagonist, the knight, returns from a crusade with his faith shaken. If God does not exist, he says, then life is "an outrageous horror. No one can live in the face of death knowing all is nothingness." He is upset by the silence that answers his prayers and wants certitude about God. He also wants to perform a meaningful act.

During the course of the film, he does perform meaningful acts and he does find something to affirm life. He gives the accused witch a potion to stop her pain, for example, and he distracts Death so that Jof's family can escape. Earlier they had shared their strawberries and milk with Block, and he had declared that his memory of communion with them would be for him "an adequate sign—it will be enough for me."

However, it may not be enough for him when Death comes at the end. He cries for mercy to a God "who must be somewhere" and is still met with silence. Is the meaning people find in the here and now all there is, and if so, is it adequate, or must there be some transcendent basis of meaning? A secular existentialist would say this world is all there is, and the only meaning we find is that which we make. A Christian existentialist would say God speaks to us through the actions and experiences of the here and now. Bergman said the allegory of *The Seventh Seal* has a simple theme: the eternal human search for God, with death as our only certainty.

Sources for Further Study

Bergman, Ingmar. *Images: My Life in Film.* Translated by M. Ruuth. New York: Arcade, 1994. Bergman discusses how some of his films came to be. *The Seventh Seal* was inspired by medieval songs and religious art as well as the conflict between his childhood piety and adult rationalism. Jof and Mia embody his concept of human holiness, but the film is not otherworldly.

Gervais, Marc. *Ingmar Bergman: Magician and Prophet.* Montreal: McGill-Queen's University Press, 1999. Considers from a contemporary Christian viewpoint how Bergman's films evolve and interact with Western culture. Analyzes a sequence in *The Seventh Seal* in depth, to show how meaningfulness emerges.

Kalin, Jesse. *The Films of Ingmar Bergman.* Cambridge, England: Cambridge University Press, 2003. Bergman's achievement is moral and philosophic. In *The Seventh Seal* God and the devil are everywhere, but the evidence is not transcendent. Places Bergman with respect to existentialism, noting his differences from Jean-Paul Sartre, Martin Heidegger, and Albert Camus.

Lauder, Robert. *God, Death, Art, and Love: The Philosophical Vision of Ingmar Bergman.* Mahwah, N.J.: Paulist Press, 1989. Finds in Bergman's preoccupation with God, death, art, and love, from *The Seventh Seal* (1957) to *Fanny and Alexander* (1982), the development of a coherent philosophic vision.

Jack Barbera

SHE WHO IS
The Mystery of God in Feminist Theological Discourse

Author: Elizabeth A. Johnson (1941-   )
First published: New York: Crossroad, 1992
Genre: Nonfiction
Subgenre: Theology
Core issues: Friendship; God; Holy Spirit; suffering; the Trinity; women

Johnson argues that the reality of God cannot be imagined, much less captured in words. Yet speech about God is necessary, and what is said matters, for speech is intertwined with thought. For most of Christianity's history, names and images of God have been weighted toward masculine imagery and a patriarchal worldview. Only by including metaphors drawn from women's experience can we reflect most fully humanity's understandings of God, or move toward a more just, peaceful human order. Such metaphors can be found, submerged, in Scripture, classical theology, images of Sophia (Holy Wisdom), the triune God, and the suffering God.

Overview

In *She Who Is*, Elizabeth A. Johnson writes that any approach to knowing a God who is beyond imagining must start with things that are known through human experience. For most of Judaic and Christian history, the names and images used for God have been masculine and patriarchal. God as Father, as Lord, as divine king or ruler, all these names are gender specific and therefore cannot help but affect believers' mental images. Despite abstract formulations that the deity is beyond gender, a male identity is implied in most God-talk. This means that women see themselves as created in the image of God only by denying their own sexual identity. The consequences go beyond the effect on individual women or even on all women: The Catholic Church also suffers.

Johnson points out that traditional speech about God draws its imagery and concepts almost exclusively from the world of ruling men. The concept of theism was developed by medieval and early modern thinkers in opposition to atheism, polytheism, and pantheism. It stresses divine transcendence, and the traits it ascribes to God are modeled on the pattern of an earthly absolute monarch—a being who is omnipotent, unmoved, and more interested in praise and obedience than in relationship or succor. Insofar as this model remains normative in Christianity, it is an idol. Like all idols, it obscures the glimpses of holy mystery that might be granted to people. It also works against the quest for a more just and peaceful human order.

After establishing the need for feminist rethinking of the names and images used to talk about God, Johnson considers how the task might be done. She rejects the solutions of some—to discard the term "God" entirely, to add "feminine" traits or dimensions to the existing list of usages for God, to reemphasize the role of the Holy Spirit and endow it with female qualities. Another solution, using male and female images equally in referring to God, Johnson supports in theory, but warns that both male and female imagery must be taken from the full reality of both genders' experience and show male and female as powerful in both public and private spheres. She doubts that any equivalent imaging of God will be possible without a long and hard effort both to find female symbolism applying to God and to use it un-self-consciously.

The rest of the book is a pioneering effort to do just that. The first source Johnson uses is women's own interpreted experience, with an introductory statement that human experience has always been used as a basis for theology. Among the diverse components of women's experience, she identifies the common one of conversion, which involves coming to recognize one's worth as a woman, finding solidarity in community, and knowing oneself through the dialectic of relationship, in which both reflections and differences are discerned. In this light, women and men are both bearers of "the image of God and Christ."

Johnson's examination of classical theology points out the richness of both tradition and the Bible in the multitude of symbols used for God. There are symbols taken from personal relationships, from human crafts, from philosophy, and from nonliving objects such as rocks. Many terms refer to the work of creation. African usage tends to honor God as "The One who. . . ." Islamic tradition has ninety-nine names for God; the hundredth name is thought to be the true one that does not exist because God is ineffable. Names multiply because none of them can express the whole nature of God.

One of the most promising symbols in Christian thought, though, is that of Sophia. Often viewed as divine wisdom, Sophia is notable for representing the active presence of God to the world. The wisdom tradition holds Jesus to be Sophia incarnate, the wisdom of God, sent into the world. Sophia appears elsewhere as the spirit that activates the world: "life, movement, color radiance . . . blowing everywhere the winds of renewal in creation" and thus representing the mystery of God. As mother, Sophia can make plausible the images of God the Mother, giving birth to the universe, caring for all her creation, being concerned with the flourishing of her whole household, which is the world. Johnson reminds us of the fierceness of a mother bear, making the point that motherhood is not to be confused with passivity.

The last quarter of the book, while not losing the original focus, explores some topics with other implications. Its title, "Dense Symbols and Their Dark Light," evokes territory not much explored by the mainstream of theology. The chapter on the triune God points out how, except for Eastern Orthodox churches, the Holy Spirit is the neglected member of the Trinity. God the Father and the Son are spoken of a great deal and usually in male terminology. The Holy Spirit is shadowy, amorphous, and ill-defined. Most thinking about the Trinity assumes that while God the first (Father figure) can be complete in "him"-self, the same is not true of the second and third members, because they devolve from God the Father. Indeed, classical theology has explained their relationship as one based on origins (Saint Augustine) and one of opposition (Thomas Aquinas). Johnson courageously suggests that neither is the only way the Trinity can be envisioned: Why not another order (Spirit-Son-Father), for instance, and why not another way of relating? She suggests that friendship, as a relationship of equals, is a woman-friendly model that might bring into view further truths. With it, a triune entity can have order without subordination. Certainly the doctrine of the Trinity and the person of the Holy Spirit, whatever they may have meant to the early Church, are little comprehended—or even thought about—by most Christians today. New feminist insights deserve at least a hearing.

A chapter on She Who Is considers the implications of "being" as a description or quality of God. Divine aliveness needs a more active term than the word "to be." The concluding chapter on the suffering God examines the uses of suffering and calls the church to account for the holocaust of women murdered as witches, mostly for the "sin" of threatening males' dominance in the realms of healing and of connection with the Spirit. For the vast numbers of women violated and tortured in the history of the world, does the concept *imago Dei* apply? Johnson answers that it does. God is Love. Love entails suffering. This is not self-evident, because the traditional God stands above it all. However, there are situations in which only a suffering God can help, and here too, women's experience can aid understanding of God.

Christian Themes

Beyond the generally accepted truth that God is ineffable and beyond comprehension, the book's most pervasive theme is that people's efforts to do so, through words and images, have not come as close as they might, because male and patriarchal thought patterns have shaped Christian discourse. Women hold up half of heaven, should images from women's experience not be equally represented when we try to define or describe God?

A secondary theme is relationships as a central model for God's connection with humanity. Subordinate/superior concepts come from cultural and historical roots, and neither correspond with transcendent reality nor prove useful in achieving a more just order on earth.

Johnson discusses at length the distinction between elements essential to Jesus' identity as a finite human on earth and those that define his humanity in Christian doctrine. Belonging to a church that ordains only men because of their supposedly more Christomorphic character, Johnson is well equipped to argue this point. Why, she asks, should maleness be a determining characteristic for the priesthood when Jesus' age, ethnic background, and other accidents of his identity are not? Like the rest of this intricate, superbly argued work, these themes it highlights call out for more attention.

Sources for Further Study

Halbertal, Tova Hartman. *Appropriately Subversive: Modern Mothers in Traditional Religions*. Cambridge, Mass.: Harvard University Press, 2002. Halbertal discusses strategies for living with dissonance practiced by Jewish and Catholic women.

Joy, Morna, and Eva K. Neumaier-Dargyay, eds. *Gender, Genre, and Religion: Feminist Reflections*. Waterloo, Ont.: Wilfrid Laurier University Press, 1995. Feminist insights into various world and tribal religions. Articles from a symposium.

Moses, Paul. "Sister Elizabeth Johnson's *She Who Is*: A Nun Vies God as 'Our Mother.'" Review of *She Who Is*. *Newsday*, July 20, 1993, p. 43. A review of Johnson's work that discusses her desire for images of God as a woman and her receipt of the University of Louisville Grawemeyer Award in Religion in 1993 for this book.

Ruether, Rosemary Radford. *Sexism and God-Talk*. Boston: Beacon Press, 1993. A companion volume to Johnson's work, this includes more historical and biblical details as well as feminist reimaging of Jesus and Mary.

Emily Alward

THE SHEPHERD OF THE HILLS

Author: Harold Bell Wright (1872-1944)
First published: 1907
Edition used: The Shepherd of the Hills. Gretna, La.: Pelican, 1992
Genre: Novel
Subgenre: Morality tales
Core issues: Atonement; redemption; trust in God

As a visitor to the Ozark Mountains, Wright was deeply affected by the simple life and the sense of religion and community that existed in that area. His novel imparts a sense of that simple living and suggests that modern people can lose their way by seeking material goods or personal glory.

Principal characters
Daniel Howitt, the Shepherd of the Hills
Grant "Old Matt" Matthews, a prosperous farmer
Young Matt, Grant's son
Aunt Mollie, Grant's wife
Sammy Lane, a young woman engaged to Ollie Stewart
Jim Lane, Sammy's father and acquaintance of Wash Gibbs
Wash Gibbs, the town bully and former leader of the Baldknobbers
Preachin' Bill, a ferry operator and philosopher
Pete, Grant's and Daniel's grandson

Overview

Harold Bell Wright's *The Shepherd of the Hills* is a straightforward story of the wilderness and the difficulties ordinary people faced on the frontier. Wright set his work in the Ozark Mountains of south-central Missouri, basing his characters on people he had met during several visits to the region. The atmosphere and story line are also drawn from his experiences. This includes the Christian fellowship exhibited when a stranger arrives in the fictional town of Mutton Hollow.

Mutton Hollow is the type of backwoods society that was part of the American frontier. The fight for survival draws families together as they battle against nature, poverty, and ruffians. Yet when a well-spoken stranger by the name of Daniel Howitt appears one day, he is welcomed and allowed to stay at the home of the prosperous Grant Matthews. Grant, or Old Matt as he is known, is mourning the death of his daughter fifteen years earlier. She fell in love with a young artist who then left her. Depressed, she died after giving birth to their son, Pete. Unknown to Old Matt, Howitt is the young artist's father, mourning the disappearance of his son and searching for the family he had abandoned in the hills. However, even with these secrets swirling around him, within a short time Howitt becomes a member of the community, taking a job as the shepherd at Old Matt's farm and becoming known as the Shepherd of the Hills.

As the Shepherd becomes part of Mutton Hollow, he begins to change the people who live there. He becomes the wise elder who provides a voice for those who suffer silently. He provides Sammy Lane with an education in both reading and speaking properly as she prepares for her life outside the hollow with her fiancé, Ollie Stewart. However, the Shepherd's efforts have an unexpected effect on Sammy: The girl is no longer dazzled by the excitement of city life. Her education has opened her eyes to the world, and she realizes that she is less interested in leaving the hollow than before. Sammy's physical distance from Ollie creates an emotional distance between them, and they find that they are incompatible. Sammy realizes the simple life is more natural for her. She is assaulted by Wash Gibbs, the town ruffian and leader of the Baldknobbers, a band of outlaws who terrorized the hollow years earlier. When Young Matt, Old Matt's son, comes to her rescue, Sammy realizes that he is the type of man she wants to marry, and she splits with Ollie.

A sudden drought threatens the hollow and its residents, destroying their crops, crippling their livestock, and bankrupting them. The community is on the edge of disintegration when the Shepherd receives a mysterious gift of gold from his unbalanced grandson. Young Pete says that "God's gold" has appeared to help the people of Mutton Hollow, but what the Shepherd does not know is that the gold comes from the much-discussed hidden mine in the hills. The gift proves to be an attempt at atonement by a mysterious stranger who wanders the woods.

The arrival of another stranger to the hollow reveals the Shepherd's past to the people who live there. It is discovered that Howitt had been a reverend at a large Chicago church. A famous man well liked by his community and parishioners, Howitt had treated the religious tradition as a means for climbing the social and economic ladder rather than as a blessing through which to spread the word of God. His pride and joy had been his son, Howard, whose artistic talent had earned him great praise and fame. This talent was what had attracted Old Matt's daughter to Howard. The young man's fame had destroyed him, and he disappeared, leaving his father to believe he was dead. The reverend had left the church and fled to the hollow both to recover his spirituality and to atone for what his son had done. His life as the Shepherd leads him to rediscover his beliefs and to a contented life as he tosses away all of his worldly concerns and material needs.

At the climax of the book, Howitt discovers that his son, Howard, has been hiding in Mutton Hollow for years, living in the hidden gold mine. His son is the mysterious apparition that has appeared to residents of Mutton Hollow through the years. Over the years, Howard has been seeking redemption for his abandonment of Old Matt's daughter and for her death. He has been spending his days in the mine looking at the painting of her that brought him so much delight and so much suffering. His quest for fame and fortune have ruined his life and turned him away from God and his father. His lonely vigil in the cave has served as punishment for his sins.

Wright's portrayal of Christian charity and his paeans to the simple life made him one of the most popular authors of the early twentieth century. His first book, a series of sermons, was *That Printer of Udell's* (1911). The book was a favorite of President Ronald Reagan, who read it as a boy but took its homilies to heart and made them a guide for his subsequent political career. The popularity of *The Shepherd of the Hills* sparked a tourist boom in the Ozark Mountains. During the 1950's informal then formal outdoor renditions of the book were presented, drawing thousands of people to the nearby town of Branson. Now a major tourist destination, Branson is less likely to be identified with the book that built its development.

Christian Themes

The Shepherd of the Hills emphasizes the simple pleasant existence that places a person closer to God. Wright suggests that only by returning to a simpler existence can men such as Daniel Howitt find the peace of mind that is lacking in the complex society in which they live. Another continuing theme of the book is that of redemption of sins. After discovering what his son had wrought in the death of Old Matt's daughter, Howitt remains in Mutton Hollow, trying to undo the harm by helping Sammy Hale. His teaching of Sammy opens her mind and may save her from the fate suffered by Old Matt's daughter. Sammy also learns from the Shepherd to value a simple life. Her engagement to Ollie Stewart promises her wealth and freedom from the drudgery and ignorance that is Mutton Hollow. However, she finds that such a change in her life will pull her away from God and her roots. Sammy rejects what would have been an easier life for one dedicated to family, community, and God.

This willingness to put aside false dreams of material goods and sophistication is another of the book's themes, as is forgiveness. Old Matt had spent fifteen years living with burning hatred for the boy he blamed for his daughter's death. However, his close relationship with Daniel Howitt and the discovery of Howard Howitt in the mine forces him to forgive past acts and to understand that both men and their children have suffered.

Sources for Further Study

Ferre, John P. *The Social Gospel for Millions: The Religious Bestsellers of Charles Sheldon, Charles Gordon, and Harold Bell Wright*. Bowling Green, Ohio: Bowling Green State University Popular Press, 1998. Examines the religious context of three early twentieth century authors who published Christian works during that period.

Green, Brian. *Shepherd of the Hills*. New York: Emerald House Group, 2001. A literary analysis of *The Shepherd of the Hills* with emphasis on the religious content of the life lessons that Wright attempted to impart.

Tagg, Lawrence. *Harold Bell Wright*. Boise, Idaho: Boise State University Press, 1994. A biography of one of the most popular authors of the early twentieth century. The book details his life outside writing and discusses how his books became popular reading before World War II.

Douglas Clouatre

THE SHOES OF THE FISHERMAN

Author: Morris West (1916-1999)
First published: 1963
Edition used: The Shoes of the Fisherman. Boston: G. K. Hall, 1991
Genre: Novel
Subgenre: Catholic fiction
Core issues: Catholics and Catholicism; clerical life; faith; grace; love; redemption

In West's novel, set at the height of the Cold War, Kyril Cardinal Lakota, tortured in the Soviet Union and imprisoned for seventeen years, is elected pope. West focuses on Kyril's self-doubt and his efforts to reconcile the human and pastoral requirements of the faith with the task of running the massive Vatican bureaucracy. Despite the skepticism of the senior Catholic hierarchy, Kyril successfully offers himself as a confidential conduit between the United States and the Soviet Union to prevent the outbreak of war.

> *Principal characters*
> *Kyril Lakota*, the protagonist
> *Valerio Cardinal Rinaldi*, the Cardinal Camerlengo who proposes Lakota's election
> *Cardinal Leone*, head of the Holy Office and dean of the Sacred College
> *George Faber*, an American journalist
> *Chiara Calitri*, Faber's mistress
> *Ruth Lewin*, an American woman who saves Faber from despair
> *Jean Télémonde*, a priest and radical theologian
> *Kamenev*, Lakota's interrogator and torturer, now the leader of the Soviet Union
> *Georg Wilhelm Foster*, Kamenev's secret agent and courier

Overview

Morris West was an Australian writer whose deep interest in and commitment to Catholicism provided the central theme for nearly all of his thirty novels. When *The Shoes of the Fisherman*, his novel of internal Vatican politics, was published in 1963, it met with mixed reviews. Some literary critics felt that the plot was too thin. The book nevertheless became enormously popular. More than twelve million copies were sold, propelling *The Shoes of the Fisherman* to the top position on *The New York Times* best-seller list for many weeks.

The novel begins with the death of the pope and the arrangements for a conclave to elect a successor. The story focuses on Kyril Lakota, who is a Catholic priest in the Soviet Union during World War II. After the war he is elevated to a bishopric and soon thereafter arrested and tortured. After Lakota has been imprisoned in Siberia for seventeen years, his chief interrogator, Kamenev, organizes an escape for him. It has become politically embarrassing for the Soviet Union to continue his imprisonment. After Lakota makes his way to Rome, he finds that the dying pope has made him a cardinal. At the conclave of cardinals convened to elect the pope's successor, Lakota is nominated and elected through the intervention of two of the most influential cardinals: Rinaldi and Leone, both of whom believe that it is time for the election of a non-Italian Pope. West's novel anticipated by fifteen years the election of Pope John Paul II (born Karol Jozef Wojtył), the first non-Italian Pope since the sixteenth century.

Despite self-doubts, Lakota accepts election and becomes Pope Kyril I. His Siberian experience and his efforts to minister to fellow prisoners have made him acutely aware of the need for the spiritual and pastoral functions of the Catholic Church. However, the Vatican is a huge enterprise in which money, size, and tradition have produced immense bureaucratic inertia. Thus Kyril is presented with a paradox: To move too quickly to serve the pastoral needs of the Church may deny him the support of the senior Vatican officials who are needed to carry reforms into reality. Yet, to move too slowly or not at all is to make the Church increasingly irrelevant to the masses of the world's people—and the Church has been losing membership. Kyril prays for guidance and strength. His attempts to deal with the central paradox of *The Shoes of the Fisherman* are revealed in the three major subplots of the novel.

George Faber is an American journalist specializing in news of the Vatican, where he has excellent sources. The middle-aged man is having an affair with a young woman, Chiara Calitri, the wife of a rising Italian politician, Corrado Calitri. The Calitris separated shortly after their wedding, so Chiara seeks an annulment so that she will be free to marry Faber. Faber, desperate to resolve the issue, seeks evidence that Corrado is a homosexual. He offers to pay witnesses to testify. His efforts become known to Corrado, who is able to ruin Faber by cutting him off from his Vatican contacts. The sordid affair becomes known to Kyril; the annulment proceeds nevertheless. Chiara breaks with Faber, who suffers both professional and personal crises. Deeply troubled by the ignominious role he has played, he considers suicide. He is rescued by the intervention of Ruth Lewin, a spiritual protégé of Pope Kyril. The story illustrates the transmission of faith and goodness to Faber through Lakota and Lewin.

Jean Télémonde is a French Jesuit and a brilliant scholar. He has spent twenty years in exile from the Vatican, forbidden by his vows of obedience from publishing his work, which some consider heretical. Now he is recalled to present his revised conclusions to the Holy Office, whose head is Cardinal Leone. Pope Kyril is hoping that his new work will be acceptable to the Holy Office and that it will introduce some more modern thinking into the Church. Télémonde is invited to speak at the Feast of Saint Ignatius Loyola. After the lecture, to Kyril's sorrow, the Holy Office decides that Télémonde's thesis contradicts fundamental Catholic doctrine. Leone, himself upset, has to bring the news to Kyril. Leone offers his resignation, which Kyril declines. The opposition to Télémonde's ideas has been principled; Kyril has learned that even the pope cannot force change too quickly. Télémonde accepts the obedience to which he is commanded but becomes ill and dies almost immediately, by implication, of a broken heart.

In the third subplot a secret channel of communication is opened between Kamenev, now the leader of the Soviet Union, and Pope Kyril. When Kamenev's agent appears, he informs Pope Kyril that Kamenev needs a private channel of communication with the president of the United States. He asks Pope Kyril for help. After much discussion of the diplomatic and political dangers of such a course, Kyril instructs an American cardinal to inform the president and show him Kamenev's letters. The establishment of this private conduit between the two leaders reduces the dangers of war as they are able to explore possible compromises freely and avoid the limiting tendencies of their own foreign affairs bureaucracies.

The last issue discussed in this book is Kyril's project to travel widely outside the Vatican. He is able to persuade the Vatican hierarchy to support such papal journeys. Here too, West anticipates historical reality by a dozen years or more. The travels of the real Jean Paul II could almost have been presaged by the fictional Kyril's desire to give Catholicism a human and pastoral face.

West's novel is rich in detail. Obviously familiar with the ambience of the famous buildings and chapels of the Vatican City, he also seems well acquainted with the structure and practices of the Vatican hierarchy. For this reason *The Shoes of the Fisherman* is both believable and enjoyable.

Christian Themes

The central theme of *The Shoes of the Fisherman* is the human and priestly struggle to understand and implement God's will. Kyril writes, "And here is the shape of another mystery: that I who am called to spend so much find myself so poor in the things that are of God. . . ." Even in the absence of explicit divine guidance, Kyril believes that his choices will forward God's aims. However, at every turning there are sound institutional or political reasons not to act. The Church has put authority ahead of charity. Ministering to simple human love and need, which are in accordance with the simple heart of Christian doctrine, seem to be dangerous to the health of the Church as an institution. Both Kyril and the senior Vatican hierarchy recognize the tension between pastoral and organizational needs—a tension that exists in the real Church just as much as it does in West's fictional Roman Curia.

Kyril's instincts are to side with the human or individual needs. His decisions do bring some personal peace and understanding to Faber and Lewin. Some amelioration of international strains does come about through his intervention. However, Kyril is unable to vanquish the bureaucracy altogether. His patronage and support of Télémonde end with the latter's death, to Kyril's grief and anger. As the story concludes, Kyril finally persuades the hierarchy to support his plan to travel to spread the Gospel. The Church will attempt to recover the faith of the masses by reintroducing itself into private and public life through works of practical charity. Kyril, although hopeful that the Church can be rebuilt to serve humanity, doubts whether he has been given the light to do so by God. He is alone, facing what West calls "his long Calvary."

West—who remained a believer and communicant until his death—was not sanguine about the prospects for reform of the Church in the real world. Several of his Vatican books hint at his personal views: an end to celibacy for the clergy, an end to the ban on birth control, and the admission of women to the priesthood.

Sources for Further Study

Confoy, Maryanne. *Morris West: Literary Maverick*. Milton, Qld.: John Wiley, 2005. A biographical and critical study of West and his work.

West, Morris. *The Devil's Advocate*. New York: Dell, 1959. The first of West's books focusing on the priesthood and Catholic hierarchy. First appearance of Valerio Rinaldi, one of the characters in *The Shoes of the Fisherman*.

_____. *Lazarus*. Boston: G. K. Hall, 1990. A conservative pope undergoes heart bypass surgery and on his recovery finds that his attitudes toward the human and bureaucratic sides of the Church have changed.

_____. *A View from the Ridge: The Testimony of a Twentieth-Century Christian*. San Francisco: HarperCollins, 1996. West's spiritual and autobiographical memoir in which he speaks in his own voice about his deep Christian beliefs.

Robert Jacobs

SHOWINGS

Author: Julian of Norwich (1342-after 1416)
First transcribed: wr. c. 1373, revised and expanded c. 1393, pb. 1670
Edition used: Showings, translated and by E. Colledge and James Walsh. New York: Paulist Press, 1978
Genre: Nonfiction
Subgenres: Meditation and contemplation; mysticism; spiritual treatise
Core issues: Creation; God; love; prayer; sin and sinners; union with God

In her account of sixteen mystical visions, Julian of Norwich, an English anchoress, creates a new and startling portrait of the divine—a motherly God, who sees his creatures as a great treasure. Her God humbly takes up his dwelling place in the human soul and regards the sinner as a mother might regard a child who has taken a fall. Sin is lamentable, but the sinner is not contemptible. Hell exists, but Julian is not certain that anyone dwells there. Prayer, divinely initiated and inspired, is coveted by God, giving him joy. The meaning of all, she discovers, is love.

Overview

In May of 1373, Julian of Norwich, at the age of thirty, suffered a grievous illness. On the seventh night of her suffering, she lay very close to death, her eyes on the crucifix held by her confessor. She had received the last rites days earlier. Now, hardly able to breathe, she believed her death was imminent. However, in a moment, all pain ceased, she tells the reader, and she felt completely sound, if a little disappointed, as she longed for release into the next life. Deprived of this, she prayed to experience the pains of Christ's passion. As if in answer to her prayer, she saw the wounded head of the crucified Christ, the first of sixteen visions or revelations that she would experience over the next twelve hours or so.

Julian went on to record her visions in a work called *Showings* (also known as *Shewings*, *Book of Showings*, and *Revelations of Divine Love*), composing two versions, the so-called short text (ST), presumably written soon after the visions occurred, and the long text (LT), written some twenty years later. In the short text, Julian provides brief descriptions of each revelation. In the long text (which this essay refers to), these descriptions are accompanied and amplified by passages of reflection on theological and devotional matters that are the result of twenty years of study and thought.

Her visions or "showings" are of three types. Some are corporeal or bodily sights like the first vision of the crowned head of the crucified Christ that appears in chapter 5 (LT) and the famous passage on the hazel nut, which Julian learns is "all that is made," sustained and held in existence by the love of God (chapter 4, ST). Others consist of words that are clearly spoken in her mind, as in the words "I thirst" from chapter 17 (LT). A third type she calls a "ghostly sighting," one that lacks both words and images. A good example of this type appears in chapter 5 (LT), where Julian describes how the Lord shows her a vision of his "familiar [homely] love," describing it as "everything which is good and comforting for our help."

What Julian discerns in the course of her visions and in the years of reflection that follow them is a vision of God and our relationship to God that is endearing, in sharp contrast to the exacting judge of medieval Christianity. Hers is a welcoming God, ready to embrace creatures even when they sin. He/she is our mother, father, brother, and loving spouse. We are "knitted in a knot" to God, "oned" with him through Christ. Consequently, because we share in the will of Christ, we can never fully assent to sin. We are the "noblest thing" God ever made, and he makes our soul his " dwelling place."

In many of her visions, Julian beholds a motherly Christ whose care for souls is tender and nurturing. Christ, the second person of the Trinity, bears us into eternal life through the labor of his death on the cross and nourishes us from the blood and water flowing from his side, as a mother might nurse the child at her breast. This maternal God appears as well in the long and complex parable of the Lord and Servant (chapter 51, LT). Although the story opens with a male servant who has been sent on an errand by his lord, it quickly moves to a more feminine scene when the servant, overly eager and speeding along to do his master's will, takes a fall from which he cannot rise or even look back to take consolation from the gaze of his lord. The lord, meanwhile, gazes with the tenderness and compassion of a loving mother on his dutiful servant and plans to reward him for his pain and suffering.

Julian's fourteenth revelation centers on prayer. The vision occurs as the words "I am the ground of your beseeching" are brought suddenly into her mind. In this vision, she comes to realize that prayer is not a human invention but is grounded in God's holy will, an expression of his generosity that desires to reward us for all eternity. God wants us to have some good thing, and he motivates us to pray for it. Knowing this should inspire us to trust and to feel secure, Julian learns, even in the midst of doubt. Effectively, what prayer achieves, she will find on further reflection, is the alignment of the will of the one who prays with the divine will.

When Julian reaches the end of her account, she hearkens back to an early reflection on the reality of sin when she wondered why God allows sin to exist. In that reflection, she ponders the possibility that God could have prevented sin, making all things well. She is assured then by the words of God that "Sin is necessary but all will be well, and all will be well, and every kind of thing will be well" (chapter 27, LT), bequeathing to future generations the most famous and comforting words of her text. As she closes her book and wants to sum up the meaning of all that she has experienced in the course of the vision, she learns that love was its meaning and that all is, indeed, well, as God promised.

Christian Themes

Very little is known about the life of Julian of Norwich, not even her real name. She adopted the name Julian from the Church of Saint Julian in Norwich, to which she attached herself when she took up life as an anchoress. However, we can tell from her writing that she was an educated woman, familiar with Scripture, the writings of Saint Augustine and Boethius, and works of contemplative monastic spirituality. Her teachings on sin, for example, show the influence of both Boethius and Augustine in their insistence that evil lacks substance: "I believe that it [evil] has no substance, no share in being...." (chapter 27, LT) and that, though sin is a necessary part of reality, God has the power to bring good out of evil, summoning the assurance "that all will be well." Her mystical visions will yield a unique theological perspective, but this perspective will be grounded in traditional Catholic Christian orthodoxy.

This is true even of her portrayal of God/Christ as mother. She is not the first to think of God this way. Others from the Middle Ages and earlier, including Saint Anselm and Saint Bernard of Clairvaux, had touched on this idea, but she offers possibly the fullest, richest, most thought-out development of the concept. Her God is close and caring. He is our clothing, she says, made of love that wraps us in a protective embrace, much as the protective womb of the mother cradles the growing baby. Through the labor pains of his passion and death, Christ births us into eternal life. He remains a doting mother, ever at our side, nourishing us with the Eucharist, always eager to hear our voices in prayer and to shower gifts on us.

Julian's interpretation of God's motherliness is derived from her exploration of the Trinity, a mystery she reflects on without apparent trepidation. Through the Incarnation, Christ shares in our human nature, both physical and spiritual, and for Julian this sharing makes him the best expression of the motherliness of divine love.

Sources for Further Study

Baker, Denise N. *Julian of Norwich's "Showings": From Vision to Book.* Princeton, N.J.: Princeton University Press, 1994. Traces the evolution of Julian's writings from the origin of her visions in affective spiritual practices to the sophisticated theology of the educated medieval woman.

Dearborn, Kerry. "The Crucified Christ as the Motherly God: The Theology of Julian of Norwich." *Scottish Journal of Theology* 55, no. 4 (2002): 283-302. Dearborn explains how Julian develops her concept of the motherliness of God without contradicting traditional teachings or sacred Scripture.

McEntire, Sandra, ed. *Julian of Norwich: A Book of Essays.* New York: Garland, 1998. Eleven essays cover a wide range of pertinent topics including genre, Julian's theology, writing style, and possible models.

Pelphrey, Brant. *Christ Our Mother: Julian of Norwich.* Wilmington, Del.: Michael Glazier, 1989. A good source for the nonspecialist; includes a useful outline of each vision.

Carol Breslin

THE SHUNNING

Author: Beverly Lewis (1949-   )
First published: Minneapolis, Minn.: Bethany House, 1997
Genre: Novel
Subgenre: Literary fiction
Core issues: Amish people; coming of age or teen life; freedom and free will; marriage; obedience and disobedience; self-knowledge; women

When an independent Amish woman at the threshold of adulthood discovers the truth about her long-ago adoption and abandons her approaching marriage to her community's minister, she experiences the devastating psychological impact of a community shunning. Lewis, in turn, exposes the harsh nature of the Amish culture that limits the possibilities of self-exploration, disenfranchises women, restricts the exercise of the heart, denies the enjoyment of aesthetic beauty, and, most troubling, thwarts the intimate experience of God's love and compassion so vital in more orthodox Christian cultures.

Principal characters
Katie Lapp, born Katherine Mayfield, the protagonist
Rebecca Lapp, the woman who raised Katie
Ella Mae Zook, Katie's great-aunt
John Beiler, an Amish bishop, a widower with five children, engaged to marry Katie
Laura Mayfield-Bennett, a wealthy woman living in New York, Katie's birth mother

Overview

At age twenty-two, headstrong Katie Lapp struggles within the Old Order Amish community of Hickory Hollow (population 253) in rural Lancaster County, Pennsylvania. Although with her love of music, her passion for color, and her dreams of elegant fashion and embroidered fabrics, she has never been comfortable within the plain-style Amish life, she was baptized at age nineteen and is preparing to marry the community's bishop, John Beiler, a forty-something widower with five children. The love of her life, Daniel Fisher, with whom she had shared her love of music, disappeared three years earlier in a boating accident in Atlantic City. She does not love Beiler (the marriage's unpromising premise is underscored by the wedding being prepared even as an unforgiving winter descends), but she is willing to accept the submissive role long assigned Amish women.

When Katie is rummaging the attic for her mother's wedding gown, she comes across a rose-colored satin infant's gown embroidered with the name "Katherine Mayfield." Her imagination ignited, she queries her mother, who tells her nothing.

The next day, Katie discovers the gown is gone.

Even as preparations for the wedding continue, Katie runs afoul of the strict Amish code that forbids performing music other than hymns. As Katie conducts the family's buggy along a back country road, she absently sings aloud a beautiful melody, the last she and Daniel had written (music, she insists defiantly, is part of what God created in her). One of Bishop Beiler's children happens to overhear her and inadvertently reveals the offense during a dinner with both families. Such willful sinning is addressed in public confession, conducted by her future husband, who lectures Katie about the need to turn away from such godless inclinations and then insists that she destroy her guitar to restore her to the faith. Later, however, Katie cannot do it.

Meanwhile community members have noticed a fancy white car with a chauffeur and a woman with auburn hair, dressed in fur, an outsider, trying to locate a mother named Rebecca with a daughter in her early twenties. The woman stops at the general store and happens to meet Katie's great-aunt, Ella Mae Zook, a wise and loving woman, nearly eighty years old. The woman gives Ella Mae a letter to pass on to the woman for whom she is looking. Ella Mae takes the letter to Katie's mother. Rebecca knows the secret that has haunted her is about to be revealed. Long ago she had been taken to a Lancaster hospital to have her baby because of complications feared to be too much for an Amish midwife to handle, and her baby daughter had been stillborn. There, Rebecca had met a distraught teenager from a privileged family in upstate New York who had just delivered a healthy girl but who could not keep her. Rebecca and Samuel had agreed to take the baby (along with five hundred dollars) and give her a loving home in the Amish country that the teenage girl had fallen in love with. The letter confirmed that the outsider was Katie's birth mother and that she was dying and wanted to find her daughter. Knowing the adoption was never legal, Rebecca burns the letter.

The wedding is now within days, and Katie again confronts her mother about the mysterious dress. Rebecca tearfully tells her the story. Katie receives the news calmly; it confirms what she had long suspected: that she did not belong among the austere Amish. During the wedding ceremony, when the minister asks if anyone objects to the union, Katie speaks up, saying that she is a sinner, willful and disobedient, and not worthy of the bishop. She flees the church and that night takes her horse to the city and goes to a dress shop, where she tries on a luxurious dress. When she returns to her home, she wants to be called Katherine and refuses to wear her *kapp*, setting free the fiery auburn hair that had always distinguished her from other Amish girls.

The community reacts quickly, imposing the harsh sanction of a *Meinding*, or shunning. Katie is to be ostracized from any social contact for six weeks and then given a chance to repent and return to the wedding arrangement. Over the next few days, Katie languishes in total isolation. Only Ella Mae breaks the imposed quarantine and tells her grand-niece that she now has the world to explore and her own self to discover. The old woman also tells her that her birth mother has been in town looking for her. When Katie's brother coldly refuses to let her even hold his newborn, Katie knows she must leave. Guitar in hand, she departs tearfully (her mother relents despite the shunning and gives her daughter the money from her birth mother, which has accumulated in the bank to eighteen hundred dollars). At the end of the novel, Katherine is renting a spare room, ready now to find out who she is. Her heart is sad, but her soul is free.

Lewis provides a closing scene in which Katie's birth mother, in a mansion in the Finger Lakes, wonders whether she will ever meet the daughter she now regrets abandoning. After Katie has departed, Daniel Fisher's sister receives a registered letter from Daniel, saying that he is alive and wants to return to the community—and to his Katie—to ask forgiveness.

Christian Themes

Before *The Shunning*, Lewis was known as a prolific writer of inspirational young adult fiction that encouraged readers to embrace the love of Christ and the good news of the Christian gospel. *The Shunning* was her first foray into adult fiction. Although she meticulously re-creates Amish ways (particularly the courtship and marriage rituals) and lovingly describes her native rural Lancaster, Lewis is not Amish. Hence, she does not endorse its lifestyle—her narrative disputes the sect's rigorous tenets, specifically its views of women, its suspicion of music (Lewis is a classically trained pianist), and its harsh xenophobia. Daniel Fisher has introduced Katie to an entirely different reading of the Christian God (he has been secretly attending a Bible study group), a reading that suggests it is faith—not works or commitment to a church community—that opens the soul to God's love. In tracking the difficult liberation of Katie Lapp, Lewis parallels Nathaniel Hawthorne's *The Scarlet Letter* (1850). As in that text, a woman of powerful emotional and artistic sensibilities is trapped within an oppressive patriarchal religious community (suggested in both cases by a wild mane of auburn hair kept under a cap), where passion must be suppressed to maintain a place (the discovery of the rose-colored infant's gown early in the novel parallels the Surveyor's discovery of the scarlet letter). Clearly Lewis cannot endorse Christianity when it becomes unyielding and cruel, suggested by the shunning, a vehicle for enforced conformity.

Here the powerful message of Lewis's Christianity must be indirectly perceived: Christianity encourages, rather than discourages, expressions of the heart, a respect for both sexes, a celebration of aesthetics (beauty, color, music), the embrace of the powerful pull of love (although Lewis shies away from sexuality), and ultimately the consecration of each individual as an expression of the love and wisdom of the Creator. Unlike Hester Prynne, however, Katie is finally freed.

Despite the lack of tidy resolution involving Katie and her birth mother and the sudden resurrection of Daniel Fisher (Lewis continues Katie's story in two subsequent volumes in the Heritage of Lancaster trilogy), the book is complete in itself—Katherine does not need her birth mother or her boyfriend to begin her journey. Rather Katie is ushered toward a moment of emancipation appropriate to Lewis's conception of the individual as a celebration of God's handiwork.

Sources for Further Study

Garrett, Ruth Irene, and Rick Farrant. *Crossing Over: One Woman's Escape from Amish Life*. San Francisco: Harper, 2003. Helpful, often disturbing nonfiction account of the oppressive conditions of women within contemporary Amish culture (set in Iowa).

Hostetler, John A. *Amish Society*. Baltimore: Johns Hopkins University Press, 1993. The landmark definitive examination of the Amish culture with particular attention to the psychology of a shunning.

Lewis, Beverly. *The Confession*. Minneapolis, Minn.: Bethany House, 1997. The second volume in the trilogy tracks Katie's reunion with her dying mother in upstate New York and her disappointing discovery of the materialism in her mother's lavish lifestyle.

_____. *The Reckoning*. Minneapolis, Minn.: Bethany House, 1998. Closing volume of the trilogy in which Katie reunites with Daniel Fisher and makes her peace with her Amish upbringing.

Ryan, Mary Beth. "Lancaster County Roots Fertile Ground for Former Residents: Contemporary Christian Writer Bases Heritage Trilogy on Amish Ways." *Lancaster New Era*, September 25, 1997, p. D1. Lewis discusses the Heritage of Lancaster County trilogy and her other writings, including books for children, as well as her beliefs and values.

Joseph Dewey

SILENCE

Author: Shūsaku Endō (1923-1996)
First published: Chimmoku, 1966 (English translation, 1969)
Edition used: Silence, translated by William Johnston. New York: Taplinger, 1979
Genre: Novel
Subgenres: Catholic fiction; historical fiction (seventeenth century); literary fiction
Core issues: Alienation from God; Asians or Asian Americans; Catholics and Catholicism; forgiveness; martyrdom; persecution; silence

The persecution and martyrdom of Japanese Christians and Portuguese missionaries in the 1640's form the frame for an exploration of God's work in the world. Endō uses God's seeming silence in the midst of suffering to point his characters and readers alike to a deeper emotional and intellectual understanding of God's redemptive work in human history and in individuals.

> *Principal characters*
> *Sebastian Rodrigues,* the protagonist, a Portuguese missionary to Japan
> *Father Garrpe,* another priest, who accompanies Rodrigues
> *Kichijiro,* a Japanese Christian who has apostatized
> *Christovao Ferreira,* Rodrigues's mentor, a Portuguese missionary who has apostatized
> *Inoue,* the Lord of Chikugo, who oversees the persecution of Christians

Overview

In Shūsaku Endō's *Silence,* when the rumor of Christovao Ferreira's public renunciation of his faith reaches his former students, they refuse to believe it and determine to travel to Japan as missionaries to discover the truth for themselves.

The first part of the novel consists of letters written by Sebastian Rodrigues, one of the missionaries. Rodrigues tells of the immense difficulty he and his companion, Father Garrpe, face in attempting to travel to a Japan that is hostile to Christianity and has closed its doors to nearly all Westerners. They manage to find a guide named Kichijiro, whom Rodrigues instantly mistrusts.

Kichijiro's story, which is gradually revealed in the course of the journey, is one of continual wavering in the face of persecution. Like Judas (or like Peter), Kichijiro is presented as having betrayed Christ and apostatized. However, he does agree to put the Jesuit missionaries in touch with underground Christians; after doing so, he becomes enormously proud of his role in bringing the priests to Japan.

The Japanese Christians have been without priests for six years, but they have managed to create a system for maintaining, as best they can, the structure of the Church and its sacraments. Rodrigues's pride begins to grow as he speculates about his own importance to the continuation of Christianity in Japan.

At this point, government officials arrive in the village where the Christians live and demand that they send three representatives to Nagasaki for questioning. The usual means for determining whether villagers are secret Christians is to ask them to step on a *fumie*, an image of Christ, usually made of bronze and designed to be stepped on. By desecrating the image of Christ in this way, the people prove that they are not Christians or are rejecting their Christian faith. The representatives (one of whom is Kichijiro) ask the priests whether they should step on the *fumie*. Surprisingly, Rodrigues immediately tells them that they should trample on it. They do so, but the officials demand that they also spit on an image of the Virgin Mary. Kichijiro is the only one able to do so—he has, once again, apostatized.

The other two Christians are brought back to the sea near the village and are martyred there. Rodrigues likens the horrible silence of the sea to the horrible silence of God during their martyrdom.

At this point, Garrpe and Rodrigues part ways—if one of them is captured, the other will be able to continue the priestly work Japan needs. The novel follows Rodrigues in his solitary journey though a silent and empty Japanese countryside. In this long section, the last of Rodrigues's letters, Rodrigues continually compares his situation to that of Christ in his final days: He wipes his face and discovers that what he thought was sweat is blood. He then likens his reflection to the face of the crucified Christ and compares his thirst to that of Christ on the cross. He recalls Christ's words to Judas at the Last Supper: "What thou dost, do quickly." Finally, he encounters Kichijiro, who, despite calling out, "Father, forgive me," has betrayed Rodrigues. The reader is left with the image of three hundred silver coins being thrown in the face of Kichijiro.

The shift to an omniscient narrator at this point mirrors a shift in the novel's concerns. Rodrigues is to be questioned by Inoue, a magistrate who was responsible for getting Ferreira to apostatize. Inoue argues that Japan is like a swamp and that Christianity is like a tree that is not suited to swampy conditions. In other words, he says that Western Christianity cannot thrive in eastern Japan.

Meanwhile, Kichijiro asks to be imprisoned with Rodrigues because he, too, claims to be a Christian. In the prison, Kichijiro confesses his sins—of weakness and of apostasy—and the priest says the words of absolution to him. Not long after, under threat of torture, Kichijiro once again tramples on the *fumie* and is set free.

Rodrigues is then called to witness an attempt to get his fellow priest, who has been captured, to apostatize. Three Christians who have already apostatized will be thrown into the sea unless Garrpe apostatizes. Garrpe drowns while shouting something that cannot be heard to the three former Christians, who also drown.

During this, Rodrigues silently encourages Garrpe to apostatize, comes to the realization that he would apostatize if he were in the same position, and angrily accuses God of being, once again, silent when he should intervene in human affairs.

Rodrigues is taken to Nagasaki, where he meets his former teacher, Ferreira, who acknowledges his own apostasy and encourages Rodrigues to apostatize. He, too, declares Japan to be a swamp in which Christianity is incapable of growing. While Rodrigues is imprisoned and awaiting the torture he expects to undergo, Kichijiro once again appears, shouts his pleas for absolution toward Rodrigues's cell, and is led away. Rodrigues silently and mechanically speaks the words of absolution but, recalling his betrayal, cannot personally forgive Kichijiro.

While he listens to the groans of other Christians undergoing torture and the arguments of Ferreira, Rodrigues prays that God will break his silence. When he is led to the *fumie*, it speaks to him, declaring that he should step on the image. As he does so, a cock crows in the distance.

The rest of the novel shows Rodrigues attempting to come to grips with his stepping on the *fumie*—an act that he does not consider apostasy, even though he knows his superiors do. Endō shows how Rodrigues works with the Japanese officials (though not necessarily willingly) to identify Christian artifacts that are being smuggled into the country. The diary of a Dutch shipping clerk and the appendix, the notes of an officer in charge of Rodrigues's residence, are quite ambiguous.

Christian Themes

Endō struggled throughout his life to understand the relationship between his identity as a Japanese and as a Catholic. *Silence* ponders whether Western Christianity (though not Christianity itself) is incompatible with Japanese culture. If it is, then Western Christianity must adapt to Japan, rather than Japan and the Japanese adapting to Western Christianity. The repeated discussion of "the swamp of Japan" reaches no neat conclusion, but Rodrigues's stepping on the *fumie* and his internal debate about its significance indicate that his Portuguese Christianity has been overcome by the swamp of Japan. However, a new understanding of Christ, Christ's work in the world, and Christianity may be at work in Rodrigues: Some form of Christianity is possible in Japanese culture.

The issue of the adaptability of Christianity applies, of course, not only to Japan in the 1600's or Japan in the 2000's but also to all cultures at all times. If Western Christianity found a swamp in Japan, as the novel suggests, might it not also find a swamp in twenty-first century America, Africa, or Asia? If it does, what would an acceptable adaptation of Christianity be for those countries?

The eponymous subject of the novel has been interpreted in two main directions. Either God remains silent throughout the novel despite the pleas of his followers for him to speak or the reader is invited to see the ways in which God communicates in or through the apparent silence. Endō supported the latter interpretation in interviews and video presentations. The novel is an extended meditation on Habakkuk 2:20: "The Lord is in his holy temple: let all the earth keep silence before him." Readers are invited to be silent so that they can hear God.

Sources for Further Study

Gessel, Van C. "Hearing God in Silence: The Fiction of Endō Shūsaku." *Christianity and Literature* 48 (1999): 149-164. Analyzes the concept of silence in the novel, exploring whether God is presented as silent or if God speaks through the silence in the novel.

Netland, John T. "From Resistance to Kenosis: Reconciling Cultural Difference in the Fiction of Endō Shūsaku." *Christianity and Literature* 48 (1999): 177-194. Argues that the novel attempts to construct a specifically Japanese Christianity, one that fits Japanese culture while remaining true to the Christ of the Bible.

Sano, Hitoshi. "The Transformation of Father Rodrigues in Shūsaku Endō's *Silence*." *Christianity and Literature* 48 (1999): 165-175. Explores the often-neglected appendix to the novel to gain insight into Rodrigues's relationship to Christianity after the main plot's conclusion.

Keith Jones

THE SILVER CHALICE

Author: Thomas B. Costain (1885-1965)
First published: Garden City, N.Y.: Doubleday, 1952
Genre: Novel
Subgenres: Biblical fiction; Catholic fiction; historical fiction (first century)
Core issues: Friendship; Holy Spirit; Jesus Christ; sacrifice

The Silver Chalice *was one of a series of American novels in the tradition of Lew Wallace's* Ben-Hur: A Tale of the Christ *(1880) and Lloyd C. Douglas's* The Robe *(1942) that chronicled events surrounding the Passion and the early years of the Catholic Church. It was widely linked with the perceived revival of orthodox religion institutions in the 1950's.*

> *Principal characters*
> *Joseph of Arimathea*, a prominent, wealthy Jew who is one of the chief backers of the early Christians
> *Peter*, the leading apostle of Christ, leader of the early Church
> *Luke*, a physician, an apostle of Christ and author of the third Gospel
> *Basil*, a Greek slave and craftsperson from a formerly aristocratic background
> *Deborra*, Joseph of Arimathea's granddaughter and Basil's wife
> *Simon Magus*, a magician who seeks to employ Christianity for his own showy ends
> *Nero*, a Roman emperor who persecutes the Christians
> *Helena*, Basil's first love

Overview

Thomas B. Costain, a Canadian who spent his adult life in the United States, was a late bloomer as far as literature was concerned. While pursuing a successful publishing career that ultimately led to him to become a senior editor at the New York firm of Doubleday, Costain began, in his fifties, to write historical novels. Featuring copious background and strong, humanistic characterization, Costain's style as well as his outlook is roughly similar to that of his friend and fellow Canadian historical novelist, Nova Scotian Thomas H. Raddall. Unlike Raddall, however, Costain focused most of his attention on the medieval period. In *The Silver Chalice*, he went back further and wrote of the period immediately after the Gospels. *The Silver Chalice* was the bestselling book in 1953 and was made into a movie in 1954, starring Paul Newman in his first leading role.

The Silver Chalice begins in Judea. Basil, a young Greek slave, is asked to craft a silver chalice to hold the cup used by Jesus and his followers at the Last Supper. Basil is the son of Ignatius of Antioch, a man of stature in his community. However, he had been tricked out of his inheritance and sold into slavery. Apprenticing himself to a silversmith, he has made the best out of his situation and learned the skills of sculpture and engraving. Basil is a skilled sculptor and soon creates a beautiful silver chalice to hold the cup.

Basil becomes educated in the beliefs of the early Christians as well as in the Jewish lore that lies behind these beliefs. Luke, one of the most stalwart of Jesus' apostles, instructs Basil in the wide disparity between the ideals Jesus exemplifies and the realities of life. Luke teaches that the Church, guided by the Holy Spirit, seeks to propagate the message of Christ amid the sordid ways of the world. Luke suggests that the beauty of the cup amid the degradation of the world is a figure for the peril Christians must successfully face to be untainted by the stain of sin. Furthering his involvement with Christianity, Basil falls in love with Deborra, the imaginative and resourceful granddaughter of Joseph of Arimathea, the wealthy Jew who had arranged for Jesus's burial, whom he marries even as her grandfather dies. He encounters a wide range of characters, from role models such as the leading Christian apostle Peter to the irresponsible magician Simon Magus, who perverts Christianity into mere self-display and entertainment, and Mijamin, the unscrupulous Bedouin bandit who is always looking for an opportunity for himself. Basil becomes a wealthy man and owns property, including slaves.

Made unhappy by Peter's spurning of him and his views, Simon Magus presents himself to Rome's decadent and malevolently self-centered emperor, Nero. The magician tries to carve out a third position between Christianity and paganism, claiming that he is Jesus' true successor as magician and wonder worker. Helena is an assistant to Simon Magus who insinuates herself into Basil's life. Though tempted by Helena's beauty and even more by the love potions she has clandestinely given him, Basil forswears this invitation to infidelity, politely dismisses Helena, and dedicates himself to a lifetime of companionship with Deborra.

In a vainglorious effort to show his magical powers, Simon Magus jumps from a tower, thinking he will be able to fly, but instead plummets to his death. Nero, pleased by Simon's failure, seeks to make the Christians scapegoats for his death. However, many of the leading Christians manage to escape and hide themselves. Nero also searches for the chalice; however, the Christian elders have craftily hidden it.

The chalice has been hidden in a humble kitchen, covered with sugar, and ignored by the Roman search parties because of its unlikely place of sequestering. While celebrating this victory, Basil remembers his own years as a slave and, in a flush of generosity, frees all his slaves. At this moment, though, the chalice is stolen by a bunch of thieves, most likely led by Mijamin. Basil and Deborra, chastened by the loss of the chalice and now impoverished by Basil's dispensing of his slaves, nonetheless vow to lead a Christian life together in the future. The book ends with the predication of an apocalyptic return of the chalice in contemporary times.

Christian Themes

In many ways, *The Silver Chalice* is a retelling of basic themes in the Christian story in an entertaining and inspirational mode, which appealed to many people in the 1950's. However, Costain's narrative has certain particular preoccupations that distinguish it from similar historical novels that seek to retell the narratives contained in the canonical Gospels and the book of Acts. One difference lies in the idea of the chalice itself, and its importance as a symbolic motif of Christian truth.

The pleasing shape of the cup exemplifies the role of aesthetic beauty in Christianity. The stress on the role of the chalice in preserving the Christian legacy and its association with artistic creativity has thematic similarities to Dan Brown's 2003 novel *The Da Vinci Code*, though Costain's materials and his perspectives are vastly more orthodox.

Women play a considerable role in *The Silver Chalice*. Deborra is a strong female character who is not just the meek ancillary to her husband, Basil, or the male elders of her community. Many of the readers who made *The Silver Chalice* such a financial success in the early 1950's were women, and the novel presents enough of an inclusive depiction of early Christian life to avoid becoming confined to a male-oriented action-adventure genre.

Whereas a previous North American novel of Christian beginnings, Lloyd Douglas's *The Robe* (1942), depicted the Roman Empire as a potential vehicle, if reformed, of Christian ideals, Costain paints a negative portrait of not only the hedonist Emperor Nero but also his adviser Petronius, who in history was the author of the acclaimed *Satyricon* (c. 60 C.E.; *The Satyricon*, 1694) as well as someone who died at the hand of Nero's persecution. There is no room for virtuous Romans in Costain's vision. Jews, however, are treated with respect and understanding, and the Jewish contribution to Christianity is given full recognition. This element of *The Silver Chalice* is cognate with the emergence in the 1950's of "the Judeo-Christian tradition" as a concept of Western civilization, particularly its spiritual components, that assimilated Jews and Roman Catholics in the United States could embrace as readily as the more established Protestant communities.

The anti-Roman viewpoint of the novel bears another message: a determination not to succumb to the things of this world, not to capitulate to Mammon. The disappearance of the chalice at the end is mandated by the fact that readers know there is no extant silver chalice. However, Costain uses the disappearance as a reminder that, for a Christian, it might be better, at least in the short term, to do without material possessions and rely on one's own emotional resources and moral values.

Sources for Further Study

Frederick, John T. "Costain and Company: The Historical Novel Today." *College English*, 15 (April, 1954): 373-379. Still the only extant scholarly article on Costain; puts him in the context of the American and European historical novel as a genre.

Fuller, Edmund. "Which Held the Blood." Review of *The Silver Chalice. Saturday*

Review 35 (August 2, 1952): 18. The most thorough of the contemporary reviews of the best-selling book.

Noonan, Peggy. Introduction to *The Silver Chalice*. Reprint. New York: Loyola Classics, 2006. Enthusiastic overview of the work by the well-known conservative and Roman Catholic commentator.

Nuzzo, Lucia J. "Thomas B. Costain." In *American Novelists, 1910-1945*, edited by James J. Martine. Columbia, Mo.: Bruccoli Clark Layman, 1981. Basic facts about the life and work of Costain.

Nicholas Birns

SIMPLY CHRISTIAN
Why Christianity Makes Sense

Author: N. T. Wright (1948-)
First published: San Francisco: HarperSanFrancisco, 2006
Genre: Nonfiction
Subgenres: Critical analysis; spiritual treatise; theology
Core issues: Beauty; church; God; Holy Spirit; Jesus Christ; justice

Wright argues that the Christian story provides not only the best account of human yearnings for justice, loving relationships, beauty, and spiritual reality but also their best satisfaction. The life of Jesus Christ is the coming near of God's kingdom; the bodily resurrection of Jesus vindicates God's promise of a resurrection that brings life in the new heavens and the new earth. God's people express the first glimmers of that future by prayer and Bible study, assembly as a church to worship, and humble service to others.

Overview

Simply Christian begins by listing reasons to believe in God: the longing for justice in a world where there is much injustice, the search for spirituality in a culture that beckons us to a wholly material world, our craving for permanence in relationships that no matter how great will end in death, and those fleeting experiences of beauty in a world where there is so much ugliness. These are "echoes of a voice" that point to a Creator. Though N. T. Wright is clear that these echoes are neither proofs that compel belief nor unambiguous pointers to the Christian God, they may open the minds of the honest to look for something more than the flat scientific materialism and drab consumerism of modern Western culture.

Not all truth is the result of observation and experiment, Wright notes. We observe the moral chaos around us but we know the world was made for justice; and we know that our thirst for spirituality, relationships, and beauty are real. Such knowledge requires resources beyond those available to the scientist and engineer. Philosophy, then, is an appropriate place to begin, but the god to whom philosophy points is ill-defined and virtually unknowable. Whatever or whoever is ultimately responsible for these echoes is not simply another element or part of this universe. So what is "God"? There are three basic options.

The first option is pantheism. Here God and the universe are one. God is everything and everything is God. (A slight variation is panentheism, where everything is God, but God is more than everything in what is called the universe.) The fundamental difficulty with this option is its inability to deal with evil. If we are all one with God, then what we call evil and tragedy must not really be bad since they are themselves divine.

The second option is that God and the universe are utterly distinct: God created the universe but now allows it to run on its own. This is the Deist position that became popular in the eighteenth century Enlightenment. Only slightly different is an "interventionist" God who spends most of his time in the supernatural realm and only occasionally intervenes. Wright fears that many Christians assume this picture. However, a god whose only connection with the universe is an occasional miracle is not a fully Christian God, nor can such a God account for the ongoing "echoes of voices."

The third option is one where God and the material universe overlap. Though the created realm is not God (contrary to option one), there are places where God's presence is continually knowable. The entire created realm is in a "close, dynamic and intimate relationship" with its loving God (contrary to option two). Wright says this is the best explanation for the echoes we continually hear.

It is the same conception of God that is produced when we listen carefully and patiently to the grand story of Scripture, Wright argues. This story begins with human rebellion and consequent corruption of God's good creation. God responds by choosing Abraham to father a nation, the Jews, to announce God's forgiveness and restoration for all nations. However, God's chosen people rebel and are sent into exile. Finally, a prophet is sent, Israel's messiah, whose vocation is to look directly into the depths of evil and become the very meeting place of heaven and earth—a place where God's beauty shows clearly, an obedient servant where the widows and orphans are given justice, a temple where the presence of God dwells palpably, and a suffering servant who seeks not his own victory through military might but prayerfully awaits the work of God. When God's prophet, Jesus the Messiah, is crucified on Friday, he suffers; when he is bodily raised on Sunday, he is vindicated.

The story gives rise to many questions. Why this story? Wright's short answer is that unless the Christian story is essentially true, it is historically impossible to account for the meteoric rise of the Church.

Why is that important? Western modernity locates history's pinnacle between 1650 and 1800, when science began to claim supremacy over philosophy and theology as the best source of knowledge, and democracy trumped monarchy as the best form of government. However, the true pinnacle came a millennium and a half earlier, Wright says. By conquering evil with love, and death by resurrection, Jesus did what Israel could not do—inaugurate God's kingdom or rule here on earth.

Finally, Wright asks: If God's kingdom has already come to earth, then what should Christians do? First, they should worship and pray. Second, they should read and study the Bible—not as a list of rules and formulas, but as a five-act drama whose first four and a half acts have been written. Christians should finish the play by working to restore justice, rediscovering relationships, and giving new birth to beauty.

Christian Themes

Wright begins with the theme of general revelation, asking, How much do we know about God through common human experience? In our desire for justice, spirituality, relationships, and beauty, we hear echoes of God's voice calling us.

Wright demonstrates his greatest strength in addressing the theme of God's specific revelation in Jesus Christ. Here his immense scholarship as a historian of Jesus offers significant payoff for grasping Jesus' message and his religious and cultural context. Jesus is best understood as a first century Jew who proclaimed the Kingdom of God and himself as the fulfillment of God's work with Israel.

On a related theme, Wright tackles the nature of the Bible. Its pages contain God's story of salvation in the history of Israel, in the ministry of Jesus, and in forming the Church as a response to Jesus' message, all of which demonstrate God's love for the world. Most important, we are called to respond to the message of the Bible. As a bishop, Wright is deeply concerned with the Christian community and exhorts it to live in the light of Jesus' message and to offer hope to a despairing world. The church's calling (or vocation) is found in God's sending it into the world for "restorative justice."

Toward the end, Wright sketches the theme of eschatology, or the final chapter of God's purpose for creation. The Creator will not give up on the world by destroying it and popping Christians into heaven, or "life after death." Instead God will renew the created world and his people, who will live eternally in the new heavens and new earth, a promise Wright calls "life after 'life after death.'"

Sources for Further Study

Lewis, C. S. *Mere Christianity*. London: Geoffrey Bles, 1952. A major influence on *Simply Christian* in its presentation of Christianity to the thoughtful reader. Bishop Wright, though, brings an insider's view in addressing problems of the contemporary church. Wright is a corrective for the times; Lewis is timeless.

Ostling, Richard N. "Modern Book Is Counterpart of C. S. Lewis Classic." *Beaumont Enterprise*, March 25, 2006, p. B1. Review of Wright's book discusses its similarities to Lewis's *Mere Christianity*.

Wells, Samuel. "Straight Talk." Review of *Simply Christian* and *The Last Word*. *The Christian Century* 123, no. 24 (November 28, 2006): 42-45. Discusses Wright's rejection of dualism and deals with the concepts included in his work.

Wright, N. T. *The New Testament and the People of God*. Minneapolis, Minn.: Fortress Press, 1992. The first volume in the series *Christian Origins and the Question of God*, it lays the groundwork for Wright's study of what can be known historically about Jesus of Nazareth as reported in the Gospels.

_____. *Jesus and the Victory of God*. Minneapolis, Minn.: Fortress Press, 1996. The second volume in the series *Christian Origins and the Question of God*, this book presents Wright's analysis of the so-called quest for the historical Jesus and argues for Jesus' self-understanding of his vocation as acting in Israel's place as the suffering servant who is vindicated by God.

_____. *The Resurrection of the Son of God*. Minneapolis, Minn.: Fortress Press, 2003. The third in the series *Christian Origins and the Question of God*, this book examines the meaning of "resurrection" in classical, Jewish, and Christian contexts and argues that the best explanation of the empty tomb and the appearances of Jesus to the disciples afterward is bodily resurrection.

Dan Barnett, Greg Cootsona, and Ric Machuga

THE SINGER TRILOGY
The Mythic Retelling of the Story of the New Testament

Author: Calvin Miller (1936-   )
First published: The Singer, 1975; *The Song,* 1977; *The Finale,* 1979; trilogy, 1990.
   Downers Grove, Ill.: InterVarsity Press
Genre: Poetry
Subgenres: Allegory; fantasy; narrative poetry
Core issues: Awakening; cause universal; good vs. evil; Jesus Christ; knowledge;
   revelation

Miller uses poetry to convey the message of the Gospels, the early history of the Christian Church, and the Christian hope for the future to those unfamiliar with the New Testament and also to help those familiar with the Bible reexamine the important messages of Christ and the Church. By placing his Christ figure and his followers in an alien yet familiar world, Miller's narrative poetry reached out to millions of readers and earned him a place of honor in the science fiction, fantasy, and Christian literary circles long before evangelical Christianity became a publishing powerhouse.

   Principal characters
      Singer, the Christ figure
      World Hater, the Satan figure
      The Singer's Mother
      Crippled Girl, Singer's disciple
      Friendship Seller, Singer's disciple
      Madman, Singer's disciple, who founds the Singerian religion
      Everyman, a student turned Singerian
      Praxis the Builder, a temple designer for Urbis and a late
         converter to the Singerian religion
      Dreamer, a Singerian with the final revelation at the end of Terra
      Ansond, the leader of the army of the Singer
      Elan, the ruler of Ellanor, the capital of the world, and the
         Antichrist Figure

Overview

   In *The Singer Trilogy,* Calvin Miller allegorizes the life of Jesus Christ, the struggles of the Christian church, and the future promise of rebirth in an alien world where the names are different but the motivations are similar to those found in the New Testament. Each character and each event mirrors a New Testament person or action. *The Singer* is much like the four Gospels, *The Song* partly mirrors the book of Acts, and *The Finale* skips ahead to an apocalyptic ending akin to the book of Revelation.
   The Singer recounts the life of a young Tradesman who fights his real nature as the

Troubadour or Singer who created the universe by his words. The events of the Gospels are collapsed, though John's ideas of transcendence and the fight between good and evil have a strong influence on this book. Throughout, Miller changes characters' names to reflect their new roles and new spiritual and emotional levels of consciousness.

The Singer encounters the World Hater multiple times as he travels, singing the Star-Song and healing the minds and bodies of those he encounters—if they wish to change and believe it is possible—including a crippled girl and a prostitute. In a retelling of the Sermon on the Mount, he sings the Hillside Song, which is rejected by his listeners, who want other ways to overcome the Canyon of the Damned, the World Hater's realm.

In a move reminiscent of Jesus' journey to Jerusalem, the Singer goes to the Great Walled City of the Ancient King, whose people practice the old, traditional religion. There he frees the Madman, who becomes his final disciple, and together they stir up a crowd. Their victory is short-lived, because the Singer has never sung the Star-Song in its entirety, and the last stanza angers the Musicians of the old religion, who with the crowd that has become enraptured by their traditions, seize, mutilate, and then kill the Singer on the Great Machine of Death, which resembles a torture rack. In the end, the Singer's Mother and the Friendship Seller go to comfort the Madman while the Singer rises and brings the Crippled Girl to them.

The Song is about the battle between the World Hater and those who hear, embrace, and try to pass on the Star-Song in a fashion similar to the acts of the Apostles. As the Madman is changed into Anthem, founder of the Singerian religion, via a Holy Spirit entity called the Invader, the World Hater renames himself Sarkon and reinvents a nature religion to compete for the hearts of the people.

After Anthem speaks to a crowd in the marketplace, the Invader enters hundreds of people in a way similar to Pentecost (Acts 2). Unlike the Bible, however, *The Song* makes a strong attack against science, which Sarkon claims he will use to distract people from the Star-Song. Sarkon's first target is Everyman, who is studying science, philosophy, religion, and other matters purely from texts. Initially Everyman is enticed by the lure of not thinking but instead relying on science while indulging his bodily desires. Eventually, Sarkon's lies are revealed through the use of the Singer's name, and Everyman rejects science to embrace the new religion.

At this point, Sarkon uses more trickery to arouse the city crowds to attack the Singerians. Given a vision, Anthem and Everyman leave the Great Walled City and head to Urbis, the capital of the world, which calls to mind Paul's going to Rome to preach. Along the way, they meet and speak to Praxis the Builder, who enjoys the thought of the Singer but cannot abandon his traditional deities, so he re-creates the story into a more acceptable variation including other gods and grand temples, something that Sarkon grabs onto eagerly.

The Song then turns into an allegory of the early centuries of the Christian Church as persecutions and corruptions of the story of the Singer occur. The most prominent event is the persecution of the Singerians, reminiscent of the short-lived attempt by

Nero to blame Rome's burning on the Christians. Among the imprisoned Singerians, an apocalyptic story, appropriately called "The Finale," circulates; it claims they will overcome Sarkon and his forces of death.

Miller closes his allegorical poem with *The Finale*, set far in the future, where science and technology are everyday facts of life while the ideas of the Singerians are widespread. The inhabitants either seem to know they are killing their world through pollution and technology but console themselves with ideas of the coming of the Singer, or they do not believe their world will be destroyed. Dreamer is one of these Singerians who works in the deadly ore mines and just tells himself that he must. The radiation he is exposed to creates visions that comfort him, and he begins actively seeking them out.

These visions, which may be thought of as an allegory to the book of Revelation, foretell of a great war between the Singer and the World Hater, who now calls himself the Prince of Mirrors. However, as Dreamer has these visions, they come true in the world around him. Elan, the greatest king, uses his small army of dragons to subjugate the rest of the world while the Prince of Mirrors corrupts their minds by issuing the Mark of Elan, which has a mirror on it to show the wearer that the only hope of the world is the wearer himself.

In the Lifeland, where the Singer resides with the faithful, there is both dread of and hopeful preparation for this great battle between them and the agents of the World Hater. Things move quickly, and soon the two armies meet in battle, where victory is certain for the Singer. However, to truly defeat the World Hater and keep him from Terra Two (the new world), it takes the might of the Singer's forces and the newly enlightened Dreamer, renamed Avenger, to capture him and imprison him in Terra One forever.

Christian Themes

Throughout the trilogy, those who become Singerians are shown to undergo an awakening to their negative selves so that they can embrace the Star-Song fully. These negative selves are searching for meaning and connection because they feel lonely and separated from the world, other people, and the forces of Good. Those who reject the Singer, though, instead undergo a false awakening to their desire for power and their ability to manipulate and harm others. In the first two poems hope is offered to even those with the false awakening so that someone like Praxis the Builder can repent before the end of his life.

While the Singer Trilogy is partly an allegory of the New Testament, early Christianity, and apocalyptic beliefs, Miller's use of this fantasy setting makes the message of separation from God and other people a universal problem. At a few points there are even mentions of other worlds and other galaxies whose people struggle with the question of self-awareness and join the battle between good and evil. These internal battles that the Madman, Praxis, and the Dreamer fight lead to an external war with those who cannot stand to hear the Star-Song.

The Singerians have one form of knowledge, based on self-awakening and the battle between good and evil. Their knowledge is shown as superior to the second type of knowledge, science, discussed at length in the second and third books. Everyman's reading and the earth-destroying technology of Elan are merely references to this inferior knowledge. Miller's poem states quite clearly on several occasions that science is false knowledge; it is so false that not even the World Hater uses it but instead relies on appealing to desires for power and physical pleasure in those he corrupts.

All the Singerians are awakened through their exposure to and acceptance of the Singer, who is clearly the Jesus Christ figure of the poem. The two journeys are wonderfully parallel in action, motivation, and even words. In some ways the Singer is even stronger, because once he accepts who he is, he can feel sorrow for what is happening around him, but he never doubts his role and what he must do.

A revelation is the unveiling of secrets or hidden plans, and there are multiple revelations throughout the Singer Trilogy. The Singer's life—present, past, and future—are revealed to him, and he shares this knowledge with those who awaken. Those Singerians who are persecuted in the second and third books receive hope in the form of "The Finale," which is a revelation that their suffering will end and that the Singer will be triumphant. Before and during this ultimate battle, Dreamer also has visions that reveal to him why it is happening and what is occurring that he cannot see with his eyes.

Sources for Further Study

Blodgett, Jan. *Protestant Evangelical Literary Culture and Contemporary Society.* Westport, Conn.: Greenwood Press, 1997. Calls *The Singer Trilogy* the most successful Christian fantasy work of the modern era and discusses several of its themes.

Miller, Calvin. *Covenant for All Seasons: The Marriage Journey.* Rev. ed. Wheaton, Ill.: H. Shaw, 1995. The story of the courtship between Calvin Miller and his wife, Barbara. Contains many biographical details.

_____. *Jesus Loves Me: Celebrating the Profound Truths of a Simple Hymn.* New York: Warner Books, 2002. Miller's book focuses on music as a way to spread the message of Christianity. Provides insight into his use of song and poetry.

Mort, John. *Christian Fiction: A Guide to the Genre.* Greenwood, Conn.: Libraries Unlimited, 2002. Discusses several trends in Christian literature and cites examples of several popular fantasy and science fiction books, including *The Singer Trilogy.*

Szalewski, Susan. "Omaha Pastor's Works Popular in Bible Belt: 'Humble' Author Has Few Local Readers." *Omaha World-Herald,* July 14, 1989, p. 9. A short profile of Miller looks at his works and life as a pastor.

TammyJo Eckhart

SINNERS WELCOME

Author: Mary Karr (1955-)
First published: New York: HarperCollins, 2006
Genre: Poetry
Subgenres: Autobiography; lyric poetry; narrative poetry
Core issues: Coming of age or teen life; Jesus Christ; love; prayer; redemption; sin and sinners; suffering

Karr's Christian poems fall into two categories: a cycle of poems that recall in contemporary and somewhat irreverent language the birth, life, death, and resurrection of Christ and poems that reflect from a Catholic Christian perspective on key personal experiences of Karr, her relationship with her teenage son, and the fate of some of her friends and some notorious strangers. The book concludes by reprinting Karr's slightly revised 2005 essay on the relationship of poetry, prayer, and Christian faith.

Overview

Mary Karr's poems in her collection *Sinners Welcome* approach their often deeply personal or biblical subjects from a clear, contemporary Christian perspective. Although her poems show occasional quibbling with official Catholic doctrine and use a casual and sometimes irreverent language toward biblical themes, Karr decisively sees herself as a Catholic poet.

The story of Karr's conversion to Catholicism at age forty is rendered in the title poem "Sinners Welcome." As the author writes in her essay "Facing Altars: Poetry and Prayer," which is included as afterword to her poems, the phrase comes from a banner hung over the entrance of Saint Lucy's Catholic Church in Syracuse, New York, where Karr embraced her new faith. It is in this church that the persona of the title poem opens her heart to Jesus' love.

Before the clearly autobiographical persona's conversion and even after, many poems in the collection tell of her spiritual agonies when faced with the sadness, chaos, violence, and tragedy of contemporary human life. Throughout these poems, the spiritual despair of the persona is expressed with great emotion and with lyrics of personal directness. Yet there is always the insistence, even if sometimes very subtle, that Jesus has provided an answer to human despondency. "Disgraceland" tells of the persona's four decades of rejecting Jesus who nevertheless "always stood/ to one side with a glass of water" while she was suffering, but she admits that she "swatted" him away for a long time.

Interspersed throughout *Sinners Welcome*, there is a series of five poems called "Descending Theology" that tell of the birth, life, betrayal, passion, and resurrection of Jesus. Derived from the author's meditations along Jesuit precepts, the five poems retell key biblical stories with lyrics built on a modern combination of naturalism and spiritualism. Here, the voice of the persona is casual and sometimes irreverent, but her trust that the biblical message is still true in the contemporary world comes across as completely genuine.

Many of Karr's poems deal with the persona's attempt to reconcile herself, to a great part out of Christian charity, with her deceased, highly idiosyncratic mother, who was an atheist artist. In "Pathetic Fallacy," like some related poems, the persona uses irony and sarcasm to describe the irrefutable fact that she can no longer communicate normally with her dead mother, who has been cremated. Yet on a spiritual level, she can still feel her mother's guardian presence. Other poems forgive the mother for once having planned to abort her unborn daughter ("Coat Hanger Bent into Halo") or to have almost attacked her with a knife when she was five. In the later instance, told in "Overdue Pardon for Mother with Knife," the persona praises God who stopped her mother's hand before she struck her terrified child.

Subject of another cycle of interspersed poems is the persona's relationship with her son, who has grown up from a helpless baby to a college-bound teenager. In "Son's Room," the persona tells how the very dependency of her baby boy saved her from losing herself in a drunken stupor, subtly alluding to the power of the infant Jesus.

In "Pluck," the persona observes with obvious irony how her responsibility for her young boy in the midst of financial distress moved her closer to God:

> I developed pluck—
> a trait much praised in Puritan texts,
> which favor the spiritual clarity
> suffering brings.

Dryly the persona continues on how she rejected the clamor of the materialistic world. When creditors called to dun her, she put the receiver next to her son's caged crickets, treating the caller to their song.

"Entering the Kingdom" tells of how, at the end of his adolescence, the persona's son is free to find God on his own. The poem delineates the limit of human guidance when it comes to personal spirituality and accepts the inevitability of children becoming people independent of their parents.

In *Sinners Welcome*, poems dedicated to friends of the author often deal with loss, suffering, disappointment, and death. Karr's poetic voice is both stark in telling of the dark side of life, yet also full of saving irony and obstinate irreverence. Most important is the poet's Christian view that seeks to put sadness and tragedy into larger perspective. "Metaphysique du Mal" chronicles the pain the persona feels on the cancer death of her friend, the fifth friend to die within five years. There is nothing more to do for her than to accept the mystery of death and embrace the life that is going on. This is symbolized by the steady ticking of the persona's wristwatch, resembling both the beat of her heart and God's enduring love.

There are a few poems that deal with violent strangers whose crimes appear to show their distance from God. Yet even for the person who murdered his father at sixteen, the persona feels hope that in jail he will find compassion for another living thing. Were this wish of the persona to come true, she feels, the murderer would be able to disencumber his heart and find his way to his divine creator's love. It is this belief in the universal power of God's love that deeply unifies the Christian poems of *Sinners Welcome*.

Christian Themes

In Karr's *Sinners Welcome*, there is a strong focus on the redemption that the love of Jesus Christ offers to those who accept him into their lives. The poems dealing with the persona before her conversion to Catholicism depict misery and despair but always hint that Jesus is ready to save those willing to be saved by him. Sadness, tragedy, and nihilism are not the only alternatives contemporary Western life has to offer, the poet suggests. Christianity is a powerful and life-saving option. This theme runs throughout her poetry.

In this vein, the title poem celebrates the persona's submission to Jesus as a key event. Religious conversion is told in highly personal as well as biblical terms. As the persona opens her shirt to show Jesus her burning heart that his love has ignited, she feels taken up by him like the proverbial lamb of Christian symbolism. Yet "Sinners Welcome" further widens its frame of reference by likening Jesus to the unlikely figure of Ulysses of Greek mythology. Like Ulysses finally coming home to Greece, the persona marvels at Christ's arrival in her own world. Out of her union with Jesus, she feels joy germinating from the seed of her newfound faith.

A strong theme is the poet's Jesuit-inspired meditation on the life of Jesus. This is told in the five poems of the "Descending Theology" cycle. Here, Karr combines naturalism with biblical spiritualism. There is the starkly realistic description of Mary experiencing the pains of childbirth and her baby boy tasting the first drops of her milk. Later, Christ's death on the cross is described medically correctly as resulting from lung collapse. Yet the poems also highlight the biblical significance of each event. In Mary's womb, Jesus is seen as already bearing the full burden of humanity's sin. His resurrection is celebrated as a return from death. The final poem of the cycle likens Jesus' abundant love for each human to the breaking of water at birth, ushering in new life, just as, according to the Christian faith, baptism brings humans the promise of eternal life.

Other themes of Karr's wide-ranging Christian poetry include the coming of age of the persona's son who has to find his own way to God, the universality of human suffering that can be ameliorated by the acceptance of Christian faith, and the persona's own plucky relationship with Jesus. Throughout, the poems of *Sinners Welcome* express the poet's firm belief in the truth of Christian salvation.

Sources for Further Study

Cunneen, Sally. "Mary Karr: Sharing the Shock of Reality." *National Catholic Reporter* 42, no. 42 (September 29, 2006): 18-19. Substantial discussion of the importance of poetry and Christianity in Karr's life; analyzes some of the poems in

Sinners Welcome and provides biographical background based on a personal interview with Karr.

Musgrove, Laurence. "*Sinners Welcome.*" *Christianity and Literature* 55, no. 4 (Summer, 2006): 618-621. Discusses relationship of the book cover's neon cross with its contemporary religious content, offers intelligent analysis of key poems, and reflects on Karr's concluding essay.

Ratner, Rochelle. "Karr, Mary. *Sinners Welcome.*" Review of *Sinners Welcome*. *Library Journal* 131, no. 1 (January 1, 2006): 122-123. Concise review focusing on the violence apparent in some of Karr's poems. Briefly places the book in the context of spiritual poetry in English.

R. C. Lutz

SIR GAWAIN AND THE GREEN KNIGHT

Author: Pearl-Poet (fl. late fourteenth century)
First transcribed: Late fourteenth century
Edition used: Sir Gawain and the Green Knight: A New Verse Translation, translated by Marie Boroff. New York: W. W. Norton, 1967
Genre: Poetry
Subgenres: Adventure; narrative poetry; romance
Core issues: Fear; forgiveness; humility; repentance; self-knowledge; truth

In his account of Sir Gawain's adventure with the mysterious Green Knight, the Pearl-Poet uses both folklore and Arthurian legend to create a lively work of fiction with religious significance. Sir Gawain must choose among the conflicting codes of chivalry, courtesy, and Christianity, often choosing wrongly. Through the character of Sir Gawain, readers learn about the sin of pride, the nature of temptation, the value of repentance, the importance of humility, and the healing power of redemption.

>*Principal characters*
>Sir Gawain, the protagonist, one of King Arthur's knights
>The Green Knight, a huge, magical knight who interrupts Christmas at Camelot
>Lord Bertilak, the host at the Castle Haut Desert; the Green Knight
>Lady Bertilak, Lord Bertilak's beautiful wife
>King Arthur, the great hero of English legend
>Queen Guinevere, Arthur's wife
>Morgan le Fay, a sorceress intent on making trouble for Arthur and his court

Overview

Written by the Pearl-Poet (also known as the Gawain-Poet), *Sir Gawain and the Green Knight* is perhaps the finest Arthurian romance in English literature. After a brief introduction connecting the events of the story to the mythical founding of Britain by the Trojan warrior Brutus, the story turns to Christmastime at Camelot where Arthur's court, a young and rowdy group, are about to celebrate a New Year's feast. Arthur refuses to eat, however, until someone tells him of some adventure or miracle. As if on cue, an enormous green knight on a green horse rushes into the court and challenges the court to a game: He will endure a blow from a knight if the knight will submit to a blow a year and a day later. Gawain leaps to the challenge and whacks the Green Knight with an axe, chopping off his head. However, the Green Knight does not die. He simply grabs his severed head and tells Gawain that to keep his honor, Gawain must find him in the Green Chapel and submit to the blow in a year and a day.

The Green Knight rides out of the room, and the stunned court returns to its festivities.

In the second part of the poem, the poet traces the cycle of the year through the liturgical calendar, moving from the New Year to Michaelmas to All Hallows Day. Just as the year grows older, Arthur's court grows heavier with trepidation for their beloved Gawain, who must ready himself for his ordeal. In some particularly lovely passages, the poet describes Gawain's preparations and gear for the journey. His shield in particular is important for the religious significance of the poem; it is adorned with a pentagram as a token of "trouthe" on the outside, and on its inner surface is a picture of the Virgin Mary.

Gawain leaves the court as Christmas approaches, facing the wilds of northern England alone in his search for the Green Chapel. When he is nearly defeated by the weather, he prays to the Virgin for help. Suddenly, the Castle Haut Desert appears, and Gawain finds himself welcomed by Lord and Lady Bertilak and an old crone. The lord assures Gawain that he knows where the Green Chapel is and that it is not very far away. He invites Gawain to stay with them for several days and enjoy their company. He invites Gawain to play a game: He says that he will give Gawain anything that he gains on each of three days he is away hunting if Gawain will give him anything he gains while staying at the castle.

On each day, Lady Bertilak comes to Gawain's bed and tempts him. Gawain is in a difficult position: The code of courtesy demands that he engage in lovemaking, while the code of chivalry demands that he honor his host. He compromises by taking a kiss, which he dutifully later gives to Lord Bertilak when he returns. On the third day, however, Lady Bertilak offers him a green girdle that she says will protect him from all harm. Fearing death at the hands of the Green Knight, Gawain takes the girdle but does not reveal this to Lord Bertilak.

When Gawain finally arrives at the Green Chapel, he finds the Green Knight sharpening his axe. He puts his head on the block to take the blow, but flinches, and the Green Knight chides him. The Green Knight begins a second blow but does not complete it. On the third attempt, he just nicks Gawain's neck. He then reveals that he is Lord Bertilak, that he came to Arthur's court at the direction of the old crone, Morgan le Fay, and that he gave Gawain the nick because Gawain did not give him the girdle he had received from Lady Bertilak. Gawain is mortified. He begs for pardon, which Lord Bertilak grants, then says he will wear the girdle on his sleeve as a sign of his shame. He returns to Camelot, humbled, and the court welcomes him home. They make light of his badge, choosing to wear green girdles themselves as a sign of solidarity. For Gawain, however, the adventure has been a learning experience: Far from the perfect knight he thought himself to be, he remains a humbled, contrite, yet redeemed man at the end of the story.

Christian Themes

Sir Gawain and the Green Knight, while overtly an exciting and humorous romance, is at heart a deeply religious work. Through the series of tests and games in the poem, the poet demonstrates Gawain's growth as a human being. Like most humans,

Gawain does not understand the real purpose of the tests to which he is subjected until after they are over. It is only in retrospect that he can understand that it is not his honor that is being tested, but his humility; not his lovemaking, but his truthfulness; and not his courage, but his faith in God.

The poem is both subtle and sophisticated as it presents the difficult choices that confront Gawain: He must choose, over and over, among the codes of chivalry, courtesy, and Christianity, codes that are often in conflict with each other. When he leaps to chop off the Green Knight's head, he believes that he is demonstrating chivalric courage; what he demonstrates is rashness and a lack of Christian charity. When he allows Lady Bertilak into his bed, he believes that he is honoring the code of courtesy; he violates, however, the chivalric response to the hospitality of his host. When he accepts the green girdle, he believes he is saving his own life; but the gift marks his fear of death and his lack of faith. Finally, when he does not give the green girdle to Bertilak at the end of the day, he breaks his promise.

The story reveals the sinful nature of even the most perfect of knights. Gawain suffers from the sins of pride, lack of faith, and dishonesty. His confession to the Green Knight of his wrongdoings allows him ultimately to be redeemed by the Green Knight's forgiveness. His return to Camelot is marked by his sincere contrition and repentance.

The heart of the poem, ultimately, is the notion of truth. In Middle English, the word "trouthe" had many more nuances of meaning than simply truth as opposed to falsehood. It also connoted a sacred promise and faithfulness. In modern English, this sense continues in the word "troth" as used in a traditional wedding ceremony or in words such as "betroth" and "betrothal." Gawain's real failure is not a failure of nerve but rather a failure to keep trouthe. Although he is the Knight of the Virgin Mary, he fails to keep trouthe with her, preferring to trust Lady Bertilak's magic. In addition, his failure to act honorably in keeping his bargain reveals a failure of trouthe with both King Arthur and Lord Bertilak. Yet, in the court's embrace of Gawain, the end of the story offers hope and redemption for all of flawed humanity.

Sources for Further Study

Anderson, J. J. *Language and Imagination in the Gawain-Poems*. Manchester, England: Manchester University Press, 2005. Places *Sir Gawain and the Green Knight* within the context of the other poems of the manuscript, looking closely at religious concepts of humility, sin, God's justice, and truth.

Boroff, Marie. *Traditions and Renewals: Chaucer, the Gawain-Poet, and Beyond*. New Haven, Conn.: Yale University Press, 2003. The noted modern translator of *Sir Gawain and the Green Knight* examines the confessional scene, noting that it is the Green Knight who pronounces judgment on Sir Gawain as opposed to a priest.

Brewer, Derek, and Jonathan Gibson, eds. *A Companion to the Gawain-Poet*. Cambridge, Mass.: D. S. Brewer, 1997. Includes many fine readings, particularly a chapter by David Aers concerning Christianity and courtly codes.

Howard, Donald R., and Christine Zacher, eds. *Critical Studies of "Sir Gawain and the Green Knight."* Notre Dame, Ind.: University of Notre Dame Press, 1968. Classic collection of critical work on *Sir Gawain and the Green Knight,* including several chapters on Christian significance, Gawain's lessons and flaws, and the meaning of the Green Chapel.

Thompson, Raymond H., and Keith Busby. *Gawain: A Casebook.* London: Routledge, 2005. Places the character of Gawain in a historical context, tracing his depictions from early medieval texts through modern day. Extensive annotated bibliography.

Diane Andrews Henningfeld

THE SOCIAL TEACHING OF THE CHRISTIAN CHURCHES

Author: Ernst Troeltsch (1865-1923)
First published: Die Soziallehren der christlichen Kirchen und Gruppen, 1912 (English translation, 1931)
Edition used: The Social Teaching of the Christian Churches, translated by Olive Wyon. Louisville, Ky.: Westminster/John Knox Press, 1992
Genre: Nonfiction
Subgenres: Church history; critical analysis; theology
Core issues: Church; ethics; Jesus Christ

In this massive and pioneering work, Troeltsch attempts to use historical and sociological tools to canvas and analyze the distinctive ethical and institutional positions taken by Christian churches and groups over and against the social, political, and economic institutions and practices within which Christian social identity and influence were formed. He argues that such a study could aid Christians in their quest for an effective mode of social engagement.

Overview

Ernst Troeltsch belonged to a pioneering generation of German social thinkers who studied value conflict in the formation of social and cultural unity. In studies of religion, they emphasized the tension within "universal" religions between world-affirming and world-rejecting impulses. The former impulse finds expression in beliefs that the cosmos is divinely created, sustained, or guided; the latter finds expression in beliefs that the cosmos stands in profound disjunction with divine purposes, triggering responses such as asceticism, expectation of divine judgment, or longing for otherworldly salvation. Focusing primarily on three periods of Christian history—early Christianity, medieval and Reformation Christianity, and early modern Protestantism—Troeltsch shows how Christians, wrestling with the ambiguities of institutional and personal value conflict, attempted to create Christian identities suitable for their times and cultures.

Because they expected the world to be quickly replaced by the Kingdom of God, these social dilemmas were especially acute for the earliest Christians. To follow Jesus meant to live wholly in terms of the coming redemption and in radical disjunction with this world. The expectation of a perpetually delayed salvation, however, could not sustain the nascent community for long, and Christianity had to adjust to life in an enduring world. Troeltsch argues that the social tensions of this dilemma permeated the ethical and theological discourse of early Christian thinkers from Paul to Augustine. Their primary response was to find in Jesus not only the announcer of future redemption but also a cosmic Christ who offers salvation within this world. In turn, redemption came to mean grace that ensures both salvation in the next world and forgiveness, personal transformation, and strength to live a virtuous life in this world, mediated by an authoritative institutional church. However, the nagging question persisted: What is to be rejected and affirmed in the life of this world? Its social ethic attuned to the world to come, Christianity borrowed from preexisting Jewish and Greco-Roman ethical and philosophical perspectives. Troeltsch argues that the expectation of a future Kingdom of God was ultimately recast into a Neoplatonic hierarchy of divinely created goods: those of this world—the state, the economy, the family—were affirmed, but only in their proper place below the higher eternal goods that call forth absolute love of God and neighbor. Combined with a Stoic theory of natural law, this perspective offered a relative Christian affirmation of secular institutions even while demoting them beneath the higher ethical demands that echoed from the Gospel.

The medieval Church broke out of this model for the simple reason that it was situated in a culture it had helped to create. To a large extent, Christianity permeated and affirmed secular medieval institutions. This circumstance found intellectual expression in the Christian-Aristotelian theology of Thomas Aquinas, which held that divine revelation, grace, and the Church perfected and completed the political, social, and economic institutions natural to the created pattern of rational human development. The underlying formal ideal of the unity of religion and culture expressed here was assumed not only by the medieval Church but by the Protestant Reformers as well.

At this point in his analysis, Troeltsch proposes one of his most famous themes: the analytical distinction between three types of religious institutional formation—the church-type, sect-type, and mysticism-type. For many readers, this distinction is the enduring heart of his book.

By the term church-type, Troeltsch means the type of religious institution, first exemplified in Christianity by the medieval Church, that affirms and stabilizes worldly institutions, seeing them as divinely ordained. Such support, in turn, increases the authority with which the Church maintains its own expansive theological and sacramental power. The price for this influence, however, is the compromise of the radical ethical requirements of the Gospel. Redemption is understood in terms of grace offered for the forgiveness of sins, including for these compromises. Those born into a given territory are automatically born into the Church by infant baptism, followed by participation in formalized sacramental observances administered by a priestly hierarchy. The world-rejecting ethic of Jesus is not denied by the church-type, however, but sponsored primarily in monitored forms of asceticism. Even here, though, the emphasis usually falls not on rejection of the world but on rejection of the pride or lust associated with worldly experience. Troeltsch argues that even though Protestant Reformers later significantly adjusted the substance of this type, they left its basic form intact, assuming the unity of culture and religion.

The dominance of the church-type during the medieval and Reformation periods, however, forced the latent world-rejecting impulse—the sect-type—into the open rebellion characteristic of such groups as the Waldensians, the Hussites, and the Anabaptists. The Christ of the sect-type was not the cosmic redeemer but the culturally disjunctive and prophetic Jesus of the Sermon on the Mount, the suffering and persecuted Lord who calls his followers to lives of simple discipleship in anticipation of the coming kingdom. In the sect-type, baptism is a voluntary adult act signifying the personal and communal commitment of the faithful few who will take up the cross of Christ. Their world rejection consists not so much in detachment from greed, lust, or pleasure, nor in monasticism, but in steadfast refusal to participate in institutions, religious or secular, that are characteristic of, or have compromised with, a corrupt world, no matter how long that world endures.

In the struggle between and within these two types, a third latent type emerged: the mysticism-type. Always a part of Christianity, mysticism was usually attuned to the internal spiritual meaning of external belief and practice. In the struggles between church and sect, however, mysticism emerged as a separate religious formation, marked by indifference or hostility to institutional religion. Mysticism calls for personal union with God. Its Christ is the inner word experienced in the depths of the soul or in visionary ecstasy. Troeltsch illustrates his mysticism-type with a bewildering array of historical figures, but this variety was precisely what he wanted to highlight. In the deadly confessional strife of the Reformation and post-Reformation periods, the individual's inward life became an attractive avenue of independent spiritual transcendence. Moreover, as modern Europeans grew increasingly wary of all institutional religious authorities, whether of church or sect, the authority of subjective religious experience only grew stronger.

Christian Themes

Which of the three types canvassed above is the correct form of Christianity? Troeltsch answers: all three. The church-type expresses the universality of Christianity, but the sect-type preserves the early meaning of Jesus' Gospel, while the mysticism-type conveys the idea of inner communion of the soul with its God. All are scriptural, legitimate, and once-united components driven asunder by the conflicts of historical development. Observing the increasingly secularized and industrialized Europe of the early twentieth century, Troeltsch wonders how Christianity would sustain itself and its culture. The greatest achievement of the early church had been the construction of the Church itself as an enduring institution grafted onto an alien pagan world that it had outlived. In the modern world, however, Christianity finds itself in the same situation, searching for its place in an increasingly alien and religiously fragmented world. The future of each of the three types does not look promising: Neither an increasingly ineffective form of hierarchical authority, nor a sectarian rejection of the world, nor an institutionally indifferent mysticism seemed to offer realistic avenues for enduring cultural engagement. The future is open, Troeltsch argues, and he ends his book wondering whether a new institutional form or a new combination of the three types would emerge soon enough to help resolve the religious and cultural dilemmas of Europe.

Sources for Further Study

Chapman, Mark D. *Ernst Troeltsch and Liberal Theology: Religion and Cultural Synthesis in Wilhelmine Germany*. Oxford, England: Oxford University Press, 2001. Detailed account of Troeltsch's program for a culturally engaged and ethically responsible form of Christianity.

Drescher, Hans-Georg. *Ernst Troeltsch: His Life and Work*. Minneapolis, Minn.: Fortress Press, 1993. Troeltsch's intellectual development; good summaries of his major works.

Harrisville, Roy A., and Walter Sundberg. "Ernst Troeltsch: The Power of Historical Consciousness." In *The Bible in Modern Culture: Baruch Spinoza to Brevard Childs*. 2d ed. Grand Rapids, Mich.: Wm. B. Eerdmans, 2002. Troeltsch's theological and methodological positions related to his interpretation of Christian history.

Liebersohn, Harry. "Ernst Troeltsch: From Community to Society." In *Fate and Utopia in German Sociology, 1870-1923*. Cambridge, Mass.: Massachusetts Institution of Technology Press, 1988. Troeltsch's sociology of religion and his underlying sense of cultural and religious crisis.

Welch, Claude. "Ernst Troeltsch: Faith, History, and Ethics in Tension." In Vol. 2 of *Protestant Thought in the Nineteenth Century*. New Haven, Conn.: Yale University Press, 1985. *The Social Teaching of the Christian Churches* in the context of an insightful overview of Troeltsch's theological work and its historical context.

Bradley Starr

THE SONG OF ALBION TRILOGY

Author: Stephen R. Lawhead (1950-   )
First published: The Paradise War, 1991; *The Silver Hand,* 1992; *The Endless Knot,* 1993
Edition used: The Song of Albion Trilogy. 3 vols. Nashville, Tenn.: WestBow Press, 2006
Genre: Novels
Subgenres: Alternate universe; fantasy
Core issues: Friendship; good vs. evil; love; myths; responsibility; spiritual warfare

Two Oxford students, an American and a Briton, slip through a home in a Scottish cairn and find themselves in Albion, an alternate world that at first appears to be a paradise. There they soon adapt to the lifestyle, which resembles that of the ancient Celts, and learn the significance of the Celtic myths. Both men are trained as warriors, but in the ensuing battle between good and evil, they take different sides. Eventually the American, who has become the high king, sacrifices his life to save both Albion and his own world from being dominated by the forces of evil.

> *Principal characters*
> *Lewis Gillies*, an American student at Oxford, Llew and the High King in Albion
> *Simon Rawnson*, a rich British fellow student, Siawn Hy and Llew's enemy in Albion
> *Tegid Tathal ap Talaryant*, Llew's friend, a bard
> *Prince Meldron*, son of Meldryn Mawr, who usurps the throne after his father's death
> *Goewyn*, the daughter of Scatha, a prophetess, and later Llew's wife
> *Professor "Nettles" Nettleton*, an elderly don and a Celtic expert
> *Meldryn Mawr*, king of Prydain
> *Ollathir*, Meldryn Mawr's chief bard
> *Paladyr*, Meldryn Mawr's champion and his murderer
> *Scatha (Pen-y-Cat, or Head of Battle)*, a woman who runs a school for warriors
> *Susannah*, Simon's fiery girlfriend and eventually Lewis's rescuer

Overview

Stephen R. Lawhead's *The Song of Albion Trilogy* is the story of a young man's venture into another world, where he attains the status of a mythical hero before returning to the time and place from which he came. The hero of the trilogy is Lewis

Gillies, an American graduate student at Oxford University, where he is specializing in Celtic studies. His cynical, aristocratic friend and roommate, Simon Rawnson, who also enters the other world, becomes one of the primary villains in the Otherworld.

The first book in the series, *The Paradise War*, begins with a startling discovery. While scanning the newspaper at breakfast, Simon sees a photograph of an aurochs, a oxlike creature that appeared near Inverness and promptly died. Because the aurochs has long been extinct, Simon persuades Lewis to drive up to Scotland with him to investigate. At Carnwood Farm, they find a cairn with a hole in it, and Simon disappears.

When Simon does not return, Lewis drives back to Oxford. There he is approached by Professor Nettleton, a don at Merton College. Nettleton, or "Nettles," informs Simon that the border between the worlds has become unstable, thereby imperiling everyone, because everything good in the real world depends on archetypes stored in the Otherworld. The two men travel to Scotland, only to find the cairn area occupied by a hostile group of "metaphysical archaeologists" headed by Nevil Weston. Eluding them, Simon flings himself into the Otherworld, where he soon finds himself in the midst of a battle. To Lewis's amazement, one of the warriors is Simon, who has just killed the enemy's champion. Simon gives Lewis the victim's head, thus buying him acceptance into the band to which Simon belongs. It is led by Prince Meldron, the son of Meldryn Mawr, king of Prydain.

Although he still means to take Simon home with him, Lewis is sent to a school for warriors that is headed by the woman warrior Scatha. On the way, the bard Tegid Tathal teaches Lewis the language, and they become friends. After seven years, Lewis, now called Llew, is released from the school so that he can attend a gathering of bards. There Llew witnesses a demonic creature's attack on the king's chief bard, Ollathir, which ends with his death. Gwenllian, who is one of Scatha's three daughters, announces that the struggle between good and evil has begun. The Phantarch, who guards the magical Singing Stones, has been killed, and the Song of Albion has been silenced. She adds that good cannot triumph until the song is restored and Silver Hand becomes the ruler.

When Llew and Tegid find the Phantarch's body, Llew spots the Singing Stones, which the Phantarch had hidden. Llew and Tegid take the stones with them and use them to help Meldryn Mawr defeat the evil Nudd. In recognition of Llew's contribution to his victory, Meldryn Mawr names him the king's champion. Before Llew can intervene, the former champion, Paladyr, kills the king. Realizing that the baleful influence of Simon, now Siawn Hy, has begun to permeate the court, Llew begs him to return home, but he refuses, and Llew goes back alone.

The second book in the trilogy, *The Silver Hand*, is told from the point of view of Tegid. With the death of Ollathir, Tegid had become the king's Chief Bard, who alone can name a king's successor. When Llew reappears, still hoping to take Siawn Hy back with him, Tegid proclaims Llew the new king of Prydain. However, Meldron seizes the throne, throws both Llew and Tegid into a hostage pit, and seizes the Singing Stones that control the Song of Albion.

Though Llew and Tegid manage to escape and are taken in by the Cruins, the king fears Meldron too much to let them remain for long. They make their way to Scatha's school, where Llew realizes that he is in love with Scatha's daughter Goewyn. Llew and Tegid again attend the gathering of the bards, who Llew hopes can help him regain his throne, but Meldron appears and slaughters all the bards. He then cuts off Llew's hand, thus making it impossible for him ever to be king, since tradition holds that a king must be unblemished. After blinding Tegid, Meldron sets the two adrift in a boat, but the men are plucked from danger by the all-powerful Creator. After a number of adventures, they build a settlement. Refugees from Meldron's tyranny soon join them there. Hearing that Meldron has attacked Scatha's camp, Llew's forces hurry to her aid, but they do not arrive in time to save her young warriors or two of her daughters. Only Scatha and Goewyn escape. Meldron next invades the settlement, but Llew magically acquires a silver hand and defeats the attackers. Meldron is killed. In the war crimes trial that follows, Siawn Hy is convicted. Attempting to escape, he is mortally wounded, but he then vanishes. Because Nettleton has found out that Simon was involved in a conspiracy with Weston that would end in the destruction of Albion, Llew is profoundly relieved. The book ends with the recovery of the Singing Stones and the recognition of Llew as king not just of Prydain but of all Albion.

The third book in the trilogy, *The Endless Knot*, is told by Lewis, now known as Llew Silver Hand. Though Nettleton again reminds him that no human being is allowed to remain in the Otherworld, Llew cannot bring himself to leave the place where he has found happiness. Furthermore, he believes that his people need him. When Goewyn accepts his proposal of marriage, Llew promises her that he will remain as long as he can, and if possible, forever.

However, evil again invades paradise. During the wedding festivities, the settlement is set on fire, and the Singing Stones are stolen. Llew prepares to lead his warriors in pursuit of the attackers, but Goewyn points out that his duty as king is to remain and rule. Llew does so. His warriors capture the malevolent Paladyr, who masterminded the raid, and bring back the Singing Stones. At his trial, Paladyr claims "naud," which means that a king must prove his greatness by granting mercy. Llew spares Paladyr's life and sends him to the Foul Land.

Although there are signs that the settlement is being watched, Llew has become complacent. When the pregnant Goewyn and another woman set out for a morning ride, he does not send anyone with them. The women are kidnapped and taken across the sea to the Foul Land. Though Tegid warns Llew not to leave his kingdom, Llew insists on going to their rescue. In the Foul Land, Llew and his warriors are trapped by Paladyr and the dreaded Brazen Man, who reveals himself as Siawn Hy. Though Llew is killed, after his death he sees a holy fire consume Siawn Hy and Paladyr and purge the Foul Land. Back in Albion, Llew is entombed but then emerges from the cairn to find Susannah waiting for him. They return to Oxford, where together they will write the story of his adventures.

Christian Themes

Lawhead's theological education and his personal commitment to Christianity are reflected in all his works. Like his other books, *The Song of Albion Trilogy* is an account of a conflict between good and evil. When Lewis first arrives in Albion, he believes it to be a paradise, an unfallen world. He notes that it is untainted by human invention and assumes that its inhabitants live in harmony with nature and one another. However, when he finds himself in the midst of a bloody battle, he realizes that Albion is not as peaceful as he had thought. In the Celtic myths related by the bards, there is evidence that like the biblical Garden of Eden, Albion has always had its serpents; in the utterances of its prophets, it is clear that it will always be threatened by evil.

Following Christian theology, Lawhead explains the presence of evil as a consequence of free will. The divine Creator, who is referred to in the novels as the Swift Sure Hand, permits his creatures to make choices. Thus though the students at the school of warriors are supposed to be thoroughly prepared for a lifelong battle against evil, some of them may choose a different course. Temptation comes to both Paladyr and Prince Meldron through their overweening pride. Similarly, it is pride that turns Simon from merely an amusing but self-centered cynic into Siawn Hy, a Judas to his best friend and an enemy of all that is good.

The good characters in *The Song of Albion Trilogy*, especially Tegid and Llew, know that winning battles against outside forces is not enough; one must also defeat the temptations that lurk within one's own heart. After Llew becomes High King, his decisions are even more difficult because they involve his responsibility to his people and to the kingship itself. He chooses rightly when he shows mercy to Paladyr and again when he sends others to pursue the raiders who burned his settlement, but by leading the expedition to the Foul Land, he puts his love for Goewyn ahead of his kingly duty. Nevertheless, in his death, Llew becomes the Christlike figure of the Celtic prophecies, who sacrifices his own life for his people. Back home, however, Lewis is once again an ordinary human being, who by writing about his experiences can be a prophetic voice in a decadent society.

Sources for Further Study

Andraski, Katie. "Through the Door." Review of *The Paradise Door* by Stephen R. Lawhead. *Christianity Today* 35 (October 7, 1991): 32-33. Admires the style and the spiritual depth of *The Paradise War*, which the reviewer calls a story of redemption.

Irwin, Robert. "From a Science Future to a Fantasy Past." *Antiquity* 69 (June, 1995): 238-239. Irwin states that though most mass-market fantasies are unimaginative and non-Christian, Lawhead's trilogy displays an impressive "imaginative conviction."

Manlove, Colin. *Christian Fantasy: From 1200 to the Present*. Notre Dame, Ind.: University of Notre Dame Press, 1992. By analyzing a number of major works, the author shows how the genre has altered over time. Extensive notes and index.

Schaap, James Calvin, ed., and Philip Yancey, comp. *More than Words: Contemporary Writers on the Works That Shaped Them*. Grand Rapids, Mich.: Baker Books, 2002. Twenty-one Christian writers, including Lawhead, pay tribute to the literary masters who inspired them.

Summer, Bob. "Crossway's Crossover Novelist." *Publishers Weekly* 236 (October 6, 1989): 28, 32. Lawhead explains to the interviewer how his theological training, his research into Celtic history, and his faith have influenced his works.

Rosemary M. Canfield Reisman

SONG OF THE SPARROW
Meditations and Poems to Pray By

Author: Murray Bodo (1937-   )
First published: Cincinnati: St. Anthony Messenger Press, 1976
Genre: Poetry
Subgenres: Lyric poetry; meditation and contemplation
Core issues: Catholics and Catholicism; prayer; service; trust in God

Bodo's meditative journal takes the reader on a journey through three seasons of the spirit, offering insights into praying, writing, serving others, and healing the soul.

Overview

Murray Bodo's *Song of the Sparrow* is a meditative journal of poetry and prose that documents the writer's progress through three seasons—autumn to spring—when nature metaphorically seems to die and then be reborn. Bodo writes of his own efforts to grow spiritually through increased recognition of one's need to pray more sincerely, to trust in and listen to God, and to serve others.

The journal begins in autumn, when Bodo finds that changes in nature are provoking spiritual musings. To Bodo, autumn is "thought-time," when falling leaves remind him of mortality and his thoughts are directed heavenward, as prefigured by the deep blue sky above. As the sky becomes more visible, Bodo finds himself more cognizant of birds flying through it, especially sparrows. The writer's sudden awareness that he has overlooked something quiet, yet ever present—something as common as sparrows—provokes similar awareness of his need to deepen his awareness of the presence of God in his life. "Like the sparrows that have always been in my life, God is so present that I take him for granted."

Epiphanies like this one are characteristic of much of Bodo's journal; his short musings and poems on seasons, birds, beaches, and so forth are offered to provoke similar moments of spiritual perception on the part of the reader. As Bodo observes:

> The God within me reveals his presence, fleetingly, and all the rest of my days are changed permanently. Something happens that I did not merit and that I cannot explain or communicate. But it is more real than any communicable experience, and I cannot formulate it or capture it in words.

In the autumn section of Bodo's work, these perceptions usually involve such human failings as pride, callousness, lack of charity, and selfishness. His meditations urge his readers to forgive others and themselves and to trust in God. To reach these goals, Bodo suggests that we reenvision and reinvigorate our prayers as well as devote ourselves more consciously and lovingly toward serving our neighbors. For many, prayer is simply repetition, a magic formula to create whatever is desired; as Bodo suggests, "prayer is not self-analysis but self liberation through concentration and absorption in God." Done humbly, prayer enables us to hear the still, small voice of God and to recognize his presence in signs, even sparrows.

The winter section of *Song of the Sparrow* continues Bodo's observations on praying and trusting in God. For example, Bodo offers a mnemonic for his way of praying—SPORT—as a way of deepening the reader's prayers. *S* indicates a need to silence oneself; *P* stands for purification, letting go of grudges and forgiving wrongs done us; *O* stands for being open to God, however he chooses to communicate; *R* stands for responding; and *T* stands for talking with God. Overall, however, the focus of this section shifts toward serving others. Once again, the season is used to indicate spiritual needs. In winter we want to stay comfortably indoors, away from the cold, but our spiritual welfare requires that we reach out to others in service. Serving others "makes tangible our union with the other, God himself." Put in more explicitly Christian terms, Bodo posits that our service to others connects us with "the Body of Christ."

As a poet and a writer, Bodo is aware that his service to others is best done through his writings, which can provide instructions and offer advice and solace to readers in spiritual torment: "I keep writing/ After midnight,/ Hoping I might/ Help you, biting/ Your fingernails,/ Sleepless, afraid."

In the spring section, Bodo subtly shifts focus from how one can serve others and thereby develop one's relationship with God to how to maintain that relationship. "The secret," Bodo observes, "is in letting go and trusting God." To Bodo, this means surrendering self-obsessions, worries about others, and nagging doubts in order to become more conscious of one's dependence on God's providence. Characteristically, Bodo describes this moment of epiphany:

> We fight that kind of surrender and resist it. Then one day we wake up and realize that letting go is the only answer. And waking up is pretty much what happens. Everything before that insight was a sleeping away of our lives in fear and trepidation. Then we jump out of bed and start living fully for the first time. Nothing matters from then on but God's will, and God himself absorbs our failures and our successes, and we praise him no matter what happens.

Spring is an appropriate time for these observations, Bodo contends, because at that time nature seems to be reborn—brighter, cleaner, more joyful. Our trust and reliance on God and our loving service to others gives birth to a deep joy in us as well.

Christian Themes

Three significant Christian themes dominate *Song of the Sparrow*. These are the separation between God and human beings, the spiritual value of service as a way of connecting with God and cooperating with his grace, and trusting in God as a loving and giving father.

Bodo spends much of his book on the existential loneliness we feel and how much we hunger for some concrete awareness of God. "Turn wherever you may, nothing and no one short of God can satisfy your longing or distract you from that gnawing in the mind and heart which speaks of an emptiness that is yet to be filled."

The autumn woods call to the writer's mind his existential emptiness: "I walk in the bleak November woods and I want to believe that I am not alone, that this loneliness is illusion only." We are all too conscious of how empty we are and how much we want God to fill our emptiness: "And so I reach out and call upon God and I am no longer alone." As Bodo suggests, God is ever-present; part of our problem as human beings is that we will not accept him on his terms. For example, while we expect a thundering voice from the heavens in answer to our prayers, what we receive is a silent stirring in the heart or an unexpected gift from another person.

> Each one of us, whether he realizes it or not, is a living symbol of the presence of God in the world. By who we are and how we act we can either build up or tear down the Kingdom of God. God has chosen to act through men, first through his son, Jesus, and then through all the members of his Mystical Body. That God is alive and well is most evident in those who live through him and with him and in him.

As Bodo puts it, it is in giving these gifts to each other that we thank God for his grace and indicate our willingness to cooperate in his will for us.

Sources for Further Study

Berger, Rose Marie. "Necessary Words." Review of *The Earth Moves at Midnight* by Murray Bodo. *Sojourners Magazine* 33, no. 2 (February 4, 2004): 46. This review of Bodo's collection of poems about his growing up finds them simple and elegant.

Bodo, Murray. *The Place We Call Home: Spiritual Pilgrimage as a Path to God.* Brewster, Mass.: Paraclete Press, 2004. The Franciscan priest writes of pilgrimage and describes several of his own.

_____. *Poetry as Prayer: Denise Levertov.* Boston: Pauline Books and Media, 2001. In this biography of another poet, one who was his friend, Bodo offers insights into how he views poetry as a means of enriching and strengthening one's prayers.

Chase, Elise. Review of *The Way of Saint Francis: The Challenge of Franciscan Spirituality for Everyone* by Murray Bodo. *Library Journal* 109, no. 1 (January 1, 1984) 102. A collection of meditations on topics inspired by Saint Francis, including one on the dynamics of psychic death and rebirth.

Michael R. Meyers

SONGBIRD

Author: Lisa Samson (1964-   )
First published: New York: Warner Books, 2003
Genre: Novel
Subgenre: Literary fiction
Core issues: African Americans; faith; forgiveness; grace; healing; marriage; preaching

The young wife of an itinerant southern preacher whose ministry finds success amid the early 1980's boom in televangelism, Charmaine Hopewell, blessed with a singing voice she sees as a way to spread God's saving message, struggles with a secret from her childhood that she has withheld from her husband and with a growing addiction to prescription medication to combat depression. In this modern-day parable, Charmaine moves ultimately to accepting her vulnerability and imperfections and in turn entrusting herself to the providential care of a loving God.

> *Principal characters*
> *Myrtle Charmaine Whitehead Hopewell*, the protagonist
> *Harlan Hopewell*, Myrtle's husband
> *Isla Whitehead*, Myrtle's mother who abandoned her
> *Hope Hopewell*, Myrtle's adopted daughter
> *Minerva Whitehead*, Myrtle's grandmother

Overview

Growing up in Lynchburg, Virginia, living modestly in a boarding house with her mother, Isla, a waitress who is given to bouts of drinking during which she curses her daughter for ruining her life, Myrtle Charmaine Whitehead learns early on the risk of trusting in the permanence of anything. At eleven, she comes home from school to find a letter from her mother with cash and a promise to return in two weeks. Abandoned, the girl eventually seeks help from her Sunday school teacher, a compassionate woman who had already noticed the girl's singing talent. Myrtle is taken into the woman's home and just begins to accept that family's love when the woman is killed in a car accident.

Dispatched into the foster care system, Charmaine (as she begins to call herself) moves through a series of loveless homes until at age fifteen she runs away with a college boy with whom she is infatuated. On her own again, she is taken in by a loving husband and wife who run a bowling alley/coin laundry in Baltimore. (Charmaine had bought a bus ticket to Baltimore as that was as far as her money would take her.) Hired as a snack-counter worker, Charmaine is given a chance to sing pop tunes for the customers, a gig that leads her to Atlantic City, where she sings in a Supremes-style trio in a sleazy casino bar.

Although she had undergone a religious conversion in an unexpected moment of expansive enlightenment in Baltimore, Charmaine never confronts the implications of her religious awakening until, on impulse, she wanders into a rescue mission off the Atlantic City boardwalk and hears the powerful preaching of Harlan Hopewell. She feels the confidence in his message. She knows now that her voice should be put to its fullest service by glorifying God. Within weeks, Charmaine and Harlan are married (although he is nearly twice her age). Charmaine joins his itinerant crusade as a singer. She tells him that her parents are both dead. The lie haunts her. She begins to be troubled by bouts of depression and insomnia.

The dynamics of her marriage alter when Charmaine is asked to care for the granddaughter of the Sunday school teacher who long ago had taken her in. She accepts the child, a beautiful girl named Hope. Then she becomes the de facto caregiver of Leo, an African American boy, when his mother, a drug addict who is part of Charmaine's singing troupe, must undergo drug rehabilitation and subsequently abandons the child. Unable to conceive (although there is no medical reason why), Charmaine evidences again and again her conviction that Christianity means extending care to others without expectation of return. As her own gospel singing career begins to blossom, Charmaine starts to take prescription medication (Tofranil) to combat her depression even as her husband gains fame for preaching against psychiatry and prescription drugs and counsels his followers to trust in Jesus.

When their crusade takes them near the town where her mother grew up, Charmaine resolves to introduce herself to her grandmother, Minerva Whitehead, a grade school teacher. The reunion is joyous. Minerva eventually agrees to move in with Charmaine after Harlan accepts a preaching position in rural North Carolina. After Charmaine finally tells Harlan the truth about her mother, she and Minerva hire a private detective to locate Isla. What follows is a difficult reunion: Isla, diagnosed with paranoid schizophrenia, has been confined to a state-run Maryland mental facility. She has stopped responding to treatment and spends her days tending a small garden. With money from her record sales, Charmaine relocates her mother to a first-class facility in North Carolina.

With regular national exposure on a cable evangelical program that is part of the burgeoning growth of Christian television during the mid-1980's, Charmaine and Harlan are caught up in the wave of scandals that rock that industry. Amid the media frenzy for exposés on any evangelist, Charmaine, shaken by newspaper inquisitions into her medical treatments as well as into the circumstances surrounding how she came to raise Leo, goes on television and admits her own program of medication and her family's history of mental illness. When Leo's birth mother reclaims the boy, Charmaine is devastated.

However, it is Lisa Samson's message that God—and trust in his presence—always has the last word. In a soaring epilogue, Harlan and Charmaine (now fortytwo) have regained their Gospel television program, a modest preaching-centered ministry that now grounds its message in the traditional embrace of God's saving love; Charmaine's depression is monitored by both medication and her faith in God;

Isla has begun to respond to Charmaine's loving attention; and most joyously Harlan and Charmaine are expecting a child of their own, a daughter whom they appropriately name Victoria. It is a crowning moment that affirms the presence of a loving God, who answers prayers despite the cynics who conceive of a world directed by the whims of contingency, whose omnipotence is manifested in what appears to be accidents, and whose love continues to sustain those who trust.

Christian Themes

Unlike much contemporary Christian literature with saintly heroes and cartoon villains, *Songbird*, which won the Christy Award for best contemporary Christian fiction, reflects Samson's background as a writer of historical romances and her admiration for realist writers—such as Anne Tyler, Larry McMurtry, and Somerset Maugham—who probe the complicated nuances of imperfect characters. Samson refuses simplistic characterization: Her Christians are noble and flawed (for instance, Harlan Hopewell, the charismatic preacher who provides Charmaine spiritual guidance, is a consummate egoist who sports a toupee and finds irresistible the siren call of televising his prayer meetings; the televangelist couple whose lavish lifestyles become the subject of the scandal that rocks Charmaine's world are the first to recognize Charmaine's gifts and give her national exposure to begin her ministry.)

That sense of authenticity is underscored by Samson's thematic use of the parable of the woman at the well (John 4:4-42). In it, Jesus stops at a well in Samaria and meets a woman, a pariah married four times and now living with a man. Jesus nevertheless offers the woman the uncomplicated gift of his healing through the symbolic offer of water, an emphatic reminder of how the lowliest sinner is significant within the dynamic of Christian forgiveness. That is crucial to Samson's Christian vision: the willingness to extend compassion to others, a reaching out that reflects God's outreach to sinners. Charmaine alters the lyrics to the familiar pop tune: People who love people are the luckiest people in the world. Samson argues that God, allowed into the emotional mayhem that defines the lives of her characters, will provide saving direction, the confirmation of his intrusive love. Samson dismisses coping mechanisms indulged in by those unwilling to ask God for help: drugs, alcohol, promiscuous sex, riches, and the busyness of friends and family. Satisfactions on the horizontal plane can never sustain happiness; it can be sustained only by the vertical vision, embracing God as the centering authority of life's unfolding narrative. Samson affirms the compelling viability of trusting in God without the distracting drama of doubt—when the lavish televangelist empire begins to collapse, Charmaine goes to the National Religious Broadcasters Convention and sings an unadorned rendition of "The Old Rugged Cross."

Sources for Further Study

Buss, Dale. "Lisa Samson: Writing at the Restaurant." *Publishers Weekly* 250, no. 37 (September 15, 2003): S9. A brief profile of the writer that sheds light on her personal life as it relates to her writing.

Higgs, Lisa Curtis. *Bad Girls of the Bible and What We Can Learn from Them.* Colorado Springs, Colo.: WaterBrook Press, 1999. Accessible readings of several morally imperfect biblical women and how they serve to promote the lessons of faith, trust, and God's directing grace. Influential text cited by Samson.

Kennedy, Douglas. "Selling Rapture." *The Guardian,* July 9, 2005, p.4. An essay on trends in Christian literature that mentions *Songbird* in passing but sheds light on the genre.

Samson, Lisa. *The Church Ladies.* Sisters, Oreg.: Multnomah, 2001. Set in the North Carolina, the narrative reflects Samson's interest in Christians handling profound emotional catastrophes. Provides an early look at Charmaine as she is involved with two families struggling to cope with moral crises involving children and child raising.

_____. http://www.lisasamson.com. Web site run by Samson featuring biographical background, inspirational messages, publication updates, reviews, interviews, and contact information.

Joseph Dewey

SONGS OF INNOCENCE AND OF EXPERIENCE

Author: William Blake (1757-1827)
First published: Songs of Innocence, 1789; *Songs of Innocence and of Experience,* 1794
Edition used: Songs of Innocence and of Experience, with an introduction and commentary by Geoffrey Keynes. New York: Orion Press, 1967
Genre: Poetry
Subgenres: Allegory; lyric poetry
Core issues: Good vs. evil; Jesus Christ; problem of evil

Lyrical poetry on the spiritual condition from the perspectives of the very young and of the more experienced.

Overview

William Blake himself used as a subtitle of his *Songs of Innocence and of Experience* (which he illustrated and printed in 1794), "Shewing the Two Contrary States of the Human Soul." Ever since, critics have debated the question of whether Blake intended to present the insoluble paradox of the human encounter with God or simply to cast into verse the contrasting experiences of the innocent and the experienced.

If one considers Blake's own moving experience as a child that he attributed to his innocent awareness of God's presence in the world and if, further, one realizes that the experiences of the very young are hardly worth a sympathetic rendering if they are nullified by the experiences of the older and the wiser, then one must take Blake as a visionary poet who knew God both as a child and as a man, wondering throughout at God's power and his glory, while comforted throughout by God's love.

Blake used his poetry to mark and define the discernible division between innocence and experience. The experience of the young and innocent is experience in the course of the movement toward evil and the struggle against evil, while the experience of the older, which includes the experience of guilt, is lightened by a kind of innocent wonder at God's love and forgiveness. The illuminating fact that Blake switched poems back and forth between innocence and experience—himself confused or struck by the ambiguity of the human encounter with God in God's world—reveals the conviction that whether a song is one of innocence or of experience, it is of the contrary states of the human soul.

For the most part, the *Songs of Innocence* are celebrations of the shepherd in his loving care of the lamb. One realizes through the child's experience that relative to God's care, all persons are lambs; relative to his knowledge, will, and power, all persons are innocent. The child's celebration of God's love is for all persons, both the innocent and the experienced; here, in the mouths of babes, are the truths experience has forgotten. Thus, in his first poem, "The Shepherd," Blake writes that the Shepherd "shall follow his sheep all the day," that "he hears the lambs [sic] innocent call," and that "He is watchful while they are in peace."

Human beings, however, are not simply lambs. In "The Ecchoing Green" (Blake's spelling), the initial image is of the sun's rising, the happy skies, the singing birds, the ringing bells, and the children's sporting on the green. But under the oak the old folk sit and, although laughing at the children's play, remember, surely with some regret, that "Such such were the joys,/ When we all girls and boys,/ In our youth time were seen,/ On the Ecchoing Green." The children become weary, the sun descends, the sports have an end, and there is no more playing "On the darkening Green." The human adventure, then, is from childhood to age, from innocence to experience, from light to darkness, from spontaneous joy to profound sorrow. This human passage, inevitable but both threatening and promising at once, is anticipated in the image of the children's returning to the laps of their parents as the playing ends and the green darkens.

Another kind of cloud, here symbolic not of the course of nature but of the inevitability of confusion and suffering, is thrown over innocence in Blake's poem "The Little Black Boy." The poem begins, "My mother bore me in the southern wild,/ and I am black, but O! my soul is white,/ White as an angel is the English child:/ But I am black as if bereav'd of light." The child's mother tells him that "we are put on earth a little space,/ That we may learn to bear the beams of love" and she promises him that "when our souls have learn'd the heat to bear/ The cloud will vanish . . ." and the child responds that when "I from black and he from white cloud free," he and the English boy will play joyfully around the tent of God: "I'll shade him from the heat till he can bear,/ to lean in joy upon our fathers knee./ and then I'll stand and stroke his silver hair,/ and be like him and he will then love me." Surely there is the experience of suffering in this poem, and there is also the affirmation of faith by which the clouds of human prejudice are dispelled. Innocence anticipates the shock of experience and the recovery through God's love.

Again, injustice intrudes upon the innocent, as portrayed in "The Chimney Sweeper." The young sweep reports that, after his mother died, his father sold him "while yet my tongue,/ Could scarcely cry weep weep weep weep./ So your chimneys I sweep and in soot I sleep." The poem tells of Tom Dacre, whose hair "curl'd like a lambs back" is shaved off so that soot cannot spoil it, dreaming of thousands of chimney sweeps locked in black coffins but liberated by "an Angel who had a bright key." The boys run leaping and laughing across the green plain to wash in the river and "shine in the Sun." They "rise upon clouds, and sport in the wind," and the Angel promises Tom that if he were a good boy he would "have God for his father and never want joy." The dream ends, and Tom rises in the dark to do his work, but he is happy and warmed by the faith that "if all do their duty, they need not fear harm."

In "The Lamb" Blake expresses the mystery of creation as grasped by the simple faith of innocence. Here the light side of creation provides a background for the dark side later to be expressed in "The Tyger." "Little Lamb who made thee/ Dost thou know who made thee?" asks the child—and answers: "Little Lamb I'll tell thee,/ Little Lamb I'll tell thee;/ He is called by thy name,/ for he calls himself a Lamb. . . ." The poem concludes, "I a child and thou a lamb,/ We are called by his name./ Little Lamb

God bless thee,/ Little Lamb God bless thee." He who made the lamb, however, also made the tiger, and Blake's "Tyger," in the *Songs of Experience*, strikes one with the mysterious creative power of God. Experience is helpless in the effort to understand the awesome signs of God's creative will. In the image of the tiger beauty and evil seem to be inextricably interrelated, but the incomprehensibility of divine creation suggests the wonder of paradoxical resolution through the dramatic workings-out of the limitless power that made the tiger possible.

> Tyger Tyger, burning bright,
> In the forests of the night;
> What immortal hand or eye,
> Could frame thy fearful symmetry?

So the poem begins, and it is evident from the beginning that the question is not the metaphysical one of who or what created the tiger; the essential question is *why* the tiger was created. Surely God created all and, hence, the tiger, but "Did he smile his work to see?/ Did he who made the Lamb make thee?" Experience wants an explanation but must be content with the God-revealing mystery of the tiger's fiery brain and heart.

There is something threatening, dark, and even evil in the image of the tiger. The tiger burns bright; the fire burns in the tiger's eyes; the tiger was somehow wrought on an anvil: "What the hand, dare seize the fire?/ . . . What the hammer? what the chain,/ In what furnace was thy brain?/ What the anvil? what dread grasp,/ Dare its deadly terrors clasp?" At the creation of the tiger "the stars threw down their spears/ and water'd heaven with their tears. . . ."

Blake's celebration of God's power through the image of the tiger is perhaps also a celebration of the possibility of love's triumph over evil. The very power that made the tiger also, and perhaps in the same act, made the lamb. The possibility of love is also the possibility of the violation of love; the power that makes evil awful is the same power that makes love awesome. The tiger is a natural beast, but Blake's genius endows the tiger with the aura of the supernatural and with all the ambiguity of the human being so created as to be capable of either destructive or purifying fire.

When the tiger appears in "Night," from *Songs of Innocence*, it appears in its natural condition, along with wolves, as howling for sheep as prey. The poem presents an image of protecting angels. As night comes, the angels visit and bless the birds and beasts and help them to sleep, but they do not stop the wolves and tigers from their prey. Despite the effort of the angels, the beasts may "rush dreadful," but the promise of the poem is that the angels will receive each spirit and escort it to the new world of eternal love, a world in which the lion (also, in the natural world, a beast of prey) will lie down with the lamb and, under the influence of divine love, guard the fold. What is true of the lion, one may presume to be true of the tiger: The possibility of love is inherent even in the dreadful.

Just as paradoxical imagery is used in both the *Songs of Innocence* and the *Songs of*

Experience to present and resolve what has been called the problem of evil, so such imagery is used to present and resolve the problem of sexual love, an aspect of the problem of evil that stems from the power of human freedom. In the *Songs of Innocence* a deceptively simple poem, "The Blossom," portrays sexual intercourse in a telling, although ambiguous, way: "Merry Merry Sparrow/ Under leaves so green/ A happy Blossom/ Sees you swift as arrow/ Seek your cradle narrow/ Near my Bosom." The next stanza, which completes the poem, is addressed to "Pretty Pretty Robin," and here the happy blossom "Hears you sobbing sobbing. . . ." Whether the "sobbing sobbing" is interpreted as a sadness evinced, a kind of joy, or an act, the element of something negative is introduced. When one moves to the *Songs of Experience*, whatever is or can be negative in sexual love is acknowledged and little of the positive remains, as in "The Sick Rose":

> O Rose thou art sick.
> The invisible worm,
> That flies in the night
> In the howling storm:
> Has found out thy bed
> Of crimson joy:
> And his dark secret love
> Does thy life destroy.

Throughout his poems Blake recognizes the positive, light, creative aspects of nature and of the human being—and also the negative, dark, and destructive aspects. The innocent respond to and delight in the brighter side; the experienced know, partly through self-knowledge, the darker—the possibility of negating the positive values made possible by the divine. This recognition, however, has its positive aspect: Through the knowledge of humanity's misuse of power, freedom, and one another, there is also knowledge, through experience, of how consciously to return to the kind of world the innocent see but cannot realize.

Christian Themes

In the *Songs of Innocence*, Blake explores how the very young in their innocence, even when suffering, recognize, accept, and delight in the presence of God. These innocents know the joys of love and sympathy, both human and divine. In contrast, the older, more experienced witnesses to God's presence and power recognize and to some degree exhibit human selfishness and know evil as the darkness of the soul in alienation from God. Like the innocent, however, experienced souls are affected by God's power and will, and they glory in the drama of life under God.

Sources for Further Study

Bentley, G. E., Jr., and Martin K. Nurmi. *A Blake Bibliography: Annotated Lists of Works, Studies, and Blakeana*. Minneapolis: University of Minnesota Press, 1964.

A definitive bibliography of writings by and about Blake. Includes a helpful introductory essay on the history of Blake scholarship.

Gillham, D. G. *Blake's Contrary States: The "Songs of Innocence and of Experience" as Dramatic Poems*. Cambridge, England: Cambridge University Press, 1966. A perceptive analysis of Blake's *Songs* in defense of the thesis that Blake dramatically expressed the contrasting attitudes of self-interest and sympathetic concern.

Hirsch, E. D., Jr. *Innocence and Experience: An Introduction to Blake*. 2d ed. Chicago: University of Chicago Press, 1975. Analyzes *Songs of Innocence and of Experience* based on perceived changes in Blake's philosophical and religious ideas while he wrote them.

Muggeridge, Malcolm. *A Third Testament: A Modern Pilgrim Explores the Spiritual Wanderings of Augustine, Blake, Pascal, Tolstoy, Bonhoeffer, Kierkegaard, and Dostoevsky*. Farmington, Pa.: Plough, 2002. Addresses the spiritual life of Blake in relationship to others.

Paley, Morton D., ed. *Twentieth Century Interpretations of "Songs of Innocence and of Experience."* Englewood Cliffs, N.J.: Prentice-Hall, 1969. A brilliant collection of critical essays by such writers as S. Foster Damon, Northrop Frye, Joseph H. Wicksteed, and Mark Schorer. The essays appear under the headings "Interpretations" and "View Points."

Phillips, Michael. *William Blake: The Creation of the "Songs," from Manuscript to Illuminated Printing*. Princeton, N.J.: Princeton University Press, 2000. A scholarly presentation of the *Songs of Innocence and of Experience*. Gorgeously illustrated, with transcriptions of the text and subsequent revisions.

Ian P. McGreal

SOON
The Beginning of the End

Author: Jerry B. Jenkins (1949-)
First published: Wheaton, Ill.: Tyndale House, 2003
Genre: Novel
Subgenres: Apocalyptic fiction; evangelical fiction
Core issues: Apocalypse; awakening; connectedness; conversion; faith; persecution

In the year 2045, religion has been abolished, and believers are strenuously prosecuted as terrorists by the National Peace Organization, of which Paul Stepola is a member. Blinded during an investigation of a pillar of fire but then miraculously healed, Paul is converted and becomes a double agent, warning the Christian underground of impending government raids. Miracles increase as the end-times arrive, and Paul has a change of heart and recommits to his marriage.

> *Principal characters*
> *Paul Stepola*, expert on religions and National Peace Organization investigator
> *Jae Stepola*, Paul's increasingly suspicious and emotionally distant wife
> *Ranold Decenti*, Paul's father-in-law, a retired army general
> *Stuart "Straight" Rathe*, a hospital volunteer and clandestine Christian
> *Angela*, a young widow and daughter of a Christian martyr admired by Paul
> *Bia Balaam*, the fanatical head of the antiterrorist task force

Overview

Soon: The Beginning of the End by Jerry B. Jenkins, coauthor of the *Left Behind* series (1995-2007) with Tim LaHaye, has a similar theme to the popular series, which deals with the end-times. In Jenkins's solo work, warring religious factions have caused World War III, which has brought devastating destruction to nations around the globe and has given birth to a world government dedicated to eradicating all religions. Thirty-six years after the war, Dr. Paul Stepola, expert on religions and investigator for the National Peace Organization (NPO), is cleaning out the effects of his deceased mother. He discovers a letter written to him by his long-dead father. The letter testifies of Christ and urges Paul to become a man of God. Horrified, Paul volunteers for the Zealot Underground, a task force formed to wipe out lingering religious believers. He gets an assignment to investigate an elderly widow in San Francisco who is rumored to be holding secret religious meetings.

In San Francisco, Paul and a team of NPO SEALs storm a building where people are praying and reading the Bible. They wipe out all the inhabitants, but a sudden earthquake kills everyone on the team except Paul. Paul's next assignment is to investigate a pillar of fire above a burning oil well in the former state of Texas. Once there, he uses Christian code words he heard in San Francisco to expose a Christian roughneck, who is then bludgeoned to death. Paul's interrogations are interrupted by another blazing gusher, and Paul is burnt and airlifted to a Chicago hospital, where he is told he will be permanently blind.

While recovering, Paul is angry at the world and at his wife, who decides to leave him. He is persistently visited by a black volunteer, Stuart "Straight" Rathe, whose wife and children were killed in a car wreck. Straight teaches Paul to play chess. Paul also spends time listening to New Testament tapes to find clues to help him unearth secret Christians.

Straight escorts Paul to Washington, D.C., to receive an award for bravery. There, Paul meets Bia Balaam, a ruthless woman who has replaced him on the task force. He also meets an attractive widow, Angela, who works at the Library of Congress and whom he asks to check out his father's letter to see if it is genuine or a government plant. There are strange happenings afoot; all the cherry trees along the Potomac River instantly shrivel. During the stormy flight back to Chicago, Paul is terrified, realizes he is a sinner, and says "Help me, God." The airplane is struck by lightning, and Paul's sight is suddenly restored.

Thinking about the New Testament, Paul becomes a believer and discovers that Straight is one, too. Straight meets with the leadership of the Christian underground, housed in a 1,400-acre former salt mine, and proposes they use Paul as an informant on government persecution. Paul accepts the proposal and decides to become a double agent. Assigned to investigate a "cursed" vault in a New York City brokerage, Paul opens the vault and discovers that a tycoon inside has turned to silver. The tycoon's brother jumps to his death but miraculously survives the fall, and Paul converts him.

Paul meets with the Christian underground and learns of their plans to clandestinely distribute Christian literature worldwide so that it will be available postrapture. His boss next sends him to Las Vegas to apprehend Jonah, a drug-and-sex cult leader. There he finds Angela, who is working to convert prostitutes. Jonah kidnaps Angela, but Paul apprehends him and his henchmen. Although Angela is attracted to Paul, he tells her he is married.

Paul's next assignment from Balaam is to go to Los Angeles, along with his father-in-law, Ranold, to crack down on the distribution of Christian literature. There Paul makes contact with "Specs" Quinn, an underground Christian hacker. However, shortly after their meeting, Quinn is exterminated by Ranold's group, as are two hundred other Christians. The task force tells the press that the unresisting victims are heavily armed zealot terrorists. Paul contacts a group of Christians who have decided to do something visible before they are all killed, concluding that God's army of angels will be on their side. They send up a drone with religious leaflets, but its controller is captured by the NPO army.

Paul gets the idea to have all Christians pray together for a miracle to dry up the Los Angeles water supply. This message is sent out over the Internet. Meanwhile, Paul's wife, Jae, flies to Los Angeles to tell Paul she wants to get back together. Then Ranold discovers Paul with the Christians and suspends him from the task force.

During an opulent banquet, the governmental oppressors suddenly notice that the water in the fountains, pools, and in their glasses has evaporated. There is not a drop left in Los Angeles. It is the beginning of the end. Underground believers will now arise with confidence and strength, boldly proclaiming the message of faith: The powers that be will stop killing the people of God, or else they will all wither like the grass and die.

Christian Themes

Although denominations are not mentioned in *Soon*, the novel expresses the beliefs of those groups who anticipate the Second Coming of Christ and the Apocalypse as discussed in the New Testament book of Revelation. By linking the novel's scenario to early twenty-first century world developments such as militant religious fanaticism, heightened antiterrorist measures, and what is portrayed as the determination to eliminate religion from the government, Jenkins heightens the reader's sense that a climate of religious persecution could indeed emerge in the United States. That such a situation might then plausibly—and swiftly—bring about the wrathful displays of the end-times is the message of *Soon*.

Another purpose of *Soon* is to point out parallels between the world of the New Testament and that of today. Paul Stepola's educational background and governmental position, as well as his name, remind readers of Paul the Apostle even before the investigator turns from persecution to discipleship. In the novel, there are seven United States, corresponding with the seven New Testament churches in Asia. For example, New York City is Ephesus, the financial port, where Paul saves Demetrius the stockbroker after a suicidal leap, just as the apostle Paul revived a man who fell from a window in Troas.

Jenkins presents Paul's professional world of rampant materialism, hedonism, and greed in contrast to the unselfish harmony of the Christian believers forced underground. Callous violence, lying, and unchecked sensuousness are shown in the lives of the government workers who, stripped of religious influence, are devoid of real love or humanity. Jenkins suggests that the solution to Paul's unhappy marriage, eroded by mistrust and selfishness, is not divorce or the replacement of his wife with a new, attractively congenial substitute. Rather, he says that Christian partners will commit to trying to make the other happy in an atmosphere of faith and trust. Through *Soon*, he shows that there can be no real humanity in a society wholly separated from God, and no ultimate survival without faith.

Sources for Further Study

Butler, Tamara. Review of *Soon*. *Library Journal* 128, no. 18 (November, 2003): 64.
    Very brief review of the novel as a fast-paced thriller likely to please fans.

Gates, David. "The Pop Prophets." *Newsweek* 143, no. 21 (May 24, 2004): 45-50. An article on Tim LaHaye and Jenkins's successful literary partnership combining religion with science fiction, with biographical information on Jenkins.

Lobdell, William. "Writer Alters Landscape of Christian Fiction: A Coauthor of Bestsellers Hopes to Reach an Even Wider Audience with His First Solo Effort." *Los Angeles Times*, October 11, 2003, p. B2. A profile of the coauthor of the *Left Behind* series that examines his beliefs and his motivations for writing *Soon*.

Lyons, Gene. "The Apocalypse Will Be Televised." *Harper's Magazine* 309, no. 1854 (November, 2004): 85-90. A critical, largely unfavorable discussion of the success of the *Left Behind* series of thrillers by Jenkins and LaHaye. Lyons objects to depicting the end-times as an action/adventure melodrama.

Thorn, Patti. "*Left Behind* Author Doesn't Stray Far." Review of *Soon*. *Rocky Mountain News*, August 29, 2003, p. 28D. Review of *Soon* that likens the work to the story in the *Left Behind* series. Brief discussion of author.

Sally B. Palmer

THE SOUL OF CHRISTIANITY
Restoring the Great Tradition

Author: Huston Smith (1919-   )
First published: San Francisco: HarperSanFrancisco, 2005
Genre: Nonfiction
Subgenres: Church history; didactic treatise
Core issues: Church; connectedness; prayer; redemption; religion

Smith argues that the loss of religion that accompanies the scientific worldview need not occur, as it is based on a mistaken premise. Science and religion deal with different realms or levels of reality and use different technical language to do so. The Christian worldview holds that there is an infinite world that encompasses the finite. The infinite shines through the finite, most perfectly in the figure of Jesus Christ, whose life, death, and resurrection bring the transcendent power called God fully into human history. This power has been mediated through the Disciples, then through the Church.

Overview

In *The Soul of Christianity*, Huston Smith, a renowned scholar of world religions, attempts to explain and defend Christianity against its secular detractors in the modern world. Although he uses symbols and analogies drawn from sources as diverse as quantum mechanics and Muscle Beach body builders, his outlook is basically that of traditional, even "establishment" Christianity, referencing the early church fathers, Church councils, and the classical tradition of Christianity's first millennium as the "gold standard" for Christian belief. Smith is, however, scrupulously fair. He readily admits that others' interpretations may differ from his and that this does not invalidate either their positions or his own. While speaking "from the inside" as a practicing Christian, he also brings the perspective of a scholar who honors the insights into the divine force held by the other great religions.

Smith asserts that the scientific revolution has been a disaster for Western culture because it has enshrined as the dominant worldview a scientific outlook, one that holds that only those things that can be seen or measured, or worked out based on observation or measurement, are real. Proof of this outlook's pernicious effects is seen in the barbaric events of the twentieth century, which far exceed the worst that happened in prior centuries, Smith argues, and even technology, the vaunted offspring of science, has removed us from the natural world and led to the poisoning of it. The things that give most people's life meaning—their thoughts and feelings, and above all, their religious faith—are devalued because of their lack of fit with the scientific belief system. That way is madness, Smith feels.

Fortunately, there is a cure for our plight, according to Smith. Once we realize what went wrong, we are free to seek what is missing. The fatal mistake, he says, is that scientism confuses the absence of evidence with evidence of absence. Because the scientific method cannot produce evidence of a divine order does not prove its nonexistence. To explore the higher level of truth that religion is concerned with, however, requires some different tools. Science and religion work with different realms, and each uses a specific technical language. Science's primary technical language is mathematics. Religion's technical language is symbol. Only symbols can negotiate the paradoxes that religion poses in exploring the multiple levels of reality.

With these preliminary guidelines, Smith takes up the task of introducing Christianity to the reader. *The Soul of Christianity* consists of three main sections: "The Christian Worldview," "The Christian Story," and "The Three Main Branches of Christianity Today."

"The Christian Worldview" lays out the structure of Christian thought. As it deals with fairly abstract concepts, many anecdotes, images, and analogies are used to clarify the ideas it discusses. One of the first concepts presented is that the world is infinite. This infinity encompasses the finite. There is a hierarchy in the finite world, and humans stand midway in it. The universe consists of nested systems, which lead into ever deeper levels of knowledge. Multiplicity increases as the infinite unrolls "downward," whereas "Everything that rises must converge,"—that is, distinctions disappear in the divine oneness, where absolute perfection is found. Absolute perfection, though, brings up the sidelight problem of evil. Smith disposes of it with the traditional Christian explanation of free will.

Smith states that God is not unilocal—contrary to logic, the divine can be both "out there" and within. The infinite is essentially opaque to our efforts to know it. Revelation is multiple, not confined to one event or religion, but reports, even of revelations, have to be interpreted, and the literal is the lowest and least reliable level of interpretation. Symbolism is the key to unlocking revelation. At best, however, it gives us only partial glimpses of a luminous universe.

Smith notes that the worldview that he has described is not exclusively Christian. It is the worldview of all revealed religions, an underlying structure that they share. "The Christian Story" unrolls upon the framework of this structure.

Although "The Christian Story" is the book's longest section, it contains the smallest amount of material unfamiliar to the average Christian. There is a brief account of Jesus' life and message. Smith places Jesus within the Jewish tradition of charismatic healers inspired by the Spirit and summarizes his ministry as "He went about doing good." He presents some discussion of Jesus' preaching and language, which he characterizes as "gigantic," casting them in such terms to cut through his listeners' cultural conditioning.

Smith describes the events of Holy Week, the Crucifixion, Resurrection, Ascension, and Pentecost. The account of post-Pentecost events summarizes Church history from the first disciples' spread across the Mediterranean world through the Council of Nicaea in 325 C.E. At this point, with Christianity officially united, Smith turns to capsule discussions of its doctrines: the Incarnation, the atonement, the Trinity, Apocalypse, life everlasting and its associated concepts, and, somewhat unexpectedly, the virgin birth. Smith does not so much put his own spin on these doctrines but rather tries to clarify them by the use of many parables and metaphors. The Apocalypse, for example, is neither a step-by-step prophecy of the world's end nor the wish-fulfillment fantasy of oppressed first century Christians. Rather, it was God's effort to stop and reverse humanity's headlong rush toward doom. Smith implies that the effort failed, and God may have decided to close history down—but he did not. Because of his love, the world goes on, with humans getting intimations of the divine power and goodness that is waiting for them at the end of history.

The final section, on the three major divisions of the faith, profiles two concepts that are the defining traits of each branch. For Roman Catholicism, the Church's teaching authority and the sacramental life of the Church function as its mainspring. Eastern Orthodoxy is defined by its corporate view of salvation: The Church as an entity is charged with sanctifying the whole world. The other pillar of Eastern Orthodoxy is the importance it gives to mysticism. On Protestantism, Smith quotes Martin Luther's "everyone must do his own believing" to explicate its key doctrine of justification by faith. Its awareness that all humans are fallible accounts for "the Protestant principle": a wariness of idolatry, of lifting anything, even a doctrine or the Bible, to the status of unquestioned truth.

Christian Themes

As a work aiming to establish the relevance of Christianity to the modern reader, *The Soul of Christianity* pays much attention to imagery. While frequently cautioning that spatial, gender-based, and similar terms do not really apply to the divine realm, the author continues to uses them fairly consistently. The result is a strong, if unintended, theme of the inadequacy of words to describe God.

In contrast, the book presents the Christian story as the way the infinite breaks through such limitations and makes itself known in the world. Jesus Christ, a man without ego, was completely open to God and God's love. His story reveals the divine nature in a way that no mere words or definitions can.

The question of whether transcendent truth or salvation can be found outside Christianity is one on which Christians today differ greatly. Even the earlier, united Christian Church had varying opinions about this, Smith says, and then points out that the Vatican makes a distinction between the church visible and the church invisible. As a student of world religions, he finds the same underlying structure and sense of the divine infusing all religions. However, the author is not willing to go beyond this in this work, which makes a persuasive case for Christianity.

Sources for Further Study

Bryan, G. McLeod. *Voices in the Wilderness: Twentieth Century Prophets Speak to the New Millennium*. Macon, Ga.: Mercer University Press, 1999. Autobiographical reflections by a religious scholar on five prophetic voices of the twentieth century: Clarence Jordan, founder of the interracial Koinonia farm in Americus, Georgia; civil rights leader Martin Luther King, Jr.; C. F. Beyers Naude, Afrikaner pastor who battled apartheid; Jaroslav Stolar, Christian leader in Communist Czechoslovakia; and Smith. Sheds light on Smith's thoughts about Christianity.

Griffin, David Ray, and Huston Smith. *Primorial Truth and Postmodern Theology.* Albany: State University of New York Press, 1989. This debate between Griffin, an exponent of process theology, and Smith, a leader perennialist, reveals their differing views of Christianity.

Holst, Wayne A. "A Devoted Christian." Review of *The Soul of Christianity. The Gazette*, May 6, 2005, p. G5. A sympathetic review of Smith's work. Notes that the author is known for his book *The World's Religions* (1958) and his television program.

Johnson, Luke Timothy. Review of *The Soul of Christianity. First Things* 163, no. 55 (May, 2006): 55-57. Reviewer sums up Smith's statements and beliefs.

Smith, Huston. *Forgotten Truth: The Common Vision of the World's Religions.* 1972. Reprint. San Francisco: HarperSanFrancisco, 1992. A powerful, personal statement that presents in depth Smith's theory of a common framework shared by most religions.

Emily Alward

THE SOULS OF BLACK FOLK

Author: W. E. B. Du Bois (1868-1963)
First published: 1903
Edition used: The Illustrated Souls of Black Folk, edited and annotated by Eugene Provenzo, Jr. Boulder, Colo.: Paradigm, 2005
Genre: Nonfiction
Subgenres: Autobiography; critical analysis; essays; history
Core issues: African Americans; faith; freedom and free will; pastoral role; racism; reconciliation; soul

Du Bois addresses black spirituality and meditates on the "Veil" that separates African Americans from European Americans and on the "deeper recesses" of black souls. He discusses black spirituality and religion and their expression through folk or spiritual music. For Du Bois, the "sorrow songs," or spirituals, are capable of transforming people because the songs emotionally transcend the sorrow that inspired them. Their purpose may be religious exaltation, but they are also a medium for expressing a desire for transcendence and enfranchisement.

Overview

W. E. B. Du Bois's classic *The Souls of Black Folk* is multidimensional text that resists classification because it contains a history of post-Civil War race relations, sociological and economical analyses, a discussion of black education, a comparative study of European American and African American cultures, a short story about a character named John Jones, and a commentary on the transformative power of "sorrow songs," or Negro spirituals, which for Du Bois are expressions of soul at the heart of African American culture. Du Bois is highly esteemed for his great sociological and historical texts, beginning with *The Suppression of the African Slave-Trade to the United States, 1638-1870* (1896); however, he also wrote poetry, five novels, an autobiography, and several volumes of essays. Of all of the works in Du Bois's oeuvre, *The Souls of Black Folk* has reached the widest audience.

Critical analyses of *The Souls of Black Folk* usually emphasize the most famous chapter, "Of Mr. Booker T. Washington and Others," to discuss Du Bois's critique of Booker T. Washington's conciliatory policies. Often the work is discussed as a sociological analysis of the problem of the color line or the line between "American" and "Negro" cultures. However, this discussion will emphasize how Du Bois presents the very personal story of his experiences on both sides of the "Veil" between himself and European Americans while deploying diverse literary techniques—rhetorical tropes, confession, autobiography, allegory, allusion, imagery, and musical motifs—to convey a spiritual and racial understanding of folk culture. As Du Bois states in "The Forethought," his text addresses black spirituality and meditates on "the two worlds within and without the Veil" and on the "deeper recesses" of black souls. Du Bois discusses black spirituality and religion and the expression of the African American soul, especially through folk or spiritual music. It is important to note, however, that Du Bois, a humanist, comments on black churches and religious leadership only briefly in *The Souls of Black Folk* and that the Marxist turn in his later works reveals a growing indifference to black religion and religious discourses.

In the first chapter, "Of Our Spiritual Strivings," Du Bois begins with an autobiographical account of his experience of the Veil as a young student in New England. He describes the Veil that exists between himself and his fellow students, who were white, saying he "held all beyond [the Veil] in common contempt, and lived above it in a region of blue sky and great wandering shadows." This concept of transcendence develops as Du Bois's intellect grows and he reflects on his own inner, psychic life and his race. Du Bois developed the concept of double-consciousness to explain the "twoness" of African American striving. He asserts that African Americans are born with a Veil that does not afford them their true self-consciousness. They can see themselves only "through the revelation of the other [white] world," which results in what Du Bois calls a "twoness," or unreconciled strivings both to be black and to be an American. Ultimately, Du Bois wants to reconcile this double-consciousness so that an African American can be "both a Negro and an American" and a "co-worker in the Kingdom of culture." This desire emphasizes the Platonic ideals of truth, beauty, and the good over materialism in the New South, which was industrializing. Du Bois felt that higher education was central for spiritual reconciliation and that enfranchisement for African Americans could be achieved if the Talented Tenth, the black intellectual elite, would enlighten the black masses while celebrating and producing African American scholarship and art.

Christian Themes

Du Bois writes very little about black religious life although he asks numerous questions that lead him to ponder the development of black religion and the black church as it grew out of pagan African rituals and voodoo. He does not add to the existing arguments and scholarship of his time but does assert that Negro spirituals were created in America but can be traced back to African forests. This points to an African home for these songs and a diaspora but does not necessarily Africanize black American culture. Similarly, he likens the black preacher to the African priest or medicine man, tracing black religion back to pagan belief systems in Africa.

Like the black preachers he admires in his chapters "Of the Faith of Our Fathers" and "Of Alexander Crummell," Du Bois has a complex status as a leader. His identification with the preacher as well as the priest or medicine man allows him to see himself as a physician and conjurer of African culture and as an artist or bardic priest capable of preaching a social gospel and expressing the sentiments of an oppressed and disenfranchised people. Du Bois felt the role of the black preacher was to facilitate a spiritual rebirth and reconciliation that would unite African Americans while helping them achieve self-assertion. He described the black preacher as "a leader, a politician, and orator, a 'boss,' an intriguer, an idealist."

Du Bois describes the segregated South as "the Valley of the Shadow of Death, where all that makes life worth living—Liberty, Justice, and Right—is marked 'For White People Only.'" While biblical allusions and imagery are scattered throughout *The Souls of Black Folk*, Du Bois most effectively deploys the traditional black identification with the children of Israel and their search for a promised land in his description of an effort to articulate the desire for freedom and spiritual reconciliation, which would allow blacks to transcend the Veil through sacrifice and intellectual pursuits rather than through passive submission to white supremacy or physical death. Ultimately, he feels that achieving transcendence requires work and effort that will produce, protect, and value black culture and art.

Grounding his notion of black folk culture in the sorrow songs forces Du Bois to consider black spirituality and belief systems as he appropriates religious texts, figures, and music. One might argue, as Theophus Smith does in *Conjuring Culture: Biblical Formations of Black America* (1994), that Du Bois stepped within the Veil of black America and used biblical allusions and imagery to conjure African culture in *The Souls of Black Folk*. A bar of music from a spiritual introduces each chapter in *The Souls of Black Folk* and celebrates the voices of the slaves, the folk who founded black American culture. Most critics agree that Du Bois meant for black culture to gain recognition through the appreciation of the "sorrow songs," but he also used the spirituals as epigraphs to place black music and art at the heart of black history. For Du Bois, the sorrow songs are transformative because they are capable of emotionally transcending the very sorrow that inspired them. Their mood and purpose may be religious exaltation, but they are also a medium for expressing a desire for transcendence and enfranchisement. The songs sing of freedom in this world as well as the next as they consciously hold onto sorrow and transcend it by transforming the negative.

Sources for Further Study
Andrews, William. "The Politics of African-American Ministerial Autobiography from Reconstruction to the 1920's." In *African-American Christianity: Essays in History*, edited by Paul E. Johnson. Los Angeles: University of California Press, 1994. Andrews discusses Du Bois's portrait of the black preacher in *The Souls of Black Folk*.
Gates, Henry Louis, Jr., and Terri Hume Oliver, eds. *The Souls of Black Folk: Authoritative Text, Contexts, Criticism*. New York: W. W. Norton, 1999. This Norton critical edition includes photographs, contemporary essays, a chronology of Du Bois's life, and historical texts and contexts for Du Bois's book.
Lewis, David Levering, ed. *W. E. B. Du Bois: A Reader*. New York: Henry Holt, 1995. This reader contains a diverse collection of Du Bois's work and situates some of the essays from *The Souls of Black Folk* within Du Bois's oeuvre.
Smith, Theophus. *Conjuring Culture: Biblical Formations of Black America*. New York: Oxford University Press, 1994. In the chapter titled "Spirituals," Smith discusses Du Bois as a "conjurational performer" as he explores conjure as a defining spirituality in black culture.

Sundquist, Eric. *To Wake the Nations: Race in the Making of American Literature.* Cambridge, Mass.: Harvard University Press, 1993. Part 3 of Sundquist's text, "W. E. B. Du Bois: African America and the Kingdom of Culture," contains a thorough discussion of Du Bois's use of the sorrow songs in *The Souls of Black Folk.*

Trisha M. Brady

THE SOURCE OF HUMAN GOOD

Author: Henry Nelson Wieman (1884-1975)
First published: 1946
Edition used: The Source of Human Good. Carbondale: Southern Illinois University Press, 1964
Genre: Nonfiction
Subgenres: Critical analysis; theology
Core issues: Freedom and free will; God; good vs. evil; knowledge; nature; reason

During the early twentieth century, Wieman argued that religion and science must be directed toward the service of what actually operates in human life, transforming and saving humanity from self-destructive propensities and leading people to the best that human life can attain. In this work, he describes this reality (God) as the creative event, or as creativity at work in the universe, and emphasizes that it alone accounts for the possibilities of new meanings and new values in human existence.

Overview

The Source of Human Good is one of Henry Nelson Wieman's most important works, in which he offers a conception of God as creative value within the context of human interactions and purposeful living. In developing his argument, Wieman introduces a key phrase, "the creative event," which connotes creativity as operating in human life and giving it qualitative meaning. For Wieman, creativity is not merely identified with the common usages often associated with it, such as solely innovative behavior on the part of individuals or achievements produced by artistic persons (although these would be included as instances of it). Rather, God *is* creativity, in the sense that God is the character, structure, or form that enables the events of human life to be creative. "The creative event" is a complex term describing a process of how the many discordant parts of our lives are reorganized into a more inclusive whole.

Wieman explains that the creative event, which results in creative good, is a concrete reality embracing four unified but distinct subevents. Briefly stated, they are

(1) the emerging awareness of qualitative meaning through communication
(2) the integration of these new meanings with those previously acquired
(3) the expanding of quality in the appreciable world and
(4) the widening and deepening of community.

The first event is the primary context from which the other three emerge. For Wieman, a stream of experience first comes to us as qualitative immediacy and then becomes cognized into knowledge relations. Qualitative meaning occurs when every organism reacts so as to break the passage of existence into units or intervals called "events" and to relate these to one another. When a single organism is able to acquire the qualitative meanings developed by other organisms and add them to its own, the human mind and its appreciable world are transformed. Wieman states that events include within their structures possibilities for developing in process. Since qualities, or values, are the things of which events are made, they are the ontological reality of an event; every event accessible to human experience is a quality or complex of qualities. Also, every event is an instance of energy. Furthermore, Wieman asserts that a conjunction is a new or more complex event made up of a strand of events. When a conjunction occurs in such a way that the qualities of the event included in the conjunction fulfill their possibilities to a greater degree, there is an increase of meaning, or qualitative meaning.

The fundamental religious significance of Wieman's philosophy of creativity emerges at this point. Since events cannot foresee the developments possible to them and the universe cannot determine whether there will be an increase or decrease of value, there must be some determining factor responsible for integrating the values of the individual events. This one process is God, or the process of progressive integration of value within the universe. Accordingly, God reveals Godself to humans in these events in such a way that we can understand and learn how to bring forth conditions that allow for an increase of value. As the creative event, God is the highest value. Creativity in humans is something produced in us as a consequence of the prior workings of the creative event. For Wieman, God is part of the cosmic whole but is not totally identified with the universe. Also, in this naturalistic framework, limitations are placed upon God by the present realities at hand. Although God can work only with what is present, Wieman insists that creative good may never be destroyed.

Christian Themes

Wieman's empirical orientation and naturalistic metaphysics compel him to refute the transcendental conceptions of the divine celebrated within the dominant Jewish and Christian theological traditions. Dismissing a supernatural God that is immaterial and residing beyond history, Wieman conceives the creative event as materially based, where matter is meant as a form of energy that determines the very structure of time and space, together with all else that exists or is possible. As a natural process, God is the continuous creator of ideals, aspiration, and value, the supreme manifestation of freedom, and the source and sustainer of human freedom. As creativity, the creative event underlies all others in the sense of being a changeless structure of felt quality and knowable order, and it is necessarily prior to every other form of experience.

According to Wieman, the creative event is always and absolutely good in the sense of creating value and must necessarily destroy values that have become too ossified in order to achieve the best possibility for new values under prevailing conditions. Wieman further suggests that sin is any resistance to creativity for which humans are responsible, or the domination of created good over creative power. As long as humans are preoccupied with seeking only the material goods of life, then creative good cannot accumulate and enrich human lives. Although his view of God as creativity does not totally rid itself of the residue of philosophic idealism, Wieman's pragmatism and scientific emphasis tend to avoid much of the subtle rationalism that characterizes much Christian process cosmology. As such, his empirical theology also confounds both traditional Western metaphysical systems and the nihilistic trends regarding the ethics of much aesthetic postmodernism that have recently come under attack.

Wieman's empirical leanings lead him away from traditional notions of Christian revelation. For him, the creative event is unknowable aside from the way it functions in relation to other events. Although human need forms the basis from which this function is delineated, the stress is on the remarkable creativity that is both discernible and elusive to reasoning individuals. With the use of such faculties as observation, rational analysis, and intuition, individuals can gain knowledge of this divine reality. Wieman also offers a unique conception of Christian faith, which he describes as a creative and liberating commitment to the creative event (or quality apprehended by way of feeling). This deeper commitment is, again, to the actuality, not merely to ideas about it. This faith commitment entails conformity of lifestyle and behavior to the overall purpose of the creative event: the increase of human freedom individually and collectively accompanied by growth of creative community.

Moreover, Wieman expresses soteriological concerns in this work. Emphasizing a primordial interrelatedness among all organisms, he suggests that transformation of individuals occurs in interactions with others. At the level most important for human living, the creative event always operates between persons. Hence, the isolated person can never experience God, or so it appears. Arguing that a healthy encounter with the other helps to promote the possibility of creative community, Wieman believes that humans are responsible for opening themselves to creative interchange as the source of good. When we do so, we may be "saved" from illusions of isolation and separation from others.

This vision of interrelatedness, organic growth, and mutual support and meaning for all who participate in the processes of creativity introduces an ethical component to Wieman's thought. Creative interchange helps provide the necessary structures for authentic communities of solidarity, care, and justice. With his emphasis on the structure of the creative event, Wieman's empirical theology foreshadows important poststructuralist insights regarding the open-endedness of our practices and struggles and the fact that we live in worlds of paradox and uncertainty. His religious naturalism rejects both traditional Christianity's triumphalism and modernism's love affair with guaranteed progress.

Sources for Further Study

Bretall, Robert W., ed. *The Empirical Theology of Henry Nelson Wieman.* New York: Macmillan, 1963. This collection of essays clarifies some of the basic themes in Wieman's unique process theology. Most of the contributors assess whether or not Wieman's empirical framework can provide an adequate conceptual base for explicating the understanding of existence implicit in Christian faith. Included is an autobiographical essay by Wieman, outlining the single problem on which his intellectual life was focused and describing significant influences that shaped his thought.

Shaw, Marvin C. *Nature's Grace: Essays on H. N. Wieman's Finite Theism.* New York: P. Lang, 1995. These essays considers Wieman as the leading member of the group of religious naturalists associated with the University of Chicago who founded the school of "naturalistic theism," the idea that the divine is an immanent and finite creativity at work in an evolving universe.

Southworth, Bruce. *At Home in Creativity: The Naturalistic Theology of Henry Nelson Wieman.* Boston: Skinner House, 1995. An introduction to Wieman for a new generation, covering Wieman's philosophical and theological ideas and placing them in the context of feminist and liberation theologies. Bibliography, index.

Wieman, Henry Nelson. *The Intellectual Foundations of Faith.* New York: Philosophical Library, 1961. Wieman reasserts his argument for a rational foundation of faith based on an empirical view of the nature of God, which alone can guide humans toward purposeful, fulfilling living. He provides a critique of various contemporary answers to the question, What can save humanity from its self-destructive propensities?

_____. *Man's Ultimate Commitment.* Carbondale: Southern Illinois University Press, 1958. Believing that individuals can be transformed into great good or great evil, Wieman emphasizes that there must be something that underlies such transformation, requiring human cooperation.

Carol Wayne White

THE SPARROW

Author: Mary Doria Russell (1950-   )
First published: New York: Villard Books, 1996
Genre: Novel
Subgenre: Science fiction
Core issues: Catholics and Catholicism; clerical life; conscience; faith; good vs. evil; problem of evil; suffering

In The Sparrow, *an expedition from Earth to Rakhat goes terribly wrong, apparently because of misunderstandings between the human space travelers and the sentient beings who live on the planet. Russell uses the science fiction genre to explore two questions important to Christianity: why horrific things happen to good, well-meaning, conscience-driven people and what the occurrence of these bad things tells us about the existence of God and the nature of deity.*

> *Principal characters*
> *Emilio Sandoz*, a Jesuit, the sole survivor of a mission to the planet Rakhat
> *Sofia Mendes* and *Jimmy Quinn*, scientists on the mission
> *Anne Edwards* and
> *George Edwards*, husband-and-wife team of scientists on the mission
> *D. W. Yarborough*, the Jesuit leader of the mission to Rakhat
> *Marc Robichaux*, a Jesuit crewmember
> *Vincenzo Giuliani*, the father general of the Society of Jesus
> *John Candotti*, Giuliani's secretary
> *Johannes Voelker*,
> *Edward Behr*, and
> *Felipe Reyes*, Jesuits investigating the aftermath of the mission to Rakhat
> *Askama*, a young Runa, one of Rakhat's sentient races
> *Supaari VaGayjur*, a wealthy merchant, a Jana'ata, the planet's other sentient species
> *Hlavin Kitheri*, a nobleman-poet of the Jana'ata

Overview

In *The Sparrow*, Mary Doria Russell employs a plot convention dear to science fiction and fantasy writers for more than a century—that of humankind's first encounter with an extraterrestrial race—to explore a lengthy roster of Christian issues and concerns: innocence and corruption; the role God does or does not play when things go horribly wrong for humanity; sex, birth control, and procreation; suffering; and confession.

Russell's narrative hops back and forth between the present (2059-2060) and the past (roughly 2019-2040). As the novel opens, the Society of Jesus (the Jesuits) is beginning an investigation into what went wrong with a mission sponsored by their order to Rakhat, an Earthlike planet recently discovered in the Alpha Centauri system, one technically advanced enough to send out radio transmissions of music, beautiful songs that delight all who hear them. The team of eight explorers consists of four Jesuits and four scientists from different backgrounds. A year after landfall, transmissions from Rakhat to Earth end. The Jesuits send a rescue mission, and these men learn that all the original explorers are dead except for the Jesuit linguist, Father Emilio Sandoz, who is found seemingly working as a prostitute. Furthermore, when the rescue team finds him, Sandoz kills the Rakhati child who led the humans to him. When this news reaches Earth, an international scandal ensues, and the father general of the Jesuits convenes a group of priests to question Sandoz and to piece together why the expedition went so horribly wrong.

Among the investigators is Father Johannes Voelker, who bitterly denounces Sandoz as a whore and a child murderer. Sandoz's account is as follows:

> Upon reaching Rakhat, the Earthlings soon make contact with a race of sentient humanoids: the Runa, herbivores who partake somewhat of both simian and canine attributes and who are pastoral traders. The humans repeatedly fail to grasp essential differences between themselves and the Runa. For example, the Earthlings assume that the largest Runa are males and the smaller are females, when the opposite is true. Likewise, the humans have trouble grasping the grammar of the Runa language, for its gender system is based not on sex but on whether the noun referred to is visible or invisible.

These misunderstandings multiply when the crew meets Supaari VaGayjur, a merchant from a nearby city who trades with the Runa but who is a member of Rakhat's other sentient race, the Jana'ata, carnivorous, catlike creatures. It is the Jana'ata who produce the radio transmissions that first attracted the notice of Earth. Having grown somewhat bored with the gentle, unprepossessing Runa, Fathers Sandoz, Marc Robichaux, and D. W. Yarborough wrangle an invitation from Supaari to visit his city of Gayjur. In Gayjur, Sandoz senses that Supaari is being less than open with them: He keeps them out of sight of other Jana'ata and is primarily interested in making trade agreements with them to secure the rights to goods and supplies they brought from Earth. Sandoz is especially haunted by a brief scene he glimpses of three Runa seemingly being executed by the Jana'ata. On their return, the three priests are saddened to learn that scientists Jimmy Quinn and George Edwards have been murdered by poachers while tending the gardens that they had helped the Runa plant.

These deaths are the harbingers of the onslaught of horrors that conclude the novel. The Earthlings have noticed that the birth rate has soared among the Runa but do not realize that this is because of the richer diet provided by the gardens that the humans have taught them to cultivate. One day, Jana'ata soldiers arrive without warning and slaughter the Runa newborn—and prepare them as food. The two races are revealed as intertwined carnivores and herbivores, both of whom have evolved into sentient beings without ever having disengaged themselves from their original relationship of predator and prey. Sofia Mendes tries to rally the Runa to resistance, crying "They are few; we are many," and in the resultant melee, all the humans are killed except for Sandoz and Robichaux, who are taken as prisoners to Gayjur. There Supaari tries to protect them by subjecting them to what is, for the catlike Jana'ata, a declawing operation. He does this because, in his culture, declawed individuals cannot hunt and therefore can be given refuge by any member of society willing to take them in. Supaari, not understanding human biology, does not realize that he is torturing the Earthlings. Robichaux dies from this operation, and Sandoz is left with grotesquely mutilated hands. Soon, Supaari, to earn the right to marry and procreate in his society, where population growth is rigorously controlled, betrays Sandoz, giving him to the aristocrat-poet Hlavin Kitheri to be a sex slave. After months of debasing sexual assaults, the priest decides to make a break for freedom by killing the next guard who opens his cell door. Unfortunately, the next person through the door is the Runa child, Askama, whom he had earlier befriended, arriving with the rescue mission from Earth.

The novel ends in a powerful sequence in which the father general of the Jesuits demands that Sandoz tell the committee of inquiry everything about his imprisonment and rape on Rakhat, holding nothing back, moving even the skeptical and sardonic Father Voelker to compassion.

Christian Themes

Russell's major theme is the inexplicability of suffering and torment, especially that of those who trust in God and, from a specifically Christian standpoint, seek to propagate the faith. Each of the Earthlings is good-hearted and well-meaning, and Sandoz has been called a saint, a favorite of God; nevertheless, all die or suffer abominably or both. However, Russell steers clear of offering an easy explanation, though she explores a number of possibilities: suffering as a test of faith, sorrow as a conduit to closeness with the deity, the necessity of God's absence to give humans space to exist as free beings. The most challenging possibility surfaces in a conversation between Fathers Giuliani and Reyes in the final chapter. Giuliani insists that God cares for his children, citing Matthew 10:29, the famous verse about God noting even the fall of a sparrow. Reyes points out God notes the sparrow's calamity but wonders whether he merely observes. Does he care about the fall? This question brings up a possibility hinted at throughout the novel in the failure of the crew to understand the alien races they encounter: Perhaps God is so different, so essentially alien in comparison with humanity, that humans cannot perceive his actions and reactions, much less grasp his motives.

Another Christian theme expressed passionately in *The Sparrow* is the call to withhold judgment as found in Matthew 7:1: "Judge not, that ye be not judged." The media as well as Sandoz's own order are quick to express disgust at his apparent lapse into carnality and child murder. Yet, by the novel's end, readers know that Sandoz is truly innocent: He fought his imprisonment and molestation, and the death of Askama was a tragic accident during a justifiable attempt at freedom.

Sources for Further Study

Hyland, Sabine. *The Jesuit and the Incas*. Ann Arbor: University of Michigan Press, 2003. Provides a worthwhile contrast between Russell's interplanetary Jesuit mission and an actual one to the Incas, who may have partly inspired Russell's Runa— a word sometimes used for speakers of the modern Incan tongue.

Pearl, Nancy. Review of *The Sparrow*. *Library Journal* 126, no. 9 (May 15, 2001): 192-193. Reviewer calls the work a philosophical novel rather than a work of science fiction as it centers on the question of what good and evil are.

Russell, Mary Doria. *Children of God*. New York: Ballantine, 1998. Russell's sequel/completion of *The Sparrow*. Less engaging than the original, but it provides a satisfying end to the story as well as exploring new religious themes.

Stableford, Brian. "Religion." In *The Encyclopedia of Science Fiction*, edited by John Clute and Peter Nichols. New York: St. Martin's Griffin, 1995. Thorough examination of the treatment of religion in science fiction prior to Russell.

Thomas Du Bose

THE SPIRITUAL EXERCISES

Author: Saint Ignatius of Loyola (1491-1556)
First published: Ejercicios espirituales, 1548 (English translation, 1736)
Edition used: The Spiritual Exercises of St. Ignatius, translated by Anthony Mottola with an introduction by Robert W. Gleason. Garden City, N.Y.: Image Books, 1964
Genre: Nonfiction
Subgenres: Didactic treatise; guidebook; instructional manual; meditation and contemplation
Core issues: Agape; Catholics and Catholicism; contemplation; daily living; devotional life; discipline; fasting; guidance; holiness; Holy Spirit; humility; Jesus Christ; monasticism; mysticism; prayer; purgation; purity; self-control

The Spanish mystic Ignatius of Loyola founded the Society of Jesus, the Jesuits, one of the most significant religious orders in the history of the Roman Catholic Church. The Spiritual Exercises *resulted from his profound spiritual experiences and his concern to impart the disciplined life of the Spirit to others.*

Overview

Born of a noble family in the Basque region of northern Spain, Ignatius of Loyola embarked on a military career, intending to become a soldier. At the battle of Pamplona in 1521, he received a severe leg wound that left him disabled. During his painful period of recovery, he spent long periods in prayer and study of the lives of the saints. Through numerous mystical experiences, he concluded that God was calling him to be a soldier for Christ. He spent several years in study and contemplation, with an extended period (1528-1535) in Paris. There in 1534, he and six of his friends constituted the Society of Jesus with a concern to extend apostolic witness wherever they went. In 1540 Pope Paul III approved the Jesuits as an official order of the Roman Catholic Church, with Loyola as its first "general." *The Spiritual Exercises*, which he began writing as early as the 1520's but revised throughout his life, served as a guide to the spiritual life of the Jesuit order. It has become a textbook for spiritual renewal and discipline used by persons throughout the Church.

The materials that make up *The Spiritual Exercises* were written over a period of several years and grew out of the religious devotion and idealism of Loyola himself. They represent a handbook of Christian spirituality intended to move the faithful to ever-increasing maturity through moral reflection, meditation, and discipline. Just as the worldly soldier prepares for warfare through an unending series of drills and exercises, the Christian soldier must prepare for the battle against evil. *The Spiritual Exercises* therefore constitute a training manual for life in the Spirit. By following this organized spiritual method, the Christian grows and matures in the faith and knowledge of the Lord.

The book is divided into basic sections, each to be practiced for one week. The time spent on each exercise may vary from a month to a few days. There is freedom to extend or restrict the time available for the observance. A brief introductory session provides "directions" for understanding the nature of the material and preparing the heart of the pilgrim for spiritual reflection. These introductory directions are aimed at purifying the person of sin and worldly distractions. Each exercise seeks to lead the believer to continuous reflection on the life, death, and resurrection of Jesus Christ to the end that Christ's love may be experienced anew. The instructions also suggest that the spiritual exercises are best observed under the guidance of a retreat master or spiritual mentor. In fact, younger Christians require such direction for the proper use of the exercises. Special instructions to the "master of the exercises" are provided throughout the book.

The first week is a time of spiritual purgation and preparation. In this section Loyola defines the purpose of the exercises as intended to help the seeker "to conquer himself and to regulate his life so that he will not be influenced in his decisions by any inordinate attachment." The pilgrim thus learns to practice Christian discipline in such a way as to reject everything that might distract from Christ. Spiritual renewal, therefore, begins with self-examination. The chief end of human beings is to "praise, reverence and serve God." Any activity that helps achieve that goal is acceptable for the Christian. Any activity that inhibits the goal is unacceptable. The "exercitants" (those who practice the exercises) are called upon to examine their lives with utmost honesty and intensity. No sin, mortal or venial, is to be overlooked. One is "to ask the grace to know my sins and to free myself from them."

The first exercise also establishes some basic spiritual steps that are repeated in all other sections of the book. These include the "preparatory prayer" and the first and second "prelude." The preparatory prayer is an invocation of divine grace upon the individual that all "intentions, actions and works" may be completely devoted to the service and praise of God. The first prelude calls the participant to focus mental attention on a particular place (location) in which the object or event of contemplation occurs. The mind thus moves back in time to significant moments in the life of the Virgin or Christ. The exercitant may be asked to create a mental image of Mary receiving the Annunciation, or of Christ in the carpenter shop, on the cross, or by the seashore.

The second prelude involves supplication, asking God for what one wants, needs, or desires. Such desires are not whimsical or self-centered but are prompted by the specific subject matter of the exercise. When reflecting on the Resurrection one asks for joy. When meditating on the Crucifixion one seeks sorrow and tears.

Participants are required to devote a portion of every day to the examining of the conscience—morning, noon, and evening. Explicit instructions are given regarding the process of confession and repentance in the continuing life of the Christian.

The use of the imagination is a major factor in the spiritual discipline of the exercises. Exercitants are required to use their imagination throughout. In the meditation on hell, for example, the reader is urged to feel the heat, smell the brimstone, and hear the screams of the damned. On another occasion, one is to imagine being bound in chains and standing before God in judgment. Through the intensity of visualization, the believer moves to spiritual sensations. The spiritual life involves the discipline of the mind.

The second week of the exercises involves meditation on the kingdom of Christ. During this week the *imitatio Christi*, the imitation of Christ, is urged upon the participant. Through reflection on Christ, his birth and activity in the world, the Christian learns to imitate his life. Meditation on the Incarnation and the Nativity provide spiritual insight into the nature of Christ, his humanity and divinity. In fact, Loyola suggests that the pilgrim read passages from *Imitatio Christi* (c. 1427; *The Imitation of Christ*, c. 1460-1530) by Thomas à Kempis or from the saints' lives during this week of meditation.

In considering the Incarnation, participants meditate on the many peoples of the world, their sins and sorrows, and the desire of God to save them. In preparing for the Incarnation, the individual considers "what I should say to the Three Divine Persons, or the eternal Word Incarnate, or to His Mother and our Lady." Those who wish to explore the nature of Christ's divinity are asked to imagine "the infinite fragrance and sweetness of Divinity" in order to secure "spiritual profit."

The intensity of the meditation is evident in the "observation" that the exercise on the Incarnation be observed at midnight, daybreak, at Mass, at Vespers, and before supper, each time for at least one hour. Instructions acknowledge that the pilgrims will experience exhaustion, physical and spiritual, after the first full week of activities. Thus some exceptions might be made: The midnight observance may be omitted.

This week of exercises also focuses on the virtues of the kingdom life. Meditations concentrate on "the two standards" for human behavior, Christ and Satan. One reflects on the evils of the demonic as contrasted with the beauty of Christ. On the same day the exercitant concentrates on "the three classes of men" and the question of attachment to the things of this world. The end of such meditations is that persons shall learn how to act as God inspires them. Those who know Christ have "broken all the attachments," desiring only those things that God permits.

After reflection on specific occurrences in the life of Jesus, the exercises turn to the "three modes of humility." Each marks a steady progression to a higher degree of humility and self-denial.

During the second week, Loyola gives serious attention to the role of free will and "choice" in spiritual life. How does one make choices to marry or remain celibate, or to discern the will of God in all things? Proper choices may be good or indifferent and may be accomplished only as God acts on the human will "to reveal to my spirit what I should do to best promote His praise and glory in the matter of choice." Such decisions are best made when one has cultivated enough other spiritual disciplines to experience "a time of tranquillity" when the soul acts "freely and calmly" in using its divine resources.

The third week of exercises is directed toward meditation on the sufferings of Christ. Exercitants reflect on the events that led up to Christ's death—the Last Supper, the Garden, his arrest and trials, his crucifixion and burial. Using the imagination, the pilgrim returns to the places and events of Christ's passion, the road from Bethany to Jerusalem, the upper room, the house of Pilate, the hill of Golgotha, the sepulchre of his burial.

Rules for the use of food and drink and the practice of fasting are included in this section. Food is never to be a distraction from the life of the Spirit. Even while eating, the Christian should focus concentration on the spiritual realm, contemplating Christ's presence at meals, the lives of the saints, and the need for temperance in all things.

The fourth and final week requires contemplation of the resurrection of Christ and the experience of divine love, the ultimate goal of all Christian spirituality. Through these exercises the believer discovers the wholeness of faith and unity with God. Contemplation becomes a means of attaining divine love expressed in "deeds rather than words." A portion of this chapter is devoted to the three methods of prayer, each leading to greater intimacy with God. The first method involves moral contemplation, using the Ten Commandments, the seven capital (deadly) sins, and the five senses as guides for purification of the self. The second method of prayer involves careful contemplation of each word of such selected prayers as the "Our Father" (Lord's Prayer), the "Hail Mary," and the Creed (Apostles'). Instructions include the position of prayer, kneeling or sitting, with eyes closed or focused on one spot, and the considerations for each word of the prayer. The third method involves a "rhythmical recitation," a process of breathing out the same selected prayers in "rhythmical measure." The major portion of this final exercise, however, is given to meditation on the "mysteries" of Christ's life, from the Annunciation to his resurrection appearances. These reflections are taken directly from the text of the Gospels.

The book concludes with a section containing various rules for Christian living. These include rules for discernment of spirits, for distribution of alms, and for proper "thinking with the church." The section on discerning the spirits gives particular attention to periods of "desolation" that may overtake the Christian. Loyola advises that during such times one should avoid all rash behavior and continue to stand firm in the faith. The Spirit brings consolation, not confusion, during such stressful times. Christians should also understand the nature of the enemy, Satan, and how he acts to entrap them. He works in secrecy, "like a false lover who wishes to remain hidden" and as an "angel of light" who entices the soul to his own evil "designs and wickedness."

"Rules for thinking with the church" provide advice on proper mental attitudes in the "Church Militant." Loyola recommends frequent participation in worship and reception of the most holy sacrament at least once a year, preferably once each week. He also urges conformity to Church doctrine and the careful study of the doctors of the Church (theology). This devotion, like all others in the exercises, provides a means of continued conformity of the soul to the image of Christ.

Christian Themes

The Spiritual Exercises of Saint Ignatius of Loyola provides the seeker with a manual of vigorous military discipline in the spiritual life. It is a guide to Christian maturity that offers instruction in the freedom of the Spirit within the security of religious

structure. A classic of the Church's devotional life, its prescriptions can be summarized as follows:
- The spiritual life is a life of rigorous discipline.
- The Christian disciple must reflect continuously upon the life, death, and resurrection of Christ.
- Continued self-examinations are necessary for spiritual growth.
- The imitation of Christ is the essence of Christian discipleship.
- Meditation on the Incarnation prepares the soul for spiritual experience.
- The experience of divine love is the ultimate goal of Christian spirituality.
- Prayer is the means to greater intimacy with God.
- All devotion is a means to conformity to the image of Christ.

Sources for Further Study

Barthel, Manfred. *The Jesuits: History and Legend of the Society of Jesus.* New York: W. Morrow, 1987. A history of the Jesuit order from its beginning to the present.

Donnelly, John Patrick. *Ignatius of Loyola: Founder of the Jesuits.* New York: Longman, 2004. An interpretive biography that places Loyola and his spirituality in the context of the Reformation. Includes a bibliography and index.

Lonsdale, David. *Eyes to See, Ears to Hear: An Introduction to Ignatian Spirituality.* Maryknoll, N.Y.: Orbis Books, 2000. A good introduction to Ignatian spirituality in general, with a chapter devoted to *The Spiritual Excerises.*

Loyola, Ignatius. *The Autobiography of St. Ignatius Loyola.* New York: Harper & Row, 1974. A spiritual autobiography.

Wulf, Fredrich, ed. *Ignatius of Loyola: His Personality and Spiritual Heritage, 1556-1956.* Saint Louis, Mo.: Institute of Jesuit Resources, 1977. Essays on Ignatius and the Jesuits on the four hundredth anniversary of his death.

William J. Leonard

"STATION ISLAND"

Author: Seamus Heaney (1939-   )
First published: 1984, in *Station Island*
Edition used: Opened Ground: Selected Poems, 1966-1996. New York: Farrar, Straus and Giroux, 1998
Genre: Poetry
Subgenres: Allegory; biography; lyric poetry; narrative poetry
Core issues: Atonement; confession; illumination; mysticism; pilgrimage; redemption

In his introductory note to Station Island, *Heaney wrote that the twelve title poems constitute "a sequence of dream encounters set on an island in County Donegal where, since medieval times, pilgrims have gone to perform the prescribed penitential exercises (or 'stations')." The poems follow the pilgrim/poet as he recollects the experiences of his life, which require a meditative exploration of his commitments and responsibilities as a man and artist.*

Overview

The Irish poet Seamus Heaney, Nobel laureate in literature in 1995, has not been a proponent of any specific theological position, but throughout his boyhood in Ireland he lived in a cultural community suffused with a deep tradition of Christian—more specifically Catholic—conventions and currents. Near his family farm in Mossbawn, he recalled, "St. Patrick, they said, had fasted and prayed there fifteen hundred years before." In "Gaelic times," the Heaney family was involved "in ecclesiastical affairs in the diocese of Derry," and in his home "of course, there were religious magazines," However, as he became prominent as a poet, he found himself torn by a divide between what he calls "the old vortex of racial and religious instinct" and a desire to seek "the mean of humane love and reason."

These two contending (and potentially complementing) perspectives demarcate the outer poles of the spiritual and literal terrain that Heaney traverses in the sequence "Station Island," the title poem of his 1984 volume of that name. As the first section of the poem opens, the narrative conscious of the penitent introduces the setting:

> A hurry of bell-notes
> flew over morning hush
> and water-blistered cornfields,
> an escaped ringing
> that stopped as quickly
> as it started. *Sunday,*
> the silence breathed

This is the Sabbath, and the pilgrim/quester meets a figure from antique Irish mythology, the legendary Simon Sweeney, whom he recognizes as "an old Sabbath-breaker/ who has been dead for years." The apparition signals the dream-scape sense of the setting, where Sweeney becomes the first in a series of guides for a mystical journey that will loosely follow the path—the stations—set by Christ on the way to the Crucifixion.

The second section, and many of those that follow, pivot on a meeting between the pilgrim and a representative figure from his life or from a current or historical Irish cultural context. Here it is an "aggavated man," a compendium of grievances whose complaint expresses the pain of Irish history. He is drawn on the personage of William Carleton, a nineteenth century activist caught up in the conflict between Catholic and Protestant factions. This is a singular source of Heaney's own burden as a man and a poet. He tries to explain that in his native county, there was an easy accommodation between sects, which is acknowledged, but as a part of an admonition to "Remember everything and keep your head." With this counsel in mind, the third section is a return to the pilgrim's religious origins, but now he has a new awareness of what was previously habitual, a developing consciousness of the full meaning of a litany that had been said almost automatically. Familiar doctrine is joined to an instinctive response to the wonders of the natural world in a widening definition of sacred ground.

The fourth section recalls the pilgrim's acquaintance years ago with a young priest who was attracted to worldly things and compelled to renounce his calling, a parallel for the pilgrim/poet's attraction to the allure of the world. He is faced with the question of what he might have to relinquish to serve his own truest calling, his poetry. This is followed by a section in which he expresses his gratitude for the masters of his craft, who have shown him the way to "the great/ moving power and spring of verse." The parallel between a religious and an artistic quest continues as his mentors are likened directly to the scholar/priests who directed him in his youth. In the sixth section, there is another transition away from a religious focus and toward the things of the world, as the pilgrim, mingling awe and astonishment, recalls the full force of the appearance of women in his life. Unable to deny or resist the ramifications of the romantic imagination, the energy source of his lyric muse, he wonders

> Freckle-face, fox-head, pod of the broom,
> Catkin-pixie, little fern-swish:
> Where did she arrive from?

The seventh section is central to the mature poet's attempt to find a way to handle the public demands of the political troubles of Irish history and present strife. Prominent enough to be faced with expectations from many quarters, he fashions an encounter with an old friend, murdered in the plague of sectarian violence, whose appearance he is reluctant to accept but whose claims of fellowship, faith, and fidelity to a humane response in his poetry lead through a harrowing narrative to the pilgrim's confession of inadequacy. "Forgive the way I have lived indifferent—/ forgive my timid circumspect involvement," he prays. As the phantom vision fades, he is offered an ambiguous absolution that is not without some succor for his guilt.

The eighth and ninth sections are immediate confrontations with men whose deaths were direct results of sectarian hatreds. First, the poet is challenged for his response to his cousin's murder by Protestant assassins, his "evasion and artistic tact" placing him in a psychological *"Purgatorio."* His recognition of his failure is one of the prime motives for this pilgrimage. He next encounters a rebel martyr who died in prison following a hunger strike. Tormented by feelings of inadequacy, he declares his hatred of "everything/ That made me biddable and unforthcoming." Nonetheless, he banishes the rebel's "unquiet soul" to an emblematic burial "in a bog," and in a version of a classic dark night of the soul reaches a point of clarity—a "different core"—establishing a spiritual foundation.

The tenth section begins to compose this base in terms of any simple object formed for beauty and utility, and the eleventh expands the idea of an object built with reverence and used with respect. In this case, it serves as an analogue for the gift of poetry, "the zenith and glimpsed jewels of any gift" understood and fully appreciated. In the final section, the gift is reformed as a "living fountain"—a symbol of the eternal renewal brought by a spiritual consciousness of the wonders of the world. Here, the poet's guide is the shade of James Joyce, whose complicated relationship with Ireland might serve as a symbol of the struggle an artist faces. His comment "The main thing is to write/ for the joy of it" is Heaney's working precept for times to be.

Christian Themes

The penitent who traces Christ's journey to the cross accepts the sins and lapses of his life as the burden of being human and attempts to reclaim and restore his faith by following the example of Christ's teaching and essence. Although Heaney does not hew too closely to a traditional version of this experience, using twelve stations rather than fourteen because the poem takes its bearings at a mid-point on the road, he is concerned with what he called "poetry as divination" in a lecture he gave to the Royal Society of Literature in 1974. During that lecture, on the poetry of Gerard Manley Hopkins, he elaborated, saying that "Christ's mastering descent into the soul is an act of love" and then added, just as "the poetic act itself is a love-act," using the poetry of Hopkins as an example of this action.

In "Station Island," Heaney is trying to reach, as Hopkins's poetry did, "a sacramental apprehension of the world," and as Hopkins did in the poem "Heaven-Haven," discover "the mystery of Christ's efficacy and action in human life" by questioning his choices and decisions in conjunction with the terminal events of Christ's life on earth. In his Nobel lecture, Heaney referred to "the Christian moralist in oneself," and as much as his poetry has dealt with the immediate impact of political demands and personal preferences, he has made a conscious effort "to make space in my reckoning and imagining for the marvelous as well as the murderous." The twelve sections of "Station Island" are a record of this impulse in action and a register of the moral and ethical standards that Heaney has tried to maintain.

Sources for Further Study

Collins, Floyd. *Seamus Heaney: The Crisis of Identity*. Newark: The University of Delaware Press, 2003. Collins puts more emphasis on the Christian aspects of Heaney's work than other scholars, covering his early life in detail, including photographs and interviews.

Corcoran, Neil. *The Poetry of Seamus Heaney: A Critical Study*. London: Faber, 1998. A discriminating, knowledgeable study of Heaney's poetry, using the poet's literary criticism, relationship to Irish culture, and participation in contemporary social and artistic issues to inform the discussions of poetry.

Heaney, Seamus. *Preoccupations: Selected Prose 1968-1978*. New York: Farrar, Straus and Giroux, 1980. An appealing account of the poet's preferences, influences, and intentions, gathered in a series of eloquent, revealing and incisive essays and lectures, notably one on the effect of Gerard Manley Hopkins's poetry on Heaney in religious and aesthetic terms.

Vendler, Helen. *Seamus Heaney*. New York: HarperCollins, 1998. An enlightening consideration of Heaney's style, form, and language in terms of an argument that Heaney is primarily a lyric poet.

Leon Lewis

THE STREAM AND THE SAPPHIRE
Selected Poems on Religious Themes

Author: Denise Levertov (1923-1997)
First published: New York: New Directions, 1997
Genre: Poetry
Subgenre: Lyric poetry
Core issues: Catholics and Catholicism; daily living; doubt; faith; sainthood; trust in God

The thirty-eight poems in The Stream and the Sapphire, *previously published in seven collections between 1978 and 1997, are from the period of Levertov's gradual conversion to Christianity. This collection, the last she saw published before her death, explores her movement from skepticism to faith, and examines the lives of various saints, especially as they confronted their doubts. Levertov also touches on the nature of worship and contemplation of God, especially as revealed through creation.*

Overview

Denise Levertov developed her theology as she wrote her poems. She sought to capture the truth of experience in poetry and gradually moved from skepticism to faith as she discovered truth in Christianity. Her father, Paul Levertoff, was an Anglican priest of Russian Jewish descent, and her mother, Beatrice Spooner-Jones Levertoff, was a devout Welsh Christian. Both parents descended from highly religious families that embraced a variety of Judeo-Christian mysticism that informs much of Levertov's poetry, especially in her sensitive treatment of nature.

While many of Levertov's poems treat religious or spiritual themes, some of her most overly religious ones are captured in *The Stream and the Sapphire*. The title of the collection is taken from her poem "Flickering Mind." The persona in this poem presents herself as a minnow whose flittering in the stream of time makes her comprehension of God—the unchanging mover of history, the gleaming sapphire in the stream—difficult. This title piece emphasizes the theme of faith seeking to reach beyond the paradoxes of experience, a theme most of the poems echo.

Levertov placed the poems in this collection in roughly chronological order and divided them into four main sections: "The Tide," "Believers," "Conjectures," and "Fish and a Honeycomb." The poems in "The Tide," named after one of the poems in this section, deal with the ebb and flow of faith. The opening poem, "Human Being," articulates Levertov's skeptical questions about why innocent children and animals suffer, but concludes with a word of thanks for the gift of life. The philosophical problem of pain was the first hurdle Levertov had to overcome before accepting belief in God.

In this first section, "Psalm Fragments (Schnittke String Trio)" and "Suspended" examine the paradox of faith in a God who is difficult to discover in a fallen and sinful world, but who nonetheless does not allow believers in God to fail or fall. God's presence is silent, intangible, and undeniable. The remaining poems in this section also explore the mystery of God's person and work in the world.

"Believers," the second section of the collection, is the most thematically unified. Both "Poetics of Faith" and "St. Peter and the Angel" deal with events in the life of Peter. The first event is Peter's failed attempt to walk to Jesus on the water, recorded in Matthew 14:28-32, and the second event is Peter's release from prison, as described in Acts 12:1-19. Both of these poems depict Peter's perplexity in experiencing the miraculous and not being able to comprehend it; conversely, Levertov notes that individual action helped make these events possible. Miracles are, after all, rooted in daily life as well as in God's eternal provision. The next three poems— "Caedmon," "The Servant-Girl at Emmaus," and "Conversion of Brother Lawrence"—treat moments when people have encountered the miraculous in ordinary circumstances. The emphasis here falls on the dignity of labor and how God can be honored through it. The next poem, "Dom Helder Camara at the Nuclear Test Site," connects Levertov's call for peace through political action with her affirmation of life in the Church. The two are inseparable in her mind. One of the most intriguing poems in this section is "Annunciation," which treats the nature of the decision Mary made to become the mother of Jesus. This poem then explores the nature of annunciations in daily life when people choose whether to give birth to God's gifts offered to them.

"Conjectures," the third section, includes three meditations, two on the teachings of Jesus and one on the nature of purgatory in daily life. The first two poems, "On the Parables of the Mustard Seed" and "What the Figtree Said," both discuss the vital role of imagination in faith. The third poem, "Heresy," weaves a discussion of purgatory into a fanciful consideration of reincarnation, chiefly as a metaphor for the translation of the dusty nature of humans into the celestial qualities of God's heaven.

"Fish and a Honeycomb," the last section, presents six poems on various aspects of the death and Resurrection of Jesus Christ. The second poem in this section, "On a Theme from Julian's Chapter XX," builds on "The Showings: Lady Julian of Norwich," a poem in the second section. This second poem examines Dame Julian of Norwich's desire to identify with the wounds of Christ, even as Christ identified with the suffering of the world. Again, the role of imagination is prominent in the exercise of faith. This section also contains a fine poem on Saint Thomas Didymus (treated earlier in "Agnus Dei"). In Levertov's poem, Thomas's demand for proof leads to illumination, not condemnation. The final poem, "Ascension," concludes the book with an imaginative meditation on how Jesus Christ felt when leaving behind the world of flesh on his return to heaven.

Christian Themes

According to Levertov, writing poetry provided her an opportunity to discover and develop theological insights. The poems in *The Stream and the Sapphire* are signposts on her way to faith. The central theme in all these poems is the nature of faith, but Levertov combines this theme with discussions about doubt, aesthetics, imagination, and sainthood.

The most prominent theme in this collection is doubt and faith. Levertov usually depicts faith as a paradox, one dependent on intangibles for people living in a physical world. Some of her most stunning treatments of this theme can be found in "Human Being," "Avowal," "Variation on a Theme by Rilke," and "Suspended." In these poems she affirms her sense of being upheld by an intangible grace.

Another prominent theme in Levertov's poems is her treatment of aesthetics and faith. Many of these poems began with aesthetic experiences, such as listening to a concert, viewing a painting, or attending a Mass. Some of her most prominent displays of this theme are "Candlemas," "Agnus Dei" (taken from "Mass for the Day of Saint Thomas Didymus"), "Psalm Fragments (Schnittke String Trio)," and "The Servant-Girl at Emmaus" (based on a painting by Diego Velázquez). Such poems underscore Levertov's realization that beauty—which is one of the three transcendentals in theology along with goodness and truth—can lead people to God. Levertov uses the Affirmative Way or Positive Way in approaching creation, seeing the love of people and creation as the beginning point for understanding God.

For Levertov, imagination is also a vital ingredient in faith. "On the Parables of the Mustard Seed" and "What the Figtree Said" are both fine examples of how imagination can function both as a tool for creating the poem and as a key to the Kingdom of God. Without imagination, the gifts from God are easily lost.

The theme of sainthood also plays a prominent role in Levertov's poetry. Saints such as Mary, Simeon, Peter, Thomas Didymus, Brother Lawrence, Dame Julian of Norwich, and more contemporary spiritual leaders such as Thomas Merton and Dom Helder Camara, populate her poems. However, Levertov's saints are paradoxically very human, having great doubts and fears while determining to be valiant for God.

Sources for Further Study

Bodo, Murray. *Poetry as Prayer: Denise Levertov*. Boston: Pauline Books and Media, 2001. A devotional treatment of poetry by Levertov. Discusses seven poems from *The Stream and the Sapphire*, various essays, and Bodo's talks with Levertov.

Gallant, James. "Entering No-Man's Land: The Recent Religious Poetry of Denise Levertov." *Renascence* 50, nos. 1-2 (Fall, 1997/Winter, 1998): 122-134. One of eleven articles in this issue by various authors on Levertov's religious poetry. This issue has one of the best collections of essays on this topic.

Levertov, Denise. *Conversations with Denise Levertov*. Edited by Jewel Spears Brooker. Jackson: University Press of Mississippi, 1998. A fine collection of previously published interviews with Levertov given between 1963 and 1995. These interviews treat Levertov's craft, social concerns, and faith.

_____. *New and Selected Essays*. New York: New Directions Books, 1992. A strong collection of essays and talks produced by Levertov between 1965 and 1991. Note especially "A Poet's View" and "Work That Enfaiths."

_____. *Tesserae: Memories and Suppositions.* New York: New Directions Books, 1995. A selection of twenty-seven memoirs about memorable events and places in Levertov's experience. These works give glimpses into the author's imaginative process.

Daven M. Kari

STRENGTH TO LOVE

Author: Martin Luther King, Jr. (1929-1968)
First published: New York: Harper & Row, 1963
Genre: Nonfiction
Subgenre: Sermons
Core issues: African Americans; connectedness; freedom and free will; good vs. evil; hope; justice; love; morality; nonviolent resistance; obedience and disobedience; problem of evil; racism; social action

Awarded the Nobel Peace Prize in 1964, King labored for racial equality in his native United States and throughout the world. Heading the Southern Christian Leadership Conference, King practiced a philosophy of nonviolent resistance and civil disobedience. He was also a masterful preacher, orator, and writer. This is a series of sermons—some written in Georgia jails—preached by King from 1955 to 1963 during the Civil Rights movement in the United States.

Overview

More than seventy million human beings were uprooted, enslaved, or killed in the twentieth century alone. What happened to those victims? Is death—utter annihilation—their end? How should we appraise such wasting of human life? Considering such questions as these moves one to reflect on the significance of evil. Why does it exist? Where does it lead? Can evil be overcome?

Raising his voice against a world that wasted human life through racial hatred, poverty, and violence, the Reverend Dr. Martin Luther King, Jr., spent his life wrestling with those questions in word and deed. King outlined part of the problem of evil in his "Letter from Birmingham Jail" (April 16, 1963):

> Lamentably, it is an historical fact that privileged groups seldom give up their privileges voluntarily. Individuals may see the moral light and voluntarily give up their unjust posture; but, as Reinhold Niebuhr has reminded us, groups are more immoral than individuals. We know through painful experience that freedom is never voluntarily given by the oppressor; it must be demanded by the oppressed.

Later, on August 28, 1963, King spoke at a massive civil rights rally in Washington, D.C. He proclaimed in his now famous "I Have a Dream" speech that

> in spite of the difficulties and frustrations of the moment, I still have a dream. It is a dream deeply rooted in the American dream. I have a dream that one day this nation will rise up and live out the true meaning of its creed: "We hold these truths to be self-evident: that all men are created equal."

His dream, King concluded, was that

when we let freedom ring, when we let it ring from every village and every hamlet, from every state and every city, we will be able to speed up that day when all of God's children, black men and white men, Jews and Gentiles, Protestants and Catholics, will be able to join hands and sing in the words of that old Negro spiritual, "Free at last! Free at last! Thank God almighty, we are free at last!"

As an orator and a spiritual-political leader for his nation, King may never have had a finer moment than on that summer day in the American capital. The point is arguable, however, because the Sunday sermons that King preached regularly were brilliant and inspiring, too. Urged to publish a sampling of them from the period 1955-1963, King expressed misgivings because "a sermon is not an essay to be read but a discourse to be heard." Nevertheless, the publication of *Strength to Love* more than fulfilled his hope that "a message may come to life for readers of these printed words."

King's sermons make clear that evil is activity, sometimes inactivity, and thus a manifestation of power. Evil powers are those that *waste*. That is, evil happens whenever power is used to ruin or squander life, or whenever it is not used to forestall those results. The kind of evil that most concerned King ignores and violates the worth of individuals. Everyone inflicts that sort of pain to some degree. Yet some people, and especially some societies, are more perverse than others. We measure them by the extent to which their actions waste human existence.

As he combated evil, King found it meaningful to affirm his love for life in Christian terms. Through Jesus, preached King, God gives reason to trust that life beyond death is in the future for people of faith. God also, however, intends that this hope should give us courage to take action now for justice, dignity, and freedom. Affirming that the world and human life are God's creation, King saw God at work in the world, striving with men and women to achieve a community in which racism has no place. The fatherhood of God, King frequently emphasized, implies the interdependence—the brotherhood and sisterhood—of humankind. All people, wrote King, "are caught in an inescapable network of mutuality, tied in a single garment of destiny. Whatever affects one directly affects all indirectly. I can never be what I ought to be until you are what you ought to be, and you can never be what you ought to be until I am what I ought to be."

Within this framework of God's love and human interdependence, King attempted to determine evil's significance. Nothing is more obvious, he thought, than the presence of evil in the universe, its chief manifestation being our brutalizing tendency to hate and oppress one another. King saw every person's existence as a mixture of and a struggle between good and evil. Created in God's image, human life is good, but it is also stained and shattered by destructive powers. King had no comprehensive theory that ultimately explained why evil exists, although he did point to humanity's abuse of freedom as a crucial factor. Instead he focused on the structure of evil, on God's action and our human responsibility in coping with it.

"Evil," asserted King, "carries the seed of its own destruction." Its forces are powerful and stubborn, never voluntarily relinquishing their hold. King argued, "evil cannot permanently organize itself." Its nature is to divide, separate, and negate. This structure suggests a sense in which evil is self-destructive. It will not destroy itself completely, he admitted. New obstacles will impede us repeatedly. The consuming force of evil, however, does not exist unchecked. Internally unstable, it is capable of being subdued by the powers of goodness—justice, freedom, and especially love—which remain vital however threatened they may be at times. "Looking back," King could say as he surveyed the battle against American racism, "we see the forces of segregation gradually dying on the seashore."

As for God's action and humanity's responsibility in coping with evil, King held that God is committed to freedom. God permits evil as part of the price to be paid for freedom in the world, but he also contended that God did not will—directly or indirectly—any specific instance of evil. God's commitment to freedom, however, does have some important ramifications for the way in which God permits evil to exist. That commitment means not only that people can diverge from the course of action that God wants them to pursue but also that trying to discern and follow God's will entails conscious choices. Furthermore, if divergence from the will of God occurs, God does not always use every available means to set things right.

Not that God is unconcerned about justice, insisted King. God is committed to justice but within the context of freedom. God's purpose for human life seems to entail our attempt to establish a community of love through our creative use of freedom, which includes both controlling the potential for evil in human existence and atoning for evil actions that do occur. "Therefore," King contended, "God cannot at the same time impose his will upon his children and also maintain his purpose for man." Yet God will not allow human beings to make a total shambles of creation. Evil is kept in check partly by its very nature. Moreover, although God will not do for us what we can do for ourselves, when people turn to God in faith, they can renew courage and strength to attempt what is just and good.

The universe is formed and finally controlled by the love of God. That love's reality and power, moreover, are revealed with special clarity in the life, death, and resurrection of Jesus. Love builds up and transforms life for the good. It also conquers death; the grave is not our end. "Love," said King, "is the most durable power in the world. This creative force, so beautifully exemplified in the life of our Christ, is the most potent instrument available in mankind's quest for peace and security."

If only men and women will give themselves to love, the universe is structured to favor that ideal. Conversely, King was also convinced that hate and violence breed more of the same even if they sow the seeds of their own destruction at the same time. The forces of evil must not be allowed to do business as usual; resistance to them is indispensable. As he pursued the cause of racial justice, King urged his followers to take up nonviolent resistance and civil disobedience. The authority of these strategies, he asserted, resides in their ability to expose and thwart evil without sacrificing persons. Suffering may be experienced in the course of such resistance, but this suffering is redemptive. It can strike the human conscience and thus produce a defense of freedom and justice. Such suffering can also lead to repentance in those who cause it.

No matter how much he had reason to despair, King retained a deep and abiding faith in the goodness and power of God. "Our God is able," he liked to say, a conviction that provided the title for one of the most popular sermons in *Strength to Love*. At the same time, King always stressed God's decision to create persons with freedom and to respect the integrity and power that freedom entails. God gives us power and then respects it. Such a God, underscored King, is one who takes risks. Such a God recognizes that things may not always function smoothly and that injustices may occur, perhaps even on a massive scale. This God apparently has a high degree of patience and self-control. When things are not going well, God could intervene directly and dramatically. If, however, King is correct, God's actions in the world are more indirect and subtle. God instills courage when people ask in faith, and God gives renewed strength when people trust and call upon God to support righteous ends. King notes that the kingdom of God for us is "not yet," and for now this life remains a scene of struggle and suffering. Improvements, however, are possible. Oppression can be relieved. Freedom and justice can be extended when, with God's help, we find strength to love.

Reviewing the racial strife that wracked Birmingham, Alabama, in the 1960's, King once observed that it was not the brutality of bad people but the silence of good people that was the greater tragedy. As a religious man, King knew that some forms of silence show a healthy respect for forces beyond our control, while others can restore human energies and prepare them for effective use—the life of prayer and the retreat for quiet meditation are not to be ignored. King also understood, however, that silence can mean failure of nerve in facing issues that do have solutions. He counted on concerned men and women to keep trying their best, not only with words but with actions. Evil is mighty, but King added that God is good and almighty. He wanted that conviction to motivate the love that is needed if we are to create a just society and thereby vindicate God's decision to respect human freedom.

Christian Themes

King's message of courage and hope was rooted in the example of Jesus Christ: As exemplified in Christ, love is the most durable power in the world. The universe is governed by a loving, personal God who is the companion of those who struggle for justice. Evil cannot permanently organize itself, for it contains the seeds of its own destruction. In the life, death, and resurrection of Jesus, we see that unearned suffering is redemptive and that evil is overcome with good. God is able to subdue all evil, but God calls on humankind to cooperate in this task and strengthens those who do so. Hence, when combined with Mahatma Gandhi's method of nonviolent resistance, the Christian doctrine of love is a potent force in the struggle for freedom.

Sources for Further Study

Ansbro, John J. *Martin Luther King, Jr.: The Making of a Mind*. Maryknoll, N.Y.: Orbis Books, 1982. Analyzes King's thought, particularly his strategy of nonviolence, with special reference to the formative philosophical and religious influences on his outlook.

Baldwin, Lewis V., with Rufus Burrow, Jr., Barbara A. Holmes, and Susan Holmes Winfield. *The Legacy of Martin Luther King, Jr.: The Boundaries of Law, Politics, and Religion.* Foreword by Clayborne Carson. Notre Dame, Ind.: University of Notre Dame Press, 2002. Discusses King's relationship to Christianity and politics, the development of his ethics, his objective moral order and moral law, and how all this expanded to a global stage. Includes bibliographical references and index.

Deats, Richard. *Martin Luther King, Jr., Spirit-Led Prophet: A Biography.* Foreword by Coretta Scott King. Hyde Park, N.Y.: New City Press, 2003. This biography examines King's life, emphasizing his faith, religious beliefs, and spirituality. Includes bibliographical references and index.

Lincoln, C. Eric, ed. *Martin Luther King, Jr.: A Profile.* New York: Hill & Wang, 1984. Useful insights into King's life and thought are brought together by a leading interpreter of black religious experience in the United States.

Moses, Greg. *Revolution of Conscience: Martin Luther King, Jr., and the Philosophy of Nonviolence.* Foreword by Leonard Harris. New York: Guilford Press, 1997. This work focuses less on King as an activist and orator than on his role as an immensely influential intellectual and philosopher.

Oates, Stephen B. *Let the Trumpet Sound: The Life of Martin Luther King, Jr.* New York: Harper & Row, 1982. A carefully done biography of a skilled scholar and writer.

Washington, James M., ed. *A Testament of Hope: The Essential Writings of Martin Luther King, Jr.* San Francisco: Harper & Row, 1986. A splendid collection, including public speeches, interviews, articles, excerpts from books (including *Strength to Love*), and autobiographical reflections. Includes a selected bibliography.

John K. Roth

THE SUBVERSION OF CHRISTIANITY

Author: Jacques Ellul (1912-1994)
First published: La Subversion du christianisme, 1984 (English translation, 1986)
Edition used: The Subversion of Christianity, translated by Geoffrey W. Bromiley. Grand Rapids, Mich.: Eerdmans, 1986
Genre: Nonfiction
Subgenres: Church history; critical analysis; theology
Core issues: Church; Holy Spirit; morality; religion; revelation

Christianity has become a perversion of the revelation of God, the body of Christ, and Christian love, according to Ellul. The historical transformation of the biblical message into religion, morality, and a sociological movement has led to a culture opposite of what one reads in the Bible. The source of the perversion is to be found in the human heart, which experiences weakness as discouragement, grace as intolerable, and freedom as unlivable. Nevertheless, the body of Christ, although entombed in sociological institutions, still lives.

Overview

Jacques Ellul was born on January 6, 1912, in Bordeaux, France, to a poor family. His French mother was devoutly Protestant, and his father, a Serbian aristocrat, came from a Greek Orthodox religious background although he was described by Ellul as being highly critical of anything to do with religion. While Ellul was attending law school at age eighteen, a year after his father lost his job and the stock market crash of 1929, he discovered the writings of Karl Marx and became enthralled with Marx's explanation for the political and economic situation Ellul was personally experiencing. Marx's basic affirmations—the centrality of the historical dialectic, the revolutionary function of certain groups of people, the emphasis on explaining the material reality surrounding people, and the overall identification with the poor—would become lifelong commitments for Ellul despite his disappointing encounter with political groups claiming to be Marxist, his disillusionment with the Communist Party, and most significant, his abrupt and brutal conversion to Christianity in 1932.

The Subversion of Christianity, like Ellul's corpus of more than fifty books, manifests the enduring tension he experienced between the reality he saw in the works of Marx and the truth he heard in the life of Christ. He describes a series of historical and sociological transformations of Christianity that oppose the revelation of God in Christ. The first of what Ellul terms perversions is the sacralization of rituals, visual images, social spaces, and nature by Christianity after its originally subversive and antinature project of desacralizing all the existing pagan and natural religions, rituals, and idols with which it came in contact.

Christianity's early success at descralizing and demythologizing natural religions was due largely to its willingness to translate the historical narrative of God's people and Jesus into philosophical and legal ideas easily understood by the Greco-Roman world. According to Ellul, however, this successful translation became another perversion in the history of Christianity—the transformation of revelation as historical event into revelation as philosophical truth. A gradual shift occurred from reading the Bible as a purely historical document recording the agreements and disagreements of God with his people to reading the Bible as a series of stories containing hidden abstract universal truths, philosophical systems, and moral codes. The result was the birth of theology, the fundamental source of error in Christian thought. Even when the theology is true and not heresy, Ellul argues that such systems ultimately lead one to intellectual, epistemological, and metaphysical questions, not to the living history of God's relation to his people.

By the end of the third century, the increase in numbers of Christians had become the source of the institutional perversion of love and grace into formalized requests for service and social action. With growth in membership came an accumulation of wealth, the need for management of that wealth, and ultimately a power hierarchy that perverted the body of Christ into an institution. Along with the division that occurred between clergypersons and laypersons, Ellul describes an additional related perversion that excluded from positions of authority the most innovative element of Christianity—women—because of the tendency toward placing men in positions of power in hierarchical structures.

As the institutions developed with the aid of theological constructions, God's revelation was gradually perverted into a morality, Ellul says. Sociologically, the subversion of Christianity into morality occurred mainly because of the need to delineate the behaviors of members of this new institution from nonmembers and the masculine tendency toward judgment and calculations of debt and credit. Theologically, the construction of any moral system is a manifestation of the Original Sin described in Genesis, where human affirmations of what is good and evil are substituted for the will of God.

During the medieval period, the Muslim affirmation of the inherent connection between nature and Islam influenced Christianity to make a stronger identification of itself as a religion conforming to nature. Ellul states that several perversions resulted from this identification. "Natural theology" emerged with the theory that a soul is by nature Christian. Consequently, baptism as a sign of active grace in one's life was perverted into baptism as an instrument of salvation, which materialized as infant baptisms, forced conversions, and the justification of the Crusades. Moreover, Christianity influenced by Islam developed the missionary/colonizing attitude of invading other cultures to secure conversions just as Muslim missionaries had for centuries been invading Africa to secure conversions to Islam.

The political perversion of the Christian spirit is the last transformation described, though it began historically with the people of Israel and their relation to state power, moved through the union of religion and state via Constantine to the end of the Middle Ages, and continues to the present in the form of religion's validation of state nationalism. Whenever the institutions of religion validate political powers and justify any authority other than God's by either becoming the state as in the Middles Ages or serving state nationalism and economic systems as they have for communism and capitalism, then Christianity the religion is the complete opposite of the body of Christ.

Despite the subversion of Christianity into religion, Ellul concludes with several historical observations that affirm the body of Christ remains sociologically active nevertheless.

Christian Themes

Several of the Christian themes Ellul presents are not new. The association of religion with power as it is used in the service of politics had been observed by Marx, if it was not already explicit in the Old Testament book of Isaiah. The distinction between Christianity as lived faith and Christianity as morality was already present in the works of philosopher Søren Kierkegaard, as was Ellul's observation of the inverse relation between the large numbers of people being institutionally identified as Christian and those actually living the difficult life of Christ: When everyone is Christian, no one is. The emphasis on revelation as the person and historical event of Jesus Christ—not the theological constructions and doctrines that emerge to explain the meaning of that event—is repeatedly affirmed in the writings of Karl Barth. Though Ellul knows such content has been voiced before, he creates a new mode for appropriating these themes. He cites Scripture in support of traditionally Marxist observations designed to undermine religion while simultaneously pointing out that such criticisms do not touch the revelation of God occurring independently of religion. When Kierkegaard discusses similar points, he heightens our sense of individuality as his reflections lead us to ever higher levels of introspection. In contrast, Ellul's use of historical events and sociological descriptions of institutional shifts to affirm Kierkegaardian insights lead us not into deeper private self-reflection but into the very public world of society and history. In relation to Barth's theological affirmation of the centrality of revelation in Christ, Ellul's descriptions of perverted sociological institutions are designed to elicit living social responses in individuals, not intellectual affirmations of a theological truth regarding revelation. His text is at once a historical analysis of the development of Christian beliefs and doctrines, a sociological study of the Church as institution and its effect on how individuals live, and a theological affirmation of the revelation of God and spirit of Christ that transcends both history and society.

Apart from Ellul's unique contextualization of existing themes, he identifies three Christian themes in need of further exploration: the negative influence of Islam on Christianity during the Middle Ages; the masculine influence on Christianity toward morality and power, away from the feminine values of love and protection of the weak that were essential elements of the pre-subverted Christian spirit; and the original opposition of Christianity to nature.

Sources for Further Study

Christians, Clifford G., and Jay M. Van Hook, eds. *Jacques Ellul: Interpretive Essays*. Chicago: University of Illinois Press, 1981. A variety of scholarly interpretations including an epilogue by Ellul, twenty-page bibliography, notes on contributors, and index.

Goddard, Andrew. *Living the Word, Resisting the World: The Life and Works of Jacques Ellul*. Waynesboro, Ga.: Send the Light, 2005. A biographical overview followed by descriptions of Ellul's theological and sociological assessments of violence, law, and politics. Includes a fifty-four-page bibliography and index.

Hanks, Joyce M., ed. *An Annotated Bibliography*. Vol. 5 in *Jacques Ellul*. Greenwich, Conn.: JAI Press, 2001. The most comprehensive source of information on published and unpublished works by Ellul with an extensive, well-organized list of secondary materials, including dissertations.

Troude-Chastenet, Patrick. *Jacques Ellul on Religion, Technology, and Politics: Conversations with Patrick Troude-Chastenet*. Atlanta: Scholars Press, 1999. A broad introduction originally published as *Entretiens avec Jacques Ellul* (Paris: La Table Ronde, 1994).

Erik Nordenhaug

SUFFERING

Author: Dorothee Sölle (1929-2003)
First published: Leiden, 1973 (English translation, 1975)
Edition used: Suffering, translated by Everett R. Kalin. Philadelphia: Fortress Press, 1975
Genre: Nonfiction
Subgenres: Meditation and contemplation; theology
Core issues: Despair; ethics; Jesus Christ; mysticism; social action; suffering

Sölle states that we must seek the causes of suffering to eliminate it and its meaning to discover our humanity. The long history of Christian masochism—suffering understood as punishment, training, or expiation—focuses wrongly on a sadistic God. Conversely, it is part of human nature to actively avoid or repress suffering and despise and marginalize those who do suffer. Given that suffering is an inevitable part of being human, the question is not about whether we can get around suffering but whether we will use it productively to increase love in this world, affirmation for life, and genuine consolation and solidarity with those who suffer.

Overview

Dorothee Sölle draws on Simone Weil's philosophy to explore the phenomenon of suffering as "affliction," involving three distinct dimensions. First is physical pain, but this is the least, because once it is gone, it is as if it never occurred. Second is psychological pain, the sense of being poured out, empty, or numbed and imprisoned by pain. These two dimensions alone do not rise to the level of affliction, however, without the third pole, social degradation, in which the sufferer is abandoned or worse, ridiculed, blamed, and despised for one's suffering state. According to Sölle, Christianity's response too often has been a type of theological sadism.

> God comes to a sufferer only with pedagogical intent. Brutality and salvation become brothers, suffering serves to teach obedience and there is a perfect alliance between repressive theism and repressive society.

Sölle traces three possible interpretations of the suffering in the story of Abraham and the (near) sacrifice of Issac: First, God takes delight in annihilation; second, religious devotion requires obedience up to the sacrifice of one's life; or third, the story writer is attempting to overcome the idea that God may be pleased with human sacrifice.

Ironically, at the same time, Christians in society assiduously avoid suffering, and therefore people become increasingly insensitive and indifferent to the suffering of others.

> People stand before suffering like those who are color-blind, incapable of perception and without any sensibility. The consequence of this suffering-free state of well-being is that people's lives become frozen solid.

Even while Christianity has promoted a theological sadism, at the same time it has proclaimed an apathetic God, in other words, a God incapable of suffering. The worst form of apathy is found not at the personal but at the political level. Sölle connects the history of the Nazi period as a foretaste of the "inability to suffer" that only became clearer in the history of Vietnam.

Sölle furthers Weil's exploration of the suffering of the oppressed working classes through meditation on the story of a fifty-five-year-old foundry worker in Dusseldorf. He suffers the physical pain of blisters, metal burns, polluted air, fatigue, and undue bodily stress. Psychological suffering includes the monotony of the work and hopelessness that conditions will ever improve. Lastly, workers fear talking openly with one another lest they lose their jobs. There is suffering that is unbearable and destructive, suffering that is mute and that excludes change and learning.

What may bring about transformation of such conditions? Sölle emphasizes the importance of searching for language of lament that is essential for stepping out of the stage of mute, numb pain. This is the language of the Psalms. At the same time, this move from passive endurance to a kind of suffering that may humanize us produces social conflict. In the Christian story we see this same dynamic in Gethsemane. Sölle's intent is to "historicize" both the passion and resurrection, so that we understand that Jesus' experience is one that may happen to anyone. In the midst of suffering, it is inevitable that we cry out with the theodicy question, "Why?" However, theodicy is only an intermediary step; a "historicized" resurrection may be described as those historical moments and places where humans demonstrate the capacity to continue to love and affirm life even in the midst of suffering and uncertainty.

The mystical question regards how people can come to accept grief as joy. Sölle says it is not that our desire to diminish suffering decreases, but what increases is our concentration on a greater cause, to put God's love into practice. In the mystical way, suffering and letting go are set against acting and having. Moreover, in the Christian understanding, suffering, mysticism, and revolution move close to one another, as Christians move past simple toleration of suffering to working on suffering so as to affirm the great love for life as a whole.

> What matters is whether the suffering becomes our *passion*, in the deep double sense of that word. The act of suffering is then an exercise, an activity. We work with the suffering. We perceive, we express ourselves, we weep. To meditate on the cross means to say good-bye to the narcissistic hope of being free of sickness, deformity and death. Then all the energies wasted on such hopes could become free to answer the call for the battle against suffering.

Sölle explores this paradoxical freedom to work with suffering in the testimony of last letters of those condemned to death by the Nazis. What is so striking about these witnesses is their lack of bitterness or anger and the deep love expressed for those they are leaving behind. Facing death they know they may not avoid, they demonstrate concern for others, a deep knowledge of the connection between sorrow and joy, and a desire to impart a mission to those who remain. In Sölle's view, Christians must see that wherever people are tormented and suffering, Jesus' crucifixion and death continue. Moreover, love, though it does not intentionally seek confrontation, nevertheless finds itself on the cross in its unequivocal insistence on the liberation of people. Humans may avoid much bitterness of suffering, but at the cost of ceasing to love.

Christian Themes

Sölle reconfigures traditional understandings of the Christian life (*imitatio christi*) and attributes of God and Jesus Christ. While Christians have been admonished to interpret their suffering as a kind of vindication of the power of God through their very powerlessness or to adopt a universal willingness to suffer as central to their Christian identity, Sölle identifies such understandings as forms of masochism. To posit a kind of righteousness behind the reality of suffering, whether by way of a God who demands the sacrifice of Isaac or uses Job as an object lesson, or by way of a Christ who stoically suffers as the necessary sacrifice or scapegoat for sin, is to move in the direction of theological sadism.

In this respect Sölle foreshadows the feminist theologians and ethicists who in the 1980's and beyond systematically began to analyze and critique traditional understandings of Christian atonement. For Sölle, the only salvation available to anyone in the context of suffering is to continue loving, or at least to desire to go on loving, even if only with the smallest part of oneself. Atonement thus is redefined. Only faith in God provides the necessary capacity to continue to affirm life in the dark night of the cross. Golgotha is the moment in which Jesus spiritually comes of age, as he must undertake the task of doing without his father. The story of Jesus' Passion reveals a kind of Christianity that moves past religion understood as a defense mechanism against disappointment. God's suffering with and in Jesus on the cross reveals the pain of God's suffering wherever creation is wounded and intensifies the cry for human hands of healing and action.

> The only choice we have is between the absurd cross of meaninglessness and the cross of Christ, the death we accept apathetically as a natural end and the death we suffer as a passion.

The strong tie Sölle develops in this work between Christian mysticism and social action is further developed in her final book, *Mystik und Widerstand* (1977; *The Silent Cry: Mysticism and Resistance*, 2001).

Sources for Further Study

Hall, John Douglas. *God and Human Suffering: An Exercise in Theology of the Cross*. Minneapolis, Minn.: Augsburg, 1986. A fully developed Lutheran Christian theological exploration of the question of suffering and its relation to Christian salvation and life. Appendix outlining alternative understandings, index.

Perkins, Judith. *The Suffering Self: Pain and Narrative Representation in the Early*

Christian Era. New York: Routledge, 1995. An interdisciplinary study of the rise of the understanding of the self as sufferer in the early Christian period. Bibliography, index.

Weil, Simone. *Waiting for God*. New York: Harper, 1973. "The Love of God and Affliction" contains Weil's threefold description of affliction, and "Reflections on the Right Use of School Studies" describes Weil's focus on prayer and attention. Weil's philosophy lays the foundation for Sölle's description of suffering.

Williams, Rowan. *Writing in the Dust: After September 11*. Grand Rapids, Mich.: Wm. B. Eerdmans, 2002. Bishop of Canterbury's narrative theological response to September 11. Readers will find his description of the Christian response to unfathomable suffering similar to Sölle's.

Kelly Denton-Borhaug

SUMMA THEOLOGICA

Author: Saint Thomas Aquinas (1224/1225-1274)
First published: Summa theologiae, c. 1265-1273 (English translation, 1911-1921)
Edition used: The "Summa Theologica" of Saint Thomas Aquinas, translated by the Fathers of the English Dominican Province. New York: Benziger Brothers, 1947
Genre: Nonfiction
Subgenres: Didactic treatise; theology
Core issues: Creation; God; Incarnation; reason; salvation; soul

Aquinas states that God reveals himself both to faith and to reason; the knowledge granted by faith in divine revelation advances beyond rational knowledge but does not contradict it, since truth can never contradict itself. The light of natural reason can reveal God's existence, several of God's attributes, and the nature of his creation, including human nature, ethics, virtue, law, and government. However, humanity's return to God in redemption is known through the revelation of Jesus Christ and through the sacraments of the Christian Church.

Overview

When Pope Leo XIII in 1879 issued his encyclical *Aeterni Patris* (on the restoration of Christian philosophy) urging that the philosophy of Thomas Aquinas be promoted and taught within the Roman Catholic Church, he ratified a view of Aquinas already held by many: that Aquinas is not only the supreme medieval and Roman Catholic theologian and philosopher but also one of the greatest philosophers of all time. Aquinas's synthesis of biblical teachings with the philosophies of Aristotle and of Neoplatonism reaches its best-known expression in his final major work, the *Summa Theologica*. Despite its daunting size, intricate structure, and occasionally difficult ideas, this "summary of theology" was actually intended as an introductory text for students.

The *summa*, or summary form, was quite common in Aquinas's time; many theologians and philosophers wrote in this encyclopedic, systematic style, and Aquinas himself had previously completed the *Summa contra gentiles* (c. 1258-1264; English translation, 1923). The *Summa Theologica* is divided into three principal parts (the second part has two sections): Prima Pars, Prima Secundae Partis, Secunda Secundae Partis, and Tertia Pars. Tertia Pars, left only about half done by Aquinas at his death (up through question 90), was supplemented by his followers with additional material based on one of Aquinas's previously written philosophical commentaries. Each part is divided into treatises on various subjects, such as the "Treatise on Law" or the "Treatise on Man," which are themselves divided into several numbered questions (extensive essays). Each question is further divided into articles. These articles deal with a single yes-or-no question, such as whether God exists. Aquinas begins each article with a series of theological and philosophical objections to the yes-or-no answer he has in mind. He follows these objections with a short statement, always beginning with "On the contrary" (*Sed contra*), presenting his answer, which is based on the authority of the Bible, the Christian fathers of the Church, or a recognized source such as Aristotle.

The heart of the article is then presented in the section beginning "I answer that" (*Respondeo dicens*), in which Aquinas logically demonstrates his answer. These parts of each article are the parts most often quoted as exemplifying Aquinas's own philosophical positions and style of argumentation. After finishing his argument, Aquinas addresses and answers, one by one, each of the objections given at the beginning of the article. Thus each yes-or-no question is given not only an answer based on authority but also a philosophical, logical defense of that answer and a refutation of the most common objections raised by Aquinas's opponents. In this highly formal structure, the *Summa* echoes the typical form of medieval scholastic debate known as the "disputed question" (*quaestio disputata*), which would have been well known to Aquinas's original readers.

Aquinas states in the *Summa* that he will present the knowledge of God as revealed in sacred doctrine. However, sacred doctrine reveals God not only as he is in himself but also as the beginning of all things and as their final goal or last end. Therefore, Aquinas must write first of God considered in himself, then of God's creation of rational creatures, including humans, and then of humans in themselves, as he does in the Prima Pars. As the reader must then consider the rational creature's advance toward God, the Prima Secundae Partis treats humanity's return to God as its last end or goal. Finally, the Secunda Secundae Partis and Tertia Pars present Jesus Christ as humanity's way of returning to God; these sections discuss Christ's Incarnation, perfect nature, divinity, humanity, and so on, as well as dealing with the sacraments of the Christian Church as the way in which Christians participate in Christ's redemptive life, death, and resurrection. Thus the overall scheme of the *Summa* is that of a movement away from God in Creation and Original Sin, followed by a return to God in Christ.

However, since they are more specifically philosophical in nature, the first two divisions of the *Summa* are by far the most extensively quoted and discussed sections in the modern world. Aquinas begins by analyzing the nature and extent of sacred doctrine, its necessity over and beyond philosophical knowledge, and the limitations of theological language. God and his attributes are the proper object of this knowledge, so next Aquinas presents logical arguments for God's existence and his attributes such as perfection, goodness, unity, eternality, and Trinity (God as Father, Son, and Holy Spirit). The most famous of the treatises that follow include discussions of Creation, human nature, happiness, virtues and vices, Original Sin, and the various kinds of law (eternal, divine, natural, and human).

Because of their profundity and interest, these sections of the *Summa* have perhaps received disproportionate attention when compared to the plan of the work as a whole. However, much scholarship now focuses on recovering Aquinas's contribution not only as a systematic philosopher but also as a deeply devout Christian theologian and writer. No matter how it is considered, therefore, the *Summa* remains one of the most important and influential Christian works in existence.

Christian Themes

According to Aquinas, no division exists between the "revealed" truth known by faith and the general, "natural" revelation known by reason; truth itself is a unity, because ultimately the same God authors all that is true. Grace does not destroy nature but rather perfects it; consequently, supernatural revelation certainly will go beyond natural revelation but will not contradict it. For example, one may know of God's existence simply because the Bible declares it, but one may also know of God's existence rationally by the Five Ways (motion, causality, contingency, degrees of perfection, and teleology). By reason, one may also know some of God's attributes, such as his unity and perfection. However, some aspects of God, such as his Trinitarian nature, may be known only by faith.

Likewise, Aquinas says moral laws may be known directly by God's commands but are also accessible to all by the "natural law" written in the human heart. God's "eternal law" disposes all things by means of God's perfect knowledge and will, and is therefore identical with what is meant by the theological term "providence." Humans cannot, of course, know completely this eternal law, but what humans can grasp of it through their reason is the natural law. The human law (civil law, criminal law) should be based on the natural law; for example, criminal penalties for murder are based on the natural law prohibiting murder.

Human nature is a hylomorphic union of soul and body, with the intellectual soul providing the human "form." The material of the body is provided by one's parents, but the intellectual soul is infused directly by God. Original Sin causes the loss of humanity's original gift of righteousness and effects the perpetual inclination toward evil within humans but does not destroy the soul's innate powers such as rationality and freedom of the will.

Aquinas's teleological vision, in some respects quite similar to Aristotle's, sees all things as directed toward some end. Humans themselves have a single last end toward which they direct their activities and desires, even if they are mistaken in how to achieve this end. The general term for this last end is "happiness," but final perfected happiness can be attained only by the beatific vision of God. Ultimate happiness therefore depends on redemption through Christ, and so Aquinas's philosophical discussion is ultimately a theological discussion as well.

Sources for Further Study

Davies, Brian, ed. *Aquinas's "Summa Theologiae": Critical Essays.* Oxford, England: Rowman & Littlefield, 2006. Contains background on the work and critical essays on the varied content of Aquinas's thought, with a special focus (four out of eleven essays) on Aquinas's description of the soul and its powers.

Farrell, Walter. *A Companion to the "Summa."* 4 vols. New York: Sheed & Ward, 1945-1949. In addition to providing more than an explanatory commentary on each consecutive section of the work, Farrell engages Aquinas's thought philosophically.

Kreeft, Peter. *A Summa of the "Summa."* San Francisco: Ignatius Press, 1990. Excerpts and explains the work's essential philosophical passages for beginning students of Aquinas. Only covers the first part and the first section of the second part.

Torrell, Jean-Pierre. *Aquinas's "Summa": Background, Structure, & Reception.* Translated by Benedict M. Guevin. Washington, D.C.: Catholic University of America Press, 2005. A brief work that nonetheless covers much material, from an account of Aquinas's life to an assessment of the *Summa*'s literary structure, historical context, and doctrinal influence.

Craig Payne

THE SUPPLICATING VOICE
Spiritual Writings of Samuel Johnson

Author: Samuel Johnson (1709-1784)
First published: New York: Vintage, 2005, edited by John F. Thornton and Susan B. Varenne
Genre: Nonfiction
Subgenres: Devotions; essays; sermons
Core issues: Charity; death; prayer; suffering; trust in God

Johnson sees this world as a place of suffering, endurable only if one trusts in God and carries out his commandments. Christians must recognize their flaws, repent and do penance for them, share in Christian worship, demonstrate their faith through acts of charity, and while holding firm to their own beliefs, exhibit tolerance toward those whose religious views are different from their own.

Overview

The Supplicating Voice is a collection of Samuel Johnson's writings and statements dealing with religion. It includes sermons, personal prayers, diary entries, poems, published essays, relevant definitions from Johnson's *Dictionary of the English Language: To Which Are Prefixed, a History of the Language, and an English Grammar* (1755), and comments made in conversation and recorded by his friend and biographer James Boswell in his *Life of Samuel Johnson, LL.D.* (1791).

Johnson did not deliver the sermons he wrote. They were intended for presentation by clergymen who, lacking the skill, the time, or the inclination to make up sermons of their own, bought them from Johnson for two guineas each. An exception was the sermon on immortality that Johnson wrote for presentation at the funeral of Johnson's wife, Elizabeth "Tetty" Johnson, on March 17, 1752. It was one of only three sermons that were dated and the only one to be published. According to Boswell, the preacher decided not to use it, but the sermon, whose subject was immortality, was printed later that month. Though Johnson believed he wrote at least forty sermons, perhaps many more, he did not keep records of his sales. Therefore only the twenty-seven in this book can be ascribed to him with relative certainty.

In all of his sermons, Johnson began with biblical texts, which he then discussed in a rational, methodical manner. In them, he often contrasted God's majesty and righteousness with the lowly, sinful state of human beings and urged the imagined congregation to avoid pride, to be compassionate, and above all, to be charitable.

Ironically, though Johnson was a loyal member of the Church of England, he seldom attended services. He was too restless, both physically and intellectually, to sit through long sermons that were so often pedestrian and uninspired. However, he valued prayer highly, and throughout his life he composed prayers in the formal style of the Anglican collects, which he used in his personal devotions. From time to time, he also kept a diary. Neither the prayers nor his diaries were intended for publication, but fortunately some of these writings survived. In them, it is evident that though even as a young man Johnson had accepted the truths of Christianity and was living according to the Christian moral system, his faith grew steadily more profound as he grew older.

Johnson's most famous poem is "The Vanity of Human Wishes: The Tenth Satire of Juvenal, Imitated" (1749). Like the Roman writer Juvenal, Johnson points out the futility of every human endeavor. Worldly power is easily lost; military glory ends in death; feminine beauty soon fades; and even intellectual prowess vanishes. However, while Juvenal maintained the Stoic position, that to be rational means to subdue every emotion, even hope, Johnson ends his poem by asserting that happiness can come to human beings as the byproduct of obedience to God and faith in Providence. Also included in this collection are the early poem "Upon the Feast of St. Simon and St. Jude" and a modern translation of a Latin poem by Johnson, "Christianus Perfectus," in which the poet outlines a Christian's spiritual progress on the road to heaven.

Between 1750 and 1760, Johnson wrote essays for his own publication *The Rambler*, then for the periodical *The Adventurer*, and finally for *The Idler*. Although many of these essays were light in tone, often satirizing foolish behavior, Johnson made it clear that his serious essays were solidly based on Christian teachings. Those selected for *The Supplicating Voice* deal with such issues as how one can live a worthwhile life, whether a Christian should live in solitude or in society, and how a believer should face old age and death.

Because Johnson was known sometimes to argue first one side and then the other, it is to be expected that the passages from Boswell's *Life of Samuel Johnson* would sometimes seem to contradict each other and that they would not always be consistent with his dictionary definitions. For example, Boswell reports Johnson's castigation of the Presbyterians for having no fixed form of worship and for dispensing with the apostolic succession, and yet he relies on the great Presbyterian writer John Milton for many definitions involving religion. On more than one occasion Johnson states his belief that the differences between Christians are trivial, that where the essentials of the faith are concerned, they agree. However, such inconsistencies demonstrate the depth of Johnson's thought. While he was too precise in his reasoning to ignore details, he also knew that even the most thoughtful human beings cannot see earthly matters as God does. It is significant that, as Boswell reports, on his deathbed Johnson declined painkillers, asserting that he wished to have a clear mind when he surrendered his soul. Not only does that incident demonstrate his unswerving faith in God, but also it shows that he hoped to have all of his questions answered when he arrived in the next world.

Christian Themes

Johnson held to the doctrines and the practice of the Church of England, which he believed was linked through the apostolic succession to the church founded by Christ. Like other Reformation churches, the Church of England believed that the Scriptures contained all that was necessary for salvation. Johnson, too, considered the Scriptures, not later doctrines or papal decisions, the ultimate authority. However, he also looked to the early patristic writings for guidance. He believed that the Roman Catholic Church was wrong in many of its actions, such as its use of purgatory to extract money from the faithful. In theory, however, Johnson saw nothing wrong with such Roman Catholic practices as believing in purgatory, praying for the dead, or making one's confession and being assigned penance.

As for the Presbyterians, Johnson not only thought their practice flawed and their system of church government erroneous but also emphatically rejected their doctrine of predestination, which, unfortunately, had been mentioned with approval in the Thirty-nine Articles of the Church of England. Johnson believed that Christ died for all people, that everyone has free will, and that salvation is available to all through grace, conditional on their having faith in God, repenting of their sins, and performing works of charity. When he referred to his "late" conversion, he did not mean that he came to faith or to Christian practice late in his life. In his Latin poem and throughout his writings, Johnson makes it clear that, in accordance with the Church of England, he thought of conversion as a gradual process, involving systematic self-examination, amendment of life, and spiritual growth, a process that ended only with death.

Johnson's lifelong preoccupation with death has been seen as evidence that his faith was not always as strong as it seemed. However, Johnson does not fear death; he fears the judgment that will follow. Ironically, Johnson was a very model of that quality he so emphasized, charity toward others. He supported a household of needy people, and he gave so generously of his substance that often he could not meet his own financial obligations. Nevertheless, his habit of self-examination kept him always aware of how far short of Christian perfection he fell. It is ironic that Johnson had such difficulty believing that God would exhibit the same compassion toward him that he routinely did toward others. In his final days, however, Johnson seemed to lose his fear of death and the subsequent judgment. He died secure in salvation through the grace of God.

Sources for Further Study

Chapin, Chester F. *The Religious Thought of Samuel Johnson*. Ann Arbor: University of Michigan Press, 1968. Traces the development of Johnson's faith and contrasts his views with that of contemporary evangelicals. Notes and index.

Clark, Jonathan, and Howard Erskine-Hill, eds. *Samuel Johnson in Historical Context*. New York: Palgrave, 2001. Essays by literary critics and historians address the controversy between critics who see Johnson merely as a moralist and those who note his intense commitment to religious and political causes. Notes and index.

Potkay, Adam. *The Passion for Happiness: Samuel Johnson and David Hume*. Ithaca, N.Y.: Cornell University Press, 2000. Argues persuasively that Johnson and Hume share a definition of happiness drawn from classical sources. However, the author fails to point out the Christian basis of Johnson's beliefs.

Quinlan, Maurice J. *Samuel Johnson: A Layman's Religion*. Madison: University of

Wisconsin Press, 1964. Explains gradual change in Johnson's beliefs, including his acceptance of the doctrine of the atonement. Notes and index.

Suarez, Michael F., S.J. "Johnson's Christian Thought." In *The Cambridge Companion to Samuel Johnson*, edited by Greg Clingham. Cambridge, England: Cambridge University Press, 1997. Johnson was an outstanding theological thinker as well as a Christian moralist. A systematic, lucid analysis.

Rosemary M. Canfield Reisman

SUTTER'S CROSS

Author: W. Dale Cramer
First published: Minneapolis, Minn.: Bethany House, 2003
Genre: Novel
Subgenre: Literary fiction
Core issues: Acceptance; redemption; surrender; trust in God

This novel, set in the small town of Sutter's Cross in northern Georgia, deals with faith and redemption. Harley, a long-haired drifter, appears one day at a church picnic. The members of the Sutter's Cross Community Church do not know how to treat him; only the elderly Miss Agnes Dewberry is able to open her arms to him. Soon, she and Harley come into conflict with the plans of ruthless developer Web Holcombe, a man used to getting what he wants, regardless of the methods or costs.

>*Principal characters*
>*Jake Mahaffey*, a construction supervisor
>*Lori Mahaffey*, Jake's wife
>*Web Holcombe*, a millionaire developer
>*Miss Agnes Dewberry*, an elderly farm widow
>*Harley*, a drifter
>*Eddie Holcombe*, Web's son
>*Marcus*, Eddie's friend
>*Orde Wingo*, a Sunday school teacher who attends church with the Mahaffeys

Overview

In *Sutter's Cross*, W. Dale Cramer tells the story of people in a small north Georgia town who find their notions of piety, holiness, and faith tested. It is a novel about people learning to place their faith in God rather than in themselves and realizing it is only through trusting in God that you can live a whole and fulfilling life. The novel opens with the Sutter's Cross Community Church picnic; Jake Mahaffey and his fellow church members and picnickers do not know what to think of the long-haired, greasy drifter, Harley, who happens by the picnic.

When Harley pounces on elderly Agnes Dewberry (to perform the Heimlich maneuver), one of the male members of the congregation mistakes his motives and smashes him in the face. When Harley is taken to the hospital, doctors discover that his jaw has already been broken in an accident not long before. Harley refuses to let the hospital hold him, and before long he has retreated into the Appalachian mountain wilderness above Agnes's farm. More than anything, Harley wants peace in which to read his Bible and to meditate on the overlook called Joshua's Knee at the edge of the high, long ridge in the territory behind Agnes's house.

Jake finds Harley to be an enigma; he sees himself as Agnes's protector and wants to make sure that Harley means her no harm. He is willing to accept Agnes's word that Harley is a good man who means well; however, other members of Jake's church—such as Sunday school teacher Orde Wingo—cannot see past Harley's long hair, beard, and dilapidated clothing. Before long, Jake has other things on his mind besides Harley; his wife, Lori, tells him she is pregnant. It is not long before Jake realizes that Harley is what he seems to be: a man seeking to become closer to God.

Juxtaposed against Harley is millionaire Web Holcombe. The son of a well-to-do developer, Web has used his experiences in Vietnam to justify a take-no-prisoners approach to building his own empire. He has single-handedly made Sutter's Cross a desirable golf resort. Married to a beautiful woman and wealthy beyond his dreams, Web sees himself as a man in control of his life, who needs no help from anyone—including the God in whom he does not believe.

Web is planning to build a country club and a series of developments, and he is courting wealthy foreign investors to come into Sutter's Cross. However, a number of farms stand in the way; Web's ruthlessness is revealed when he is willing to resort to hiring a henchman to blackmail one of the farmers. Yet, despite his ample resources, Web's relationship with his twelve-year-old son, Eddie, is tenuous. Web misses Little League games to attend meetings and is never around when Eddie and his best friend Marcus go on adventures in the woods.

Eddie and Marcus have their own problems. Eddie is starting to like girls and Marcus has no faith in himself and cannot seem to get anything right—his baseball swing, or building a treehouse. Both of the boys are taunted by a bully and his cronies.

Web's world comes crashing into Harley's when Web realizes that his ability to enjoy his favorite sport of gliding in his sailplane will be greatly complicated with the closing of the closest airstrip to house sailplanes. Before long, Web has settled on a ridge of territory behind Agnes's house—and owned by her. Web asks Agnes to sell him her land, and when she refuses, he tries to have both Harley and Jake intercede for him. Jake's integrity is challenged when Web hires him to develop houses and Jake soon realizes that it is only because Web wishes to take advantage of Jake's relationship with Agnes. Jake passes the test of his integrity even as he and Lori must endure twin tragedies: They have lost their baby and discovered that Lori has cancer.

When Web finally realizes that he cannot gain Agnes's land through proper methods, he chooses others: He has the area rezoned so that she cannot pay her property taxes, and eventually he even hires an arsonist. Even as Web continues to bulldoze his way toward his own goals, others find their eyes being opened and their hearts touched by Harley. Harley is a man with a past filled with tragedy and sorrow who has found a measure of peace only through surrendering his will to God's; in this surrender he has gained a strength and wisdom that helps the people he comes in contact with, such as Agnes and young Marcus.

Events eventually come to a head in *Sutter's Cross* when the edge of a hurricane passes through the region and causes massive flooding of the river. Harley's secrets have been revealed to the sheriff, and even as Jake searches the hills to save Harley, Orde Wingo and a group of armed vigilantes are combing the woods for him as well.

The flooding places Web's son Eddie into great danger, and it is only through miraculous acts of heroism by Harley and Jake that disaster is averted. Through the intervention of God in his life and Harley's example, even Web Holcombe comes to see the error of his ways.

Christian Themes

Cramer uses Web's sailplane as the perfect metaphor for his life. Flying in it gives him the illusion that he is in control, above everything else, master of his fate and of all he surveys. Through one nearly tragic flight, Web discovers that he is subject to the will of God and that his vain pride in his mastery of his environment will come up short in the end. In contrast, Cramer uses the accident that brings Harley to Sutter's Cross to symbolize the path forward. Drunk and racing on mountain roads at night to flee a tragic past, Harley drives his motorcycle over a precipice and falls into the river. Falling through space, he has no control of his motorcycle or his body. Later, spending his time in the mountain recesses and on Joshua's Knee, reading the Bible left behind by Agnes's son, who died in Vietnam, Harley realizes that he has never had any control and for him to reach any fruition in his life, he must place it in God's hands. The plunge into the river serves as a kind of baptism; afterward, he is reborn.

The novel is also about acceptance. Harley does not fit Orde Wingo's vision of what a Christian should be. Therefore, despite Harley's obvious eagerness to discuss the Bible and to become part of the church community, Orde makes it clear that he does not welcome Harley. In a few short meetings, Harley is able to help Marcus see the power of prayer and surrendering his will to God's; Jake, too, learns about strength and faith in God from Harley. Even Web Holcombe is eventually touched to the core by Harley's ultimate, Christ-like sacrifice; yet, Orde, devout churchgoer, is not a participant in the spiritual growth sparked by Harley's appearance.

Sources for Further Study

Butler, Tamara. Review of *Levi's Will* by W. Dale Cramer. *Library Journal* 130, no. 10 (June 1, 2005): 108. Review of the third book by Cramer mentions his tendency to create fallen heroes.

Crosby, Cindy. "Spiritual Misfits." Review of *Sutter's Cross*. *Christianity Today* 47, no. 3 (March, 2003): 79. A brief review that describes the spiritual challenges the novel's characters must meet.

Mort, John. Review of *Sutter's Cross*. *Booklist* 99, nos. 9/10 (January 1/15, 2003): 845. Review praises Cramer's first novel.

Publishers Weekly. Review of *Sutter's Cross*. 249, no. 51 (December 23, 2002): 46. Review that focuses primarily on the style of the novel and its place in the tradition of southern literature.

"W. Dale Cramer." *Contemporary Authors Online*. Farmington Hills, Mich.: Thomson Gale, 2007. A short biography of Cramer that discusses *Sutter's Cross*.

Scott D. Yarbrough

SYNOPTIC GOSPELS

Authors: Matthew (fl. first century C.E.), Mark (fl. first century C.E.), and Luke (fl. first century C.E.)
First transcribed: Euaggelion kata Matthaion, Markon, Lucan, c. 140 C.E. (English translation, c. 1380)
Edition used: Revised Standard Version of the Holy Bible. New York: Oxford University Press, 2002
Genre: Holy writings
Subgenres: Biblical studies; spiritual treatise; theology
Core issues: The cross; discipleship; Gospels; Jesus Christ; scriptures; suffering

The Synoptic Gospels of the Bible—Matthew, Mark, and Luke—provide the most comprehensive view of the life, death, resurrection, and teachings of Jesus of Nazareth, called Jesus the Christ by believers. Written as faith summaries rather than biographies, they focus on the sayings and deeds of Jesus in his public ministry, which lasted for three years. Although some of the letters of Saint Paul predate the Synoptic Gospels, most Christian sects rely almost exclusively on these books as a cornerstone for their theological beliefs, rituals, and codes of ethics.

Overview

The Gospels (literally, good news) of Matthew, Mark, and Luke have been called Synoptic (seen together) Gospels since the end of the eighteenth century because they contain similar details in the life of Jesus of Nazareth. In addition, the three Gospels have a linguistic resemblance in the Greek in which they were written, which is not thought to be coincidental given that Jesus himself spoke Aramaic and the Gospels purport to be a written record of his teachings. The fourth Gospel, attributed to John, is set apart from the others because of its late composition and the author's use of figurative and symbolic language that is not found in the three Synoptics.

From the eighteenth century, scholars have debated various theories as to why there is so much similarity among the three Synoptic Gospels. At least one-third of the Gospel material is repeated in the other Synoptics. This question is referred to by biblical scholars as the Synoptic problem. The most obvious explanations are that the writers, or evangelists, copied from one another or witnessed the same events.

These theories have been discounted for a number of reasons. First, it is improbable that the evangelists were apostles in close proximity with Jesus. Because the earliest of the three Gospels (Mark) was not written until approximately 65 C.E. and the two others up to twenty years later, any copying would probably have been from Mark's earlier document. Because most scholars do not believe that Matthew and Luke copied from each other, the most prevalent theory has been that the Synoptic authors drew on a number of existing documents. It has been proposed that there was a document or an early source (called Q for *quelle*, or source) of one-line sayings of Jesus that Matthew and Luke both used for their information. In addition, some scholars believe that both Matthew and Luke had their own private sources of material about Jesus and also drew on Mark's Gospel for some of their content.

The Synoptic problem is of special interest to students of the Bible engaged in the quest for the historical Jesus. This quest focuses on determining which details of Jesus' life, deeds, and words are the most likely to be historically accurate. For example, because only two of the Gospels (Matthew and Luke) begin with the birth of Jesus, it is widely held that details of Jesus' birth are unknown. The accounts rendered by Matthew and Luke differ greatly from each other and contain a number of elements that biblical scholars consider to be either symbolic or indicative of the evangelists' theological objectives. With the exception of the inclusion by one evangelist of an incident recounting Jesus' being lost on the way to the temple at age twelve (Luke 2:39-52), all three of the Synoptic Gospels follow Jesus closely during the three years of his public ministry before his execution. Because there are extrabiblical attestations to the events recorded in the Synoptic Gospels, this material is considered to be, for the most part, historically accurate.

Because the Gospels are summaries of beliefs about the messiahship of Jesus written to specific audiences for specific theological purposes, there are differences in focus, details, and symbolic significance among the three Synoptic Gospels. Matthew, for example, wrote predominantly to Jewish Christians living after the destruction of the temple in 70 C.E. Employing many Old Testament allusions, Matthew attempts to show Jesus to be the fulfillment of Old Testament messianic prophecies. He stresses parallels between Jesus and Moses, the major liberator of Jewish tradition, which would be especially important for the Jewish followers of Jesus who were concerned about their relationship to Judaism and, in particular, their obligation to Jewish law. In fact, Matthew presents the Pharisees (the staunch supporters of traditional Judaism) as Jesus' main opponents, echoing the tension that existed between various segments of the Jewish community at the time he wrote. Matthew's deliberate appeal to a Jewish audience can be seen in his careful tracing of Jesus' genealogy back to Abraham, the father of the Jewish faith.

Tradition holds that the author of Luke's Gospel (and the Acts of the Apostles) was a physician and traveling companion of Saint Paul. Although none of this can be historically verified, Luke's Gospel appears to be directed toward Gentile Christians living in a Hellenistic culture (perhaps Greece or the Greek cities of Asia Minor), who were not as familiar with Jewish traditions and customs. In an attempt to present Christianity as no threat to the governing Roman authorities, Luke traces Jesus' lineage back to their common ancestor, Adam. The focus of his Gospel is to present Jesus as the universal savior. Concerned with the inclusion of the marginalized in the Kingdom of Heaven that Jesus proclaimed, Luke emphasizes Jesus' compassion, including many stories about how he interacted with and embraced the outcasts of society.

The Gospel of Mark is believed to be the earliest of the four Gospels and, as such, possesses an authenticity that the others do not. Held by tradition to have been a disciple of the apostle Peter, Mark wrote to an audience of persecuted Gentile Christians.

This focus is reflected in his emphasis on the suffering and cross of Jesus and highlights Jesus' exhortations to his disciples to "take up their crosses" and follow him. Perhaps as a way of defending the lack of insight on the part of the apostles with regard to Jesus' status as Messiah, Mark employs a literary technique referred to by biblical scholars as the Messianic secret. After performing miracles or exorcisms, Jesus admonishes the onlookers to say nothing to anyone. He silences demons who recognize his divine nature and instructs his apostles in private as to the real meaning of his parables. Although scholars have had different theories as to why Mark uses this technique (which is not found in the other Synoptics), the most commonly accepted explanation is that Mark is challenging common assumptions about the role of a Messiah. By avoiding quick labeling, Jesus forces his followers to reach their own conclusions about his nature and salvific role.

Jesus' messiahship is not political but characterized by suffering. This can be seen clearly in the pivotal chapter 8 of Mark's Gospel, in which Peter "confesses" Jesus to be the Messiah. When Jesus goes on to remark that the Son of Man (a title used by Jesus most often for himself in Mark's Gospel) must suffer, be put to death, and rise three days later, Peter protests this fate, thereby indicating a false understanding of the nature of Jesus' messiahship. Jesus immediately rebukes Peter, saying angrily to him, "Get behind me, Satan! For you are not on the side of God but of men" (Mark 8:33).

All three Synoptics relate the numerous miraculous healings Jesus performed and his discourses and instructions to his disciples, and recount the altercations with Jewish leaders leading to his arrest and crucifixion. These biographical details provide Christian sects with a firm basis for their doctrinal beliefs about the nature of the God-man Jesus and a model of ethical perfection for their followers.

Christian Themes

Although the Synoptic writers emphasize different characteristics of Jesus as Messiah, they all present Jesus as wonder worker, sage, teacher, and Son of God. From depictions of his humble birth in a manger in Matthew and Luke's Gospels, all three Gospels go on to record the numerous miracles of Jesus (healings, exorcisms, and nature miracles) and the effects the words and deeds of Jesus had on his many followers.

Growing up as a practicing Jew in first century Israel, Jesus followed the customs and rituals of his religious tradition. Rather than offer a new religion, Jesus reinforced the message of the Old Testament prophets by demanding a change of heart that would have a liberating effect on people as well as on the unjust social order in which they lived. The main theme of Jesus' teaching was that the Kingdom of God announced by the Old Testament prophets had indeed arrived. This kingdom, ushered in by Jesus, would bring with it the liberation of the oppressed as foretold by the prophet Isaiah. Although the kingdom had officially arrived, it had to be realized within the hearts of all those willing to undertake the necessary conversion to enter this kingdom.

Jesus summarized his message as the Great Commandment: Love God with all of your heart, mind, and soul, and love your neighbor as yourself (Mark 12:30-31, Matthew 22:37-39). The fact that this is a reiteration of two Old Testament passages (Deuteronomy 6:5 and Leviticus 19:18) illustrates Jesus' respect for his Jewish religious background and his attempt to promote love as the guiding principle of all ethical action. His close relationship with God, his *abba* (an Aramaic word commonly translated as "father" but more accurately translated as the more intimate "daddy"), can be seen in his penchant for private prayer and his countless attempts to portray God's love through parables. The love that Jesus preached was a self-sacrificing love that put the welfare of others before all else. The Greek term for this type of selfless love is *agape*, sometimes referred to as Christian love. The rewards of practicing this type of love are manifold, according to Jesus. Many of the paradoxes he used resound with this theme. ("For whoever would save his life will lose it; and whoever loses his life for my sake and the gospel's will save it" Mark 8:35, Matthew 16:25, Luke 9:24.) In fact, Jesus' willingness to subject law to the overriding consideration of love not only led to his occasional breaking of established Jewish laws but also antagonized some influential Jewish leaders, ultimately resulting in his arrest and death.

The many miracles of Jesus recorded in the Synoptic Gospels not only attracted many followers but also divulged Jesus' true nature and identity. Although there exists a difference of opinion among Christian denominations as to the true nature of Jesus (for example, Jehovah's Witnesses and Mormons do not believe Jesus to be a distinct person in the triune Godhead as do most Christians), the biblical stories of Jesus' acts of power provide modern Christians with evidence of Jesus' supernatural essence. These miracles, which amazed onlookers at their occurrence, indicated to early Christians Jesus' mastery over both the physical and spiritual realms. Because illness was believed to be caused by sin, the idea that Jesus could heal physical ailments indicated a power over sin that was reinforced by Jesus' overtly proclaiming to various recipients of miracles that their sins were forgiven (Mark 2:5, Luke 5:20, Matthew 9:2). His mastery over nature (for example, the calming of the sea in Matthew 8:23-27, Mark 4:35-41, Luke 8:22-25) hinted at his divine status. The authority with which he ordered demons to come out of those possessed evoked awe in onlookers.

These acts involved what many Jewish leaders regarded as an appropriation of divine authority and culminated in their leveling a charge of blasphemy against him, seen by scholars as a significant factor in Jesus' subsequent arrest and execution. The greatest of all of Jesus' miracles, his own resurrection, is recounted in the Synoptic Gospels along with numerous accounts of post-resurrection appearances. His followers and generations of Christians who came after them believed that this act illustrated for once and for all Jesus' divinity and identified him as the son of God.

Sources for Further Study

Brown, Raymond. *An Introduction to the New Testament.* New York: Anchor Bible, 1997. A preeminent biblical scholar guides the reader through the sociohistorical background of the Gospels and their philosophical and theological significance. Provides resources for further study.

Brown, Raymond, Joseph Fitzmyer, and Roland Murphy, eds. *The New Jerome Bibli-*

cal Commentary. Englewood Cliffs, N.J.: Prentice Hall, 1987. A serious academic guide to individual passages of Scripture. Provides background, interpretation, and resources for more in-depth analysis. Catholic perspective, but more academic than denominational.

Malina, Bruce, and Richard Rohrbrough. *Social Science Commentary on the Synoptic Gospels.* 2d ed. Minneapolis, Minn.: Augsburg Fortress Press, 2002. Provides the reader with fascinating sociological background to the world in which Jesus lived and a deeper insight into the meanings of his words and actions.

Sanders, E. P., and Margaret Davies. *Studying the Synoptic Gospels* Philadelphia: Trinity Press International, 1990. Surveys the various scholarly debates about the purpose, authorship, and interrelationship of the Synoptic Gospels for the interested layperson. Clear explanations of abstract theories.

Senior, Donald. *Jesus: A Gospel Portrait.* Rev. ed. Mahwah, N.J.: Paulist Press, 1992. Senior combines biblical scholarship with a reverential study of the person of Jesus, his world, and his significance for Christians today. Contains a valuable bibliography.

Throckmorton, Burton H. *Gospel Parallels: A Comparison of the Synoptic Gospels.* 5th ed. Nashville, Tenn.: Nelson Reference, 1992. Handy tool first published in 1949. Illustrates clearly how the material of the Synoptics lines up. Gospel passages are copied in parallel columns for clear comparison.

Mara Kelly-Zukowski

THE TASKS OF PHILOSOPHY

Author: Alasdair MacIntyre (1929-)
First published: Vol. 1 in *Selected Essays.* Cambridge, England: Cambridge University Press, 2006
Genre: Nonfiction
Subgenre: Essays
Core issues: Ethics; knowledge; reason

MacIntyre argues that philosophical and moral theories must be understood in the context of particular cultures and traditions as efforts to provide a rational justification for the theorist's understanding of truth. Philosophical and moral progress results not from knowledge of truth but from the discovery of theories and justifications that are closer to truth.

Overview

Through essays written from 1972 to 2002, Alasdair MacIntyre provides an overview of his philosophical project with particular applications of his version of Thomistic philosophy to modern issues. In MacIntyre's view, the philosophies of Saint Thomas Aquinas and Greek philosopher Aristotle depict philosophical discourse as occurring within the context of a tradition. Thus, philosophy is a craft in that it requires a teacher who can provide an understanding of the principles and purposes (ends) of the craft and yet also allows the student to move beyond the teacher's understanding of those principles and purposes.

MacIntyre emphasizes that each person exists within the context of a particular tradition or culture. Moreover, a person's ability to understand others and to be understood is provided by tradition and culture in the form of a dramatic narrative. The dramatic narrative, by providing a background and structure, organizes thought such that it can be rational and comprehensible. It provides the philosopher with particular theses and arguments that circumscribe the scope of possible rational discourse within the tradition. Thus, the dramatic narrative both makes rational inquiry possible and, at the same time, limits the extent of that inquiry.

At times, however, an individual enters into an epistemological crisis because the dramatic narrative is insufficient. This insufficiency can be discovered because of conflicts inherent in the tradition or because of an encounter with rival traditions. This results in a breakdown in the relationship between what seems to be true and what is true. Progress within a particular tradition is characterized by the ability to identify, solve, and explain problems and difficulties within the tradition. If these problems result in a sustained incoherence in the tradition, it becomes more likely that an individual will begin to doubt the sufficiency of the tradition. Having made this realization, the inquirer must either stagnate, defending the deficiencies of his own viewpoint against the attacks of rival viewpoints, or else attempt to engage the imagination to understand a rival view from the standpoint of that rival. To the extent an individual is able to make this imaginative leap, it becomes possible to reexamine one's original tradition in light of the rival tradition, in hopes that the rival tradition will provide a more coherent understanding of truth, including an explanation for why the original tradition failed in precisely the ways that it failed.

True reconciliation occurs through the creation of a new narrative that enables individuals to understand both how they could have intelligibly believed the earlier narrative and how they were misled. This process, while leading to a more adequate narrative, does not lead to a philosophy that is not subject to further questioning. In other words, it does not lead to absolute truth. However, it also should not result in relativism.

To understand the problem with relativism, it is important to distinguish between truth and rational justification. Individuals who hold to a particular moral viewpoint necessarily distinguish between these two concepts, whereas a relativist necessarily conflates them. Truth is the *telos* or final end of all philosophical and moral inquiry. Rational justifications are intended to provide support for belief in a particular moral view. The practice of rational justification aims at a progress toward truth that is characterized as a movement from what is local, partial, and one-sided toward conformity of the intellect with truth. This possibility of progress, however, presupposes the possibility that the particular rational justification will be found insufficient and will be revised. Thus, any recognition of the changeability of rational justifications cannot serve as a basis for accepting relativism. This would not be the case if rational justification was essentially synonymous with the truth at which it aims.

This understanding of rational justifications as necessarily rooted in traditions and of truth as the final end of all theoretical inquiry is of fundamental importance for recognizing how MacIntyre's thought stands in relation to modern and contemporary philosophy. Modern or Enlightenment thought, following French philosopher René Descartes, attempts to avoid the danger of skepticism by attempting to doubt everything that need not be accepted by every person in every place or time. It claims not only that we can provide a foundation for philosophy but also that we can provide this foundation independent of any final end. MacIntyre, following the German philosopher Friedrich Nietzsche and his successors, contends that no such skepticism is possible and that, to the extent that it is possible, it leads to madness and unintelligibility. Skepticism asks certain questions, and radical doubt makes it increasingly difficult to even understand the questions that are being asked.

In addition, Enlightenment thought fails because it presupposes that it is possible to have first principles independent of a final end. MacIntyre points out that it is only because there is a final end that it is possible to understand anything in the way of first principles. In other words, the process of inquiry and the existence of humans as creatures that enquire presupposes that there is truth toward which such inquiry can aim. This acceptance of first principles and final ends, however, distinguishes MacIntyre not only from Enlightenment thought but also from contemporary philosophy. While MacIntyre generally accepts Nietzsche's critique of the Enlightenment conception of rationality, he rejects Nietzsche's failure to recognize that final ends are necessary to provide a coherent theory of truth and rational discourse.

Christian Themes

Questions concerning the relationship between philosophy and Christian belief are perennial, and MacIntyre's attempt to revive the Aristotelian and Thomistic tradition of virtue-based ethics is an important contribution to discussions that have become mired in the debates between Enlightenment thought and the followers of Nietzsche. In the final essay of the book, however, MacIntyre addresses an issue of particular interest to the Christian philosopher.

In the 1998 encyclical *Fides et ratio* (on the relationship between faith and reason), Pope John Paul II presupposes that truth is a good and is the good of the human intellect. This presupposition, in turn, requires a rejection of certain philosophical theses such as relativism. At the same time, he states that philosophy must remain autonomous and that if it did not proceed according to its own principles and methods, it would be of little use. MacIntyre argues that this conjunction of attitudes has led to a caricature of the encyclical as promoting free inquiry only as long as that free inquiry comes to the conclusions already predetermined by Christian faith.

Building on the Thomistic tradition, MacIntyre emphasizes that the Christian understanding of rational inquiry is closely connected to the Christian understanding of human nature. It is not enough to recognize that truth is the final end of rational inquiry, but it is also important to acknowledge the significance of the nature of human beings as creatures who engage in rational inquiry, as creatures who are truth seekers. Philosophy, MacIntyre explains, seeks rational answers to questions posed by human beings. This seeking, moreover, is an essential part of the nature of all humans. As a result, it is precisely because of the encyclical's commitment to truth as the good of the human intellect that it acknowledges the independence of philosophy. It is only through philosophy's independence that reason is capable of making the unforced assent to truth that is essential to rational inquiry. Divine revelation, while it does provide answers and it does help illuminate false reasoning, does not end rational inquiry. Instead, it provides additional resources and goals for inquiry.

Sources for Further Study

MacIntyre, Alasdair. *After Virtue: A Study in Moral Theory*. 2d ed. Notre Dame, Ind.: University of Notre Dame Press, 1984. The landmark book in which MacIntyre analyzes the decay of modern thought and its inability to provide any unifying framework for reconciling rival views and philosophies.

_____. *Three Rival Versions of Moral Enquiry: Encyclopaedia, Genealogy, and Tradition*. Notre Dame, Ind.: University of Notre Dame Press, 1990. Focuses on the nature of the conflict between current types of moral inquiry and how to bring them into dialogue.

_____. *Whose Justice? Which Rationality?* Notre Dame, Ind.: University of Notre Dame Press, 1988. A discussion of the development of Western moral philosophy, focusing on the ways in which different conceptions of justice and rationality interacted.

Murphy, Mark C., ed. *Alasdair MacIntyre*. New York: Cambridge University Press, 2003. A helpful collection of essays discussing MacIntyre's work. Essays include discussions of the relationship between history and philosophy, the significance of tradition, and MacIntyre's impact on the social sciences, moral philosophy, and political philosophy.

Rowland, Tracey. *Culture and the Thomist Tradition: After Vatican II*. New York: Routledge, 2003. Drawing heavily from MacIntyre, attempts to provide a theological analysis of culture and particularly of modern culture.

Joshua A. Skinner

THE TEMPLE

Author: George Herbert (1593-1633)
First published: 1633
Edition used: The Temple, in *The Works of George Herbert,* edited by F. E. Hutchinson. Oxford, England: Clarendon Press, 1941
Genre: Poetry
Subgenre: Lyric poetry
Core issues: Church; faith; pastoral role; virtue

Herbert collects his poems of a lifetime into an architectural setting, with its "porch," "supreliminary" (a passageway into the main sanctuary), and the church "proper," with its "altar" providing the focus for worship.

Overview

George Herbert was born into a noble family; his elder brother was Lord Herbert. George became public orator at Cambridge University in 1620, and he was a friend of the crown prince. The death of King James in 1625 turned his attention to spiritual matters, much influenced by the godly community of Nicholas Ferrar in Little Gidding. Herbert relinquished his worldly opportunities, and for the last three years of his life he pastored a small church at Bremerton, near Salisbury. His famous account of a pastoral model, *A Priest to the Temple: Or, The Country Parson His Character and Rule of Holy Life,* was published posthumously in 1652. *The Temple,* a volume of his lyrical poems, embodies expressions of his personal struggles of faith and was used as a device of pastoral teaching.

Just as the Book of Common Prayer sets the frame for the corporate devotion and worship of Anglicanism, so Herbert collects his poems of a lifetime into an architectural setting, with its "porch," "supreliminary" (a passageway into the main sanctuary), and the church "proper," with its "altar" providing the focus for worship. As Herbert cites from Psalm 29:9, "in His Temple, does every man speak of His Honor," so the life of the Christian is subsumed within a corporate sharing in the faith, fellowship, and ordinances of the Church.

Seeing the need of unity in all of one's life before God, Herbert identifies, in the first section of his poems, the individual's need of right conduct before God. In the second section, Herbert seeks to deepen the Christian's life by reviewing the spiritual virtues. In the third section, possibly composed before the poet's scheme for *The Temple* had been formulated, Herbert traces the history of the "Church Militant." Thus the book has a threefold structure in considering the significance of the symbols of the church architecture, the virtues of the Christian life, and the events of the Church's history.

The simplicity of Herbert's poems is deceptive, as each of the 162 poems has very varied patterns of line and rhyme. Self-reflection and scriptural meditation are inextricably bound together for the poet, for as Jesus told the tempter, "Man shall not live by bread alone, but by every word that proceeds from the mouth of God" (Matthew 4:4). Accordingly, Herbert offers a number of explicitly biblical poems that meditate on some verse or thought of the Bible, and frequently in *The Temple* God's words—"Thy words"—become the poet's—"my words"—to guide human beings beyond their own, blind, inadequate resources, to know the will of *God*.

Like Solomon, Herbert prefaces his collection with a prayer of dedication: "Lord, my first fruits present themselves to Thee;/ Yet not mine neither: for from Thee they came." His first poem in the opening section, "The Church Porch," is entitled "Perirrhanterium," the Greek term for the instrument used for sprinkling holy water, to suggest that the poem is a preparatory ritual of cleansing before entering "the Church" section of *The Temple*. For remember "when once thy foot enters the Church, be bare/ God is more there, than thou; for thou are there/ only by His permission." Likewise, contrary to the Puritan tradition that makes so much of the sermon, "resort to sermons, but to prayers most:/ praying is the end of preaching."

In "The Church," we enter the major collection of the poems. Appropriately, we begin with "The Altar," "made of a heart and cemented with tears" of the supplicant. "The Sacrifice" then follows, the focus of worship being on Christ, whose refrain is repeated in sixty-four verses, "was ever grief like Mine?" The conclusion is, "never was grief like Mine." "Thanksgiving" then spells out the spirit of gratitude in the worshiper. Other Lenten themes follow through to "The Passion" of Good Friday and the Resurrection of Easter. "Baptism," "Sin," and "Repentance" follow.

Major elements of the life of the Christian then are delineated: "Faith," "Prayer," "Holy Communion," "Love," "The Tempter," "The Holy Scriptures," "Grace," and "Affliction." It is as if the Lord himself teaches us between his risen appearance at Easter and his ascension at Pentecost. After this seasonal rhythm of devotional training, there follows the daily rhythm of worship in "Matins" and "Evensong" and the habitual problems of "Sin." "Church Monuments," "Church Music," "Church Lock and Key," "Church Floor," and "The Windows" all add their contribution to the maturing character of the Christian, so that "doctrine and life" combine and anneal as one faith in the Lord.

There follows the need to cultivate the virtues of the Christian life: "Contentment," "Humility," "Frailty," "Constancy," the serenity of "The Star," the restful composure of "Sunday," the depression of "Avarice," and the exercise of self-"Denial." Further recitations bring us to "Christmas" and once more to "Lent." Biblical poems follow, such as "Colossians 3:3," "The Pearl" (Matthew 13:45), "The Quip" (Psalms 38:15), "Love Unknown" (Psalms 51), "Ephesians 4:30," "Praise II" (Psalms 116), "Self-Condemnation" (Luke 23:18-19), "Mary Magdalene" (Luke 7:37-38), "The Odor, 2 Corinthians 2:15-16," and "The Rose" (Song of Songs 2:1). However, the range of emotional and spiritual experiences and needs that Herbert articulates is impossible to do full justice to in such a summary. He concludes with "Love (III)," "Love bade me welcome: yet my soul drew back,/ guilty of dust and sin," a poem that Simone Weil thought was the most beautiful in the English language. At the end of the Anglican service of Holy Communion the *Gloria in excelsis* is sung, and with these words, "Glory be to God on high, and on earth/ peace, goodwill toward men," Herbert concludes "The Church."

The third section, "The Church Militant," celebrates the presence of God's provident deeds in history, commencing with the patriarchs and Old Testament times. Then it proceeds to trace the impact of Christianity on the classical world, the Reformation, to the present time. The collection closes with the words: "Blessed be God alone,/ Thrice blessed Three in One."

Christian Themes

In the poems of *The Temple*, Herbert is doing many things. At one level he is autobiographical, expressing his personal realization of what it means to be a priest in God's house. Sometimes, as in "The Quip," the poet is defenseless before his assailants, with only the repeated reply on his lips, "But Thou shalt answer, Lord, for me." In "The Sign," the poet knows the depth to which he must yield himself to God. As a pastor, he reminds himself, "Christ purg'd His temple; so must thou thy heart." Indeed, "look to thy actions well:/ for churches are either our heav'n or hell."

At another level, Herbert represents the claims and value of the visible church. In "The Invitation," all are invited to share in the Communion "supper," to a feast which is God himself. For "where is All, there All should be." In the "Church Militant," having described the corruption of past false institutions, Herbert anticipates "then shall Religion to America flee:/ They have their times of Gospel, ev'n as we." However, he believes it will be accepted by dint of their poverty, "for gold and grace did never yet agree:/ Religion always sides with poverty."

At a third level, Herbert senses the contradictions of life, of nature and grace, of continuity and renewal, of humankind's natural existence and God's purposes. In day-to-day living, balance and theological resolution are needed, in the experience of faith by tension. In "Vanitie," he sees the immediate presence of eternal life within a fleeting world of death. In "The Tempter (II)" he suffers the inconsistencies of life. In "The Glimpse" he lives with spiritual desertion. Tension, however, is resolved when I can see "My life is hid in Him that is my treasure." So Herbert sees theology in practice, as a daily challenge. For as "The Forerunners" reiterates, "Thou art still my God." The mystery of God's presence is life's resolution.

Sources for Further Study

Clarke, Elizabeth. *Theory and Theology in George Herbert's Poetry: Divinitie, and Poesie, Met*. New York: Oxford University Press, 1997. Several chapters in this analysis of Herbert's Christian poetics address *The Temple*. Bibliography, index.

Malcolmson, Cristina. *Heart-Work: George Herbert and the Protestant Ethic*. Stanford, Calif.: Stanford University Press, 1999. Several chapters address *The Temple*: "Gentility and Vocation in the Original *Temple*"; "*The Temple* Revised: 'Selfnesse' and Pollution"; and "The Character of Holiness in *The Temple*." Illustrated; bibliography, indexes.

Summers, Claude J., and Ted-Larry Pebworth, eds. *"Too Rich to Clothe the Sunne": Essays on George Herbert.* Pittsburgh, Pa.: University of Pittsburgh Press, 1980. Sympathetic essays on Herbert's Christian faith as expressed in his poems.

Thekla, Sister. *George Herbert, Idea and Image: A Study of "The Temple."* Normanby, Yorkshire, England: Greek Orthodox Monastery, 1974. A specifically Christian appreciation of *The Temple*, in contrast to many fine scholarly works on George Herbert that do not take this theological perspective.

Wall, John N., ed. *George Herbert: "The Country Parson," "The Temple."* New York: Paulist Press, 1981. This edition provides a particularly useful introduction.

James M. Houston

THEIR EYES WERE WATCHING GOD

Author: Zora Neale Hurston (1891-1960)
First published: 1937
Edition used: Their Eyes Were Watching God. With a new foreword by Mary Helen Washington. New York: Perennial Library, 1990
Genre: Novel
Subgenre: Literary fiction
Core issues: African Americans; coming of age or teen life; compassion; fear; justice

Hurston's coming-of-age novel differs from earlier examples of this tradition in that the person coming of age is a black woman. Given the racial climate of 1930's America, this was a crucial distinction.

Principal characters
Janie Crawford, the narrator of the story
Phoeby Watson, Janie's friend
Nanny Crawford, Janie's grandmother
Logan Killicks, Janie's first husband
Jody Starks, Janie's second husband
Tea Cake Woods, Janie's third husband

Overview

Their Eyes Were Watching God is narrated in third person, but as Henry Louis Gates, Jr., and other critics have noticed, Zora Neale Hurston is careful to give the novel the feel of first person. She accomplishes this by having the main character, Janie, tell the story to her friend Phoeby on the front porch. The novel opens with Janie returning to Eatonville at around the age of forty after having wandered. People up and down the streets are gossiping not only about what she has done on her journey away from home and her relationship with a younger man but also about the audacity of a woman her age wearing long hair and dressing provocatively. As Janie tells her story to Phoeby, she establishes the parameters of the coming-of-age pattern that the novel will follow.

In most novels of this sort, the main character leaves home and discovers love and fortune out in the world. Janie experiences love, but she returns without a man and without any large amount of money. Despite the absence of these things, she is satisfied with what she has gained and tells Phoeby, "Ah done been tuh de horizon and back and now Ah kin set heah in mah house and live by comparisons." The trajectory of the novel is circular rather than linear, allowing the author to focus the reader's attention on self-discovery rather than world discovery. Indeed, Janie discovers herself through the men with whom she becomes involved. When the novel ends she has only herself.

Janie's first husband is chosen by her grandmother Nanny after she recognizes Janie's dawning sexuality, symbolized in the novel by a blooming pear tree. Nanny finds Janie kissing Johnny Taylor under the pear tree and immediately arranges a marriage for her with Logan Killicks, a much older man who has forty acres of land and more material possessions than any other man in the community. Nanny explains to Janie that "De nigger woman is de mule uh de world," and therefore, she must take what she can find. Logan will provide Janie what Nanny calls "protection." He will provide for her, and he will not beat her. To Nanny, the marriage is ideal. To Janie, it "desecrates the pear tree," in that she can find no romantic or sexual satisfaction in Logan. Though Logan treats Janie well, he treats her as a possession.

Janie leaves Logan for Joe Starks. Joe (or Jody) is a man of great ambition, planning "to be a big voice." He coaxes Janie to go with him, and when they find themselves in Eatonville, a "colored town," without a mayor, he immediately takes charge. With his own money, he expands the town. When the people appoint him as mayor, he settles into office, building a large house and opening a store. Janie becomes "Mrs. Mayor" and runs the store. Jody forces Janie to keep her hair under a cloth, and he will not allow her to gossip or play checkers with any of the townspeople who sit on benches outside the store. Thus, though Jody is initially attractive to Janie, and his ambition allows him to bring about change in the town that none of the citizens could have imagined, Janie is still a possession of her husband. Janie discovers, in the narrator's words, that "the spirit of the marriage left the bedroom and took to living in the parlor." When Jody dies, Janie is once again on her own. Symbolizing her freedom, Janie takes the kerchief from her head and proclaims to the town, "Come heah people! Jody is dead. Mah husband is gone from me."

Janie's final relationship is the best of the three, but significantly, it does not last nor is it perfect. In fact, Janie is able to survive this relationship only by killing her last love, Tea Cake. Tea Cake is unlike Logan or Jody in that he grants to Janie a measure of freedom. He loves for her hair to hang free, and he teaches her to play checkers and to fish, even to shoot a gun—all activities not normally associated with women in the community of which Hurston writes. However, Tea Cake is the opposite of Logan and Jody also in his lack of traditional responsibility. He gambles away a portion of the money Janie had left from her relationship with Jody. He is, in fact, the prototypical blues singer, playing the guitar and living hand-to-mouth. With Tea Cake, Janie goes to the Everglades, where she works as a fruit picker. It is there that their relationship ends.

Janie, Tea Cake, and various friends wait out the hurricane that threatens the area, ignoring the example of the Seminole Indians, who, having lived in the area for eons, know it is better to flee the storm. In staying, they follow the example of the white people. In the words of the narrator, "The folks let the people do the thinking. If the castles thought themselves secure, the cabins needn't worry." Only later when the storm pounds the house in which they are staying, when Lake Okechobee begins to "roll in his bed," "The time was past for asking the white folks to look for through that door. Six eyes were questioning *God*."

In the aftermath of the storm, amid dead bodies, starvation, and mayhem, Tea Cake is bitten by a snarling dog while defending Janie. Weeks later Tea Cake exhibits the symptoms of rabies. When Tea Cake tries to attack Janie, she must use her skill with a gun to protect her life and end his. By teaching her to shoot like a man, Tea Cake has given Janie the ability to live and thereby the ability to free herself from him when she has no other choice. Janie is tried for murder in the white community, but ultimately she is acquitted.

Janie concludes her story by telling Phoeby, "Ah done been tuh de horizon and back." She concludes that every person must ultimately experience the world and God for herself: "You got tuh *go* there tuh *know* there. Yo' papa and yo' mama and nobody else can't tell yuh and show yuh. Two things everybody's got tuh do fuh theyselves. They got tuh go tuh God, and they got tuh find out about livin' fuh theyselves."

Christian Themes

In *The Sermon and the African American Literary Tradition* (1995), Doland Hubbard has argued that African Americans were forced to redefine Christian experience to make it applicable to their particular experience in the United States. White Christians had argued that slavery was justified by the Bible, and later that segregation and Jim Crow laws were biblically ordained through the stories of Cain and Abel and of Noah's descendants. African American ministers, on the other hand, identified slave experience with the experience of Jews in Egypt, so that God working through Moses to free the Hebrew children was analogous to civil rights leaders working to bring equality to African Americans. Clearly, to black Christians, God was ultimately even and square in his dealings with people—white, black, man, woman, they were all children of the same father.

Hurston's novel demonstrates this point long before the Civil Rights movement, for what Janie learns in both her relationships and in her experience in the hurricane is that all must face God in the same manner. Whites are not the ones who watch God and then tell African Americans what to do. All eyes watch God. Furthermore, Janie ultimately concludes that God sees each individual as unique: Everyone has to go to God, she concludes. We may assume, therefore, that she is justified in learning to do the things that men do and also in defending her life at the expense of her lover's.

In addition to being a God before whom each individual must stand, the God Hurston presents is overwhelming and terrifying in much the same way that God is portrayed in the Old Testament. The God that Janie and Tea Cake ultimately watch in the storm reminds the reader of the God who speaks in a whirlwind and who says to Job that he should gird up his loins and speak for himself. Hurston is unclear on the true nature of this God, reminding the reader that the Hebrews of the Old Testament were unable to say the name of God because God (or Yahweh, the name they substituted for God) was too big for them to know completely. Hurston's prose even echoes the Old Testament when she describes death in these haunting words:

Death, that strange being with the huge square toes who lived way in the West. The great one who lived in the straight house like a platform without sides to it, and without a roof. What need has death for a cover, and what winds can blow against him? He stands in his high house that overlooks the world. Stands watchful and motionless all day with his sword drawn back, waiting for the messenger to bid him come. Been standing there before there was a where or a when or a then.

The suggestiveness and ambiguity of these words echo the King James version of the Old Testament, reminding readers that God was to Adam a voice walking in the garden, that the void before the world was formed was "the face of the deep" on which God moved, and that God commanded Abraham to slay Isaac.

Hurston embeds in her novel a palpable sense of the wonder of God as well as the fear he and his world invoke. As the controlling image in the novel, the horizon is the place where one must go to know God, but even in knowing God, one does not understand fully the power of God. Along with the terror of death comes the power of sunrise expressed in these unforgettable lines: "She [Janie] knew that God tore down the old world every evening and built a new one by sun-up. It was wonderful to see it take form with the sun and emerge from the gray dust of its making." Ultimately Janie's journey to the horizon and back is worth all it costs her in that she comes to know the unknowable in life. It is with this paradox that Hurston leaves the reader.

Sources for Further Study

Boyd, Valerie. *Wrapped in Rainbows: The Life of Zora Neale Hurston.* New York: Scribner, 2003. Very readable and complete, it draws on the groundbreaking biography by Robert Hemenway.

Gates, Henry Louis, Jr. "Zora Neale Hurston: A Negro Way of Saying." Afterword in *Their Eyes Were Watching God*, by Zora Neale Hurston. New York: Perennial Library, 1990. Originally a book review in the April 21, 1985, issue of *The New York Times*. Gates explores the language of the novel, establishing a context in which to understand Hurston's approach to language and culture.

Hubbard, Dolan. *The Sermon and the African American Literary Tradition.* Columbia: University of Missouri Press, 1995. Hubbard's excellent study of the tradition of the sermon in African American literature is indispensable to understanding African American Christianity in the context of literature.

Hurston, Zora Neale. *Dust Tracks on a Road.* 1942. Reprint. New York: Harper Perennial Modern Classics, 2006. Hurston's autobiography gives readers a sense of Hurston's life as well as an understanding of autobiographical components of the novel.

H. William Rice

THEODICY
Essays on the Goodness of God, the Freedom of Man, and the Origin of Evil

Author: Gottfried Wilhelm Leibniz (1646-1716)
First published: Essais de théodicée sur la bonté de Dieu, la liberté de l'homme, et l'origine du mal, 1710 (English translation, 1951)
Edition used: Theodicy: Essays on the Goodness of God, the Freedom of Man, and the Origin of Evil, translated by E. M. Huggard, edited with an introduction by Austin Farrer. La Salle, Ill.: Open Court, 1985
Genre: Nonfiction
Subgenres: Critical analysis; essays; theology
Core issues: God; problem of evil; reason; suffering

The existence of evil presents a severe problem for both Christianity and theism in general. The difficulty of the problem of evil—that is, how evil can persist if God is morally perfect and omnipotent—has prompted many theologians and philosophers to see only two viable responses, in the form of atheism or theism based on faith and divine revelation. Leibniz, by contrast, argues that there is another alternative: theism based on reason that rationally reconciles the existence of God and the existence of evil.

Overview

Gottfried Wilhelm Leibniz's *Theodicy* was published six years before his death and has the distinction of being his only book-length philosophical work published during his lifetime. Leibniz coined the term "theodicy," which means "vindication of the justice of God." For Leibniz, a product of the French Enlightenment, the proper way of vindicating the justice and goodness of God in the face of evil was through reason, not faith. The overarching theme of the *Theodicy* is that at least some religious doctrines can be rationally demonstrated and need not be taken as articles of faith.

The problem of evil involves the apparent inconsistency of the existence of a morally perfect and omnipotent God and the existence of evil. If God were morally perfect, it seems that God would want to eliminate all evil, and if God were omnipotent, then it would be within God's power to eliminate evil. Thus it seems that evil could not exist if God does. However, since evil obviously does exist, it appears that God either does not exist or is not both morally perfect and omnipotent. Leibniz, who wanted to retain the orthodox conception of God as a morally perfect and omnipotent being, thus needed to explain why God allows evil. In the context of Leibniz's philosophy and his fundamental theological principle that God always chooses the best, the challenge thus became one of explaining how the actual world, with all of its evil, is nevertheless the "best of all possible worlds," to use Leibniz's phrase.

Theodicy / LEIBNIZ

Leibniz begins by distinguishing three types of evil: metaphysical evil (the evil involved in the existence of any finite and imperfect thing), physical evil (pain and suffering), and moral evil (sin resulting from human free will). Metaphysical evil is a problem for theism because it may seem that a perfect God would create a perfect world, and so the fact that this world is not perfect shows that such a perfect being does not exist. Leibniz's response is that while God can do anything that is logically possible, it is not logically possible for God to create a perfect world because such a world would be indistinguishable from God. Thus, to avoid the heresy of pantheism (the view that God and the world are one), it follows that the world created by God must be an imperfect world, one containing metaphysical evil.

Explaining why the world must contain some evil does not yet explain why this, the best of all possible worlds, should contain such a vast amount and variety of evil. It might be suggested, for example, that God could have created a world with no suffering and sin by creating a world without sentient creatures. While God could have created such a world, Leibniz insists it would not have been a better world than the actual world. His criterion for ranking possible worlds involves two factors: variety (or diversity of phenomena) and order (or simplicity and elegance of its laws of nature). The best world, then, is one that exhibits the maximum variety and diversity while at the same time being governed by the simplest laws. Leibniz argues that an orderly world governed by simple laws of nature inevitably involves the suffering of sentient creatures. If God were to miraculously intervene any time a creature was about to suffer, this would not be an orderly world describable by simple causal laws. If humans were incapable of sin because they lacked free will, their psychological, moral, and spiritual lives would be impoverished. It is not implausible that a world with moral agents who sin of their own free will is a better, more valuable world than one containing human "machines" that have been programmed to act in the way God has chosen. Leibniz acknowledges that when one focuses on individual examples of evil, it is hard to see this as the best of all possible worlds. However, just as the overall beauty of a piece of music can be enhanced by a dissonant chord, the world may be made more valuable by having parts that seem evil when viewed by themselves. The failure to see that this is the best of all possible worlds is due to our finite and limited human perspective.

Leibniz's position that this is the best of all possible worlds commits him to the further claim that any change in the actual world will result in a worse world. Of course it seems rather implausible to say that a world without the Holocaust, for example, is a worse world than one with it. Leibniz responds to this sort of objection by appealing to his doctrine that each individual thing has a "complete concept" that includes everything that is true of it, and any change in that concept would result in a different individual. Thus, while there could be a world without the Holocaust, such a world would also be without Mother Teresa, since her complete concept includes that she existed in a world with the Holocaust. Leibniz's suggestion, then, is that one cannot simply imagine a world without the evils of this one and then criticize God for not creating that world. According to the complete concept doctrine, a world without the Holocaust is also a world without Mother Teresa; in general, it is not possible simply to eliminate the bad while retaining the good.

Christian Themes

The problem of evil obviously presents a severe problem for versions of Christianity that purport to be based on reason rather than faith. Leibniz's attempt rationally to reconcile the existence of God with the existence of evil, while influential and ingenious, faces formidable objections. As noted above, Leibniz blocks the objection that there surely seem to be better possible worlds than this one, with his doctrine of the complete concept of the individual substance, arguing that a world without the Holocaust is also a world without Mother Teresa. However, even if the questionable complete concept doctrine is accepted for the sake of discussion, thus granting it is not possible to have the actual Mother Teresa without the Holocaust, this does not mean there could not be a very similar individual who ministers to the poor of Calcutta. What reason can Leibniz give for thinking that this alternate Mother Teresa is inferior to the actual one? In addition, Leibniz now has a problem making the complete concept doctrine consistent with the role free will plays in his solution to the problem of moral evil. According to Leibniz, Mother Teresa has a complete concept that includes the truth that she devoted her life to ministering to the poor of Calcutta. However, then this is a necessary truth about her, and so it was unavoidable that she would spend her life in this way—yet if it were necessary and inevitable that she would spend her life in this way, she cannot be thought of doing this of her own free will. Thus, in using the complete concept doctrine to solve one problem in his theodicy, Leibniz creates another.

One reason the phrase "best of all possible worlds" has entered the public consciousness is that Leibniz's optimism was ridiculed in the French writer Voltaire's eighteenth century comic novel *Candide: Ou, L'Optimisme* (1759; *Candide: Or, All for the Best*, 1759). In that novel, Dr. Pangloss (the character representing Leibniz) keeps reassuring his naïve protégé Candide—as they endure natural disasters, disfiguring diseases, and unspeakable cruelty—that this indeed is the best of all possible worlds. At one point, a bewildered Candide exclaims, "If this is the best of all possible worlds, what must the others be like?" Many modern readers of *Theodicy*, after the moral horrors and natural disasters of the twentieth century, no doubt have a similar reaction to Leibniz's philosophy.

Sources for Further Study

Jolley, Nicholas. *Leibniz*. New York: Routledge, 2005. Includes extensive coverage of topics from the *Theodicy* such as free will and the problem of evil by a leading Leibniz scholar.

_____, ed. *The Cambridge Companion to Leibniz*. New York: Cambridge University Press, 1995. Contains interpretive and critical essays by leading scholars who assess Leibniz's philosophical and theological doctrines. Includes essays on topics in the *Theodicy*.

Theodicy / LEIBNIZ

MacDonald Ross, G. *Leibniz*. New York: Oxford University Press, 1984. A short yet comprehensive account of Leibniz's philosophy. Develops the objection that Leibniz's thesis that this is the best of all possible worlds is meaningless.

David Haugen

A THEOLOGY FOR THE SOCIAL GOSPEL

Author: Walter Rauschenbusch (1861-1918)
First published: 1917
Edition used: A Theology for the Social Gospel. New York: Abingdon Press, 1945
Genre: Nonfiction
Subgenre: Theology
Core issues: Capitalism; church; ethics; love; poverty; social action

Rauschenbusch argues that social ills such as poverty, harsh industrial working conditions, impure foods and drugs, racism, political corruption, abuses of the criminal justice system, and war are manifestations of sin. Christians and the Church must address these issues by working to achieve the Kingdom of God: a human community based on love, justice, and mutual aid. The theological foundation must move beyond individual piety, worship, and repentance to concern for the material and emotional condition of all people. Religion and ethics must be blended.

Overview

Walter Rauschenbusch held a pastorate in a rough part of New York City for eleven years and knew firsthand about the many varieties of social problems. Too often, according to Rauschenbusch, people strongly condemn activities such as drinking alcohol, dancing, playing cards, and going to the movies as sins but do not adequately condemn the impoverishment of peasants and industrial workers by "the parasitic classes of society." The most glaringly sinful activity is war, so painfully evident in 1917 during World War I. Rauschenbusch is scornful of Christianity's traditional emphasis on Original Sin and the fall of Adam and Eve rather than on Jesus and the prophets. To him, sin is selfishness, and selfishness is a major source of social evils, among them despotic government, war and militarism, landlordism, predatory industry, and finance.

In *A Theology for the Social Gospel,* Rauschenbusch argues that mainstream theology has wandered far from the social and ethical teachings of Jesus. "Individualistic theology" concentrates unduly on personal repentance and salvation:

> The doctrine of the Kingdom of God was left undeveloped by individualistic theology and finally mislaid by it almost completely.... What a spectacle, that the original teaching of our Lord has become an incongruous element in so-called evangelical theology....

Rauschenbusch's ideal is the Kingdom of God, to which people can aspire in this life: "The institutions of life must be fundamentally fraternal and co-operative if they are to train men to love their fellow men as co-workers." In this kingdom, human beings are all called to labor for the common good.

The sins of selfishness are preserved and transmitted by social organizations and institutions, customs, and habits. Rauschenbusch sees the Church as having degenerated into a force for evil in pre-Reformation times.

According to Rauschenbusch, salvation should involve a strengthened commitment to loving and serving others. He rejects the isolation of mystical religious experience—but acknowledges the importance of prayer and meditation as resources for renewal. Christ's teachings focus on love, not as attitude or feeling but as the energetic and zestful participation in social life characterized by service and equality. While the Jewish priestly elite concentrated on rules and rituals, Jesus envisioned the Kingdom of God as loving interactions among all people, women as well as men, Gentiles as well as Jews.

Rauschenbusch condemns the punitive approach to criminal justice, advocating instead greater attention to teaching, discipline, and rehabilitation. He also speaks sharply against capitalism (particularly the modern corporation), preferring cooperatives as the chief form of productive enterprise. Born to German immigrant parents, he had studied in Germany and was strongly influenced by the religious and economic ideas prevalent there. Many of these ideas had migrated to the United States through people such as economist Richard T. Ely, a pillar of the Social Gospel movement. Rauschenbusch had also been strongly influenced by Henry George, by Edward Bellamy's book *Looking Backward: 2000-1887* (1888), and by British Christian socialism.

In *A Theology for the Social Gospel*, Rauschenbusch does not undertake to provide systematic analysis of social and economic problems or to outline a detailed agenda of political and social remedies. However, he is strongly critical of those aspects of theology that have strayed from the central social teachings of Jesus—in particular, the implication that one's eternal salvation can be achieved by "faith."

Many of Rauschenbusch's goals were achieved over the ensuing century. The Catholic Church, which came in for much condemnation in his writings, became much more attentive to social and economic matters. Racial and gender equality advanced. The Reverend Martin Luther King, Jr., acknowledged that he was influenced by Rauschenbusch. Socially concerned Christians were one of many powerful political forces helping bring about the creation of welfare-state programs in Europe and America. However, much of the improvement came through the process of economic growth, generated by the capitalistic institutions that he denigrated.

In *Christianity and the Social Crisis* (1907), Rauschenbusch presents in much more detail his conception of Jesus as an advocate of social justice and social reform. He calls attention to the radical social wing of the primitive Church, praising the epistle of James as a strong statement of that viewpoint. This emphasis was derailed by a growing preoccupation with the eternal life to come, along with pessimism about the possibility of improving life in the here and now. Praise for the ascetic ideal denied many of the comforts and consolations of earthly life. Although presented in a historical context, these issues were still of importance in the early twentieth century.

Rauschenbusch articulates an effective case for separation of church and state: An "established" church is bound to be a captive of the same social classes that control the state. Only if the church is a free agent can it effectively pressure the state to adopt measures of social reform.

Christianity and the Social Crisis spelled out in detail Rauschenbusch's gloomy perspective on the capitalist economy of the early twentieth century. It reflected his distress at the conditions in New York's Hell's Kitchen. The book ends with a passionate call for the Church to support socialism—a theme not evident in *A Theology for the Social Gospel*—which created a hail of public criticism of Rauschenbusch. One would not know from his exposition that real wages had increased significantly since the Civil War and that the favorable U.S. labor environment was attracting a million immigrants a year, immigrants who hoped that, after initial hardships, they would obtain a better life for themselves and their children.

By the time *A Theology for the Social Gospel* was published, the first Pure Food and Drug Act had been adopted, the Federal Trade Commission had been established, the income tax had become a permanent part of the financial system, the Clayton Act had begun protection for labor unions, and the United States was well on the way to authorizing voting by women. The spread of the Social Gospel certainly contributed to the reform atmosphere of the Progressive Era.

Christian Themes

Christian love, as expressed in the words and especially the actions of Jesus, is the foundation of Rauschenbusch's approach. Matthew 25:31-46 presents the basis for Christian living by individuals and for the activities of the Church. This love undertakes to heal the sick, to provide food and clothing for the needy, to welcome strangers, to comfort widows and orphans, and to transmute war into peace.

Rauschenbusch traced his litany of social evils to selfishness. He felt that capitalist greed was at the base of poverty and the attendant evils of poor housing, bad sanitation, child labor, alcoholism, political corruption, and even war. These evils are directly the outcome of the actions of sinful institutions, especially business corporations. Rauschenbusch's institutional focus anticipates the work of Walter Wink (*The Powers That Be: Theology for a New Millennium*, 1998).

In conjunction with Saint Paul's admonitions in 1 Corinthians 13, this view is also the basis for Rauschenbusch's criticism of the Church—its failure to take the lead in combating the social problems he enumerated. He condemned asceticism, monasticism, mysticism, and excessive churchly preoccupation with ritual and dogma. His emphasis was on social action and only secondarily on the possibility that people might be experiencing sinful thoughts and feelings. Likewise, concerns for salvation and the afterlife were subordinate to opportunities and responsibilities to improve the social conditions experienced here and now. Rauschenbusch states that social action is needed to bring about the Kingdom of God: actions—not merely thoughts, feelings, and ritual observances—and working in fraternal collaboration with others.

Rauschenbusch presents an image of Jesus that stresses his life as a process of growth and discovery. He was not merely acting out a script that was presented to him early in life. The social concerns that he articulated were at the center of early church life, until the Church was compromised by its union with political power.

Sources for Further Study

Evans, Christopher Hodge. *The Kingdom Is Always but Coming: A Life of Walter Rauschenbusch*. Grand Rapids, Mich.: Wm. B. Eerdmans, 2004. While not neglecting personal matters (his relation with his father, his affinity to matters German) the book stresses the social as well as theological context of Rauschenbusch's work.

Fishburn, Janet. "Walter Rauschenbusch and 'The Woman Movement': A Gender Analysis." In *Gender and the Social Gospel*, edited by Wendy J. Deichmann Edwards and Carolyn De Swarte Gifford. Urbana: University of Illinois Press, 2003. Rauschenbusch felt strongly that a woman's place was in the home as wife and mother.

Rauschenbusch, Walter. *Christianity and the Social Crisis*. New York: Macmillan, 1907. Detailed evidence on the social emphasis of the Bible and the early church; describes how the Church deviated from this. Develops his socialist perspective in detail.

Smucker, Donovan E. *The Origins of Walter Rauschenbusch's Social Ethics*. Montreal: McGill-Queen's University Press, 1994. Emphasizes influences relating to pietism, Anabaptist sectarianism, social and religious liberalism, and Christian socialist transformationism.

Paul B. Trescott

A THEOLOGY OF LIBERATION
History, Politics, and Salvation

Author: Gustavo Gutiérrez (1928-)
First published: Teológia de la liberación: Perspectivas, 1971 (English translation, 1973)
Edition used: A Theology of Liberation: History, Politics, and Salvation, edited by Sister Caridad Inda and John Eagleson. Maryknoll, N.Y.: Orbis Books, 1973
Genre: Nonfiction
Subgenre: Theology
Core issues: Ethics; freedom and free will; justice; Latin Americans

This work is considered to be one of the most important contributions to the development of liberation theology, a theological movement that developed in Latin America and argued that the heart of Christianity is the search for social justice. Gutiérrez, a Peruvian priest and professor, argues not only that theology must have new concerns but also that there must be a new way of doing theology. Most important for Gutiérrez is that salvation must not be simply concerned with an otherworldly reality or the afterlife.

Overview

A Theology of Liberation consists of four parts, which include thirteen chapters and cover more than three hundred pages. Part 1 includes one chapter that discusses the purpose of theology. According to Gutiérrez, the classic task of theology was to seek after wisdom and pursue rational knowledge. Throughout history, however, some have seen the task of theology as a meditation on proper human action. Gutiérrez sees his theological method as a reflection on circumstances and actions that should be taken. Chapter 2 considers the liberation as a theological concept. Gutiérrez argues that liberation must be connected to the proper development of individuals and social orders and that liberation is not merely concerned with otherworldly issues or the afterlife.

The second part, called "Posing the Problem," contains three brief chapters about the social task confronting Christianity. Gutiérrez argues that Christians in Latin American are looking for support from the Catholic Church for the social problems faced by people in developing countries. Gutiérrez argues that the problem of the poor must be considered both on the pastoral level and on the level of theological reflection. On the pastoral level, lay movements must be given particular attention so that laypersons are supported in the struggle for social justice.

The third part, titled "The Option Before the Latin American Church," examines the development of theological ideas in Latin America regarding social life. Gutiérrez asserts that for a very long time theologians in Latin America had no real awareness of economic problems faced by everyday residents. In the 1950's, however, theologians began addressing the social plight of Latin Americans. He also includes a brief discussion of the theory of dependence as an explanation for the poverty in the Americas. This economic theory argues that Latin American nations never developed vibrant domestic economies because trading partners purchased raw materials at very low prices from Latin American nations and then sold finished goods to these countries at higher prices. Reformist movements were not enough to counter the economic colonialism practiced by northern nations. In light of the failure of European nations, liberation theology was a born as a challenge to the situation.

Finally, Gutiérrez offers a chapter outlining the tasks before the Latin American Church. Laypersons and priests alike must participate in social reform movements. Priests who engage in social reform efforts must not be seen as subversives but as true supporters of the people. Moreover, bishops must be supportive of these social movements. Gutiérrez applauds the efforts of Latin American bishops, particularly those at Medellín Conference in 1968, which called for the liberation of Latin Americans from economic servitude. Gutiérrez rejects the label that liberationists are merely communists operating under the guise of religious terminology. Instead, he calls his views and those of others promoting liberation as socialism informed by Christianity and maintains that the broad participation of the oppressed is essential for proper social change.

Part 4, "Perspectives," includes five chapters. The first considers the relation between liberation and salvation. Here Gutiérrez agrees with the central concern for salvation in the Christian tradition but asserts that we must think anew about the meaning of salvation: "Salvation is not something otherworldly," but rather "salvation is something that embraces human reality, transforms it, and leads it to its fullness in Christ." He calls this a qualitative approach to salvation. He says that the political liberation called for will be a "self-creation of man." According to Gutiérrez, this was the case with ancient Israel, and it is the case with the developed world at the time of his book. He rejects the customary focus on otherworldly liberation and asserts that the promises of God are directed toward earthly realities. In support of his position, he cites passages from documents approved at the Second Vatican Council (1962-1965) which refer to the temporal progress of God's kingdom. Christ is presented as a liberator who calls for a radical reordering of human life.

The next chapter argues from biblical texts that God works in history through the acts of those called by him. God's followers, then, are to work for justice. Gutiérrez lists passages from both the Old and New Testaments in support of his call to work for justice. Finally, Christ is presented not as a teacher of otherworldly realities but as one who called his followers to love their neighbors in a radical way.

Another chapter in this section considers the meaning of the end times, or the eschaton, and the hope one has for the new reality. Gutiérrez argues that Revelation informs that we can have hope for a transformed world and that this hope is founded upon God's promises to those who follow him.

There follows a chapter titled "The Church: Sacrament of History" in which Gutiérrez says that the Church itself, as a sign of God's presence in the world, must be an instrument of social transformation. This involves a new understanding of the

Church. The Eucharist must be seen as a means of nourishing Christians for social action. Finally, all Christians must engage in class struggle as an expression of Christian brotherhood.

The final chapter of the work argues that the Catholic Church must in all of its actions and in its theological teachings side with the poor and attempt to alleviate their condition. Gutiérrez calls material poverty a sin that must be confronted.

Christian Themes

The first theme expressed in this work is the new mode that theology must undertake to address the social conditions of the poor. Theology is no longer about knowing; rather, it is about action, or praxis as Gutiérrez calls it. Scriptural passages from both the Old and New Testaments and other theological documents of the Catholic Church are interpreted in light of this viewpoint. Thus, passages on the poor in Scripture are given new attention. Christ is presented as a radical social reformer and liberator of the poor. Passages suggesting otherworldly realties are interpreted in the light of worldly conditions.

Another theme is the new meanings of "liberation" and "salvation." These terms become interchangeable, because the work of bringing liberation to the poor will also bring salvation to the poor, salvation from the material poverty forced upon those in less developed countries. Liberation and salvation will occur in this world. Gutiérrez further argues that it is appropriate to have eschatological hope for this to occur.

Another theme developed by Gutiérrez is the theological justification for Christians, including laypersons and priests, to become social revolutionaries who seek to overturn existing social and economic arrangements. Gutiérrez recognizes the Marxist tone of this language but rejects the notion that his social vision must accept the Marxist atheism and materialism. He calls for all to overturn the unjust social structures in place in the world. Gutiérrez is certainly pleased that many have accepted this role in the years immediately preceding the publication of his work.

In the same vein, a significant theme of the work is the critique of capitalism and the argument that socialism is most compatible with Christianity. Gutiérrez asserts that dependency and capitalistic exploitation explain poverty. He embraces socialism as compatible with a Christian vision for society.

Sources for Further Study

Bokenkotter, Thomas. *Church and Revolution: Catholics in the Struggle for Democracy and Social Justice.* New York: Image Books, 1998. Examines Catholics who have promoted social reform. Includes two chapters that consider the humanist vision of the Jacques Maritain.

Novak, Michael. *Will It Liberate? Questions About Liberation Theology.* Mahway, N.J.: Paulist Press, 1986. Provides a largely critical perspective of liberation theology, questioning Gutiérrez's use of Marxist ideology and his understanding of economic development as being ill-conceived and ill-considered. Gutiérrez is discussed throughout the work.

Rowland, Christopher, ed. *The Cambridge Companion to Liberation Theology.* New York: Cambridge University Press, 1999. Eleven significant essays, including one by Gutiérrez, survey the basics of liberation theology and explain the development of its core ideas.

Michael L. Coulter

A THEOLOGY OF THE JEWISH CHRISTIAN REALITY

Author: Paul M. Van Buren (1924-1998)
First published: Vol. 1, *Discerning the Way,* New York: Seabury Press, 1980; vol. 2, *A Christian Theology of the People of Israel,* New York: Seabury Press, 1983; vol. 3, *Christ in Context,* New York: Harper & Row, 1988
Genre: Nonfiction
Subgenre: Theology
Core issues: African Americans; God; revelation; scriptures; the Word

A multivolume work intended to explore the Christian relationship to Judaism in terms of what the author believes will be a new period in Jewish-Christian relations in the wake of the Holocaust.

Overview

Discerning the Way, the first volume in Paul M. Van Buren's ambitious theological work *A Theology of the Jewish Christian Reality,* is intended to portray both Christianity and Judaism as legitimate ways to God. In the author's view, Christianity has not superceded or replaced Judaism as a way to God. Instead, he sees the Jewish people as the elder siblings of the Christians, establishing the path that the latter should follow. He discusses how Christians and Jews should walk together along this path and considers the identity of Christians, as Gentiles who worship the God of Israel, in terms of the path they walk together with the Jews. He looks at theology as a conversation about God, which must recognize that Christians converse about the God of Israel. In this conversation, Christians are responsible to God and to the saints and to all of those who have walked the way. Van Buren examines the nature and attributes of God, the Bible and the Church, and the authority of the Bible in terms of the tradition of the God of Israel. He discusses the revelation of Christianity as a historical phenomenon and considers how the Christian redemption is related to Israel's hope for creation.

The second volume, *A Christian Theology of the People of Israel,* attempts to establish a Christian theology of Israel. This is both difficult and necessary, according to Van Buren, because Christianity has a long anti-Judaic tradition that culminated in the horrors of the Holocaust. It is also difficult because it is a theology of other people. Van Buren maintains that his theology cannot simply be a report of Jewish teaching nor can it be a Jewish theology. Instead, this theology should ask about the duty and the ability of the Christian Church to hear the testimony of the Jewish people to God.

Van Buren asserts, in this central second volume, that a Christian theology of Israel is necessary because of the tradition of Israel's election by God and because the scriptures of Israel have served as the canon of Christianity. Christianity must also deal with the Jewish rejection of Christ, as understood by the Church. Through examination of the Hebrew Scriptures in the Christian Bible, Van Buren looks at Israel's testimony to creation. He discusses the creation of human beings in the image of God. Creation was good but unfinished and therefore involves risk. By its testimony to the creation, Israel has provided hope for creation.

The election of Israel and the relevance of this election to the nations, or Gentiles, receive special attention. Van Buren discusses the nature of election and covenant. He considers the covenant of Noah and the covenant of Abraham in the Scriptures. Van Buren then looks at the people of Israel under the covenant and election, and he looks at the historical meaning of this people. Applying the historical concept of Israel to the present day, Van Buren considers what Israel might mean for the people of the Third World and for African Americans.

Van Buren examines the land of Israel, both in the past and in the present, finding Israel an exception among nations, facing special challenges and problems, as well as a special mission. He explicates the Torah and the relationship of the Torah to Jesus. He looks both at how Jesus arose as a rabbi within Israel and at how Israel's rejection of Christianity can be considered as a form of witness. He sets forth Israel's mission as maintaining a living covenant with God and looks at the ways in which Christianity can be thought of as having a mission to the people of Israel.

The third volume, *Christ in Context*, offers a historical approach to Christology. Van Buren's intent in this part of the work is to understand Christ in terms of the Jewish background. Here, he argues that Christology, thinking about Christ, must acknowledge that Christianity has existed within a developing historical background. Christ and the church around Christ were, in the earliest historical period, inside Israel. Then, from the first century C.E. through the Holocaust, the Christian Church defined itself as being against Israel. In the years since World War II, the Church has been understood as existing with Israel. Van Buren argues that a proper understanding of Christ must acknowledge not only that Israel had a covenant with God in the past but also that this covenant continues to exist in the present and into the future.

Christian Themes

The relationship of Christianity to Judaism has been one of the great themes in the history of Christianity. Christianity began as a movement within Judaism, and the question of whether non-Jewish converts to Christianity should also become Jews or conform to Jewish religious regulations concerned many early Christians, notably Saint Paul. Some early Christian sects argued that Christianity had replaced Judaism, which should be repudiated altogether. Mainstream Christianity's adoption of the Hebrew Bible as the Old Testament, followed by the New Testament, implied continuity between Judaism and Christianity. For many believers, though, this also implied that Judaism had been replaced or superceded by Christianity and that Jews should therefore convert to the newer faith. Moreover, some interpretations of the Gospels implied that the Jewish people were responsible for the crucifixion of Christ.

Over the centuries, the question of the relationship between Judaism and Christianity has resulted in a long tradition of anti-Jewish ideas and persecution. As Europe became identified as Christendom from late antiquity through the early Middle Ages,

Jews were left as the primary religious outsiders within a civilization that recognized itself as Christian. Christian churches and Christian theology often contributed to the persecution of the Jews.

During World War II, the Nazis in Germany attempted to exterminate the Jews of Europe, a program known as the Holocaust or the Shoah. Some of the Christian denominations in Germany actively cooperated with the Nazis; others passively accepted the Holocaust. The Roman Catholic Church is sometimes accused of failing to act to protect the Jews, and some thinkers argue that this alleged failure was rooted in theological tradition and culture. After the war, the experience of the Holocaust led many Christian thinkers to reconsider the relationship between Christianity and Judaism.

Sources for Further Study

Haynes, Stephen R. *Prospects for Post-Holocaust Theology*. Atlanta, Ga.: Scholars Press, 1991. An examination of Christian theology in the years following the Holocaust that considers how theologians Karl Barth, Jürgen Moltmann, and Van Buren have attempted to reexamine Christianity and Christian theological views of Judaism.

Haynes, Stephen R., and John K. Roth, eds. *The Death of God Movement and the Holocaust: Radical Theology Encounters the Shoah*. Westport, Conn.: Greenwood Press, 1999. A collection of essays on responses to the Holocaust among the radical theologians of the 1960's, with whom Van Buren is often associated. Essays by John K. Roth and John J. Carey, in particular, provide consideration of Van Buren's early thinking and affiliation with radical theologians. The book also contains an essay by Van Buren that describes his movement away from a secular reading of the Scriptures and discusses how his discovery of Judaism led him to give such a prominent place to the Jewish people in his theology.

Lindsay, Mark R. *Covenanted Solidarity: The Theological Basis of Karl Barth's Opposition to Nazi Antisemitism and the Holocaust*. New York: Peter Lang, 2001. A study of the theology of Karl Barth, a thinker who greatly influenced Van Buren, and how this theology led Barth to stand against Nazi policies during World War II.

Ogletree, Thomas W. *The Death of God Controversy*. Nashville, Tenn.: Abingdon Press, 1966. An account of theologians associated with the so-called Death of God movement during the 1960's. Ogletree looks at Van Buren, along with others associated with this movement, such as Thomas J. J. Altizer. Van Buren distanced himself from the Death of God label and from the secularizing tendencies of his early thought.

Carl L. Bankston III

THE THEORY OF MORAL SENTIMENTS

Author: Adam Smith (1723-1790)
First published: 1759, revised 1790
Edition used: The Theory of Moral Sentiments, edited by D. D. Raphael and A. L. Macfie. Oxford, England: Clarendon Press, 1976
Genre: Nonfiction
Subgenres: Critical analysis; didactic treatise
Core issues: Compassion; humility; morality; responsibility; self-control; wisdom

Drawing on Stoic philosophy (and its emphasis on natural law) as well as Christian doctrine, Smith created a complex analysis embracing sociological, psychological, moral, and ethical elements. According to Smith, individuals draw a personal moral outlook largely from their sensitivity to an "impartial spectator," the internalized reflection of peer-group and reference-group opinion. Smith undertook to evaluate both the intention (motivation) behind an action and the consequences of that action.

Overview

Adam Smith, a leading member of the late eighteenth century movement known as the Scottish Enlightenment (a period of intellectual questioning in which a Scottish humanism developed), is best known for *An Inquiry into the Nature and Causes of the Wealth of Nations* (1776; commonly known as *The Wealth of Nations*), which more than any other work created the modern intellectual discipline of economics. Much earlier, in 1759, however, Smith published another work, *The Theory of Moral Sentiments*, while he was a professor of moral philosophy at the University of Glasgow; he produced a revised edition of this work in 1790, well after publishing *The Wealth of Nations*.

Most of the subsequent study of Smith's work has been conducted by economists. Some have suggested inconsistency between *The Theory of Moral Sentiments* and *The Wealth of Nations*, with the former giving much more attention to the sources of virtues such as benevolence, while the latter allegedly praises self-interest. In fact, both books give much attention to the unintended consequences of actions, with *The Theory of Moral Sentiments* giving much more praise to good intentions. Smith inherited from the ancient Greek Stoic philosophers the idea that social affairs manifest the workings of natural laws that produce beneficial and harmonious results, even when people's motives are less than virtuous.

Although Smith was apparently a Presbyterian, *The Theory of Moral Sentiments* does not contain many overtly Christian points of reference. Smith did not take the Ten Commandments, the Sermon on the Mount, or other obvious biblical references as his basis for discussion. Emphasis in *The Theory of Moral Sentiments* is, rather, very much on moral sentiments—that is, people's attitudes and feelings about right and wrong. Smith's emphasis is congruent with modern psychology and sociology. Each of us is conditioned ("socialized," in modern discourse) by the family environment of childhood and by peer groups to accept attitudes about right and wrong. These views are personified in an "impartial spectator," an imaginary judge who watches and evaluates what we think and do—essentially our conscience. Smith, however, acknowledges that each of us is also concerned about the way our friends and associates judge us. Smith's analysis thus covers both the "inner-directed" and "other-directed" personalities made famous by sociologist David Riesman (*The Lonely Crowd: A Study of the Changing American Character*, 1950). Smith is also confident that each individual is inclined to feel "sympathy" for others, which he defined as the capacity to identify with other people's thoughts and feelings.

Smith drew examples largely from his own social circle. He did not try to analyze the concepts of right and wrong formed by people raised in dysfunctional households or the kind of people depicted by Smith's contemporary, artist William Hogarth, in his scathing illustrations of lowlife in London's slums. Smith was confident that, as societies evolved over time, standards would converge toward moral laws of nature that would promote the welfare and happiness of the entire society. These might be biblical principles; they might also be the "agreeable" principles Smith attributed to "commercial society" in *The Wealth of Nations*.

Smith emphasized three elements of natural morality: prudence, justice, and benevolence. Prudence embraces the dimensions of self-concern and self-interest; it occupies center stage in *The Wealth of Nations*. However, Smith clearly expected that most people would also develop a strong sense of justice, being prepared to treat others fairly and honestly. He expected, finally, that they would feel and act on sentiments of benevolence toward others. (Christian doctrine would probably rank these virtues in inverse order.)

Smith entertained no illusions about human perfectibility. Though he did not dwell on sin as a category, most of the varieties of sin passed in review, not all equally condemned. For Smith, vanity is, perhaps, less objectionable than pride, and it may be better to be too proud than too humble. Smith followed the Stoics in giving much praise to self-command, to virtuous attention to one's duty.

The central theme of *The Wealth of Nations*—that the self-serving pursuit of wealth by individuals can lead to public benefits through productivity and economic growth—was clearly foreshadowed in *The Theory of Moral Sentiments*. Smith also warned against a "spirit of system" that could lead to the sort of fanatical and violent radicalism unleashed in the French Revolution.

Christian Themes

The Theory of Moral Sentiments was not presented as a set of rules or instructions about how to behave or how to think. Rather, Smith speculated on the way in which people formed their ideas on these subjects. His idea that we should assess our thoughts and feelings as the impartial spectator would see them parallels the biblical advice to judge other people as we would judge ourselves. He cites the Decalogue (the Ten Commandments), but only in reference to honoring parents.

Smith did not make many references to overtly Christian writers; there are many more references to Greek and Roman authorities. A rare exception is a section dealing with the "casuistry" of such Roman Catholic authorities as Saint Thomas Aquinas. The tone is not very respectful: The practice of confession is associated with "superstition." Smith's illustration of rules of casuistry asks, Suppose a robber extracts from his victim a promise to pay him a large sum of money on his release. Is the victim morally bound to pay it?

Jesus' name never appears, but Smith affirms that "to love our neighbor as we love ourselves is the great law of Christianity," adding "so it is the great precept of nature to love ourselves only as we love our neighbor." A rather inconclusive passage examines the impulses of benevolence in relation to the commandment to love God and one's neighbor. A more sympathetic rendering of the same theme refers to Greek philosophers as well as "many ancient fathers of the Christian church." Smith is skeptical about the contribution to happiness from more goods, but he articulates the important view that the quest for material wealth can lead to productive actions and (unintended) benefits for the entire society.

Smith's own sentiments appear to differ from mainstream Christian doctrine at many points. A notable example is his opinion that "the futile mortifications of a monastery" appear far less worthy than "the ennobling hardships and hazards of war." Smith assumes that it is proper for our benevolence to be primarily directed toward our inner circle of family and friends. He commends the sentiments of universal benevolence but suggests that is God's concern. Mere mortals should direct their concern toward persons whose needs and conditions they know at firsthand. We find no counterpart of Christ's command that we love our enemies. At the same time, Smith was a consistent internationalist, condemning attitudes of rivalry and antagonism between nations. This was to become a major theme of *The Wealth of Nations*, in which Smith vigorously defended free trade and condemned the idea that another nation's improvement was somehow one's own loss.

Some critics have classed Smith as a Deist for references that emphasize the wisdom and benevolence of the Creator and imply that he saw God as the "divine watchmaker" who, after Creation, now sits back and lets the system operate spontaneously according to the natural laws he set in place. Smith refers approvingly to

> the idea of that divine Being, whose benevolence and wisdom have, from all eternity, contrived and conducted the immense machine of the universe, so as at all times to produce the greatest possible quantity of happiness. . . .

Finally, Smith examined the promises of life after death somewhat skeptically, noting that the greatest rewards were promised for acts and attitudes of faith and devotion in a manner often opposed to our moral sentiments.

Sources for Further Study

Ekelund, Robert B., Robert F. Hebert, and Robert D. Tollison. "Adam Smith on Religion and Market Structure." *History of Political Economy* 37, no. 4 (2005): 647-

660. A concise review of Smith's rather detached and skeptical views of religion.

Bibliography.

Fitzgibbons, Athol. *Adam Smith's System of Liberty, Wealth, and Virtue*. New York: Oxford University Press, 1995. Argues that Smith set out to overthrow the prevailing traditional (Christian, Aristotelian, authoritarian) approach to morals with a more liberal view derived from the Stoics, consistent with the kind of natural law represented by Sir Isaac Newton.

Fleischacker, Samuel. *On Adam Smith's "Wealth of Nations": A Philosophical Companion*. Princeton, N.J.: Princeton University Press, 2004. Despite the title, there is extensive discussion of *The Theory of Moral Sentiments*. Religious sentiments receive only a brief commentary, but there are chapters on moral philosophy, vanity, and distributive justice.

Griswold, Charles L., Jr. *Adam Smith and the Virtues of Enlightenment*. New York: Cambridge University Press, 1999. Primarily focused on *The Theory of Moral Sentiments*, but effectively blends this with *The Wealth of Nations* to stress Smith's concern for individual freedom (against religious dogma as well as slavery and political autocracy).

Taylor, Overton H. *A History of Economic Thought*. New York: McGraw-Hill, 1960. Devotes chapter 3 to *The Theory of Moral Sentiments*, stressing the central roles of prudence, justice, and benevolence, and noting Smith's confidence that the spontaneous evolution of moral sentiments works to promote the welfare of society.

Paul B. Trescott

"THEY ARE ALL GONE INTO THE WORLD OF LIGHT!"

Author: Henry Vaughan (1622-1695)
First published: 1655, in *Silex Scintillans*
Edition used: Norton Anthology of Poetry, edited by Alexander W. Allison et al., with an essay on versification by Jon Stallworthy. New York: Norton, 1983
Genre: Poetry
Subgenres: Lyric poetry; meditation and contemplation
Core issues: Death; faith; God; mysticism; nature; soul

In this metaphysical poem, the poet Vaughan, alone on a hill, glimpses the souls of the departed walking in a spiritual light. This fragmentary vision makes his earthly life seem drab by comparison, and he yearns to know what really lies beyond death. He remarks that no one can penetrate the mystery intellectually, but that in sleep people sometimes get a "peep" into transcendence. The poem ends with a plea to God to show him, either in this life or in death, what lies beyond death.

Overview

"They Are All Gone into the World of Light!" considered one of English poet Henry Vaughan's best poems, consists of ten stanzas of quatrains altering lines of iambic pentameter and iambic trimeter. The poem deals with Vaughan's mystical revelations concerning such Christian topics as death, eternal life, faith, God as Father/Creator. An important feature of the poem is a traditional Christian contrast between a better "other world" and this life as a "vale of tears."

The poem begins as a lament: "They" have departed the poet's world for a "world of light," presumably the Christian heaven, while the poet remains, abandoned and unable to join those whom he desperately wishes to join. During the course of the poem, the poet's lament over this separation (from whom, specifically, is never stated) shifts to contemplation about what that other world must be like ("What mysteries do lie beyond thy dust/ Could man outlook that mark!") and ultimately a plea to the "Father of eternal life" to "Resume [his] spirit from this world of thrall/ Into true liberty." As befits the theme of separation and departure, the entire poem is studded with contrasts that mark the division between the poet in his dark, befogged world and the departed's world of light. Intellectual inquiry and wonder over the mystery of the holy realm contrast with frustration in the final stanzas, where the poet demands that God either answer his doubts or take him to where he can find out for himself.

Despite his fleeting visions of the departed "walking in an air of glory," the poet craves certainty as to what happens to people after death. The first four verses of the poem contrast his momentary vision of the dead in a "world of light" with his own earthly existence, which is "at best but dull and hoary." The poet speculates that he may have been allowed these heavenly glimpses to "kindle my cold love." The fifth stanza changes direction to probe into the mystery of "beauteous Death"—an image that, paradoxically, joins darkness with light:

> Dear, beauteous Death! the jewel of the just,
> Shining nowhere, but in the dark;
> What mysteries do lie beyond thy dust
> Could man outlook that mark!

The structure of the poem here suddenly makes the equation of "death" and "light" evident to the poem's listener, if not the poem's speaker himself: Death occupies the same position as the "world of light," "air of glory," "glow," "glitter," and "holy Hope" of previous stanzas; Death even "shines" (in the dark) and is recognized as a pathway (dust) rather than a final end.

The sixth stanza emphasizes this mystery by drawing an analogy between the poet's question and the fact that a person can realize a bird has flown its nest but not know where it has flown. Stanza seven admits the possibility of another dimension, heaven, of which, in sleep, mortals are granted a "peep." The eighth stanza moves from intellectual inquiry and recognition of the irrational to faith when the poet speculates that if a star were locked in a tomb, it would be invisible to him but nevertheless would burn and ultimately shine when released.

The last two stanzas directly address a traditionally Christian God, "O Father of eternal life." The poet asks God to free him from "the world of thrall," presumably from earthly limitations. The poem's conclusion thunders with the demand that God either show him clearly what lies beyond—in an allusion to Paul's expression "Now we see through a glass darkly, but then we will see face-to-face"—or else take him to heaven where he "shall need no glass."

"They Are All Gone into the World of Light!" rests on light and dark imagery. As is Vaughan's custom, the spiritual visions are expressed in words that denote light. The dead are shining; the beyond is a realm of light; angels bring "brighter dreams." Nouns such as "sun," "stars," "flames," and "beams" are used in connection with the soul. Even death is a "jewel" as far as the righteous are concerned. Verbs such as "glows," "glitters," "glimmering," "shining," and "shine," further emphasize the happier state of those in "the world of light" and contrast with the "thrall," "gloomy grove," "decays," and mists of earthbound life.

The poet's mix of iambic tetrameter with iambic trimeter evokes a conversational tone. The pentameter is sometimes varied with anapests and the trimester punctuated with an extra syllable. This irregularity serves to break up any rhythmic monotony in which content is obscured by pattern. The poem is saved from platitude by alternating mystical revelation with intellectual curiosity, and by expressing a frustration with ambiguity.

Christian Themes

The primary poem's Christian theme surrounds Vaughan's struggle to understand the human-God relationship. The poet begins in a state of sorrow, frustration, and even anger at his state of being "alone" but over the course of the poem comes to understand, accept, and yearn for the union with God that will lift him out of a world of sin and reunite him with the Creator. Death, which stands at the center of this transformation, is transformed from a state to be feared to a doorway to salvation.

Vaughan's work has a freshness that prefigures the Romantics and strikes a chord in modern readers because of its simplicity, striking imagery, and honest recognition of complication. It therefore continues to resonate with readers, particularly Christians, who can recognize in the poet some of the struggles and doubts they face in daily life.

Sources for Further Study

Clements, Arthur L. *The Poetry of Contemplation: John Donne, George Herbert, Henry Vaughan, and the Modern Period.* New York: State University of New York Press, 1990. This book attempts distinctions between the terms "mysticism," "meditative," and "contemplative." Clements addresses their blurring definitions and makes the point that Vaughan's varied philosophical interests and his Gnostic leanings always appeared in the context of orthodox Christian mysticism.

Hutchinson, F. E. *Henry Vaughan: A Life and Interpretation.* Whitefish, Mont.: Kessinger, 2005. This biography also deals with the philosophical sources of Vaughan's mysticism as well as his unification, in the sense of creating correspondences, between the heavenly and terrestrial. Hutchinson notes that Vaughan, unlike the poet Herbert, sees animals and other parts of creation as worshiping God in their blind obedience.

Skulsky, Harold. "The Fellowship of Mystery: Emergence and Exploratory Metaphor in Vaughan." *Studies in English Literature 1500-1900*, no. 27 (1987): 89-107. This article asserts that Vaughan's emergent metaphors (a metaphor that develops as a result of something else) express Gnostic Christian longings through use of allusion and utterance, the establishment of an intimate, conversational tone.

Mary Hanford Bruce

THE THIRD SPIRITUAL ALPHABET

Author: Francisco de Osuna (c. 1492-c. 1540)
First published: Tercer abecedario espiritual, 1527 (English translation, 1931)
Edition used: The Third Spiritual Alphabet, translated with an introduction by Mary E. Giles. New York: Paulist Press, 1981
Genre: Nonfiction
Subgenres: Meditation and contemplation; mysticism
Core issues: Mysticism; prayer; purgation; recollection; union with God

Osuna's work is not only a personal statement of belief in the prayer of recollection but also its most eloquent description and its boldest defense.

Overview

Little is known of the author of a work that was to influence one of Spain's most famous mystics, Saint Teresa of Ávila, and through her, countless others. Francisco de Osuna was ordained about 1519-1520 and three years later entered a Franciscan monastery, where, as a guide for meditation, he formulated maxims and arranged them in alphabetical order. He composed three such alphabets, each with twenty-three distichs to correspond with the twenty-two letters and tilde of the Spanish alphabet, and later glossed them as treatises on the Passion (1528), prayer and ascetic practices (1530), and recollection (1527). A total of six alphabets appeared, though not all follow the alphabetical format: *Ley de amor* (1530; law of love), fifty-one rules of love; *Norte de los estados* (1531; the North Star of ranks), advice to people in all social ranks on Christian ideals; and *Gracioso convite* (1530; gracious banquet), on the Eucharist. Osuna's life was devoted to preaching and writing in both Spanish and Latin during a time of religious renewal and ferment in Spain. His work in the Franciscan order took him to France, Belgium, and Italy.

Osuna wrote during a fertile yet dangerous time in Spain. Mysticism was in the air in the sixteenth century, fostered by translations in Spanish of the writings of early and later mystics such as Pseudo-Dionysius the Areopagite, Meister Eckhart, Bernard of Clairvaux, and John Gerson; translations of the New Testament; the ideas of Desiderius Erasmus and interiorized Christianity; and the practice and teaching of mental prayer in and out of monasteries. In the forefront of the push for a Christianity purified of extraneous external practices were laywomen who, with laymen and religious, especially Franciscan priests, inspired small gatherings for the purpose of prayer. Among the charismatic women leaders were Francisca Hernández and Isabel de la Cruz, both of whom were brought before the Inquisition on charges that included teaching quietist doctrines.

The practice that was sure to arouse the suspicion of the Inquisition was mental prayer, which, defined briefly, is to think about the meaning of words that are said, whether aloud or silently. On the basis of this definition, mental prayer sounds innocent, but when some advocates professed their utter inability to do anything whatsoever in prayer except abandon themselves to divine grace, the ranks of the prayerful split and the stage was set for the Inquisition to attack. On one side were the advocates of *dejamiento* (abandonment), who went so far in the abandon to God's grace that they denied the efficacy of virtuous deeds, vocal prayer, external devotion, penitence, and even the Eucharist, claiming, in the last instance, that the Eucharist was more effectively present in the heart than in a bit of bread. Opposing them were the defenders of *recogimiento*, or recollection, who accepted the sacramental and devotional life of the Church while nourishing an inner prayer that at least in the beginning stages required mental effort.

Osuna clearly was in the camp of the second group; his *Third Spiritual Alphabet* is not only a personal statement of belief in the prayer of recollection but also its most eloquent description and bold defense. To appreciate the vigor of the treatise and its author's courage, we need to remember that only two years before its publication, the Inquisition had made its first public statement against the *alumbrados* (enlightened ones), condemning their practice of *dejamiento*.

The twenty-three treatises of *The Third Spiritual Alphabet* trace the journey inward in terms of recollection. The initial five treatises are a preparation for the journey, which is to be made primarily through the heart. Osuna first clarifies that the goal of union with God is proper to all Christians; he then counsels as appropriate to understanding our relationship with God the response of gratitude for the general work of Creation, particular blessings we receive, and favors bestowed by God that we do not discern. Our general response is to be affective, with the understanding blind, the will deaf to all but love for God, and the memory dumb. The fifth treatise is an exhortation to a careful examination of conscience—counsel the pilgrim is to heed not only at this point of beginning recollection but all along the journey as well.

The sixth treatise is among the most important of the alphabet. Osuna emphasizes first that, although each must find an individual path to God, all should practice recollection in imitation of our Lord Jesus Christ who went into the desert to pray alone. He states that recollection is the term for mystical theology, or wisdom infused into the soul, and offers several other names for it: the art of love, union, profundity, concealment, abstinence, drawing near, enkindling, welcome, consent, the marrow and fat of sacrifice, attraction, adoption, arrival, height, spiritual ascension, and the third heaven. In general, recollection gathers together the senses, sensuality and reason, bodily members and virtues, the soul's three powers with its highest faculty, and God and the soul.

Treatises 7 through 12 develop recollection as the art of emptying the heart from within. Osuna recommends first purgation of thought (treatise 7), actions and speech (9), memory and will (11), and understanding (12). In the order of purgations, Osuna's methodology is similar to that of Saint John of the Cross, reflective perhaps of the Scholastic training they had in common.

Osuna also details reasons for learning and teaching recollection; offers practical advice on the choice of a spiritual director (8); and advises how to respond when the intensity of love erupts in outcries and gestures (9). His discussion of sighing, groaning, and bodily movements during prayer suggests that these phenomena may be a mark of progress in prayer; his commonsensical advice, however, is to control the outbursts unless in doing so interior devotion wanes. Anticipating the teaching of later Carmelite mystics, Osuna refused to measure spirituality by extraordinary phenomena that affect the senses and emotions.

The tenth treatise is a beautiful exposition of the favors God bestows along the journey, including the gifts of tears, teaching, and healing. In distinguishing the tears of beginners, proficients, and perfects, Osuna once again honors the tripartite division of the mystical way and the movement from active to passive consciousness.

The inward journey intensifies in subtlety as in the eleventh and twelfth treatises Osuna describes the purgation of the higher faculties of memory, will, and understanding. Memories of worldly pleasures are to be erased, leaving only images of the Sacred Humanity and of God on a general, universal level. Purgation of the will is accomplished both actively, as the soul strives to desire only God, and passively, when the heart inexplicably is moved to desire God. The twelfth treatise in its entirety is a culminating point in *The Third Spiritual Alphabet* as the soul is taught to rely not on natural knowledge or even understandings that come in a supernatural way—as when one hears voices from the outside—but on knowledge received in the darkness of unknowing.

Having described the process whereby the senses and higher faculties are recollected, Osuna explains in following treatises experiences that come to the soul well along the mystical way. His topics include vocal prayer, prayer of the heart, and mental or spiritual prayer (13); the need for gentle discipline in the practice of prayer and the purgation of passions, especially joy and sadness (14); and general and special recollection (15). His descriptions of prayer are perceptive, as when he distinguishes between general recollection as a state of alertness to God and special recollection as moments of retiring into the heart (he recommends at least two hours each day of special recollection). In regarding recollection as a process of prayer, Osuna differs from Teresa, for whom recollection was one kind of prayer.

Treatise 16, on love, is a second culminating point in the alphabet. Osuna's advice is that we learn to draw love from everything in creation and refer it to God.

The remaining treatises are unified by a pattern of alternating themes; Osuna treats now prayer, now problems and obstacles: love and infused prayer; suffering and imitating Jesus Christ in hardship as well as glory; spiritual prayer; humility and temptations; the heights of prayer wherein the soul understands in darkness; and zeal and perseverance.

Just as treatises 12 and 16 are climactic points, so also is treatise 21. Culminating all the preceding material in the treatise, Osuna expounds the role of understanding in the *vía negativa* of recollection, elaborating the doctrine of the negative way and clarifying misunderstandings about the practice of *no pensar nada* (stopping thought). Osuna supports the belief of affective mystics that it is the will rather than the understanding that enables wisdom to be received into the soul. In the third degree of silence, the soul is transformed in God, its understanding quieted so that it understands nothing happening about it. In the highest part of the soul, God's image is imprinted and there are received divine understandings which the understanding cannot understand. Although the understanding is asleep and the will at rest in this union of soul with God, the perfection is not the *no pensar nada* condition of the quietists. Osuna maintains that not only must one learn to quiet oneself by mental discipline during the purgative and illuminative stages of the journey, but even the most advanced souls must always exercise their understanding. Recollection is a process that requires unceasing vigilance.

Christian Themes

A summary of the main Christian concerns of Osuna's *The Third Spiritual Alphabet* includes the following points:

- Recollection is a general term for prayer, including vocal prayer accompanied by thinking, mental prayer, and passive prayer.
- Recollection is also the process of prayer wherein the soul becomes increasingly passive with respect to God.
- Eventually recollection is an ongoing alertness to God intensified by moments of acute awareness of God when the soul is infused with wisdom beyond rational understanding.
- The way of recollection is primarily affective, but recollection is not quietism.
- Recollection is open to everyone, including women and married people.

Osuna's *Third Spiritual Alphabet* is important in its own right as a detailed description of the interior journey as well as a source of inspiration for both Saint Teresa of Ávila and Saint John of the Cross. The fusing of the affective and intellectual that is a hallmark of later Carmelite spirituality informs the alphabet. The structure of the alphabet is not as rigorous as that of Saint John's treatises, but the ascent away from the known to the unknown that Osuna traces through increasingly subtle forms of recollection is similar to Saint John's. If Saint Teresa is a favorite with spiritual pilgrims today, it is in large part because her appealing style is enlivened by images she met in Osuna's work. A traveler on the mystical way and spiritual director for many others, Francisco de Osuna, like Saint Teresa and Saint John, drew on rich experiential resources to create a treasure house of practical advice, wisdom, and love of God.

Sources for Further Study

Beaumont, David Joseph. "Prayer and the Contemplative Life in Francisco de Osuna's *Third Spiritual Alphabet*." Master's thesis. Berkeley, Calif.: Dominican School of Philosophy and Theology, 1988. A rare study of the work, by a student of the Dominican order.

Calvert, Laura. *Francisco de Osuna and the Spirit of the Letter*. Chapel Hill: North Carolina Studies in the Romance Languages and Literatures, 1973. A careful and illuminating study.

Mary E. Giles

THIS PRESENT DARKNESS

Author: Frank E. Peretti (1951-   )
First published: 1986
Edition used: This Present Darkness. Rev. ed. Wheaton, Ill.: Crossway Books, 2003
Genre: Novel
Subgenres: Apocalyptic fiction; evangelical fiction; thriller/suspense
Core issues: Apocalypse; evangelization; faith; good vs. evil; Holy Spirit; mysticism; prayer; spiritual warfare

Peretti's first novel is an evangelical tale of spiritual warfare and the power of prayer to overcome demonic influences. In line with fundamentalist beliefs, Peretti highlights how non-Christian doctrines such as those found in New Age philosophies draw people away from biblical truths. The story is recognized as one of the leading late twentieth century novels to influence the boom in overtly Christian fiction.

> *Principal characters*
> *Juleen Langstrat*, a psychology professor
> *Lucius*, prince of Ashton, the head demon
> *Tal*, an angel who is captain of the host of angels
> *Alf Brummel*, chief of the Ashton police
> *Oliver Young*, the pastor of the Ashton United Christian Church
> *Henry L. "Hank" Busche*, pastor of Ashton Community Church
> *Mary Busche*, Hank's wife
> *The Remnant*, praying members of the Ashton Community
> *Bernice Krueger*, a reporter for the *Ashton Clarion*
> *Marshall Hogan*, owner and chief editor of the *Ashton Clarion*
> *Sandy Hogan*, Marshall's daughter
> *Ba-al Rafar*, prince of Babylon
> *Susan Jacobson*, the Maidservant

Overview

In the small college town of Ashton, demonic forces have been covertly working to take control of the town. The evil plot is to manipulate Whitmore College into bankruptcy and then assume ownership, use this control of the college to control the town of Ashton, and thereby spread Satanic influence in society. Led by the ruling demon Lucius, a gaggle of smaller demons known by their vices begin a subtle attack to control and manipulate the town's residents in order to weaken their Christian strength and prepare the community for total domination by dark forces. People who are weak in their faith are easy targets; those who are strong in Christian faith are either targeted for elimination or forced out of the town through deceptive or illegal practices.

In preparation for the town's destruction, Juleen Langstrat is maneuvered into place as a new psychology professor at Whitmore College. As a servant to the dark forces, she begins to aid in the takeover by teaching and promoting New Age philosophies, Eastern religious practices, and witchcraft. Juleen is part of a larger organization known as the Universal Consciousness Society, which is a worldwide front organization for Satan. She practices, promotes, and teaches a type of meditation that facilitates communication with demonic spirit guides. She is able to influence other key members of the community, such as Alf Brummel, the chief of police, and Oliver Young, the pastor of the Ashton United Christian Church. Both Alf and Oliver are recruited by Juleen to help weaken the community's Christian strength.

While the demonic takeover efforts are under way, the Holy Spirit, aided by the subtle efforts of the angels, begins to position key people in preparation for the impending spiritual battle. Led by Tal, the captain of the host, they work quietly behind the scenes, at times revealing themselves as helpful figures and at other times whispering subliminal suggestions to their charges. The angels are strengthened through the prayers of the Remnant, members of the community who are strong in their faith or who have recently been led by the Holy Spirit to accept Jesus Christ. Hank Busche and his wife, Mary, are divinely brought into the community to pastor at the Ashton Community Church. Hank is strong in his faith and, despite a few demonic attacks, stands strong in leading the Remnant in continual prayer.

Bernice Krueger, a reporter for the local newspaper, the *Ashton Clarion*, initiates the investigation of the demonic takeover as a result of an angelic suggestion. Working with Marshall Hogan, the new owner and chief editor of the paper, she begins to realize that there is something underhanded going on in the town. They are led on an arduous and at times treacherous investigation to uncover the deceptive and illegal practices that have forced so many townspeople out or ended in their untimely deaths. Hogan, in particular, is susceptible to demonic attacks because of his neglect to develop a stronger Christian faith. He also has a deteriorating relationship with both his wife and his daughter because he puts work ahead of everything else. Because of these broken relationships, his daughter Sandy becomes an easy target for the Universal Consciousness Society.

Shortly after the arrival of Tal, Ba-al Rafar, prince of Babylon, descends on the scene in preparation for the final spiritual battle for the town. As a ruling demon, Rafar usurps Lucius as the prince of Ashton and assumes responsibility for the final takeover of Ashton. Tal and some of the other angels have battled Rafar in the past; the angels are continually concerned that enough prayer coverage from the Remnant is in reserve to ensure a victory in the final battle. After demonic efforts have succeeded and the town is spiritually weakened, the demonically influenced humans are positioned and manipulated for the final possession of the town. At the same time, the angels and demons are inconspicuously positioned for the final spiritual battle.

Unbeknownst to the demonic forces, the angels have been able to influence several key people. Susan Jacobson, who is known as the Maidservant, awakens to the call from the Holy Spirit and works to gather key documents that are instrumental to Bernice and Hogan in proving the many illegal and deceptive practices that have forced people out of the town. The records Susan brings forth are enough to stop the sale of the college. In the final battle between good and evil, Lucius, who is jealous of Rafar, betrays the satanic cause by influencing Alf to resist his orders from Juleen. As a result, Alf unknowingly begins to aid Hank and Hogan. Lucius, in his jealous rage, severely wounds Rafar. When Rafar and Tal finally engage in battle, Tal, strengthened by the prayers of the Remnant, is ultimately able to defeat the demonic foe.

Christian Themes

This Present Darkness is representative of apocalyptic, evangelical Christian fiction of the late twentieth and early twenty-first centuries. It tells a story of spiritual warfare in which the forces for good, here aided by "prayer coverage," battle innumerable odds to beat the forces of evil. In line with evangelical beliefs regarding the importance of prayer to aid in spiritual warfare, it also highlights many Christian beliefs regarding the importance of listening to and obeying the will of God spoken through the Holy Sprit. It also emphasizes the need to evangelize to those who may be weak in spirit or plagued by their own "demons" but hear the call from God to repent and accept Jesus Christ as their savior.

The title of the work, *This Present Darkness*, is a subtle description of current societal influences that many Christians have come to see as forces of evil, particularly those New Age philosophies that attract followers under the guise of being a new form of religion. The New Age religions may offer watered-down versions of Christian values but are seen as being more lenient, accepting sinful behavior and thus deceiving followers into leading sinful lives. Other New Age movements, represented in the novel by the Universal Consciousness Society, promote something greater than God.

Characters like Juleen and Sandy illustrate the influential yet detrimental effects of New Age philosophies. Frank E. Peretti uses the character of Hogan Marshall to show how self-focus can be a form of sin that leads to broken relationships. Hank and Mary Busche and the Remnant highlight the importance of developing Christian faith—following God's will even when one may question it—and the importance of prayer to thwart Satan's continual efforts to lead people into sin and away from God.

Peretti would continue the spiritual warfare in a sequel, *Piercing the Darkness*, in which demonic influences, in the form of organizations promoting liberal, non-Christian views, threaten to undermine fundamentalist Christian beliefs about parenting and education.

Sources for Further Study

Blodgett, Jan. *Protestant Evangelical Literary Culture and Contemporary Society.* Westport, Conn.: Greenwood Press, 1997. *This Present Darkness* is used to illustrate points regarding the content and publishing of religious fiction and how it supports protestant beliefs.

Howard, Jay R. "Vilifying the Enemy: The Christian Right and the Novels of Frank Peretti." *Journal of Popular Culture* 28, no. 3 (1994). Notes how *This Present*

Darkness and *Piercing the Darkness* promote the beliefs of the new Christian Right.

Jensen, Arden E. *Prophet in the Wasteland: A Critical Biography of Frank Peretti.* Tallahassee: Florida State University, 2000. Offers a critical examination of Peretti, the makeup and beliefs of his readers, and a critical analysis of his works.

Jorstad, Erling. *Popular Religion in America: The Evangelical Voice.* Westport, Conn.: Greenwood Press, 1993. Brief analysis of *This Present Darkness* and its sequel, *Piercing the Darkness*, noting some of the criticisms and cultural significance.

Simolke, Duane. *This Present Darkness and Its Influence.* Abilene, Tex.: Hardin-Simons University, 1991. Discusses Peretti's work in the context of Christian fantasy, relying heavily on other published Christian fantasy works in his analysis.

Stedman, Barbara A. *The Word Become Fiction: Textual Voices from the Evangelical Subculture.* Muncie, Ind.: Ball State University, 1994. Analyzes the texts of Janette Oke and Frank Peretti with a focus on the reasons for their appeal among Christian evangelicals.

Susan E. Thomas

THE THORN BIRDS

Author: Colleen McCullough (1937-   )
First published: New York: Harper & Row, 1977
Genre: Novel
Subgenres: Literary fiction; saga
Core issues: Catholics and Catholicism; guilt; healing; priesthood; repentance

Three generations of the Cleary family display the evidence of lives well and badly lived in this saga, which spans fifty-four years. The novel deals with the consequences of one's choices and the visitation of the sins of the fathers (and mothers) on their children. The failure to honor commitments is examined in some detail, especially the notion that one is free to make choices, but one cannot control the results of those choices.

Principal characters
Ralph de Bricassart, a priest and later cardinal in the Catholic Church
Meggie Cleary, the only daughter of the Cleary family
Fiona Cleary, Meggie's mother
Padraic "Paddy" Cleary, Meggie's father
Mary Carson, Paddy's sister, owner of Drogheda
Frank,
Hugh,
Jack,
Bob,
Stuart,
James, and
Patrick Cleary, Meggie's brothers
Luke O'Neill, Meggie's husband
Justine O'Neill, Meggie's daughter
Dane O'Neill, Meggie's son
Rainer Moerling Hartheim, Justine's lover

Overview

The Thorn Birds considers three generations of a sprawling Irish family, the Clearys. At the novel's beginning, Fiona and Paddy Cleary are eking out a meager living from Padraic's work as a sheepshearer in New Zealand. The life is hard, especially for Meggie, the only girl among Fiona and Paddy's children. However, the Clearys receive a notice from Paddy's wealthy sister, Mary Carson, in Australia, that she wants them to move there and learn to run the operation on Drogheda, her Australian homestead. She tells Father Ralph de Bricassart that they will inherit the property when Mary dies.

Mary does not explicitly promise the Clearys that they will inherit Drogheda, although that is implied in her offer to them. Mary loves Father de Bricassart, though he does not return her love, and she is jealous of the attention he pays to Meggie. She deliberately places Father de Bricassart in a dilemma that will test his character. She leaves two wills: One has been filed with her lawyer, leaving Drogheda to the Clearys. The other she leaves in her house with a letter to the priest; in this will, she leaves her estate to the Catholic Church. Her fortune, in excess of thirteen million pounds, is a huge amount in the 1920's. It will buy Father de Bricassart's place in the Catholic hierarchy. Father de Bricassart has the option of destroying the second will and leaving in place the will that leaves Drogheda to the Clearys—but he does not. He puts the second will into effect, ensuring that he will rise in the Church. He eases his conscience by noting that Mary has left a considerable income to the Clearys, as well as residence in her home. The management of Drogheda goes to Paddy, his sons, and eventually his grandsons. Although Father de Bricassart suffers some guilt, he never looks back.

In the 1934, Meggie marries Luke O'Neill, a stockman on Drogheda. Luke takes her to Queensland, where he plans to work in the sugarcane. He puts Meggie to work as a housemaid, takes control of all her money, and generally treats her as the acquisition he sees her to be. Luke is obsessed with making and saving money. He makes every effort to prevent Meggie from getting pregnant; he goes off and works for weeks on end without seeing her. Meggie does eventually manage to get pregnant, but she has a difficult pregnancy and a difficult delivery. She names the baby girl Justine. Luke does not bother acknowledging the birth of his daughter. Meggie is having such a difficult time recovering from the pregnancy that she accepts the offer of a vacation on Matlock Island, a gift from her friends and employers. Her friends' plan is to send Luke to join her when he shows up, but Luke is not interested. When Father de Bricassart arrives for a visit and asks where Meggie is, they send him to join her. They believe him when he says he only wants to see her. Father de Bricassart and Meggie have an affair that lasts long enough for Meggie to become pregnant. When she realizes that she is expecting a child that is most likely Father de Bricassart's, she arranges to visit Luke for what is to be their last encounter. Then she returns to Drogheda.

In 1938, Meggie gives birth to a son she names Dane. She swears never to tell de Bricassart that the child is his. By this time, de Bricassart is an archbishop working in the Vatican, and the unrest that will become World War II is beginning to gather force. Fiona, who lost Paddy years before in a fire, works with Meggie to maintain life at Drogheda. When Dane is seven, Fiona tells Meggie that she knows who fathered the boy; she also tells Meggie that she will pay for what she has done.

In time, de Bricassart becomes a cardinal. When Dane decides he wants to be a priest, his mother is horrified, believing that the Church has robbed her of both the men she loves. Ultimately, however, she sends him to seminary in Rome, putting him under the care of de Bricassart. Justine, who has become an actress and something of a star on the London stage, visits Dane in Rome. They have tea in the Vatican with de Bricassart, and she is introduced to Rainer Moerling Hartheim. Rainer is a friend of de

Bricassart and something of a self-made German magnate. He and Justine begin a long friendship, although at first Justine refuses to allow the relationship to become romantic.

When it is time for Dane to be ordained as a priest, all of the uncles on Drogheda attend the ordination, but Meggie refuses. After the ordination, Dane plans to take a holiday in Greece, and Justine is to join him there. She receives notice of a chance to play a part she covets, however, and returns to London, while Dane continues his stay in Greece. On the beach, he sees some tourists caught in the undertow. In rescuing them, he loses his own life. Dane's death is hugely devastating to his family. Justine blames herself for not being there and ends her relationship with Rainer. Meggie flies to Rome and secures de Bricassart's help to transport Dane's body home for burial. At this point she tells him the truth about Dane's parentage, and de Bricassart helps her; he even goes to Drogheda to officiate at Dane's funeral, but he dies of a heart attack while there.

Justine decides to leave the stage to return to Drogheda for good. Ultimately, however, Meggie knows that the move will be destructive for Justine, and she writes to her, urging her to stay in London. Justine reunites with—and marries—Rainer.

Christian Themes

One of the strongest Christian themes in *The Thorn Birds* appears to be that the wages of sin is death. Those who engage in sinful activities lose someone dear to them. Fiona had a child before she was married to Paddy Cleary; that child, Frank, eventually winds up in prison for thirty years. Meggie loses both de Bricassart and Dane. De Bricassart loses the son he never knew and eventually his life. God, as envisioned by Colleen McCullough, is not only a jealous God; he is a vengeful one, as well.

However, other sins seem less frequently punished. De Bricassart can do the Clearys out of their inheritance with impunity; he rises in the Church anyway. If he suffers pangs of conscience, those pangs do not deter him from his clerical ambitions. Dane is presented as perhaps the most pure-hearted character in the story, and for that and his heroism, he drowns, the sins of the parents visited upon him.

It remains for Justine, not presented as a likable character at all, to effect a degree of healing in the family. She suffers great guilt when Dane dies, though she was not responsible. Meggie finally rises to an unselfish act by freeing her from her need for repentance, allowing healing to come to the women in the family and allowing Justine finally to love and be loved.

Sources for Further Study

Cassill, Kay. "The Thorned Words of Colleen McCullough." *Writer's Digest*, March, 1980. Looks at the way McCullough works, particularly how she went about creating the story and the characters in *The Thorn Birds*.

DeMarr, Mary Jean. *Colleen McCullough*. Westport, Conn.: Greenwood Press, 1996. Examines nine novels by McCullough, including *The Thorn Birds*; includes a biography of McCullough.

Morris, Gwen. "An Australian Ingredient in American Soap: *The Thorn Birds* by Colleen McCullough." *Journal of Popular Culture* 24, no. 4 (Spring, 1991): 59-69. Compares the novel to similar American works, pointing out those elements that are distinctly Australian. Also considers religious themes, noting the novel's Puritanical slant.

June Harris

THR3E

Author: Ted Dekker (1962-   )
First published: Nashville, Tenn.: W Publishing Group, 2003
Genre: Novel
Subgenres: Evangelical fiction; mystery and detective fiction; thriller/suspense
Core issues: Daily living; freedom and free will; good vs. evil; heart; innocence; psychology

Dekker uses fiction to present an interpretation of biblical teaching about the struggle between good and evil within a person. By personifying the abstract, he demonstrates the capacity for evil resident in any person and the need for God's goodness and grace to rescue us from that evil.

> Principal characters
> *Kevin Parson*, the protagonist
> *Richard Slater*, a stranger who calls Kevin
> *Samantha*, Kevin's best friend
> *Jennifer Peters*, an FBI agent assigned to Kevin's case
> *Belinda Parson*, Kevin's adoptive mother and aunt
> *Dr. John Francis*, a professor and spiritual mentor to Kevin

Overview

Thr3e opens with a conversation between seminary student Kevin Parson and Dr. John Francis, his philosophy professor and mentor, on the relationship between human nature and evil, the subject of a paper Kevin is writing. They discuss the possibility that all people have an equivalent, inherent capacity to do evil as part of their human nature. Driving home after leaving the seminary, Kevin receives a cell phone call from a stranger identifying himself as Richard Slater, who claims to know what Kevin is hiding and says it is time to expose him. Slater gives him three minutes to confess his sin to the newspapers before Slater blows up the car. He also leaves Kevin with a riddle.

Unaware what sin Slater could mean, Kevin abandons the car just in time to escape the explosion. More bomb threats and riddles follow, always escalating in destructiveness, always with time limitations or clues involving the number three. Kevin contacts his closest friend and soul mate, Samantha, whom he has known since childhood, to visit and help him solve the mystery. The Federal Bureau of Investigation (FBI) assigns agent Jennifer Peters to the case at her earnest request; the case resembles the pattern of a riddling bomber who killed her brother a year before, and she seeks to avenge his death. With the help of Samantha and Jennifer, Kevin seeks to discover Slater's identity and motive while they seek to solve his riddles and thwart his explosions.

The second riddle and bomb lead Kevin to visit the home in which he was raised by his Aunt Belinda after his parents' death—the home he left at his earliest opportunity eight years earlier. The involvement of Kevin's home arouses memories and emotions associated with the highly abnormal, mentally tortuous first twenty-three years of his life. Though Kevin is too conflicted to discuss or dwell on his relationship with Belinda, Jennifer's investigation eventually reveals that Belinda created an artificial experience of the world by not allowing Kevin interaction with or exposure to anything she disliked or of which she disapproved. She created a fantasy world by physically cutting out what in her view were undesirable sections of newspapers and books, and she sought to limit Kevin's intellectual development so he would not shame her retarded son, Bob. Kevin was not allowed to interact with other children, and he made friends with Samantha at age eleven only by sneaking out his window at night. One result of this upbringing, Jennifer comes to realize, is that Kevin had no significant exposure to worldly evil until he left home. Another consequence that plagues Kevin increasingly as the emotional tension of Slater's riddle-bombing games escalates is his hate-love for Belinda. He despises her small-mindedness and the memories of growing up in her house, but the very world she created for him as a child also made him emotionally dependent on pleasing her, and he discovers that his years away have not entirely freed him.

Another inner struggle for Kevin is aroused by Slater's insistence that he confess to having committed an unspecified sin. This demand and the mystery of Slater's motive and identity force Kevin to relive a memory of the only person he can imagine who might have a cause for hatred or revenge. A cruel boy threatened him and Sam when they were eleven, and—unbeknownst to Sam—Kevin locked him in an abandoned warehouse one night, leaving him, as far as Kevin knows, to die. After more riddles and bomb threats, Kevin concludes that Slater must be this boy and confesses this sin to the media, grieving internally over his own capacity to commit evil. The confession and report of it on the evening news do nothing to stop the riddles and bombs, however.

Kevin's internal struggle with his past, his conscience, and his unresolved hate-love for Aunt Belinda become crucial to the resolution of mystery of Slater's threats and riddles. The plot culminates with Slater's kidnapping Belinda in order to lure Kevin to her rescue and force him to choose between killing her and killing Samantha. This moment of decision and the inward journey Kevin has undergone through the events leading up to it create an inner crisis in which Kevin must come to a clearer understanding of his evil and good natures and of their relationship to his actions. If he fails to comprehend and master his own evil, he will destroy others and himself.

Christian Themes

In the novel's opening dialogue, Dr. Francis tells Kevin, "Evil is beyond the reach of no man," to which Kevin counters, "But can a man remove himself beyond the reach of evil?" The ensuing dialogue establishes the novel's central argument: The spiritual nature of human beings hosts a constant battle between good and evil. In this conversation, Kevin tells him that for his paper about human nature—which we later learn is entitled "On the Three Natures of Man"—he has, following the example of Christ, chosen to use fiction as a vehicle for his main point. This comment is extraneous to the plot itself (for the reader never actually glimpses the text of Kevin's paper), but it indicates that Ted Dekker's use of narrative in the novel will serve the same purpose. A phrase from Dr. Francis that Kevin has appropriated sums up this trinity: "the good, the bad, and the beautiful," the latter referring to the human soul caught in the middle of the struggle between the two moral extremes. The relationship to this battle of human free will and consciousness is the primary philosophical question of the novel and the foundation for the tension that fuels the action.

Throughout the novel, inner faith in Christ and the practical outward life of the Christian are mentioned only briefly in a few conversations. However, Dekker's development of this theme is rooted, he makes explicit, in Romans 7:15-25. Dr. Francis alludes to the passage in a conversation with Jennifer about Kevin's case and his theory of human nature, and Dekker excerpts the passage for the reader on the last page of text after the novel's conclusion as a kind of postscript. In this passage the apostle Paul describes his own struggle between "the good I want to do" and "the sin living in me . . . the evil I do not want to do." This passage is often interpreted to describe and account for the struggle with sin experienced by the Apostle Paul and, by extension, any regenerated Christian's new nature in Christ trapped within an old, sinful nature. However, the interpretation of the passage offered by Kevin and Dr. Francis through Dekker's tale is that Paul's struggle applies to all humans, believers in Christ and nonbelievers. Dr. Francis tells Jennifer he believes the good-me-evil triad exists in everyone, including her, and Dekker portrays her distinctly as a non-Christian. In Kevin and Francis's view, which seems to be Dekker's as well, all people—regenerated in Christ or not—have free will to choose good or evil, and this freedom is continuously poised in the midst of the battle between the two.

Sources for Further Study

Byle, Ann. "Christian Author Thrills, Chills Fans: Ted Dekker Has Not Been a Published Author for Long, but His Novels Are Consistent Best-Sellers." *The Grand Rapids Press*, May 3, 2003, p. B7. Provides some background on Dekker and his popularity, with key quotations from the novelist.

Dekker, Ted. http://www.teddekker.com. The author's Web site offers a brief biography, a list of his other fiction, his Web log, a chat forum about Dekker's fiction, and features promotional trailers for some of his books and the film adaptation of *Thr3e*.

_____. *The Slumber of Christianity: Awakening a Passion for Heaven on Earth*. Nashville, Tenn.: Thomas Nelson, 2005. Dekker criticizes the Church for its reluctance to pursue pleasure in God and calls the Church—believers in Christ—to awaken to God-centered pleasures in the midst of the darkness and dryness that can dull the spiritual senses to God's goodness and hinder the Christian from walking in freedom, hope, and joy.

Zaleski, Jeff. Review of *Thr3e*. *Publishers Weekly* 250, no. 15 (April 14, 2003): 50. Recommends the novel, noting that Dekker's "spiritual message is subtle and devoid of the theologically and politically conservative agenda present in other novels."

Christopher E. Crane

THREE ESSAYS

Author: Albrecht Ritschl (1822-1889)
First published: Philadelpha: Fortress Press, 1972, translated with an introduction by Philip Hefner
Genre: Nonfiction
Subgenres: Essays; philosophy; spiritual treatise; theology
Core issues: Calvinism; Lutherans and Lutheranism; Protestants and Protestantism; social action

Ritschl, a late nineteenth century German thinker, took a Kantian sense of the constitutive and categorical nature of religion and intertwined it with a sense of confessional identity and social responsibility.

Overview

Three Essays, published and translated in its present form in the United States in 1972, is a distillation of the most seminal work of the late nineteenth century German theologian Albrecht Ritschl. It should be noted that *Three Essays*, edited by Philip Hefner (who supplies a lengthy introduction that situates Ritschl in the history of Christian thought), exists as such only as an English-language book.

The first essay, "Prolegomena to a History of Pietism," was originally a prologue to a longer history of the Pietist tendencies in Protestantism (those tendencies emphasizing fervent and performed expression of belief as the mainstay of religious devotion). Though strongly Protestant (in fact Ritschl's great motivation, in wishing to combine Lutheranism and Calvinism and to give a total sense of Christian history, was to provide a Protestant rival to the universal and ecumenical tendencies of Catholicism), Ritschl criticizes his historical precursors for scanting the proto-Protestant tendencies already present in late medieval Catholicism. In Franciscan devotion, for instance, Ritschl finds a sense of piety that both tried to define monastic piety as something distinct from the word and sought to present it to people outside the Church as a model for their own piety. The very concept of reformation, Ritschl argues, was endemic to Catholicism, as Catholicism, unlike Eastern Orthodox Christianity, did not have the Byzantine model of the civil ruler maintaining a theoretical suzerainty over the Church. This Western difference has both historical and theological origins, but it virtually ensures that there will always be reforming tendencies, as there is no external political organism to keep these in check.

On the Protestant Reformation itself, Ritschl distinguished between Lutheranism, which did not expect the Church to be any purer than the surrounding society; Calvinism, which sought to reform the surrounding society by bringing it to the level of the Church; and Pietism, which placed the individual achievement of moral perfection above all. This moral perfection, the expression of the Holy Spirit, could be achieved through religious feeling, through the effect of piety. Whereas Lutheranism and Protestantism continued the Catholic stress on discipline as a way to achieve perfection (although placing the instrument of discipline less in the Church as an institution than in divine grace and the confessing community), Pietism, in its call for perfection, rejected the world in its entirety, not wishing either to reform the world or to use worldly instruments to help achieve religious reform. Ritschl admires the spiritual dedication and sense of mission of Pietism. However (and this is a characteristically Ritschlian move), he admonishes Pietism for losing any social dimension—not because he values society as such, as a substrate undergirding and subtending all human forms of expression, but because he fears that the Pietist striving for human perfection will jettison any sense of sin. Assuming a social context for piety, as both Lutheranism and Calvinism do in different ways, allows, in a sense, for the sinfulness that has always characterized Church history to be exposed and foregrounded, so it can be acknowledged and internalized to check man's potentially excessive pride. Pietism, which seeks to sweep away particularities of human sin in the fervent rush to individual perfection, does not mean to escape from a moral consciousness. Ritschl worries, however, that it ends up evading moral categories that make Christian experience meaningful.

In "Theology and Metaphysics," Ritschl contrasts "revealed religion" with "natural religion"; the latter is religion that innately springs up in the human mind, whereas "revealed religion" is that disclosed by a specific scripture, act of divine revelation, or collective historical or cognitive belief experience. Strongly influenced by Immanuel Kant's belief that truth does not exist outside framing constitutive categories, Ritschl argues that there is no such thing as natural religion. For religious experience to mean anything, it must be public; there cannot be a private religion (in much the same way as the twentieth century philosopher Ludwig Wittgenstein later argued that there cannot be a private language). Revealed religion is a collective act that is historically disclosed in a defined community.

Recollection, or continuity, is the basis for such a community. We believe today because we have remembered we have believed in the past and affirm the continuity of our beliefs. Similarly, when we adhere for the first time to a set of religious doctrines, we vow to carry that belief forward and affirm it in the future. Once again Ritschl is trying to define the historic attributes of Catholicism—its sense of a magisterium or tradition-defining exposition of doctrine—in a way that does not presuppose an institutional structure presided over by bishops. Whereas liturgical Christianity secures the guarantee of continuity through a succession of bishops traceable in historical time, Ritschl stresses that the collective memory of the confessing community, as passed along within and by individuals, is the historical glue. Ritschl thus dismisses any ontological guarantee of religious identity, rejecting it as a secular remnant of pagan Greek philosophy and not properly germane to Christian thought. Ritschl becomes an antimetaphysical thinker who does not see it worth laboring to define a horizon of being as such. The only horizon that is worthwhile for him is one that is ecclesiastical and confessional.

The final chapter of *Three Essays* is "Instruction in the Christian Religion." A document originally written to enlighten high school students, it is one of the most accessible of Ritschl's works. Ritschl begins by sharply distinguishing Christian meanings of concepts, such as human equality, that might have superficial analogues in pagan philosophies such as Stoicism. Ritschl sees everything important in Christianity, including the forgiveness of sins, as transpiring within a community. In the father-son relation of God and Jesus, he finds the prototype of the social bond that links all Christian believers. The God of the Bible is not given his true identity unless one understands him as the God who is the Father of Christ. The baptized Christian is not initiated into individual salvation by Christ but linked in a constituted community that expresses collectively the kinship with Jesus that God has disclosed.

Ritschl ends by discussing theories of Communion. He cites the Catholic, Lutheran, and Calvinist views with respect to the concepts of the body and blood of Christ in the act of Communion, and he ends with the recognition of a tacit pluralism in practice and with the realization that, when Christ originally instituted this sacrament, it was to promote unity, not division.

Christian Themes

Albrecht Ritschl was born into a long line of ministers in the Prussian Union Church, which was officially Lutheran but incorporated Calvinist elements. Ritschl's intellectual curiosity led him to be influenced by figures ranging from the philosopher Georg Wilhelm Friedrich Hegel (1770-1831) to the New Testament critical scholar Ferdinand Christian Baur (1792-1860) to the church historian Adolf von Harnack (1851-1930). Compared to some of his influences, Ritschl was practical-minded. He believed that the world around him could be gradually improved and that what people did in their daily lives mattered in a theological sense. He was not, however, interested in isolated gestures or concrete events without a greater historical horizon.

Reacting against both present-minded social activists and textual historians who looked carefully only at selected segments of biblical text or of church history, Ritschl insisted on considering the entire history of the Church, from its earliest Israelite beginnings to the present day, as the overall ground against which ethical and moral judgments must be made.

Though Ritschl understood that the Kingdom of God, as proclaimed in the New Testament, was partially reserved for a future eschatological state—in other words, for the end-time after the Day of Judgment—he also maintained that part of the Kingdom of God was realizable in our own day, expressed by concrete ethical action within a community confessing belief in God and acknowledging the salvation of Jesus Christ as a prerequisite for all morality and judgment. Ritschl is hardly a household word outside college theology departments, but he influenced scores of better-known later thinkers and has provided Christians with one of the most satisfactory accounts of what it means to live a Christian life in community.

Sources for Further Study

Clark, Christopher. *Iron Kingdom: The Rise and Downfall of Prussia, 1600-1947.* Cambridge, Mass.: Harvard University Press, 2006. Gives background on the

Prussian Union Church so important to Ritschl's thought, as well as on the history of German unification that provided the political background for Ritschl's theology.

Dorrien, Gary J. *The Making of American Liberal Theology: Idealism, Realism, and Modernity, 1900-1950.* Louisville, Ky.: Westminster John Knox Press, 2003. Canvasses Ritschl's underestimated influence on later American Social Gospel and reformist thinkers.

Lotz, David W. "Albrecht Ritschl and the Unfinished Reformation." *Harvard Theological Review* 73, nos. 3/4 (July, 1980): 337-373. Views Ritschl as anticipating some of the major themes of twentieth century Protestant theology; reasonably accessible in its approach.

McCulloh, Gerald W. *Christ's Person and Life-Work in the Theology of Albrecht Ritschl.* Lanham, Md.: University Press of America, 1990. An occasionally dense exploration of the sometimes explicit, sometimes tacit Christological emphasis in Ritschl's work; also contains useful biographical detail.

Richmond, James. *Ritschl: A Reappraisal.* London: Collins, 1978. A seminal text in the attempt to rescue Ritschl from the opprobrium placed on him by neo-orthodox theologians such as Karl Barth; particularly concerned to rebut accusations of "liberal optimism."

Nicholas Birns

THE THREE HARDEST WORDS IN THE WORLD TO GET RIGHT

Author: Leonard Sweet (1947-   )
First published: Colorado Springs, Colo.: WaterBrook Press, 2006
Genre: Nonfiction
Subgenres: Critical analysis; philosophy
Core issues: Discipleship; Jesus Christ; love

The postmodern attempt to give meaning to life while at the same time destroying the notion of a grand narrative has resulted in a culture of people who merely exist instead of living abundantly. Jesus Christ proclaimed a grand narrative, the Kingdom of God as a Presence among humanity, in which he himself was that necessary Presence. The Presence of Jesus as the Kingdom of God gives the Christian a new identity, new integrity and new intimacy which is then made active through the Presence in the words "I love you."

Overview

In *The Three Hardest Words in the World to Get Right*, Leonard Sweet proposes that the phrase "I love you" is the hardest group of words in all of human language to live out. The phrase is fundamental to the Christian life, but its meaning and significance have become hidden by the regular and familiar way with which we use and misuse the words.

Sweet argues that the full power of the phrase "I love you" is being undermined by the culture in which we live. Postmodern society has embraced a lifestyle of selfishness, living purely for the pleasure and prosperity that life can provide right now. However, though it is called a lifestyle, selfishness is really only a meager attempt to survive life instead of fully living. Though society denies the value of a metanarrative, Sweet believes that we must again embrace a grand narrative as the necessary foundation on which the difficult phrase "I love you" is built.

The narrative to which Sweet points is the biblical story of redemption, proclaimed by Jesus Christ with the phrase "Your Kingdom come." Sweet argues that the Kingdom is not an organization that we are to create on earth, but a reality, the Presence of Jesus, which is already in place and in which we are to join. When we join this narrative, we discover that the phrase "I love you" is the central concept of the Presence on earth, and each word represents an area of life where the Presence must make us new, thus enabling us to live a biblical lifestyle, an abundant, meaningful life.

"I" indicates the new identity that the Presence of Jesus brings. Humanity makes "I" the central component of daily living. The human tendency is to demand selfishly what we want, when we want it, often without regard for others. Some have responded to this tendency by attempting to demolish the self, to remake people into uniform, identical beings; however, the Presence creates a much different change. Instead of trying to make our own identities, we surrender our identities to Jesus, and he enables us to be our real selves. By giving up ourselves, we find ourselves. Then, instead of being created by or conformed to culture, we are free to interact with and find fellowship in community, especially a community made up of others who have also found this true identity in the Presence. We are free to give of ourselves and live out the power of the phrase "I love you" when we have been given a new identity.

In order to live out the word "love," the Presence gives us a new integrity. To explain this concept, Sweet uses the Apostle Paul's description of the love of Christ as architecture; it is three-dimensional. Length assures us that God will do whatever is necessary to reach the one he loves. God is love, and he loves us limitlessly, thus enabling us to respond to his love. Breadth reveals a love that reaches everywhere and everyone. It is intimate, and though such intimacy will break our hearts, in giving up control and embracing the pain of love, we discover that such surrender guarantees that no one is left outside his love. Depth of love penetrates to the core of our being to make us holy. Rather than emotional love, God's love is willful, a choice to love us until, like a fire, his Presence has purified us completely. These three aspects combine to give us an integrity that allows us to live in response to God's love for us, choosing to love as he does, because he has chosen to love us.

"You" is the creation, by the Presence, of a new intimacy. The combination of a new identity and a new integrity means we can reach out in a new way to the world around us. We were created for community, but it is not until we are renewed by the Presence that we can truly exist in community, purposely thinking less of ourselves and ministering more to others. This community, too, is threefold. We must have intimacy, a living relationship, with God himself. Such intimacy also requires caring for and reaching out to our neighbors and our world. Finally, this intimacy means caring for the created world with as much concern as we show for people in our community.

The final truth, Sweet contends, is that the grand narrative is true for every person in every culture in the world. However, it will not always appear in precisely the same manner everywhere. The Presence of Jesus makes us more individual, not more alike. Every human is a multifaceted personality. Differences of perspective and interests give us greater ability to understand truth and be more fully human. God speaks the same truth in every culture, but always in a language that culture can understand. The Presence is a cross-cultural reality, and we must embrace that reality, instead of trying to control it, so that the biblical lifestyle, depicted in the metaphor of the body of Christ, may be fully perfected, hastening the revelation of Jesus Christ.

Christian Themes

In the Gospel of John, Jesus Christ promised the world salvation and life to the fullest. In *The Three Hardest Words in the World to Get Right*, Sweet contends that such abundant life is missing from the culture as well as from the Church. Instead, most people are caught up in a mind-set that glorifies the present over the eternal. Spiritually adrift, we substitute selfish consumption and mindless entertainment for true meaning and security. Unfortunately, the Christian Church has not stepped forward to reverse this trend, retreating instead into the safety of traditional Christianity, where everyone looks and acts the same in church but lives identically to the world around them everywhere else.

Sweet is convinced, however, that such abundant life is actually attainable. In our postmodern society, what we are missing is the Who, the source of this life, and the How, the manner in which it is revealed. Sweet argues that the Who is Jesus Christ, the central character in the grand narrative of Christianity and the one who creates this promised life in us. The How is "I love you"—a three-word description of the biblical lifestyle that is based on a true identity, motivated by a true love, and results in a true community. Jesus Christ lived this life for us; secure in his identity, he loved others selflessly, by choice, and connected with people, without being controlled by them, and with culture, without being absorbed into it.

Not only did Jesus live this lifestyle for us; he intends to create it in our daily lives. As we develop a relationship with Jesus, his Presence radically changes us so that we can live as he did. He changes our "I" by giving us a new identity that is not based on who we are but is secure because of Who he is. He gives us a new integrity that enables us to "love" as he did, choosing to put others first and selflessly going as far as is necessary to reach everyone in the world who still needs this life. Finally, Jesus recalibrates our understanding of "you" so we can have true community, intimately relating to God, our fellow human beings, and our planet in a context of love and holiness. When all three are put together, Christians are enabled to live out the same abundant life that Jesus portrayed, a life best described by the phrase "I love you."

Sources for Further Study

Allender, Dan B., and Tremper Longman. *Bold Love*. Colorado Springs, Colo.: NavPress, 1992. Describes the power of forgiving love and the call to, like God, risk ourselves in order to love the people around us.

Carson, D. A. *The Difficult Doctrine of the Love of God*. Wheaton, Ill.: Crossway Books, 2000. Attempts to delineate the common ideas and misconceptions about God's love and reexamine them in light of the biblical texts.

Jacobsen, Douglas, and Rodney J. Sawatsky. *Gracious Christianity: Living the Love We Profess*. Grand Rapids, Mich.: Baker Academic, 2006. God's love is a gracious love, and Christians must be characterized by these virtues in order to reach out to the unbelieving world.

MacArthur, John. *The Love of God*. Dallas, Tex.: Word, 1996. Discusses the biblical doctrine of the love of God and attempts to answer some specific questions about God's love.

Shannah Hogue

"THREE VERSIONS OF JUDAS"

Author: Jorge Luis Borges (1899-1986)
First published: "Tres versiones de Judas," 1944 (English translation, 1962)
Edition used: "Three Versions of Judas," in *Labyrinths: Selected Stories and Other Writings*, edited James E. Irby and Donald A. Yates. New York: New Directions, 1962
Genre: Short fiction
Subgenre: Literary fiction
Core issues: The Deity; Gnosticism; Jesus Christ; Latin Americans; martyrdom; sacrifice

In "Three Versions of Judas," Borges documents the fictional career of a deeply troubled theologian, Nils Runeberg, who reasons himself into heresy and death. In extrapolating from biblical truths, Runeberg offers increasingly bizarre yet logical versions of the nature of Judas and of Christ. Borges's work both mimics and mocks theological reasoning, demonstrating that the human or divine nature of Christ might be no more than the language used to describe that nature.

Principal characters
The narrator, an unnamed speaker who recounts the story of Runeberg
Nils Runeberg, a Swedish theologian

Overview

In "Three Versions of Judas," Argentine writer Jorge Luis Borges presents a very short story that does not seem much like a story at all. Borges's stories are often criticized for being overly philosophical and devoid of character, plot, and setting. Those who offer such critiques, however, often miss the parodic and playful nature of Borges's writing.

Certainly, "Three Versions of Judas," complete with lengthy footnotes and filled with the language of theological debate, seems more an academic article than fictional short story. It is in his creation of a fully fictional article, however, that Borges calls attention to the power of language to create alternate realities that exist nowhere but within language. Borges seems to suggest that readers need to take care in what they believe or disbelieve; if he is able to create an academic article peppered with quotations of both those who exist and those who do not, if he is able to patch together biblical text to make it say something very different from standard interpretation, what else is possible in the labyrinth of language? Are all belief systems nothing more than arguments built on faulty initial assumptions? Is there any ultimate reality behind the language that describes it—or is language all that there is?

The story opens with an unnamed narrator connecting an early twentieth century

Swedish theologian, Nils Runeberg, to the Gnostic heresies of the second century, suggesting that Runeberg lived too late. Had he lived earlier, he would have been known as one of the great heretics of his day. Nevertheless, the narrator contends that Runeberg was a man of deep religious faith whose writing ultimately ruined his life.

"Three Versions of Judas" purports to be the summary of Runeberg's reasoning concerning the natures of Jesus and Judas. Runeberg begins with an epigraph from Thomas De Quincey (a real nineteenth century English writer) that says that everything written about Judas previously was false. Runeberg picks up this theme; whereas De Quincey argues that Judas's role in the betrayal of Christ was necessary in order for Christ to reveal his divinity and that Judas should therefore be celebrated, Runeberg argues that Judas's role was completely unnecessary logically, since any Roman guard would have had no trouble identifying Jesus, with or without Judas's intervention. Consequently, Runeberg reasons, since Judas *did* betray Christ, it could not be an error or an accident. Thus, it must have been a preordained act. Just as the Word lowered itself to human condition, Judas lowered himself to become a criminal worthy of the deepest pit of hell.

The narrator further reports that Runeberg's book *Kristus och Judas* (Christ and Judas) met with refutations from theologians all over the world. (As Borges often does, he mixes the names of fictional theologians and works with the real, making it difficult for readers to distinguish between the two.) As a result, Runeberg revised his doctrine, expanding his notion of the nature of Judas. Runeberg argues here that because Judas was chosen by Christ to be one of his disciples, his actions must be viewed as having the best motives possible. Consequently, Judas chose the worst possible crime out of deep humility. He willingly chose hell, just as Christ willingly chose his role in the redemption of humanity.

Runeberg, however, pushes his reasoning one step further. Because God's sacrifice must have been perfect in order to redeem humankind and because God himself is perfect, God must have become fully a man, capable of pain, suffering, sin, and deceit. God's choice of the man he would become, therefore, is inextricably bound up in the nature of the sacrifice. Christ's sacrifice, Runeberg reasoned, was not perfect, because it was too brief. The perfect sacrifice would be an eternal sacrifice, an eternity spend in hellfire. Thus, the perfect sacrifice would require God to become the vilest man he could be: Judas.

According to the narrator, when Runeberg's book was published, his work was dismissed by theologians and the public. For Runeberg, this was simply evidence that he had uncovered the truth about God, Christ, and Judas. God, he reasoned, did not want the secret to be known. Consequently, Runeberg realized that he had committed a sin even greater than that of Judas; he had revealed the secret name of God.

The story concludes with the description of Runeberg screaming his wish to go to hell, and with the report of his death from an aneurism in 1912. The implication is that Runeberg's knowledge drove him insane before killing him. The narrator suggests that few, other than some scholars of heresies, would remember him. He also suggests, however, that Runeberg has significantly complicated the concept of the Son.

Christian Themes

In "Three Versions of Judas," Borges, an Argentine of Jewish descent and Christian upbringing but not a religious man himself, brilliantly parodies the overwrought reasoning of theological debate. In particular, he uses one of the oldest heresies, the Gnostic doctrines, to create an argument that elevates Judas to the role of God. While this story can be read as a humorous, tongue-in-cheek send-up of an academic battle having no connection to reality, it also can be read as a serious discussion of the nature of Christ, a theological debate that has raged for more than two thousand years.

These debates tore the early church apart, leading to schisms and the distinction between orthodoxy and heresy. Christology, the study of the nature of Christ, was born in these debates. The essential question is this: Was Christ completely divine, was he completely human, or was he some combination, and in what proportions? The answer to this question is essential for people of faith; if Christ's sacrifice is necessary to redeem all humankind, then it must truly be a sacrifice. If Christ is wholly divine, then is there a sacrifice at all? If Christ is wholly human, then does he have the power to redeem all humankind?

Borges pushes the debate away from Christ in this story, however, and has his protagonist focus on the nature of Judas. The three versions of Judas that Runeberg offers are these: Judas as betrayer for the glory of God, Judas as betrayer for his own extreme abnegation, and Judas as the secret incarnation of God. Because, according to Jewish mystical thought, even uttering the name of God is a sin, Runeberg, by naming Judas as God, commits one of the most serious of all sins himself.

Borges, the master manipulator, stands just outside the story, demonstrating the relative nature of all judgments. For Borges, orthodoxy and heresy alike are created by language rather than by ultimate reality; through language, Borges offers a mirror of reality in which all values are reversed.

Sources for Further Study

Bell-Villada, Gene H. *Borges and His Fiction: A Guide to His Mind and Art*. Rev. ed. Austin: University of Texas Press, 1999. An updated and expanded edition of Bell-Villada's 1981 study. Excellent chronology, bibliography, literary analysis, and biographical detail.

Bossart, W. H. *Borges and Philsophy: Self, Time, and Metaphysics*. New York: Peter Lang, 2003. A thorough discussion of the philosophical constructs that inform Borges's work, including Gnosticism, heresy, nominalism, and relativism.

Lindstrom, Naomi. *Jorge Luis Borges: A Study of the Short Fiction*. Boston: Twayne, 1990. An accessible introduction to Borges, with a chronology and bibliography.

Williamson, Edwin. *Borges: A Life*. New York: Viking, 2004. A readable and compelling biography; Williamson chooses a psychoanalytical approach to reading Borges's life. Less about the works and more about the man, the book offers historical context for Borges's prose and poetry.

Diane Andrews Henningfeld

TIGER IN THE SHADOWS

Author: Debbie Wilson (1956-   )
First published: Grand Rapids, Mich.: Kregel, 2004
Genre: Novel
Subgenres: Evangelical fiction; thriller/suspense
Core issues: Communism; evangelization; hope; persecution; social action; trust in God

In post-Tiananmen China, ruthless government suppression of Christianity as a cult that fosters superstition and foments cultural instability has created a heroic underground movement that resembles the first-generation Christian movement in its courage and its willingness to endure suffering. When a Chinese American journalist accepts a teaching position at Beijing University as part of a plan to negotiate the release of her preacher-grandfather after forty years of imprisonment, she learns not only about herself and her faith but about Christianity and international politics as she becomes enmeshed in an intrigue involving satellite technology.

> *Principal characters*
> *Stefanie Peng*, the protagonist
> *Troy Hardigan*, a covert CIA operative who loves Stefanie
> *Peng Chongde*, Stefanie's grandfather
> *Lao*, also known as *the Brother*, a preacher in the underground Chinese Christian movement
> *Kong "the Tiger" Qili*, a ruthless agent in China's Public Security Bureau
> *Ren Shaoqi*, a student leader during the 1989 Tiananmen Square protest

Overview

When Stefanie Peng's grandmother receives a dire breast cancer prognosis, Stefanie, a twenty-four-year-old journalist living in Illinois, promises to reunite her grandmother, who fled mainland China during the bloody Cultural Revolution of the 1960's, with her husband, Stefanie's grandfather Peng Chongde, a charismatic Christian preacher who subsequently endured a lifetime sentence in remote government labor camps. With surprising ease, Stefanie secures a post teaching English at Beijing University, never suspecting that she is being lured to China by the shadowy Public Security Bureau, whose agents are certain that threatening Stefanie with imprisonment will convince the aged Peng to cooperate in the government's efforts to track down an elusive Christian preacher known only as Lao, the Brother.

Troy Hardigan, a longtime Peng family friend whose life has been redefined by his recent embrace of Christianity after a lifetime of indifferent worship, works for an international communications corporation involved in delicate negotiations across Asia concerning satellites with intelligence-gathering capabilities. As Stefanie, once in Beijing, begins to negotiate her grandfather's release, Troy acts as her protector even as he falls in love with her. With her instincts as a journalist, Stefanie becomes involved with free union agitators but, more important, with the Christians in the underground movement. Rejecting the government-sanctioned Christianity—which cannot baptize, cannot reference Revelation, and cannot preach Christ's miracles—this underground movement thrives only by painstakingly translating smuggled Bibles and then copying them by hand. These valiant converts conduct services in caves, warehouses, and barns, always under the threat of police raids, usually prompted by informants, and the inevitable exile to "reeducation" camps.

Kong Qili, introduced initially to Stefanie as a university administrator, is actually a career government agent involved not only in the campaign to eradicate the underground Christian menace but also in a sinister plot to coopt Western communication satellite software to gather critical strategic weapons information. The suave Kong is known as the Tiger for relentlessly tracking enemies of a Chinese government still dealing with the repercussions of the student uprisings that climaxed in the bloody riots at Tiananmen Square in 1989. A student himself at the time, Kong turned in several student leaders, one of whom, named Ren Shaoqi, has long vowed murderous revenge. A bureaucratic mistake frees Shaoqi along with Peng while they are being transported from the labor camps (although the ancient Peng sees the mistake as God's Providence). In flight, they come under the protection of the underground movement and eventually Lao himself. During their harrowing journey, eluding Chinese soldiers (Peng likens their escape to Elisha's miraculous escape after the blinding of the Syrian army), Peng counsels the angry Shaoqi about the dangers of vengeance and the power of Christian forgiveness.

When she inadvertently comes across classified computer files, Stefanie realizes Kong's true identity. Despite Kong's dismissal of her as a soft Western girl, Stefanie proves resourceful and courageous: She destroys computer files, eludes capture in a series of harrowing chases, hides with cunning cleverness. Ultimately, however, she is imprisoned. Troy, who is in fact an accomplished covert agent for the Central Intelligence Agency (CIA), frees her in a dramatic break.

Troy determines that to optimize their chances for getting out of China with both Stefanie and her grandfather, they must head to the port of Shanghai. Government agents, tipped off by an informant, press their chase. Here the quiet courage of Lao emerges—knowing of the government's interest in his arrest, he creates a diversion by agreeing to be bait in an arranged meeting with the same informant, aware that agents will swarm in for his capture and be too preoccupied to bother with Troy, Stefanie, and her grandfather as they make their way to a waiting boat in the Huangpu River. Indeed, Lao is shot and drops into the river, and the agents assume the charismatic preacher at last is dead. The Tiger, however, does not go with his agents but confronts Troy, Stefanie, and Peng as they attempt their escape. After a vicious martial arts fight with Troy, Kong shoots and wounds the American, but Stefanie heroically upends a load of heavy crates on Kong, and the three complete their escape to the river—the desperate Kong pursuing them but drowning, as he has never mastered his fear of water.

A radiant epilogue relates that Troy, recovering stateside from his wounds, professes his love for Stefanie, who has kept her promise to reunite her grandparents (the grandmother's cancer is in remission). The far more celebratory close is offered in a muted moment back in China between Shaoqi and Lao (who has survived the shooting and drifted downriver where he secured help). Together, they read the promises made by Christ in the Beatitudes, and Shaoqi, his festering anger against Kong at last stilled, asks the Christian preacher to explain such logic to him. That is the promise of Christianity in the communist world: Persecution itself becomes a vehicle for a difficult kind of hope, specifically the will to convert an entire people, one soul at a time.

Christian Themes

A tireless advocate for international human rights (*Tiger in the Shadows* was Wilson's first foray into fiction and was not published until she was in her late forties), Wilson champions the Pauline vision of a single universal Christian Church manifested by a diversity of cultures that—once they have embraced the Christian message—will be like individual cells within a single, vast, cooperative body. Ignoring this missionary imperative, so central to the Christian vision, has left entire reaches of the globe unexposed to Christianity's saving message. This imperative, which compels the narrative, is designed to inspire lax Western Christians, whose tepid commitment to their religion is juxtaposed to that of the underground Chinese movement, with its hours-long services driven by emotional outpourings, carried out in primitive conditions under the threat of arrest, torture, and execution. Indeed, the elaborate secondary plot involving the theft of satellite technology (for which Wilson acknowledges a debt to the espionage thrillers of Alistair MacLean and Tom Clancy) metaphorically suggests the Chinese subversion of this universal Christian message, its disruption of what it dismisses as a "cult" that distracts from the ongoing political and economic revolution envisioned by China's leader of the Cultural Revolution, Mao Zedong. Such secularism, embodied in the cult of Mao (Stefanie views Mao's glass-encased corpse off Beijing Square), has given contemporary Chinese culture flawed, disposable gods divorced from the grand, transcendent arc of the Christian vision.

Uninterested in the elaborate subtlety of literary analysis, Wilson, a graduate of Bob Jones University and a fundamentalist Baptist, uses broad, accessible symbols that draw on familiar archetypal Christian emblems with parable-like directness: illness and health, darkness and light, burial and resurrection, food and hunger, fire and water. Similarly, the extended love story is defined within a Christian context: Stefanie has broken off a relationship with a man who could not be faithful to her, and her growing attraction for Troy, not compelled by sexual activity, builds upon a Christian foundation of respect, trust, and concern. For Wilson, narratives instruct, heroic characters inspire Christian action, and events foster Christian hope. It is an ongoing mission for Christian literature. As such, the narrative certainly indicts the

Chinese government. The novel, which reflects Wilson's meticulous research and the novel's nearly decade-long evolution, won the 2005 Christy Award in the suspense category. Above all, it teaches the dynamic of Christian hope, the logic of forgiveness, the psychology of conversion, and, ultimately, the power of evangelical faith.

Sources for Further Study

Aikman, David. *Jesus in Beijing: How Christianity Is Tranforming China and Changing the Global Balance of Power.* Washington, D.C.: Regnery, 2003. Compelling account of Christianity's impact on post-Tiananmen China that fleshes out the complex tensions central to Wilson's novel.

Alcorn, Randy C. *Safely Home.* Wheaton, Ill.: Tyndale House, 2001. Cited by Wilson, a novel about an American executive who, on a mission to exploit cheap Chinese labor, reclaims his Christianity after witnessing horrific conditions.

Bays, Daniel H., ed. *Christianity in China: From the Eighteenth Century to the Present.* Stanford, Calif.: Stanford University Press, 1996. Helpful, accessible collection that examines the historic implications of the Christian mission to China.

Flinchbaugh, C. Hope. *Daughter of China.* Minneapolis, Minn.: Bethany House, 2002. Cited by Wilson, an inspirational novel of a Chinese orphan whose conversion to Christianity and subsequent commitment to evangelization draws her into conflict with the oppressive Chinese government.

Publishers Weekly. Review of *Tiger in the Shadows.* 251, no. 11 (March 15, 2004): 53. Concludes that, despite Wilson's lack of skill in plotting, she "succeeds in showing the abuses and restrictions imposed on Christians in China" and the novel will appeal to Christian readers.

Wilson, Debbie. http://www.onlyinternet.net/boundtogether. Wilson's Web site features articles on her human rights initiatives as well as reviews, inspirational messages, and updates on her writing projects.

Joseph Dewey

TIME LOTTERY

Author: Nancy Moser (1954-   )
First published: Uhrichsville, Ohio: Promise Press, 2002
Genre: Novel
Subgenres: Adventure; science fiction; time travel
Core issues: African Americans; awakening; contemplation; memory; psychology; self-knowledge; time; truth

Three winners of the Time Travel Corporation lottery, unhappy with aspects of their lives, explore their pasts while being induced into weeklong comas, reliving and adjusting memories of significant periods in their lifetimes to determine whether their decisions in the past were appropriate or if they should have made different choices. Their memories reveal connections the three characters shared in the past. The winners question their faith and religious attitudes as they contemplate whether to remain in the past and physically die or return to the present and resume their lives and the future with new awareness and spirituality.

Principal characters
Alexander "Mac" MacMillan, a marketing consultant
Phoebe Winston Thurgood, a housewife
Dr. Cheryl Nickolby, a surgeon
Roosevelt Hazen, a preacher
Leon Burke, a con artist
Colin Thurgood, Phoebe's husband
John Wriggens, an executive with Time Travel Corporation

Overview
Marketing expert Alexander MacMillan, known as Mac, mourns his murdered wife, wishing he could have intervened to save her life and prevent his toddler son from being injured when an intruder attacked them nine months ago while Mac was away from home. Mac's cousin, Bob Craven, urges him to consider working for Craven's new employer, Time Travel Corporation (TTC). TTC executive John Wriggens entices Mac with the incentive that he will eventually be allowed to experience time travel. Mac realizes if he could travel to the day his family was assaulted, perhaps he can achieve spiritual peace. He agrees to publicize TTC's debut "Time Lottery."

Before announcing the three winners' names, Mac explains how they will be medically supported while temporarily comatose for immersion into their memories. Scientists manipulate the brain loop, which stores and processes memories, with electricity to initiate dual consciousness, the phase during which time travelers are aware of both their past and their present and choose whether to stay unconscious and die or awaken to resume their lives. Mac stresses that the time travelers' decisions made while experiencing what TTC refers to as Alternity will not affect their present situations but notes that their awareness of their time travel experience enables them to reevaluate and possibly alter their perceptions, which will shape their futures.

One winner, Phoebe Winston Thurgood, a San Francisco housewife in her fifties, is eager to return to memories of her early twenties in 1969, when she met affluent executive Colin Thurgood and was employed as his secretary. Although she enjoys a luxurious lifestyle, Phoebe wonders if she could have made better career and personal choices instead of settling for marriage with the emotionally cold, unethical Colin, who mistreats her and constantly denounces her as unworthy. Greedy Colin pressures Phoebe to give him her winning ticket, insisting that he deserves to time travel more than she does.

Another of the winners, Dr. Cheryl Nickolby, a forty-seven-year-old Colorado surgeon, is professionally successful but emotionally unfulfilled. Promiscuously indulging in brief flings with colleagues, she yearns for a long-term commitment. Nickolby hopes to develop a relationship with a former high school classmate, Jake Carlisle, whom she admired, by returning to Lincoln, Nebraska, where she lived as a teenager in 1973.

The third winner, Roosevelt Hazen, is a sixty-nine-year-old former African American preacher living in a Memphis, Tennessee, homeless shelter. He is unaware of the Time Lottery announcement declaring him a winner. In the shelter, another homeless African American man, sixty-four-year-old Leon Burke, who has survived by deceiving people (including Hazen, who does not remember him) and stealing their money, takes advantage of Hazen's innocence, killing him and assuming his identity to claim the Time Lottery prize. Leon, dying of cancer, wants to return to 1962, the year he conned Hazen, in an attempt to reform his unlawful ways.

Cheryl begins her memories as a high school senior riding in a car with her closest friends, Pam and Julie. They stop to assist an injured African American man, coincidentally Leon, on the side of the road. Jake Carlisle and his friends stop to talk to the girls. Jake praises Cheryl's skills in first aid and suggests she become a physician, but Cheryl says her mother—who has been married several times, moving Cheryl to a new town with every new husband—has discouraged her, considering that field too difficult for women. In her attempt to win Jake's approval, Cheryl agrees to steal a history test so he can pass and remain on the school's football team. Upset when Jake rapes her, Cheryl seeks healing through prayer. She accepts a cross necklace from pious Julie to reinforce her newfound faith.

Phoebe starts with memories of her first day working for Colin. Hoping to qualify for a better-paying internship, Phoebe works to pay for her grandmother's nursing-home expenses. She tries to follow her grandmother's advice: to refuse to cooperate with the world and avoid being used by others while sacrificing her interests and integrity. Living frugally, Phoebe, in reliving her memories, is not tempted by Colin's patronizing romantic overtures. She refuses to fix his careless mistakes and lie for him, instead exposing his deceptive business practices. Phoebe's honesty earns her supervisor's approval and hope for advancement. She meets young Cheryl after her mother's third wedding. As Phoebe maneuvers through her memories, she chooses to reject materialism and finds comfort in reading the Bible and regaining her faith.

Leon initiates his memories by feeling remorse for his crimes against Roosevelt and vowing to rectify his mistakes. He arrives in Hendersonville, Tennessee, initially intending to win Roosevelt's confidence by making small repairs at Roosevelt's Baptist church, where young Phoebe and her father visit one day. While working as a handyman, Leon damages the church roof so that it leaks. Roosevelt gives him his savings to purchase supplies to repair it. Leon's plan to rob Roosevelt by leaving town permanently, pretending to drive to a Nashville hardware store, is disrupted when a boy asks to accompany him. Leon later rebukes the boy for stealing from the offering plate. When Leon sees a cross shine, he considers it a sign that God approves of Leon's rejection of crime.

The three lottery winners consider their pasts and how their staying or returning might impact their families and friends. They reflect on how returning to the past deepened their faith and moral courage and how memories might change their futures. Two choose life; one stays.

Christian Themes

Winner of the Christy Award for Best Christian Fiction in the Futuristic category, *Time Lottery* was Nancy Moser's first novel the the Time Lottery series. In the novel and the series as a whole, the relationship of religion and science concerns critics of Time Lottery, who believe that God's plans for people should not be artificially manipulated. Mac acknowledges the validity of that argument, while he emphasizes that scientific achievements represent the power of God. Explaining that God has created everything, including time travel, Mac argues that God wants people to experience and benefit from science, stressing that God ultimately controls those processes. Mac suggests that God enables time travel to help people evaluate their purpose and secure redemption to grow and seek new opportunities. Each winner undergoes a personal genesis during the seven days of his or her memory experience, resulting in the creation of a spiritually new person.

Faith guides the lottery winners as they trust God to help them realize their destiny. Somewhat like an apostle, Mac serves as an adviser, offering words of comfort and support. He reminds people that although TTC has no Christian affiliations or spiritual motivations, he considers the selection to undergo such intense, focused self-examination a divine gift from God. Mac suggests that the lottery will reveal the role God intends for the winners and help them comprehend that discovery and their uniqueness. Such knowledge of their purpose offers salvation and forgiveness for past mistakes and hope and rebirth for the future.

Mac blesses each winner, while TTC medical staffers prepare them to lose consciousness and begin their adventure. Prayer gives characters strength as they overcome their despair and doubts confronting flaws in their lives. By seeking spiritual guidance, whether talking to God or reading the Bible, the characters contemplate their lives and replace fear with faith and hope as they achieve self-knowledge and accept themselves. They seek friendships that reinforce their newfound faith. Forgiving their immorality or their weaknesses, the characters permit themselves to choose more spiritual lives, whether awakening to the present or remaining in a changed past, which frees them.

Sources for Further Study
Kaplan, H. Roy. *Lottery Winners: How They Won and How Winning Changed Their Lives*. New York: Harper & Row, 1978. Sociological study of lotteries, including a chapter discussing religious aspects. Examines how lotteries change lives, choices confronting winners, and winners' interactions with family and friends.
Moser, Nancy. http://www.nancymoser.com. Moser's Web site lists her books and discusses her themes.
_____. *Second Time Around*. Uhrichsville, Ohio: Promise Press, 2004. Moser's second novel in the Time Lottery series portrays the spiritual adventures of three more lottery winners.
Olson, Laura R., Karen V. Guth, and James L. Guth. "The Lotto and the Lord: Religious Influences on the Adoption of a Lottery in South Carolina." *Sociology of Religion* 64, no. 1 (2003): 87-110. Although this study analyzes attitudes toward monetary lotteries, its findings regarding spiritual concerns can be applied to other games of chance, such as the Time Lottery.
Reading, Anthony. *Hope and Despair: How Perceptions of the Future Shape Human Behavior*. Baltimore: Johns Hopkins University Press, 2004. A chapter explores the relationship of science, religion, and time. Examines how memory influences people's expectations, emotional responses, and decisions.

Elizabeth D. Schafer

TO KILL A MOCKINGBIRD

Author: Harper Lee (1926-)
First published: 1960
Edition used: To Kill a Mockingbird. New York: Warner Books, 1982
Genre: Novel
Subgenre: Literary fiction
Core issues: African Americans; coming of age or teen life; compassion; guilt; justice; morality; truth

This award-winning coming-of-age novel explores several basic Christian principles, particularly love, compassion, forgiveness, and sacrifice. Throughout the novel, Atticus Finch attempts to teach his children, Scout and Jem, Christian values by exercising them himself. Unlike Atticus, most members of their community find it difficult to demonstrate Christianity when race is a factor. Lee suggests that Christians, regardless of race or class, serve the same God and should adhere to the same principles. Yet, she acknowledges that within the hearts of humans, Christian ideals are often at odds with hate, prejudice, and hypocrisy.

Principal characters
Jean Louise "Scout" Finch, the precocious narrator
Atticus Finch, Scout's father, a lawyer and role model for his children
Jeremy Atticus "Jem" Finch, Scout's knowledgeable older brother
Charles Baker "Dill" Harris, Scout and Jem's friend from Meridian, Mississippi, who challenges them to encourage Boo Radley to come out of his home
Arthur "Boo" Radley, a reclusive neighbor
Tom Robinson, a black man accused of raping Mayella Ewell
Mayella Violet Ewell, a woman who accuses Tom Robinson of raping her
Robert E. Lee "Bob" Ewell, a poor, uneducated, alcoholic who accuses Tom Robinson of raping his daughter, Mayella

Overview

To Kill a Mockingbird won the Pulitzer Prize in fiction and the Brotherhood Award of the National Conference of Christians and Jews in 1961. It was adapted into a movie starring Gregory Peck in 1962. The movie earned an Academy Award for the script, and Peck won an award for best actor. Critics have pointed out the autobiographical elements of the novel, suggesting that Harper Lee, while growing up in Monroeville, Alabama, was affected by racial tensions resulting from the lack of employment opportunities for blacks and poor whites during the Depression. Her father was a lawyer and Lee attended law school before deciding to write full-time. Biographers maintain that when Lee was Scout's age, she became aware of the case known as the Scottsboro trials, in which nine young black men were tried on rape charges involving two white women, Victoria Price and Ruby Bates.

In the book, an adult Scout reflects on growing up during the Depression in fictitious Maycomb, Alabama, with her older brother, Jem, and her father, Atticus. Calpurnia, their black maid, has taken care of Scout's family since her mother died when Scout was two years old. During the three-year span of the novel, Scout and Jem, with Atticus's guidance, learn about the world around them.

The first section of the novel, which is divided into two parts, begins with the narrator reflecting on the year that her brother's arm was broken, and she attempts to trace the events that led to the accident. She describes her lineage, the major families that make up Maycomb, and the caste system that is deeply embedded into the psyche of all who live there. When Scout is six, she and Jem meet Dill, a boy who has come from Meridian, Mississippi, to spend the summer with his aunt. Together, the children devise plans they hope will get their reclusive neighbor, Arthur "Boo" Radley, to come out of his home. They have heard rumors about his life, and they begin to make up stories of their own. When Atticus learns that the children are bothering the Radley family, he encourages them to stop, but their fascination with Boo never diminishes. Boo also becomes interested in them. He leaves them small gifts in the knothole of a tree, mends Jem's pants when they are caught in a fence, and surreptitiously covers Scout with a blanket while she stands watching fire consume a neighbor's home. As the novel progresses, the children's image of Boo slowly evolves from that of an oddity to that of a human being capable of love.

At Christmas, Scout and Jem are given air rifles and a dictum: "Shoot all the bluejays you want, if you can hit 'em, but remember it's a sin to kill a mockingbird." Atticus's command foreshadows the sins of the immoral townspeople presented in the second section of the novel. Some critics have found that the statement is used to teach the children to do good rather than evil. Atticus also tells Scout and Jem that it is evil to take advantage of people who are disenfranchised.

The second part of the novel reveals the children's growing maturity as they watch the events unfold when Atticus agrees to defend Tom Robinson, a black man who is accused of raping Mayella Ewell, a poor, white woman. Atticus tells Scout, "I couldn't go to church and worship God if I didn't try to help that man," suggesting that it is his Christian duty to help those in need regardless of their race or class. When Scout and Jem visit Calpurnia's church, they learn that segregation extends to religious practices though Calpurnia maintains that whites and blacks serve the same God. This part of the novel also shows Scout's growing understanding of the contradictory behavior of the adult women she trusts and is told she must learn to emulate. Aunt Alexandra moves into the Finch home in Maycomb to help Scout develop into a young lady. The women at Aunt Alexandra's Maycomb Ladies' Missionary Society gathering speak of the love and compassion they feel for Africans though they seem to despise the descendants of Africans who live in Maycomb and work for them.

Atticus clearly proves Tom Robinson's innocence by arguing that a left-handed person abused Mayella and by showing that an accident during childhood left Tom's left hand useless. Despite this, Tom, a symbolic mockingbird, is convicted and sentenced to prison. The children are surprised and hurt to learn that the people in their community allow racism to prevent justice from prevailing. Mayella's father, Bob, enraged by Atticus's ability to reveal that he and his daughter falsely accused Tom, tries to stab Scout and Jem. Though Bob breaks Jem's arm, Boo Radley defends the children, killing Bob in the process. In an effort to protect this particular mockingbird from public scrutiny, the sheriff decides he will not arrest Boo. Echoing the beginning, the end of the novel focuses on Atticus and Scout as they sit by Jem's bed waiting for his broken arm to heal.

Christian Themes

To Kill a Mockingbird examines southern religious practices and beliefs, revealing the tension that exists within a society that discriminates against select neighbors rather than loving them. Atticus uses Christian values to raise Scout and Jem. Serving as their primary example, he teaches the children to be ethical, moral, and just. He demonstrates compassion, morality, and forgiveness. Atticus encourages Scout and Jem to forgive relatives, classmates, and neighbors who make offensive remarks about him. Yet, Scout struggles to refrain from pummeling anyone who decides to hurl insults at her. When Bob Ewell spits in Atticus's face, it affords Atticus the opportunity to show Jem and Scout what he has tried to teach them all along: A Christian must turn the other cheek.

As a lawyer and state representative, Atticus is respected in the community and known for his honesty and moral standing. Judge Taylor purposely chooses Atticus to defend Tom Robinson, a black man accused of raping Mayella Ewell, a white woman, because he knows Atticus will work hard to prove Tom's innocence. This case places Atticus is the position of being a Christ-like figure, bearing the sins of the community. "Let this cup pass from you, eh?" Atticus's brother says. Miss Maude argues, "We're so rarely called on to be Christians, but when we are, we've got men like Atticus to go for us." Critics suggest that Atticus's courage to defend Tom stems from his strong spiritual foundation and his need to make the truth of Tom's innocence evident to the community.

Lee also uses the action around the case to illustrate the tension between Christianity, bigotry, and hypocrisy. Hypocrisy and hatred are learned behaviors, suggests Lee, just as love and compassion are. Tom feels compassion for Mayella, a poor, uneducated young woman physically abused by her father. Similarly, Atticus shows love and friendship to Tom when he helps protect him from a mob intent on hanging him for a crime he did not commit. Compassion sets both men apart from other members of the community and is the catalyst for most of the conflict that surrounds them.

Sources for Further Study

Champion, Laurie. "Lee's *To Kill a Mockingbird.*" *The Explicator* 61, no. 4 (2003): 234-236. Examines the connotations of right and left used within the novel and surmises that characters such as Atticus, Tom, and Jem, who all have healthy right body parts, represent moral virtue, while Mayella and Bob, who have healthy left body parts, represent moral inequity.

Shaffer, Thomas L. "Christian Lawyer Stories and American Legal Ethics." *Mercer Law Review* 33, no. 3 (Spring, 1982): 877-901. Positioning Atticus as a heroic Christian lawyer, Shaffer discusses Atticus's ability to be moral and good while performing his duties as an attorney.

_____. "The Moral Theology of Atticus Finch." In *To Kill a Mockingbird*, edited by Terry O'Neill. New York: Greenhaven Press, 2000. Shaffer, in an article that originally appeared in the *University of Pittsburgh Law Review* in 1981, argues that Atticus is a hero because he has a sense of moral integrity that exposed the values of Maycomb's citizens.

Warshaw, Thayer S. "Teaching the Bible as Literature." *English Journal* 58, no. 4 (April, 1969): 571-576. Warshaw maintains that English teachers can employ several approaches to teaching the Bible, including teaching various Bible stories, people, and events referenced in literary works such as *To Kill a Mockingbird*.

KaaVonia Hinton

TO SCORCH OR FREEZE
Poems About the Sacred

Author: Donald Davie (1922-1995)
First published: Chicago: University of Chicago Press, 1988
Genre: Poetry
Subgenres: Lyric poetry; meditation and contemplation
Core issues: Daily living; faith

The influential poet-critic Davie wrestles with the certitudes of his Christian convictions. To underscore the spiritual restlessness, the poems are stylistically much looser than his previous work and reveal a wide range of influences from Ezra Pound to Basil Bunting.

Overview

Donald Davie was born in Barnsley in Yorkshire, England. His father, a deacon in the Baptist Church, operated a shop in a working-class neighborhood. His mother, ambitious for her son, introduced him at an early age to the British literary canon, for which he maintained a healthy respect over his long career. He attended Cambridge University, where he became a student of F. R. Leavis, whose close reading of poetry and attention to a poem's moral implications profoundly influenced Davie's career as poet and critic. In the 1950's he became identified with The Movement, a British literary movement that included Thom Gunn and Philip Larkin. The Movement, dominated by poets from Northern England, sought to recover the Britishness of British literature—its traditional forms, provincial language, and English values—which had been displaced by the internationalism and moral relativism of literary modernism. Davie supported his wife and daughter through a successful career as a college professor in both England and the United States. Though he maintained a residence in his beloved "shires" region of England, he spent the last twenty-five years of his teaching career in the United States, and a sense of displacement, both physical and spiritual, imbues much of his poetry written from the mid-1960's to his death. Although he joined the Anglican Church, he maintained a strong interest in the dissenting voices of Christian literature—perhaps hearkening back to his own Baptist roots.

Davie was both the heir to and a rebel from modernist poetry. He admired the literary techniques of modernists such as Ezra Pound and brought attention to less heralded innovators such as George Oppen and the Objectivist group. He also identified with the modernist rejection of the self-absorption of the Romantic movement. Like T. S. Eliot and W. H. Auden, Davie was a practicing Christian, comfortable as a person and an artist with Anglican Church orthodoxy. Yet while Davie's literary style was modernist, his sensibility was closer to that of Samuel Johnson, John Wesley, or other eighteenth century poets and hymn writers who saw the primary function of poetry to be moral and didactic. In his edition of *The New Oxford Book of Christian*

Verse (1981), Davie leans heavily on hymn writers at the expense of well-known Christian poets such as William Blake who were more unorthodox in their religious views.

Davie's early works of criticism, *Purity of Diction in English Verse* (1952) and *Articulate Energy: An Inquiry into the Syntax of English Poetry* (1955), set the course for his later poetry and criticism. Both volumes argue that plain diction, directness of approach, and the rational avoidance of excess (key literary values of the eighteenth century) are the hallmarks of the true British literary tradition. Ezra Pound had argued that the degeneration of the language led to the inevitable degeneration of culture. Davie gives Pound's argument a religious twist: A degenerate language is no longer an effective vehicle for the Christian Logos or word. The lack of "proper words in proper order" (to paraphrase Jonathan Swift) leads to the decay not only of art and culture but also of organized religion and the soul.

To Scorch or Freeze is more personal than Davie's earlier work and freer in its diction and syntax. Though hardly confessional, the poems provide a glimpse of a poet struggling for a sense of relevance in the late twentieth century and to create a foundation for his own religious beliefs. The opening poem, the modernist "The Thirty-Ninth Psalm, Adapted," finds its speaker bewailing a writer's block that is both literal and spiritual. The certainty of the literary polemicist has evaporated as the speaker recognizes the insignificance of his earlier poetry as "a tabloid column for crazies." He beseeches the Lord to "consider my calling" as a poet and provide the inspiration to write work of more value than poems that are mere "squawking/ and running off at the mouth."

In the poem "Ordinary God," Davie wrestles with the idea of God's intervention in human affairs. The speaker declares that while God has the power to intervene in history, he typically abjures such interference. The poem closes with an Audenesque image of God as an "ultimately faithful/ but meanwhile preoccupied landlord." Davie seeks to reconcile the notion of a rational deistic force driving the universe with that of the personal God of Christian orthodoxy. The depiction of the Supreme Being as an absentee landlord, however, seems to undermine Davie's faith in his ordinary God.

The figure of King David stands in opposition to Davie's speakers throughout *To Scorch or Freeze*. King David, although a sinner, remains God's chosen, and his verse reflects the simplicity and joy of that union with the Divine Presence. Davie's speakers are born too late, out of time, and out of touch with that presence. The poem "Sing Unto The Lord a New Song" closes with a couplet that demarcates the world of King David from that of Davie: "Praise the Lord upon the harp/ sing to him on the damnable steel guitar!" The "damnable steel guitar" becomes a symbol of the brash shallowness of the modern culture. It is not an accident that the "him" in the second line is not capitalized because, for Davie, the modern world has alienated itself from God's majesty.

Christian Themes

The title of *To Scorch or Freeze* vividly captures the work's major theme. The modern world is caught between the scorching flames of self-centered desire and the freezing distance from the Divine Presence. Davie seeks to identify the roots of this destructive dichotomy. In "Standings," for instance, he lashes out at the heterodoxy of William Blake. Davie excoriates political correctness in which the "Albion of William Blake" has become a "tesselation of ghettos." No advocate of cultural diversity, he blasts the notion of "the white man's truth/ then the black's."

The poem on the page facing "Standings" is "Church Militant," a title borrowed from seventeenth century English Christian poet George Herbert. (The poems on the facing pages throughout To Scorch or Freeze comment on each other—reinforcing its dichotomous title.) Davie imagines God as celestial commander in chief, who despite the materialism of the modern age still manages to recruit Christian soldiers in his eternal army of the faithful.

While much of To Scorch or Freeze laments modern faithlessness, the jeremiad is broken by transcendent moments such as "David Dancing." Here Davie contrasts the attempts of modern art and history to come to terms with the past with the image of David dancing before the Ark in a time outside time:

> Neither to move nor console
> he dances, not in a dream
> but exceptionally wakeful
> in a recurrent morning.

The dichotomy of "neither to move nor console" offers an answer to that of "To Scorch or Freeze." David creates his poetry in a dancing union with God in a state not of befuddled mysticism but of articulate energy enacting the Word that it glorifies.

Sources for Further Study

Bedient, Calvin. *Eight Contemporary Poets: Charles Tomlinson, Donald Davie, R. S. Thomas, Philip Larkin, Ted Hughes, Thomas Kinsella, Stevie Smith, W. S. Graham*. London: Oxford University Press, 1974. Bedient offers a good book-length study of the Movement poets and articulates Davie's position as the central critical theorist and polemicist within this loosely affiliated group.

Davie, Donald, ed. *The New Oxford Book of Christian Verse*. Oxford, England: Oxford University Press, 1981. Davie's introduction provides a typically orthodox definition of what constitutes Christian verse; his selection of works shows his favor for plain style and moral didacticism over literary preening and mystical fuzziness.

Dekker, George, ed. *Donald Davie and the Responsibilities of Literature*. Manchester: Carcanet New Press in Association with The National Poetry Foundation, University of Maine, Orono, 1983. A selection of essays, although written prior to the publication of *To Scorch or Freeze*, provides ample insight into Davie's didactic purpose as a writer and the evolution of his view of modern poetry as a means of articulating religious belief.

Jarman, Mark. *Body and Soul: Essays on Poetry*. Ann Arbor: University of Michigan

Press, 2002. Jarman, Davie's friend and colleague at Vanderbilt University, provides an intimate and reverential view of Davie's often cantankerous beliefs, both religious and poetic. While Jarman's work considers poets outside Davie's personal canon of religious poets (for example, Robinson Jeffers and William Carlos Williams), Davie's influence on the work is profound.

Vendler, Helen. *Soul Says*. Cambridge, Mass.: Harvard University Press, 1995. This work is a collection of reviews by a premier critic of modern poetry. Her review of Davie's *Collected Poems* pays homage to Davie as poet and critic and places him at the forefront of the second wave of modernist writing following the initial wave of Pound, Eliot, and Yeats.

Luke A. Powers

TRANSGRESSION

Author: Randall Scott Ingermanson (1958-   )
First published: Eugene, Oreg.: Harvest House, 2000
Genre: Novel
Subgenres: Historical fiction (first century); science fiction; time travel
Core issues: Atheism; doubt; good vs. evil; Judaism

Transgression follows the adventures of two physicists and an archaeologist as they journey back in time through a wormhole to Jerusalem in 50 C.E. There they encounter the apostle Paul at a pivotal moment in history, one that could determine the very future of Christianity. The clandestine mission of one time traveler is to murder Paul, thereby altering the course of history. When the would-be assassin's secret is revealed, the other two set aside personal differences and join forces to save Paul, themselves, and perhaps Western civilization.

> *Principal characters*
> *Rivka Meyers*, an American archaeology student and practicing Messianic Jew
> *Ari Kazan*, an Israeli theoretical physicist and lapsed Orthodox Jew
> *Damien West*, an American experimental physicist and atheist
> *Hana*, a prostitute who befriends Rivka
> *Baruch*, a faith healer who aids Ari
> *Paul*, an apostle

Overview

Set in both modern-day and first century Israel, *Transgression* chronicles the time travels of one woman and two men and their encounters with Jesus' early followers. The first novel in Randall Scott Ingermanson's City of God series, *Transgression* received a Christy Award for futuristic fiction. *Retribution* (2003) and *Premonition* (2004) continue the chronicles of Rivka Meyers and Ari Kazan, characters introduced in *Transgression*.

The novel begins with American Rivka Meyers participating in a summertime dig in modern Israel. Eventually her journey takes her back to 50 C.E., a time when the ruins she explores were products of architecture, not fodder for archaeology. A fellow archaeologist introduces her to Ari Kazan, an Israeli scientist interested in the theoretical possibility of time travel. In his university laboratory, Ari collaborates with American physicist Damien West. Building on Ari's theoretical knowledge, Damien creates a wormhole that allows him to journey back to first century Jerusalem, a trip planned to coincide with Paul's historic visit to that city. Damien's desire is not to meet the apostle but to assassinate Paul before he spreads Christianity to the Gentiles.

The scientist hopes his intervention will alter the course of Western civilization.

Incongruously, Damien seeks, by killing Paul, to destroy the very technology that allows him to traverse time. He believes Christianity is linked to the rise of Western civilization and to the development of modern science, both of which he disdains; therefore he must nip this religion in its infancy. Damien is an avowed atheist and a disciple of Theodore John "Ted" Kaczynski, the infamous Unabomber. Kaczynski's published manifesto, with its mandate to destroy technology and save the earth, appeals to the scientist's own predilection for a return to an agrarian society where humans, without the aid of machinery, labor to survive.

Rivka becomes an unwitting pawn in Damien's plan to alter history. Damien uses Rivka as a guinea pig to test his invention's safety. If she survives the crossing, he will follow. As she engages in a virtual reality game in the laboratory, he guides her toward the untested wormhole. Rivka passes through this conduit from modern times and arrives in ancient Israel. To her eyes, the setting resembles one more feature of the game she is playing. Only after escaping an attempted rape does she realize she has been physically transported through time. Inappropriately dressed for the culture she has entered, Rivka is mistaken for a woman of ill repute. A prostitute, Hana, rescues Rivka from the streets and provides this traveler from afar with appropriate attire, food, and shelter. Thus, the ostracized Hana enacts Jesus' edict to clothe the naked and feed the hungry. The two women are able to communicate because of Rivka's knowledge of ancient Aramaic.

As a Messianic Jew, Rivka believes in Jesus as the Son of God but follows Judaic practices. Entering ancient Jerusalem provides her a double thrill: As an archaeologist, Rivka views intact structures previously known to her only through their remnants, and, as a twenty-first century Jewish follower of Jesus' teachings, she finds herself circulating among the first of her kind.

When Ari enters ancient Jerusalem in an attempt to locate Rivka and return her to her rightful historical era, her belief in Jesus and his rejection of Christianity clash. Unlike Damien, Ari does not wish to kill the apostle Paul, though the scientist blames Christianity for atrocities committed against the Jewish race over the centuries. Furthermore, Ari does not believe history can be rewritten. He reasons that their presence in a past age will not change the future; it will only reinforce events that will unfold as scripted. His idea is fully realized in the mosaic tiles that Rivka unearths in present-day Jerusalem early in the novel. Later, with Rivka stranded in ancient Jerusalem, fellow archaeologists at the modern site continue her excavation. The recovered tiles form a mosaic depicting Rivka and Ari's wedding, an image of a present-day couple unearthed from the past.

These visitors from the future need helpmates to survive in a culture at once foreign and familiar to them. Rivka relies on Hana, and Ari finds his mentor in Brother Baruch, a Jewish healer. Although Baruch includes the teachings of Rabbi Jesus in his faith, Paul's desire to share the good news with Gentiles strikes Baruch as too radical a break with Jewish tradition. Ari develops a renewed appreciation for his heritage through participation in Baruch's observance of rituals. Additionally, the men's friendship follows a parallel vein in their development of a love that must transcend the barriers of prejudice: Baruch's for Hana, the reformed prostitute, and Ari's for Rivka, the devout Messianic Jew.

Although Rivka and Ari succeed in subverting Damien's attempt on Paul's life, their efforts strand them in the past. In an ultraorthodox act of Sabbath observance, the electricity that sustains the wormhole is shut off by religious officials in modern Israel. Because Rivka refuses to return before assuring that Paul is safe, and Ari refuses to go back without the woman he loves, they remain together in the city of Jerusalem in a time before they were born.

Christian Themes

The time travels of an Orthodox Jew, a Messianic Jew, and an atheist allow all three to witness the development of the Christian religion fifty years after Jesus' death and resurrection. During this period, Jewish followers of the Rabbi Jesus were circulating his teachings in the streets of Jerusalem. The novel's title, *Transgression*, refers to a number of transgressions, chief among them the characters' violation of time, but there are also breaks with moral codes and religious laws. The novel addresses a number of religious themes, including the nature of good and evil and the divide between faith and doubt. Additionally, the novel offers a look at Judaism and its relationship to early Christian practice.

Randall Scott Ingermanson (a practicing physicist as well as a writer) allows faith in God and in science to coexist comfortably in *Transgression*. Science is presented as God's contribution to humankind, another channel through which to understand God's marvels and power. The true disbeliever in the novel is Damien, the sole character who disavows both God and science, and he is depicted as a villain. His very name identifies him as a demon intent on destroying Western civilization, both its predominant religion, Christianity, and its scientific body of knowledge. However, Ari and Rivka embody Judeo-Christian ethics when they set aside their differences (religious, political, and cultural) to aid each other and to thwart Damien's scheme.

Rivka believes that Jesus is the true Messiah, but Ari's doubts about God in general are more difficult to overcome. Raised in an ultraorthodox Jewish household, Ari saw his father killed by Christians during a street riot. Wary of conservative practices, Jewish or Christian, Ari places his trust in Albert Einstein and science; God and faith appear to him less reliable. However, faith overcomes doubt in ancient Jerusalem when Ari is the recipient of a miracle. Stung by a wasp, his supply of epinephrine destroyed by Damien, Ari suffers what should be a fatal bout of anaphylactic shock, until the prayers of Brother Baruch save him. This validation of the power of faith is sufficient even for the most skeptical of scientists.

Sources for Further Study

Ingermanson, Randall Scott. *Who Wrote the Bible Code? A Physicist Probes the Current Controversy*. Colorado Springs, Colo.: WaterBrook Press, 1999. The author of *Transgression* examines the theory that the Bible contains a code that can predict today's events and concludes that such a code does not exist. Sheds light on his beliefs.

Mort, John. Review of *Transgression. Booklist* (June 1, 2000): 1854. Emphasizes the thriller's clever blend of science, history, and theology. Provides commentary on the novel's accurate and insightful rendering of events in first century Jerusalem, as well as its compelling storyline.

"Randall Scott Ingermanson." *Contemporary Authors Online*. Farmington Hills, Mich.: Thomson Gale, 2006. Offers information about the author's career and a synopsis of *Transgression*.

Salm, Arthur. "Laws of Physics Are on His Side." *The San Diego Union-Tribune*, August 12, 2001, p. Books 6. An interview with the author that describes several of his works, including *Transgression*.

Dorothy Dodge Robbins

TRAVELING MERCIES
Some Thoughts on Faith

Author: Anne Lamott (1954-   )
First published: New York: Pantheon Books, 1999
Genre: Nonfiction
Subgenres: Autobiography; essays; meditation and contemplation
Core issues: Attachment and detachment; children; conversion; friendship; self-knowledge

In relating her journey to Christianity, Lamott offers both insight into her personal faith and a path others may choose to follow. Ultimately, she feels a deep sense of awe considering the places we all begin and end. Humor and balance make the work attractive to both Christian and non-Christian audiences, as Lamott offers an unexpectedly liberal view of Christianity.

Overview

In *Traveling Mercies*, Anne Lamott describes her faith journey as "a series of staggers from what seemed like one safe place to another." Her chapter titles frequently show evidence of her Christianity, with titles that either describe religious principles, such as "forgiveness," or the importance of family, such as "Mom" and "Dad." However, as she shows, she began life in a home where emotions were repressed and religion was heavily disparaged. She has strong secular roots as well, and she freely admits to being a liberal who supported George McGovern's presidential campaign in 1972. Because her own journey was so capricious, she recognizes and respects plurality, transforming even her most intense religious experiences into moments with which all her readers can identify through the use of humor and vivid description. Many of these essays originally appeared in slightly different form online in *Salon* magazine.

Lamott begins with her childhood: She experiences an emotional distance from her parents in childhood, loving the feeling of belonging at a Catholic mass with a friend's family. Later, moving to a castle whose emptiness echoes her family's emotional repression, she becomes close to another friend's mother, this one a Christian Scientist. This mother believes that God is a mother as well as a father, and that she, Anne Lamott, is beautiful, down to the wild and kinky hair that elicits her father's friends' racist jokes about her supposed mulatto heritage. Playing tennis with this woman's daughter, Shelly, and sleeping over at her house, Lamott hides from the rest of her life. As her teen years progress, she becomes increasingly involved in drugs and alcohol, even getting drunk with her father one night while her mother is studying for a law exam. One college class draws her closer to God, and a group of Jewish friends celebrate her mock bat-mitzvah, but she drops out of college.

Lamott feels drawn to St. Andrew's Presbyterian Church at the height of her addiction because the singing touches the places in her soul that those religious moments of childhood had reached. She cannot, however, bear to stay for the sermons, not wanting to be preached at about Jesus. After a weeklong alcohol and drug binge following an abortion, she starts hemorrhaging badly, and fear sobers her. Lying in bed after the bleeding stops, she realizes Jesus is there, invisible in the room with her. After that, though she does not stop drinking immediately, she senses Jesus as "a little cat" following her. After accepting Jesus, she begins gaining control of her addictions. She gets sober and a year later is baptized. She then fights her way through bulimia.

A second pregnancy brings her to a new turning point. After deciding not to have an abortion, she finds she can rely on her friends at St. Andrew's to help her with her baby son, Sam. Similarly, after her best friend, Pammy, dies, Lamott realizes she must live joyfully in spite of death. Her faith carries her through the struggles of motherhood and the loss of her friend. It also gives her insights into everything from friends coping with a terminally ill child to another child's overcoming a little of her fear of dogs to learning how to forgive.

Before her conversion, Lamott's religion was "sewn together from bits of rag and ribbon, Eastern and Western, pagan and Hebrew, everything but the kitchen sink and Jesus." Even after choosing the Christian path, Lamott's spirituality is unorthodox. Her moment of conversion was almost anticlimactic, but typically Lamott. She surrenders to her repressed religious yearnings with a curse followed by a resigned, "All right [Jesus]. You can come in." After her formal baptism, she refuses to ignore the wisdom she finds in other religions, taking advice from Buddhists as willingly as from Christians. More than that, though she clearly takes her religion seriously, her sense of humor creates an open atmosphere where more than literal biblical interpretations have meaning.

Because her work lacks the moralizing critics might expect from a Christian author, Lamott's message reaches a broad audience, even as it embodies the faith she expresses. Her writing draws on some of Christianity's core themes, particularly that God loves everyone and grieving is a lifelong process, endurable only with God's love. She also believes she can hear God in the deep quiet part of her soul, and several of the essays plumb the depths of that silence. Considered as a whole, *Traveling Mercies* represents a new kind of Christian literature, one that is open to faith of all kinds while still committed to strong religious values.

Christian Themes

Lamott's most powerful messages include the strength of God's love for all people, forgiveness, and miracles. She describes her own flaws unflinchingly; she feels God loved her even when she was an addict living on a houseboat and recovering badly from her abortion. She describes a priest friend's coming to Christ as feeling like an unwanted article at a pawnshop who is, unexpectedly, given a reprieve because Jesus agrees to take his place on the shelf. She comes to faith herself only after experimenting with several religions, which leaves her with a powerful respect for wisdom from a variety of sources.

Particularly in her emergence from addiction and bulimia, she relies on outside guidance. A priest helps her begin dealing with her alcoholism and drug addictions, and a therapist assists her in finding ways to cope with bulimia. When she becomes pregnant a second time (with Sam), a minister tells her to listen to the quiet parts of her soul when deciding whether or not to have an abortion. This guidance carries her through other crises, and she even makes a "help" box, where she puts the problems she is turning over to God and letting go of herself.

Without preaching to her audience, Lamott suggests that she could never have emerged from her addictions, from her bulimia, or from her lost childhood without God's love, even if she did not know it at the time and even if she could not know who his agents would be. She repeatedly relies on God's love and forgiveness to find herself, and she repeatedly describes events—even small things, such as Sam's enjoyment of an inner-tube trip on his birthday—as miraculous, recognizing God's presence in the smallest parts of her life.

In coming to terms with her father's and her friend Pammy's deaths, Lamott conveys the significance of God as a comfort in times of strife. After Pammy's death, she goes on vacation with Sam to Ixtapa, Mexico, where she realizes that it is a fallacy to believe grief passes quickly, but we must live with joy anyway. She realizes that grieving is necessary, that we carry pieces of our lost loved ones with us for our entire lives, and that God helps when the grieving hurts too much. Still brokenhearted twenty years after her father's death, she nevertheless realizes that the mud to which we will all return is wonderful for itself, and she can live, enjoy life, and write because of love, because of God, and she is grateful.

Sources for Further Study

Jones, Malcolm, Patricia King, Sherry Keene-Osborn, and Mike Hendricks. "Touched by the Angels." *Newsweek* 133 (May 3, 1999): 71-72. Focuses on Jan Karon, Iyanla Vanzant, and Anne Lamott as three best-selling mainstream religious authors.

Lamott, Anne. *Plan B: Further Thoughts on Faith.* New York: Riverhead, 2005. Continues Lamott's spiritual journey. Essays cover topics ranging from faith in the face of turning fifty to her mother's death to Sam's teenage years.

Merwin, W. S. *The Rain in the Trees.* New York: Knopf, 1988. Merwin's poetry resonates with Lamott; here the poems discuss love and the loss of Eden through progress. Lamott introduces *Traveling Mercies* with an excerpt from Merwin's "Thanks."

Pearlman, Mickey, and Katherine U. Henderson. "Anne Lamott." In *Inter/view: Talks with America's Writing Women.* Lexington: University Press of Kentucky, 1990. While pregnant with Sam, Lamott discusses her Northern California roots and how all of her books are about being lost and found.

Tennant, Agnieszka. "'Jesusy' Anne Lamott." *Christianity Today*, January 21, 2003. A sympathetic perspective on an iconoclastic and challenging writer whose radical Christianity is, perhaps surprisingly, rooted in tradition.

Tippett, Krista, host. "The Meaning of Faith." *Speaking of Faith.* St. Paul, Minn.: American Public Media, originally aired in October, 2004. Streaming audio available at http://speakingoffaith.publicradio.org. An interview with Lamott and individuals from three other religions discussing the meaning of faith in their lives.

Jessie Bishop Powell

A TREATISE CONCERNING RELIGIOUS AFFECTIONS

Author: Jonathan Edwards (1703-1758)
First published: 1746
Edition used: A Treatise Concerning Religious Affections, edited by John E. Smith, in *The Works of Jonathan Edwards*, edited by Perry Miller. New Haven, Conn.: Yale University Press, 1959
Genre: Nonfiction
Subgenre: Spiritual treatise
Core issues: Awakening; guidance; heart; holiness; Holy Spirit; soul; virtue

Edwards addresses the problem of distinguishing true religion from false, genuine piety from the counterfeit, sainthood from hypocrisy, and Christian spirituality from religious zealousness.

Overview

An early convert to Calvinism, Jonathan Edwards was ordained minister of First Church, Northampton, Massachusetts, in 1727, and through such provocative sermons as "God Glorified in Man's Dependence" (1731), "A Divine and Supernatural Light" (1733), and "Justification by Faith Alone" (1734) became a central figure in the religious revival in New England that came to be known as the "Great Awakening." Among his other important works are *Freedom of the Will* (1754), *The Great Christian Doctrine of Original Sin Defended* (1758), and *The Nature of True Virtue* (1765).

In the preface to his *Treatise Concerning Religious Affections*, Edwards contends that there is no more important question than that concerning the distinguishing features of those who are truly religious and pious. The practical problem of distinguishing the truly pious from the fervent pretenders to piety arose in the spiritual excitement of the Great Awakening, during which it became difficult, if not impossible, to separate the truly holy from those whose emotional intensity and frenetic activity gave them the appearance but not the reality of virtue and piety.

Edwards was troubled, both spiritually and intellectually, by the confusion of emotionalism with true virtue. "There is indeed something very mysterious in it," he writes, "that so much good, and so much bad, should be mixed together in the church of God." Mysterious as it is, however, the coexistence of the true and the false in religion is something that must be acknowledged. "'Tis no new thing," he adds, "that much false religion should prevail, at a time of great reviving of true religion; and that at such a time, multitudes of hypocrites should spring up among true saints." The problem for Edwards, then, was that of distinguishing true religion from false, genuine piety from the counterfeit, sainthood from hypocrisy, and Christian spirituality from religious zealousness.

Edwards begins the task of resolving the problem by remarking on the love and joy of the Christian victims of religious persecution to whom Peter (in 1 Peter 1:8) wrote (with reference to Christ), "Whom having not seen, ye love; in whom, though now ye see him not, yet believing, ye rejoice with joy unspeakable, and full of glory." Although the persecuted Christians did not see Christ, they loved him; although they suffered, they knew the joy of loving the divine. These religious affections—love and joy, founded in the divine—sustained and spiritually transformed these early Christians and thus were signs of their true piety, arising from the grace of God. Edwards's reflections on Christian love and joy lead to the statement of his central proposition: "True religion, in great part, consists in holy affections."

In writing of the "affections," Edwards was not referring to sentiments, feelings, or passions; he was writing of the "inclination and will" of the soul, the active tendency to embrace some things and turn away from others. He conceived of the spiritual affections pragmatically; he regarded them as dispositions to act, as established inclinations showing themselves in action.

A distinction is drawn by Edwards between the soul's understanding, which is dependent upon perception and speculation, and the soul's inclination, its capacity and tendency to approve or reject, to like or dislike, to be for some things and against others. When an inclination determines action, it may be called "will," and when the mind is affected by inclinations, it may be called "heart." The religious affections, then, are active inclinations affecting the will and the heart; and when they do so under the influence of the divine, they are true religious affections.

Since the affections are either positive or negative—either inclinations to approve or inclinations to reject—they involve either a "cleaving to . . . or seeking" something or, on the other hand, being averse to or opposed to something. Of the inclinations for something, Edwards gives as examples love, desire, hope, joy, gratitude, and complacence; as examples of inclinations against something, he cites hatred, fear, anger, grief, and the like. Some of the affections, Edwards points out, involve both positive and negative inclinations. Pity, for example, involves a positive inclination toward the sufferer and a negative inclination toward the suffering.

Although the religious affections are often of the mixed sort, involving love of the divine and hatred of sin and of Satanic influences, the love of God—that is, love directed toward the divine—is "the chief of the affections, and fountain of all other affections." The two commandments given by Christ—to love God and, accordingly, to love one's neighbor—"comprehend all the duty prescribed," Edwards writes. Thus, "the essence of all true religion lies in holy love."

In support of his general doctrine that true religion consists in the holy affections, Edwards emphasizes "vigorous and lively actings"; our wills and inclinations, he writes, must be "strongly exercised." The affections are springs of human action, to be sure, but unless that action be earnest and enlist all our strength, it cannot be a sign of true piety.

Edwards argues that it is of no help in determining whether a person having religious affections has *true* religious affections, signs of true piety, to discover that the religious affections are intense ("in a very high degree"); nor is it significant if the affections appear to have bodily effects, such as trembling or fainting. Further, if someone having religious affections is "fluent, fervent and abundant" in talking about religious matters, it does not follow that such a person is truly pious, or not: Fervent protestations prove nothing. Nor does the fact that religious affections may arise in a person without any effort on that person's part prove that the affections are supernaturally and divinely caused—nor that they are not. Finally, even if passages of Scripture come to mind and give rise to religious affections, nothing is shown either way about the truth of the affections.

One might suppose that the appearance of love could be taken to be significant in appraising the religious affections, but although love is "the chief of the graces of God's spirit," Edwards writes, it can be counterfeited, and hence no mere appearance of love proves that the reality of spiritual love is present.

Nor, Edwards continues, can one determine whether or not religious affections are "gracious," signs of God's grace, by noticing that, in a given case, the affections are many and varied, or that some persons experience comfort and joy after awakenings of conscience, or that people spend a great deal of time in zealous religious activity, or that they have their mouths full of praise for God, or that they are confident that their experience has a divine origin, or that what they do is pleasing to the truly godly.

If all these presumed indicators of true religion are false signs, what signs are reliable? Edwards offers twelve signs of holy affections, but he warns that no set of signs could enable anyone to determine with certainty whether someone enjoys true affections. The difficulty is not with the signs but with the use of them, with seeing clearly whether or not the signs are present. Nevertheless, the signs are useful in seeking understanding even though they can hardly be employed to convince hypocrites.

The true affections, first of all, arise from influences that are "spiritual, supernatural and divine." Edwards states that "true saints" are "spiritual persons," and he explains that by a "spiritual" person is meant one in opposition to a "natural" person, the latter being without benefit of the influence of the Spirit of God. To be spiritual is to be of the Spirit of God, and true spirituality consists in being affected by God's grace.

The second sign of the true affections is that they have as their objective ground the excellence of divine things, not any benefit that might come to the person and thereby satisfy self-love. That is, God is loved as God and because of the glory and excellence of God, not because God might benefit those who love him.

One may take it as a sign of true affections that they are based on a love of the "beauty and sweetness" of the "moral excellency" of divine things. By "moral excellency," Edwards means what we might call "spiritual" excellency, for the morality with which he is concerned does not relate to the practical benefits of certain modes of conduct in society but to the requirements of holiness or virtue. The moral excellency of God *is* God's holiness; to love God for his holiness is to find his moral excellency beautiful and sweet and, hence, to take delight in that holiness.

The fourth sign of the true affections is that they arise from an enlightenment of the mind that consists in a true spiritual understanding of divine things. Spiritual understanding, Edwards avers, involves "a sense of the heart," a heartfelt sense of spiritual beauty. Such understanding is not speculative; it involves a "taste" of the moral beauty of divine things—that is, a sense of their reality and a delight in their apprehension.

The spiritual conviction of the reality of divine things is a fifth sign of the true religious affections, provided that the conviction is "reasonable," that is, that it arises from a spiritual understanding, a sense of the excellence and beauty of the divine.

Gracious affections, Edwards writes, "are attended with evangelical humiliation," the sixth sign of the true affections. Edwards explains that by "evangelical humiliation" is meant "a sense that a Christian has of his own utter insufficiency, despicableness, and odiousness, with an answerable frame of heart." Again, to be significant, the sense of one's insufficiency must proceed not from the natural observation that one is limited in various ways but from a spiritual understanding of the difference between the perfections of God and the imperfections of the self, an understanding achieved through the influence of the Spirit of God.

The seventh sign of the true religious affections is that they are accompanied by a transformation of the soul brought about through spiritual understanding. Such transformation or "change of nature" is abiding; it is the permanent effect of the encounter with the Spirit.

The eighth sign is that, if the religious affections promote "the lamblike, dovelike spirit and temper of Jesus Christ," their doing so is a sign of their being true and holy religious affections.

The ninth sign is that the religious affections soften the heart; they lead to a tenderness of spirit. Persons so affected become as little children.

The tenth sign is that truly gracious affections are proportionate to their objects; they exhibit "beautiful symmetry." Some persons make a great show of loving God, but they show little love or benevolence in their relationships to other persons: In such persons there is an imbalance of concerns, a disproportion that is a sign of false affections.

The eleventh sign is that true affections give rise to an increase in spiritual appetite: "The more a true saint loves God with a gracious love, the more he desires to love him, and the more uneasy is he at his want of love to him." The increase in spiritual longing is Edwards's eleventh sign of the true affections.

The twelfth and final sign discussed by Edwards involves Christian practice: "Gracious and holy affections have their exercise and fruit in Christian practice." Christian practice, Edwards emphasizes, is "the chief of all the signs of grace"; it is the "principal sign" by which one can determine the truth or falsity of religious affections. Edwards argues at great length in support of this final definitive sign; he quotes extensively from Scripture, and he places special emphasis on Christ's insistence that "Ye shall know them by their fruits" (Matthew 7:16). Unless the religious affections make a profound and Christian difference in practice, they are not signs of true piety.

Christian Themes

In a time of revivalism, when distinguishing between the truly pious and the merely exercised was paramount, Edwards worked to identify genuine "religious affections" both as a means of making that distinction and as a means of instructing. For Edwards, "affections" (corresponding to what we would now call emotions) were positive and negative inclinations of the soul; among the former are love, desire, hope, joy, gratitude, and complacence; among the latter are hatred, fear, anger, and grief. True religion consists, for the most part, in the true religious affections.

Love is the paramount religious affection. The preeminent virtue of Jesus Christ was expressed in the exercise of the holy affections. Among circumstances that cannot be taken as signs of true grace in persons having religious affections are their making fluent and fervent religious protestations, their spending much time in worship and other religious activities, their confidence about their own piety, and their happening to be pleasing to the truly godly.

Although there is no way of being certain about the piety of persons, there are twelve signs of the true religious affections: (1) They arise from spiritual, supernatural, and divine influences; (2) they are grounded in the excellence of divine things; (3) they are founded on the appeal of the moral excellence of divine things; (4) they arise from the mind's enlightened understanding of divine things; (5) they are attended with a reasonable and spiritual conviction of the reality of divine things; (6) they are associated with honest humility; (7) they accompany a spiritual transformation; (8) they promote the spirit of love that Christ made evident; (9) they soften the heart; (10) they exhibit a beautiful symmetry and proportion; (11) they lead to an increase in the spiritual appetite for holiness; and (12) they have their exercise and fruit in Christian practice.

Although Edwards offers twelve signs of the true affections and, hence, of true religion, the argument for any one is but a special emphasis on a feature of a basic argument that covers them all; the spirit of a person may, through God's grace, be affected by the Spirit of God; the sense of God gives rise to the holy affections; the holy affections, in turn, are springs of actions that reflect the beauty and holiness of their divine inspiration. To be truly religious and pious, then, is to be transformed by the religious affections arising from and reflecting the moral excellence of divine things: It is to love God.

Sources for Further Study

Crisp, Oliver D. *Jonathan Edwards and the Metaphysics of Sin*. Burlington, Vt.: Ashgate, 2005. Chapters include "The Divine Decrees," "Adam's Fall," "The Authorship of Sin," "The Secret and Revealed Will of God," "Temporal Parts and Imputed Sin," and "Inherited Guilt." Bibliography, index.

Edwards, Jonathan. *Freedom of the Will*. Edited by Paul Ramsey. Vol. 1 in *The Works of Jonathan Edwards*, edited by Perry Miller. New Haven, Conn.: Yale University Press, 1957. First published in 1754, this is Edwards's philosophical masterpiece. In it, he argues for Calvinism against Arminianism and for the doctrine that freedom of the will is not only compatible with determinism but also requires it.

_____. *The Nature of True Virtue*. Foreword by William K. Frankena. Ann Arbor: University of Michigan Press, 1960. First published in 1765 (written in

1755), this statement is consistent with Edwards's *Treatise Concerning Religious Affections*; here he argues that true virtue consists in benevolence to being in general, that is, "love to God," and consequently that "virtue is the beauty of the qualities and exercises of the heart."

Gura, Philip F. *Jonathan Edwards: America's Evangelical.* New York: Hill and Wang, 2005. A full biography of Edwards from the early years to Princeton. Illustrated; bibliography, index.

Larsen, Dale. *Jonathan Edwards—Renewed Heart: Six Studies for Individuals or Groups with Study Notes.* Downers Grove, Ill.: InterVarsity Press, 2002. Offers six lessons on Christian living based on Edwards's life and passages from Scripture.

Miller, Perry. *Jonathan Edwards.* Introduction by John F. Wilson. Lincoln: University of Nebraska Press, 2005. Wilson's introduction sets the stage for students of Edwards. Bibliography, index.

Simonson, Harold P. *Theologian of the Heart.* Grand Rapids, Mich.: Wm. B. Eerdmans, 1974. A careful, detailed, and rewarding study of Edwards's conviction that virtue requires a "sense of the heart" as affected by the grace and glory of God.

Ian P. McGreal

TREATISE ON DIVINE PREDESTINATION

Author: John Scotus Erigena (c. 810-c. 877 C.E.)
First published: De divina praedestinatione liber, 851 C.E. (English translation, 1998)
Edition used: Treatise on Divine Predestination, translated by Mary Brennan. Notre Dame, Ind.: University of Notre Dame Press, 1998
Genre: Nonfiction
Subgenres: Didactic treatise; theology
Core issues: Grace; predestination; problem of evil; sin and sinners; soul

In his treatise, Erigena states that philosophy is a form of religious expression whose proper exercise can reveal religious truths. God cannot predestine humans for evil and punishment. Foreknowledge is not equivalent to predestination. Free will is meaningless unless humans have the capacity to reject God's goodness. Evil, being solely the absence of good brought about by free will, has no real existence. All descriptions of the transcendent Deity are necessarily metaphorical.

Overview

John Scotus Erigena's *Treatise on Divine Predestination* is the product of religious controversies that raged during the Carolingian renaissance of the ninth century. He wrote it in response to a request by Hincmar, bishop of Rheims, for a refutation of the teachings of Gottshalk of Fulda. Gottschalk, a Saxon monk, stirred up controversy in the West Frankish kingdom of Charles the Bald by teaching that there were two divine predestinations, one toward virtue and salvation and one toward evil and damnation. Concerned that this misinterpretation of Saint Augustine appeared to condone wrongdoing as inevitable and to render attempts at reform futile, Charles summoned a synod of bishops to Quierzy in 849. The synod ordered Gottschalk imprisoned, but his doctrines continued to be propagated despite the efforts of Hincmar and Hrabanus Maurus, the kingdom's foremost theologians.

Hincmar then appealed to John Scotus Erigena, an Irish scholar. Neither a monk nor a cleric, Erigena was better equipped than any contemporary to evaluate Saint Augustine as a philosopher. Now considered to be the only Western philosopher of any stature between Boethius in the sixth century and Saint Anselm in the eleventh, Erigena had already established a reputation for learning.

The *Treatise on Divine Predestination* went far beyond simple refutation of Gottshalk's doctrines. In its nineteen chapters, Erigena addressed broader considerations of good, evil, and the nature of the afterlife. In his emphasis on free will and the essential goodness of human nature, his arguments approached the position of fellow Briton Pelagius, founder of the Pelagian heresy, which maintained that humans were capable of achieving salvation through free will alone, without the necessity of Christ's sacrifice. The *Treatise on Divine Predestination* was condemned by French bishops at the Councils of Valence (855) and Langres (859). Detractors referred to it as *pultes scotorum*, or "Irish porridge." It passed into obscurity, surviving to modern times in a single manuscript copy. Protected by the patronage of the Frankish king, Erigena continued to write, producing translations from the Greek that introduced Christian Neoplatonism to the Latin-speaking world and an original philosophical work, *De divisione naturae* (c. 862-866, also known as *Periphysion*; best known in partial translation as *On the Division of Nature: Book 1*, 1940; complete translation, *Johannis Scotti Eriugenae Periphyseon [De divisione naturae]*, 1968-1981).

Erigena begins his treatise by stating that true philosophy is true religion and outlining the four-part model of philosophical disputation he intends to follow. This consists of division of the question into parts (*divisoria*), determining one from many (*definitiva*), indicating the hidden from the manifest (*demonstrativa*), and resolution (*resolutia*). In the first three chapters he presents a series of logical arguments against the doctrine of two predestinations. God, being the supreme cause of all things, is not subject to necessity, and therefore predestination to evil does not necessarily follow from predestination to good.

God is unity, Erigena argues. The ineffable cause of all things is indivisible into genera and species. The terms of theological discourse are merely verbal symbols imparting understanding to a person in his ascent toward God. "Predestination" is such a symbolic term, describing imperfectly one aspect of the Deity. A symbol divided into mutually exclusive parts cannot represent something indivisible; therefore, the doctrine of dual predestination is, in Erigena's words, fabulous, like the legend of Icarus.

Therefore there can be only one divine predestination, one toward human happiness and salvation. The role of free will in the divine plan occupies much of the remainder of the book. Following Saint Augustine, Erigena sees free will as a gift from God, without which humanity would not bear the complete image of its creator. Free will would not be free without conferring the capacity to reject God. This rejection and the evil resulting from it were not created by God but are composed of individual voluntary acts of people. Evil is the absence of good. It has no substance; like darkness and silence, it is defined by what it is not. God did not create it, and God does not compel or predestine any person to commit evil acts.

Erigena distinguishes between foreknowledge and predestination. God has foreknowledge of many things of which he is not the cause. Christ's selection of Judas as a disciple illustrates the distinction. Christ knew that Judas would betray him, but he did not cause that betrayal. Because God is eternal, past and future have no meaning for him; his foreknowledge is equivalent to memory and, like memory, does not imply causation.

Gottschalk cited numerous writings of Saint Augustine containing explicit references to God predestining sinners to punishment. According to Erigena, these are to be understood as arguments by contrariety, that is, stating the opposite of what is intended to point out its absurdity. The heretical potential of applying such a line of reasoning to sacred texts was not lost on contemporary or subsequent guardians of Church orthodoxy.

The book concludes with a philosophical treatment of the afterlife reminiscent of that of the heretical third century Greek writer Origen, who envisioned all of creation returning to God at the end of time. This scenario precludes the existence of a separate Hell reserved for the punishment of the wicked. Erigena offers several explanations for biblical references to the fires of judgment. He likens the Heavenly Kingdom to a sumptuous palace, and condemned sinners to visitors so ill that they experience nothing but misery despite their surroundings. The fiery torments of Hell may also be a metaphor for extreme psychological pain caused by separation from God. That interpretation, however, seems to be contradicted by a physical explanation of eternal flames through which all souls pass during the process of being reunited with God and in which unredeemable sinners become permanently lodged, as unchanged as asbestos.

Christian Themes

Erigena's *Treatise on Divine Predestination* is notable for its paucity of references to the specific role of Jesus Christ in human salvation. It is hardly surprising that Hincmar—who commissioned it—repudiated it, contemporary church councils labeled it as heretical, and the Vatican placed the first printed edition of Erigena's work on its list of banned books. The work provides an early solution to the much-debated problem of reconciling the existence of evil with the concept of an omnipotent and benevolent God—by no means an exclusively Christian debate. Its approach to biblical inerrancy and literal interpretation of sacred texts is radical even by modern standards. If God is fundamentally indescribable in human terms, everything relating to God becomes metaphorical, and the aptness of every metaphor open to question.

Gottschalk saw predestination as a divinely ordained master plan that determined, before people were born, the course of their lives and the outcomes of all the decisions determining whether their lives led to salvation or to sin and damnation. This comes close to John Calvin's concept. For Erigena, God, standing outside of time, simply has foreknowledge of the outcome. He no more compels a person to sin, than a chronicler relating the evils of the past causes those evils to have occurred. Erigena attributed the decision to sin to excessive preoccupation with matters of the flesh. These matters are not inherently evil, but belong to a lower order of creation. Redemption depends on directing one's intellect and understanding toward contemplation of the divine, not to earn grace, but as a means of rendering one susceptible to the workings of grace to which all people, by reason of their humanity, are already predestined.

Sources for Further Study

McGinn, Bernard, and Willemien Otten, eds. *Erigena: East and West*. Notre Dame, Ind.: Notre Dame University Press, 1994. A collection of conference papers mostly dealing with the influence of Eastern Christian thought on Erigena; focuses on *On the Division of Nature: Book 1*.

Mathew, H. C. G., and Brian Harrison, eds. *Oxford Dictionary of National Biography: From the Earliest Times to the Year 2000*. Oxford, England: Oxford University Press, 2004. The entry on Erigena contains summaries of his major philosophical works. An invaluable reference for recent scholarship on British historical figures.

Moran, Dermot. "Origen and Eriugena: Aspects of Christian Gnosis." In *The Relationship Between Neoplatonism and Christianity*, edited by T. Finan and V. Twomey. Dublin: Four Courts Press, 1992. Contains analyses of the philosophy of Origen, Saint Augustine, and Gregory of Nyssa; useful for understanding Neoplatonic concepts of substance and nature.

_____. *The Philosophy of John Scottus Eriugena: A Study of Idealism in the Middle Ages*. Cambridge, England: Cambridge University Press, 1989. Idealism used here in the Platonic philosophical sense: the observable universe as a manifestation of an ideal existing in the mind of God.

Martha A. Sherwood

THE TRIP TO BOUNTIFUL

Author: Horton Foote (1916-   )
First produced: pr. 1953, pb. 1954
Edition used: The Trip to Bountiful, in *Horton Foote's Three Trips to Bountiful,* edited by Barbara Moore and David Yellin. Dallas, Tex.: Southern Methodist University Press, 1993
Genre: Drama
Subgenre: Literary fiction
Core issues: Acceptance; compassion; faith; resignation; suffering

Initially a television play and later a motion picture, Foote's The Trip to Bountiful *typifies his major themes as played out by small-town rural Texas characters who undergo loss and sacrifice, particularly when leaving home, often for urban settings. The drama's central character is a Christian widow, fond of singing hymns, who rises from suffering to an act of self-determination to achieve a calming sense of resignation to a situation she cannot change.*

> Principal characters
> *Mrs. Watts,* an elderly widow
> *Ludie Watts,* Mrs. Watts son, a Houston accountant
> *Jessie Mae,* Ludie's wife
> *Thelma,* a woman Mrs. Watts meets in the bus station
> *The sheriff,* a lawman of Harrison, Texas

Overview

The Trip to Bountiful opens in the Houston apartment of the Wattses: Ludie, his wife Jessie Mae, and Mrs. Watts, Ludie's mother. The play tells the story of Mrs. Watts, an elderly widow not without pride, who has left her rural Texas home to live with her hardworking and self-effacing son and his lazy, selfish wife. Jessie Mae likes beauty shops and movie magazines, and she insists on controlling her mother-in-law's small government check. She also registers irritation at Mrs. Watts's habits (such as quietly singing hymns), and she considers Mrs. Watts crazy to wish to return to her home, the small town of Bountiful, Texas. Mrs. Watts previously has made several unsuccessful attempts to return home, and when she again privately expresses this need to her son, she is told that he can make a living only in Houston. Awake on a moonlit night as his wife still sleeps, Ludie is comforted by his mother, who sings him a childhood song and tells him of another moonlit night in Bountiful when she relieved his childhood fear of death; he claims not to remember the occasion. Ludie's wife awakens and quarrels with Mrs. Watts before returning to bed. The next day, chafing under the shrewish supervision of her daughter-in-law, Mrs. Watts hides her government check from Jessie Mae and plans her escape to Bountiful. The next day, she leaves with her bag after Ludie and his wife have left the apartment.

As act 2 opens, Mrs. Watts arrives at a Houston bus station, where she can only purchase a ticket to Harrison, a town near Bountiful. There she meets a friendly and lonely young woman, Thelma, who is going to her parents' home until her husband returns from overseas. Mrs. Watts, seeing her son and his wife approach the station, hides. Ludie learns that his mother has been there and leaves with Jesse Mae, who asks the police to help them retrieve Mrs. Watts.

In the next scene, Mrs. Watts talks to a sympathetic Thelma on the bus about her problems and plan to stay in Bountiful with her childhood friend, Mrs. Callie Davis. Then she unsuccessfully tries to lift the lonely young woman's spirits by quoting Psalm 91. When Thelma states her deep love for her husband, Mrs. Watts confesses that she never loved her husband but had loved another man, whom her father prevented her from marrying.

The next scene is the Harrison bus station, where Mrs. Watts learns from the ticket agent that no one has lived in Bountiful since the last resident, Callie Davis, recently died. Shattered by the news, Mrs. Watts resolves to continue her trip and to spend the night in the station until morning. Thelma helps her retrieve a purse and leaves for her bus, bidding an affectionate good-bye to the older lady, who soon falls asleep on a bench. Upon awaking, she encounters the local sheriff, who has been asked by the Houston police to hold her there until her son arrives. She begs the sheriff to let her visit her old home. On the verge of collapse, she tells the lawman that she has endured a loveless marriage, the death of two children, and years of petty bickering, but now she must see her old home again, even if briefly, to help her understand why her life has grown empty. Moved by Mrs. Watts's desperate plea, the sheriff determines to drive her to Bountiful and wait there for Ludie and Jesse Mae to arrive.

In the next scene the sheriff and Mrs. Watts stand before her now dilapidated home. Ludie arrives and thanks the sheriff, who leaves. Mrs. Watts apologizes to Ludie for causing him trouble. As they reminisce, he tells his mother that it does no good to remember the past. When he refuses her final plea to remain, she realizes the pain she is causing and determines to accept what must be. Like her son, she must accept the inexorability of change. Jessie Mae enters and presents a list of rules to control her mother-in-law's behavior. Mrs. Watts consents to return quietly and acquiesce to Jessie Mae's demands. When Jessie Mae demands the pension check, Ludie asserts himself and reminds his wife that she has promised to live in peace with his mother. After Mrs. Watts hands her the check, Jessie Mae uncharacteristically returns it to Mrs. Watts. As her son and his wife leave to go back to their borrowed car, Mrs. Watts falls behind, kneeling to feel the earth in her fingers and gain the sense of the strength and dignity that will allow her to survive. Secure in the knowledge that her remaining existence will be sustained because of her last contact with Bountiful, she bids it good-bye.

Christian Themes

Christian faith implies a belief in the scriptural narrative and the acceptance of God's favor extended to humanity through Christ. It accepts the immutable truth, goodness, and power of God. Also it can encompass a dependence on the truthfulness of another. That the protagonist knows by heart Psalm 91, which proclaims that God is a refuge of strength and protection, suggests that she is a woman of faith. Suffering, as a Christian theme, is something to be endured patiently, in the realization that present travail cannot be compared with the life and glory that will be later revealed. Jesus and Job are lucid examples. Both endure great suffering, accept it as God's will but question it, and ultimately are rewarded by God, who ends their suffering.

To Mrs. Watts, like Job, the Lord has given and taken away. She has lost a comfortable rural livelihood, marital love, independence, and much more, and she questions her current plight. Although she does not achieve Job's salvation, she does reach a state of acceptance. The hymn "There's Not a Friend Like the Lowly Jesus," recurs throughout the play, underscoring Mrs. Watts's faith and ultimate acceptance.

Themes of acceptance and resignation are intertwined. Protestant theologian Reinhold Niebuhr in "The Serenity Prayer" (1934) clearly defines the former concept: "God, give us grace to accept with serenity the things that cannot be changed, courage to change the things that should be changed, and the wisdom to distinguish the one from the other." Foote's central character does not serenely accept her conditions, until she recognizes the intensity of her son's suffering and his need not to look back when he begins to develop a new inner strength. Resignation, from a strict Christian perspective, accepts that conditions are determined by God's will. Both Jesus and Job proclaim that the Lord's will, not their own, be done. Like suffering, it is to be endured patiently with the hope of a better tomorrow. Mrs. Watts, revitalized by her trip to Bountiful, accepts resignation but has gained self-knowledge.

The Christian theme of compassion implies empathy—suffering with, and having pity for, another—and also assumes that God is compassionate and forgiving. The Bible offers the example of the Good Samaritan. In *The Trip to Bountiful*, Mrs. Watts practices compassion, as do other characters, such as Ludie, Thelma, and the sheriff. When Mrs. Watts compassionately understands her son's unhappiness, her recognition brings her greater wisdom. Horton Foote, a Christian humanist who saw the world with a clear eye, believed in the healing power of loving connection.

Sources for Further Study

Briley, Rebecca. *You Can Go Home Again: The Focus on Family in the Works of Horton Foote*. New York: Peter Lang, 1993. Places special attention on family dynamics and values and Foote's work.

Foote, Horton. *Beginnings: A Memoir*. New York: Scribner, 2004. The playwright's informative narrative of his professional life, from young actor to award-winning writer.

_____. *Genesis of an American Playwright*. Edited by Marian Castleberry. Waco, Tex.: Baylor University Press, 2004. Insightful chapters on the author's experiences as a writer for stage and screen. Includes a chronology and a bibliography of published and produced work.

Moore, Barbara, and David G. Yellin, eds. *Horton Foote's Three Trips to Bountiful*.

Dallas, Tex.: Southern Methodist University Press, 1993. In-depth study of the play's evolution, from teleplay to stage to film. Includes texts of the three versions with production and interpretative information, illustrations, artist interviews, and bibliography.

Wood, Gerald C., ed. *Horton Foote; A Casebook.* New York: Garland, 1998. Essays by twelve writers address significant aspects of Foote's life and work. Contains a chronology and a valuable annotated bibliography of both the author's works and critical works about him.

Christian H. Moe

THE TRIUMPH OF LOVE

Author: Geoffrey Hill (1932-   )
First published: Boston: Houghton Mifflin, 1998
Genre: Poetry
Subgenres: Lyric poetry; meditation and contemplation
Core issues: Faith; forgiveness; good vs. evil; love; memory; redemption

Hill's difficult book-length poem concerns itself with the twentieth century, the bloodiest century in history, and is a consideration of all those who have perished in war and in other unnecessary and violent ways. Above all, the poem deals with the great injustices done to the memories of those who have gone before us—who have suffered so that we may live—as their names are erased from the pages of history and as their faces and all that they stood for disappear from our hearts and minds. In the end, Hill focuses on love as it stages a protest against evil.

Overview

Born in Bromsgrove, Worcestershire, Geoffrey Hill's work is defined by his working-class upbringing (his father and grandfather were police officers), his early memories of World War II, his views of European history, and his Christian vision of the world. Hill, who is deaf in one ear, was educated at Bromsgrove High School. He went on to attend Keble College, Oxford, where he studied English literature and first began to publish his poems. After graduating from Oxford, Hill taught at Leeds University for the better part of three decades. During this time, he also taught in Michigan and Nigeria. After leaving Leeds University, Hill taught at Emmanuel College and Boston University. He retired from Boston University in August, 2006, and assumed the title of professor emeritus. A revered poet, Hill has published numerous poetry collections, including *The Mystery of the Charity of Charles Péguy* (1983) and *Canaan* (1996). *The Triumph of Love* is widely considered his finest work.

Hill is popularly considered an inaccessible poet, a poet whose work can be appreciated only by a chosen few. This speaks to a profound decline in cultural literacy, as readers are less and less willing to invest themselves wholly in a work of literature. Like T. S. Eliot and Ezra Pound, Hill is a poet who demands every bit of his readers' attention. His work is littered with majestic and esoteric allusions and with foreign words and phrases. To the common reader, Hill's unannotated work is murky, but to the curious and invested reader, his work is rich and rewarding.

The Triumph of Love is no exception to this rule. It seems to have divided readers and critics. A profound work (and a profoundly difficult one), *The Triumph of Love* is a book-length poem that spans 150 cantos and seeks to make sense of the explosive and violent twentieth century. It is a meditation on ruination and forgiveness, and Hill confronts the great questions in a dark and humorous way. Hill's humor stands in direct contrast to the bleak subject matter, but he has chosen his sharp-tongued persona as a means of indicting all purveyors of wreckage, all enemies of love. As the poem builds in intensity, Hill's speaker grows angrier and angrier, promising "thirty/ vicarious rounds of bare-knuckle."

The poem is a great challenge, no doubt. Struck by the force of Hill's language, the reader is immediately pressed into action. The epigraph from Nehemiah 6:3 introduces the notions of distance and separateness that inform the poem. The speaker is self-conscious and, at times, absurd. His reflections waver between manic glee, disturbed invective, and gentle questioning. Even the reader who is lost in Hill's thick language, in the narrow maze that he has constructed, finds something to celebrate here: the sense of urgency and solemnity that inhabits these lines. In this poem, Hill calls on Petrarch, simultaneously paying homage to him and announcing that he is working in the same tradition. He writes:

> Vergine bella, as you
> are well aware, I here follow
> Petrarch, who was your follower,
> A sinner devoted to your service.

Yet the work is not solely indebted to Petrarch. The title itself calls to mind Edward Holmes's 1902 sonnet sequence and H. B. Hoffman's epic of the Great Northwest from 1923, both called *The Triumph of Love*. Still, Hill draws his greatest inspiration from Petrarch and from biblical writers such as Daniel and Ezekiel, and he also owes an obvious debt to Marivaux's *Le Triomphe de l'amour* (pr., pb. 1732; *The Triumph of Love*, 1994), a work first performed in 1732. Like Marivaux, Hill dismisses lust for leisure and pleasure, slothfulness, and other sinful behavior, as he sets out to prove that love alone can tame brutish humanity and heal the world.

Hill's triumph in this grandiose poem is his vision of the twentieth century as tragic, as the ultimate representation of the universe's cyclical nature: Violence begets violence writ large. Modern war is enormous, atrocities inescapable, and forgiveness and redemption real. Hill looks to the time before our time for answers to the questions we no longer seem capable of answering: Why are we here? What is this function of poetry? Where and how can we see God's hand at work in the world? Hill knows that the answers lay well in the past, in the ecstatic and genuine belief of our ancestors, our exemplary models of faith and endurance. The twentieth century, Hill writes, is a "fire-targeted century" that has spawned a new generation of ignorant and contemptuous victims. Indictments such as this do not leave us without hope, though. We are never far from understanding that there is solemn and serious work to be done, that there is something to atone for or someone to console.

Christian Themes

Though the fact is often overlooked, Hill is a Christian with a profound understanding of theological thought, and like Ernest Hemingway's priest in *A Farewell to Arms* (1929), he knows that it is through suffering, through defeat, that humans become Christian and ultimately persevere as Christians. On that note, Hill's primary function in *The Triumph of Love* is to promote human endurance, to declare (in a very mystical manner) that love always—even when the most bestial acts are being committed—conquers evil.

Hill is deeply concerned with exultation and mysticism, and he heartily identifies with writers such as Saint Augustine, John Milton, and William Blake, wildly exuberant and mystical figures who also confront notions of redemptive faith. Hill's Christianity is evident in his understanding of justice, judgment, and forgiveness. He writes: "To know all/ is to forgive all." Significantly, Hill's concept of sympathy stems from his understanding of forgiveness. He states that Christians must be engaged, that they must suffer, and that they must, at their core, be sympathetic to those who mourn instead of angry at the aggressors. In this manner, Hill acknowledges that humans must have "daily acknowledgement/ of what is owed the dead." This is a sentiment that ties him to other Christian writers whom he greatly admires: Charles Péguy, Georges Bernanos, Saint-John Perse, and Paul Claudel.

At one point in *The Triumph of Love*, Hill expresses the desire to "grasp once, in emulation,/ work of the absolute, origin-creating mind," an expression of the most basic Christian ambition: to understand God and his work, if only for a moment. Knowing his limits as a human, Hill settles on seeking out some sort of religious experience in this most secular of ages. He prays for "our arrival/ at a necessary salvation."

Addressed to the Virgin Mary ("Vergine bella"), *The Triumph of Love* offers a Christian vision of guilt and redemption, and it is an attempt to reconcile the evils of the past through gentleness and understanding. Most important, there are 150 cantos in the poem, and it should be noted that the same number of Psalms are in the Bible. This is not mere coincidence, as Hill draws much inspiration from the Bible, calling on Daniel and Ezekiel and Ruth, deeply influenced not only by their stories but also by their literary styles. Like so much of the best Christian literature, *The Triumph of Love* is, finally, a song of praise.

Sources for Further Study

Bloom, Harold, ed. *Geoffrey Hill: Modern Critical Views*. Philadelphia: Chelsea House, 1986. Bloom declares that Hill is the strongest British poet active at the time.

McNees, Eleanor Jane. *Eucharistic Poetry: The Search for Real Presence in John Donne, Gerald Manley Hopkins, Dylan Thomas, and Geoffrey Hill*. Lewisburg, Pa.: Bucknell University Press, 1991. McNees's exploration of the Christian notion of presence in Hill's work, as compared with poets with whom he shares much in common.

Milne, W. S. *An Introduction to Geoffrey Hill*. Vol. 3. London: Agenda/Bellew, 1998. An introductory account of Hill's work.

Roberts, Andrew Michael. *Geoffrey Hill: Writers and Their Work*. Tavistock, England: British Council & Northcote House Educational, 2004. This introductory account of Hill's work combines close readings of poems with reviews of critical debates.

William Boyle

TRUE HONOR

Author: Dee Henderson
First published: Sisters, Oreg.: Multnomah, 2002
Genre: Novel
Subgenres: Adventure; romance
Core issues: Attachment and detachment; constancy; good vs. evil; love; responsibility; service

Former Central Intelligence Agency agent Darcy St. James goes back into service in the wake of assassinations and terrorist plots connected with the 9/11 attacks. Navy SEAL Sam Houston gives her protective cover after she is stabbed. As she builds a case against a terrorist financier, they end up working in tandem, her covert activities meshing with his team's direct actions. The pair, who share a deep faith in God, come to love each other. Their target is finally brought down in Nassau but in an unexpected way. They look forward to sharing their future together.

Principal characters
Darcy St. James, a CIA agent and questing Christian
Sam "Cougar" Houston, a Navy SEAL, Chief Petty Officer in Special Operations
Gabriel Arneau, a longtime CIA agent, Darcy's former partner and immediate supervisor
Sergey Alexandrov, a former KGB station chief and Russian spy, now officially retired
Luther Genault, a former Czech intelligence agent, now an investor and "arranger" for various terrorist acts
Vladimir Kurst, Luther's number-two man
Tom "Wolf" Yates, Sam's teammate, newly married
Amy Bond, Darcy's sister, a sheriff in North Dakota

Overview

In *True Honor*, the third installment in Dee Henderson's Uncommon Heroes series, Darcy St. James is enjoying retirement after a danger-studded career as a Central Intelligence Agency (CIA) agent. Still energetic and idealistic at age thirty-five, she is renovating a large old house in North Dakota, near her sister's home. However, Darcy's country needs her one more time.

Her former partner Gabriel calls, requesting her to take on one last mission—meeting with Sergey, a retired Russian spy, to convey a message through unofficial channels. Reluctantly, she agrees to go back on duty for only as long as it takes to complete this task. Waiting at an upscale Florida resort for Sergey to appear, she falls into conversation with Sam Houston, a Navy SEAL who is attending his teammate Tom's wedding. Darcy and Sam like each other immediately but seem unlikely to meet again.

Sergey hands Darcy the confidential message. Then suddenly he comes at her with a knife. Darcy, caught off guard, manages to block his arm and prevent him from hitting his mark, but she is still injured. A moment later, Sam sees Darcy floundering in the bloody water of the resort's swimming pool. He dashes over to pull her out.

Darcy's first impulse is to chase after Sergey and her second to get to a place of refuge. The first is impossible; Sergey has disappeared. As for the second, Sam insists on going with her. A hectic flight from one secret location to another follows. Gabriel orders her back to Washington, D.C.; two other agents have been taken out that night, and attempts had been made on others' lives. Sam's security clearance is as high as Darcy's, so he goes back with her in the role of guard.

Neither Darcy nor Gabriel can make sense of Sergey's action or the puzzling message he gave Darcy: "It was necessary." The following Tuesday, the assaults on the World Trade Center and the Pentagon take place. Intelligence services learn that Luther Genault, a former Czech intelligence agent turned investor, had advance knowledge of the terrorists' attacks and made stock deals profiting from them. He is now recruiting snipers to target European security officers. Darcy signs on to another tour of duty with the CIA to help nail Luther's organization.

She and Sam find themselves working on the same project. Using powerful new technology, Sam and his teammate Tom "Wolf" Yates covertly record a conversation on a Lebanese beach between Dansky, Luther's operations man, and Battihi, an Egyptian terrorist. Darcy decodes the transmission. Sam's unit sets up demolition devices at a Moroccan compound that serves as a storage area for explosives and a refuge for terrorist operatives.

This raid goes off with textbook perfection, but Luther and his assistant Vladimir remain at large, hidden through false identities and dummy financial entities. Darcy and Gabriel begin the tedious task of monitoring stock-market movements and other data, seeking clues to Luther's activities.

Meanwhile Darcy ponders other puzzles. Sergey's stabbing of her remains out of character and bizarre. Intelligence agents typically do not kill agents working for other countries. When she learns his family had been assassinated, she realizes he was acting under duress. Also, her relationship with Sam is deepening, and she does not know what, if anything, she should do about it. Being part of a strange and interminable "war" makes pursuing a romance seem irresponsible. Still, as they discover the many values they share, above all their faith and sense of duty to country, she concludes that she could find no better husband than Sam, if things work out that way.

During a surreptitious meeting with Sergey—which everyone warned her against—Darcy learns that Luther has probably bought an island. Sergey is on his own personal mission to extract vengeance from Luther for his family's deaths. To find the island, he needs more resources than he can command alone. They make a deal, each trading information that the other needs.

The final search for the terrorist financier begins. The SEALs are brought in, this time to track munitions that Luther has hidden on a rocky Caribbean islet. Eventually both a CIA team and the SEALs converge on the Pierre Hotel in Nassau, where Luther and Renee are hosting a giant birthday party. Plans are in place to keep the suite under heavy surveillance, then nab Vladimir and Luther when the weeklong party breaks up.

However, Luther and Vladimir escape the hotel disguised as German tourists. Darcy realizes that the pair are fleeing the island via a charter helicopter. After rushing to the building's roof, Sam and Darcy see the helicopter bearing Luther and Vladimir fly away, then see it explode in midair. They dash back to the current CIA quarters, only to dodge a barrage of bullets from across the street.

Luther's career and life is over, but somehow it feels all wrong to Darcy. Luther's death is not the result of her months of intensive work, but the act of one man with a personal grudge and a Stinger. Sergey got to Luther first. Darcy cannot begrudge Sergey his revenge, but she still feels cheated. The sense of "unfinished business" will probably always haunt her about this case, but she knows that this is the way God often works.

Christian Themes

True Honor is an unusual blend of post-Cold War spy thriller, military romance, and study of the Christian response to the worldwide terrorist threat. By using a fictional framework, Henderson avoids heavy issues such as whether one should take a pacifist stance or view the war as a just war, or whether the terrorism is the result of a "clash of civilizations," a centuries-old struggle between Christianity and Islam. Indeed, the novel's villains are not motivated by ideology or religious zeal, but by greed for riches and by a fascination with blowing things up. That they are willing to kill indiscriminately in pursuit of these goals makes them evil. Both Darcy and Sam see themselves as warriors in one small battle of the age-old struggle of good against evil.

However, their roles in this struggle and their personalities make them approach it in two different ways. Darcy is dogged and totally focused on her objectives while working on a case. This enables her to endure the boring parts, the days of scanning monotonous data for one clue. Along with her penchant for analysis, she has frequent doubts. She wonders if the struggle will ever be over, if God will help her endure yet another scene in which innocent people die, and if she is missing something right before her eyes that is the key to a larger puzzle. Her doubts are voiced in frequent short, silent prayers. Sam does not deal in doubt. He has supreme trust in God and his cause—a marvelously useful attitude for a soldier. He simply assumes that if he does his best, right will prevail.

There is a recognition that other loyalties also have claims in a Christian's life. The famous "render unto Caesar" admonition allows for the loyalty to country that is so large a part of both main characters' motivations. Similarly, loyalty to family is important. One of Sergey's thematic functions is to show the universality of such claims. Although Sergey served another country and his family is unknown to Darcy, he is basically a moral man. In contrast, the terrorists and their backers are detached from any loyalties beyond themselves.

Love between Darcy and Sam develops out of shared tasks, goals, and values. At their very first meeting, Darcy notices the motifs on Sam's ring—the SEAL emblem and a cross—clues to what is important in his life. The closeness among SEAL Team Nine members is similar to that she has known within small intelligence task forces. All these things form a good basis for their future life together.

Sources for Further Study
Duncan, Melanie C. Review of *True Valor* by Dee Henderson. *Library Journal* 127, no. 2 (February 1, 2002): 78. A review of the second book in the Uncommon Heroes series, which traces the romance that develops between a Navy lieutenant and an Air Force major as they perform exceptional tasks.
Henderson, Dee. *True Devotion*. Sisters, Oreg.: Multnomah, 2000. The first book in Henderson's Uncommon Heroes series contains Sam's teammate Joe "Bear" Baker's story. Many glimpses of SEAL life and work and the motif of God as refuge.
Kiesling, Angie. "Love—and Then Some: With a Handful of Spin-off Genres, Inspirational Romance Just Got a Whole Lot Trickier to Shelve." *Publisher Weekly* 250, no. 37 (September 15, 2003): S4-6. A general article on Christian romance that says Henderson "owns" the romance suspense genre.
Zaleski, Jeff. Review of *True Honor*. *Publishers Weekly* 249, no. 33 (August 19, 2002): 68. Praises the work as an exciting thriller.

Emily Alward

THE TRUTH TELLER

Author: Angela Elwell Hunt (1957-   )
First published: Minneapolis, Minn.: Bethany House, 1999
Genre: Novel
Subgenres: Science fiction; thriller/suspense
Core issues: Acceptance; children; trust in God

Lara Godfrey learns to trust in the will of God as she tries, with the aid of modern reproductive science, to have her dead husband's child. She also has to trust in God while battling a billionaire who wants to prove his bizarre theories of eugenics by using Lara's child and his unique talents.

> *Principal characters*
> *Lara Godfrey*, a physician's assistant
> *Michael Godfrey*, Lara's late husband, a painter
> *Dr. Olivia Densen-Braun*, Lara's boss at the clinic
> *Dr. Helmut Braun*, Olivia's husband, a genetics expert
> *Devin Sloane*, a billionaire villain and eugenicist
> *Connor O'Hara*, Lara and Michael's next-door neighbor
> *The Iceman*, a fifty-three-hundred-year-old Copper Age corpse
> *Hunter Shephard*, Lara's son

Overview

With *The Truth Teller*, Angela Elwell Hunt creates a kinder, gentler techno-thriller in the mold of the works of Michael Crichton. Although some murders do take place, the level of violence is not ratcheted up to the point of gruesomeness, and all the violence is driven by the demands of the plot as well as the necessity of making the villain look suitably callous. Also, the plot presupposes the existence of God, not merely in the minds of the main characters, but as a verifiable event, which rarely if ever happens in a genre that exalts the efficacy of modern science while at the same time warning of its Faustian dangers.

In *The Truth Teller*, Lara Godfrey, a health-care worker in the women's clinic in Charlottesville, Virginia, has just lost her husband from bone cancer and plans to bear his child, using the sperm he had frozen before his death. The villain, Devin Sloane, is an eccentric billionaire whose handsome face makes him attractive to the media. According to Sloane, modern society along with humanity is not evolving but devolving, and the main cause of this general debasement is the variety of pollutions throughout the modern environment, ranging from the physical to the cultural. Thus, when the frozen body of a Copper Age man, *Homo Tyrolensis*, is discovered in the Alps, Sloane obtains a tissue sample in the hopes of siring a new type of human being with it—a purer, less debased human being, whose genetic material would have been closer in time to "the divine spark" that created humanity. Sloane is also a practical eugenicist:

The charity hospital he underwrites not only studies patients to find ways to genetically eradicate their diseases but also sterilizes them so they cannot pass on their imperfections and, it is hinted in the narrative, probably exacerbates their conditions, since nearly 80 percent of them die after they are released.

The character who links Lara to Sloane is Dr. Helmut Braun, who is married to Dr. Olivia Densen-Braun, Lara's boss at the clinic, and is a genetics expert. Sloane pressures Braun to implant Lara with an egg fertilized with material taken from the Iceman; when she comes to term, she will be sedated, her child taken from her, and then raised by Sloane in a physically and culturally antiseptic environment. After she has been implanted with the embryo, Lara discovers this attempt, and escapes with the help of her next-door neighbor, Connor O'Hara, who is a librarian and information specialist.

Lara and her son, the aptly named Hunter Shephard (after his hunter-shepherd "father"), live in Florida for five years, until Sloane's minions discover them, and they return to Virginia, where Connor convinces her to stop fleeing and to fight Sloane; Connor also becomes her husband. During this courtroom battle, the fact that Hunter is a living lie detector, the truth teller of the title, emerges, and after several carefully prepared plot reversals and revelations, the book ends, not with a superficial fairy-tale ending, but an ending in which all the main good characters do live happily ever after, but in the Christian sense.

Christian Themes

The chief religious denomination mentioned in the novel is the Baptists. Lara's benevolent and Santa Claus-like lawyer is a deacon in his Baptist church, and a crucial plot point is highlighted with a reference to the nineteenth century split between the Lying Baptists and the Truthful Baptists, a congregation that split over the question of lying to save lives. Connor O'Hara's father is a minister, and while his denomination is not given, he is said to be still preaching in Lynchburg, Virginia, home to Jerry Falwell and Liberty University.

Almost all the good characters pray, and even Helmut Braun prays for Lara at one point. Sloane himself seems to be religious in that he wants the mother of the Iceman's child to be a "spiritual person," but his use of the word "spiritual" rather than "religious" betrays him. Sloane does not believe that the Iceman was closer to the Christian God, but to all the gods of earlier humankind. His beliefs are rootless and ungrounded, and thus he becomes a kind of anti-father figure in the novel, wishing to control Lara's child totally. Sloane stops at nothing in his pursuit of the tree of knowledge.

The good characters, and Lara in particular, struggle to learn God's will and to accept it. She has to learn this in her strategy to oppose Sloane and in her marriage with Connor. Most of the religious judgments about reproductive therapy are based on a primary belief in the sanctity of human life. Lara will allow only one of her eggs to be fertilized at a time, and her boss Olivia's clinic is known for its respect for the right to life. All of Lara's further decisions about reproductive therapy are based on whether it seems as if God has permitted humans to develop the procedure. The entire question of gene therapy and genetic manipulation to cure diseases seems to be accepted, although in terms of the plot, they become moot points.

Even if Lara cannot be absolutely sure of the rightness of the procedures, she puts their result in God's hands—if it is his will, they will be successful. Thus she permits herself to be impregnated with what she thinks is an embryo created from Michael's sperm and her egg. When Hunter is born, she knows that it is God's will that it happened, and she views Hunter as the tree of life. A small inconsistency here is Lara's refusal to have Hunter's DNA tested to ascertain his parentage. She says she does this because she does not want Hunter to be treated like a piece of property, but the real reason is to complicate the plot. If Hunter is tested, the conflict collapses.

The question that the novel never fully answers is why Hunter has been given the gift of truth telling. He not only can detects lies but also can discern "*absolute* truth," as Lara puts it. Even though she regrets calling Hunter a "little prophet," that is exactly what he is. One of the truths that he proclaims is that God loves everyone, a fact universally accepted by most Christians, and thus almost a greeting-card sentiment. However, when a Buddhist tells Hunter that "All paths lead to God," Hunter answers, "You have believed a great big lie." Hunter is not merely a child who makes adults uncomfortable by pointing out their hidden selves; he denounces the modern tendency to acknowledge the validity of all religions. The main problem for the author at the end of the novel is what to do with this prophet after he has been revealed to modern America, and Hunt's solution is predictable and might seem evasive, but the reader has to admit that dealing with the career of Hunter Shephard O'Hara would require a volume all its own—and prophets are without honor in their own country.

However, the main message of the book is hope. When Lara struggles over whether to have Michael's child, she reads in Proverbs: "Hope deferred makes the heart sick, but when dreams come true, there is life and joy." A woman on a bus (who disappears like an angel) leaves Lara a handwritten copy of lines from Psalm 139, a hymn of hope. The tree of life defeats the tree of knowledge in this world, and certainly in the next.

Sources for Further Study

"Angela Elwell Hunt." *Contemporary Authors Online*. Farmington Hills, Mich.: Thomson Gale, 2007. A short biography of Hunt that lists her many works.

Butler, Tamara. Review of *A Time to Mend* by Angela Elwell Hunt. *Library Journal* 131, no. 6 (April 1, 2006): 78. This romance between a nurse and a doctor examines what happens when an oncology nurse gets breast cancer.

Hunt, Angela. "To Hollywood with Jesus, Mary, and Joseph." *Tampa Tribune*, December 10, 2006, p. 1. Hunt describes her experiences writing a book to accompany the film *The Nativity Story* (2006). She talks about the process of writing.

Moore, Waveney. "Prolific Writer's Goals Are Lofty, and So Are Her Themes." *St. Petersburg Times*, August 21, 2005, p. 11. Article describes Hunt's methods as a writer and her work on a novel about Mary Magdalene.

William Laskowski

THE TWILIGHT OF COURAGE

Authors: Bodie Thoene (1951-   ) and Brock Thoene (1952-   )
First published: Nashville, Tenn.: T. Nelson, 1994
Genre: Novel
Subgenre: Historical fiction (twentieth century)
Core issues: Compassion; constancy; courage; ethics; good vs. evil; Judaism; redemption; sacrifice; self-abandonment; suffering

This historical novel weaves together certain events surrounding the beginning of World War II—from the destruction of Warsaw in the fall of 1939 until the fall of Dunkirk in the spring of 1940—with the lives of its characters, confronting the reader with both the moral failure and moral victory of nations and individuals.

>   *Principal characters*
>   *Josephine Marlow*, the protagonist, an American journalist
>   *Mac McGrath*, a cameraman with Movietone News
>   *André Chardon*, a French army colonel
>   *Horst von Brockman*, a major in the German army
>   *Katrina von Brockman*, Horst's wife
>   *Richard Lewinski*, a Polish Jew and genius mathematician
>   *David Meyer*, an American pilot who volunteers for the Royal Air Force
>   *Trevor Galway*, a British navy lieutenant aboard HMS Intrepid
>   *Yacov Lubetkin*, the infant son of Etta and Aaron Lubetkin, victims of the Nazis

Overview

In *The Twilight of Courage*, the husband-and-wife team of Brock and Bodie Thoene explore the interplay of political events in Europe at the start of World War II as they imprinted themselves upon the lives of the novel's principal characters and how the frayed moral fabric of the time brought people to personal crises just as it brought the continent to war. The novel begins with Rabbi Lebowitz, in Jerusalem, praying for the safety of his granddaughter, Etta Lubetkin, and her family in Warsaw, Poland. Rabbi Lebowitz's granddaughter, Etta, her husband, Aaron Lubetkin, and their children—the smallest of whom is the infant Yacov—have been arrested for trying to leave Warsaw's Jewish ghetto without permission. They are taken captive by the Nazis to be incarcerated. Etta is able to hide Yacov with a Christian Polish woman just before the Lubetkin family is herded aboard a train for the slave camps.

Josephine Marlow, an American news correspondent assigned to Europe, realizes that she has waited too long to leave Warsaw. She finds herself working as an emergency relief worker for the wounded in a Warsaw's bombed-out St. John's Cathedral.

Just before Poland surrenders to Germany, Marlow is placed in German custody as an American press neutral to be questioned and shipped to the Netherlands; from there she ultimately finds her way to London.

Horst von Brockman, a German army officer who is not an official member of the Nazi Party and does not agree with all Nazi political positions, witnesses the brutality of the Nazis' methods of dealing with enemy prisoners in Warsaw. Von Brockman is aghast at what he sees, but he is warned to suppress his moral outrage for the sake of his career and the personal safety of his family as well as himself.

Meanwhile, the entire world sits on its hands as Nazi Germany and Russia both attack and virtually destroy the national identity of Poland. The nation's leaders are either imprisoned or killed, and the country is carved into pieces as spoils for the aggressors. England and France are afraid to confront German chancellor Adolf Hitler, not because they are not powerful enough to engage the Nazi army but simply because they are willing to sacrifice Poland and other Eastern European countries to appease the aggressor and, they hope, avoid war altogether. The United States sees the struggle as a purely European matter, choosing neutrality as the economically prudent course.

David Meyer, a young American crop duster, disagrees with his country's neutrality stand. Besides, he likes the idea of flying the incredibly fast and maneuverable Hurricane fighter planes that the British Royal Air Force (RAF) has developed. Meyer decides to renounce his U.S. citizenship and flee to Canada, where he joins the RAF. He soon finds himself on a transport ship headed for England, where he will be trained to fly the Hurricane and then be assigned to combat. After undergoing the RAF's intense training program, Meyer flies combat sorties from a base in France that borders the neutral state of Belgium.

In a semi-covert operation, intelligence officer Colonel André Chardon has secretly invited Polish mathematical genius Richard Lewinski to his home to attempt to break the code of the infamous Nazi Enigma cryptograms. Lewinski was a ranking operative in Poland when the Enigma machines were being designed, but because of his Jewish heritage he was designated as undesirable when the Nazis came to power. Consequently, Lewinski is the object of a Nazi manhunt as a Jewish escapee as well as a potential intelligence saboteur.

American Mac McGrath, a cameraman for Movietone News, escapes Warsaw just before the Nazi invasion. An associate and would-be paramour of Josephine Marlow, McGrath believes that Marlow is safely on her way out of Poland as he is making his own escape from the invading Nazi assault. After his escape from Poland, Movietone News reassigns McGrath to cover the "Phony War," as it is known among the Allied countries. McGrath continues to develop his already keen skill for inserting himself into the front lines of every combat situation. He ultimately chooses the adventure of his life as a war correspondent over a life as the lover and husband of Marlow.

As the continuing aggression of Nazi Germany pushes the West toward war, the lives of the characters begin to face moral dilemmas that mirror those of the nations on the brink of war. Von Brockman sees the clear moral void of his country's policies and the depravity of the atrocities committed by the Gestapo's SS (Nazi police) units in the field. On the other hand, his identity as a man is invested in his role as a warrior, not merely a professional soldier. These forces collide in a crisis of honor when, after being sickened by the treatment of Jews in Poland, von Brockman agrees to save a single Polish Jewish infant, Yacov Lubetkin. This decision saves not only the baby's life but also von Brockman's soul.

Chardon is on secret assignment in England when he learns that his lover, Elaine Snow, has been murdered by the Nazis, allegedly for conspiring to assassinate Hitler at a Munich beer hall. Chardon not only grieves over the death of Snow but also faces his own failure to confront the anti-Semitic bigotry of his family by marrying Snow and accepting the child he has fathered as his own.

England finally rejects the failed leadership of Prime Minister Neville Chamberlain and embraces the bold resistance against Nazi aggression advocated by Winston Churchill. Consequently, England enters the fray to assist France as Germany makes its "end-run" around the Maginot line. France makes drastic changes in its military leadership, albeit almost too late. As Germany invades through Belgium, the Netherlands, and the Ardennes Forest, it virtually surrounds the British and French fighters and nearly destroys them, driving them into the sea and a devastating rout at Dunkirk.

Just as the nations of France and England suffer disaster and are nearly defeated as a consequence of their lax moral strength in resisting evil, the novel's characters—Chardon, Lewinski, McGrath, and even the innocent Yacov Lubetkin—endure catastrophic pain and anxiety, escaping only with their lives.

Christian Themes

The foundational Christian theme of *The Twilight of Courage* is the ongoing necessity to resist evil in order to allow good to survive and triumph. The novel juxtaposes this struggle at two levels—personal and national—as both characters and nations are torn by their desire for "peace at any price" and the need to identify and confront evil for what it is.

At the personal level, Horst von Brockman and André Chardon illustrate this internal moral battleground, played out on a physical battleground. Von Brockman, a Nazi officer, and Chardon, a French officer, are beset by their respective moral cataclysms as they simultaneously function as players in the wartime drama of their homelands. Appalled by the utter brutality and depravity of the Gestapo forces during the invasion of Poland, von Brockman is shaken to his core as he tries to find honorable footing on which to continue as a professional warrior. Chardon, an officer in the French army, which is standing against the Nazis' abominable treatment of the Jews, has fallen in love with a Jewish woman whom he refuses to marry and fathers a child he is reluctant to claim as his own in the face of his family's anti-Semitism. This story brings these men face-to-face with the truth of their real characters as they decide how they will conduct their lives.

On the field of nations, a similar moral dichotomy unfolds at the beginning of the war. Germany, rising out of a period of economic recession and poverty to regional prominence, has become aggressive toward its neighbors, embracing a totalitarian form of government that is heavily invested in military might. As Germany flexes its military muscles in Europe, the traditional standardbearers of freedom and democracy, England and France, take a weak, conciliatory approach to German foreign policy. The French and English find, to their consternation, that the more they placate Hitler, the more aggressive he becomes. Finally turning from appeasement to resistance, the Allies engage evil in a just war.

Sources for Further Study

Carrigan, Henry, Jr. Review of *The Twilight of Courage. Library Journal* 119, no. 18 (November 1, 1994): 65. A brief review of the novel.

Cooper, Ilene, and Sally Estes. "Upfront: Advance Reviews." *Booklist* 91, no. 2 (September 15, 1994): 84. Recommended novels for young adults, including *The Twilight of Courage*.

Groot, Tracy. "Thoenes Hinge Their Books on Small Details." *Grand Rapids Press*, November 13, 1994, p. J11. Brief overview of the Thoenes, from their discovery by actor John Wayne.

Holmes, Cecile S. "Exploring Ethics Through Fiction: Husband-Wife Writing Team Is a Novel Success." *Houston Chronicle*, December 17, 1994, p. 1. A profile of the husband-and-wife team, the Thoenes, authors of historical and Christian fiction, which praises their "meticulous research." Photo.

Mort, John. Review of *The Twilight of Courage. Booklist* 91, no. 2 (September 15, 1994): 84. A lukewarm review.

Joseph P. Pendergast

TWO FROM GALILEE
A Love Story

Author: Marjorie Holmes (Marjorie Mighell; 1910-2002)
First published: Old Tappan, N.J.: Revell, 1972
Genre: Novel
Subgenres: Biblical fiction; historical fiction (first century)
Core issues: Courage; faith; guidance; illumination; Incarnation; Judaism; revelation; trust in God; virginity

A portrayal of the lives of two young Jewish people, Mary and Joseph, from their marriage until the birth of Jesus, this novel allows readers to live the human drama of teenagers in love in first century Palestine—perhaps the most significant love story in human history. Mary and Joseph strain the customs and mores of their religion and their society to follow God as he directs their lives in the most mundane details. The familiar story is retold in the fresh light of real human emotion, apart from the traditional trappings of religion.

Principal characters
  Mary, the protagonist, daughter of Hannah and Joachim, wife of Joseph, and mother of Jesus
  Hannah, Joachim's wife, Mary's mother
  Joachim, Hannah's husband, Mary's father
  Joseph, Mary's husband, the son of Jacob and Timna
  Elizabeth, sister of Hannah and aunt to Mary

Overview

Novelist Marjorie Holmes explores the emotions of young romance through the biblical characters of Mary and Joseph in *Two from Galilee*. As the story begins, Mary, the eldest child of Hannah and Joachim of the village of Nazareth in Galilee, has just experienced her first menstrual period, ushering her into womanhood. As would be the case in first century Palestine, the next phase in Mary's life, and the family's main concern, is a proper and fitting marriage.

Mary is not interested in the more prosperous of her prospects. Rather, she insists on marrying the man of her girlhood dreams, Joseph the carpenter. In a culture where love is perhaps the least valued consideration in choosing a marriage partner—a function left to parents rather than the participants in the marriage—Mary's feelings are not given serious consideration. Mary, however, demonstrates some of the courage and constancy that will characterize her life as she digs in her heels and persuades her father to entertain Joseph as a serious suitor for her hand in marriage. Hannah, heretofore always a dominant force in the affairs of the family, finds herself at odds with her daughter, who has the impertinence to interfere in affairs between her parents.

Hannah also has much at stake personally in the social value of Mary's nuptial union, since she has long touted Mary as one of Nazareth's most desirable young women because of her natural beauty, grace, and quick wit. Therefore, Hannah is utterly opposed to Mary's choice of a carpenter, of all people, as a husband.

In the midst of arranging the marriage, matters go from tense to unbearable. After Mary has held her ground, persuading her father to accept the marriage proposal of Joseph, suddenly Mary receives a revelation from God that she has been chosen to become the mother of the Messiah. This news is not unsettling until the angel who delivers the message tells Mary that Joseph is not going to be the father, but God is. Mary must now confront not only Hannah, a mother who is very disappointed with her daughter's choice of husbands, but also the prospect of becoming the "secret" mother of God, because no one will believe in the possibility of this virgin birth. Mary must deal with the social stigma of being pregnant out of wedlock and with the prospect of convincing her betrothed that she has not been cheating on him. Mary's courage, faith, and trust in God are tested to the breaking point during the following months.

In her embarrassment, Hannah, hoping that Mary's lack of a menstrual period has been caused by stress or emotional turmoil, suggests that Mary go to visit her aunt, Hannah's older sister, Elizabeth. Elizabeth, the wife of Zachariah, a Levite priest in the Jerusalem Temple, lives on the outskirts of Jerusalem in a dwelling much more luxurious than that of Hannah and Joachim. Mary is comforted by Elizabeth, herself pregnant in old age. The two women—aunt and niece—form a friendship that proves to be providential for Mary. Nevertheless, she is continually anxious about how Joseph will react to her conundrum. Will he accept her as his wife, or will he divorce her as unfaithful? Knowing that the social circumstances preclude the celebratory wedding that the families have planned, and realizing that, as a tradesman, her soon-to-be husband will face the brunt of villagers' disapproval daily, Mary is caught between the desire to be with her family and the need to know the mind and heart of Joseph.

Mary and Joseph begin their married life together under the cloud of social censure, but also in the euphoria that brings joy to the hearts of all newlyweds. They are at last together as husband and wife, awaiting the birth of their firstborn, when Joseph hears the news that the Roman emperor has decreed that a census be taken of the entire empire and that each male head of household be counted in the location of the family's ancestral home. Thus begins the journey of the very pregnant Mary and Joseph to Joseph's ancestral home, the city of David: Bethlehem.

Holmes marvelously paints the lives of these two singular humans, with whose story her readers are so familiar, in moving and palpable detail until the months just following the birth of the child.

Christian Themes

Two from Galilee is a story of family life, especially as that relates to young adults in the culture of first century Judaism. The societal mores and strong familial bonds cementing the culture are all in evidence here. Layered on this depiction of Jewish culture and daily life is the overarching belief in the centrality of God to life. God as the center is foundational, not only to Judaism but also to the followers of Jesus.

This is dramatically evidenced in the character of Mary as she places herself totally in God's hands, even to her obvious social peril and detriment. God is also at the center of Joseph's life: Joseph opens himself to the guidance of God's spirit and accepts circumstances—a virgin birth—totally beyond his comprehension. Joseph goes about his daily work of making a living and preparing a home for his family in a community that is well aware that he is not the father of Mary's baby. He overcomes his masculine pride, dealing with both with his own doubts and with social ostracism, to maintain his faith in Mary and in God. Although it takes some time for Mary's parents to accept God's will, they eventually do, Joachim with some initial wavering and Hannah, the controlling manipulator, finally accepting that God has truly chosen her daughter to bear the Messiah. Each of these exemplifies true faith in God. This faith is depicted with a realism that reveals the daily struggles to accept God's will—as a faith that is lived out every day in ordinary life, in the dust of the farm, the carpenter shop, and the kitchen.

Sources for Further Study

Holmes, Marjorie. *Three from Galilee*. San Francisco: Harper & Row, 1985. In this sequel, Holmes portrays the daily life and struggles of the Holy Family, Mary, Joseph, and Jesus, during the Nazareth years. The author applies her insightful character development not only to the humanity of Mary and Joseph but also to the Savior himself.

_____. *The Messiah*. New York: Harper & Row, 1987. The third novel in the series portrays Jesus' ministry and Passion.

Nixon, C. Robert. Review of *The Messiah*. *Library Journal* 112, no. 15 (September 15, 1987): 94. This review of the third novel of the series concludes that, "on the whole, Holmes has done a remarkably good job, giving us a believably divine human and nicely drawing the characters that surround him."

Widmer, Cynthia. Review of *Three from Galilee*. *Library Journal* 110, no. 15 (September 15, 1985): 93. A review of Holmes's first sequel to *Two from Galilee*.

Joseph P. Pendergast

UNATTAINABLE EARTH

Author: Czesław Miłosz (1911-2004)
First published: Nieobjeta ziemia, 1984 (English translation, 1986)
Edition used: Unattainable Earth, translated by the author and Robert Hass. New York: Ecco Press, 1986
Genre: Poetry
Subgenres: Lyric poetry; spiritual treatise
Core issues: Beauty; Catholics and Catholicism; doubt; good vs. evil; life; memory

In this collection of poetry and meditation, Miłosz engages the contradictions of being. He celebrates the richness of the sensuous world (which he casts in Edenic terms) while simultaneously contemplating the insufficiencies of language, intrusions of history, and the individual shortcomings of his private spiritual development. Miłosz's judicious praise is an attempt to embrace the real, in all its multiplicity and fleetingness, by seeking to draw together as many voices and human perspectives as possible against the inexorability of time.

Overview

In *Unattainable Earth*, Czesław Miłosz's first collection of poetry published after receiving the Nobel Prize in 1980, he sets himself a task that he acknowledges is unachievable: to create a literature that embraces a world too immense for our limited vision and insufficient language. In his preface, Miłosz notes that the Polish title for the collection means "earth too huge to be grasped," which provides both a central thematic figure and a sense of scale for the poet's ambition "to transcend my place and time, searching for the Real."

In his poems, the writer not only shrugs against the limitations of consciousness and humanity's fallen state but also struggles against the constraints of form. Rather than simply a collection of poems, *Unattainable Earth* is much more. It is filled with aphorisms and philosophical pronouncements as well as lyric poetry, and the book expands its formal boundaries by mortaring what Miłosz calls "Inscripts"—prose fragments and full poems by other authors, even letters he received—into the architecture of the collection.

These interpolations are wide-ranging but consistent. They include passages from the third century *Corpus Hermeticum* (a collection of Greek texts from a more extensive group of works containing secret wisdom known as Hermetica), as well as writings by Miłosz's more immediate spiritual forebears, such as the philosopher Simone Weil and his cousin, the French poet and mystic Oscar V. de L. Miłosz. The inscripts, including poems by D. H. Lawrence and Walt Whitman, were initially translated by Miłosz into Polish, but remain in their original form in the English version as "an homage to tutelary spirits."

Taken together, this anthology—or "mosaic," as Miłosz puts it—makes up a kind of individual spiritual autobiography. Its variety of voices, both in terms of the authors incorporated into the body of the book and the numerous personas addressed and adopted by the poet, only underscores the focus of its mediation. What does it mean, the writer questions, to be an individual in the world?

On one hand, his tactic is a mode of protection and self-preservation; as Miłosz acknowledges, his efforts offer a means of countering mortality. This is achieved not through literary glory, or even certainty in an eternal reward, but through an imaginative association with others: "I invent stories, similar to my own, a lifted elbow, the combing of hair before a mirror. I multiplied myself and came to inhabit every one of them separately, thus my impermanence has no power over me."

Even more, however, the act of connecting with others is an act of compassion, an attempt to remember and to recognize the worth of a single existence, "to embrace the poor lives of beings." In numerous poems, Miłosz asserts the value of individuals by sketching them: a former teacher, Father Chomski; a fellow poet from his youth whose obituary he had received; numerous anonymous or scarcely recollected figures. The particularity of these lives leads to a universal recognition of the plight and the splendor of what it is to be human.

Similarly, Miłosz describes his fascination with art objects, though his response is not that of an aesthete; instead, he finds in them the pulse of past existences. "The witnesses are old things, undimmed, dense/ With the life of human hands: the intense reds/ in stained glass, stone lacework, marble heads. . . ." It is the sturdy wooden table at which he senses the touch of other fingers that captures his sympathy and leads him to recognize that he, like those before him, will pass through mortality without leaving more than a trace of the essential quality of his selfhood.

The poet acknowledges that, despite his struggles to resurrect figures both known and imagined, he fails to represent the true richness of human lives. This failure is largely due to his own insufficiencies and the inability of language to capture actuality. Miłosz continually laments that he is unable to express the always elusive quality of lives, admitting in one of his prose fragments that "every one of my efforts to say something real ended the same way, by my being driven back to the enclosure of form, as if I were a sheep straying from the flock." Language, he says, is weak, and he regrets his inability to write with the kind of purity and detachment demanded by the pressures of suffering and history.

Yet the poet's lament at the instability of language is voiced with a contradictory, balancing impulse: the poet's astonishment at his own being. "What use are you? In your writings there is nothing except immense amazement." Despite the relentlessness of mortality, the poet is able to assert his ego in the face of human tragedy and decline. He is given a space in which time loosens its power, in which language may be enough. Such an eternal instant appears in the poem, "At Dawn," a grace note in which he is able to write, "Only this moment at dawn is real to me./ The bygone lives are like my own past life, uncertain./ I cast a spell on the city asking it to last."

Christian Themes

Unattainable Earth is a confession of doubt and a prayer that the poet's offering, however insufficient, may still be accepted. Despite his firm Catholic imagination, Miłosz admits to his inability to achieve an unshaken belief, a struggle that characterizes his spiritual engagement: "sometimes believing, sometimes not believing,/ With others like myself I unite in worship." He minimizes the quality of faith within himself, claiming that "I was not a spiritual man but flesh-enraptured,/ Called to celebrate Dionysian dances."

Miłosz links the presence of *eros* in his imagination with his attentive observance of the sensuous world, a quality that informs his understanding of Christian theology and biblical myth. Thus, when he turns to the story of Adam and Eve in his collection's first section, he does not retell the account in Genesis as an investigation of innocence and sin. Instead, Eden becomes an allegory of consciousness; Miłosz, marveling at the "otherness and sameness" of his lover, wonders that "Not one, divided in two, not two, united in one:/ The second I, so that I may be conscious of myself.// And together with you eat fruits from the Tree of Knowledge/ And by twisting roads make our way through deserts."

Even more central to his theological thought is the problem of suffering. In a poem entitled "Theodicy," he addresses "my sweet theologians" who debate the existence of pain in a world created by a benevolent God. "A decent man cannot believe that a good God wanted such a world," he exclaims. Because of the weight of this empathy, and despite his public position as a Catholic intellectual, Miłosz described himself as a Manichaean.

Yet above all else, Miłosz's poetry is an effort to praise God and champion being against the powers of "the Great Spirit of Nonbeing,/ The Prince of this World." His effort at seeking the real is itself an act of worship. The collection ends with the affirmation,

> To find my home in one sentence, concise, as if hammered in metal. Not to enchant anybody. Not to earn a lasting name in posterity. An unnamed need for order, for rhythm, for form, which three words are opposed to chaos and nothingness.

Sources for Further Study

Fiut, Aleksander. *The Eternal Moment: The Poetry of Czesław Miłosz*. Berkeley: University of California Press, 1990. A book-length study that offers an investigation into Miłosz's philosophy and poetry, including his efforts to respond to the "erosion of the Christian imagination."

Miłosz, Czesław. *Conversations*. Edited by Cynthia L. Haven. Jackson: University Press of Mississippi, 2006. Collection of interviews from 1980 to 2001, including conversations about the challenges of writing poetry in what the poet calls "a largely post-religious world."

_____. *Native Realm: A Search for Self-Definition*. Translated by Catherine S. Leach. Garden City, N.Y.: Doubleday, 1968. Autobiography that introduces both the author's life and his philosophy, displaying ways in which Miłosz's experiences shaped and were enriched by his theological strivings.

Miłosz, Czesław, and Thomas Merton. *Striving Towards Being: The Letters of Thomas Merton and Czesław Miłosz*. Edited by Robert Faggen. New York: Farrar, Straus and Giroux, 1997. Correspondence between Miłosz and the Trappist monk and writer, Thomas Merton, illuminating the spiritual elements of Miłosz's poetry and thought, including their role in his political writing.

Todd Samuelson

UNCLE TOM'S CABIN
Or, Life Among the Lowly

Author: Harriet Beecher Stowe (1811-1896)
First published: 1851-1852 (serial), 1852 (book)
Edition used: Uncle Tom's Cabin: Authoritative Text, Backgrounds and Contexts, Criticism, edited by Elizabeth Ammons. New York: W. W. Norton, 1994
Genre: Novel
Subgenre: Romance
Core issues: African Americans; *agape*; church; ethics; freedom and free will; martyrdom; social action

Stowe's romance was written to protest the Fugitive Slave Act of 1850 and criticize Christians for failing to condemn slavery in the North and South.

> *Principal characters*
> *Uncle Tom,* the protagonist, a pious slave
> *Arthur Shelby,* Tom's owner
> *Emily Shelby,* Mr. Shelby's wife
> *George Shelby,* the Shelbys' son
> *Eliza Harris,* Mrs. Shelby's maid
> *George Harris,* Eliza's husband
> *Tom Loker,* a man hired by Arthur Shelby to retrieve Eliza and her son
> *Augustine St. Clare,* Tom's master in New Orleans
> *Evangeline,* called Little Eva, St. Clare's daughter
> *Simon Legree,* a cruel master
> *Cassy* and
> *Emmeline,* slaves on Legree's plantation

Overview

Harriet Beecher Stowe's *Uncle Tom's Cabin: Or, Life Among the Lowly* (1852) is a romance that protests the Fugitive Slave Act (1850). As part of the Compromise of 1850, the Fugitive Slave Act made the federal government, via federal commissioners, responsible for apprehending runaway slaves and returning them to their alleged owners in the South. The federal commissioners were allowed to deputize citizens and force them to seize and report fugitive slaves, even against their wills, or face fines and imprisonment. This act galvanized opinions in the North against slavery and fueled the movement for abolition. Stowe's novel uses abolitionist rhetoric to criticize Christian churches, particularly the Presbyterian Church, for failing to condemn slavery in the North and South. Stowe's representation of slavery and of fugitive slaves calls on readers to respond to the question of slavery and the Fugitive Slave Act with an ethics rooted in Christian love and civil disobedience.

Arthur Shelby, in debt and facing dispossession and bankruptcy, decides to pay his mortgage by selling two slaves, Uncle Tom and Harry, to a trader named Mr. Haley. When Mr. Shelby tells his wife, Emily, about his agreement with Mr. Haley, she is angry and refuses to be her husband's accomplice. Mrs. Shelby despises the institution of slavery because it is incompatible with her Christian values. She is upset by her husband's business deal with Mr. Haley because two families will be divided. Through Mrs. Shelby's voice, which condemns complicity with slavery as hypocritical, Stowe appeals to Christian mothers who, like Mrs. Shelby, thought that they could "gild" slavery, cover it over with "kindness, and care, and instruction." Mrs. Shelby's conscience and sympathies are moved by the emotional devastation caused by the separation of families. She represents Stowe's notion that mothers have the ability "to love and feel for all mankind" because of the love they "learned" to feel for their own children.

By representing the slaves' responses to the violation of their families under the institution of slavery, Stowe humanizes slaves by showing their familial bonds. Eliza, Mrs. Shelby's maid, tells Uncle Tom and Aunt Chloe of Mr. Shelby's plans and explains that she will flee with her son, hoping to prevent a separation she cannot bear. She is heading north to find her husband, George Harris, also a fugitive slave. While Uncle Tom's wife encourages him to flee with Eliza rather than be sold down the river, he tells her: "It's better for me alone to go, than to break up the place and sell all." Putting the good of the slave community ahead of his own desires, Tom leaves his family to go to a Mississippi slave market with Haley.

Haley chases after Eliza, but forewarned, she miraculously escapes Haley when she crosses the Ohio River. Haley, refusing to accept the loss, hires Tom Loker to bring Eliza and her son back to him under the statutes of the Fugitive Slave Act. Eliza and Harry eventually make their way to a Quaker settlement where George and Eliza find each other but are still being hunted by Loker. While George eventually shoots Loker to avoid being captured, Eliza convinces George and the Quakers to give Loker medical attention at another settlement.

On a steamboat headed for Mississippi, Tom befriends a young, white girl named Evangeline, called Little Eva, whose father, Augustine St. Clare, buys Tom from Haley. Now, Tom is in New Orleans and a slave in the St. Clare household. Two years later, Eva becomes very ill and dies. After her death, St. Clare decides to set Tom free; however, St. Clare dies before completing the legal paperwork. Tom is sold by Marie Clare, Augustine St. Clare's wife, to Simon Legree, who takes Tom to rural Louisiana. Legree abuses Tom, especially after Tom refuses to beat fellow slaves when Legree commands him to do so. Cassy and Emmeline, also slaves on Legree's plantation, devise a plan to escape. When they hide in Legree's house, Legree assumes that they have fled and thinks Tom knows where they are. Tom prays and refuses to reveal Cassy and Emmeline's stratagem. Legree orders his overseers to beat Tom. Rather than listen to the sneering words of hate, Tom hears "a higher voice" saying, "Fear not them that kill the body, and, after that, have no more that they can do," which is an allusion to Christ's words to the Apostles in Matthew 11:28. Legree threatens Tom's life and demands to know where Cassy and Emmeline are. When Tom refuses to reveal their location, Legree strikes him. Tom, near death, forgives Legree and the overseers. The suffering black slave extends forgiveness to his murderers, bestowing the gift of love on his tormentors and becoming a Christlike figure of absolute good. George Shelby arrives at Legree's plantation hoping to buy Tom's freedom, but he is too late. Tom tells George, "O, Mas'r George, ye're too late. The Lord's bought me, and is going to take me home." Tom's martyrdom convinces George to free his slaves and pay them for their work.

Heading toward freedom, Cassy and Emmeline travel to Canada. The Harris family is further reunited when Cassy realizes and reveals that Eliza is her long-lost daughter. After going to France, the Harrises adopt the idea of African colonization and decide to emigrate to Liberia. George hopes to strengthen the nation of Liberia, "which shall have a voice in the council of nations," in hopes of gaining visibility and a voice in the public sphere.

Christian Themes

Uncle Tom's Cabin was written during the crisis of the 1850's, when the nation was divided over the question of slavery—an institution that had become so ingrained in the nation's (particularly the South's) economy that it would lead the country into civil war. The inhumanity of slavery had been legitimated in 1789 with the ratification of the Constitution and its "three-fifths" clause (Article I, section 2, paragraph 3), which gave slaveholding states disproportionate power within the federal government. The clause, later superseded by the Fourteenth Amendment, embodied an earlier compromise over the formula used for collecting taxes and apportioning representation in Congress. The passage of the Compromise of 1850 became a powerful weapon in the antislavery discourse of Christians and abolitionists because it gave slavery extraterritoriality and made slavery a national institution in states where slavery had been abolished. The "compromise" of the Fugitive Slave Act required Northern citizens to enforce the slave laws of the South as a constitutional obligation. Thus, Northern citizens were forced to choose between obeying the law, which required them to remand fugitive slaves, and transgressing it.

Stowe charges each scene of her novel with abolitionist and religious rhetoric that describes slavery as un-Christian and immoral. In chapter 45, Stowe, speaking of the Fugitive Slave Act, says that for many years she avoided the subject of slavery but could not continue to be silent on the subject once she witnessed "Christian . . . people actually recommending the remanding of escaped fugitives into slavery, as a duty binding on good citizens." She describes the legalization of slavery as a system that makes the slave owner an irresponsible despot corrupted with absolute power. She chides Christians for their complicity with slavery by asserting that "the people of the free states" are "guilty . . . before God" for their complicity with slavery because "they have not the apology of education or custom." Speaking of slaves, she writes, "how much more they [slaves] might do, if the Christian church would act toward them in the spirit of her Lord!" Stowe recommends that the Christian church lift up the slaves by educating them before helping them leave the country for Liberia or Canada. Stowe's jeremiad warns Americans and the "Church of Christ" to recognize the "signs of the times" and refuse to perpetuate the injustice of the status quo. The self-proclaimed prophetess, who asserted later in life that as the author of *Uncle Tom's Cabin* she was but a humble instrument of God's words, begs her Christian readers to repent of their injustice and accept God's grace. She asks them: "[C]an you forget that prophecy associates, in dread fellowship, the day of vengeance with the year of his redeemed?"

Writing to a Protestant audience, Stowe dramatizes the opposition between the institution of slavery and the ideologies supporting it against Christian ethics and values. She asserts, in the final chapter of *Uncle Tom's Cabin* ("Concluding Remarks"), that no Christian who understands the horrors of slavery should be able to tolerate it. For Stowe, Christianity and Christian sentiment rests on a principle of universal love, or *agape*—redemptive goodwill toward all people. This form of love surpasses *eros* and philia because it asks for nothing in return. *Agape* has the power to call out to consciences and call people to responsibility. Thus Stowe points the way to social transformation through a story that represents the power of Christian love.

Sources for Further Study

Kazin, Alfred. *God and the American Writer*. New York: Alfred A. Knopf, 1997. Chapter 3, "Christians and Their Slaves (Harriet Beecher Stowe and Others)," provides excellent historical context for Stowe's literary works and religious ideas.

Sizer, Lyde Cullen. *The Political Work of Northern Women Writers and the Civil War, 1850-1872*. Chapel Hill: University of North Carolina Press, 2000. Discusses Stowe as a religious visionary while comparing and contrasting her work with texts by Lydia Child and Fanny Fern.

Wilson, Edmund. *Patriotic Gore: Studies in the Literature of the American Civil War*. New York: W. W. Norton, 1994. The first chapter of Wilson's book is devoted to a discussion of Stowe's religious influences and beliefs within the context of the debates leading up to the Civil War.

Trisha M. Brady

THE UNEASY CONSCIENCE OF MODERN FUNDAMENTALISM

Author: Carl F. H. Henry (1913-2003)
First published: Grand Rapids, Mich.: Wm. B. Eerdmans, 1947
Genre: Nonfiction
Subgenres: Essays; theology
Core issues: Ethics; poverty; racism; social action

Because Fundamentalism has retreated from social involvement and focused on individual salvation and personal morality, Henry calls Christians who believe in the supernatural to engage the world and lead the movement for social reform. Modern Fundamentalism has an uneasy conscience because it knows it is called to this role and has shirked this duty.

Overview

In the first half of the twentieth century, division arose among Protestant denominations between people who believed the Bible was God's word about humanity (Fundamentalists, a term Carl F. H. Henry capitalizes in his book) and those who believed it was a human world about God (Liberals). On a denominational level, the Fundamentalists lost most of the battles, and the Liberals came to dominate the larger denominations. Because the Liberals emphasized the social aspects of Christianity, the Fundamentalists retreated to individual concerns. In response to Henry's challenge, the National Association of Evangelicals was strengthened, Fuller Theological Seminary was founded, and ther periodical *Christianity Today* was established. Henry not only called for these developments but also was instrumental in all three institutions.

The Uneasy Conscience of Modern Fundamentalism contains eight addresses that Henry originally delivered at Gordon College of Theology and Missions in Boston. In the first, "The Evaporation of Fundamentalist Humanitarianism," he says that Fundamentalists make much of the embarrassment of religious Liberalism. Two world wars and an intervening depression have shown the Liberal Christians' belief in human goodness and inevitable progress to be false. Seeing that one's opponents are wrong does not, however, make one's own position right. Fundamentalism has withdrawn from society and has no agenda for confronting the problems of aggressive warfare, racial hatred and intolerance, the liquor traffic, and the injustices of management and labor. Moreover, Fundamentalists no longer even point out these evils in their preaching. Some have concluded from the silence of the Fundamentalists that they have no plan for social improvement because their pessimism about human nature leads them to believe that no social progress is possible.

In chapter 2, "The Protest Against Foredoomed Failure," Henry notes that nothing could be less true than the idea that the biblical view of humanity precludes social improvement. Indeed, only the biblical estimate of humanity's sinfulness and need for regeneration is sufficiently realistic to offer a cure for social ills. The reason Fundamentalists refuse to endorse Liberal programs for social reform is that they know that those programs are foredoomed to failure. Fundamentalists realize that the Liberals' naïve and misplaced confidence in humanity grows out of a superficial view of reality. They understand that the key to world betterment is to insist on human "lostness" and God's ability to restore the responsive sinner. Instead of leading the way, however, Fundamentalists spend all their energies resisting the programs of Liberals. In doing so, they have abandoned their heritage and narrowed their world-changing message to a world-resisting one. No twentieth century Fundamentalist has produced a contemporary version of Saint Augustine's *De civitate Dei* (413-427; *The City of God*, 1610).

In chapter 3, "The Most Embarrassing Evangelical Divorce," Henry describes how, during the first protracted period in its history, Fundamentalist Christianity stood divorced from the great social reform movements. Hebrew-Christian thought historically involved the social aspects of human life. In the Old Testament, Adam's sin makes all humanity fall, Abraham's covenant is to bless the whole world, the Mosaic law promises blessing for obedience and punishment for sin to nations as well as to individuals, and the Prophets lash out with uncompromising vigor against the social evils of their day. The New Testament continues the theme of social involvement as Jesus meets the needs of the whole person as well as the global person. Fundamentalism has betrayed this heritage because it does not explicitly sketch the social implications of its message. It fails to be biblical when it fails to challenge the injustice of totalitarianism, the secularism of modern education, the evils of racial hatred, the wrongs of current labor-management relations, and the inadequate bases of international dealings. Fundamentalism must make it clear that Christianity opposes every personal and social evil, and that it offers the redemptive work of Jesus Christ and the regenerative work of the Holy Spirit as the only hope for the solution of social evils.

Chapter 4, "The Apprehension over Kingdom Preaching," notes that, while in the past Fundamentalists preached that the kingdom of God would come in this world, recently they have hesitated to preach about it. Fundamentalists resist "kingdom now" preaching, which identifies God's kingdom with any present earthly social order. While many of them preached "kingdom then" before World War II, the non-fulfillment of the prophecies they thought they understood has disenchanted them with this kind of preaching as well. Fundamentalists cannot, however, avoid preaching about the kingdom, because Jesus preached about it. Jesus' message involved both "kingdom now" and "kingdom then," so Fundamentalists should show how the preaching of the kingdom is relevant to the predicament of the world, quit squabbling among themselves about the details of the coming of the kingdom, and discard the misapprehension that because perfection waits for the full coming of the kingdom, nothing can be improved in the present.

In chapter 5, "The Fundamentalist Thief on the Cross," the two thieves between whom Jesus was crucified are compared to symbolize Liberalism, which thinks Jesus cannot change the world, and Fundamentalism, which thinks that Jesus will have an effect only on the indefinite future. Both are wrong, because Jesus said, "Today thou shalt be with me in paradise." Because Jesus' words rang with the present tense, Fundamentalists must confront the world now, with an ethic to make it tremble and with a dynamic to give it hope.

In chapter 6, "The Struggle for a New World Mind," Henry exhorts Fundamentalism to present a complete worldview that deals with political, economic, sociological, and educational issues. To this end, Fundamentalists must develop a competent literature in every field of study that presents the implications of a Christian worldview and shows how it differs from a non-Christian perspective. Fundamentalism must also develop an educational system that teaches its worldview to children and adults. In addition, Fundamentalism must be lived out in every area of life, including the political arena.

Henry states in chapter 7, "The Evangelical 'Formula of Protest,'" that when Fundamentalists (or as this chapter calls them, evangelicals) run their own organizations, they should work for social improvement. When they are part of larger organizations that include Liberal elements, they should join their voices in denouncing evil. When these mixed groups propose solutions to social problems that cannot work because they ignore the problem of human redemption, Fundamentalists should suggest better solutions. Only when these redemptive solutions are disallowed should the Fundamentalists break with the larger group. An even better way, however, would be for all Fundamentalists to unite to work for social reform.

In chapter 8, "The Dawn of a New Reformation," Henry asserts that the need for a vital Fundamentalism today is as great as it was in the corrupt emperor Nero's Rome. Fundamentalists must realize that while perfection cannot be achieved in this world, some societies are better than others, and so they must work for social improvement. When the twentieth century Church begins to "outlive" its environment as the first century Church outreached its pagan neighbors, then the world will see that Christianity will solve the problems of the individual and of society.

Christian Themes

Christians who believe in the supernatural—Fundamentalists, as Henry calls them—have found the solutions of world problems offered by Liberals to be inadequate and so have refused to join them the promoting these solutions. Sadly, however, these Fundamentalists have done nothing to offer or to work for better solutions. This quiescence is a betrayal of biblical Christianity, which redeems people and renews society. Fundamentalists must join together to discover truly Christian responses to the obvious needs of the day, such as aggressive warfare, racial hatred and intolerance, the liquor traffic, and the injustices of management and labor. While some Fundamentalists seem blissfully unaware of these problems, Henry hopes that his work will awaken them and spur them to action.

Sources for Further Study

Henry, Carl F. H. *Confessions of a Theologian: An Autobiography.* Waco, Tex.: Word Books, 1986. Henry explains his involvement in the creation of evangelicalism.

Larsen, Timothy, ed. *The Biographical Dictionary of Evangelicals.* Downers Grove, Ill.: InterVarsity Press, 2003. Defines the evangelical movement as having arisen in Britain in the 1730's and covers the lives and achievements of famous evangelicals and their precursors, from John Wyclif in the fourteenth century to modern figures born as late as 1935.

Marsden, George. *Reforming Fundamentalism: Fuller Seminary and the New Evangelicalism.* Grand Rapids, Mich.: Wm. B. Eerdmans, 1987. An insider's history of the movement and institutions Henry helped to lead.

Patterson, Bob E. *Carl F. H. Henry.* Waco, Tex.: Word Books, 1983. A theological biography explaining Henry's work in its historical setting.

Zoba, Wendy Murray. *The Beliefnet Guide to Evangelical Christianity.* New York: Three Leaves Press, 2005. Contains a good article on Henry.

Charles White

UNSPEAKABLE
Facing up to Evil in an Age of Genocide and Terror

Author: Os Guinness (1951-   )
First published: San Francisco: HarperSanFrancisco, 2005
Genre: Nonfiction
Subgenres: Critical analysis; handbook for living; history; philosophy
Core issues: Problem of evil; suffering

Writing after the September 11, 2001, terrorist attacks on New York and Washington, D.C., Guinness engages his readers in a review of the perennial questions surrounding the presence of evil and suffering in our world, invoking every individual's responsibility to confront these issues as an integral dimension of living an authentically examined life. Guinness ultimately encourages his readers to take a realistic attitude toward the extent of modern evil and at the same time to embrace the goodness that exists alongside it.

Overview

Throughout his career as a speaker and writer, Os Guinness has sought to provide a contemporary audience with a foundation for Christian faith marked by an intellectual solidity that is often sorely lacking among popular Christian authors today. Since as far back as the early 1970's, as a member of Francis Schaeffer's L'Abri community in Switzerland, Guinness's approach to apologetics has been marked by his attention to the necessity of grounding and legitimizing Christianity in ways that directly confront the diversity of competing worldviews. For example, Guinness rejected the 1960's youth culture's turn to the East for spiritual inspiration, arguing that the Eastern path offered escape but no real answers to their longings. However, instead of a predictably Eurocentric appeal for Christianity, he offered an analysis of Eastern-influenced spirituality that revealed the failure of the gurus and their disciples to confront the fullness of the Eastern traditions, an approach that is echoed in *Unspeakable*. Similarly, in books such as *The Call* (1998) and *Fit Bodies, Fat Minds* (1994), Guinness has attacked the anti-intellectual spirit of many American evangelicals and instead has pursued a rearticulation of the basics of the Christian faith sparked with insights drawn from a wide range of sources, both religious and secular.

Guinness's 2005 *Unspeakable* provides its readers with an approach to the age-old questions of evil and suffering that are firmly planted in the context of a post-9/11 pastoral theology. From the outset, Guinness insists on a realistic confrontation with the monstrosity of evil in the modern world. This insistence upon a full awareness that evil does, indeed, exist may be the most important contribution of the book. Guinness's emphasis on the reality of evil and suffering often makes for a difficult reading experience, and many readers may find themselves pressed to abandon the book because of its relentless accounting of atrocities. At the same time, the book's pressing concern with a wide range of modern horrors—from the Holocaust and the Chinese

Cultural Revolution to ethnic cleansing in the former Yugoslavia and the Rwandan genocide—underscores Guinness's dissatisfaction with both evangelical Christianity and the secularism of Western intellectual elites. In Guinness's view, both have failed to provide answers to the problems raised by the history of the twentieth century in a way that can provide us with a guide to living a fully examined life.

Guinness begins his book by considering the parallels between the terrorist attacks of September 11, 2001, and the great Lisbon earthquake of 1755. The earlier catastrophe, which constitutes a central incident in Voltaire's *Candide: Ou, L'Optimisme* (1759; *Candide: Or, All for the Best*, 1759), shocked the West out of its early modern complacency and forced Europeans to rethink their general belief in a benevolent and all-powerful God. As Voltaire so eloquently demonstrated in his novel, disillusioned believers were left with no alternative but to reject their belief in the best of all possible worlds and to cultivate their individual gardens in a universe abandoned by Providence. For Guinness, the principal consequence of the Lisbon disaster was to usher in the Enlightenment's rejection of a personal God and the West's embrace of rationalism and humanism. In reverse fashion, Guinness believes that the events of 9/11—coming at the end of a century marked by mass murders on a previously unimaginable scale—will serve as a cultural impetus to rethink postmodernism's embrace of relativism and to reconsider the traditional Christian approach to the problem of evil as the one view that offers the most meaningful answers for a world that has been made numb to the suffering of humankind.

Guinness's call to rethink the problem of evil and suffering emerges from the recognition of four facts, which he identifies in the introduction to his book. First, "the scale and scope of evil has increased in the modern world." As Guinness's own examples throughout the book demonstrate, it would be easy to maintain that no more persuasive case against the existence of God could ever have been devised than the history of the twentieth century. Second, "modern people have demonstrated a consistently poor response to modern evil." Guinness cites numerous incidents, from the Holocaust to the Rwandan massacres of the 1990's, when the world has chosen to remain silent and inactive in the face of horrors perpetrated by humans against other humans. Third, Guinness contends that "modern people have shown a chronic inability to name and judge evil and to respond effectively." In one of the most controversial examples in the book, Guinness refers to the Abu Ghraib prison scandal, in which American soldiers were accused of engaging in the systematic torture of Iraqi prisoners, all within the confines of one of former Iraqi dictator Saddam Hussein's most notorious prisons. The failure of American political leaders and citizens to name and indict torture as evil when perpetrated by their own is a prime instance of a typically postmodern relativism that has rejected notions like sin and judgment in favor of moral equivocation. Fourth, Guinness goes on to argue that "the worst modern atrocities were perpetrated by secularist regimes, led by secularist intellectuals and in the name of secularist beliefs." This last point is particularly significant because of attempts by the American intelligentsia to lay the blame for 9/11 and other evils at the feet of faith itself. Guinness is quick to point out that the mass murders committed by

Joseph Stalin, Mao Zedong, and Pol Pot were perpetrated by avowedly secularist revolutionaries.

Christian Themes

After reviewing the different explanations for evil and suffering offered by the Eastern and secularist traditions, Guinness turns his attention to the answers provided by the third modern family of faith, the Judeo-Christian. Highlighting Saint Augustine's formulation of the trilemma (If God is both all-good and all-powerful, how can evil and suffering exist?), Guinness reviews three principal reassurances that a biblical worldview offers to a modern world beset by evil. First, "the world should have been otherwise." The essence of the story of the Creation and the Fall is that sin and evil are an intrusion into the world, not a natural fact of human existence, as in the Eastern or secularist worldview. Second, as Guinness asserts from his own Christian perspective, "no other god has wounds." Here, the cross serves as the most eloquent testimony possible of a God who chooses to share in the fullness of human suffering. For Guinness and all who share his faith, "the crucifixion of Jesus is the supreme pattern of innocent suffering in history." Third, Guinness calls on his readers to recognize that "the resistance leader knows what he is doing and victory day is coming." For Christians, Jesus of Nazareth is the resistance leader with the plan of salvation and the promise of eternal rest.

According to Guinness, the biblical response to evil and suffering consists of three profound attitudes. First, a biblical perspective requires us to acknowledge that evil resides in each of our hearts. Guinness singles out both American exceptionalism, the attitude that the United States in its so-called defense of freedom around the world can do no wrong, a common theme of American evangelicals, and utopianism, as manifested in the secular insistence on the perfectability of humankind, as twin lies that deny the reality of evil in our world. Second, the biblical worldview entails "a commitment to forgive the evildoer appropriately, though without ever condoning the evil deed." For Guinness, the attitude of forgiveness performs a dual function, freeing the past for both the one who forgives and the one who is forgiven, as well as freeing the future and thus ever re-creating the possibility of renewal and a new beginning. Finally, with a host of examples of the actions of people of faith, Guinness emphasizes the biblical approach's ongoing commitment to reform.

Sources for Further Study

Cooper, Ilene. Review of *Unspeakable*. *Booklist*, February 1, 2005, p. 919. A descriptive review.

Karel, Thomas A. Review of *Unspeakable*. *Library Journal* 130, no. 6 (April 1, 2005): 112. Brief review that assesses Guinness's book as "unpleasant but probably necessary" and a good starting point for discussion of the issues it addresses.

Publishers Weekly. Review of *Unspeakable*. 251, no. 51 (December 20, 2004): 55. Brief review that concludes that the book "makes a compelling case for faith, and courage, in the face of evil's dark reality."

Wachter, Paul. "Confronting a Culture of Fear." *America* 192, no. 12 (April 4, 2005): 32-33. Negative review of *Unspeakable* in which the assistant editor of the Catholic Near East Welfare Association's *One* magazine concludes that "In times of bad fortune, people tend to cling to their beliefs, whatever those may be. Guinness provides no compelling reason to do otherwise."

Tony Rafalowski

THE UNUTTERABLE BEAUTY
The Collected Poetry

Author: G. A. Studdert Kennedy (1883-1929)
First published: 1927
Edition used: The Unutterable Beauty: The Collected Poetry. London: Hodder and Stoughton, 1964
Genre: Poetry
Subgenres: Lyric poetry; narrative poetry
Core issues: Alienation from God; compassion; the cross; good vs. evil; Incarnation; suffering

God does not stand apart from his suffering creation. This is particularly evident in times of war, when suffering seems to overwhelm normal certainties and Christian faith. According to Studdert Kennedy, only an understanding of how God also suffered and continues to suffer, especially through Christ's cross, can generate answers to the urgent questions that come to those involved.

Overview

World War I generated a great deal of literature, much of it detailing the horrors of the trench fighting in northern France. Best known is the verse of poets such as Wilfred Owen, Siegfried Sassoon, Isaac Rosenberg, and Rupert Brook. However, many other poets wrote verse that was probably more popular at the time but less literary and therefore was not anthologized in later collections.

One such poet was G. A. Studdert Kennedy, better known as "Woodbine Willie" by the troops. He was a chaplain with the British forces in Flanders from 1915 to 1919 and, during that time, received the Military Cross for his bravery under fire in rescuing wounded men at Messines Ridge. His first volume of poetry, *Rough Rhymes of a Padre* (1918). was a collection of verse that had appeared in magazines and newspapers during the war. This was followed by *Peace Rhymes of a Padre* (1920) and *Songs of Faith and Doubt* (1922). However, the volume that was to become his most popular, selling by the thousands for years after, was *The Unutterable Beauty*.

His early life does not seem to have given him any preparation for ministering to common soldiers under fire. His father was a vicar in the Church of England of St. Mary's, Quarry Hill, Leeds, in Yorkshire. Studdert Kennedy attended a prestigious school, Leeds Grammar School, then went to Trinity College, Dublin, Ireland, to major in classics and divinity, graduating in 1904. After several years as a schoolteacher, he attended Theological College at Ripon, Yorkshire. He was appointed first as curate of Rugby Parish Church and then, in 1912, of Leeds Parish Church. In 1914 he married Emily Catlow and became vicar of St. Paul's, Worcester. This training and these appointments were typical of a professional minister of religion within the Church of England.

It was the experience of meeting common soldiers, many of whom had no church connection at all and only a nominal Christian faith, in the shared danger of enemy fire, that completely changed his life. From then on, Studdert Kennedy became a passionate advocate for the common man, and after his demobilization, became heavily involved in various organizations promoting social justice, often working at a political level. His poetry was a by-product of his advocacy of the common man, rather than a second vocation. His best-known postwar activity was setting up the Industrial Christian Fellowship and becoming an itinerant preacher and crusade leader for it. He died in 1929 while participating in a crusade in Liverpool. Archbishop William Temple described him as "the finest priest I have known," and Studdert Kennedy's friend, the Reverend Dick Sheppard, called him "the biggest little man of our day," referring to his small stature.

All of Studdert Kennedy's poetry is popular, in that it is meant to appeal immediately to the ordinary reader. Its verse form is simple and modeled on traditional forms, using an everyday vocabulary. It is meant to persuade and convince, and it expresses much of his strong feelings for his subject matter. The poetry in *The Unutterable Beauty* can be divided into three sections. The first consists of poems coming directly out of Studdert Kennedy's wartime experiences; the second, of more general poems, most generated by convictions and perspectives gained by his wartime experiences; and the third, a series of poems modeled after Rudyard Kipling's *Barrack-Room Ballads, and Other Verses* (1892), verse meant to be spoken by common soldiers, using their own dialects of English to put forward their way of seeing the world and particularly the Christian faith.

Studdert Kennedy was particularly impressed by the natural unspoken bravery and loyalty of the common soldiers, even in the most appalling conditions. "Solomon in All His Glory" is such a poem: The ragged uniforms of the soldiers are more beautiful than Solomon's garments, symbolizing the inner worth of the soldiers. "Non Angli sed Angeli" is another long poem commenting on, among other things, the bravery of the English soldier under fire. This comes out more dramatically in the "Dialect Poems," the monologue form giving direct voice to the soldiers. "Passing the Love of Women" concerns the comradely love the soldiers had for one another, and "To Stretcher Bearers" suggests the rough but genuine compassion they had for the wounded.

The chaplains were, of course, expected to maintain the status quo of the military hierarchy and the air of patriotism, at the expense of preaching their own convictions. In his poetry, at least, Studdert Kennedy refuses to do this. Some of his poems, such as "Waste," are as antiestablishment as Wilfred Owen's. "Dead and Buried" is a passionate political commentary on the betrayal of the Versailles Treaty of 1919. He even mocks the typical chaplain's sermon, either directly or through the mouth of his soldiers, as in "Well?" In one poem, "Woodbine Willie," he celebrates his nickname, deriving from a cheap brand of cigarettes issued to the men, Wills' Woodbines. He always carried packs of these cigarettes around with him to give to the soldiers. In a very real sense, the name gave him a new identity and definition.

However, not all the poems were either theological or related to war. There are a number of poems delighting in nature. Others talk of general social evils and the need to fight these actively or the temptations to the Christian life, especially posed by sex and erotic love.

Christian Themes

The most significant Christian theme that emerges from the volume is that of the suffering of God. The official theology of the Church of England taught the "impassibility" of God, that God was not affected by human emotions and was beyond suffering. Christ had entered into the world and had undergone suffering but was now in glory. Studdert Kennedy violently opposed this view of God. To him, the only Christian answer to the suffering of the soldiers was that God was down there with them, suffering along with them. That was the basis for his theodicy. The many "Calvaries," roadside crucifixes set up by the Catholic churches, became symbols of this suffering God in Christ. Christ continued to suffer. The "once for all" suffering of Christ at his crucifixion was challenged. It was not "once"; it is always, as Studdert Kennedy makes clear in "The Suffering God."

The centrality of the cross and its suffering is used to oppose the typical teaching that this is the will of God because it is patriotic. Faith and doubt are closely linked in his poetry: Much received truth is shown to be grossly inadequate; old questions have to be re-posed and new answers found. Studdert Kennedy's theology is worked out at an emotional level, as in "Tragedy," "Faith," and "The Truth of May." One of his difficulties is maintaining the transcendence of God. His stress on God's suffering leads him to emphasize his immanence, his presence, even in the fighting men. In a poem such as "Right Is Might," Christian orthodoxy is strained to its limits. The title poem, "The Unutterable Beauty," expresses Studdert Kennedy's belief in the pastoral and prophetic role of his poetry. There is a passionate mysticism in much of his verse.

Sources for Further Study

Edwards, D. "'Woodbine Willie' Was a True Prophet." *Church Times*, June 24, 1983. A modern reassessment of the prophetic role of Studdert Kennedy's poetry and preaching.

Fuller, Roy. "Woodbine Willie Lives." In *Owls and Artificers: Oxford Lectures in Poetry*. Oxford, England: Oxford University Press, 1971. A modern poet revisits Studdert Kennedy's verse, and reinstates the worth of popular poetry.

Grundy, Michael. *A Fiery Glow in the Darkness: Woodbine Willie—Padre and Poet*. London: Osborne Books, 1997. The most recent and certainly most detailed biography of Studdert Kennedy. It deals both with the larger-than-life man and his immensely popular poetry.

Purcell, William. *Woodbine Willie*. Oxford, England: Mowbray, 1983. This is one of Mowbray's Religious Reprint series, being a reprint of an earlier, but still very useful, biography.

David Barratt

THE VARIETIES OF RELIGIOUS EXPERIENCE
A Study in Human Nature

Author: William James (1842-1910)
First published: 1902
Edition used: The Varieties of Religious Experience: A Study in Human Nature, edited with an introduction by Martin E. Marty. New York: Penguin Books, 1983
Genre: Nonfiction
Subgenres: Essays; philosophy
Core issues: The divine; mysticism; psychology; religion; soul

James examines testimony concerning concrete religious experiences, experiences that involve a sense of an unseen reality yet are as convincing as any direct sensible experience can be. It is with this sense of the unseen and the variety of reactions to it that James is concerned here, not with the various ways in which the unseen has been conceptualized. He finds a variety of reactions—and consequently, "varieties of religious experience."

Overview

William James was the son of Henry James, an American Swedenborgian, and the brother of Henry James, Jr., the American novelist. James was trained as a physician, but he turned to psychology and later to philosophy. His contribution to psychology, *The Principles of Psychology* (1890), has become a classic in the field. James early became the most popular spokesman of the American philosophical movement pragmatism. Among his other important philosophical works are: *The Will to Believe, and Other Essays in Popular Philosophy* (1897), *Pragmatism: A New Name for Some Old Ways of Thinking* (1907), *The Meaning of Truth: A Sequel to "Pragmatism"* (1909), and *Essays in Radical Empiricism* (1912). The present work was compiled from his Gifford lectures.

James begins his series of lectures by characterizing the kind of study and the subject matter with which he is concerned. His concern is a psychological study of religious experiences, but he is not concerned with the physiological and neurological conditions that may underlie religious experiences. Such conditions, he argues, underlie all mental states, and consequently, are irrelevant in describing and evaluating religious experience. In fact, they are as irrelevant in evaluating religious opinions as they are in evaluating opinions in the natural sciences and in the industrial arts. No one accepts or rejects an opinion in the sciences on the basis of the author's neurological type, and the same should be the case with religious opinions. James readily admits that many striking religious personalities are eccentric, even pathological; but such personalities, for this kind of study, function as microscopes and enlarge, for easier viewing, the subject matter of religious experience. The criteria for the evaluation of the experiences, however, must be kept distinct from these pathological considerations. Immediate luminousness, or philosophical reasonableness, and moral helpfulness James takes to be the only two relevant criteria for evaluating the religious phenomena with which he is concerned.

As for delimiting the subject matter as such, that is, deciding which experiences are to be called religious, James eschews an attempt to define the term "religion" as such. He is not concerned with "the essence of religion," but with describing and evaluating those experiences usually classified as religious. He is, likewise, not concerned with the institutional aspects of religion, but with the personal aspects. He ignores the ecclesiastical organization with its rituals and creeds, its systematic theologies, and its ideas about the gods, and confines himself to examining "the feelings, acts, and experiences of individual men in their solitude, so far as they apprehend themselves to stand in relation to whatever they may consider the divine."

The term "the divine" is here taken to refer to what one considers the most primal, enveloping, and real, and religion is the person's attitudes and reactions to it. James wishes "the divine" to be interpreted broadly enough to include the godless, or quasi-godless, religion of an Emersonian optimism and a Buddhistic pessimism. On the other hand, James does not wish to include, as religious, all attitudes concerned with a total reaction to life, for this would make the subject matter too broad and strain the ordinary use of language. After all, there are trifling and sneering attitudes toward the whole of life, attitudes that would hardly qualify as religious. "There is something solemn, serious, and tender," he tells us, "about any attitude which we denominate religious. If glad, it must not grin nor snicker; if sad, it must not scream or curse." As a consequence, James limits "the divine" to "the most primal, enveloping and real which an individual feels impelled to respond to solemnly and gravely, and neither by a curse nor a jest."

James is still not quite satisfied, however, with his characterization of the religious attitude, for it does not clearly distinguish the religious attitude from what might be called the purely moral, such as the stoic attitude. The solemn and serious reaction and attitude of the religious person is distinguished by an element of joy or happiness. It is not a simple joy that results from a person's being liberated from oppressive moods; it is a solemn joy, or happiness, that embraces within it the negative, or tragic, side of life and holds it in check. The religious reaction and attitude, which is the subject of these lectures, as a consequence, has a depth and strength that is lacking in the purely moral.

After delimiting the kind of experiences with which he is concerned in his study, James turns to the testimony concerning concrete religious experiences, and this occupies the bulk of his lectures. The amount, as well as the variety, of the testimony that he has collected is phenomenal and any summary will appear a lifeless skeleton compared to the richness of his concrete cases and his own colorful commentary. In this main section, however, James is primarily concerned with reporting what religious persons concretely describe, not with an evaluation of the experiences. These experiences by and large involve a sense of an unseen reality—that is, a reality that is not present to the special and particular senses—yet these experiences are as convincing to the person who has them as any direct sensible experience can be. In fact, one could say, James tells us, that "the life of religion . . . consists of the belief that there is an unseen order, and that our supreme good lies in harmoniously adjusting ourselves thereto." It is with this sense of the unseen and the variety of reactions to it that James is concerned here, not with the various ways in which the unseen has been conceptualized. The latter are creedal and theological, and, consequently, primarily institutional concerns. His concern is with the concrete personal experiences, including the reactions of the person having the experience. In addition to the solemnity, seriousness, and joy that he sees characterizing these experiences in general, James finds a variety of reactions—and consequently, "varieties of religious experience."

It is an underlying thesis of these lectures that this variety of reactions to the divine, and consequently, the varieties of religious experience, is due to the varieties of human personality. The solemn joy of which we spoke earlier will exemplify a continuum of responses depending, for example, on how sanguine or somber the personality of the person experiencing is. For the two extremes here, the more optimistic one and the more pessimistic one, James coined the colorful phrases "the healthy-minded" ("the once born") and "the sick soul" ("the twice born"). Either extreme can be quasi-pathological, he tells us; but it is the extremes that interest James for, as was mentioned earlier, there one can see the religious reactions enlarged.

The healthy-minded, or optimistic, response can be either immediate and involuntary, or systematic and voluntary. In either case, the person looks on all things, finds them good, and refuses to admit their badness or ignores their presence. "The sanguine and healthy-minded," he writes, "live on the sunny side of their misery-line, the depressed and melancholy [the sick souls] live beyond it, in darkness and apprehension." He includes among his collection of reports of the sick souls, experiences of the vanity of all mortal things, a very deep sense of sin, and a general panic fear of the universe. To the sick soul, the healthy-minded appears blind and shallow; to the healthy-minded, the sick soul appears unmanly and diseased. It is only natural to expect these two extreme types of personality to react to the presence of the divine in quite different ways.

Having already suggested that the sick soul perhaps has a deeper sensitivity to evil in the universe and, as a consequence, perhaps a deeper religious insight, James devotes three lectures to the "divided self" and the process of its unification and conversion, summarizing and quoting from the testimonies concerning these experiences and loosely classifying them in terms such as "sudden" or "prolonged" and "unconscious and involuntary" or "conscious and voluntary." From the wealth of testimony, James finds three general characteristics of the converted state: The first is the loss of all worry, the sense that ultimately all is well with one, and a willingness to be, even though outer conditions may remain the same; the second is the sense of perceiving truths that one did not know before; and the third is that the world itself appears to undergo an objective change, a newness seems to beautify every object. The converted state is almost the precise opposite of the state of "the sick soul" or "the divided self."

In the fact that James devotes three lectures to saintliness and two more to the value of saintliness one can observe something of James's pragmatic interest in religious experience. He has told us that immediate luminousness, or philosophical reasonableness, and moral helpfulness were the only relevant criteria of evaluation. Saintliness, the "fruits of genuine religion," and frequently the fruit of conversion, provides the factor in religious experience for the application of the "moral helpfulness" criterion to religious experience. Consequently, saintliness is very important for James in evaluating religious experience, and he devotes five lectures just to this one topic, by far the most allotted to any one topic in the series. In examining the lives of the conventional religious saints, James finds that the saintly characteristics are frequently taken to excess, excesses of devotion, purity, charity, and asceticism. These excesses, however, are, he thinks, the result of an imbalance within the individual due to a weakness of the intellect.

James now turns to the possible data for the other criterion of evaluation of religious experience, namely, immediate luminousness, or philosophical reasonableness, and he devotes two lectures to mystical experiences and one to religious philosophy. James lists four marks for what he takes as mystical states: ineffability, noetic quality, transiency, and passivity. By their very nature, these experiences, James concludes, are invulnerable: The mystic has been there, the nonmystic has not. By virtue of this same fact, however, the experiences can have no authority over the nonmystic. What these experiences can do is to offer us a hypothesis of another world or of a wider world than is given to us in sensation. However, James then points out, the religious experiences of the nonmystic also offer us such a hypothesis. Consequently, mystical experiences offer us no more for the application of the criterion of philosophical reasonableness than religious experience in general does.

What James appears to mean by "religious philosophy" is a philosophical attempt to prove or to justify religious belief by some form of coercive argument. Here James is probably more emphatic than at any other point in his series of lectures: "We must conclude that the attempt to demonstrate by purely intellectual processes the truth of the deliverances of direct religious experience is absolutely hopeless." The history of the apparent failure of this attempt is perhaps now well known. Before giving us, however, his own conclusions concerning the evaluation of this vast testimony concerning the phenomenon of religious experience, James treats in one lecture a number of more minor elements in religious experiences, such as aesthetic elements, sacrifice, confession, prayer, and automatism.

As James looks at the reports of religious experiences of the previous lectures, he finds them containing three general beliefs and two psychological characteristics. The beliefs are: (1) that the visible world is a part of a more spiritual universe from which it draws its chief significance; (2) that union, or harmonious relations, with that higher universe is our true end; and (3) that prayer or communion with the spirit thereof is a process in which spiritual energy produces effects, psychological or material, within the phenomenal world. The two psychological characteristics are: (1) a new zest that adds itself like a gift to life; and (2) an assurance of safety and a temper of peace, and, in relation to others, a preponderance of loving affection.

Before evaluating these beliefs and psychological characteristics, James considers the position that religion, from the standpoint of modern science, is an anachronism because of its concern with personal destiny and the preponderance of feeling involved. He rejects this thesis on the grounds that it is precisely here that we deal with realities in the completest sense of the term. "Individuality is founded in feeling; and the recesses of feeling, the darker, blinder strata of character, are the only places in the world in which we catch real fact in the making, and directly perceive how events happen, and how work is actually done."

As suggested earlier, the psychological characteristics are evaluated on the basis of their moral helpfulness; but James here raises the question of the objective "truth" of the religious beliefs, the philosophical problem of evaluation. They must at least, he suggests, be in harmony with our scientific beliefs and not conflict with them. This James finds to be the case with these three general religious beliefs in their above vague formulation. He takes the existence of such a spiritual universe to be a hypothesis evoked to explain the religious effects, particularly the above two psychological characteristics. Here he falls back on what he calls "the instinctive belief of mankind," that something is real if it has real effects. To be a good hypothesis, however, the beliefs must be spelled out and related to facts other than the ones the hypothesis is invoked to explain. It is in the spelling out of the religious hypothesis in more specific ways, which he terms "over-beliefs," that we find the religious beliefs frequently conflicting with each other and with our accepted scientific beliefs.

Christian Themes

In his attempt to identify the psychological basis for the variety of religious experience, James delineates the following principles, which reflected a growing need to explain spirituality in general, and Christian spiritual life in particular, in the context of a growing secularism at the beginning of the twentieth century:

- Neurological and physiological conditions are as irrelevant in evaluating a person's religious experiences as they are in evaluating a scientist's physical hypothesis.
- Religious experiences should be evaluated in terms of their philosophical reasonableness and moral helpfulness.
- A person's psychological makeup contributes to the more specific characteristics of a person's religious experiences, and this accounts for the variety among religious experiences.
- An examination of the reports of religious experience discloses three general beliefs and two psychological characteristics. The beliefs are: (1) the visible world is part of a more spiritual universe from which it draws its significance; (2) that union or harmonious relations with that higher universe is our true end; and (3) that prayer or communion with the spirit thereof is a process in which spirit energy produces effects within the phenomenal world. The two psychological characteristics are: (1) a new zest that adds itself like a gift to life; and (2) an assurance of safety and a temper of peace, and in relation to others, a preponderance of loving affection.

- The differences between religious beliefs are differences in over-beliefs, the way in which the vaguer and more general beliefs are made specific and the spiritual is related to the cosmos.
- Religious experiences are primarily concerned with individual feelings and destinies, but this is not to be deplored; such experiences deal with realities in the completest sense of that term.

Sources for Further Study

Carrette, Jeremy, ed. *William James and "The Varieties of Religious Experience": A Centenary Celebration.* New York: Routledge, 2005. A collection of more than a dozen scholarly essays examining James and the history of psychology; James, psychology, and religion; and James and mysticism. Illustrated; bibliographical references, index.

James, William. *The Meaning of Truth.* New York: Longmans, Green, 1909. This is James's more mature and systematic position on truth, which is quite relevant to his suggestions at the end of the present work and *The Will to Believe.*

_____. *The Will to Believe, and Other Essays in Popular Philosophy.* New York: Dover, 1956. Particularly in the title essay, James virtually takes up where he disappointedly left off in *The Varieties of Religious Experience*, with an evaluation of the truth of religious beliefs.

Richardson, Robert D. *William James: In the Maelstrom of American Modernism.* Boston: Houghton Mifflin, 2006. A major biography of James, a comprehensive tome at 622 pages, with plates, illustrations, maps, bibliographical references, and index. Includes several chapters on James's religious thought, including one on *The Varieties of Religious Experience.*

Bowman L. Clarke

VELMA STILL COOKS IN LEEWAY

Author: Vinita Hampton Wright (1958-   )
First published: Nashville, Tenn.: Broadman & Holman, 2000
Genre: Novel
Subgenres: Evangelical fiction; literary fiction
Core issues: Compassion; faith; forgiveness; healing; love; redemption; sin and sinners

In this character-driven novel, Wright creates an authentic cast whose faith in God and church does not prevent the normal human flaws and failings. Local citizens weather trials of sickness and sin as they journey toward forgiveness and God's grace at work in their small community.

> *Principal characters*
> *Velma Brendle*, the protagonist, owner of the town diner
> *Doris Pines*, a neighbor
> *Shellye Pines*, a neighbor
> *Len Connor*, the father of Shellye's baby
> *Jack Thomas*, a pastor
> *Howard*, an ailing relative
> *Grady Lewis*, an abusive husband

Overview

In Vinita Hampton Wright's novel *Velma Still Cooks in Leeway*, the title character, Velma Brendle, operates the only restaurant in the small town of Leeway, Kansas. The regular crowd feels like family, and Velma prays for her customers. People's stories and struggles weigh on Velma, so she works a few hours a week as janitor at Jerusalem Baptist Church seeking quiet. The past two years have been tough. She feels that God has not come through for her town, but she senses a revelation approaching.

In spring, 1996, Velma's eighteen-year-old neighbor, Shellye Pines, "turns up" pregnant. Two months before, Shellye had come to Velma teary-eyed and bruised. Len Connor, the youth group's golden boy, had taken her virginity. When Shellye names the father, "good ol' boy" Pastor Jack Thomas (in whom Velma has never placed her trust) asks if she is sure. Riled, Shellye maintains that Len was the only man who could have caused the pregnancy and that he forced her. Len denies it.

Hurt that she is not believed, Shellye stops going to church. Her mother, Doris, unsettled since her husband's desertion years ago, is emotionally absent, adding to Shellye's stress. Velma often welcomes the girl into her home, offering her the emotional support that Doris does not. Cousin Howard calls in late May. Thirty-eight, fighting cancer, and without a job or insurance, he needs a place to live. He moves in and thanks Velma but seems removed from his feelings about his nearing death.

Howard likes Velma's church friends, however, and notes he is seeing what he has missed.

At a revival meeting, the evangelist preaches that God supplies grace moment by moment. Shellye goes forward at the invitation. She says God is giving her the grace to raise her own baby. When the evangelist asks who will stand with Shellye, more than half the church and Pastor Thomas stand. Shellye then returns to the church, and Grady Lewis spends time with her. Although Velma would not have chosen him, he seems godly, and he proposes in late July. Velma feels disturbed when Grady insists that she wear a cream dress (denoting that she is not a virgin). Shellye, having been raped, believes that she remains a virgin because the rape was against her will. Despite her occasional misgivings about Grady and his rigid standards, Velma delights in catering the wedding reception. She watches Grady's looks of love and scolds herself for worrying about this pairing.

In October, Len comes to Velma's front door. Velma reminds him that there are some hurts to clear. Len and Shellye agree to talk at Velma's home, but Shellye makes Velma promise not to tell the overprotective Grady. Len apologizes for his actions and confesses to his father and Pastor Thomas that he raped Shellye. Grady confronts Pastor Thomas about letting Len off without prosecution, but the pastor is thankful that Len and Shellye have found some resolution.

Shellye's daughter is born. Doris, though delighted, feels unprepared to be a grandmother. At Christmas, Shellye brings homemade candy to Velma. As Shellye prepares to leave, Velma notices that she has a big, ugly bruise; after she departs, Velma realizes that the bruise is shaped like fingers. At about the same time, Pastor Thomas asks Velma to talk to Shellye about her attitude: Grady is frustrated by Shellye's not cooperating with his spiritual leadership. Velma responds that Grady may be expecting too much of the tired new mother and then speaks with Shellye—almost asking her if Grady is hurting her but allowing Shellye to gloss things over. The next time Shellye comes to her house, Velma asks about the red mark on her cheek, and Shellye admits that Grady slapped her as a reflex when she overstepped. Pastor Thomas and Grady appear, and Grady apologizes repeatedly. Velma almost asks Thomas if this has happened before, but she lets it ride because the couple are apparently making progress.

When Velma cooks German dishes, Howard devours them and urges her to serve them at the diner. He, Shellye, and Doris brainstorm about decor and names. They work hard to persuade Velma that a change is possible. In the meantime, throughout the winter months and into the spring, Velma and Doris both provide Shellye and the baby shelter whenever she flees Grady's temper. During such episodes, Shellye instead seeks counsel with Pastor Thomas and ends by going home to Grady. Velma prays to God on behalf of her troubled friends.

The deacons vote not to make Grady a deacon and ask him to step down from teaching to focus on his marriage. Shellye cries all the way to the car. Pastor Thomas implies to Velma that he does not want Shellye hurt, as she was when he and others refused to believe Len raped her. Four days prior to the opening of Velma's new restaurant, Little Germany, another bad spell drives Shellye to her mother's and then back home to Grady. This time, Pastor Thomas counsels her to stay away from Grady longer.

At a celebration of the restaurant's opening, Velma notices how good Howard looks. In the midst of Shellye's struggles and Velma's worries, she has not noticed that God is healing Howard. After the restaurant closes, Howard and Velma take leftovers by Grady and Shellye's house. No one answers the door, so they slip into the kitchen. Velma smells blood. They spot a trail of blood, which leads to Doris's body. Howard calls 911 and searches for Shellye. The police come, and Shellye and the baby are found outside. At the hospital, the horrifying details emerge: Her mother suspected trouble and arrived when Grady was abusing Shellye. He turned on Doris. In the end, therefore, Doris saved her daughter, vindicating her role as Shellye's mother by giving her own life for Shellye.

In August, Howard gathers his things to return home. He says that Shellye has forgiven Len and the church people and probably will forgive Grady, too. Shellye truly knows how to love. In her journals, Velma addresses God to work through bad memories and find sense and solace. Velma still cooks in Leeway and she observes the Lord's love slipping in wherever it can.

Christian Themes

An overtly Christian novel—with each chapter introduced by an epigraph from the book of Ezekiel and ending with a recipe from Velma's restaurant—*Velma Still Cooks in Leeway* nevertheless speaks to nonbelievers as powerfully as it does to believers. Although the small community of Leeway, Kansas, appears to be a quiet town, events of eternal proportion rock Velma's secluded world. Velma finds herself surrounded by family, neighbors, and customers who wrestle with sin in their lives. Much needs to be forgiven in this close-knit community, and on many levels. Velma must forgive her neighbor, who deserted his wife and daughter. She must forgive the abandoned wife, Doris, who never recovered emotionally and is initially unable to meet her daughter's needs. The community must forgive Len, the young man who date-raped the daughter, Shellye. Velma must forgive the church members who let Shellye down in her time of need. She must also forgive herself for doing the same. Subplots also call for mercy and forgiveness adding depth and creating a poignant, echoing call for Christians to extend God's grace to each other.

When Grady, Shellye's new husband and presumed rescuer, abuses her, the people of Leeway—like ordinary people everywhere—are surprised by their own blindness. They operate as though the troubling things in life will correct themselves as long as people doing the best they can. It takes Doris's murder to shake them awake, and in hindsight they finally perceive their own complicity in the abuse, realizing that they should have acted on the little warnings they thought they saw instead of making allowances for a man who seemed devoted to God. Velma realizes that she, too, has been locked into a dangerous pattern. Like her mother and her grandmother before her, she did not speak when she had the power to do so.

A forerunner of Wright's edgier Christian fiction, *Velma Still Cooks in Leeway* presents a disturbing yet reassuring exploration of the basic need for forgiveness and people's corresponding need to grant forgiveness. Both actions are rooted in God's love and sacrifice. Even when sin and its consequences invade lives, God's divine forgiveness and love gently sustain his people.

Sources for Further Study

Mort, John. Review of *Velma Still Cooks in Leeway*. *Booklist* 97, no. 3 (October 1, 2000): 304. Touts Wright as a "rarity" in the world of Christian fiction writers.

Publishers Weekly. Review of *Velma Still Cooks in Leeway*. 247, no. 30 (July 24, 2000): 66. Recognizes Wright's novel as a "bona-fide work of literary fiction" worthy of readership inside and outside the Christian market.

Winner, Lauren F. "The Wright Stuff." *Christianity Today* 45 (April 23, 2001): 84-87. Discusses Wright's books and her opinion on changes in the caliber of Christian fiction and the level of artistry developing among Christian writers.

Wright, Vinita Hampton. "A Life of Quiet Grace." Interview by Jana Reiss. *Publishers Weekly* 247, no. 38 (September 18, 2000): 82. Wright comments on her choice to write about Christians as ordinary, not idealized, people.

Kimberly T. Peterson

VERITATIS SPLENDOR

Author: John Paul II (Karol Jozef Wojtyła; 1920-2005)
First published: 1993 (English translation, 1993)
Edition used: Encyclical Letter "The Splendor of Truth," translated by the Vatican. Boston: Pauline Books and Media, 1993
Genre: Nonfiction
Subgenres: Encyclical; exegesis
Core issues: Conscience; ethics; freedom and free will; good vs. evil; morality; truth

In this landmark papal encyclical, Pope John Paul II addresses certain fundamental questions of the moral teachings of the Catholic Church. In response to various modern philosophies obscuring moral norms, John Paul asserts traditional Christian belief in universally binding moral laws, which the Church teaches competently and authoritatively. Reason and faith oblige humans to direct their free actions to pursue this moral law. Authentic goodness and truth are fully revealed in Jesus Christ, shine forth in the life of the saints, and are to be constantly proclaimed by the pastors of the Church.

Overview

Veritatis Splendor, one of the major encyclicals written by Pope John Paul II, addresses the question of moral truth from a Christian perspective. In response to new controversies, John Paul proposes to answer certain fundamental questions regarding the moral teachings of the Catholic Church.

John Paul begins his essay with an exegesis of the famous dialogue of Jesus with the rich young man in chapter 19 of the Gospel of Saint Matthew. In this dialogue, the young man asks Jesus what good he must do to inherit eternal life. Jesus answers so as to link moral good with the fulfillment of human destiny and to relate the moral life to acknowledgment of God. Humans are bound to obey the natural law that God has implanted in the human heart. The natural law is first given expression in the Decalogue and reaches fulfillment as the new law of the New Testament. The complete moral path for Christians is to follow Jesus, especially in the new commandment that he gave his disciples: "This is my commandment, that you love one another as I have loved you" (John 15:12). Humans are able to give a free response of love for God and for neighbor by the grace of the Holy Spirit.

Because of this relationship between the moral good of human acts and eternal destiny, the Church has developed a special aspect of theology referred to as moral theology. In moral theology, the Church assesses what is good and evil in human actions. Humans find answers to these questions in God alone, who gives the moral law. Humans have freedom in their beliefs and actions, but it is a freedom to embrace what is good, not to determine what is good or evil.

Humans discover this moral law through their reason, whereby the eternal, divine law, and human law intersect. Because humans participate in God's eternal law through their reason and autonomous will, their freedom is magnified, not negated, by obedience to divine law. Pure statistics and empirical study cannot determine morality. Likewise, moral theology cannot be described as mere physicalism or naturalism because it properly takes into account the place of the human body in deciding moral questions, such as those relating to the sexual act and marital relations. A person is composed of both spirit and body, and the morality of an act cannot be disassociated from its physical dimension.

Because the moral order is inscribed in the rational nature of a person, it governs all human beings. This universality and immutability of the moral law does not violate the individuality of persons and cultures. Rather it transcends them, thereby presenting an objective standard by which all human actions can be measured. The application of the objective moral law finds expression in a person's conscience, which judges in a concrete situation the practical application of the rational truth to do good and avoid evil. Conscience is a sanctuary where the will of God is heard, calling for acts consistent with what is ethical. Conscience should be followed but should also be well-formed.

The obligation to form one's acts in conformity with the concrete demands of each situation is not excused by a fundamental intention or "option" to live fully for God. Mortal sin—that is, a gravely immoral act, deliberately and freely chosen—can sever one's relationship with God. In a related fashion, the morality of human acts depends on both the intention and the consequences deliberately sought (in contrast to unacceptable teleological theories of consequentialism or proportionalism, which would evaluate actions solely by assessing the possible consequences). In the nuanced but classical language of Catholic moral ethics, John Paul defines the morality of the human act as depending "primarily and fundamentally on the object rationally chosen by the deliberate will." These judgments apply to believers and nonbelievers alike. Some acts are intrinsically evil and cannot be remediated by a subjectively good intent; evil cannot be done so that good may come of it (Romans 3:8).

Moral questions ultimately command both freedom and truth. "You will know the truth and the truth will set you free" (John 8:32). Faith is likewise inexorably linked to morality. In Christian faith and the teachings of the Church, humans learn the truth about universal and immutable moral norms. Authentic freedom calls humans to embrace the good that is revealed by God, manifested in the person of the crucified Christ. The legacy of the martyrs and saints exemplifies the fidelity of persons who witness to truth and the moral order, even preferring death to a single grave sin. Utilitarianism, extreme pragmatism, and relativism all constitute an obscuring of the transcendent moral order, as does public dissent by theologians. The Church, its pastors, its theologians, and its members must embrace and proclaim the truths of the moral life, thereby converting personal lives and renewing the social, economic, and political spheres of society.

Christian Themes

"What is truth?" Pilate asked Jesus. John Paul answers Pilate's question in this highly complex and profound encyclical. As John Paul notes in the preface, "The Splendor of Truth shines forth in the works of the Creator and, in a special way, in man created in the image and likeness of God." In this one sentence are evoked traditional themes of Christian and Catholic teachings. The moral and natural law of God is revealed in the physical world and in the human, and is accessible to human reason. Morality has a universal and unchangeable nature that can be known by all persons who are suitably disposed, although the Church teaches the fullness of the moral laws with conviction and clarity.

These teachings have been historically criticized as impinging on human freedom; in modern times, they have been criticized for opposing empirical research, democracy, positivism, and individual and cultural identity. The pope leaves the task of assembling a complete and systematic presentation of Christian morality to the then recently published *Catechism of the Catholic Church* (1992). Nevertheless this is the first papal document addressing the philosophical and theological foundations of moral law, and John Paul uses it to reply to controversial tendencies leading to extreme individualism, pragmatism, utilitarianism, and relativism. Although focusing on these specific tendencies, he does so while reflecting on the whole of the Church's moral teachings. Appropriately for this profound examination, John Paul draws extensively on the major Catholic theologians Saint Thomas Aquinas and Saint Augustine and the teachings of the milestone Second Vatican Council (1962-1965). The traditional Catholic assessment of concrete actions according to the Decalogue is ratified, although enriched by a modern emphasis on the disposition of the human person toward God.

Jesus fulfills and does not negate the commandments by "interiorizing their demands" and enhances and does not destroy freedom by connecting it to obedience to the law of God. Thus the pope is able to classify certain acts, historically condemned by Catholics—such as homicide, genocide, abortion, euthanasia, suicide, torture, slavery, prostitution, contraception, and oppression of workers—as intrinsically wrong. John Paul expresses in modern and philosophical fashion the Christian belief in objective norms of truth and morality. Jesus Christ proclaimed himself to be "the way, and the truth, and the life" (John 1:14). In freely pursuing what is true and what is good, humans find a loving relationship with God.

Sources for Further Study

Allsopp, Michael E., and John J. O'Keefe, eds. *"Veritatis Splendor": American Responses*. Kansas City: Sheed and Ward, 1995. A collection of twenty essays, both critical and supportive, on *Veritatis Splendor* by American authors.

Dinoia, J. A., and Romanus Cessario, eds. *"Veritatis Splendor" and the Renewal of Moral Theology*. Huntington, Ind.: Our Sunday Visitor, 1999. With contributions by ten well-known scholars, including Avery Dulles, S.J., and Alasdair MacIntyre, this collection of essays addresses perspectives on the encyclical, issues raised by the encyclical, and the reception of the encyclical.

Miller, J. Michael, ed. *The Encyclicals of John Paul II*. Huntington, Ind.: Our Sunday Visitor, 2001. A collection of the thirteen encyclicals issued by Pope John Paul from 1979 to 1998; editor Miller includes helpful and extensive introductions and bibliographies relating John Paul's encyclicals to his papacy and to the Catholic magisterial tradition.

Howard Bromberg

THE VICAR OF WAKEFIELD

Author: Oliver Goldsmith (1728/1730-1774)
First published: 1766
Edition used: The Vicar of Wakefield, vol. 4 in *Collected Works of Oliver Goldsmith*, edited by Arthur Friedman. Oxford, England: Clarendon Press, 1966
Genre: Novel
Subgenres: Humor; romance
Core issues: Clerical life; marriage; virtue

Goldsmith shows how innocence becomes prey in a world of deceit and how the seven cardinal virtues are the only reliable moral guides to regeneration and happiness.

> *Principal characters*
> *Dr. Charles Primrose*, the vicar of Wakefield, the protagonist
> *Deborah Primrose*, Charles's wife
> *Olivia Primrose*, the Primroses' elder daughter
> *Sophia Primrose*, their younger daughter
> *George Primrose*, their eldest son
> *Moses Primrose*, their gullible second son
> *Dick Primrose* and
> *Bill Primrose*, their last sons, young boys
> *Mr. Wilmot*, a church dignitary
> *Arabella Wilmot*, Mr. Wilmot's daughter
> *Sir William Thornhill*, a rich and benevolent baronet initially disguised as Mr. Burchell, a vagrant
> *Farmer Williams*, a sturdy rustic
> *Squire Ned Thornhill*, a rake
> *Lady Blarney* and
> *Miss Carolina Wilelmina Amelia Skeggs*, procuresses disguised as fine ladies
> *The Flamboroughs*, innocent and unpretentious neighbors
> *Ephraim Jenkinson*, a sharper and later an aide to Dr. Primrose
> *Wilkinson*, a butler posing as a squire
> *Mr. and Mrs. Arnold*, uncle and aunt of Arabella Wilmot

Overview

Oliver Goldsmith's novel *The Vicar of Wakefield* centers on Dr. Charles Primrose, the village priest, and his wife, Deborah, who live with their six children in affluent happiness in Wakefield. All look forward to the marriage of the Primroses' eldest son, George, to Arabella Wilmot, daughter of a wealthy church dignitary. Dr. Primrose heatedly defends one of his favorite subjects, monogamy, with Arabella's father, Mr.

The Vicar of Wakefield / GOLDSMITH

Wilmot, a man three times widowed and about to marry his fourth wife. When news arrives that Dr. Primrose has lost all his money through his broker's embezzlement, Mr. Wilmot breaks the engagement of Arabella and George. George leaves to recoup the family fortune, and the other Primroses set out for a distant village to live more humbly. On the way, they meet Mr. Burchell, a wanderer who saves the Primroses' young daughter Sophia from drowning. For his act, the family promises hospitality to Burchell.

The Primroses rent a cottage from Squire Thornhill, a loose-living young gentleman, who takes an immediate liking to elder daughter Olivia. Recognizing the advantages of a marriage between Olivia and the squire, Deborah strives to bring it about. Squire Thornhill, however, does not propose, while Burchell pays modest court to Sophia. Events reach a hopeful peak when two ladies, friends of Squire Thornhill, visit the Primroses. These ladies are amenable to taking Olivia and Sophia to London as companions. Squire Thornhill encourages the plan, but Burchell objects.

To improve the family's finances, Dr. Primrose and his second son, Moses, go to a fair to sell their horses, but each is duped by the sharper Ephraim Jenkinson. Meanwhile, in spite of his repeated visits, Squire Thornhill refuses to propose marriage to Olivia. Dr. Primrose suggests that she then consider a proposal from Farmer Williams. Disappointed in Thornhill's reluctance, Olivia agrees to marry Williams, but four days before the wedding she runs off. Because of an ambiguously worded letter, Dr. Primrose thinks that Burchell has abducted her.

A sad Dr. Primrose resolves to search for his daughter. Falling ill, he finds himself by chance in the house of the Arnolds, Arabella's uncle and aunt, whom she is visiting. Now courted by Squire Thornhill, Arabella still loves George, who by greater chance arrives penniless at the Arnolds to tell of his wanderings, during which he met with continual deceit and shameless behavior. Squire Thornhill then arrives and, to get rid of George, buys him a commission in the army. Still in love with George, Arabella promises to wait for him.

Disappointed at not finding Olivia, Dr. Primrose leaves for home. En route he discovers her, abandoned at an inn. Olivia tells him that her seducer was not Burchell but Squire Thornhill, who married her before a Roman Catholic priest. The forgiving father and repentant daughter reach home, only to find their house ablaze. Most of the family having escaped, Dr. Primrose rushes into the flames to save his two youngest sons. Soon after, Squire Thornhill appears to announce his plan to wed Arabella and arrange a marriage for Olivia with hopes that she will also keep a lover. After Dr. Primrose rages against him, Thornhill demands his rent. Destitute and unable to pay, Dr. Primrose is sent to jail. There Dr. Primrose delivers sermons to the other prisoners. At first they mock him, but his preaching and concern make them reform their ways. One of the prisoners is Ephraim Jenkinson, the sharper who had defrauded Dr. Primrose and Moses at the fair. Now contrite, he vows to help Dr. Primrose.

More misfortunes befall the vicar when a report arrives that Olivia has died and Sophia has been abducted. Then George arrives in chains, jailed because he had wounded a man in a duel to redress the family's honor, besmirched by Squire Thornhill's seduction of Olivia. Coincidences tumble one after another: Burchell, revealing himself as the good Sir William Thornhill, arrives with Sophia, whom he has saved. Squire Thornhill (who is revealed to be Sir William's nephew) arrives, only to be admonished by Sir William. Arabella arrives and reunites with George. Jenkinson appears with Olivia, whose reported death was erroneous, and a valid marriage license attesting that she is married to Squire Thornhill. Returning home, Dr. Primrose learns that the thief of his money has been caught and that his fortune will be returned. The next day, the family celebrates the double wedding of George and Arabella and Sir William and Sophia at church.

Christian Themes

Goldsmith writes of his protagonist, Dr. Primrose, "The hero of this piece unites in himself the three greatest characters upon earth; he is a priest, an husbandman [farmer], and the father of a family." With Primrose also the narrator, the novel becomes a spiritual autobiography of a Christian hero, whose warning is a Latin epigraph on the title page: "Take heart ye who are miserable; take heed ye who are happy."

From this spiritual journey of a fall and a rise, three Christian themes emerge. The first is marriage. Because so much in eighteenth century England depended on rank and station, marrying well was crucial to the hopes of every family. After Primrose loses his money, it becomes hard for his children to marry well, so he relies on farming as a second income to cultivate marriage proposals from Squire Thornhill and Farmer Williams. More than its social consequences, marriage has religious significance. Primrose argues that priests should marry only once (the "Whistonean Controversy"), and throughout the novel Primrose's own strong marriage sustains him. That the novel closes with the recognition that Olivia's marriage to Squire Thornhill is legal and the double wedding of two of Primrose's other children affirms the importance of the marriage theme as more religious than romantic.

Clerical life is another Christian theme. The novel shows that the life of a country parson was hard. Even with his university education, the learned Dr. Primrose must struggle as a farmer to provide for his family. Priestly pay—Queen Anne's Bounty, dating from the early 1700's—was so low that many parsons had to work to supplement it. Never complaining, Primrose exemplifies the Christian idea of the dignity of labor. Another difficulty for a priest was his allegiance to two "families," one by marriage, the other by holy orders. Just as Primrose balances the two demands of preaching and labor, he balances the demands of family and congregation. Still another obstacle to the clerical life is the prominence that the Church had lost under the Whig government by mid-century. Primrose complains that "sacred power . . . has for some years been every day declining, and losing its due share of influence in the state." As the established religion, the Church of England had been devalued by a Whig government, composed largely of "Dissenters," Presbyterians and others who refused to join the national church.

A third theme is virtue, exemplified throughout by Primrose. With the seven cardinal virtues as its ethical architecture, the novel is a monument to Christian morality. Goldsmith measures Primrose first by the criteria of the four classical virtues: prudence, justice, fortitude, and temperance. On prudence, Primrose too often falls short. An intellectual virtue, prudence is crucial to piercing the frauds that beset Primrose. His lack of prudence leaves him open to deceptions by Squire Thornhill, the "ladies," Wilkinson, and Ephraim Jenkinson. Believing the best in people, the gullible Dr. Primrose too often fails to suspect their worst. Justice prevails, however, in Primrose's character. Despite his powerlessness, the parson stands squarely against the powerful Squire Thornhill to denounce him as a whoremonger. In fortitude, Primrose is a modern Job. He searches, despite his illness, for his daughters when they are abducted; he stands firm when he and his son are imprisoned; and he courageously rushes into the fire to save his children. While Primrose's temperance leaves something to be desired as it leads to the detriment of his family, his zeal is driven by righteousness in incriminating Wilmot and inveighing against Squire Thornhill.

While his vanity about his prowess in preaching and arguing is a minor vice, Primrose is an exemplar of the three theological virtues: faith, hope, and charity. His faith is unimpeachable, expressly in his justifying the many coincidences as acts of providence. His hope is constant. Even in his darkest hours—his home lost, daughters lost, son lost, himself imprisoned and injured—hope allows Primrose to endure. Charity, Saint Paul's greatest virtue, is Primrose's in full measure. He deeds his salary to the families of deceased clergy; he loves everyone; and he forgives all, from Olivia, who brings shame to the family, to the hard-boiled prisoners he meets in jail.

Sources for Further Study

Battestin, Martin C. *The Providence of Wit: Aspects of Form in Augustan Literature and the Arts*. Oxford, England: Clarendon Press, 1974. Accounts for the biblical allusions, Christianity, and providence in the design of the novel.

Bellamy, Liz. *Commerce, Morality, and the Eighteenth-Century Novel*. New York: Cambridge University Press, 1998. Addresses several eighteenth century novels, including *The Vicar of Wakefield*, in an attempt to see the rise of the novel as a genre in the context of the century's concern with economic theory, public versus private morality, and commercial versus anticommercial ethics.

Emslie, Macdonald. *Goldsmith: "The Vicar of Wakefield."* Great Neck, N.Y.: Barron's Educational Series, 1963. Assesses the vicar, nature and society, wealth and charity, and language.

Ferguson, Oliver. "Dr. Primrose and Goldsmith's Clerical Ideal." *Philological Quarterly* 54 (1975): 323-332. Examines Primrose in the context of the eighteenth century Church and clergy.

Goldsmith, Oliver. *The Vicar of Wakefield*. Edited by Arthur Friedman with an introduction and notes by Robert L. Mack. New York: Oxford University Press, 2006. Mack's introduction to Friedman's edition provides context and background for the novel.

Hopkins, Robert H. *The True Genius of Oliver Goldsmith*. Baltimore: Johns Hopkins

University Press, 1969. Argues that the novel is more satiric than comic and sentimental.

Quintana, Ricardo. *Oliver Goldsmith: A Georgian Study*. New York: Macmillan, 1967. Explains the comedy in the novel.

Rothstein, Eric, and Howard D. Weinbrot. "*The Vicar of Wakefield*, Mr. Wilmot, and the 'Whistonean Controversy.'" *Philological Quarterly* 55 (1976): 225-240. Argues that this controversy on marriage was quite minor and that Primrose's disputing it so heatedly is comic.

H. George Hahn

A VIEW OF THE EVIDENCES OF CHRISTIANITY

Author: William Paley (1743-1805)
First published: 1794
Edition used: Paley's Evidences of Christianity, with Notes and Additions by Charles Murray Nairne, M.A. New York: Robert Carter, 1874
Genre: Nonfiction
Subgenres: Biblical studies; didactic treatise; history
Core issues: Knowledge; reason; scriptures

Written as an answer to the skeptical empiricism of contemporary David Hume, A View of the Evidences of Christianity presents scholarly arguments for accepting the New Testament as divinely inspired, historically accurate, and uniquely authentic in its representation of God's will for humankind. It draws on comparisons between Gospels and Epistles and on a number of classical nonbiblical sources.

Overview

William Paley's *A View of the Evidences of Christianity* (1794) stands both chronologically and conceptually between his two better-known works, *The Principles of Moral and Political Philosophy* (1785) and *Natural Theology: Or, Evidences of the Existence and Attributes of the Deity* (1802). The latter, a well-reasoned treatment of the arguments for intelligent design, begins with the often quoted analogy of inferring the existence of a watchmaker from finding a watch in a field. In the introduction, Paley suggests that the three works build on each other in reverse chronological order. Moral philosophy is built on the premise that God wishes the happiness of his creatures and that to ensure the virtue necessary for happiness, an adequate system of future rewards and punishments must exist. To accept that the New Testament contains an accurate description of that system, one must be convinced of its authenticity as divine revelation and historical record. Such conviction in turn requires belief in a deity who cares for and communicates with humankind.

As a philosopher, Paley was an empiricist who considered all human knowledge to be based, ultimately, on things sensed and experienced directly. For a Christian empiricist, that basis consisted foremost of the testimony in the New Testament and the writings of early Church fathers. Paley wrote *Horae Paulinae: Or, The Truth of the Scripture History of Saint Paul as Evinced by a Comparison of the Epistles Which Bear His Name* (1790) and *Evidences of Christianity* as an answer to David Hume's skepticism, particularly with respect to miracles.

Horae Paulinae is the more original work. In *A View of the Evidences of Christianity*, Paley draws heavily on Nathaniel Lardner's *The Credibility of Gospel History* (1727), which was the earliest major work to examine biblical texts in their historical context. Paley's contribution consists of reducing a diffuse scholarly work to a form accessible to an audience of parish clergymen and undergraduates at Cambridge University, where he taught moral theology, and of integrating biblical scholarship with a practical system of morality.

A View of the Evidences of Christianity is divided into three sections. The first part discusses the miracles attributed to Christ in the New Testament and presents arguments for accepting them as real occurrences. The second part, "Auxiliary Evidences of Christianity," presents other evidence from the Old and New Testaments and ancient writers supporting the veracity of the Gospels. The third part, "A Brief Consideration of Some Popular Objections," systematically examines eighteenth century arguments against either the historical accuracy of Christianity or its value as a guide to the conduct of human affairs.

Paley sets the stage with a series of rhetorical questions: Suppose the entire human race has lost sight of the divine means of obtaining future happiness. Suppose that God wishes to reveal his plan and that miracles are necessary to make that plan acceptable. The miracles, he concludes, are no less plausible than the revelation itself.

David Hume cast doubt on biblical miracles, maintaining that unreliable testimony was a far more probable explanation than an occurrence seemingly violating natural laws. He cited the lack of recent, well-documented instances of a similar nature to bolster his position. Paley counters by saying that this in no way violated the principle that like circumstances beget like results; because there is now no messiah spreading the message of salvation, no miracles are required.

The apostles and early Christian evangelists maintained their story in the face of severe persecution; moreover, with a few minor exceptions, it was always the same story. This would be unlikely if any part of it were a fabrication, Paley asserts. Ancient lists of the books of the orthodox canon include the same texts used throughout the Christian world in the eighteenth century, indicating that the selection process was not far removed in time or location from the events described. In contrast, other miracle stories cited by skeptics were based on testimony of solitary witnesses, promulgated by people who stood to profit by it, or described events explicable as natural phenomena.

Under the heading of auxiliary evidence, Paley cites Old Testament prophesies relating to Jesus and Jesus' own vision of the destruction of the Temple of Jerusalem. He accounts for the low proportion of specific moral precepts in Jesus' teachings by saying that the morality of actions depends entirely on their effects and that this has always been a subject of human experience rather than divine revelation. There is a long section juxtaposing Gospel passages with excerpts from contemporary writers, principally Flavius Josephus's *Bellum Judaium* (75-79 C.E.; *History of the Jewish War*, 1773), illustrating a high degree of accuracy in historical details. Paley cites the early rapid spread of Christianity and the successes of missionary activity in his own day as evidences for the essential truth of the message. The section concludes with a thoughtful, informed discussion of Islam. Paley uses Islam's militancy and its emphasis on literal hellfire to bolster his vision of Christianity as having spread through persuasion rather than coercion.

In "A Brief Consideration of Some Popular Objections," Paley first addresses discrepancies between the Gospels, maintaining that they are minor, consisting mainly of omissions, and arise from each evangelist having written his Gospel with a specific design in mind. Demonic possession, an "erroneous opinion" attributed to the apostles, reinforced the message at the time but had become irrelevant. Paley speaks contemptuously of Voltaire and others who would "make Christianity responsible in its own credibility for every narrative contained in the Old Testament." Much of the Old Testament does not meet the standards for plausibility that Paley applied to the New Testament, and he feels confident in relegating it to a place of secondary theological importance.

Saint Paul mentions miracles infrequently, as do second century Christian apologists, who indicate that contemporary pagans accused Christ of having been a magician. Emphasizing miracles to sophisticated ancients, reasons Paley, would have weakened the Gospel message.

In answering criticisms based on the supposed ill effects of Christianity in human history, Paley maintains that the role of Christianity in history is to be measured in the inner lives of humble people and not in the deliberations of princes, whose actions are based on the principle that those who are in power do whatever they can to keep it. While not denying that Christianity has been the excuse for persecution and oppressive laws, he considers that the root cause lies elsewhere. He thinks the persecution has been exaggerated, stating "The Slave trade [whose abolition was a personal cause to Paley] destroys more men in a year, than the Inquisition does in a hundred." He cites the French Revolution, then in the throes of the Reign of Terror, as an example of the havoc occurring when Christian values are repudiated.

Christian Themes

Although Paley was far from an original thinker, his three major works were extremely influential in shaping mainstream English thought in the nineteenth century. *A View of the Evidences of Christianity* was required reading for all Cambridge University undergraduates from 1822 to 1920. Charles Darwin, who eventually repudiated the doctrines embodied in *Natural Theology*, considered them two of the most worthwhile texts he had encountered during his education. The techniques of historical analysis and cross-comparison used by Paley are standard among Roman Catholic and mainstream Protestant biblical scholars today. Although the entire work deals with Christian themes, its core might be characterized as advice to educated Christians on how to read the Bible. In particular, it strikes a reasonable balance between total skepticism about anything failing to meet modern standards of scientific or journalistic accuracy and complete insistence on biblical inerrancy and a literal interpretation of every chapter and verse of the Old as well as the New Testament. The principle, that humans have no need of divine revelation to perceive what they can learn from the senses and their collective experience, and that this applies to the specifics of moral behavior, provides a very useful yardstick against which to measure the myriad provisions of Hebrew law and the less numerous prohibitions contained in the Epistles of Saint Paul, by weighing whether an additional two millennia of experience lead to a different conclusion.

Sources for Further Study

LeMahieu, Dan L. *The Mind of William Paley: A Philosopher and His Age.* Lincoln: University of Nebraska Press, 1976. A comprehensive biography covering the genesis and content of Paley's major works; good chapter on Paley's impact in the nineteenth century.

Matthew, H. C. G., and Brian Harrison, eds. *Oxford Dictionary of National Biography: From the Earliest Times to the Year 2000.* Oxford, England: Oxford University Press, 2004. Contains biographies of Paley and Hume that evaluate the impact of their writings.

Sweet, William. "Paley, Whately, and Enlightenment Existentialism." *International Journal of the Philosophy of Religion* 45, no. 3 (1999): 143-166. Traces the efforts of two rational Christian theologians to attack rational Deism with its own weapons. Richard Whately wrote *Historic Doubts Relative to Napoleon Bonaparte* (1819), a satire on skeptical treatments of the Bible as history.

_____, ed. *God and Argument.* Ottawa, Ont.: University of Ottawa Press, 1999. A collection of conference papers. The chapter "Evidentialism and Its Origins and the Anglo-American Philosophy of Religion" contrasts Paley with William Clifford, an American agnostic. Contains a chapter on philosophical approaches to miracles.

Martha A. Sherwood

VIOLENCE AND THE SACRED

Author: René Girard (1923-   )
First published: La Violence et la sacre, 1972 (English translation, 1977)
Edition used: Violence and the Sacred, translated by Patrick Gregory. Baltimore: Johns Hopkins University Press, 1977
Genre: Nonfiction
Subgenres: Biblical studies; critical analysis
Core issues: Gospels; Jesus Christ; morality; sacrifice

Literary critic and anthropologist Girard looks at societies over history to attempt to answer the question of how violence and religion have been so repeatedly and integrally intertwined throughout the centuries. His answer is that the violent is the sacred, and that the sensation of transcendence we experience as holiness is nothing other than our innate violence, disassociated from ourselves and transfigured by religion. Religion exists to control the violent impulses inherent in humans, to harness and redirect them into the sacred.

Overview

René Girard begins *Violence and the Sacred* by looking at works of literature such as *El ingenioso hidalgo don Quixote de la Mancha* (1605, 1615; *The History of the Valorous and Wittie Knight-Errant, Don Quixote of the Mancha,* 1612-1620; better known as *Don Quixote de la Mancha*) by Miguel de Cervantes, *Le Rouge et le noir* (1830; *The Red and the Black,* 1898) by Stendahl, *A Midsummer Night's Dream* (pr. c. 1595-1596) by William Shakespeare, and *Bratya Karamazovy* (1879-1880; *The Brothers Karamazov,* 1912) by Fyodor Dostoevski. In all of these, Girard says, the same concept of desire and an impulse toward violence prevail. We tend to want what other people want; in other words, desires are mimetic, primarily stirred by the desires of others rather than internal forces. Rivalry and violence are thus created by exposure to other human beings. Mimetic desire is not an entirely bad thing; it can be a constructive force, if our shared desires move us toward something that is good and can be shared. However, more often than not, it is a source of jealousy, anger, and violence.

Girard turns this concept outward to look at how it plays out with a larger social group. In early human history, small groups of hunter-gatherers wandered across the land and seas, rarely encountering each other. However, as time passed, the groups became larger stationary communities, and as the amount of daily interaction with other humans increased, rivalries leading to violence increased.

According to Girard, violence is mimetic. People witnessing it tend to act violently in turn, and more and more are drawn into the mimetic frenzy. Mimesis is not the issue, but the direction in which it leads people is. The only way to stop the wave of violence and keep societies from destroying themselves is through a sacrifice.

A sacrifice is a surrogate victim, animal or human, that acts as a scapegoat and dispels the violence. The scapegoat must have certain qualities. First it must be both part of the community yet somehow apart from it. Second, it must be similar to the target of rivalry that started the mimetic violence. Third, it must be a victim that can be sacrificed without fear of retribution.

Moreover, the ones enacting the sacrifice, the sacrificers, cannot be aware that they are making a scapegoat out of the victim. So that the sacrificers can perform the act without recognizing it for what it is, a misunderstanding must arise. Therefore, Girard argues, religion was invented in the form of a supernatural being demanding the sacrifice. In most societies, animal sacrifice became a substitute for human sacrifice. However, if the catharsis of animal sacrifice was not enough to maintain a society, then human sacrifice was employed. The culture that arises from this religious impulse will have sacrificial ritual, myth, and prohibitions.

In looking at mythology, Girard finds myth after myth acknowledging its violent origins while trying to cover them up, with deity after deity creating the world through its own dismemberment. Common prohibitions reflect the same mimetic crises, because often the most available and accessible objects are prohibited. As the most likely to provoke mimetic rivalries among members of the group, these objects are strictly regulated or forbidden. Societal hierarchies also work to lessen mimetic crises: When a desired object is not attainable because of class, the feeling of rivalry is reduced.

If, Girard asks, the solution to societal crises requires a social act whose meaning must be concealed, how can society see the truth of sacrificial violence and abolish it? For a way out of this dilemma, Girard turns to the Hebrew Bible, which records a slow transition away from the mechanism of sacrifice. In the Bible, the victim is given a voice for the first time: The blood of Abel, for instance, "cries from the ground." Joseph, the target of collective violence by his brothers, becomes an agent of reconciliation. In the story of David, Jonathan rejects the mimetic rivalry with David that his father, Saul, attempts to draw him into, and with the renunciation of that rivalry, Jonathan demonstrates a new way for human beings to interact with each other. In addition, after a time, animal sacrifices begin to be denounced in the Hebrew Bible, because if the basic structure of the sacrifice is a repetition of the urge toward violence as social mechanism, it cannot move away from it. Instead, ethical structures begin to develop in place of the tradition of animal sacrifice.

Jesus represents the final movement away from this tradition, Girard says. He renounces the rival messianic model of a victorious warrior appearing to slay all enemies of God and warns his followers away from the connection between mimetic rivalry and violence: "You have heard that it was said, an eye for an eye and a tooth for a tooth. But I say to you, do not resist an evildoer. But if anyone strikes you on the right cheek, turn the other one also."

Jesus unmasks the violence and deception inherent in the old social mechanisms. Because of his ethical challenge to the sacrificial cult and the economy built around its tradition, demonstrated in his cleansing of the temple, Jesus is killed by the agents of those forces. His death demonstrates that in the craze of mimetic violence, truth is lost: The crowd that cheered Jesus now stones him, the disciples flee, and Peter denies him.

Jesus' death, though, is not an appeasing sacrifice to an angry god as a punishment for human sin. Instead, Jesus is returned to life by God. Moreover, he does not return to avenge himself on those that killed him, but rather witnesses to his disciples that sacrificial violence can be short-circuited. Jesus becomes the bridge between the world of violence and the brighter kingdom of Heaven.

Christian Themes

Girard argues that Jesus has exposed sacred violence permanently and, in doing so, has moved us into a precarious time in which we splinter society because we continue to rely on the structure of the sacrificial tradition. Groups are organized around a victim or group of victims, decentralizing society by not having a single central victim. Furthermore, because humans have a tendency to avenge victims in a way that creates more victims, violence escalates and social chaos ensues.

At the same time, we are drawn to the Kingdom of God by witnessing Jesus' statement regarding the sacrifice and its true meaning: that the sacrifice is no longer necessary. In doing so, we renounce rivalry, realizing that the Kingdom of Heaven is open to everyone and that to follow Jesus is to become an advocate for all of humanity. This brings us again to the concept of mimetic desire. Girard says that the more our human desires are patterned after the desires of Christ, the more we desire the life offered us by God be offered to others in turn.

By offering forgiveness and strength to resist violence, Girard argues, Jesus counters the worldly impulse to resolve conflicts through the competitive use of power. Jesus' refusal to enact violence on those who had acted against him short-circuits the cycle of violence and removes the need for the mechanism of the sacrificial victim. Jesus has modeled the right way to act on the human impulse toward mimesis, a way urged on us by God.

In the same way, it is important for us to model Christ for others, serving as an example, Girard notes. The members of the Holy Trinity imitate each other with love, with no rivalry, in the same way that Jesus urges us to love.

Sources for Further Study

Bailie, Gil. *Violence Unveiled: Humanity at the Crossroads*. New York: Crossroad, 1995. Bailie uses Girard's theory of mimetic desire and phenomena ranging from Aztec mythology to Bob Dylan to explore the power of Christian revelation.

Girard, René. *Deceit, Desire, and the Novel*. Baltimore, Md.: Johns Hopkins University Press, 1965. Girard analyzes the novel in terms of mimetic desire, setting the groundwork that he later draws on in *The Violence and the Sacred*.

Hamerton-Kelly, Robert G.: *The Gospel and the Sacred: Poetics of Violence in Mark*. Minneapolis, Minn.: Fortress Press, 1994. Uses biblical texts to interpret the modern social situation using a framework that draws heavily on Girard's theories.

Schwager, Raymund. *Must There Be Scapegoats? Violence and Redemption in the Bible*. San Francisco: HarperCollins, 1978. Applies the scapegoat theory to biblical theory to create a new frame for it.

Williams, James G. *The Bible, Violence, and the Sacred: Liberation from the Myth of Sanctioned Violence*. 1991. Reprint. Valley Forge, Pa.: Trinity Press International, 1995. Approaching Girard's theory from the viewpoint of a biblical scholar, Williams points out numerous places where the Gospels rely heavily on sacrificial violence.

Cat Rambo

VIRGIN TIME

Author: Patricia Hampl (1946-   )
First published: New York: Farrar, Straus and Giroux, 1992
Genre: Nonfiction
Subgenres: Journal or diary; meditation and contemplation
Core issues: Catholics and Catholicism; contemplation; faith; pilgrimage; prayer; silence

Hampl explains how she discovered the meaning of prayer as practiced by Roman Catholics through the ages. She travels to holy sites in Italy, where she learns about the lives of saints and nuns, and visits a retreat in Northern California, where she engages in spiritual silence and contemplation. She clears up her confusion about her strict Catholic childhood and makes startling connections between the power of prayer and the origins of poetry.

Overview

Virgin Time is organized into three sections: "Faith," "Miracles," and "Silence." "Faith" begins as Patricia Hampl flies from the United States to Europe to explore the origins of Catholicism. Although raised Roman Catholic, Hampl has been doubtful and confused about the concept of faith. How does one sustain faith? How does one reconcile childhood rebellion with a current need for spirituality? Hampl is interested in prayer and contemplation, especially as practiced by contemporary nuns. Her friendship with an American nun, Sister Mary Madonna (from the San Damiano Monastery near Hampl's hometown of St. Paul, Minnesota) provides the springboard for the trip. Hampl recognizes the similarities to a traditional pilgrimage; she will be traveling far to visit holy sites.

She begins her trip literally and figuratively in Italy. Hampl has signed up for an Italian walking tour called The Road to Assisi. The tour is based on the nomadic travels of Saint Francis, a prominent saint. In metaphorical terms, Hampl is mimicking Geoffrey Chaucer's *Canterbury Tales* (1387-1400), in which an odd assortment of pilgrims make their way to a religious site. After a few days of walking, Hampl realizes that she is more concerned with watching her traveling companions than taking notes about what it is like to traverse the old trails of Catholicism. She becomes wrapped up in their assumptions and personalities.

Her observations of her companions segue into memories of influential people. She categorizes her childhood as one of elitism. Parents and authority figures taught her that Catholics are better than people who belong to other Christian denominations and that they were pre-chosen for positions of divine exultation. Along with elitism came rites and rituals that Catholic children were to perform and respect, yet never question. She recalls that her favorite subject in school was literature, taught with fervor by nuns. Her early education in literature was one of the first areas of friction. While

Catholic school was pushing her toward the old-fashioned role of the passive and obedient wife, the heroines in literature were anything but that sort of woman.

The walking tour culminates in a rigorous climb to the summit of Subasio, a mountain near Assisi that Saint Francis had climbed. Hampl completes the hike and tour, but she feels that her understanding of spirituality remains incomplete.

In "Miracles," Hampl spends a few days at the Poor Clare monastery of Santa Chiara. There she meets briefly with a young American nun, Sister Agnes, who has come to Santa Chiara for more intense work with a stronger commitment to ending poverty. Hampl is curious about the sister's path to contemplation. Before coming to Europe, Sister Agnes was a physician in Detroit, Michigan. She began the process of entering a monastery in Michigan, but backed out. Some years ago, she visited Santa Chiara and unexpectedly decided to pursue taking her vows. Now, Hampl discovers, the young Sister Agnes plans to stay at the cloister of Santa Chiara, simply pursuing prayer and God. As the two women depart, Hampl is surprised to learn that Agnes desperately wants a calligraphy kit, and that, ironically, Agnes's name before entering the cloister was Patricia. Later, Hampl hears that Agnes has left the Santa Chiara cloisters and returned to Detroit.

Next she meets up with a lively group of nuns and friars who are quick to embrace comparisons to *The Canterbury Tales*. In contrast with the mostly secular participants who were on vacation on the walking tour, this new group is deeply religious, taking part in the trip as a form of study, contemplation, and reunion. The nuns and friars talk about Saint Francis and Saint Clare as peers who, despite their long-ago deaths, are still part of modern life.

Hampl continues to be intrigued by the decisions and personalities of her traveling companions. Her new roommate, Elsie Pickett, is unhappy with the trip because she thinks that the others are not focusing on the most important aspect of prayer. Elsie has latched onto the fact that when Saint Francis prayed, it was with groans and sighs, as if he were consumed by spirit. She is disheartened by how modern Catholics are afraid to contend with this deep aspect of prayer—that it is not silent, but it also is not comprehensible. It is inarticulate, which is a new idea to Hampl.

In the final section, "Silence," Hampl attends a retreat at a Cisterian women's monastery in a Northern California redwood forest. The retreat is a popular destination for two reasons. First, the monk Thomas Merton, known for his vow of silence, visited it once. Many of his contemporary admirers follow his travels, not unlike how people also follow Saint Francis's travels. Second, the retreat is located in an old-growth redwood forest that neighbors lumber-company land. As a result, there is an air of divine stewardship.

Hampl realizes, at the week's end, that she does know what prayer is. It masquerades as language, but in reality it is a state of being. She counters the usual notion that silence says something to us; instead, she realizes that silences helps us sort through what needs to be said. This awareness bridges the remaining gaps between silence and the composition of poetry. She even interprets Psalm 90 as referring to the type of contemplation that turns time into poetry.

Christian Themes

Like many women of her generation and vocation (she is a college professor), Hampl is at odds with her Catholic upbringing. She is frustrated with the pronouncements from the Vatican, such as the official church positions on marriage, abortion, and homosexuality. However, she is intrigued by the silent, prayer-based contemplation of the nuns. Can one engage in the private, spiritual aspects of Catholicism without compromising morals? Thinking about privacy and spirituality leads Hampl to the concepts of prayer and time.

The title of her book, *Virgin Time*, refers to the monk Thomas Merton's awareness that outside of the human world of time, there is the time between moments, such as the moment between night and day, or the moment that was the original beginning of time. This is virgin time. It is time without forward motion, or time that is paradoxically timeless, a state simply known as being.

An implicit suggestion in the narrative is that practicing prayer, contemplation, and silence may be a way to experience virgin time. For Hampl, poetry is also a natural result, and its creation is linked to contemplation. The book covers many examples of how Catholics approach prayer. Some make it their life's work; others approach it as personal and private; stories of Saint Francis claim that he sighed and groaned while praying. She disputes the notion that prayer is akin to surrender, explaining instead that prayer can be the stimulus for what needs to be said, a figurative song of expression. Despite her fervor for understanding prayer, she believes that prayer is dead. Much of the memoir is about her search for ways to reinvigorate her personal understanding of prayer and how it is an integral foundation for poetry.

Because Hampl's travels take her to the thresholds of holy sites, she writes about Roman Catholic history and how contemporary friars and nuns view their holy duties. She describes the varieties of Catholic orders (Franciscan compared with Dominicans, for example). Nothing is idealized; Hampl finds fault not only within herself, but also with her traveling companions who have their own idiosyncrasies that, on occasion, eclipse their divine duties. It is this conflict of the modern world with the old world that interests her. As an educated, independent woman, she found it easy to leave the church; now she encounters people like herself who have returned on their own terms, and she is fascinated by how people find their inner integrity. Hers is the archetypal search for private religious virtue.

Sources for Further Study

Hampl, Patricia. "In Memory of Me." Interview by Maureen Abood. *U.S. Catholic* 71, no. 9 (September, 2006): 24-29. Hampl discusses writing, her life, and her views on several Christian topics.

_____. *A Romantic Education*. Boston: Houghton, 1981. Hampl visits Prague to learn about communism, religion, and her Czech ancestors. A precursor to the similar discovery narrative of *Virgin Time*.

McCarthy, Mary. *Memories of a Catholic Girlhood*. New York: Harcourt, 1957. Recounts McCarthy's struggles after her parents' deaths in 1918. Worth comparing with Hampl's first memoir; also considered a classic of the genre.

Ohlson, Kristin. *Stalking the Divine: Contemplating Faith with the Poor Clares*. New York: Hyperion, 2003. Ohlson accidentally discovers the Poor Clare nuns engaging in continual prayer in a Cleveland, Ohio, neighborhood. Most of the nuns in Hampl's book are part of the Poor Clare network.

Spoto, Donald. *Reluctant Saint: The Life of Saint Francis of Assisi*. New York: Viking Compass, 2002. This historical book includes details about Saint Francis's method of prayer and contemplation, which are a focus in Hampl's memoir.

Jen Hirt

THE VOCATION OF MAN

Author: Johann Gottlieb Fichte (1762-1814)
First published: Die Bestimmung des Menschen, 1800 (English translation, 1848)
Edition used: The Vocation of Man, translated, with an introduction and notes, by Peter Preuss. Indianapolis, Ind.: Hackett, 1987
Genre: Nonfiction
Subgenres: Meditation and contemplation; spiritual treatise
Core issues: Conscience; doubt; faith; knowledge; morality; reason

Fichte argues that humans can know only what is in their mind, such as thought and sensory experiences. What exists outside the mind, in the natural world, is merely the product of intuition and reasoning responding to sensory impressions. Humans inhabit two realms: the sensuous, which binds them to the laws and conditions of the natural world, and an invisible world that inspires faith in an eternal Spirit. The vocation of humankind is to live according to the eternal plan of this Spirit, which speaks through our moral conscience and guides our spiritual lives to a state of perfection.

Overview

Johann Gottlieb Fichte begins his search for the source of human knowledge with "Doubt," the title of his first section. We humans, he argues, infer the existence of objects in the natural world from sensory impressions and from thoughts about those impressions. Everything in nature, including humans, obeys a universal law of cause and effect and is the product of an unwavering necessity. Because all we know is the product of thought, we can know only what occurs or exists in our consciousness. It is in the nature of humans to think, and we are free to choose how we think, but the way we think is determined by our nature. We cannot be other than what we are, just as objects in nature cannot be something else. From this analysis of the human intellect, Fichte arrives at two conflicting views of human existence: Humans are subject to the cause-and-effect laws of nature, yet their ability to reason will raise humans above the strict necessity that controls the natural world.

In the second section, "Knowledge," Fichte seeks to resolve this dilemma. He does so by conducting a dialogue between "I," representing his own, questioning self, and "Spirit," who guides him in his quest for truth and understanding of the nature and activity of human consciousness. Through meticulous analysis of inner experience and the processes of thought, he concludes that humans synthesize mental activities, which consist of spontaneous thinking and the passive receptivity of sensation. We infer the existence and behavior of objects in the external world by combining sensation with the law of causality, but because this mental activity never extends beyond the intellect and the laws of our nature, we can never know more than ourselves. Sensation produces an image of an external object, but how we see this image is determined by the laws of our intellect, and therefore what we "see" is only ourselves "seeing." Human consciousness is the result of this combination of reception, inference, and intuition. Our understanding of the external world grows because reasoning enables us to apply what we already know to new experiences. In this way, what we know is determined by what we already know, yet this knowledge has no actual reality. It is only an abstraction existing in our mind.

In the final section of the book, "Faith," Fichte asserts that humans must act on the belief that knowledge has validity and that other humans exist in the external world, which is the arena of our actions. Further, we must accept others as independent beings and respect their freedom to act and think as they choose. Faith includes the belief that we share a bond with all other rational beings in the world of spirit. Fichte's faith also compels him to believe that a universal, benevolent will directs all existence and speaks to him through his moral conscience. Remaining steadfastly true to this will, he flows toward spiritual perfection. Progress toward this ideal is not achieved all at once, however; rather, it evolves as humans improve their understanding of nature. In time, humans will lose their temptation to do evil, developing cultures that benefit both nature and humankind. As these cultures expand their influence, they will ultimately encompass all of existence.

Evil exists in the world because humans have not yet achieved a universal community of good will, but they will, for a divine will directs everything toward everlasting goodness; even evil serves this purpose, for eventually its futility and destructiveness will teach humans to embrace only goodness.

To give meaning and purpose to his life, Fichte accepts on faith the existence of a higher power who wills goodness for all things. The natural world is bound by endless repetition that has no meaning for him. The fact that humans possess reason and spirit makes them a part of the spiritual world. Fichte has finally found his vocation: While on earth he shall resolutely and unwaveringly obey the divine will, which tells him how to act at every moment. The faith that his reason discovers not only explains the relation of the spiritual world of the mind to the world of the senses but also turns despair into hope and joy by convincing him that the spirit underlying all existence leads to eternal life and spiritual perfection. While on earth, he will continue to experience pain and illness, for he inhabits a physical world in which suffering and other misfortunes are inescapable, but his faith in the goodness of the universal will and in the existence of an eternal spiritual life enables him to look on evil and suffering in the physical realm without dismay or dread. Even death is not fearful to him, for he regards it as a transition from the world of the senses into the spiritual world of everlasting goodness.

Christian Themes

Moral goodness derives from a faith in the perfection and purpose of an eternal Spirit, whose nature is infinite, perfect, and benevolent. Fichte does not turn to organized or traditional religion or to the Scriptures for his moral guidance. He comes to his faith through a rational examination of the nature of the human intellect, which uses reason, intuition, and inference to discover the nature and extent of human knowledge. Although his understanding is based on indirect knowledge, through his inner responses to sensuous experiences, Fichte posits a world outside his own mind, and he believes that growth and renewal in the natural world mirror a similar progress in the spiritual realm, through which humans, by virtue of their innate moral conscience, are allied.

Unlike the objects in the natural world, humans are not the product of cause and effect, Fichte argues. Because humans have the freedom to think and act, they are capable of improvement, and their nature is such that they grow toward perfection, guided by their moral conscience, which mediates between them and the eternal Spirit. Humans are by their nature good, or strive to be good, because they are part of the eternal Spirit, but they must have faith in the divine Spirit, which, through each person's moral conscience, guides humans toward goodness. In the natural world, of which humans are a part, death and birth signify endless renewal; in the spiritual realm, all humans share a common alliance with the divine Spirit and progress toward a state of perfection.

It is humankind's vocation to obey the moral conscience steadfastly. Fichte's faith and morality are not sectarian, but they are consistent with Christian principles and practices in the sense that the individual is guided toward a state of spiritual perfection by a faith in an all-powerful Spirit whose divinity is unquestioned. Self-examination is the basis of Fichte's faith, and his reasoning guides him to a spiritual awareness very much like the awakening of the Christian seeker. Through philosophical reasoning, Fichte comes to the spiritual awareness, and faith, that a devoted Christian might discover in biblical study.

Sources for Further Study

Baur, Michael. "Self-Measure and Self-Moderation in Fichte's *Wissenschaftslehre*." In *New Essays in Fichte's Foundation of the Entire Doctrine of Scientific Knowledge*, edited by Daniel Breazeale and Tom Rockmore. Amherst, N.Y.: Prometheus Books, 2001. Discusses Fichte's theory about how the human mind operates, illuminating the ideas in *The Vocation of Man*.

Breazeale, Daniel. "Bibliography." In *Fichte: Historical Contexts/Contemporary Controversies*, edited by Daniel Breazeale and Tom Rockmore. Atlantic Highlands, N.J.: Humanities Press, 1994. An entire chapter lists the essential studies of Fichte's work, including *The Vocation of Man*.

La Vopa, Anthony J. *Fichte: The Self and the Calling of Philosophy, 1762-1799*. Cambridge, England: Cambridge University Press, 2001. Explains Fichte's concept of God, which underlies *The Vocation of Man*, in relation to the charge against him of atheism.

Radrizzani, Ives. "The Place of *The Vocation of Man* in Fichte's Work." In *New Essays on Fichte's Later "Jena Wissenschaftslehre,"* edited by Daniel Breazeale and Tom Rockmore. Evanston, Ill.: Northwestern University Press, 2002. Besides Radrizzani's essay, this volume includes Rockmore's discussion of Fichte's use of the term "representation" in *The Vocation of Man*.

Zöller, Günter. *Fichte's Transcendental Philosophy: The Original Duplicity of Intelligence and Will*. Cambridge, England: Cambridge University Press, 1998. Clarifies Fichte's major concepts, giving special attention to the meaning of "faith" in *The Vocation of Man*.

Bernard E. Morris

WAITING FOR GOD

Author: Simone Weil (1909-1943)
First published: Attente de Dieu, 1950 (English translation, 1951)
Edition used: Waiting for God, translated by Emma Craufurd with an introduction by Leslie A. Fiedler. New York: Harper & Row, 1973
Genre: Nonfiction
Subgenres: Essays; letters
Core issues: Agape; Baptism; church; conversion; faith; God; love; mysticism; suffering

In this collection of letters and essays on the love of God and the spiritual demands of such love, Weil offers the most direct way of comprehending her iconoclastic faith and, by extension, an intellect's reading of her faith.

Overview

Simone Weil was born in Paris on February 3, 1909, to an agnostic Jewish family. She was graduated in 1931 from the École Normale Supérieure as a teacher of philosophy. In 1934, she took a year's leave from her teaching to take a job at the Renault Works in order to learn through her own experience the hard conditions of the workers there. After another period of teaching, she spent several weeks on the Catalonian front sharing the sufferings of the Republican army there during the Spanish Civil War. She wrote for various journals of the political left and periodically took on manual labor without asking for or receiving any concessions because of her social status, education, or health, which was often poor.

In June, 1941, Weil met the Reverend J. M. Perrin, O.P., and through him Gustave Thibon, a Catholic writer, both of whom had a profound influence on her. In 1938 she had undergone a mystical experience in which, as she reported it, "Christ came down and took me," and in letters to Father Perrin she told of this experience and of the anguishing reflections that her persistent spiritual search provoked. In May, 1942, she left France with her family to escape from the Nazi-installed Vichy government's anti-Semitic policies; she traveled to the United States from Casablanca. She was then asked to work with the French provisional government in London and went there in November, 1942. She became ill in England but refused to take the food she needed to survive so that she would not be in a more favored position than the French suffering under the German occupation. She died on August 29, 1943.

In his introduction to the American edition of *Waiting for God* (the British edition has the title *Waiting on God*), Leslie Fiedler describes Simone Weil as "the Outsider as saint in an age of alienation, our kind of saint." Born into an agnostic Jewish family, she became a political leftist, probably more out of love for the oppressed than from the influence of any political philosophy. She became devoted to God through an entirely unexpected and, were it not for the fact of its happening, incredible mystical experience, one in which, as she described it to Father Perrin, "Christ himself came down and took possession of me."

Despite her mystical encounter with Christ, a spiritual marriage that was repeated frequently when she recited the poem "Love" by George Herbert (the recitation of which had first brought Christ to her) or the Lord's Prayer in Greek, she never was baptized into the Church. She remained outside the Church and insisted (in letters to Father Perrin) that "the will of God is that I should not enter the Church at present." By remaining outside the Church, she identified herself with those who, through the accidents of personal history, lived their lives in suffering and isolation, in poverty and rejection, also outside the Church. Her death from starvation was a consequence of her refusing to eat more than her compatriots, who were suffering under the Germans during the occupation of France.

Waiting for God consists of letters and essays sent or entrusted to Father Perrin. Weil's letters are represented by a set of six letters, beginning with one concerned with her hesitations concerning baptism, including her significant "spiritual autobiography," and concluding with her "last thoughts." The essays that follow are "Reflections on the Right Use of School Studies with a View to the Love of God," "The Love of God and Affliction," "Forms of the Implicit Love of God," and "Concerning the Our Father." Together these letters and essays, as presented in *Waiting for God*, enable the reader to come to focus on Weil's unique faith and brilliant intellect.

In her letter to Father Perrin concerning baptism (dated January 19, 1942), Weil writes that she has been wondering how to reach the point of conforming herself to God's will. She argues that it is necessary, if one is to clarify the matter, to distinguish three domains: that which is independent of human beings (the past, present, and future beyond the reach of any finite person); that which is under the rule of the will; and that which, although not under the will, is nevertheless in some way and to some degree dependent upon us. As for the first domain—the domain of the facts beyond our power—"everything that comes about is in accordance with the will of God," she argues, and she contends that accordingly we must "love absolutely everything," including evil, our past sins, our sufferings, and "what is by far the most difficult," the sufferings of others.

The second domain is the domain of duty; here the intelligence and the imagination reign. In the third domain, however, "we experience the compulsion of God's pressure, on condition that we deserve to experience it." (Here the idea central to her faith and thought is expressed for us: that we are to love God by attending to him, by waiting for him attentively and with love.) "God rewards the soul that thinks of him with attention and love," she writes; ". . . we must go on thinking about God with ever increasing love and attentiveness." God's reward comes in the form of a "compulsion," a "pressure," to which, she declares, "we have to abandon ourselves . . . to run to the exact spot whither it impels us and not go one step farther, even in the direction of what is good." The culmination of this process of submitting oneself to the divine pressure is reached when "the pressure has taken possession of the whole soul" and "we have attained the state of perfection."

Weil makes it clear to Father Perrin that God has not by his will led her to enter the Church. She suggests that she may not be at the level of spirituality that would be adequate for one to be worthy of the Sacraments. However, she declares her readiness to submit to the God on whom she attends: "If it is God's will that I should enter the Church, he will impose this will upon me at the exact moment when I shall have come to deserve that he should so impose it," and, again, "But one thing is absolutely certain. It is that if one day it comes about that I love God enough to deserve the grace of baptism, I shall receive this grace on that very day, infallibly, in the form God wills."

The second letter is also concerned with the problem of her entering the Church. Here she expresses her misgivings concerning the Church as a "social structure." She confesses that she is very easily influenced, and that the Church, through its power as a community of enthusiastic persons, might very well have the effect on her of winning her allegiance through her emotions rather than by way of her independent will to love God. She declares that the thought that she might come to regret having been baptized with sentiments "other than those that are fitting" fills her with horror. The degree of her submissiveness to the will of God, the strength of her determination to wait for God to move her, is shown by the following declaration near the end of her letter: "If I had my eternal salvation placed in front of me on this table, and if I only had to stretch out my hand to take it, I would not put out my hand so long as I had not received the order to do so."

Weil's determination to be moved only by God is also expressed in the third letter of the collection in *Waiting for God*, a letter written to Father Perrin on April 16, 1942. She tells him that she will be leaving France at the end of the month, and she writes: "It seems to me as though something were telling me to go. As I am perfectly sure that this is not just emotion, I am abandoning myself to it." Abandonment of this kind (submission to the will of God) will bring her to "the haven," she writes, and she goes on to tell him that, for her, the haven is the cross. She adds: "If it cannot be given me to deserve one day to share the cross of Christ, at least may I share that of the good thief." She envies the good thief: "To have been at the side of Christ and in the same state during the crucifixion seems to me a far more enviable privilege than to be at the right hand of glory." (At the close of her next letter, the "spiritual autobiography," she repeats the idea: ". . . every time I think of the crucifixion of Christ I commit the sin of envy.")

In her letter of May 15, 1942, from Marseilles (letter four in the book, entitled "Spiritual Autobiography"), Weil begins her account of what might be called her spiritual pilgrimage by reminding Father Perrin that he neither brought her the Christian inspiration nor brought her to Christ; by the time she met him, "it had been done without the intervention of any human being." She tells him that she had never sought God; for her the "problem of God" was a problem to be let alone. (She was already, one might presume, "waiting for God"; in any case, the tendency on her part to let problems resolve themselves whenever there was nothing she could do about it was later manifest as the tendency to await God's "pressure," to be ready for but not to anticipate his action on her.) Despite her having put the problem of God aside, she adopted (for as far back as she could remember) the "Christian attitude," and she declares that from childhood "I always had . . . the Christian idea of love for one's neighbor, to which I gave the name of justice."

Through her year's experience in the factory (she tells Father Perrin) she became intimately aware of the *malheur* (the French word is translated as "affliction") of others: ". . . the affliction of others entered into my flesh and my soul." She suddenly came to regard herself and the others in affliction as slaves, and "the conviction was suddenly borne in upon me that Christianity is preeminently the religion of slaves, that slaves cannot help belonging to it, and I among others."

In 1937 in Assisi, in the chapel of Santa Maria degli Angeli, "something stronger than I was compelled me for the first time in my life to go down on my knees," she writes Father Perrin. In 1938 she found that during the liturgical services at Solesmes she was "able to rise above" her migraine headaches (from which she often suffered) and to find joy in the service. She realized then "the possibility of loving divine love in the midst of affliction," and she came more and more to understand and to appreciate (and even, in a sense, to share) the passion of Christ.

A reading of George Herbert's "Love" led to her first encounter with God, and she explains that "in this sudden possession of me by Christ, neither my senses nor my imagination had any part; I only felt in the midst of my suffering the presence of a love." She is careful to tell the father that "God in his mercy had prevented me from reading the mystics, so that it should be evident to me that I had not invented this absolutely unexpected contact."

In the close of her autobiographical letter Weil writes to Father Perrin, "Good-by, I wish you all possible good things except the cross; for I do not love my neighbor as myself, you particularly, as you have noticed." (For herself, of course, she wished the cross; she wished to wait in extreme suffering for God, to share the passion of Christ.)

In letter five to "S" (entitled "Her Intellectual Vocation"), she remarks that her vocation requires her to remain outside the Church "in order that I may serve God and the Christian faith in the realm of the intelligence."

The idea that "God's mercy is manifest in affliction as in joy" and that both joy and affliction are signs of the contact with God is developed in her very significant letter of May 26, 1942 (letter six, "Last Thoughts"), again to Father Perrin. After declaring to the father that "in affliction itself . . . the splendor of God's mercy shines," she writes: "If still persevering in our love, we fall to the point where the soul cannot keep back the cry 'My God, why hast thou forsaken me?' if we remain at this point without ceasing to love, we end by touching something that is not affliction, not joy, something that is the central essence . . . : the very love of God."

Christian Themes

The letters of *Waiting for God* offer the most direct way of comprehending (to some degree only, of course) the iconoclastic faith of Simone Weil, for they are personal and go directly to the heart of her affliction and her faith. (We know her personal anguish when she describes herself in the letters "Last Thoughts" as "a barren fig tree for Christ" and tells Father Perrin that "for other people, in a sense I do not exist. I am the color of dead leaves, like certain unnoticed insects.")

The essays are valuable, however, as an intellect's reading of her Christian faith. In "Reflections on the Right Use of School Studies with a View to the Love of God," Weil develops the central idea that prayer consists of attention and that, accordingly, Christian study is fundamentally a matter of giving full attention and developing the power of attention. "In every school exercise," she writes, "there is a special way of waiting upon truth, setting our hearts upon it, yet not allowing ourselves to go out in search of it," and she underscores the spiritual seriousness of her message by writing: "Only this waiting, this attention, can move the master to treat his slave with such amazing tenderness." Even the love of neighbor requires attentively looking at the neighbor to know the neighbor as one who suffers. If one goes at Latin or geometry with the right kind of attentiveness, she concludes, one may on that account "be better able to give someone in affliction exactly the help required."

The essay "The Love of God and Affliction" is a careful statement of her view that both joy and affliction are necessary if one is to know God, and she describes affliction as "a marvel of divine technique," and adds the reassuring comment that although affliction is the most depressing and painful kind of suffering, if one loves—that is, persists in turning toward God—one finds oneself "nailed to the very center of the universe. It is the true center; . . . it is God." We cannot go to God, she declares, but if we love God whatever our affliction, "Over the infinity of space and time, the infinitely more infinite love of God comes to possess us."

If one is inclined to suppose that Simone Weil was urging an attitude that calls for isolation and self-absorption in the effort to make contact with God, one has only to read her essay "Forms of the Implicit Love of God," in which she argues that the love of God includes and requires love of neighbor, love of the world's order, love of religious practices, and friendship. Although she argues that "contact with God is the true sacrament," she immediately adds that "We can, however, be almost certain that those whose love of God has caused the disappearance of the pure loves belonging to our life here below are no true friends of God."

Sources for Further Study

Cabaud, Jacques. *Simone Weil: A Fellowship in Love*. New York: Channel Press, 1964. Based on careful research and extensive interviews, this biographical account, with its numerous revealing photographs, provides a vivid picture of the dedicated but tortured life of Weil.

Doering, E. Jane, and Eric O. Springsted, eds. *The Christian Platonism of Simone Weil*. Notre Dame, Ind.: University of Notre Dame Press, 2004. A collection of essays on Weil's Christian Platonism. Bibliography, index.

Fiedler, Leslie A. Introduction to *Waiting for God*, by Simone Weil. New York: Harper & Row, 1973. Fiedler, of Montana State University, provides an excellent introduction in an edition that also includes letters, essays, and a biographical note translated from the French edition.

Panichas, George A., ed. *The Simone Weil Reader*. New York: David McKay, 1977. A well-produced, representative selection of Weil's writings.

Perrin, Joseph Marie, and G. Thibon. *Simone Weil as We Knew Her*. Translated by Emma Craufurd. New York: Routledge, 2003. Includes an introduction by J. P. Little; bibliography.

Pétrement, Simone. *Simone Weil: A Life*. Translated from the French by Raymond Rosenthal. New York: Pantheon Books, 1976. A monumental biography by one of Weil's closest friends, who as a doctor of philosophy and letters was well equipped to handle the sometimes elusive thought of Simone Weil. A detailed biographical account, with many photographs.

Rees, Richard. *Simone Weil: A Sketch for a Portrait*. Preface by Harry T. Moore. Carbondale: Southern Illinois University Press, 1966. Sir Richard Rees's account of Weil's life emphasizes her ideas in an intelligent and sympathetic way.

Weil, Simone. *The Need for Roots*. Translated by Arthur Wills with a preface by T. S. Eliot. New York: Putnam, 1952. Published in French as *L'Enracinement* (Gallimard, 1949), this is a thoughtful but not always successful attempt to develop a Christian social ethics, particularly aimed at France.

_____. *Notebooks*. Translated by Arthur Wills. London: Routledge & Kegan Paul, 1956. Reflects the original and inquisitive intellect of Simone Weil.

Ian P. McGreal

WAITING FOR GODOT

Author: Samuel Beckett (1906-1989)
First published: En attendant Godot, pb. 1952, pr. 1953 (English translation, 1954)
Edition used: Waiting for Godot, with a revised text. Edited with an introduction and notes by Dougald McMillan and James Knowlson. New York: Grove Press, 1994
Genre: Drama
Subgenres: Literary fiction; parables and fables
Core issues: Alienation from God; attachment and detachment; despair; loneliness; resignation; suffering

In this tragicomedy in two acts, Beckett presents two tramps on a nearly empty stage, containing only a dead tree and a small mound. The tramps arrive near twilight, stay till dark, and return the next day. This cycle has repeated itself for many years and appears endless. Almost nothing happens except when Pozzo and Lucky arrive in both acts, followed by a boy who denies that he is the same boy who came the day before. The tramps return to this place because they expect or hope that Godot will come and save them.

Principal characters
Vladimir, a tramp and optimist who believes in Godot
Estragon, Vladimir's cynical partner
Pozzo, a landowner and slave master
Lucky, Pozzo's slave
A boy, Godot's messenger

Overview

Waiting for Godot is an unremitting picture of despair and futility. It established a new direction for modern theater and made Samuel Beckett one of the foremost dramatists of that new trend in theater. In each act, two tramps, Vladimir and Estragon, longtime friends, appear at twilight on a desolate country road in the middle of nowhere to wait for an obscure figure named Godot, whom they have never seen, but whom they believe will rescue them from their otherwise empty and banal lives. The play may be understood as a metaphor for the human condition in the modern world.

Designed to cope with the banality and emptiness of their lives, this behavior is ritualistic. Every day they return to the same place to wait for the mysterious Godot. To pass the time and to fill the emptiness, they engage in comic banter and vaudevillian shtick. In act 1, just as the two tramps discuss whether they are tied to each other, this place, and to Godot, two others, Pozzo and Lucky, arrive, tied together by a long rope. Their arrival provides a grotesquely comic interlude that dramatizes the tramps' condition. Bound together and inseparable, Pozzo and Lucky share a common fate: Neither can do without the other. Metaphysically, all these "ties" represent the desperation of humans bound to a meaningless existence they cannot abandon. Figuratively speaking, the tramps are at the end of their rope.

Aware that language has failed them, their thinking is disorganized and fragmented, their memories inconsistent and unreliable, and their lives insignificant and absurd, the tramps struggle to find a reason to go on living. Their lives are reduced to the barest essentials: They own nothing, eat only carrots and turnips, sleep in ditches, and wear frayed and worn-out clothing. Although Godot has never come, they continue to wait. The two acts appear to repeat themselves: The tramps arrive and engage in various banters; Pozzo and Lucky appear; and at the end of each act, a boy materializes, a messenger from Godot but never the same boy. As the curtain closes in both acts, the tramps announce their intention to leave but do not move.

Despite the apparent repetition, significant differences define the two acts. In act 1, Vladimir, optimistically, and Estragon, cynically, wait for Godot. When Pozzo and Lucky, tied to each other with a long rope, arrive instead, the tramps, desperate to believe that Godot has arrived, confuse Pozzo with Godot. Amused by their misidentification, Pozzo denies he is Godot. Nonetheless, the tramps see in them an opportunity for diversion and for company. Gregarious, pompous, and somewhat formidable, Pozzo tells them they are trespassing on his land. In direct contrast, Lucky, his degenerate slave, is completely submissive. Devoid of human expression, obsequious, and pitiful, he cannot speak unless prompted by Pozzo. In sympathy, the tramps ask Pozzo to make Lucky speak. At Pozzo's command, Lucky begins an incomprehensible speech filled with fragmentary and oblique references to academic issues, history, and the Bible. Gradually his speech increases in tempo and finally dissolves into incoherent phrases and words. The others, totally frustrated by what sounds like the ravings of a madman, silence him by knocking him down and physically restraining him. When Pozzo and Lucky depart, the tramps are alone again to face the reality that Godot has not arrived. While they are in the pit of their despair, a boy messenger arrives and announces that Godot will not come today but surely tomorrow. Disillusioned and frustrated by the fact that they have heard all this before, the tramps declare their intention to leave. The curtain comes down, but the tramps do not move.

In act 2, some slight but significant changes occur. The tree has sprouted a few leaves, Pozzo is blind, Lucky is dumb, the boy messenger claims he is not the same boy who appeared yesterday, and Vladimir's optimism is shattered. As a result, he staggers under the weight of the hopelessness of their situation, whereas Estragon's cynicism is confirmed.

In structuring the play in two acts, Beckett was influenced by Saint Augustine's remark: Do not despair; one of the thieves was saved. Do not presume; one of the thieves was damned. Fascinated by their symmetry, Beckett borrows the structure for *Waiting for Godot*. Act 1 builds on a slight, but perceptible, movement toward hope. Act 2, on the other hand, moves from guarded optimism to despair. To Vladimir, the fact that the tree has grown leaves is a sign of hope. However, this hope is destroyed when Pozzo turns up blind and Lucky dumb, and a new messenger arrives denying he appeared previously. Frustrated and exhausted by his struggle to maintain hope and to make sense out of these events, Vladimir reaches a level of despair not seen before. He questions whether life has meaning, and more frantically, whether meaning is possible. Like Estragon, he entertains the thought that he can no longer endure his life. Throughout the two acts, he has attempted to convince Estragon and himself that salvation is possible. By the end of act 2, that hope has faded.

Christian Themes

Although Beckett claimed he was not a Christian, the quest for salvation is the cornerstone of the play and frequent Christian allusions serve as its subtext. However, in *Waiting for Godot*, these allusions serve not to assert belief, but to dramatize its decadence. Once Christianity provided Western civilization with a construct of meaning and hope, but now, decimated by the horrors of two world wars and the deconstruction of reality and meaning in modern philosophy, it is no longer credible. Because the characters no longer believe in Christianity or in anything, they are helpless and alone in a meaningless universe. Yet because the language and values of Christianity are the only ones they know, it serves them as a point of reference for their urgent need to find meaning and purpose. Thus, Estragon compares himself to Christ as the model for his own suffering. Waiting for the mysterious Godot can be understood as humankind waiting for redemption from an otherwise unbearable life. Although Beckett strenuously denied that Godot was God, in *Waiting for Godot*, as the object of the characters' ultimate longings and their hope for salvation, he serves a similar function as God. In act 1, Vladimir and Estragon speak of addressing Godot with a kind of prayer. At the end of act 2, the boy-messenger—a possible allusion to Christ—describes him as an old man with a white beard. This description evokes from Vladimir the plaintive cry, "Christ have mercy on us!" an echo of one made by Estragon in act 1 when he and Vladimir ask God and Christ to have mercy on them.

Other references to the Gospels abound. Early in the play, Vladimir speaks of the Gospel of John in which one of the thieves crucified with Jesus was saved, one damned. Although Vladimir does not say so, this Gospel represents the possibility that he and Estragon might also be saved. The tree is the most prominent Christian symbol. Much of the action centers around the tramps' desire to hang themselves from it, an allusion to crucifixion. Another Christian reference occurs in act 1, when Vladimir alludes to Proverbs 13:12. He tries to recall the lines that speak of hope as a "tree of life," an allusion that relates directly to the play's tree. In another example, Vladimir asks Estragon whether he has ever read the Bible. In act 2, frustrated by the inability to identify Pozzo and Lucky, Estragon calls Pozzo "Abel," and Lucky "Cain." Taken together, these and many more similar references tell us that Beckett's characters struggle to find meaning through the only language they know.

Sources for Further Study

Byden, Mary. "Beckett and Religion." In *Samuel Beckett Studies*, edited by Lois Oppenheim. New York: Palgrave Macmillan, 2004. A short but detailed study of the way various critics have responded to Beckett's use of religion.

_____. *Samuel Beckett and the Idea of God.* New York: St. Martin's Press, 1998. The most comprehensive book to study Beckett's work and his use of God.

Damashek, Richard. "Samuel Beckett's *Waiting for Godot*." Ph.D. diss., Columbia University, 1965. A study of the play that considers not only the Christian references but also the relation of the play to Simone Weill's *Attente de Dieu* (1950; *Waiting for God*, 1951).

Pattie, David. *The Complete Critical Guide to Samuel Beckett.* New York: Routledge, 2000. Contains both biographical information on Beckett and critical analysis of his works, including *Waiting for Godot.*

Richard Damashek

WALKING BY FAITH
The Diary of Angelina Grimké, 1828-1835

Author: Angelina Emily Grimké (1805-1879)
First published: Columbia: University of South Carolina Press, 2003, edited by Charles Wilbanks
Genre: Nonfiction
Subgenres: Autobiography; journal or diary
Core issues: Communion; perfection; Quakers; racism; self-knowledge; silence; women

Grimké, along with her older sister Sarah, was one of the few Southerners from slaveholding families to denounce slavery publicly and leave the South before the Civil War and the most intense period of abolitionism. This seven-year diary covers, first, the period of Angelina Grimké's life when she was wrestling with the decision to leave the Presbyterian Church in Charleston and become a Quaker (she had already left the Episcopal Church of her parents), and, secondly, her decision to leave Charleston and join her older sister Sarah in Philadelphia, never to return to South Carolina.

Overview

Angelina Grimké's religious struggle is activated by her growing revulsion with slavery and her ultimate decision to become an abolitionist speaker. The diary is more a spiritual delineation of the scriptural justifications for her changing positions than it is a daily diary; every entry is filled with biblical quotations. Her method is perpetually to find biblical analogies to her situation, and she seems to be able to find comfort in this kind of "proof-texting" when the Presbyterian minister, a friend, or a family member castigates her for her position.

Grimké's self-doubts are clearly laid out as she decides to take up Quaker practices: "plain speaking" (thee and thou, using "First Day" and "Second Day" instead of Sunday or Monday, "Fifth Month" instead of May, and so on), and the prohibitions against eating rich foods or wearing a lace-trimmed shawl or dress. She describes her destruction of her beloved novels of Sir Walter Scott, her denunciation of her brother for his treatment of his slaves, and her worries about her vexed relationship with her mother over slavery, the expense of redoing the drawing room (her father, an Oxford-educated judge, having died when she was very young), and her other siblings (especially a brother who did not contribute to his own upkeep). All of this is written in amazing particulars. The reader feels as if Grimké were in the room speaking directly to the reader about her spiritual journey of self-doubt to self-knowledge.

Grimké arranges to go to Philadelphia, first for a visit of several months. On returning to Charleston, she thinks she will rejoin the Quakers in Philadelphia within several months but is unable to return until about a year later. Because by this time she had left the Presbyterian Church and was speaking out against slavery to friends and family, she worried daily about the trials of continuing to live in the slave-holding society of South Carolina. Additionally, she was changing her dress, her speech, her eating and social habits, and she agonized over each difficulty with her acquaintances and family. She believed that she was called on to speak out against her brother's partying and drinking, her mother's orders to slaves, and her sister's use of lace and silks. She herself cut the lace off her dresses, refused rich cakes and wine, adopted Quaker speech by using thee and thou, refused to stand for prayers, and did not take communion.

Grimké's diary is filled with scriptural references on each matter, and her arguments against slavery become more sophisticated. She communicates with the Presbyterian minister about leaving the church and is ultimately satisfied that he understands. However, the Presbyterian Session then calls her to account on two charges: that she has absented herself from Sunday services and that she has not taken communion. By this time she has been attending the Quaker meeting in Charleston and has decided that this silent meeting is better than Sunday worship. When she appears before the session, her argument is that she believes that if she did indeed take communion and attend services, she would be doing a greater blasphemy than if she absented herself, believing as she now does that neither practice was demanded of Christians (supported of course by scriptural references).

Finally, Grimké is told she has a place to stay in Philadelphia and a position taking care of a child in the home of a Quaker there. So at the end of October, 1829, she travels by ship to Philadelphia, but she worries about leaving her mother. Applying for membership in the Society of Friends in Philadelphia, she is castigated for leaving her mother in Charleston, agrees to return to Charleston if necessary, but finally is accepted into the Arch Street Quaker meeting.

In 1831, Grimké travels with friends to New England, having been invited by Catherine Beecher, head of a girls' school in Hartford, Conn. Grimké is trying to determine her life work and learns that she could become a teacher in six months. She also visits prisons, factories, and an insane asylum, as well as natural wonders such as mountains and waterfalls. However, she is dissuaded by her Quaker community from pursuing teaching, since Beecher's seminary is Presbyterian and people there know nothing about Quakers.

For over a year, both before and after her trip to New England, Grimké is courted by Edward Bettle, son of a prominent Philadelphia Quaker family. Grimké is decidedly ambivalent in her attitude toward him, sometimes enthusiastic, sometimes worried that marriage will take her away from her "great work" (details of which she did not yet know). When Bettle is taken ill and dies within two weeks in late 1832, Angelina ultimately feels relief. She is reading abolitionist literature, making her clearest arguments against slavery, and preparing mentally for her entry into the public world as an abolitionist speaker and organizer, beginning with her letter to William Lloyd Garrison in 1835, published in *The Liberator*.

Christian Themes

The years of this diary cover Grimké's struggles with denominational differences and her conversion to Quaker beliefs and practices, especially while she was still living in Charleston with her family. So each step, from cutting the lace off her mantle to using Quaker speech to refusing to participate in family prayers and beginning to attend Quaker (silent) meeting on "First Day," is met with great conflict and self-doubt in her diary. Even when she first travels to Philadelphia, she is assailed with doubts about the spiritual correctness of her decisions; when she returns to Charleston, she is confronted by those wishing to dissuade her at every turn—her mother and brother, the Presbyterian minister, and her friends and acquaintances.

The Doctrine of Perfection (1810) is an early Methodist belief noted by the Reverend John Fletcher that asserts that humans were once perfect. If humans were once perfect, it is possible to again attain perfection, and humans must attempt to become perfect again. For Grimké, this perfection was a kind of enlightenment, so she attempts in all things to see her faults and try to change them. The doctrine is in essence a rejection of the doctrine of Original Sin. Believing in the doctrine of perfection leads Grimké closer to the Quaker belief in humanity's inherent goodness.

Grimké's arguments against slavery become more sophisticated in the years of her diary, as she notes the reasons why the usual biblical injunctions for slavery will not stand. She uses the Golden Rule in her debates with friends and family in Charleston, asking if that person would like to be a slave. When the answer was no, then she would quote, "Do unto others as you would have them do unto you." She learns to argue with biblical accuracy and to preach in Quaker meetings, and she is especially influenced by Elizabeth Evans, a woman preacher in Philadelphia. Note that the Hicksite Quakers, which Grimké first disagreed with, accepted women as preachers (such as the great Lucretia Mott) whereas other (Orthodox) Quakers and most other denominations did not. However, Grimké came by her rhetorical power by means of her prodigious biblical knowledge, her experiences teaching Sunday School in the Presbyterian Church, and the education she received from her older sister Sarah and the books in her father's library.

Sources for Further Study

Birney, Catherine. *The Grimké Sisters: Sarah and Angelina Grimké, the First American Women Advocates of Abolition and Women's Rights.* Reprint. Westport, Conn.: Greenwood Press, 1969. First published in 1885 by a contemporary, the work is remarkably free of nineteenth century laudatory rhetoric.

Browne, Stephen Howard. *Angelina Grimké: Rhetoric, Identity, and the Radical Imagination.* East Lansing: Michigan State University Press, 1999. Study of Grimké's rhetoric and language in diary, letters, and speeches.

Lerner, Gerda. *The Grimké Sisters from South Carolina: Pioneers for Women's Rights and Abolition.* Rev. ed. Chapel Hill: University of North Carolina Press, 2004. This expanded edition, by the women's history scholar who wrote the first twentieth century biography of the sisters, includes a new introduction and bibliography, as well as speeches and essays of both sisters.

Lumpkin, Katherine DuPre. *The Emancipation of Angelina Grimké*. Chapel Hill: University of North Carolina Press, 1974. Important biographical work with detail from years covered in Angelina's diary.

Margaret H. McFadden

WAR IN HEAVEN

Author: Charles Williams (1886-1945)
First published: 1930
Edition used: War in Heaven. Grand Rapids, Mich.: Wm. B. Eerdmans, 1970
Genre: Novel
Subgenres: Mystery and detective fiction; thriller/suspense
Core issues: Good vs. evil; mysticism; myths; spiritual warfare

The body of a murdered man in a London publishing house and a mysterious silver chalice in an obscure English village represent the two plot lines that Williams weaves together in this supernatural thriller. The victim's identity continues to elude police, and the chalice, which turns out to be the Holy Grail, changes hands several times between people who desire it for very different purposes. In the end, the murder is solved, the Grail and its keeper vanish, and good overcomes evil.

> *Principal characters*
> *Julian Davenant,* an Anglican archdeacon of Fardles
> *Gregory Persimmons,* a retired London publisher
> *Prester John,* the legendary keeper of the Holy Grail
> *Kenneth Mornington,* an editor in the Persimmons family firm
> *Duke of North Ridings,* an aristocrat living near Fardles
> *Lionel Rackstraw,* Kenneth's coworker
> *Barbara Rackstraw,* Lionel's wife
> *Adrian Rackstraw,* Lionel and Barbara's son
> *Dmitri Lavrodopoulos,* the owner of a London pharmacy

Overview

War in Heaven begins with the discovery of an unidentified corpse under the desk of Lionel Rackstraw, an editor at the Persimmons family firm. A few days later, Julian Davenant, the archdeacon of the village church in Fardles, visits Kenneth Mornington, a young editor at the firm, who shows him a copy of *Historical Vestiges of Sacred Vessels in Folklore* by Sir Giles Tumulty. Tumulty's manuscript suggests that the Holy Grail (the chalice Jesus and his disciples drank from at the Last Supper) is at the Fardles church. Gregory Persimmons, the firm's retired owner who is involved in the occult and has read the manuscript, determines to possess the Grail at any cost as a source of power for black magic.

Gregory moves to Cully, a country house near Fardles, to begin his quest. After a mysterious break-in at the church, and after Gregory unsuccessfully tries to purchase the chalice from the archdeacon, Gregory's henchman attacks the archdeacon and steals it. Lionel and Barbara Rackstraw and their son, Adrian, are vacationing at Cully at Gregory's invitation. Realizing that his occult power will be enhanced if he can corrupt an innocent child by initiating him into black magic, Gregory befriends the four-year-old boy and plans to take him and the chalice out of England.

A few weeks later, Mornington and the Duke of North Ridings, a local aristocrat, visit the archdeacon, who is convinced Gregory has the chalice. When they visit Cully, the archdeacon grabs the Grail from where it is prominently displayed and flees with his two friends. Despite a frenzied car chase, Gregory is unable to catch them, and the three men spend the night at the duke's London home. Although Gregory wants the chalice for black magic, his allies in black magic, Manasseh and Dmitri Lavrodopoulos, want to destroy it. When the archdeacon senses that someone is trying to destroy the Grail through supernatural means, he enlists Mornington and the duke for an all-night prayer vigil, and the chalice remains intact.

Gregory regains the Grail through manipulation. He scratches Barbara's arm when she is playing with Adrian, and he applies ointment he had used for occult purposes to her wound. When Barbara reacts with extreme mental, spiritual, and physical distress, Gregory offers to have his supposed doctor-friend Manasseh heal her in exchange for the Grail. Although Mornington and the duke believe they must protect the chalice, the archdeacon is willing to exchange it to save Barbara. For the archdeacon, although God is manifested in and through all created objects, a human being is worth more than any object.

Gregory has the chalice again, and Barbara is healed, but in a mysterious, supernatural way that baffles Gregory and Manasseh. Her healing coincides with the arrival in Fardles of a young man named John who had suddenly appeared after the all-night prayer vigil. (Prester John, the legendary medieval priest-king whose task is to protect the Holy Grail, is the novel's only supernatural character.) The two groups of people interested in the Grail—those who desire to manipulate supernatural power and those who seek instead to serve it—are clearly demarcated by their reactions to him: the archdeacon and his friends welcome the new visitor warmly, while Gregory and his acquaintances experience hostility and fear.

When Mornington and the duke arrive at Dmitri's shop in London to retrieve the chalice Gregory brought there in preparation to leave England, Mornington is killed by occult powers, and the duke is made to summon the archdeacon. Freely offering himself in service to God's will, the archdeacon is stretched out on the floor and bound, with the Grail on his chest in preparation for an occult ritual. He experiences desolation and separation from God, but when evil seems at the height of its power, the chalice begins to emit blazing light and energy, Prester John appears and releases the captives (the archdeacon, the duke, and Adrian), and Gregory hands himself over to the police for the murder of James Pattison, the unidentified victim at the beginning of the story. (Gregory had employed Pattison to commit petty crimes, but after Pattison's conversion and desire to confess his wrongdoings, he needed to be silenced.)

In the closing scene, Prester John celebrates Mass in Fardles, with the archdeacon assisting and the Rackstraws and the duke in attendance. At the end of the service, John is transformed as light comes forth from the Grail, filling the whole church. The archdeacon dies peacefully on the steps of the altar, and John and the Holy Grail disappear.

Christian Themes

Although the story takes place on earth, the phrase "war in heaven" describes the conflict between Michael the archangel and the devil in Revelations 12:7. The novel's title points to Charles Williams's recurring theme that the supernatural is always imminent in the physical world and can break through into ordinary life at any time. Williams stretches the boundaries of conventional realistic fiction to dramatize his belief that divine and demonic powers can become manifest in various ways on earth and interact with and through human beings.

Given this premise, even the most ordinary people can become agents of supernatural powers—whether good or evil. The archdeacon is a small, plump man who quietly sings hymns as he goes about his daily tasks, but it is through his prayer and submission to God's will that the lives of Adrian and the duke are spared and the Grail ultimately restored. Gregory, who seems to be a typical retiree pursuing his hobbies, is responsible for a murder, for Barbara's (temporary) psychic disintegration, and the nearly successful corruption of Adrian. Williams is less concerned with presenting his characters in their social interactions with one another than he is in presenting their cosmic dimension, their choices and interaction with the forces of good and evil.

Adapting the Arthurian Grail myth to a modern setting, Williams traces people's reactions to the chalice as an indicator of their spiritual condition. The archdeacon views it as a symbol that represents but does not contain God's presence in the world, so he has no desire for it and acts only in accordance with the guidance he receives in prayer. However, Gregory perceives it as a magical object that can be used to increase his power and is willing to harm others to obtain it. Unlike the archdeacon, Mornington sees it as an important Arthurian symbol, and the duke sees it as a sacred object of veneration, but both feel impelled to protect it from evil, a choice that leads to Mornington's death.

Williams's technique of intertwining the supernatural and the natural in a credible way reflects his belief that because of the Incarnation, the world has changed forever and is filled with God's presence. With this novel, William affirms God's providence, revealing his power and goodness and the ultimate impotence of evil.

Sources for Further Study

Hadfield, Alice Mary. *Charles Williams: An Explanation of His Life and Work*. New York: Oxford University Press, 1983. Expanded, revised version of a 1959 work by Williams's coworker at Oxford University Press, the book is a commentary on his novels, plays, poetry, and theology, woven into the context of his life. Index.

Horne, Brian, ed. *Charles Williams: A Celebration*. Herefordshire, England: Gracewing, 1995. Eighteen essays by colleagues, former students, and critics on various aspects of Williams's life, theology, and writing. Index.

Howard, Thomas. *The Novels of Charles Williams*. New York: Oxford University

Press, 1983. Plot summaries with running commentary on Williams's seven novels; very helpful clarifications of some of his more difficult passages, symbols, and theological concepts.

Huttar, Charles A., and Peter J. Schakel, eds. *The Rhetoric of Vision: Essays on Charles Williams*. Lewisburg, Pa.: Bucknell University Press, 1996. Essays by British, American, and Canadian critics focused primarily on literary analysis of Williams's fiction, poetry, and critical works; very detailed index.

Marsha Daigle-Williamson

WARRANTED CHRISTIAN BELIEF

Author: Alvin Plantinga (1932-   )
First published: New York: Oxford University Press, 2000
Genre: Nonfiction
Subgenres: Critical analysis; hermeneutics; theology
Core issues: Doubt; faith; reason; religion; truth

How rational and intellectually justifiable is Christian belief? Plantinga attempts to answer this question by casting doubt on one of the fundamental epistemic principles of the Enlightenment and offering instead a new model of rationality and intellectual acceptability known as reformed epistemology. He contends that Christian beliefs are warranted to the extent that they are formed by properly functioning natural cognitive faculties. These faculties can be dulled and damaged by sin, but restored by faith to lead believers to produce warranted Christian belief.

Overview

In the Enlightenment of the late seventeenth and eighteenth centuries, there emerged the idea of a religion rationally grounded in the deliverance of reason and experience. This was one of the central theses of the Enlightenment concerning religious belief, which itself was underwritten by the more universal claim that we are under obligation to govern our belief-forming faculties to the end of arriving at truth and avoiding mistake and error. To secure truth and shun falsehood, we must have reason for believing; we must believe or disbelieve as reason dictates. Under the rational ethics of belief, we are not, therefore, exempt from the obligation to govern our assent in the domain of religious beliefs.

Confronted with such a claim about the primacy of rationality in belief retention or rejection, religious believers have two options. Either they can abide by the obligation and set out to provide the requisite grounding for their religious beliefs, or they can abjure the requirement by challenging its legitimacy. If they pursue the first option and succeed in providing the rational grounding, they can continue what they were doing, though now they will be doing it on this new basis; otherwise, in case of failure, they must abandon their beliefs. There is also the possibility of partial success and partial failure where, again, believers have to purge their belief system downward to jettison beliefs that cannot be rationally grounded. However, rather than engaging in the grounding endeavor, reformed epistemologists such as Alvin Plantinga opted for the second of the two main alternatives: They challenged the religious epistemology of the Enlightenment on its pivotal principle. In particular, according to *Warranted Christian Belief*, religious beliefs do not have to be rationally grounded to be rational.

As a reformed epistemologist, Plantinga's challenge to the epistemological account of the Enlightenment is mounted on several fronts. He claims that a great many religious beliefs are not in fact rationally grounded in the deliverance of reason and experience. A vast number of them are not rationally grounded in anything at all; they are neither acquired nor maintained on the basis of other beliefs. They are, in Plantinga's phrase, basic beliefs or immediate beliefs, on the ground that they are not formed by the mediation of inference. Some beliefs are evoked, for example, by mystical experience and others by a person's experience of some aspect of the world or human experience. Religious beliefs can thus be properly basic and not held on the basis of any inferential evidence at all.

Also, the psychological act of believing is very much a situated phenomenon in the sense that for almost any proposition that people are entitled to believe in their situation, there will be others in other situations who are not entitled to believe that proposition. To the question "Is one entitled to believe P?" the answer must almost always be "It all depends." The underlying thought is that there is an irreducible plurality of fundamental perspectives on reality, where people's acceptance of one of them is strongly influenced by their prephilosophical beliefs and commitments. Moreover, it is claimed that it is not in general possible to show, by neutral philosophical argument, that a particular perspective is correct and all the others are mistaken. In view of this, it is perfectly appropriate and in no way irrational for people to philosophize on the basis of their own perspective, even if they have not been able to demonstrate the correctness of that perspective in a way that is convincing to others. In particular, Christian philosophers are entitled to their own perspective, or, in Plantinga's term, to their own sets of examples, by which they determines the criteria for properly basic beliefs.

Although the Enlightenment model of religious belief may not be unproblematic, there are still serious misgivings about Plantinga's reformed epistemology. On his epistemological account, our beliefs about the external world are formed by certain psychological processes that occur immediately, without inference or any kind of argument. For instance, I believe that I am seeing a tree when "I am appeared to treely." However, one can be "appeared to" as often as one likes, yet the fact remains that this is compatible with not seeing the tree. The question is how to separate veridical from illusory/delusory beliefs. Also, the claims that there is an irreducible plurality of fundamental perspectives on reality and it is not irrational for people to philosophize on the basis of their own perspective seem to usher in a self-defeating radical relativism. Such a pervasive perspectival point of view does not leave much room for differentiating between genuine and spurious systems of religious belief.

Nonetheless, the central contention of Plantinga's reformed epistemology is that belief in the existence of God—along, perhaps, with some other crucial religious beliefs—is properly basic. It is a belief that people can be justified in accepting without basing it on other beliefs. Although Plantinga readily concedes that there is no general criterion for proper basicness, he maintains that some of our religious beliefs can be accepted as properly basic. To support his position, Plantinga proposes that humans have been given, in John Calvin's terminology, a *sensus divinitatis*—a God-given disposition to believe in God in certain circumstances. For example, when contemplating a butterfly or reflecting on a misdemeanor, an individual may be moved to believe "God has made this wondrous thing" or "God disapproves of this mean behavior." Plantinga then extends this claim that belief in God can be properly basic to the claim that the central truths of Christian faith can be held in a properly basic way, if they are maintained on the basis of the instigation of the Holy Spirit. However, Plantinga's anthropological claim that human beings are naturally disposed to form immediate beliefs about God is highly controversial. For one thing, there are many individuals who do not have any natural inclination to form such beliefs, and for those who have, it can be explained away in terms of cultural conditioning and social habituation. For another, how can one account for the incompatible and contradictory beliefs about God that believers of different religions have, notwithstanding believers of various denominations of the same religion?

Christian Themes

Plantinga's *Warranted Christian Belief* can be properly appreciated against the Enlightenment criticism that faith involves belief without evidence or with deficient evidence. He attempts to overturn the underlying Enlightenment assumption that rational religious beliefs must be based on evidence. However, what is distinctive about his position is the conditional character of his argumentation. That is, Plantinga does not claim to be able to demonstrate that beliefs about the *sensus divinitatis* and the instigation of the Holy Spirit are true, but, rather, if they are true, then it is likely that some individuals are reasonable to believe them. Such a position is intellectually inadequate for many thinkers—whether religious or not—whose desire is to establish what is true on the basis of some neutral epistemological position that provides a basis for probing the propriety of such claims.

Plantinga is effectively arguing that such an epistemological stance may be beyond our human capacities. What we can know depends on the truth about our world and our capacities, and what we believe we can know may depend on our beliefs about the world and our capacities. There may be no neutral epistemological stance, because what we think we can know may depend on what we believe about our relation to the world we are trying to know, and that in itself is subject to variation.

Sources for Further Study

Baker, Deane-Peter. "Plantinga's Reformed Epistemology: What's the Question?" *International Journal for Philosophy of Religion* 57, no. 2 (April, 2005): 77. Baker examines the criticisms against *Warranted Christian Belief.*

_____, ed. *Alvin Plantinga.* New York: Cambridge University Press, 2007. A collection of essays on Plantinga, including one on his model of warranted Christian belief.

Beilby, James K. *Epistemology as Theology: An Evaluation of Alvin Plantinga's Religious Epistemology.* Burlington, Vt.: Ashgate, 2005. An examination of Plantinga's religious epistemology, with discussion of his model of warranted Christian belief.

Moser, Paul K., ed. *The Oxford Handbook of Epistemology*. Oxford, England: Oxford University Press, 2002. Philip L. Quinn's "Epistemology in Philosophy of Religion" offers a critical examination of Plantinga's epistemological account of warranted Christian belief.

Stackhouse, John G., Jr. "Mind Over Skepticism." *Christianity Today* 45, no. 8 (June 11, 2001): 74-77. This profile of Plantinga examines his philosophy in depth. Contains discussion of whether belief can be proven on the basis of reason and experience.

Wainwright, William J., ed. *The Oxford Handbook of Philosophy of Religion*. Oxford, England: Oxford University Press, 2005. The handbook contains a number of detailed surveys of issues in philosophy of religion that also discuss the contribution and significance of Plantinga's *Warranted Christian Belief* to those issues.

Majid Amini

THE WAY OF ALL FLESH

Author: Samuel Butler (1835-1902)
First published: 1903
Edition used: Ernest Pontifex: Or, The Way of All Flesh, edited by Daniel F. Howard. London: Methuen, 1965
Genre: Novel
Subgenre: Literary fiction; satire
Core issues: Clerical life; coming of age or teen life; faith; obedience and disobedience; reason

This very unorthodox Christian novel rejects conformist Christianity (in the form of Anglicanism) and celebrates a heterodox faith that inverts many Victorian-era beliefs. Now it is the child who is wise, the adult who is foolish. Now it is discipline that is harmful, leniency that is beneficial. Now it is dogmatism that is sinful, broadmindedness that pleases God. Through his novel, Butler exhorts Christians to think about their faith and to assess its claims in the light of science and logic, and argues for a rational Christianity.

> Principal characters
> Ernest Pontifex, the hero
> Theobald Pontifex, Ernest's unjust father; an Anglican cleric
> Christina Pontifex, Ernest's mother
> Edward Overton, the narrator; Ernest's godfather
> Alethea Pontifex, Ernest's kindly aunt
> George Pontifex, Ernest's grandfather; a self-centered publisher
> Pryer, a curate and a swindler
> Ellen, a servant; later Ernest's wife
> Towneley, an admired friend
> Hawke, an evangelist
> Shaw, a free-thinker

Overview

Often autobiographical in nature, a Bildungsroman depicts a protagonist's coming of age, following the protagonist from youth to maturity while focusing on the forces shaping the young person's character. While lesser examples of this genre explore just one aspect of a hero's development—intellectual growth, for instance—the best examples of the genre touch on many areas of growth. By this measure, Samuel Butler's *The Way of All Flesh*, which investigates with equal vigor its hero's intellectual growth, emotional maturation, and spiritual flowering, ranks among the very best of the genre.

The hero who grows, matures, and flowers in *The Way of All Flesh* is Ernest

Pontifex, the pitiable son of a cruel and self-righteous Anglican clergyman. (That Butler was the son of an Anglican cleric hints at the autobiographical nature of the novel.) At birth Ernest is endowed with many positive qualities common to children—cheerfulness, curiosity, self-confidence—but over time these qualities are exorcised (like demons) by a bullying father, to such an extent that by age twenty Ernest has utterly lost his way, living not as his own soul or spirit (his "true self") counsels but as his parents—representatives of an uncaring society—dictate. However, Ernest will recover, abandoning his father's path (ordination, marriage, respectability as a clergyman) to map his own way.

At the heart of *The Way of All Flesh* is a depiction of two sets of forces, one set furthering Ernest's deterioration, another set contributing to his recovery. The immediate cause of Ernest's decline is his father, Theobald, a brutish disciplinarian who, having been bullied himself into becoming a cleric (the bully was Theobald's own father, a miserly publisher who would "shake his will"—that is, threaten disinheritance—to get his way), works to break Ernest's spirit, the better to make him docile and compliant. Shaping events within the Pontifex household, however, is a vastly more powerful force: the Anglican Church. As presented in *The Way of All Flesh*, the Anglican Church epitomizes all that is soul-destroying in Victorian society. Staffed (the appropriate word) by careerist clergymen with no interest in spiritual matters, the church exists not to guide the wayward, nor to comfort the distraught, but to prop up an unjust social order. To this end, the Anglican Church espouses a strictly hierarchical view of human existence in which God (through the Bible) dictates to clergyman, clergyman dictates to parent, and parent dictates to child, with the entire system demanding blind obedience by subordinate parties. In effect, the church, through its teachings, encourages in every social sphere a credulous trust in "superiors," sanctioning such trust by reference to biblical injunctions against disobedience. Within *The Way of All Flesh*, the harmfulness of church doctrine is evident whenever parent clashes with child, for in all such instances the parent feels duty-bound to crush the child's will—the ultimate justification being that obedience is a virtue pleasing to God.

The Way of All Flesh presents Victorian England in the worst possible light. In recording Ernest's deterioration, the novel depicts many important social institutions—the family, the Anglican Church, the educational system—as unjust and not nurturing, with particular scorn aimed at the institutions society holds in highest regard. Yet, *The Way of All Flesh* is not entirely pessimistic. Indeed, the novel ends with Ernest not defeated but triumphant, or at least in a state of emotional, intellectual, and spiritual equilibrium. How Ernest reaches this state is the novel's second focus of interest.

Having fallen as far as an honest man can fall—shunned by his parents, disgraced in his profession, imprisoned for a sordid crime—Ernest takes stock of himself, working out how he—an unselfish man who only wanted to do good—ended up a felon and an outcast. What Ernest realizes is that faith did him in, specifically blind faith vested in unworthy people and institutions. In brief, Ernest grasps that he has trusted too much and thought too little, mindlessly adopting his father's understanding of life (itself inherited from the Anglican Church) rather than reasoning out his own understanding. Unwilling now to take anything on faith, Ernest begins to think for himself, forging an idiosyncratic worldview. This is Ernest's life-changing discovery: that every sound belief is rooted in reason, not faith.

Reasoning leads Ernest to doubt much that his society takes for granted. No longer does he accept that parents know what is best for children, that clergymen are endowed with spiritual insight, or that the Anglican Church is an earthly expression of God's will. In rejecting so much that his compatriots hold dear, Ernest—his reticence notwithstanding—becomes the very model of a rebel.

Christian Themes

The Way of All Flesh testifies to Butler's abiding interest in Christianity. By the time Ernest Pontifex is ordained as a cleric, he has learned (as have we) to distinguish between high and low Anglicanism, between Anglicanism and Roman Catholicism, and between ritualism and evangelicalism. Although anti-Anglican, *The Way of All Flesh* is by no means anti-Christian. To the contrary, the novel celebrates Christianity—of a certain type—as the best of all religions.

The celebration, however, is subdued. What most concerns Butler in *The Way of All Flesh* is not exaltation of his own version of Christianity but condemnation of another version: Anglicanism. As presented in Butler's work, Anglicanism is arrogant in its demands and contemptuous in its offerings, demanding absolute faith while offering only a mishmash of unscientific and self-contradictory teachings. While all religions require faith ("faith" is another word for "religion"), Anglicanism, in Butler's view, requires a faith so childish and complete as to be a form of abject credulity. In effect, the Anglican Church requires adherents to eschew rationality, accepting even those Church teachings contrary to science or logic. How old is the earth? Geologists, Ernest learns, say many millions of years. Despite this, the Anglican Church posits the earth as mere thousands of years old—with believers told to take this on faith. Here, as elsewhere, Church doctrine is unscientific, and so is, for Butler, unreasonable in the most literal sense. The Anglican Church features in *The Way of All Flesh* as a hive of unreason. Worst of all, the Church not only generates much nonsense but also conflates acceptance of the nonsense with moral goodness.

However, *The Way of All Flesh* is not anti-Christian. Scattered through the novel are passages characterizing another Christianity, a rational, humble, and life-affirming creed. To call this Christianity "rational" is to highlight both its commitment to coherence and its grounding in the physical sciences. Beliefs must not only fit together but also be compatible with the findings of geologists and paleontologists. Also characterizing this unorthodox Christianity is humility, evident in a willingness to rethink matters in the light of new information. Finally, this Christianity—Ernest's Christianity—is life-affirming, counseling people to embrace pleasure and reject suffering.

Cohering around Ernest Pontifex's journey as a Christian, *The Way of All Flesh* charts its hero's intellectual pilgrimage from youthful disinterest to adolescent orthodoxy to middle-aged heterodoxy.

Sources for Further Study

Cole, G. D. H. *Samuel Butler and "The Way of All Flesh."* London: Home & Van Thal, 1947. Treats Butler's major works, with a chapter (mostly on *The Fair Haven*, 1873) devoted to discussion of Butler's evolving views on Christianity.

Daniels, Anthony. "Butler's Unhappy Youth." *The New Criterion* 23, no. 5 (January, 2005). Takes issue with many views expressed in *The Way of All Flesh*, arguing for instance that Ernest's Christianity is narcissistic and self-absorbed.

Furbank, P. N. *Samuel Butler.* Hamden, Conn.: Archon Books, 1971. Perhaps the best study of Butler's life and publications. Describes *The Way of All Flesh* as belonging to the literature of conversion, a body of works including Bunyan's *Pilgrim's Progress from This World to That Which Is to Come* (1678) and Saint Augustine's *Confessiones (397-400; Confessions,* 1620).

Raby, Peter. *Samuel Butler: A Biography.* London: The Hogarth Press, 1991. A sound biography, better on the facts of Butler's life than the content of his works. Discusses in some detail Butler's decision not to be ordained as an Anglican priest.

Zemka, Sue. "*Erewhon* and the End of Utopian Humanism." *English Literary History* 69, no. 2 (Summer, 2002). Analyzes the key themes in Butler's other well-known work, relating the themes to Butler's critique of Victorian society. Addresses in passing Butler's interest in various types of religious hypocrisy.

Matt Brillinger

THE WAY TO CHRIST

Author: Jakob Böhme (1575-1624)
First published: Der Weg zu Christo, 1623 (English translation, 1647)
Edition used: Jakob Böhme's "The Way to Christ," translated by John Joseph Stoudt with a foreword by Rufus M. Jones. London: J. M. Watkins, 1953
Genre: Nonfiction
Subgenres: Meditation and contemplation; mysticism; spiritual treatise
Core issues: Conversion; the Fall; humility; illumination; Jesus Christ; mysticism; reason; soul

In this collection of tracts on the mystical way, written during a period of revivalist intensity, Böhme himself had experienced a new illumination and had assumed the role of a lay evangelist. The three tracts that made up the original collection were clearly intended for the newly converted.

Overview

In his twenty-fifth year, Jakob Böhme, a cobbler, saw in a vision the origin of all things. When the manuscript in which he tried to expound the vision (later named "The Aurora") came to the attention of the local pastor, he was forbidden by the civil authority to write anything more. This was 1612. Although he complied, he became the center of a growing circle of admirers, kept up a wide correspondence, and was active in a secret brotherhood. Except for village schooling, he was self-taught. Among his friends, however, were persons of quality who lent him books and introduced him to theosophical and alchemical writings. About 1619 he resumed writing and allowed his manuscripts to circulate. *The Way to Christ,* comprising three short devotional pieces, is the only one of his manuscripts that was published during his lifetime. Written in 1622, it shows him turning back from theosophical speculation to the tradition of German mysticism. Böhme intended no break with official Lutheranism, it but is clear that his affinities lay elsewhere, and it comes as no surprise that English Behmenists allied themselves with the Quaker movement.

Böhme's *The Way to Christ* originally consisted of three tracts: "Of True Repentance," "Of True Resignation," and "Of Regeneration." In subsequent editions, from three to five additional tracts written during the same period were always included. The period was one of revivalist intensity: Böhme himself had experienced a new illumination and had assumed the role of a lay evangelist. The three tracts that made up the original collection were clearly intended for the newly converted. The same might be said of the "Dialogue Between an Enlightened and an Unenlightened Soul" (1624). "The Supersensual Life" (1622), however, was addressed to the mature disciple.

"Of True Repentance," as the author wrote to a friend, was the outgrowth of a new conversion that Böhme himself had lately experienced. "As this tract will lead you to the *Praxis,* you will experience its good since it was born through the fire of an anguishable twig, and it was and still is my own process through which I have attained the Pearl of divine knowledge." It is an awkward composition. Addressing persons who feel an inclination to repent but were unable to act, he begins by recounting reasons for repenting and follows these with various considerations that ought to lead one to take the needed steps, among them the enormity of the Fall. Consider, he says, "the noble image in which God fashioned [human beings] to his likeness." (Böhme is thinking not so much of Adam as of the Heavenly Man, rival of Lucifer, described in the *Cabala*.) Then consider what the human being has become instead, "a formless grub, like a hellish worm or abominable animal, an enemy to God, to heaven, and to all holy angels and men; and that his intercourse is—and forever shall be—with devils and hellish worms in gruesome darkness." Böhme intersperses persuasion with prayer, and through the whole he weaves an allegory of the soul engaged in knightly combat, hoping to receive a crown from the hand of the Virgin Sophia. What is the Way? Even the same as Evangelist showed Christian (though Böhme never achieves anything approaching John Bunyan's pathos): "He who does not forsake wife, children . . . even his earthly life, is not worthy of me." "Gracious reader, this is no joke," Böhme warns; "Better to be judged early in youth before the Devil has bastioned his robber's castle in the soul!" Of the Sophia-tale, he advises, "Dear reader, Do not consider this an untrue myth. This is the . . . sum and substance of Sacred Scriptures . . . clearly presented to the eyes just as it became known to the author, for this has been his whole process."

In "Of True Resignation," the second tract, Böhme makes use of the term *Gelassenheit* (from *lassen*, leave alone), which Tauler had helped to popularize. In more ordinary speech, what is here demanded is humility or, as the Psalmist expressed it, "a broken and a contrite heart." The examples of Lucifer and of Archetypal Man show what happens when God grants reason to even the most promising of his creatures. Reason is the best of treasures, but "we also see that in our technically trained men, when they acquire the light of external reason as their own, nothing results but pride." Böhme translates into his own jargon Christ's parable about the unclean spirit which, returning to finding his old quarters empty and garnished, reoccupies them together with seven other spirits more foul than himself. Says Böhme:

> As the creaturely will-spirit rises with the rational light into the center, that is, into selfhood, and begins self-delusion, it again departs from God's light. Now the Devil finds a gate opening up into him, and a garnished house, or rational light, for habitation. Then he appropriates to himself the seven forms of the life-properties which have departed from God into selfhood. Then he becomes self-conscious and sets his desire into the inclination toward his own self and into a false imagination.

In short, those who think that the light of reason is sufficient for salvation are easy game for the Devil. Instead of looking to external reason, one must descend into oneself and become dead to the world, resign oneself to Christ, and do what Christ wishes to do with his own instrument. This is the *praxis*; but Böhme is always ready with the *theoria*. The question how the creature can have any will at all, as distinct from that of its Maker, was one that Böhme was prepared to answer. There are two poles in God, as Böhme had been shown: his Love-will and his Wrath-will. These same two poles are present in every creature also. When God created Lucifer and Heavenly Man (a glorious androgynous being), he did so out of love and looked for love in response. The rest of the story is well known: The two splendid creatures got what they chose—and what they still choose even when they are aware of the error of their choice. For Lucifer, there is no hope. For the human race, the only hope lies in appropriating Christ's Passion. "Any meditative scheme leading to God" is fruitless apart from a regeneration of the mind; and for that to take place, the soul must "envelop its will in Christ's death, so that the soul's mind no longer wills sin."

The third tract, "Of Regeneration: Or, The New Birth," is concerned with the conflict that Christians experience within themselves as a result of their union with Christ. How can one be the Temple of God and at the same time a sinful mortal? To answer this question, Böhme must go back to the beginning and explain how man was created (Scripture does not tell all!); how he "stood in heaven as well as in the external world" (this was paradise); how the Devil overcame man through his imagination; how man originally begat offspring in the way God created heaven and earth (by fiat); how Adam slept (for the first time!), therein exchanging his angelic life for the life of a beast. Desolation followed, but also a covenant, which was fulfilled when "the divine Vitality introduced heavenly, living essence, and reawakened the distorted essence in Mary's seed and brought it to life." Much of the tract is directed against false Christians and against the "stone churches," which is not surprising in view of the slanders he endured from the pulpits. Their preaching and sacraments would be good, he says, if spiritually used. Still, how many there were who had attended church for decades, heard the sermons, received the sacraments, and been absolved, but remained as much beasts and children of the Devil as before! "A true Christian brings his holy church into the congregation; his heart is the true church in which one should practice the worship of God."

"A Dialogue Between an Enlightened and an Unenlightened Soul" has the makings of a morality play. Soul, in her innocence, leaves paradise in order to satisfy her curiosity about the world of creatures. The Devil offers his services and promises her all knowledge and power on condition that she break off from God and focus her desires on the serpent image. This image (which is the circle formed by the serpent biting its own tail, and also the magical fire-wheel of Mercury) ignited Soul's egocentric passions, thereby liberating Arrogance, Avarice, Envy, and Wrath—the very "foundation of Hell." So, Soul began to rule on earth in a bestial manner. Then Soul met Christ, who had come into the world to destroy the works of the Devil. When Christ offered to free Soul from her wormlike image, Soul repented and sought God's grace. However, the properties of the astral spirit that the Devil had formed in her would not let her will remain with God. Meanwhile, the Devil reappeared and drew her back into worldly things. "What are you troubling yourself about? Just look how the world lives in joy! Hasn't Christ paid the ransom and satisfied for all men? All you need to do is to comfort yourself that it has happened . . . Don't you ever think what will happen to you if you become so melancholy and insane? You will be everybody's fool." Soul was disconsolate. She decided to forsake the world and engage in charitable works—but to no avail. Then Troubled Soul met Enlightened Soul, who assured her that there was an ointment that would remove the serpent image and restore the paradisal image. "You yourself shall do nothing except surrender your self-centered, self-calculating will. Then your evil qualities will weaken and begin to die, and you will sink your own will back into the One out of which you originally came." After Enlightened Soul preached her a long sermon on following Christ and walking the straight way, Troubled Soul resolved to forsake her egocentric will and to surrender to Christ. Bewailing her wormlike form and the presence in her of the four passions, she embraced the death of Christ as her own and, permeated by God's love, broke into joyful prayer. "The marriage-feast of the Lamb was now celebrated, and the espousal of the noble Sophia with the Soul. The signet ring of Christ's Victory was impressed upon her essence and she was received again as a child and heir of God." The tract is interesting mainly because in it one can overhear the arguments and discussions, admonitions and counsels, that must have engaged Böhme and his friends in their evangelical activities.

"Of the Supersensual Life: A Dialogue Between a Scholar and His Master," dated 1622, was obviously written for Böhme's more intellectual friends. "How," the disciple asks, "may I come to the supersensual life so that I can see God and hear him speak?" The master answers: "When you can leap for a moment into that where no creature dwells then you can hear what God speaks." Salvation, in this dialogue, is presented less as a matter of embracing Christ's death than of sinking oneself into the No-thing out of which everything has come and to which it will return. Human beings fell when they separated themselves from the All, emerging as ego-centered selves in the midst of a world of severed things known to them through sensible images. In this condition, they rule externally over other creatures, led by the desires of their bestial nature. If one wants to see and hear God, one must forsake the world of images and no longer desire to claim things as one's own. Then one becomes like all things—a no-thing among no-things.

There follows an example of what Böhme calls his "deep writing." The talk has turned to love, which, the master says, is a no-thing. He explains that all things have emerged from one source, the Supersensual Unconditioned (*Ungrund*). Because it is potentially all things the Source is actually no-thing. God's being and that of his creatures are things, differentiated in virtue of an order superimposed on the *Ungrund*—but only the limited degree of order that the *Ungrund* can receive. Hence, there remains in God himself and in each of his creatures a residual no-thingness. In this no-thingness love resides, but also hate; for, one member of a pair of opposites cannot exist without the other. Human beings, for example, must love the divine that is within them but must hate the I-ness that has raised itself against God. This consideration helps the master explain to the disciple why it is that though so many people seek love, so few are able to find it. "Though Love offers itself to them it can find no place within them to live, for the imaginativeness of selfish inclinations wants to own it. Love flees, however, for it lives only in the no-thing, and therefore the ego-centric will cannot find it."

It also helps the master answer the disciple's questions about heaven and hell. These are not places but states of men's souls. Heaven operates everywhere, for it is "nothing more than a manifestation of the Eternal One wherein all works and wills in love." Hell is its counterpart: It is active everywhere God and love are excluded. "What then is an angel," asks the disciple, "and what is man's soul, that they become manifest in God's love or in his wrath?" The master's explanation is that they are projections of God's knowledge into objects of his love. "They come out of the eternal ground from which Light and darkness arise. As darkness lies in the employment of ego-centric desire, so Light consists in a similar willing with God." As for one's body, and the visible world in general, they are external manifestations of the inner spiritual world, whether good or evil. With this in mind, the master is able to answer the disciple's questions concerning life beyond the grave, the resurrection of the body, the Last Judgment, and the eternal separation of the children of darkness from the children of light. One last question: "Why does God allow such strife in this time?" There must be strife for life to exist and for wisdom to become manifest and for joy to triumph. "For this the Eternal One assumed sensibility and divisibility, and by sensibility brought itself forth again through death into the mighty Kingdom of Joy, so that there might be an eternal play in the endless unity."

Christian Themes

Böhme's Christian message in *The Way to Christ* can be summarized in the following points:

- True repentance is a lifelong struggle between the good and the evil forces in human beings.
- In true resignation, egocentric knowing and willing is replaced by God's love.
- Only as Christ restores to a soul the divine vitality lost to humankind in Adam's fall can this renewal take place.
- Heaven and hell are not places that human beings enter after death but present states of their souls.

Sources for Further Study

Böhme, Jakob. *Six Theosophic Points, and Other Writings*. Ann Arbor: University of Michigan Press, 1958. The introductory essay, "Ungrund and Freedom," by Nicolas Berdyaev, offers a convenient introduction to Böhme's general philosophical position.

Erb, Peter, ed. *Jacob Boehme: The Way to Christ*. New York: Paulist Press, 1977. Erb's introduction reaffirms that this work "provides the best introduction to [Böhme's] thought and spirituality."

Jones, Rufus M. *Spiritual Reformers in the Sixteenth and Seventeenth Centuries*. London: Macmillan, 1909. Chapters 9 through 12 offer an introduction to Böhme's life

and thought and to his influence in England, by a noted modern Quaker.
O'Regan, Cyril. *Gnostic Apocalypse: Jacob Boehme's Haunted Narrative*. Albany: State University of New York Press, 2002. Assesses Böhme's thought as a return to Gnosticism after a millennium. Although O'Regan questions the nineteenth century arguments for this stance, he agrees that in the modern period Böhme's discourse does represent a return of Gnosticism. Bibliography, index.
Stoudt, John Joseph. *Sunrise to Eternity: A Study in Jacob Böhme's Life*. Preface by Paul Tillich. Philadelphia: University of Pennsylvania Press, 1957. Traces the growth of Böhme's thought, which is seen as a new, personalist type of mysticism. Useful mainly for biographical details.
Weeks, Andrew. *Boehme: An Intellectual Biography of the Seventeenth-Century Philosopher and Mystic*. Albany: State University of New York Press, 1991. An overview of Böhme's life and thought suitable for both serious and beginning students. Bibliography, index.

Jean H. Faurot

WE HOLD THESE TRUTHS
Catholic Reflections on the American Proposition

Author: John Courtney Murray, S.J. (1904-1967)
First published: 1960
Edition used: We Hold These Truths: Catholic Reflections on the American Proposition, foreword by Walter Burghardt and critical introduction by Peter Lawler. Lanham, Md.: Rowman & Littlefield, 2005
Genre: Nonfiction
Subgenres: Critical analysis; essays
Core issues: Communism; freedom and free will; justice; morality; reason; social action

The United States is historically unique insofar as it is a free nation that, from its inception, was religiously and culturally pluralist. Nevertheless, to cohere, every nation needs a common vision, a consensus, strong enough to guide the shared aspects of its life, Murray says. The American consensus has eroded considerably, with dangerous results. American leaders must reinvigorate an ethical and political humanism that can respect Christianity's objective contributions to the nation's life and at the same time expand the secular common ground on which diverse groups can meet and contribute to public affairs.

Overview

A key architect of Vatican II's declaration on freedom of worship, *Dignitatis Humanae*, John Courtney Murray is probably the most important Catholic theologian yet to hail from the United States. *We Hold These Truths*, however, is a work of Christian political philosophy, not a theological treatise. Addressed to all thinking Americans, smartly written, and first published the same year that the United States elected its first Roman Catholic president, the book garnered national attention and has since established itself as a twentieth century classic.

We Hold These Truths is a selection of essays woven together around a central question: "What are the truths that we as Americans hold?" That is, what is the basic agreement beneath America's pluralism that holds American society together and gives the government its basic sense of direction? What are the truths on which the nation was successfully founded, what is the consensus on which it stands today, and how will this "American Proposition" need to develop if it is to endure the weight of contemporary American civilization?

Murray's book is divided into three parts. The essays in the first part introduce the basic features of the American proposition. Murray contends that the founding fathers forged a successful Constitution because they were astute lawyers and policymakers, well formed in traditional English jurisprudence. Unlike the French revolutionaries, they did not govern in the spirit of doctrinaire rationalism; instead, they built the public consensus on the shared heritage of constitutionalism and common law. This tradition was especially unifying because it was based on key truths about human society, on a sense of natural laws that were both broadly discernible and imminently practical. It taught, to pick a characteristic example, that political legislation cannot create a virtuous or educated society "from the top down," and therefore that the common good hinges on society's ability to sustain virtuous citizens with a full spectrum of free and flourishing nongovernmental institutions (families, schools, charities, churches, and so on). With the nation united by such a philosophy of "a free people under limited government," religious and cultural pluralism did not render political union impossible. Even the federal amendment resolving to "make no law respecting the establishment of any religion" became acceptable to all groups (including Roman Catholics), it being nothing more than the obviously prudent application of traditional principles of limited government.

Murray argues that the "public philosophy" grounding the American consensus has become particularly weak during the twentieth century. Increasingly, coherent political philosophy and social ethics have been neglected, as has the (chiefly Christian) intellectual tradition that originally gave meaning to the American ideal of freedom. Universities in particular have failed to disseminate the kind of reflection on experience that could reinvigorate principled consensus, focusing instead on the material and social sciences and on activist ideologies. This silent neglect of philosophy and history, together with many outward changes as the decades rushed by, has washed away almost all intelligent agreement about what America stands for and, therefore, almost all footing for healthy cultural debate.

In the second part, "Four Unfinished Arguments," Murray sets aside his general contention about public philosophy to demonstrate the concrete value of natural law; that is, of the humanistic and philosophical idea that human nature is something real that can be discovered by observation and analysis and that has laws that need to be obeyed. This concrete value he demonstrates by giving incisive arguments that illustrate how a knowledge of history, informed by a strong sense of human nature and its laws, can cut through the cacophony of public opinion on four contemporary topics: the justice of government funding for religious schools, the legitimacy of censorship, the relationship between Christian ideas and healthy citizenship, and the prospects for political freedom in a postmodern and post-Christian world.

In the third part, "The Uses of Doctrine," Murray moves from domestic policy to foreign policy and further justifies his insistence on America's need for a rational consensus about its own principles and objectives. Focusing on the Cold War and the nuclear arms race, Murray illustrates, in significant depth, how the United States' international relations have been ultimately rudderless and reactionary, with the result that maximum armament, combined with a no-first-strike pledge, falsely passes for a foreign policy that is ethically and strategically coherent.

Murray then turns to the general question of moral thought in contemporary culture and finds the American mind confined between simplistic biblical fundamentalism at one extreme and hazy philosophical relativism at the other. This circumscribes the entire spectrum within a helter-skelter individualism; direct application of private standards of altruism to global politics is manifestly naïve, so the current lack of concern for the unique moral norms that regulate human nature in its collective aspects (such as society and state) ends up abandoning national policy to be guided by material self-interest alone.

Murray concludes with an essay specifically on the philosophical tradition of natural law, illustrating it alongside the other potential sources of guiding principles for the future of the United States. He insists that it is experiential without becoming ideological (without exalting one dimension of the human person, such as its individuality, to the exclusion of others) and pragmatic without being amoral (without being so focused on the "how" of science and technique that it is deaf to the "why" of justice and charity), and therefore that the classical tradition of natural law offers the "last best hope" for American cultural leaders wishing to offer the nation a healthy sense of direction.

Christian Themes

Written from the particular perspective of Catholic and, more particularly, Thomistic and Jesuit (Suarezian) philosophy, *We Hold These Truths* offers one of America's foremost attempts to think through the encounter between the United States and Christianity. This relationship is more nuanced than American Protestantism has sometimes realized, and the questions of how politics should be influenced by faith (and Church) have emerged as increasingly vexing with the loss of national consensus. Murray's use of the Catholic tradition to suggest that there is such a thing as a strong and thoughtful humanism that is nevertheless not necessarily Christian is pertinent to the situation of a pluralistic democracy, and it suggests possibilities far exceeding common Protestant and secular evaluations of Catholic thought.

The leading theological criticism of Murray has been that he underestimates the need for specifically Christian symbols in American public life. The seriousness of this criticism being granted, it remains significant that in the midst of proposing a "secularized" Christian humanism as America's proper public philosophy, Murray clearly maintains that constitutional liberalism will prove unsustainable if it is hostile or indifferent to the Christian religion. Though American democracy is justifiable in terms of the natural law alone, its emergence from the heritage of Christian political philosophy is not happenstance. Murray elaborates two key reasons: First, Christian spirituality, with its simultaneous focus on heaven and earth, promotes a helpful mind-set that avoids both withdrawn indifferentism and monomaniacal ideologism. Second, insistence that God's Church is an institution with a right to exist and a calling to invoke transcendent authority has historically formed an unparalleled bulwark against state tyranny.

A further important theme of Murray's book is his Christian and philosophical response to the American ideal of freedom. By arguing that political freedom is precious precisely because it is ordered toward genuine responsibility, he issues profound challenges both to Americans whose notion of freedom is hollow and to various reactionaries who are tempted to view political freedom as a merely specious value.

Sources for Further Study

D'Elia, Donald J., and Stephen M. Krason, eds. *"We Hold These Truths" and More: Further Catholic Reflections on the American Proposition—The Thought of Father John Courtney Murray, S.J. and Its Relevance Today.* Steubenville, Ohio: Franciscan University Press, 1993. A late twentieth century re-examination of Murray's viewpoints and their relevance for modern times.

Ferguson, Thomas P. *Catholic and American: The Political Theology of John Courtney Murray.* Kansas City, Mo.: Sheed & Ward, 1993. An examination of Murray's thoughts about Catholicism and its connection to politics.

Hooper, J. Leon, and Todd David Whitmore, eds. *John Courtney Murray and the Growth of Tradition.* Kansas City, Mo.: Sheed & Ward, 1996. Essays by twelve Murray scholars look at his thought and beliefs and examine them for solutions to modern problems.

Weigel, George. *Catholicism and the Renewal of American Democracy.* Mahwah, N.J.: Paulist Press, 1989. An extension of Murray's project, showing how it can be used to restore rationality and civility to general debates between conservatives and liberals, as well as to several particular topics.

Joseph Van House, O.Cist.

WHAT ARE PEOPLE FOR?

Author: Wendell Berry (1934-   )
First published: San Francisco: North Point Press, 1990
Genre: Nonfiction
Subgenres: Critical analysis; essays
Core issues: Capitalism; connectedness; freedom and free will; justice; love; nature

Industrial capitalism has enslaved Western civilization, destroyed community connectedness, endangered freedom and justice, and led to the devastation of much of the natural world, according to Berry. The only solution is to reject the monetary imperative underlying capitalism and technological objects and return to small farm-based communities held together by common memories, shared and interdependent work and social activities, sensitivity to and conservation of the natural world, and love of God, family, neighbors, and the community itself.

Overview

What Are People For? is a collection of essays written between 1975 and 1990 by Wendell Berry—novelist, poet, social critic, and moral philosopher—that touches on the proper way of life for people in Western civilization. The essays include literary criticism and meditations on problematic "improvements" to nature, the decline of farming communities, the dangers of constant technological innovation, the shortcomings of organized religion, and religion's centrality in a proper moral economy. Taken as a whole, they reveal Berry's firm conviction that Western civilization has lost its way and has followed industrial and technological innovation into a self-indulgent, immoral, environmentally destructive, dehumanizing, monolithic, and unjust way of life. He warns that this way of life can only end in apocalypse: When the rape of the land for minerals to fuel the artificial, wasteful lifestyle is complete and no natural resources are left to fuel the industrial beasts (and nations), they will turn on and destroy each other in the fight for what little remains.

In "Harry Caudill in the Cumberlands," for example, Berry praises Caudill, the author of *Night Comes to the Cumberlands: A Biography of a Depressed Area* (1963), for his indictment of strip mining for coal because of its destruction of Kentucky's streams, lakes, roads, forests, and sometimes even people. He notes the destructiveness of the military-industrial state in "A Few Words in Favor of Edward Abbey," and in "A Poem of Difficult Hope," he analyzes Hayden Carruth's "On Being Asked to Write a Poem Against the War in Vietnam." In this essay, Berry says that today's world is the most destructive and therefore the most stupid period in human history.

Berry traces that destructiveness back to the Industrial Revolution, noting in "The Work of Local Culture" that William Wordsworth, in his poem "Michael," first captured the fundamentally destructive changes brought to rural communities by the Industrial Revolution. Industrialization broke the eons-old pattern of young persons leaving rural communities to then return mature and equal to the task of joining and continuing those communities because it took the jobs from the rural areas and forced these young people to leave to seek their life's work in the ever-growing urban areas. Berry's essays document the continuing decline and disappearance of small farms and small communities as rural areas become merely natural resources to be exploited and destroyed for the sake of city dwellers' artificial, consumption-driven pleasure and comfort. To Berry, the only real pleasure, and the only real way to combat the destructiveness of the industrial, technological, energy-consumptive society, is a return to the small farms and interdependent rural communities that proliferated prior to the Industrial Revolution.

In "A Remarkable Man," Berry extensively praises Nate Shaw, a black farmer in Alabama in the early twentieth century who was "a mule farmin' man to the last," despite the advent of the era of tractor farming late in Shaw's life. Furthermore, in Berry's view, Shaw's principled life as a small farmer—which led to him being imprisoned for twelve years because he defended a neighbor's stock against attachment by local authorities—made him a man of character. Shaw possessed self-respect, love of work, pride in his accomplishments, and high standards for his own work and behavior, all qualities Berry feels are woefully lacking in today's technological, urban-centered society. Therefore, Shaw is emblematic of Berry's solution to the misdirection of today's society.

As described in "The Work of Local Culture," the only solution is the revival of rural communities with interdependent, local produce production and distribution; with ecologically sound, regenerative farming practices that sustain the natural world rather than destroy it; and with cultural memories and traditions preserved by productive relationships with friends and neighbors. Only then, Berry believes, can humans be spared the eventual destruction implicit in Western civilization's direction since the Industrial Revolution. Of course, as the author himself realizes, the key question is how to bring about this reversal of direction, as he notes in "Feminism, the Body, and the Machine." He admits his own dependence on modern technology (automobile, airplane, and chainsaw) and offers no simplistic solution, just his belief that the reversal will have to begin with the revival of rural communities brought about by the residents of those communities themselves, based on the longstanding principles of neighborliness, love of that which is precious, and the desire to be at home.

Christian Themes

Christian themes are of course implicit throughout Berry's essays; the most important themes are a religiously sound relationship to nature, a moral economic system, and the primacy of love. In "God and Country," he indicts those pseudo-Christians who have read no more of the Bible than Genesis I:28, concerning subduing the earth, and who use that passage as rationalization for destroying the natural world.

Emphasizing the "replenish the earth" language of Genesis I:28, Berry contends that humans possess the earth only in trust for God. Therefore, humans cannot ethically destroy any of the natural world but must preserve and protect it from waste.

Berry also turns to Revelation 4:11 to buttress this view, emphasizing that all of the natural world was created for God's pleasure and therefore humans must safeguard it. Of course, such safeguarding is the opposite of what the Industrial Revolution and current technological innovation have done with nature. Berry's deeply held, biblically based beliefs about nature are fundamental to his dissatisfaction with modern, urban, industrial life. Berry also believes, based on Revelations, that humans must be attentive to the natural world and work to strengthen all living things as long as possible.

Further, a moral economic system is central to Berry's beliefs, and he notes this moral economy in "God and Country." In "A Practical Harmony," he argues that a moral economy, one obedient to nature's laws and based on replenishing of natural resources, was the norm throughout history until the Industrial Revolution, when elaborately rationalized rape and plunder of the natural world became the norm. Fundamental also to a moral economy is diversity rather than specialization, as is the modern norm. In "Nature as Measure," he explains that one-crop agriculture depletes the soil, but rotation of many types of crops is more consistent with what nature does without human interference.

Another central theme in Berry's essays is the primacy of love, in an all-inclusive, biblical sense that encompasses love of nature, love of other species, and love of fellow human beings. The importance of love is evident in Berry's indictment of capitalistic competition, which presupposes losers in the competition but ignores them as an embarrassment. Berry notes in "Economy and Pleasure" that the "losers" in capitalism are also the children of God and deserve more than being told to just go into another line of work. Love is also implicit in Berry's criticism that proponents of capitalistic competition always have very little to say about honesty, the fundamental economic virtue, or about community, compassion, and mutual help, all of which of course derive from Christian love. Further, in "Word and Flesh," Berry notes that only love can bring the intelligence necessary to do what must be done to reverse the destructive direction of Western civilization. This includes, as he says in "Nature as Measure," farmers tending farms they know and love—farms small enough to know and love—using tools they know and love in the company of neighbors they know and love. Finally, Berry ends the collection by stating that rape of nature has continued too long, and now it is time for marriage, based of course on love.

Sources for Further Study

Angyal, Andrew J. *Wendell Berry*. New York: Twayne, 1995. Best analysis of Berry's life, ideas, poetry, fiction, and essays to date, with excellent bibliography of writings by and about Berry.

Berry, Wendell. *The Long-Legged House*. New York: Harcourt, Brace, & World, 1965. His initial collection of essays, critical of strip mining and the Vietnam War, which established the themes of his later essays.

_____. *The Way of Ignorance*. Shoemaker & Hoard, 2005. Berry's most recent collection of essays, continuing themes of community and nature and addressing constitutional issues generated by responses to terrorism.

Goodrich, Janet. *The Unforseen Self in the Works of Wendell Berry*. Columbia: University of Missouri Press, 2001. Goodrich looks at the five personae of Berry—autobiographer, poet, farmer, prophet, and neighbor—as they are expressed in his poems, stories, and essays.

Trachtman, Paul. "Berry Wendell." *Smithsonian* 36, no. 8 (November, 2005): 54-56. A profile of Berry, who farms 125 acres in Connecticut with his family. His philosophical outlook is discussed.

John L. Grigsby

WHAT I THINK I DID
A Season of Survival in Two Acts

Author: Larry Woiwode (1941-   )
First published: New York: Basic Books, 2000
Genre: Nonfiction
Subgenre: Autobiography
Core issues: Memory; time

Woiwode slowly reveals his faith and his life story through a narrative that alternates between past and present and is divided into two acts and an intermission. In the intermission, through a remembrance of a childhood walk in the woods, his faith rises to a triumphant affirmation of the power and immanence of God.

Overview

The organization of Larry Woiwode's autobiography is unconventional; instead of presenting a chronological, step-by-step account of his life, he presents a series of incidents from the past and present divided into two acts and an intermission. This pattern is suggested by the book's subtitle, "A Season of Survival in Two Acts." The main season of survival is the winter of 1996-1997, in which Larry Woiwode and his family must struggle not only with their isolation on a farm in southwestern North Dakota during savage storms and inclement weather, but also with learning (and overcoming) the inadequacies and vagaries of a newly installed outdoor wood-burning heater, which they had installed in hopes of becoming more self-sufficient. Interspersed throughout the first act are his early experiences: the meaning of his name; his birth in Carrington, North Dakota; his childhood in Sysketon, North Dakota; the early, traumatic death of his mother; and his move to Illinois.

The overall movement throughout the two juxtaposed narratives is from the past to the future, but past life and present struggle are linked by association or metaphor. The reader soon becomes used to the rhythm that propels each of the stories. Images in the present summon memories of the past: A tractor wheel in the rain recalls a summer of work on a farm. The title of the first act indicates its pulse: "Snow with Tints of Then." It is a visual metaphor, with the tactile connotations that the word "snow" carries, as well as a linguistic play. The word "Snow" contains the word "now" and suggests that the storehouse of memory is an intricate puzzle box, the word nesting within the image, and the writer unpacking each carefully.

The second act's title also reflects its structure: "Then with Tints of Snow." It covers Woiwode's college career at the University of Illinois at Urbana; his success there both as a writer and actor; his move to New York and his initial success with the stories he published in *The New Yorker* magazine; his friendship with his editor, William Maxwell; his marriage; the birth of his first child; and the acceptance of his first novel. The first act ended with a question grounded in the present, "How can I live like this?"; the second act ends with a declarative affirmation, "I'm launched," as both his family and his literary career take flight. The rhythm of the temporal discontinuities is much slower in this section: In the first section, the past and present seem more equally matched, more in search of a balance, while in this section, the past quietly asserts its gravitic pull.

This section also satisfies the reader who is hoping to glimpse the more famous personages that often flit through memoirs, literary celebrities such as John Updike, Truman Capote, Eudora Welty, Robert Lowell, and James Wright. Woiwode includes what he terms an appropriately Borgesian moment with Jorge Luis Borges, and a meeting with a young actor at the start of his career, Robert De Niro. Woiwode had considered an acting career, having had collegiate success in the roles of Feste in William Shakespeare's *Twelfth Night: Or, What You Will* (pr. c. 1600-1602) and the title role in Shakespeare's *Richard II* (pr. c. 1595-1596), but when he moved to New York, he found that his skill in acting was congruent with, and perhaps even akin to, the talents of impersonation and skin inhabiting that are necessary to the fiction writer's art.

Charles Shattuck at the University of Illinois had introduced Woiwode first to the works and then to the person of William Maxwell, fiction editor at *The New Yorker*, who becomes Woiwode's literary father and "kindness in the flesh." In a particularly symbolic act, Woiwode house-sits for Maxwell while working on his first novel, his only real duty to keep Maxwell's beloved roses trimmed. Woiwode learns through Maxwell that fiction has its own underpinnings in the "real" that no fact checker can uncover or discover.

The final juxtaposition of the book implicitly indicates the importance of family to Woiwode's life: In the past, his first child is born, while in the present, he agonizes over the wounding of his son in a freak gun accident. Like the best autobiographies, Woiwode's gives pleasure in two ways—by displaying to readers the inner life of someone other than themselves and by linking them to their universal life.

Christian Themes

Examples of Woiwode's faith are sprinkled throughout his narratives of the present. He and his family use the phrase "The Lord be with you" and the response "And with you" in their everyday speech. He mentions that he and his wife chose their farm's location because they wanted their family to be within fifty miles of a Presbyterian Church. When he is doing a book signing and meets a nun who babysat him, it causes what he terms "a jolt of grace" to pass between them. His present belief also tinges his evaluation of the past. A friend's compliment in the past now strikes him as "the working of the Spirit." Most intriguing, when he meets the poet James Wright in New York near the end of the book, and Wright asks him, "Do you think Jesus is God?" Woiwode does not tell us the answer he gave Wright. Since this exchange occurs not long before the end of the book, it almost evokes the feeling of an eschatological cliffhanger.

By far the most important declaration of Christian themes occurs in the book's central section, "Intermission." It begins as a concrete metaphor, as Woiwode and his wife, Carole, move through the figurative lobby of his mind, but it is well to remember that the word "intermission" is made up from Latin words that mean "to be sent among." Soon Woiwode remembers a time when he was twelve years old and wandering to a special place in the countryside, a woods where he feels "the presence of God," which causes him to recall Paul's words in Colossians 1:17, "in Him all things consist." This phrase leads Woiwode to recall how Russian-born poet Joseph Brodsky, while in the gulag, remembered a line from "In Memory of William Butler Yeats" by W. H. Auden, "Time . . . worships language." The immanence of God is not merely spatial, in the sky and the hedge apples and the earth, but also temporal. His memory of Brodsky's quoting Auden leads Woiwode back to those woods, where he experiences what he calls a communion and then to a more recent time when he had difficulty praying.

The whole section is a series of interlocked epiphanies, not only in the Joycean sense, but in the original religious denotation of the word, an emergence of the inner meaning through the mundane and quotidian. Time worships the word because the word—the words in this book—can conquer time, and the Word become flesh has conquered time. The self that remembers its past is different from the past self, yet the same; it judges, sees the larger patterns, and cannot help but attempt to impose meaning. For a Christian writer, composing an autobiography involves a search for the evidence of grace in one's life, each instance of which Woiwode delicately notes, and an acknowledgment of the central interconnected mystery of God, time, and the self.

Sources for Further Study

Block, Ed, Jr. "An Interview with Larry Woiwode." *Renascence* (Fall 1991): 17-30. Wide-ranging interview in which Woiwode discusses the effects of being labeled a regional writer, the importance of ethics in teaching and writing, and the difficulty of describing a conversion experience.

Cheaney, J. B. "Taming Memory: The Fiction of Larry Woiwode." *The World & I* 17, no. 10 (October, 2002): 256. A profile of Woiwode that discusses *What I Think I Did* and the writer's life.

Woiwode, Larry. *Acts*. New York: HarperSanFransico, 1993. An outgrowth of an article written on the acts of the Apostles, this book may considered a precursor to *What I Think I Did*, as it is part autobiography, part current memoir, and part biblical and spiritual commentary.

_____. *What I'm Going to Do, I Think*. New York: Farrar, Straus and Giroux, 1969. Woiwode's first novel, the writing of which is recounted in *What I Think I Did*, and which also suggested the latter's title.

William Laskowski

WHAT JESUS MEANT

Author: Garry Wills (1934-   )
First published: New York: Viking, 2006
Genre: Nonfiction
Subgenres: Critical analysis; theology
Core issues: Faith; Gospels; Jesus Christ; salvation; sin and sinners; truth

Wills states that modern religion commonly ignores the radicalism of Jesus. He notes many ways in which Jesus challenged the authorities of his day and asserts that though Jesus had no particular political agenda, he was adamantly opposed to all religious formalism. Wills concludes that true believers must not merely adopt the rules of an organized religion but rather seek to understand the meaning of Christ's words and deeds as revealed in the Gospels and apply them rationally to modern life, keeping in mind Jesus' concern for those disenfranchised by the traditional religion of their day.

Overview

Garry Wills opens by making the bold assertion that Christ was not a Christian and that if modern Christians seek to emulate his behavior in the manner of What would Jesus do? bracelets, they are ignoring the fact that they can never truly be like Christ because they are not divine. He points out that if one seeks to understand what Christ would have humans do, one must look at his words and deeds and then attempt to understand them in the context in which they occurred. The best source for these deeds are the Gospels, because they were written most contemporaneously with his actual life. He also notes that many modern theologians cleanse the Gospels of the descriptions of Jesus they find unappetizing, and these are chiefly his very radical statements about religion. Jesus was, Wills believes, adamantly and often violently opposed to the formalized religious structures of his day, so much so that the religious leaders who recognized the danger he posed to them conspired to have him killed.

Wills follows Jesus' life chronologically, beginning with the Annunciation to Jesus' childhood status as displaced person, on the run from Herod. Wills remarks that Jesus probably was educated by religious radicals, as he would not normally have enjoyed any education at all, coming from a working-class home. Jesus' connection with John the Baptist confirms his association with radicals who were seeking to reform what they viewed as a dissolute and corrupt church. Wills interprets the testing of Jesus in the desert by Satan as a metaphor for his entire spiritual education and the assumption of his mission. He overcomes the temptations put before him and is ready to take up the heavy burden of bringing salvation to humanity.

When Jesus began his ministry, he took as his followers those who were social outcasts or from the working classes, people who were explicitly outside the power structures of their day. He purposely associated with those who were despised and unclean according to the dictates of traditional Judaism. Wills comments that all Jesus' miracles were performed in times and places where they could teach particular religious lessons to his followers; many of those he healed were considered unclean by their community, yet Jesus did not reject them. Wills points out that any distinctions among people based on money, social position, political alliance, religious observance, or anything else are false in Jesus' opinion, and he acted in a way that showed his disdain for such divisions. Wills notes that modern distinctions between those who are acceptable or not acceptable according to religion are often based on very selective readings of Old Testament texts, particularly Leviticus, which Jesus pointedly and repeatedly spurned in word and deed.

The radicalism of Jesus regarding religious leaders is revealed in his many statements about the dire plight of Scribes and Pharisees, and his complete rejection of any titles of rank for himself or his followers. Jesus also believed in equality between men and women, and Wills points out that this was the most difficult of his positions for even his disciples to comprehend. Nevertheless, women were a constant presence among Jesus' followers, and many are named in the Gospels as supporters of his work and apostles. Women also remained with Jesus when the male disciples deserted him. Additionally, Jesus discarded utterly any use of violence or warfare to advance his aims, though many wished him to lead an uprising against Rome. His overriding teaching is summed up in his statement that whatever one does to one of his followers, one does to Jesus himself. This is a powerful injunction against judgmental behavior and a strong call for servant leadership by those who would follow Christ.

Jesus' most excoriating criticism was reserved for religious authorities, as previously noted, and Wills examines in detail the many ways Jesus rejected the religious legalism of his day. He broke the Sabbath regularly by traveling, obtaining food, healing, and other practices. Also, he disdained the practice of sacrifice. This rejection of a formal, ritualized forgiveness, as opposed to a true inner examination and change of heart, marked him as treacherous to the priests of his day. Jesus noted that the temple of Jerusalem would be destroyed, and Wills interprets this as a positive development from Jesus' point of view because he opposed the pompous official religious observance it represented. There is no historical evidence that Jesus wanted his followers to have an organized priesthood of any kind, in Wills's opinion.

The church Jesus founded, Wills asserts, is the gathering of true believers in a community of love and support. Any other organization, especially one that controls money, political power and influence, or any social hierarchies is antithetical to what Jesus stood for. Jesus suffered a painful death at the hands of those who represented established religion. The God he represented and was united with was one whose love for humanity was so great as to be incomprehensible. Jesus sought to eliminate all barriers between people, and between people and God. The image for the final communion of God and humans in Heaven is a banquet, at which all are welcome who enter in the spirit of true love and service.

Christian Themes

By analyzing Jesus' life and ministry in detail, Wills advances the theory that religions that purport to be Christian are not, in fact, based on the true teachings of Christ. Though churches call themselves Christian and look to Jesus as their spiritual leader, they ignore the key concepts of Jesus' ministry.

Jesus was an extremely radical individual whose life was singular because of his special relationship to God the Father. However, he made very clear by his actions and words that he was drastically opposed to the hierarchies that circumscribed the world in which he lived. His excoriation of the traditional religious authorities of his time should not, in Wills's view, be seen as a repudiation of Judaism or Jews, a mistaken interpretation often used by the Christian church. Rather, Jesus' rejection of animal sacrifice, cleansing rituals, intercession of priests, and so on indicates his desire for complete egalitarianism of humans—socially, sexually, politically, and financially. Any system in which some people are privileged over others for any reason is the exact opposite of what Jesus taught and represented in his life on earth.

Traditional Christian beliefs of caring for the unfortunate of the world and self-abnegating service were certainly recognized by Jesus as positive behaviors. However, Wills asserts that the social and political conservatism of many modern churches would appall Jesus and is just the sort of action he came to oppose. The sanitized version of Jesus preferred by many churches is a nonexistent figure who allows people to feel superior or to control money and power. Jesus himself, however, time after time rejected such ideas and gave the example of truly Christian behavior by embracing with love all those who came to him in the spirit of trust.

Sources for Further Study

Chesterton, G. K. *The Collected Works of G. K. Chesterton*. Ft. Collins, Colo.: Ignatius Press, 1986. Traces through his three major works the development of Chesterton's theology, which was extremely influential on Wills's thought.

Guardini, Romano. *The Essential Guardini: An Anthology of the Writings of Romano Guardini*. Edited by Heinz R. Kuehn. Chicago: Liturgy Training, 1997. Includes excerpts from Guardini's major works, grouped by subject. Gives a general overview of his beliefs regarding Christ, which strongly influenced Wills.

Holan, Angie Drobnic. "What Garry Wills Means." *St. Petersburg Times*, November 12, 2006, p. 12L. Examines Wills's views as revealed in *What Jesus Meant* and *What Paul Meant* (2006), a work that disputes Saint Paul's reputation as a misogynist.

Wills, Garry. *Papal Sin: Structures of Deceit*. London: Darton, Longman, and Todd, 2000. Summarizes Wills's basic beliefs regarding papal authority, as well as the crucial difference between religion and true faith.

_____. *Why I Am a Catholic*. Boston: Mariner Books, 2003. Answer to those who inquired about his devotion to the Catholic faith based on his earlier book *Papal Sin*. Explores ideas about Jesus' true intentions.

Vicki A. Sanders

WHEN JESUS CAME TO HARVARD
Making Moral Choices Today

Author: Harvey Cox (1929-   )
First published: New York: Mariner Books, 2006
Genre: Nonfiction
Subgenres: Biblical studies; critical analysis; handbook for living
Core issues: Daily living; ethics; guidance; Judaism; morality

Cox relates his experiences during two decades of attempting to teach the moral relevance of Jesus to undergraduate students at Harvard University, students who came from many diverse religious and cultural backgrounds and who had different professional and personal goals.

Overview

In the 1980's, the Harvard College faculty introduced a moral reasoning curriculum into its undergraduate program in response to a perceived increase in professional corruption and unethical behavior (even among Harvard graduates) and a belief that a focus on facts in education had diminished the importance of values and morality. Harvey Cox, a professor at the Harvard Divinity School and the author of *The Secular City: Secularization and Urbanization in Theological Perspective* (1965), was asked to teach a course on Jesus in the new curriculum. He reluctantly agreed, despite wondering whether morality was something that could be taught in an academic environment and believing that moral reasoning did not necessarily lead to moral actions. In addition, any college class would include more than just believing Christians. How would they respond to Jesus as a moral exemplar? However, Cox accepted the challenge, teaching the course for two decades, with considerable personal fulfillment. *When Jesus Came to Harvard* is his account of that experience.

One of the challenges Cox faced with his varied Harvard students was making Jesus, who lived two millennia ago in a preindustrial rural environment, relevant to the moral quandaries of the late twentieth century, a much different world. Also, what could a morality linked to Christian theology offer to Muslims, Buddhists, Hindus, agnostics, or atheists? Cox, from a Baptist background, did not interpret the Bible as always being literally true.

Cox did not believe that the quest for the historical Jesus was ultimately satisfactory as it left Jesus only as a product of the early Roman Empire in the province of Judea, a Palestinian Jew and a rabbi who preached about the imminent coming of God, attracted a following among the underclass in Galilee, inflamed the religious and political authorities, and was arrested and subsequently crucified, the usual Roman method of executing troublemakers. His followers, believing he rose from the dead, became the earliest Christians, initially forming a sect within Judaism. Jesus' life as re-created by historians did not answer the question of what Jesus would do in any given circumstance in the modern world. Cox's response to determining what Jesus would do was to begin with the fact that Jesus was a rabbi steeped in Judaic theology and tradition and that he relied on narrative stories rather than abstract principles and precepts to convey morality. Cox notes that history and myth often intertwine, ritual can be more revealing and truthful than chronicle, and ritualized stories enrich historical fact.

Throughout *When Jesus Came to Harvard*, Cox emphasizes that Jesus was a rabbi and his knowledge of Jewish doctrines and law was extensive. Also, as a rabbi, Jesus' ministry reflected the rabbinic tradition of using narrative storytelling to convey moral and ethical issues. Cox argues that awareness of a moral issue is in itself insufficient: One must decide what moral response to make to the situation, and one has to have the courage to actually implement a response. The process, the author claims, is less a matter of abstract principles or general moral theories and more a consequence of imagination sparked by stories, or case studies, in which often Jesus himself was the central figure. As Cox notes, these stories, those that Jesus told and those that were told about him in the Scriptures, did not have to be factual in a scientific historical sense, but they had to be "true." What was of great significance with Jesus was that morality was universal, therefore his stories frequently focused on people outside mainstream Jewish society.

Although Cox's Harvard class centered on the applicability of the moral examples exemplified by Jesus, other aspects of the Jesus narrative frequently entered the discussion, such as whether the stories of the virgin birth or the Garden of Eden were historically "true." Cox does not express a literal belief in these stories but instead responds to such questions about biblical "miracles" by noting that Jesus himself was born, lived, and died, and that God encompasses every aspect of human experience, including joy, pain, and morality. Regarding the story of the Garden of Eden, Cox interprets it as Adam and Eve refusing to accept their human condition, wanting even more, similar to the conflict between the aspirations and limitations of many people in today's world. Cox points to the tradition of the *midrash* in the stories told by Jewish rabbis, likening them to the riffing of jazz musicians when they perform variations on the main theme, and claims that there is no single meaning or interpretation to the biblical stories. The author argues that moral reasoning in the abstract, in the absence of imagination and stories, limits or reduces morality's significance and impact.

In the chapter "A World Without God?" Cox explores the meanings of Jesus' imploring cry from the cross, "My God, my God, why has thou forsaken me?" Jesus' words invariably puzzled many students, who saw Jesus as a moral man abandoned by God. Why did God desert Jesus and why did Jesus feel deserted? Cox's answer is that God refuses to compromise human freedom by becoming merely the deus ex machina who rescues humanity at times of crisis. To be fully human, as Jesus was on the cross, is to face life's crises, including responding to the moral issues life presents.

Christian Themes

The author claims that the theme in Jesus' Sermon on the Mount as recorded in the book of Matthew is the major underlying message of the entire Bible, the culmination of many earlier versions of that text. However, its application in today's world, when supplemented with the account of the sermon as given in Luke, where Jesus seemed to condemn the rich and successful, was challenging to many of Cox's students, committed as they were to achieving professional success in a material world. Through discussion, however, Cox was able to give the Beatitudes modern relevance. The meek are not passive and weak but faithful and patient, and peace is not necessarily the world of a Pax Romana or a Pax Americana but rather the inner peace of *shalom*. Therefore the story of Jesus and his stories with their moral center can and have appealed not only to committed Christians but also to many non-Christians such as India's Mahatma Gandhi.

When Jesus Came to Harvard is a book about morality rather than theology. In it, Cox, a believing Christian, stresses Jesus as an observing Jew, a rabbi who taught the Torah, noting that even the Lord's Prayer is more traditionally Jewish than uniquely Christian. The stories that Jesus told, the sixty-odd parables, which make up about one-third of the first three Gospels, are not overtly about God but about wedding feasts (guests invited in from the highways), muggings (the Good Samaritan), and the activities of farmers and fishermen. However, the stories, like Zen koans, are not always easy to interpret, such as the story of the condemnation of the late-invited guest who was not properly dressed for the wedding banquet and who was thrown "into the dark, a place of wailing and grinding of teeth." Be prepared, be properly dressed, for the imminent coming of God, or be always aware of the many moral choices that life presents.

Throughout the history of Christianity, believers have looked forward to the Second Coming of Jesus and the end-times, as evidenced in the popularity of the *Left Behind* series (1995-2007), but Cox ignores those eschatological issues, referring to a Hasidic rabbi, who when asked what he would do if he knew that the Messiah was coming today, responded that he would simply continue to water his garden. When discussing Christ's Resurrection, Cox admits that he does not know what it means or what he believes about it. In fact, he doubts that "believe" is the correct word. "Confidence," "hope," and "trust" more accurately reflect his own feelings. Cox describes Jesus as an elusive "friend," today still talking and eating with humanity irrespective of rank or status. As the story of the Exodus of the Israelites from Egypt has had an inspiring impact on non-Jews, so Jesus can have a moral if not a theological meaning for non-Christians.

Sources for Further Study

Campbell, Colleen Carroll. "Jesus Christ Superfluous." Review of *When Jesus Came to Harvard. First Things* 152 (April, 2005). Campbell criticizes Cox for stressing the importance of Jesus as a moral teacher over Jesus' divinity as the Son of God.

Gula, Richard M. "Rabbinical Thinking." *America* 192 (January 2, 2005): 24. Gula argues that Cox succeeds better at introducing Jesus through the biblical stories than connecting Jesus to present-day moral choices.

Heinegg, Peter. *Cross Currents* 55 (Spring, 2005): 138. Finds Cox's work as thoughtful and relaxed rather than being rigorously analytical.

Lawton, Kim. "Interview with Harvey Cox." *Religion and Ethics*. Episode 935, April 28, 2006. In this Public Broadcasting System program, the author and Cox discuss the Pentecostals and other similar movements.

Eugene Larson

1941

WHILE MORTALS SLEEP

Author: Jack Cavanaugh (1952-   )
First published: Minneapolis, Minn.: Bethany House, 2001
Genre: Novel
Subgenres: Evangelical fiction; historical fiction (twentieth century)
Core issues: Children; fear; good vs. evil; pastoral role; persecution; sacrifice

This work of historical fiction set during Adolf Hitler's rise to power explores how Christians respond when evil arises. Sometimes fear dictates a course of inaction, and sometimes courage prompts sacrificial acts that allow good to triumph.

> Principal characters
> *Josef Schumacher*, a pastor and the protagonist
> *Mady Schumacher*, Josef's wife
> *Lisette Janssen*, a member of the church youth group
> *Konrad Reichmann*, a Hitler Youth member
> *Victor Meyerhof*, a Jewish professor
> *Wilhelm Olbricht*, Josef's father-in-law
> *Martin Wolff*, an SS officer
> *Adolf*, Wolff's collaborator

Overview

In December, 1939, the Reverend Josef Schumacher intervenes when a young man from his church reports his father for listening to the British Broadcasting Corporation. Josef is taken for interrogation, making him late for the young people's Christmas gathering. He determines to influence the members of the church youth group, including Lisette Janssen and Konrad Reichmann. At the party, he gives each youth a coin inscribed with a verse from Scripture. He encourages the young people to carry the coins and think about their verse. When Josef's Hebrew teacher arrives as the youth depart, Konrad rudely bumps into Professor Meyerhof because he is Jewish.

In April, 1940, the Hitler Youth members are summoned during a Sunday service. Josef dislikes the disrespect the timing exhibits, so his father-in-law Wilhelm Olbricht suggests he attend a Hitler Youth meeting. Josef attends the Führer's birthday celebration. The outstanding unit of the year includes some boys from Josef's church youth group, and the Führer's speech stirs Josef's German patriotism. However, he cannot reconcile the inspiring words with the harshness of the Nazis. He interferes in the beating of an elderly man and absorbs a few blows until Konrad recognizes him and calls the altercation to a halt. Josef discovers the injured Jew is Meyerhof. He escorts him home and finds his professor has been granted permission to live in his former pantry since he can no longer own property. In his cramped quarters, Meyerhof keeps a photo of his wife and Josef's mother-in-law; the women grew up together.

1942

In May, Josef exclaims that they will not use the Nazi salute in church but greet each other as Christians. Josef locates Konrad on patrol. He leads him to Meyerhof's living quarters. Konrad agrees to spend five minutes with the Jew, but when Josef knocks, no one answers. He finds Meyerhof hanging from the rafters. Later, SS agents haul Josef to Gestapo headquarters. They use torture to force him to practice the Nazi salute. Olbricht picks him up and warns him to leave the struggle to unmarried ministers. Mady, Josef's wife, accuses him of being irresponsible, saying his actions will not change anything. Josef agrees. However, when Mady wants him not to cross the Nazis again, he maintains that it is his responsibility to speak against actions and beliefs that lead people away from God. The next Sunday, his in-laws and two SS officers attend services. He asks for casket bearers for Meyerhof's funeral, but no one volunteers. The rest of the service progresses well, and Josef greets everyone with the obligatory "Heil Hitler." At home, Josef stews about the cowardice of his congregation. He realizes he is no different than his church members. Josef wonders how to effect change without endangering his family. He recalls a note saying if he is a friend of Martin Luther to use the word "bulwark" in a sermon. The next Sunday, Josef refers to Martin Luther, then quotes from "A Mighty Fortress Is Our God," including the word "bulwark."

After an intense test of his intent, Josef meets his contacts—Adolf and Martin Wolff, one of the SS officers who had enforced the salute. Wolff reveals that the Führer has authorized infanticide. Josef is drafted for Operation Ramah, a plan to rescue as many children as possible. Two weeks later, Josef, Wolff, and Adolf steal the file on the children involved. They learn that Wolff's mentally disabled son, who was taken by the Nazis, died two days earlier: He was starved to death. Despite the death, they proceed with their plan to rescue children. Josef explains to Mady that he has to go, and she is to get Lisette to stay with her.

Josef is successfully admitted to the hospital in Hadamar where the children are being held. Attendants take Josef's coin, and he berates himself that he still carried it. Two days later, a disturbance allows Josef to find the children's ward just before he is apprehended. Wolff comes to interrogate him, and Josef reports finding more than two dozen children too weak to talk or cry. By the time Wolff leaves, they have devised a plan for the next morning. As Josef is led through the hallway, he encounters his father-in-law, who is trying to determine Wolff's plan. Olbricht claims the mercy killings help people reach eternity when they have no more place in this world. Josef realizes that Olbricht had been with Meyerhof and "helped" him to a better place. Because Olbricht's wife, daughter, and grandchild are Jewish, eliminating Meyerhof makes life safer. Olbricht will not allow Josef to endanger his family. He renames Josef for the records and marks him for death.

Mady goes into labor, and Lisette helps her deliver a baby girl. During a reception for the baby, four SS agents come to confiscate Josef's papers. After they depart, Olbricht lies to Mady, telling her he does not know Josef's whereabouts. In mid-July, Wolff informs Mady that Josef is dead. He asks if the midwife noted anything questionable about the new baby. Mady admits a concern about her daughter's hearing.

In late July, Wolff shows Mady paperwork he had stolen. The baby had come close to being taken from Mady. Wolff seems to think Josef might still be alive. Mady demands to know more about Josef's disappearance, and Wolff gives her a fragment of information. Mady remembers her father's connection to that name and realizes he has compromised Josef's identity. She calls the number and uses the code word to get help.

In August, Wolff, Adolf, and Mady ask the members of the youth group to help rescue Josef. Wolff briefs them on the need and the risk. Lisette convinces Konrad to help. Konrad dresses as an SS officer. Inside the hospital, he and Adolf bluff their way past the attendant and through a meeting with the doctor to rescue Josef from the newly installed gas chamber. Josef refuses to leave without the children. They locate a truck to transport the children. Josef is grief-stricken when they discover that only six of the two dozen children survived. They carry the emaciated children to the truck. Olbricht follows them in his powerful car and blocks their escape route. Josef barters himself for the freedom of the boys as well as the others and the children. Mady and Wolff pull up, and Olbricht appears incredulous on seeing his daughter. When he still tries to take Josef, Mady confronts him and forces him to acknowledge that his choices kill people. She tells him his granddaughter will be one of the dying children since her hearing loss marks her as unsuitable. The thought that he might be involved in his granddaughter's death staggers Olbricht. He trades his vehicle for their truck and sends them to freedom.

On Christmas Eve, Wolff visits the secluded hills north of Berlin. There, Josef and Mady, with Lisette's help, run Ramah Cabin. Together, they shelter ten children unwanted by the Third Reich.

Christian Themes

In *While Mortals Sleep*, Jack Cavanaugh examines the moral choices Christians were forced to make when confronted by Adolf Hitler's policies. Josef first intervenes on behalf of a church member, then rails against the Hitler Youth movement when it draws young men from Sunday services. In both instances, the Nazis punish him. Throughout the book, somewhat minor infractions progress into clearly moral choices about outright evil, and each character must overcome or give in to that individual's fears.

Josef's father-in-law, Olbricht, compromises to protect his family. He rationalizes away the value of Jewish and infirm lives and joins in the Nazis' heinous activities. Josef's wife, Mady, avoids calling attention to her family to preserve their safety. Her stance often creates conflict with Josef because he champions what is scripturally right.

When the Nazis purge unwanted races and infirm individuals, the Christians at the center of this story resist evil at great sacrifice, fighting for those who cannot protect themselves. Konrad endangers his leadership in the Hitler Youth to help his pastor. Wolff jeopardizes his SS position to prevent the horrors. Josef risks his life to save children from infanticide. Mady realizes evil that is ignored does not go away; she cannot remain silent. To rescue her husband and protect her daughter's life, she must act. These fictional characters illustrate the plight of Christians in Nazi Germany who faced danger yet left behind a powerful legacy of doing right in the face of adversity.

Sources for Further Study

DeLong, Janice, and Rachel Schwedt. *Contemporary Christian Authors: Lives and Works*. Lanham, Md.: Scarecrow Press, 2000. Biographical sketch details Jack Cavanaugh's credentials and writing accomplishments.

Duncan, Melanie C. Review of *While Mortals Sleep*. *Library Journal* 126, no. 18 (November 1, 2001): 74. Categorizes the novel in terms of books written in a similar vein.

Mort, John. Review of *While Mortals Sleep*. *Booklist* 98, no. 3 (October 1, 2001): 281. Evaluates the novel and recognizes Cavanaugh's abilities.

Kimberly T. Peterson

1945

THE WIND IN THE WHEAT

Author: Reed Arvin (1951-   )
First published: Nashville: T. Nelson, 1994
Genre: Novel
Subgenre: Literary fiction
Core issues: Conscience; humility; service; simplicity

Gifted church musician Andrew Miracle is discovered in a rural Kansas town and goes to Nashville, where he quickly becomes a popular singer-songwriter of Christian and pop music. He feels trapped by his own success, having lost the sense of ministry that made him a musician in the first place and become uncomfortably obligated to his manager, the record label, and his many fans. With the help of a young woman, Andrew rediscovers his roots and frees himself to follow his true calling.

>*Principal characters*
>*Andrew Miracle*, the protagonist, a contemplative, devout young man and gifted church musician from Kansas
>*Cy Mathews*, Andrew's pastor in Kansas
>*Alison Miracle*, Andrew's mother
>*John van Grimes*, a music manager from Nashville who discovers Andrew
>*Carolyn Hemphill*, John's assistant who becomes Andrew's girlfriend

Overview

In *The Wind in the Wheat*, novelist Reed Arvin demonstrates the nobility of following one's own calling, as well as the perils of power, fame, and wealth, even in a religious context. His protagonist, twenty-year-old Andrew Miracle, begins the story as a somewhat naïve idealist, adrift in a world of ordinary people. In the beginning of the novel, Andrew has just received a brief and simple vision from God, in the form of a voice saying that Andrew is love. Andrew lives with his mother and works on the farm built by her and his deceased father near the small town of Rose Hill, Kansas.

Andrew's faith finds expression in the intimate, spiritual music he composes and performs at his church, where he has quietly become a small-town attraction. Andrew's obvious talent prompts the church's enthusiastic pastor, Cy Mathews, to arrange for Andrew to meet Cy's friend, John van Grimes, who comes to the church accompanying Heaven's Voices, a group of young musicians managed by John and his small Nashville company. After the concert, the three men meet, and Andrew plays and sings for John. Extremely impressed, John arranges for the group to have breakfast at the Miracle farm the next morning. With his mother's blessing, Andrew agrees to move to Nashville and join Heaven's Voices.

On his arrival at the Nashville airport, Andrew is met by John's young assistant, Carolyn Hemphill, who introduces him to the city and to some of the workings of the Christian music business. The two form an immediate friendship that quickly evolves into romance.

At his first meeting with John in Nashville, Andrew is surprised not only to be joined by two executives from Dove Records, a Christian music label, but also to be informed that John would like Andrew not to join Heaven's Voices as planned but instead to become a solo recording artist. Andrew eventually signs a management contract with John and a recording contract with Dove. Both contracts contain unusual provisions not beneficial to the inexperienced and trusting Andrew, and John secretly pockets an extraordinary finder's fee from Dove.

Andrew's success continues, and his life becomes a whirlwind with promotional parties, photo shoots, radio airplay, a music video, and a slot on another artist's concert tour. Dove hires a big-name producer to oversee the recording of Andrew's debut album and his trademark song, "Lost Without You," which becomes a hit. Andrew and his song gain the attention of Atlantic Records, a secular label that releases selected Dove albums to the general music marketplace. Atlantic agrees to commit a large amount of money to the promotion of Andrew's record, with the stipulation that the word "Jesus" be removed from "Lost Without You" so that it would then strike most listeners as an inoffensive love song, not as a song directed to God. Andrew reluctantly agrees, when his manager John urges him to accept, reassuring him that Atlantic's money and promotion will allow Andrew's ministry to reach others it otherwise would not.

After his first tour, Andrew takes time off to visit his hometown. There he learns that his mother has cancer. Within weeks, forgoing radical treatment for the chance to plant flowers, to refinish some tables built by her husband, and to see her son play at church, Alison dies, leaving Andrew feeling even more isolated than before. Even his relationship with Carolyn, once a great comfort, becomes strained and distant, and John angrily confronts Andrew about the singer's reticence in the events of his career, many of them outside of Andrew's control.

Riding a wave of stardom and ignoring his own misgivings, Andrew headlines his own concert tour. On the day of the final concert, Carolyn secretly flies out to see him before the show and tells him how much she misses the Andrew she first met, who success has turned into a withdrawn and irritable person. This encounter affects Andrew's performance on stage, and during the speaking portion of the concert, he departs from his normal script and reveals his uncertainties to the audience. This prompts an emergency visit from John the next day, during which Andrew declares his intention to end his music career and John threatens to sue him if he does. Their meeting is ended by a phone call from Carolyn, who has accidentally discovered the unfair terms of Andrew's contract with John.

Armed with this information, Andrew seeks legal recourse of his own, and a lawyer persuades John to dissolve the contract, though John keeps a substantial amount of money at Andrew's request. With Carolyn as his new representative, Andrew embarks on the final event of his short but brilliant music career, an appearance on a national television talk show, where Andrew performs "Lost Without You" with all its original lyrics intact. Andrew soon returns to Kansas, this time with Carolyn, where they are quietly married by Cy on the night they arrive and become the new caretakers of the Miracle farm.

Christian Themes

Andrew's struggle to follow his own conscience provides a framework for the narrative of *The Wind in the Wheat*. In the beginning, Andrew is captured by his vision from God and motivated by his desire to serve others, but he soon sees the talents he wants to be used by God being used by others to bring gain to themselves and to Andrew. The resulting power, fame, and wealth are all benefits he does not seek but that he decides to accept when John and others convince him they will enable his ministry to reach more people. In the end, Andrew finds this path to service unacceptable, and he abandons it to pursue a simpler life.

The author uses the image of a larger-than-life promotional poster of Andrew to comment on humility and self-image. As the unassuming young man from Kansas begins his climb to fame, John and Dove Records hold a large party to introduce Andrew and his album to members of the media and music business insiders. One of the items revealed at the party is a nine-foot-square poster featuring a retouched photograph of Andrew, in clothes and with a facial expression not of his own choosing. Several times later, the author contrasts the poster version of Andrew, seemingly perfect and full of power in his self-confidence, to the genuine Andrew, confident but humble in his calling from God.

In one of his confrontations with John, Andrew speaks of the handful of people in his hometown church who faithfully stack chairs after each service, important work, but mundane and thankless. Andrew relates the work of these chair stackers to his own former playing at the church and at the local nursing home, often for those who did not understand his talents. He envies the simplicity of the chair stackers and speculates whether it is they, and not he, who are truly serving God and already rule the world in God's eyes.

Sources for Further Study

Arvin, Reed. "Romeo Must Die: Christian Publishers Censor More than Profanity in Their Quest Not to Offend." *Regeneration Quarterly* 8, no. 1 (Spring, 2002): 6-8. Arvin's first-person critique of editorial censorship at evangelical publishers, suggesting much of classic literature would not meet their narrow standards.

Mort, John. "The Christian Alternative." In *Christian Fiction*. Greenwood Village, Colo.: Libraries Unlimited, 2002. Sets the background for contemporary Christian fiction and evangelical novels in particular; *The Wind in the Wheat* is cited as a distinguished example.

Riess, Jana. "Fiction's Growing Pains: The Awkward Adolescence of the Christian Novel." *Publishers Weekly* 249, no. 24 (June 17, 2002): S4-S9. Comments on the quality of Christian fiction; Arvin compares editorial direction from religious and secular publishers.

Clint Wrede

"THE WINDHOVER"

Author: Gerard Manley Hopkins (1844-1889)
First published: wr. 1877, pb. 1918, in *Poems of Gerard Manley Hopkins, Now First Published, with Notes by Robert Bridges*
Edition used: "The Windhover," in *Poems and Prose of Gerard Manley Hopkins*, selected with an introduction and notes by W. H. Gardner. Baltimore: Penguin Books, 1968
Genre: Poetry
Subgenre: Lyric poetry
Core issues: Beauty; Jesus Christ; nature

In this classic lyric poem, Hopkins's dense spiritual imagery pays tribute to God, Christ, and nature: The world is filled with the grandeur of God, and all reality is interconnected; God, humanity, and the universe are inseparable. Each person, each object in the world, is unique and glorifies God in its uniqueness.

Overview

The eldest of nine children of a well-to-do middle-class family, Gerard Manley Hopkins alienated family and friends when he converted from Anglicanism to Catholicism under Cardinal John Henry Newman. He joined the Society of Jesus in 1868 and became a priest nine years later, serving in slum parishes before taking a post as a classics professor in Dublin. He studied music and painting and wrote poetry, almost none of which was published until several decades after his death. He shared his verse with his poet-friend Robert Bridges through a correspondence of many years. A breakdown shortly before his death may have resulted from the tension in his life, which he considered nearly unresolvable, between his wanting to be a poet and his striving for sanctity.

To understand Hopkins's poetry, the reader must know something of his poetic theory. His three main concepts are found in the terms "inscape," "instress," and "sprung rhythm." The first two terms are closely related. By "instress," a term that Hopkins coined, is meant the principle of the physical uniqueness of an object (natural or artistic) that distinguishes it from all else that is, was, or shall be. The term is derived from *haecceitas*, as used by the Catholic philosopher John Duns Scotus (1266-1308), and is sometimes translated as "thisness." Hopkins's "inscape" may be defined as the outward manifestation of the interior integrity of a thing.

"Instress" is described in terms of energy: the force by which inscape is revealed. Instress is that which acts on the mind of the beholder in such a way as to allow the beholder to comprehend the inscape. It is, as Hopkins himself wrote, the energy by which "all things are upheld."

"Sprung" (or abrupt) rhythm is a difficult concept that commentators have tried to make comprehensible, not always with success. It is measured by feet of one to four syllables in length, regularly, although for certain effects any number of unstressed syllables may be used. If there is but one syllable, it receives the stress. If there are more syllables, the stress is on the first and different sorts of feet will result. There are four possibilities: a monosyllable, accentual trochee, dactyl, and first paeon. In this respect, sprung rhythm differs from running rhythm because sprung rhythm may use rests, monosyllabic feet, and the first paeon, whereas running rhythm (if it is scanned from the first stress in a line) can be made up only of trochees and dactyls. "Sprung rhythm" is meant by Hopkins to convey emotionally charged speech.

Hopkins's best use of sprung rhythm may be found in his famous sonnet "The Windhover." The poem, named after a small hawk, a kestrel, known for hovering in the wind, is set in the morning, when the narrator first sights the bird. Hopkins names the winged creature by the more aristocratic term (which he significantly capitalizes) *Falcon* and calls it "daylight's dauphin" to stress its royalty. The creature circles in air and, when it seems to come into conflict with the wind in a kind of crisis, experiences ecstasy in a movement resembling a skater's figure eight, a movement combining hurl and glide. The bird's control enables it to overcome the wind's force, intelligence defeating physicality, as it were. This skill excites the narrator:

> My heart in hiding . . .
> Stirred for a bird,—the achieve of, the mastery of the thing!

The triumph over the blind force of nature is exhilarating. Thus the first eight lines of this sonnet come to a close. In the sestet, Hopkins summarizes the hawk's attributes—its beauty, courage, and energy—all of which "buckle," a deliberately ambiguous term suggesting both a collapse (or submission) and a fastening together. The poem closes with an acknowledgment of the almost dangerous beauty of the bird, which, in its violence, may reflect the ambiguity of the Crucifixion: violence culminating in salvation.

Christian Themes

"The Windhover" exemplifies much that is both spiritual and explicitly Christian in Hopkins's work: that all reality is interconnected; that God, humanity, and the universe are inseparable; that each person and each object in the world is unique and glorifies God in its uniqueness; and that the revelation of individual uniqueness is found in the energy that each person or object emits.

The bird was one of Hopkins's favorite images. In "The Windhover," the hawk gives glory to God by being fully itself, but in the poem the image also suggests Christ as well as one who would use Christ as a model for life, probably the narrator of the poem. The bird is a Christlike image of self-sacrifice and in being true to itself is shown as part of the great unity of the cosmos. Everything is connected with everything, and the incorporating energy for this is signified in the concept of inscape, which reconciles the individuated creature with the rest of the universe.

The poet experimented in how exactly to present his thoughts and moods, frequently having to invent words ("wimpling," "achieve" as a noun), unique verbal combinations ("gash gold-vermilion"), and hyphenations ("dapple-dawn-drawn") and to revive words long out of use (sillion). Influenced by both Welsh and medieval verse traditions, Hopkins was determined to render meaning and feeling through his highly personalized view of poetic language.

The music of his poems was developed through use of alliteration, internal rhyme, and repeated syllables as well as words. The first two lines of "The Windhover" illustrate this:

> I caught this morning morning's minion, king-
> dom of daylight's dauphin, dapple-dawn-drawn Falcon, in his riding

It has been noted by critics that the arrangement of Hopkins's words is not based on that of ordinary speech but is rather for the effect of communicating meaning and tone. This tends to give a high energy level to his poetry when read aloud. It has further been said that the priest's interest in painting contributed to his concern for beauty and the form that establishes it. This is reinforced by his attraction to John Duns Scotus's philosophy, with its emphasis on the uniqueness of each individual person and object. It is not difficult, then, to see how Hopkins came to develop his theories of inscape and instress.

It should not be thought, however, that Hopkins wrote from a spiritually comfortable soul. His poetry often exhibited the tension he experienced between his religious faith and his poetic skills. His work reflects pain and joy, excitement and agonized interpretation. Critics have found that Hopkins, living in the era of Victorian literature in England, was separated from the literary and religious mainstream in England, and at least one critic has argued that the introverted nature of his poetry is in part a reflection of this. His poetry has also been seen as offering a kind of meeting place for orthodox Catholic theology and secular poetry—an inestimable feat, perhaps on the level of achievement in verse of what Pierre Teilhard de Chardin accomplished in science. The work of the Jesuit is clearly self-conscious; he appears continually to be asking questions such as "Who am I?" "What is the world?" "What is my place in the world?"

In spite of all of his inventiveness, Hopkins may have entrapped himself in forms; this is possibly why his later poems seem to lose the energy apparent in earlier ones. Personal illness may have contributed to a certain decline as well. One writer has considered Hopkins as self-victimized in a symbol of his own making, that of a restricted bird. Christianity is a religion of constant struggle for Hopkins, and his poetry clearly reflects his ongoing attempt to discover meaning in that struggle.

Sources for Further Study

Cutter, James Finn. *Inscape*. Pittsburgh: University of Pittsburgh Press, 1973. Cutter still offers some of the best insights into the Christology and poetry of Hopkins.

Delli-Carpini, John. *Prayer and Piety in the Poems of Gerard Manley Hopkins: The*

Landscape of a Soul. Lewiston, N.Y.: Edwin Mellen Press, 1998. Addresses Hopkins's spirituality by reading the poems as prayers, the outgrowth of his relationship with God.

Muller, Jill. *Gerard Manley Hopkins and Victorian Catholicism: A Heart in Hiding*. New York: Routledge, 2003. Places Hopkins and his beliefs in the context of his industrializing and securalizing, anti-Catholic social milieu. Sees Hopkins's introversion as an expression of the larger deflation of Catholicism in Victorian England.

Roberts, Gerald. *Gerard Manley Hopkins: A Literary Life*. New York: St. Martin's Press, 1994. A concise (153-page) introductory guide to Hopkins's poetry. Roberts maintains that Hopkins's conversion to Catholicism matured his poetic style as well as his vision.

Ward, Bernadette Waterman. *World as Word: Philosophical Theology in Gerard Manley Hopkins*. Washington, D.C.: Catholic University of America Press, 2002. Explicates twenty-nine poems in an effort to understand Hopkins's philosophical engagement with the Trinity, the Incarnation, and other Christian mysteries, revealing his struggle to express moral as well as intellectual truth in an age of religious sentimentalism and burgeoning scientism.

Harry James Cargas

THE WINTER GARDEN

Author: Johanna Verweerd (Joke Verweerd; 1954-)
First published: De wintertuin, 1995 (English translation, 2001)
Edition used: The Winter Garden, translated by Helen Richardson-Hewitt. Bloomington, Minn.: Bethany House, 2001
Genre: Novel
Subgenre: Literary fiction
Core issues: Grace; guilt; healing; reconciliation; responsibility; self-knowledge; truth

Estranged from her family for fifteen years, Ika finds her carefully insulated world shaken when her sister writes to tell her their mother is dying. Now Ika must confront not only her mother's death but also the feelings of guilt, bewilderment, and pain that characterized her childhood, growing up as an illegitimate child with a mother and stepfather who slighted her and doted on her younger sister. Ika returns home to care for her mother and cultivates a new relationship with her family that enables her to forgive and heal.

> *Principal characters*
> *Ika "Ikabod" Boerema*, the protagonist
> *Nelly Boerema de Haan*, Ika's mother
> *Dirk de Haan*, Ika's stepfather
> *Nelly Peters-de Haan*, Ika's younger sister
> *Willem Peters*, Nelly's husband
> *Abe Peters*, Nelly and Willem's older son
> *Dirk-Willem Peters*, Nelly and Willem's younger son
> *Grandfather de Haan*, Ika's maternal grandfather
> *Granddad Boerema*, Ika's paternal grandfather
> *Klaar de Haan*, Ika's aunt
> *Bart Hogerveer*, a boy who introduces Ika to gardening
> *Mr. Molenaar*, Ika's grade-school teacher
> *Dr. Spaan*, Ika's mother's doctor
> *Mrs. Wamers*, the district nurse
> *Simone Berger*, Ika's friend and employer, owner of Berger's Landscape Gardening

Overview

In *The Winter Garden*, Johanna Verweerd relates the story of Ika Boerema's personal growth, juxtaposing events of the past and present to highlight significant events. Ika's life has been shaped by her memories of a narrow sphere of childhood circumscribed by her mother and stepfather's bitterness toward and resentment of her, an illegitimate child; Grandfather Boerema's oft-repeated references to his fallen daughter; and the villagers' collective antipathy toward Ika, the evidence of Nelly Boerema's youthful indiscretion.

It has been fifteen years since Ika Boerema left her family and hometown. During that time, she and her younger sister Nelly have corresponded sporadically through letters. Ika's stepfather died some time ago, but Ika did not attend the funeral. Nelly has married and has two sons, Abe and Dirk-Willem. Ika is living in the city and has been working as a landscape designer for some time. Into her well-ordered life comes a letter from Nelly, bearing the news that their mother is terminally ill with lung cancer and dragging the past back to envelop Ika in an almost paralyzing cloud of anxiety.

To begin dealing with the situation and her own complicated relationship with her family, Ika turns to her friend and employer, Simone Berger, owner of Berger's Landscape Design. Although Simone says that Ika's family members do not deserve her friend's sympathy, she does suggest that Ika contact Dr. Spaan, her mother's doctor. When Ika does, the doctor uses her given name, Ikabod, which means "shame," and reminds her that her mother had chosen this name for her.

Ika begins designing a winter garden for the Promenade Hotel, a project that will sustain her as she struggles to reconcile the past with the present and to forge a new personal understanding. She remembers the baby turtledove she rescued years ago and suddenly needs to know if the dove still lives at her mother's house; its presence seems to assure her of a comforting link with the past and a promise for the future. A secret visit to see her mother, the refuge Ika takes in creating the plans for the winter garden, and the dove's presence at her mother's house enable Ika to commit to reconnecting with her family and staying with her mother to the end. Of increasing importance is the possibility that her mother might at last reveal the identity of Ika's father.

After returning to her mother's house, Ika learns she must let others into her experience and that life at her old home will never be as it was during her childhood. Although Ika and Nelly cautiously dip into the past and begin forging a new adult relationship as sisters, it is Abe, Nelly's teenage son, with whom Ika finds a special bond in their similar sense of humor and love for gardening and Granddad de Haan's farm. Ika quickly begins to learn what the physical demands of her mother's illness will be and what her mother's dying will require of her emotionally and spiritually.

While caring for her mother, Ika works on her design for the winter garden and tries to find a new understanding of her life and her future. Although she presses her mother for information about her biological father, her mother refuses to reveal anything about him. Her mother's illness reaches a crisis one day, and Dr. Spaan warns Ika and Nelly that they must be prepared for her death. During that long dark night, the two sisters watch over their mother as the reality of her imminent death sinks into both of them and draws them together.

Ika continues to struggle with the memories of her mother's coldness to her as a child and her growing desperation to have her questions about her father answered. In the end, though, those are not the things that matter in her relationship with her mother; Ika finds she and her mother are both in need of the same thing, to heal from the past and to look with faith to the future. For Ika's mother, the future comes on an afternoon following a visit by Nelly, Willem, and their two boys. To shield her mother from winds caused by military planes flying low over the house, Ika wraps her mother in her arms. At that moment, her mother dies, and in the silence after, the dove calls seven times.

The formalities of the funeral follow. Nelly's will causes some strife when it is discovered that she has left a prized red coral necklace to Ika, who promptly gives it to the complaining Nelly. In their mother's note, Ika learns that her former grade-school teacher, Mr. Molenaar, has been asking after her. She goes to visit him and learns the truth about her parentage, that Dirk de Haan, the man she called father all her life was, in fact, her biological father, and that the circumstances of her parents' courtship had been dictated by her Grandfather Boerema, the village minister, on discovering his daughter's disgraceful actions and condition.

Even before learning the answers to all her questions, Ika returns to the city to complete her design for the winter garden. Simone, who has been a steadfast friend from the beginning, announces that although Berger's Landscape Design will provide the design and construction for the winter garden, the maintenance contract has been given to a company from Ika's hometown, the Morning Star, whose owner happens to be Bart Hogerveer, the boy who helped Ika start her own first garden. For lonely Ika, the reunion with her old friend is the best of steps toward her new future.

Christian Themes

The Winter Garden reflects Verweerd's Reformed Christian perspective, thematically and symbolically. Ika's journey from a childhood marked by her mother's sin to personal growth and recognition of grace in her own life drive the spiritual arc of the novel. At the heart of the narrative lie the need for reconciliation and expiation of sin, and these themes are represented through the opposition of two Scriptural verses.

Samuel 4:19-22 recounts the Israelites' loss of the ark of the covenant and the naming of a child, Ichabod, "the glory is departed." Choosing such a name for her illegitimate daughter serves as a perpetuating self-punishment for Nelly de Haan, especially given her minister father's condemnation and the disapproval of the village.

Ika finds solace in prayer and reading the Scriptures, particularly the consolatory verses of Isaiah 43, the assurance of the constancy of Christ. It is these lines that give her strength to confront her mother's illness and stubbornness and bring the two women together in a moment of understanding and forgiveness. When Nelly de Haan dies in Ika's arms, they are the first words her daughter whispers.

The dove symbolizes the constancy of Christ and serves as a reminder of the possibility of grace, negotiating the two Scriptural verses that bookend Ika's relationship with her mother. The bird also keeps her company as she designs the winter garden that represents a mother holding a baby in her arms, the final image of emotional and spiritual reconciliation of the novel.

Sources for Further Study

"Joke Verweerd." *Gale Literary Databases: Contemporary Authors.* 2002. Provides biographical information and discusses her two novels, *A Winter Garden* and *Paradiso* (2001). Highlights are excerpted from an interview with the author on attaining forgiveness and the parallel growth of the author and her characters.

Mort, John. Review of *The Winter Garden. Booklist* 97, no. 22 (August, 2001): 2088. A brief review of the work that finds it a "fine, subtle story."

Zaleski, Jeff. Review of *The Winter Garden. Publishers Weekly* 248, no. 14 (April 21, 2001): 38-40. Zaleski's brief review effectively evaluates the book and provides a thoughtful consideration of the way it negotiates the impact of the past through flashbacks.

Jennie MacDonald

1957

WISE BLOOD

Author: Flannery O'Connor (1925-1964)
First published: 1952
Edition used: Wise Blood. New York: Farrar, Straus and Giroux, 1993
Genre: Novella
Subgenres: Humor; literary fiction
Core issues: Atonement; the Fall; grace; redemption

O'Connor's first novel was, by her own description, a darkly comic story about a person who is a Christian in spite of himself. Her grotesque characters exemplify her own Catholic convictions that without the redemption offered through Christ, human life is absurd and meaningless. Although the protagonist of the novel, Hazel Motes, is an abrasive and outrageous character, he alone comprehends the dreadfully serious claim that humanity requires a redemption that can be accomplished only through the death of Christ.

Principal characters
Hazel Motes, the protagonist and eventual preacher of the Church Without Christ
Enoch Emery, companion to Hazel
Asa Hawks, a "blind" street evangelist
Sabbath Lily Hawks, Asa's daughter
Hoover "Onnie Jay Holy" Shoats, a would-be disciple of Hazel's and later competitor
Solace "The Prophet" Layfield, Hazel's preaching double
Mrs. Flood, Hazel's landlady

Overview

Wise Blood opens with Hazel Motes on a train to the city of Taulkinham. His bright blue suit and broad-brimmed hat make people mistake him for a "preacher," but it soon becomes evident that although Hazel is consumed by the idea of redemption, he is not a Christian in any ordinary sense. For Hazel, Jesus is not a loving savior but rather "a wild ragged figure" who moves "from tree to tree in the back of his mind," always beckoning him to step into the dark. This image had been planted by his grandfather, a circuit preacher who had often used his grandson as an object lesson, declaring that even for the unworthy child, Jesus would have died "ten million deaths" to redeem him. In the city, Hazel intends to demonstrate that he needs neither Jesus nor the sanguine redemption he provides.

In Taulkinham, Hazel meets Enoch Emery, an oafish young man who becomes an unwelcome companion. Together, they encounter a street evangelist, Asa Hawks, and his homely young daughter Sabbath Lily. Hazel is drawn to Hawks, whose name seems to mock the fact that he is blind. In an effort to demonstrate his rejection of both the necessity for redemption and the idea of sin that requires it, Hazel decides to seduce Sabbath, and on the following day, he seeks out Enoch to obtain Hawks's address.

Enoch is driven instinctually by his "wise blood," and he cannot surrender the information until Hazel agrees to accompany him in his daily routine, which culminates in the MVSEVM in a park in the heart of the city. Here, Enoch leads Hazel to a mummified dwarf, the central mystery in Enoch's constricted world. Frustrated by this diversion, Hazel attacks Enoch and sets out alone to find Hawks.

That evening, Hazel locates the boarding house where Asa and Sabbath live, but before he confronts them, he decides to mimic Hawks's ministry. Climbing on the hood of his Essex—a "rat-colored" rattletrap—Hazel preaches his first sermon for the Church Without Christ, "where the blind don't see and the lame don't walk and what's dead stays that way." Despite his blatant sacrilege, Hazel understands better than his auditors—who regard him with mild amusement if they regard him at all—the seriousness of his message. Redemption is unnecessary if sin is denied; therefore the blood of Jesus need not "foul" the Church Without Christ. Over the next few evenings, Hazel continues to preach from the hood of his Essex, which becomes both his pulpit and his symbol of freedom from Christ and sin. "Nobody with a good car," he claims, "needs to be justified."

There is significant irony in Hazel's inability to "see" that his "good car" is a decrepit piece of junk, since "sight" is an important metaphor throughout the book. Hazel's nickname is "Haze," a metonym for his spiritual blindness, and his earliest recalled sin involved his "seeing" a forbidden sideshow. He still keeps his mother's glasses, although he used them only when he used to read from her Bible. Most important, Asa Hawks's physical blindness fascinates Hazel, especially when he discovers that Hawks has blinded himself deliberately as a public display of his faith that Christ had redeemed him.

Things are not as they appear, however. As Hazel discovers, Hawks is not blind; a failure of nerve (and faith) left him scarred but with sight. Neither is Sabbath the innocent child that Hazel had presumed. The offspring of an illicit union, Sabbath is convinced that as a "bastard" she can never enter Heaven, and so she has determined to take full advantage of her inevitable damnation. She begins to pursue Hazel with her father's blessing.

Although frustrated in his plans to corrupt Sabbath and disgrace Hawks, Hazel continues his activities as "preacher and member" of the Church Without Christ. Paradoxically, he decides that his church needs a "new jesus," one without any blood to waste. The idea of the new jesus attracts a potential disciple, but Onnie Jay Holy mistakes Hazel's earnest blasphemy for a confidence scam. When Hazel rejects Holy's facile hypocrisy, Holy hires a haggard man called The Prophet who, as a mirror image of Hazel, becomes the preacher for the competing Holy Church of Christ Without Christ.

Hazel's message of a new jesus also inspires Enoch. He has stolen the mummy from the MVSEVM and hidden it in a specially gilded cabinet. Now, driven by his blood, he removes the mummy from its tabernacle and delivers it to Sabbath. His mission complete, Enoch dons a gorilla suit and loses what remains of his human nature. When Hazel—wearing his mother's glasses—sees Sabbath holding the mummy, he violently destroys the dust-filled corpse. Later that same evening, he tracks down The Prophet and kills him by repeatedly running over him with the Essex.

The following day, Hazel attempts to leave town and continue his ministry, but he is stopped by a police officer who inexplicably destroys the Essex. Hazel returns to the boarding house with a bucket of lime and blinds himself. This act, and other self-imposed mortifications, hold a strange attraction for his landlady, Mrs. Flood, who has to summon the police to find Hazel after he wanders away. Although the police who find him also beat him to death, Mrs. Flood places his body in her bed where she stares into his empty eye sockets.

Christian Themes

The Christian themes of this work are informed by three considerations: Flannery O'Connor's own Roman Catholic faith, her use of the grotesque style, and the southern agrarian tradition.

O'Connor wrote from the perspective of a Catholic author who viewed humanity as "fallen" and thus in need of the redemption that can come only through Christ. In Catholicism, such redemption was accomplished through the sacraments, which were the visible and physical signs of invisible and supernatural grace. What O'Connor insightfully grasped was the "violence" that lay at the heart of these rituals. Baptism was not just a rite of cleansing; it was the destruction of the old self that must precede the birth of the new. The Eucharist was not simply a shared meal of bread and wine; it both symbolized and actualized the crucifixion of Christ as the perpetual action of redemption. Although none of the characters in *Wise Blood* are Catholic (Hazel assures his landlady that the Church Without Christ is indeed Protestant), they represent fallen humanity to whom grace must come through physical violence. Thus, the senseless demolition of his car is the "sacrament" that brings redemption to Hazel, who then symbolizes his new "spiritual sight" by the destruction of his physical ability to see.

By her use of the grotesque style, O'Connor emphasized this sacramental perspective in which the physical world is intermeshed with, and therefore reflects, spiritual realities. Southern writers such as William Faulkner had utilized grotesque characters to challenge cultural stereotypes; but O'Connor uses the exaggerated and distorted style of the grotesque to represent universal images of humanity's unredeemed condition. Her grotesque characters became the medium of her own evangelistic message in her *Mystery and Manners* (1969): "to the hard of hearing you shout, and to the almost-blind you draw large and startling figures."

The grotesque had also been used by Southern writers to underscore the existential problems of modern urban society, a principal concern of the agrarian movement of the 1930's. In *Wise Blood*, the city of Taulkinham provides the antithesis not of agrarian values but of the Christian ethos, symbolized by the bloodless "new jesus" who inhabits the heart of the city. Similarly, the Essex, "built by people with their eyes wide open that knew where they were at," is a modern machine that proves unable to transport Hazel beyond his existential angst; therefore its destruction must precede his redemption.

Sources for Further Study

Kreyling, Michael, ed. *New Essays on "Wise Blood."* New York: Cambridge University Press, 1995. Four essays (plus an introduction) that offer new methodological approaches to *Wise Blood*, ranging from feminist psychoanalysis to theology.

O'Connor, Flannery. *Mystery and Manners.* New York: Farrar, Straus and Giroux, 1969. A collection of some of O'Connor's nonfiction; absolutely essential for any understanding of O'Connor's own perspective on her literary work.

Srigley, Susan. *Flannery O'Connor's Sacramental Art.* Notre Dame, Ind.: University of Notre Dame Press, 2004. O'Connor's key works interpreted from the perspective of theological analysis, particularly focused on what the author terms O'Connor's "ethic of responsibility."

Wood, Ralph C. *Flannery O'Connor and the Christ-Haunted South.* Grand Rapids, Mich.: Wm. B. Eerdmans, 2004. An analysis of O'Connor's Catholic theological vision within its Southern milieu.

Rodger M. Payne

1961

WITH HEAD AND HEART
The Autobiography of Howard Thurman

Author: Howard Thurman (1900-1981)
First published: New York: Harcourt Brace Jovanovich, 1979
Genre: Nonfiction
Subgenre: Autobiography
Core issues: African Americans; clerical life; mysticism; racism

In his autobiography, Thurman takes his place in the pantheon of twentieth century African American civil rights leaders. In a straightforward voice, Thurman, the grandson of slaves, tell how through faith, curiosity, and tenacity, he fought against the racism of the world and rose to become one of the best known and loved preachers in the United States. He used his vocation as pastor, his gifts as a writer, and his commitment to inter-religious and multiracial dialogue and community to teach Americans about a God much too big to be contained in one race or faith tradition.

Overview

Born in Daytona, Florida, in 1900, Howard Thurman lived a life that both witnessed and significantly contributed to the radical transformation of race relations in the United States. As a young boy, he experienced firsthand the heat of Jim Crow and the Deep South. By the time of his death in 1981, though racism was still a reality in the United States, the nation was in a very different place, and Thurman had taken his rightful place alongside the civil rights pioneers who led the way for all people of color.

With Head and Heart is a seminal book for anyone who wishes to learn more about one of the often forgotten leaders of the struggle for racial justice in the United States. Most historians do not consider Thurman to be on the same level as Martin Luther King, Jr., Malcolm X, or Rosa Parks. However, the dignified and quiet Thurman might just be comfortable with that second-level designation, for from the time of his birth, he took an unusual inward path toward God, one that would shape him as a pastor, mystic, poet, and thinker, and set him apart from many other civil rights leaders.

Thurman writes that his path to God began under a backyard oak tree he often visited as a child. That tree is as good a metaphor as any for the God Thurman grew to know, love, and teach about to any and all who would listen.

> When the storms blew, the branches of the large oak tree in our backyard would snap and fall. But the topmost branches of the oak tree would sway, giving just enough to save themselves from snapping loose. I needed the strength of that tree and like it I needed to hold my ground. Eventually I discovered the oak tree and I had a unique relationship. I could sit, my back against its trunk and feel . . . peace. . . . I could reach down in the quiet places of my spirit . . . and know that I was understood.

From an early age Thurman revealed himself to be a man on a mission, one marked by the passionate pursuit of spiritual and academic wisdom and a commitment to using his life to build bridges of tolerance and understanding among diverse peoples and beliefs. His journey was unrelenting in its single-mindedness as he set out to acquire as much knowledge as possible about his God and his world.

Thurman relates that his early years were a struggle. His father died young. He attended a "blacks-only" church-sponsored high school at a time when few if any African Americans got much beyond grade schools. "There was never enough food and my health began to suffer," he recalls. Yet Thurman always found a way to excel and carry on—whether writing a letter appealing for tuition money to a man he had never met (and receiving it) or drilling African American World War I recruits as a way to pay for Morehouse College. Thurman thrived, always seeming to be in the right place, meeting the right people just at the opportune time, and taking every chance he was given.

Choosing church ministry as a vocation, Thurman finally escaped the South of his youth and went north to Rochester Theological Seminary in 1926 where, along with learning to pastor, he challenged the racial assumptions of his day, rooming with two white men, forging deep friendships across the color line (as he would throughout his life), and causing a minor scandal. Thurman always seemed too busy and on the way to pay too much attention to his critics.

As Thurman dug deeper into his traditional faith, he found it lacking and began his lifelong habit of challenging orthodoxy in all its forms. Post-seminary, still thirsty for knowledge, he sought out Quaker philosopher Rufus Jones as his mentor and doctoral adviser at Haverford College. Then, after serving two years as a pastor in Ohio, Thurman was appointed in 1932 as professor of theology and the dean of Rankin Chapel at Howard University. During twelve years there, Thurman nurtured a generation of young black men and women and undertook a groundbreaking tour of India, where he met Mahatma Gandhi, and he revolutionized worship at Howard.

In 1944 in San Francisco, Thurman helped found a radically new kind of faith community, the Church for the Fellowship of All Peoples. Thurman describes the vision that called it into being: "We [the founding pastors] were sensitive to the immorality and amorality of the Christian Church in its ineffectiveness in the face of racial discrimination in its own body, as well as in the general society.... [W]e were convinced that a way could be found to create a religious fellowship worthy of transcending racial, cultural, and social distinctions." These were controversial ideals for 1944, when the United States was still greatly divided along clearly defined racial, religious, and cultural lines. However, as Thurman declares in reflecting on this new kind of church and community, "What is true in any religion is in the religion because it is true; it is not true because it is in the religion." For nine years Thurman and his church community created a brand-new kind of spiritual body, filled with men and women from a wide variety of racial and religions, all religious seekers of truths.

In 1953 Thurman was named dean of Marsh Chapel at Boston University, a post he held until his retirement in 1965. The final sixteen years of his life were devoted to the

Howard Thurman Educational Trust, an enterprise that promoted and financially supported the college education of young African American women and men. As he did most of his life, Thurman wrote extensively at this time. At his death in 1981, he was the author of twenty-one books on a wide variety of subjects, including prayer, theology, and the African American religious experience in the United States.

Christian Themes

Thurman's autobiography gives the reader a powerful look into a life lived in the crucible of race in the United States and at the roles of churches and academia in both advancing and blocking the progress of racial justice in the United States. It is sobering to remember that Thurman was but one generation removed from the slavery of his ancestors, and yet with a fierce energy and an almost matter-of-fact tone, Thurman uses the book to describe his herculean efforts to succeed: as a pastor and preacher, an author, and a leader on campus and in society as a whole. Though Thurman is largely forgotten by mainstream historians, it is important to note that during his lifetime, he was named one of the fifty most influential figures in African American history by *Ebony* magazine and one of the twelve best preachers in the United States by *Life* magazine.

Thurman's autobiography reveals above all a religious curiosity and a willingness, almost from the start of his spiritual journey, to question the religious norms and push the boundaries of what passed for religious orthodoxy. Thurman visited the social radical Gandhi in India, long before he became a safe icon for the world. That encounter caused Thurman to consider truth in light of the religious diversity of India. His founding of the Fellowship Church during World War II and its intentional embrace of diversity, including a besieged and persecuted Japanese American community, was brave and far ahead of its time.

Thurman pushed the bounds of traditional worship and introduced extended silent prayer and liturgical dance when such practices were considered outside of the bounds of "normal" religious practice in Christian churches. Thurman was a mystic before religious America really understood that term. He looked for God not just outside in ritual but also within his mind and heart, in a deep and personal relationship with the universe's Creator.

Sources for Further Study

Smith, Luther E. *Howard Thurman: The Mystic as Prophet*. Richmond, Ind.: Friends United Press, 1992. This spiritual biography seeks to interpret the theological and philosophical ideas and the thinkers who most influenced Thurman's life and thoughts. It is a valuable introduction to Thurman by the scholar who has studied the man and his life more than any other person.

Thurman, Howard. *The Search for Common Ground*. Richmond, Ind.: Friends United Press, 1971. This slim volume delves into the mystical side of Thurman's hope for common ground among religious seekers in the search for God and meaning in this life.

Thurman, Howard, and Luther E. Smith, eds. *Howard Thurman: Essential Writings*. Modern Spiritual Masters series. Maryknoll, N.Y.: Orbis Books, 2006. This book is a good introduction to many of Thurman's best writings and contains a good cross-section of his thoughts on prayer, God, and race in the United States.

John F. Hudson

WITH THE GRAIN OF THE UNIVERSE
The Church's Witness and Natural Theology

Author: Stanley Hauerwas (1940-)
First published: Grand Rapids, Mich.: Brazos Press, 2001
Genre: Nonfiction
Subgenres: Critical analysis; essays; theology
Core issues: Doubt; ethics; faith

Hauerwas draws on the ideas of theologians and philosophers William James, Reinhold Niebuhr, and Karl Barth to argue that theology must take modernity seriously, but the meeting between theology and modernity must take place on its own terms, rather than on terms dictated by modernity.

Overview

With the Grain of the Universe contains the Gifford Lectures presented by Stanley Hauerwas in 2001. The aim of the Gifford Lectures, established by the will of Adam Lord Gifford, is to "promote and diffuse the study of Natural Theology in the widest sense of the term—in other words, the knowledge of God." The term "natural theology" in the context of the lectures means theology supported by science and not dependent on the miraculous.

Hauerwas begins by pointing to the contradictory circumstances of his being chosen as the presenter of the Gifford Lectures, given that he intends to speak against natural theology and the endeavor to apply scientific logic and reasoning to theology. Hauerwas uses the writings of William James, Reinhold Niebuhr, and Karl Barth (also presenters of Gifford Lectures) to support his arguments against natural theology. He points to what he calls the "meanness," or insignificance, of the scientific method and the circumstances that it examines and states that the type of God who can be "proved" via the methods of science is "not worthy of worship" and that the theologian must trust in a God that exists beyond such methodology.

Hauerwas positions philosopher James and theologian Niebuhr as reflections of each other, saying that they draw on the same basic framework. In addressing Niebuhr, he criticizes natural theology for paying too much attention to what the world is willing to hear. In doing so, he argues, natural theologians lose their ability to challenge that world with what it does not want to hear. Hauerwas asserts that Niebuhr's views were developed to be consistent with those of William James, the author of *The Varieties of Religious Experience* (1902).

Neibuhr claimed that the historical Jesus and his teachings were meaningless to contemporary society except as symbols that remind us of our distance from God. However, in the process of borrowing from contemporary science, a process that fails for both political and theological reasons, Hauerwas says, Niebuhr lost the ability to speak prophetically to the world and influenced a generation of theologians to follow in his footsteps. The ability to speak in a way that is directed by the Divine Spirit depends not on an intellectual understanding of the historical Jesus and his teachings but on a deeper acknowledgment and surrender to the historical that in turns leads to a deeper connection with God.

Christian ethics is a result of modernity: Before the Enlightenment, philosophers did not distinguish between the ethical and theological issues implicit in daily Christian living. With the Enlightenment, humanity tried to find a basis for action that was independent of theological knowledge. Theology became a kind of metaphysics, and sections of it could be dismissed or embraced, depending on the makeup of one's metaphysical beliefs.

To correct this "humanistic reduction of theology," Hauerwas turns to Protestant theologian Karl Barth, who believed that natural theology is a worldly enterprise that is too influenced by a desire to fit in with the world and its anti-Christian assumptions, and argued, as Hauerwas does in *With the Grain of the Universe*, that liberal theologians have abandoned the primary duties of theology in their desire to reconcile it with current scientific philosophies. Like Barth, Hauerwas says that because natural theology has led the field astray, it is best avoided entirely. He points to Barth's attempts to overturn the epistemological prejudices of modernity and says that the question "Who is God?" must be answered before we ask "How do we know about God?" We cannot explore our beliefs unless we begin by building and acknowledging them; otherwise they are never formed and the endeavor becomes an abortive one.

In the course of *With the Grain of the Universe*, Hauerwas looks not just at the writings and ideas of the theologians and scientists he addresses, but their lives as well. To understand Barth, he says, one must know something of his struggle against the Third Reich as well as other efforts that Barth felt subordinated Christianity in the interest of the status quo. In this way, the Christians of today need to do more than experience their theology in a mental arena. They need to live out its principles in daily existence, and nowhere more so than the area of politics. Christians cannot approach politics ethically without being willing to guide their existence in the political and historical world according to Christian tenets.

In the end, Hauerwas claims that because of the nature of Western culture, it is necessary for Christians to disown the world and its standards, including the standards of reasoning that natural theology has tried to employ, as they live their lives. In making this movement toward a belief system, he draws from theologian John Howard Yoder and Pope John Paul II as well.

Christian Themes

One of Hauerwas's central themes in *With the Grain of the Universe* is the responsibility of Christians to renounce the standards of the world when examining their own philosophy. The truth of modern theology is not proved by natural reason but lies in the church's witness in the world. The relationship between divine and human is created by the revealed nature of God rather than by human intellectual thought.

A major goal in Hauerwas's work is to provide an account of modern theology that provides guidance but does not rest on modernist assumptions. It should reframe the discourse so that scientific processes are left to science, rather than theology.

Hauerwas feels that a central crisis facing modern Christians is how to accommodate the fact that they live in a world that has different demands than the ones facing the original audience of the Bible and to resist the urge to give into the "forces of modernity" that favor actual sensory, measurable results over transcendent knowledge. This effort is not simply an intellectual effort but one that also must be lived out in the course of one's political existence.

Before we can turn to examining how we know to believe in God, Hauerwas asserts, we must be able to assert that we believe in him. Natural theology subverts the actual purpose of theology and turns it to measuring belief rather than actually believing. The responsibility of the church in the modern world is not to justify itself with endeavors like natural theology, but rather to provide moral and spiritual guidance for its congregation in a movement that allows them to acknowledge a connection with God that is centered in the heart rather than the mind.

Sources for Further Study

Hauerwas, Stanley. *Disrupting Time: Sermons, Prayers, and Sundries*. New York: Cascade Books, 2004. This collection of short pieces explores Hauerwas's basic themes, including how to live one's life in a Christian manner.

_____. *The Peaceable Kingdom: A Primer in Christian Ethics*. South Bend, Ind.: University of Notre Dame Press, 1984. Early work by Hauerwas that prefigures a number of the themes he explores in *With the Grain of the Universe*.

Hauerwas, Stanley, Michael G. Cartwright, and John Berkman. *The Hauerwas Reader*. Durham, N.C.: Duke University Press, 2001. Presents a sampling and overview of Hauerwas's writings, exploring a range of social issues over a broad span of time.

Katangole, Emmanuel. *Beyond Universal Reason: The Relation Between Religion and Ethics in the Work of Stanley Hauerwas*. Notre Dame, Ind.: University of Notre Dame Press, 2000. Latangole examines Hauerwas's views on ethics and Christianity and provides a background that helps readers understand Hauerwas's views.

Thomson, John B. *The Ecclesiology of Stanley Hauerwas: A Christian Theology of Liberation*. Burlington, Vt.: Ashgate, 2003. Addresses Hauerwas's thoughts and ideas, particularly on the character of Christians.

Cat Rambo

THE WOMAN OF THE PHARISEES

Author: François Mauriac (1885-1970)
First published: La Pharisienne, 1941 (English translation, 1946)
Edition used: The Woman of the Pharisees, translated by Gerard Hopkins. New York: Carroll & Graf, 1988
Genre: Novel
Subgenres: Catholic fiction; literary fiction
Core issues: Chastity; loneliness; love; redemption; self-knowledge; suffering

Brigitte Pian, believing herself a paragon of Christian virtue, takes on the mission of directing other people's lives. She fulfills the roles of director, judge, and executioner. Her interference in the lives of others results in repeated tragedies and unhappiness. It is only at the end of the novel that she begins to have self-doubts, and as a result of turning her thoughts inward and examining her own motives, she becomes susceptible to the grace of God and finds redemption, love, and peace.

> Principal characters
> *Brigitte Pian*, the protagonist
> *Octave Pian*, Brigitte's husband
> *Louis Pian*, Brigitte's stepson and the narrator
> *Michèle Pian*, Brigitte's stepdaughter
> *Jean de Mirbel*, Louis's best friend
> *Comte de Mirbel*, Jean's uncle
> *Comtesse de Mirbel*, Jean's mother
> *Monsieur Calou*, curate of Baluzac
> *Léonce Puybaraud*, the assistant schoolmaster
> *Octavia Tronche*, Puybaraud's wife

Overview

In *The Woman of the Pharisees*, François Mauriac recounts the life of Brigitte Pian and her influence on the lives of her stepchildren Louis and Michèle, her husband Octave Pian, Jean de Mirbel, Monsieur Puybaraud and Octavia Tronche, and Monsieur Calou, the curate of Baluzac. Mauriac tells his story through the voice of Louis Pian, Brigitte's stepson.

The story opens with an incident of mistreatment at the boarding school where Louis is a pupil. Louis's friend Jean de Mirbel is under the guardianship of his uncle, Colonel Comte de Mirbel, a brutal man who regularly visits the school to discipline Jean in the most cruel ways. Determined to maintain discipline over Jean and keep him away from his mother, whom he loves obsessively, the colonel arranges for Jean to remain at Baluzac for the summer under the tutelage of Monsieur Calou, the local curate who has a reputation for reforming boys such as Jean. Monsieur Calou's methods, however, are the exact oppositive of his reputation for toughness. At his home, Jean experiences kindness and understanding. Jean also experiences romantic love with Louis's sister Michèle.

During this summer, Jean is cruelly disillusioned by his mother. The colonel has finally permitted Jean's mother to visit him. Jean insists on spending the night with her, but she absolutely refuses him. Jean stubbornly sneaks out of Monsieur Calou's house and goes to her. Although she is not staying where he believes she is, he eventually finds her: She is with her lover. Jean's discovery leaves him not only emotionally devastated, but also gravely ill with pleurisy from the rigors of his journey.

During Jean's illness, Brigitte Pian takes measures to thwart his love affair with Michèle. After being informed of secret meetings between Jean and Michèle, she forbids her stepchildren to see Jean. Brigitte arranges for Michèle to go to boarding school and forbids even written communication between her and Jean. Monsieur Calou attempts to help Jean and Michèle. He delivers a gold locket to Jean, which the young man always wears around his neck. Seriously worried about Jean's physical and emotional health, the curate arranges for Michèle to write to him so that Jean will have news of her. A letter addressed to Jean but sent to Monsieur Calou is intercepted, and all correspondence is stopped. Eventually, the despondent Jean becomes the victim of Hortense Voyod, the wife of the local pharmacist. Hortense does not believe in God; yet she hates him and his church. She seeks vengeance against Monsieur Calou because some years earlier, he thwarted her attempt to seduce a young schoolmistress. Jean becomes the instrument of her revenge. He succumbs to her seduction, quarrels bitterly with the curate, steals money from him, and runs off with her. Her revenge accomplished, she abandons Jean.

The love affair between Jean and Michèle is not the only one to come to the attention of Brigitte. Louis reveals to her the plans of Léonce Puybaraud, the assistant schoolmaster, and Octavia Tronche to marry. Monsieur Puybaraud is a member of a celibate lay order and has devoted his life to charitable work and teaching children. Brigitte cannot accept the marriage and sets about convincing Monsieur Puybaraud and Octavia of their error, even going so far as to imply the devil may be playing a trick on them. Unable to stop the marriage, she manages to prevent either of them from being employed. Monsieur Puybaraud is forced to accept the most meager allowance from her. The hardships imposed on them result in Octavia's having a miscarriage and dying. Monsieur Puybaraud severs all ties with the Pian family, is for a time editorial secretary of an anarchist weekly newspaper, and finally retires to a Trappist monastery.

Brigitte becomes a controlling force in the life of Octave even before she becomes his wife. She is the cousin of Octave's first wife, who had given Octave reasons to suspect her of infidelity. Brigitte became his confidante and adviser in regard to his marital difficulties. After the supposedly accidental death of his first wife, Octave marries Brigitte but the memory of her cousin remains alive and constantly preoccupies Octave. Brigitte eventually leaves a letter that corroborates Louis's illegitimacy where Octave may find it. Octave, left alone in the country house, begins to drink excessively and is found dead; the letter is no longer in the drawer.

Brigitte also interferes in the life of Monsieur Calou, who makes the very serious mistake of not only approving of but also encouraging the love affair between Michèle and Jean. She is convinced that Calou is no longer fit to fulfill his office and sends a damaging letter about him to his superiors. This letter results in his removal as the curate of Baluzac. He is also forced to leave the parish.

After the deaths of Octavia Tronche and her husband Octave, Brigitte begins to have self-doubts. She questions her motives in controlling the lives of others and is tormented. She follows Louis's advice to consult Monsieur Calou. A reconciliation occurs between them, and the former curate is able to help her find through confession the forgiveness of sins that she seeks. She also meets Dr. Gellis, with whom she experiences a reciprocal love.

Christian Themes

The doctrine of Catholicism permeates Mauriac's novel. The religious and moral beliefs of the rural Bordeaux community portrayed are those taught by the Catholic faith. The character of Brigitte Pian elucidates the constant struggle between free will and obedience to God's will. Brigitte in her self-righteousness fails to realize that she has mistaken her will for God's will. She does not consider that God may be directing the choices made by the other characters even though she would have them make other choices. This is especially true in the case of Monsieur Puybaraud and Octavia. Any male-female love relationship alerts her immediately to suspect the "Evil One" is at work. For her, sexual passion is synonymous with sin or at the very least with temptation away from the higher calling of God and his church. In the final episodes of the novel, Mauriac presents the doctrine of grace. Brigitte stops seeing herself as a superior Christian with the mission of enforcing God's will on earth. She begins to turn her thoughts inward and to question her acts. She is overwhelmed with guilt for the deaths of Octave and Octavia and the misery she has caused others. She is no longer the Pharisee who thanks God that she is not like the others, but now she comes to God seeking forgiveness and grace. Having accepted herself as a sinner and, with the help of Monsieur Calou, having confessed her sins and found the forgiveness necessary for her to be at peace, she comes to a true understanding of Christian love.

Sources for Further Study

Bracher, Nathan. *Through the Past Darkly: History and Memory in François Mauriac's Bloc-Notes*. Washington, D.C.: Catholic University of America Press, 2004. Discusses Mauriac's thoughts as a Christian humanist on subjects of social justice, war, and human rights as he expressed them in his editorials in the 1950's and 1960's.

Jarrett-Kerr, Martin. *François Mauriac*. New Haven, Conn.: Yale University Press, 1954. Discusses the influence of Mauriac's religious upbringing on his writing. Also reviews his novelistic talent.

O'Connell, David. *François Mauriac Revisited*. Boston: Twayne, 1995. Good for a general introduction to Mauriac as a writer and to his work.

Turnell, Martin. *The Art of French Fiction: Prévost, Stendhal, Zola, Maupassant, Gide, Mauriac, Proust*. New York: New Directions, 1959. One of the best critics on nineteenth and twentieth century novelists. Presents Mauriac as a French Catholic novelist.

Shawncey Webb

1972

WONDERFUL WORDS OF LIFE
Hymns in American Protestant History and Theology

Editors: Richard J. Mouw (1940-) and Mark A. Noll (1946-)
First published: Grand Rapids, Mich.: Wm. B. Eerdmans, 2004
Genre: Nonfiction
Subgenres: Church history; critical analysis; theology
Core issues: Catholics and Catholicism; evangelization; faith; Protestants and Protestantism

Wonderful Words of Life *provides a history of Protestant hymnody and insights into worship practice. The first section cites Isaac Watts as a major influence from the time he composed hymns for eighteenth century British congregations, through the adaptation of his hymns by eighteenth and nineteenth century American Protestants, and continuing to the present. In the second section, contributors discuss contemporary Christian music in relation to the Youth for Christ movement and other revivalist programs. The last section looks at hymns as transmitters of theology.*

Overview

Wonderful Words of Life, edited by Richard J. Mouw and Mark Holl, is part of the Calvin Institute of Christian Worship Liturgical Studies series and focuses on the history and significance of hymns in Christianity. It is the product of the Hymnody in American Protestantism project, a three-year study conducted by the Institute for the Study of American Evangelicals. As part of the project, Stephen Mariani of Wellesley College compiled a list of three hundred of the most frequently published American hymns.

Hymns provide concise theology, often expressed in memorable poetic imagery; they both teach and delight. Generally grounded in orthodoxy, hymns allow greater understanding of saints throughout history and of the church universal. The work contains eleven essays divided into three sections. The first section examines the work and influence of hymn composer Isaac Watts. The second section looks at the role of hymns in the Protestant life, examining how hymns are used by evangelists, the Youth for Christ Movement, and the Catholic church and how white churchgoers are using gospel music. The third section focuses on the message of hymns that deal with various parts of Christian doctrine and topics such as death and divine rescue.

The first three chapters are devoted to Isaac Watts (1674-1748), an English Noncomformist pastor who wrote hymns central to British and American evangelical revivals of the eighteenth century. Perhaps his best-known hymn is "Joy to the World." Watts wrote hymns on foundational, unifying doctrines: sinfulness, faith as battle, Christ's love and redemption, and the yearning for Heaven. His hymns brought together people of various classes and races, provided a "public voice" for female composers, and promoted unity. Reformed singing had used Bible texts set to music in literal translation so that congregations might learn Scripture, but Watts appropriated the Psalms for singing through his method of "Psalm imitation," departing from literal translation to allow a poetic, emotive rendering in English, expressive of modern Christian experience. He encouraged singers to relate Scripture to their lives, both individual and communal, with political and social references. His Psalter provides a "national" background to the narrative of the relationship between God and his people. His hymns spread from their native England to the Americas. By 1800 many Watts texts had been revised to reflect an American sensibility, including the shift from Calvinism to evangelicalism.

Chapters 4 to 7 examine the popularity of hymns and their role in evangelization. Hymns played an important role in missionary work, whether in converting individuals or promoting the mission to the public. Missionary hymns frequently used battle imagery depicting the power of American Christianity and culture to subdue heathen ignorance and unbelief; they also emphasized evangelization in relation to Christ's return. Both attitudes were compelling in the growth of nineteenth century missions.

Hymns were also used in Canadian revivals, where evangelists' focus was on repentance, conversion, and commitment to Christian living. Emotionally engaging, sentimental gospel songs invited participants into the joys of salvation. While they disapproved of secular entertainment, evangelists often used the same theatrics to draw crowds to alternative entertainment venues with well-known celebrity preachers.

The Youth for Christ movement similarly took cues from popular music to create Christian music that attracts young people while promoting religious values. In the beginning, the movement struggled to define modern Christian music as separate from secular music. Its leaders denounced rock music in the 1960's as a dangerous substitute for a relationship with Christ, but modern Christian music has borrowed elements from rock and pop music to create music that is largely indistinguishable from its secular counterpart except by the lyrics, which bear a Christian message. Essay author Thomas E. Bergler states that the Youth for Christ movement, through music, has moved Protestant worship from fundamentalist to evangelical. Christian music continues to grow in popularity, with radio stations and record labels devoted to the genre, and youth evangelists use it to attract both non-Christians and Christians.

The popularity of Protestant hymns has led to their inclusion in Catholic hymnals. Essayist Felicia Piscitelli says that this is not surprising, as borrowing occurred even during the Reformation. The Second Vatican Council regularized worship in vernacular languages, along with greater lay participation and interaction with non-Catholic Christians. Piscitelli theorizes that an "evangelical" trend in Catholicism may account for increased Catholic use of praise songs and contemporary Christian music.

Along with more formal hymns, Christians have enjoyed gospel music. Gospel music is sometimes thought of as having two separate branches, black gospel and southern, or country, gospel. Black gospel music has influenced modern jazz and rock as well as country gospel and contemporary Christian music. White singers have also begun performing what has been regarded as traditional black gospel music. Essayist Virginia Lieson Brereton examines white perceptions of black gospel singers and decides that most whites who write about black gospel are "indulging in a bit of mythmaking and romanticizing," but she says that examining the white gaze can be instructive of what speaks to whites in this music.

The final section in this work deal with the theology in the hymns. Essayist Susan Wise Bauer identifies seventy-seven narrative and fifty-six systemic hymns from Marini's list. The narrative hymns trace the Christian's journey, while the systemic hymns express various aspects of Christian doctrine. Bauer concludes that numerous composers, including Watts, wrote both types, and she calls for more acceptance of narrative hymns by sometimes suspicious evangelicals.

The remaining essays deal with two common topics in hymns: death and rescue. Many American hymns refer to death in relation to historical attitudes regarding death and the afterlife. Many consolatory hymns exalt a blissful heavenly existence in contrast to a trouble-filled earthly life, while monitory hymns caution us about our mortality.

Mouw examines the topic of rescue hymns by evaluating Sandra Sizer's *Gospel Hymns and Social Religion* (1979) and Peter Selby's *Rescue: Jesus and Salvation Today* (1995). Although he finds valuable insights in Sizer, Mouw believes Selby is more correct and recommends examining rescue hymns in light of liberationist theology. The listener, he says, must understand that all people (the oppressed and the oppressors) need divine rescue and that two responses are necessary: a passive obedient waiting on God who rescues and an active faithful endeavor to rescue others through individual salvation and the removal of systems of oppression.

Christian Themes

One major theme in this work is the importance of Psalms and hymns in congregational singing and worship. Singing binds worshippers together in the expression of theological truths and encouragement to persevere in Christian living and faith. Although the authors of the essays in *Wonderful Words of Life* see value in praise songs and contemporary Christian music, they call for a valuing of historic, evangelical traditions in hymnody. If Christians ignore the Psalms and hymns of the past, they lose valuable resources for the maintenance of Christian devotion and instruction in orthodox doctrinal traditions. Collectively, hymns teach about the Scriptures of both Old and New Testaments as well as the experiences and faith of saints throughout history. Because they tend to focus on foundational, biblical truths, they can help bring appreciation, acceptance, and unity across doctrinal, denominational lines; they provide a common denominator of faith.

A second significant theme is the valuing of important contributions from a variety of doctrinal views. While liberal and conservative Christians tend to emphasize different aspects of faith, hymns address both the individual Christian's experience and the importance of adherence to the teachings of Scripture. Because traditional hymns address issues and beliefs of the universal, catholic church, they are valuable in bridging differences between Roman Catholic and Protestant Christians. This unifying effect also draws together believers of different social classes, races, and nationalities.

Sources for Further Study

Bishop, Selma L. *Isaac Watts, Hymns and Spiritual Songs, 1707-1748: A Publishing History and a Bibliography.* London: Faith, 1962. A definitive work to begin researching this innovator of Protestant hymnody; it provides sources for additional avenues of research.

Brown, Candy Gunther. Review of *Wonderful Words of Life.* The Journal of American History 91, no. 4 (March, 2005): 1457. Review examines the book's attempt to analyze the social and theological effect of hymns.

Noll, Mark A., and Edith L. Blumhofer, eds. *Sing Them Over Again to Me: Hymns and Hymnbooks in America.* Tuscaloosa: University of Alabama Press, 2006. Eleven essays examine hymnody and American Protestant life. Includes the history of the hymn "Amazing Grace" and an analysis of how the content of hymns and hymnals has changed.

Rhoads, Mark. Review of *Wonderful Words of Life.* Christian Scholar's Review 34, no. 2 (Winter, 2005): 271-272. In addition to reviewing the work, Rhoads discusses the hymnal he used as a child, the influence of gospel music, revivalism, and contemporary Christian music.

Stricklin, David. Review of *Wonderful Words of Life.* The Journal of Southern History 71, no. 2 (May, 2005): 508-509. Stricklin reviews the work and discusses its significance for Southern history.

Patricia Ralston

"A WORD MADE FLESH IS SELDOM"

Author: Emily Dickinson (1830-1886)
First published: pb. 1955
Edition used: The Complete Poems of Emily Dickinson, edited by Thomas H. Johnson. New York: Little, Brown, 1960; *The Poems of Emily Dickinson*, edited by R. W. Franklin. Cambridge, Mass.: Belknap Press of Harvard University Press, 1998
Genre: Poetry
Subgenre: Lyric poetry
Core issues: Celebration; Incarnation; Jesus Christ; redemption; the Word

This poem alludes both to Jesus as the incarnation of God and to poetry—"words that breathe distinctly" and do not die, and are available to every person, in spite of the restrictions of institutional religion. Dickinson pictures the poetic experience as similar to the sacrament of communion. The experience strengthens, even if it must be done in "ecstasies of stealth." For Dickinson, in this and some other poems, love of God and Jesus is contained in her love of language and poetry.

Overview

The second child of a prominent Amherst family, Emily Dickinson spent most of her life in the town (and the house) where she was born. Her conservative father, Edward Dickinson, generally considered to be a strict tyrant, was an important influence on his daughter, who considered home to be a holy place. Her early religious experience was in the Calvinistic Congregational Church, where the sermons on damnation terrified her as a child. She rejected the idea of sin and gradually overcame her terror, largely because of the influence of her friend, the Josiah Gilbert Hollands, whose theology was more liberal than that of her father. However, she was never comfortable with organized religion, and that attitude is reflected in many of her poems.

Also important to Dickinson's poetry is her knowledge of the Bible, which was extensive, and her interest in religious reform and the new, more imaginative sermon style of the mid-nineteenth century. Her father disapproved of this new style, which included a mixing of the sacred and the secular, but her friend Charles Wadsworth was an important innovator and practitioner. His sermons plus the popular writing of women such as Fanny Fern (Sara Willis Parton) influenced Dickinson to apply the language of religion plus her love of paradox, humor, and ambiguity to a wide variety of subjects. It also allowed her to focus on the human side of Jesus.

Dickinson's rhythm and rhyme have a religious connection as well. Many of her poems use common measure, also known as hymn stanza (the rhythm of many nineteenth century Protestant hymns), and variations on this regular rhythm. These are often used to contain controversial subjects or ironically undercut traditional ideas. "A Word made Flesh is seldom" uses the regular rhythm of iambic trimeter, with the added unstressed beat of the anaphora at the end of every other line, which adds to the lightness of the rhythm. Dickinson's regular rhyme schemes are also undercut by her use of slant or near rhyme with its resultant shift in emphasis.

"A Word made Flesh is seldom" is just one of a number of poems in which Dickinson presents God and religion as contained within poetry. In "I reckon—when I count at all—," she lists what is important to her: poets, the sun, summer, and "the Heaven of God." However, when she looks at the list, she concludes that poetry is so comprehensive, it makes the rest of the list "look a needless show," so she writes "Poets—All." In "I dwell in Possibility," she equates poetry with the possible; as her occupation, it encompasses "the spreading wide my narrow Hands/ To gather Paradise—." This also connects Dickinson to Transcendental authors of the time, including Ralph Waldo Emerson and Henry David Thoreau, who privilege poets as the ones who see and who can interpret spiritual reality to their fellows.

"A Word made Flesh is seldom" illustrates some of the difficulties of interpretation caused by the editing of Dickinson's poetry. The capitalization of "Word" in the first line of the poem is an editorial change made by Thomas Johnson; Franklin's text omits it. It is not clear whether Dickinson intended this emphasis because the original manuscript of this poem is lost. The current texts are based on Susan Dickinson's copy of the poem. Some scholars consider the poem a note, with Susan as the intended audience.

Susan's copy includes five introductory lines, transcribed as verse and separated from the poem by a line. This introduction is not usually published with the poem, but the lines do suggest the poem's occasion. Dickinson seems offended by someone's (a clergyman's?) casual, obtuse reference to the passage from John. Her poem is an attempt to correct this attitude.

Dickinson's use of her poetry as a corrective to problems she sees in institutional religion recurs in numerous poems, often more openly than in "The Word made Flesh is seldom." One of the most familiar examples is "Some keep the Sabbath going to Church—." Here Dickinson expresses her preference for nature, with a bird for her choir, wings replacing a surplice, and a sermon from God, "a noted Clergyman," who has the good sense to keep the sermon short.

Christian Themes

Both Dickinson's strict Calvinist upbringing and her awareness of changes to the religion of her time figure in her poetry. She uses the language of the Bible and Congregational theology, but she is not uncritical in her examination of religion and its relationship to life's problems. She portrays a God who seems both awe-inspiring and arbitrary, but her real spiritual connection is to a Christ who is kind and human. "A Word made Flesh is seldom" considers Christ's courageous act of becoming human, with all that entails, and the analogous act of poetry, which allows Dickinson to question, to dramatize her spiritual quest, and to express both her belief and disbelief.

For Dickinson, the unknown is both necessary and troubling; her poetry dwells in uncertainty much of the time. "This World in not Conclusion" exemplifies this. Here

Dickinson pictures what lies beyond our knowledge as both beckoning and baffling—a riddle that cannot be solved by the philosopher or the scholar. The narcotic offered by the preacher does not dull the feeling either. The poem ends with the possibility of an afterlife still "nibbling" at humanity.

The experience of possibility is significant to Dickinson. She is uncertain about many elements of religion, but she is sure of the power and lasting importance of poetry and the word. In "A Word made Flesh is seldom," she expresses how it feels to experience the power of words. This ritual needs to be approached carefully, perhaps, but it is ecstasy, and the taste of this "food" strengthens one. The fact that she parallels this experience to that of approaching Jesus through the religious sacrament of communion illustrates Dickinson's openness and questing spirit.

Sources for Further Study

Burr, Zofia. "The Canonization of Emily Dickinson." In *Of Women, Poetry, and Power*. Urbana: University of Illinois Press, 2002. This study of five American women poets begins with how Emily Dickinson's poetry has been edited and received since the 1890's, how this connects to her relationship to audiences, and how the critical expectations of other women poets have been affected by what critics have valued in Dickinson's work.

Doriani, Beth Maclay. *Emily Dickinson, Daughter of Prophecy*. Amherst: University of Massachusetts Press, 1996. Using feminist and historic readings, Doriani examines Dickinson's use of Judeo-Christian scriptures and new sermons of nineteenth century Protestants to claim her place as a woman prophet among self-proclaimed male prophets such as Ralph Waldo Emerson and Walt Whitman.

McIntosh, James. *Nimble Believing: Dickinson and the Unknown*. Ann Arbor: University of Michigan Press, 2000. In a letter to Judge Lord, Dickinson notes believing and not believing "a hundred times an hour" as the basis for nimble believing, which McIntosh defines as having an intense spiritual life without embracing any specific belief system. He examines variety in Dickinson's religious experience.

Monte, Steven. "Dickinson's Searching Philology." *The Emily Dickinson Journal* 12, no. 2 (2003): 21-51. Monte reviews current material criticism of Dickinson, then argues for reading her poetry philologically; he does an extended philological reading of "A Word made Flesh is seldom" to illustrate.

Smith, Martha Neel. *Rowing in Eden: Rereading Emily Dickinson*. Austin: University of Texas Press, 1992. Smith analyzes the conventional picture of Dickinson, then reexamines her approach to publication and the importance of her relationship with Susan Dickinson.

Stronum, Gary Lee. *The Dickinson Sublime*. Madison: University of Wisconsin Press, 1990. Stonum views Dickinson's work as focused on the sublime. He analyzes how Dickinson's sublime, which he sees as a stimulant to her reader's imagination that does not provide closure, differs from the romantic view.

Elsie Galbreath Haley

BIBLIOGRAPHY

Anchor Bible Commentary series. Garden City, N.Y.: Doubleday, 1964- . The continuously updated Anchor Bible Commentary series presents expositions of books from the Hebrew Scriptures, the New Testament, and the Apocrypha. Each of the more than eighty volumes presents a chapter-verse summary, notes on historical interpretations and translation issues, lists of key events and themes, and a bibliography of works related to the topic. Edited and written by leading scholars in religious studies and theology.

Bakken, Peter, et al. *Ecology, Justice, and Christian Faith: A Critical Guide to the Literature*. Westport, Conn.: Greenwood, 1995. Part of Greenwood's religious bibliography series, this work lists books by Christian authors and publishers that address themes related to stewardship of the environment and human rights. Short annotations follow each entry.

Barton, John, and John Muddiman, eds. *The Oxford Bible Commentary*. Oxford, England: Oxford University Press, 2001. More than one thousand pages of commentary on the books that make up the Hebrew Scriptures, the New Testament, and the Apocrypha, with independently written chapters for each book. Most chapters include introductory remarks on the book, including its title, author, date, and location. Each chapter discusses the book's major literary themes, historical references, theological views, and literary-critical approaches. Also included are chapter-verse summaries, intertextual comparisons, and extensive bibliographies.

Batchelor, Mary, comp. *A Treasury of Christian Poetry: Seven Hundred Inspiring and Beloved Poems*. New York: Gramercy-Random House, 1995. Collection of poems arranged by religious themes such as "Daily Life" and "Time and Eternity." Includes scriptural texts, well-known poems (by Emily Dickinson and Madeleine L'Engle, for example), anonymous verses, and less common works.

Bettenson, Henry, and Chris Maunder, eds. *Documents of the Christian Church*. Oxford, England: Oxford University Press, 1999. Includes primary source material and commentary on important documents from the beginnings of Christian history. Of special interest are passages containing references to Christ by non-Christian authors. Also includes creeds, work from early Christian apologists, and documents pertaining to the divergent views about the divinity of Christ, the place of the sacraments, and the authority of Rome. The last half of the book covers bulls, decrees, and conciliar documents on the eventual schism, the investiture controversies, and various heretical teachings with extensive coverage of documents related to the Protestant Reformation. Ends with church writings on such contemporary themes as liberation theology, the ordination of women, the modernization of the Mass and the ecumenical movements.

Blodgett, Jan. *Protestant Evangelical Literary Culture and Contemporary Society*. Westport, Conn.: Greenwood, 1997. Blodgett's work provides an analysis of the contemporary Christian publishing industry and an annotated bibliography of popular contemporary Christian works. The bibliography section includes not only brief synopses but also an examination of themes and even theological approaches contained in the works.

Bush, L. Russ. *Classical Readings in Christian Apologetics.* Grand Rapids, Mich.: Zondervan, 1983. An anthology of classic pieces by Christian apologetics from the second through the seventeenth centuries. Begins with excerpts from the writings of Saint Justin Martyr and includes the writings of Origen, Saint Augustine, and Thomas Aquinas. Concludes with an essay on nineteenth and twentieth century figures.

Carlen, Claudia. *The Papal Encyclicals, 1740 to 1981.* 5 vols. Reprint. Ann Arbor, Mich.: Pierian, 1990. Chronological anthology of two centuries' worth of encyclicals with introductory notes, commentaries, cross references, and guide to sources. Also available as a searchable digital database.

Chase, Elise, comp. *Healing Faith: An Annotated Bibliography of Christian Self-Help Books.* Westport, Conn.: Greenwood, 1985. Part of Greenwood's religious reference series. A bit dated, but includes classics arranged by theme.

Cohn-Sherbock, Lavinia. *Who's Who in Christianity.* 2d ed. London: Routledge, 2001. Follows the traditional Who's Who series format with biographical information about major and lesser-known figures in Christian history. Includes family and early life, important contributions, and some historical interpretation.

Counsell, Michael, comp. *Two Thousand Years of Prayer.* Reprint. New York: Morehouse, 2002. Includes written prayer texts from first century apologist Saint Ignatius of Antioch as well as other church fathers, then moves through the centuries to include prayers from eastern and western rites, religious inscriptions, monastic and mendicant prayers, prayers from around the world, and religious words from Fyodor Dostoevski, Johann Wolfgang von Goethe, Alfred, Lord Tennyson, Charlotte and Emily Brontë, and an unknown Confederate soldier, among others.

Cross, F. L., and E. A. Livingstone, eds. *The Oxford Dictionary of the Christian Church.* 3d ed. Oxford, England: Oxford University Press, 1997. A large volume with alphabetical entries on people, places, events, doctrines, and major themes from church history.

DeLong, Janice A. *Contemporary Christian Authors.* Lanham, Md.: Scarecrow, 2000. Survey of biographical data on contemporary authors of inspirational Christian fiction.

Detweiler, Robert, and David Jasper, eds. *Religion and Literature: A Reader.* Louisville, Ky.: Westminster John Knox, 2000. Though not explicitly Christian, this work is an anthology of excerpts from world (mainly Western) literature that address theological and/or existential questions. Includes the book of Genesis and the Gospel of John, writings from recent Christian philosophers such as Paul Tillich and Thomas Merton, and commentary by Jacques Derrida and Simone Weil. Arranged thematically with introductory essays and lists of sources for further study.

Freedman, David Noel, ed. *The Anchor Bible Dictionary.* 6 vols. New York: Anchor-

Doubleday, 1992. Definitive reference series for biblical terms, place names, and concepts related to biblical interpretation; also available on CD-ROM.
Gaustad, Edwin S., and Mark A. Noll, eds. *A Documentary History of Religion in America to 1877.* 3d ed. Grand Rapids, Mich.: Eerdmans, 2003. A collection of writings, arranged chronologically, that explore religious themes, trends, and movements in American history. Begins with Native American creation stories and accounts from European missionaries, then moves to accounts from the Salem witch trials to the religious debates of American revolutionaries. First volume concludes with slavery debates and nineteenth century religious revival literature.
_____. *A Documentary History of Religion in America Since 1877.* 3d ed. Grand Rapids, Mich.: Eerdmans, 2003. The second volume in this history includes writings from transcendentalists and early twentieth century reformers and from major movements such as Fundamentalism and Zionism. Sections on religion and contemporary politics and Y2K/millennial fever.
The Greatest Sermons Ever Preached. Nashville, Tenn.: W Publishing Group, 2005. Gift-book style presentation of important sermons from Jonathan Edwards and Martin Luther King, Jr., among others. Includes several familiar quotations and memorable passages.
Gutjar, Paul C. *An American Bible: A History of the Good Book in the United States, 1777 to 1880.* Stanford, Calif.: Stanford University Press, 1999. Discussion of the importance of the Christian Scriptures during America's "Christian Century." Pays special attention to the role of Christian publishers during debates about authority and doctrine.
Hammond, Pete, et al. *The Marketplace Annotated Bibliography: A Christian Guide to Books on Work, Business, and Vocation.* Downer's Grove, Ill.: Intervarsity, 2002. Almost two hundred pages worth of reviews and annotations of books about business and industry from a Christian perspective, published by an evangelical Christian press.
Harris, Stephen L. *Understanding the Bible.* 6th ed. Boston: McGraw Hill, 2003. Textbook-style presentation of books from the Hebrew Scriptures, the New Testament, and the Apocrypha. Concise summaries of most scriptural books, with discussion of important themes and areas of scholarship. Outlines widely accepted theories of contemporary biblical literary criticism such as the documentary hypothesis and the synoptic problem.
Hastings, Adrian, et al., eds. *The Oxford Companion to Christian Thought.* Oxford, England: Oxford University Press, 2000. Outlines of key teachings of major Christian philosophers, including divergent interpretations and controversial pieces.
Hillerbrand, Hans. *The Protestant Reformation.* New York: Harper Perennial, 2007. Includes treatises by Martin Luther, Ulrich Zwingli, the Anabaptists, and English reformers such as William Tyndale.
Jeffrey, David Lyle. *People of the Book: Christian Identity and Literary Culture.* Grand Rapids, Mich.: Eerdmans, 1996. A sophisticated analysis of contemporary literary theory with an eye toward answering the question of whether there is a

place for a Christian literary criticism. While offering powerful critiques of Marxist and deconstructionist approaches to literature with Christian themes, Jeffrey also chides his fellow Christians for not engaging seriously enough in the study of the Logos—the word within the texts they value.

Keller, Rosemary Skinner, and Rosemary Radford Ruether, eds. *In Our Own Voices: Four Centuries of American Women's Religious Writing.* Louisville, Ky.: Westminster John Knox, 1995. This work contains thematically arranged excerpts from literary works such as missionary society writings and memoirs. Includes commentary and background from contemporary scholars in the field.

Koester, Helmut. *Ancient Christian Gospels: Their History and Development.* Harrisburg, Pa.: Trinity, 1990. Well-known theology professor Koester discusses the Gospel tradition with special attention to the form and audience not only of the four Gospels now in the New Testament canon but also of several extracanonical works. Koester shows how stories from the oral tradition as well as hymns, poetry, and prayer are woven together alongside miracle stories and passion narratives. Compares related passages and discusses the synoptic problem.

_____. *Introduction to the New Testament: History and Literature of Early Christianity.* Berlin: Walter de Gruyter, 2000. Koester examines the diverse texts that make up the New Testament and connects many of the writings with the cultural context in which they were produced.

McGrath, Alister, ed. *Christian Literature: An Anthology.* Oxford, England: Blackwell, 2001. Edited anthology of literature that includes documentary sources from Church history (for example, Gregory of Nyssa and John Calvin) and excerpts from classic Christian literature. Each entry includes a brief summary, a list of other works by the author, and some questions for study and discussion.

Manser, Martin H., comp. *The Westminster Collection of Christian Quotations.* Louisville, Ky.: Westminster John Knox, 2001. Comprehensive collection of quotations from several translations of Scripture and from Christian teachers, saints, authors, and world leaders on a variety of topics ranging from ability, acceptance, and action to worship, youth, and zeal.

Metzger, Bruce M. *The Bible in Translation: Ancient and English Versions.* Grand Rapids, Mich.: Baker, 2001. Metzger, a published translator and interpreter of Scripture, discusses the nature of the process of translation—the stakes, the arguments, and the politics. He advises readers on the strengths and weaknesses of each of several versions and does some side-by-side comparative analysis.

_____. *The Canon of the New Testament: Its Origin, Development, and Significance.* 1987. Reprint. Oxford, England: Oxford University Press, 1997. An interesting study of New Testament books and related works that did not make the "final cut" into the modern canon of twenty-seven works. Discusses reasons for selecting particular works and includes information on contemporary research related to extracanonical works.

Metzger, Bruce M., and Michael David Coogan, eds. *The Oxford Companion to the Bible.* Oxford, England: Oxford University Press, 1993. Alphabetical listing of

important themes and topics from Scripture with discussion of and references to other works of literature.
Mort, John. *Christian Fiction: A Guide to the Genre.* Greenwood Village, Colo.: Libraries Unlimited, 2002. Guide to Christian fiction for librarians with sections organized by genre and religious group.
Music, David W. *Christian Hymnody in Twentieth Century Britain and America: An Annotated Bibliography.* Westport, Conn.: Greenwood, 2001. Extensive bibliography that includes books, book chapters, and journal articles related to hymns both as texts and as religious experiences. Arranged thematically and then alphabetically.
Neal, Lynn S. *Romancing God: Evangelical Women and Inspirational Fiction.* Chapel Hill: University of North Carolina Press, 2006. Examines the ways in which evangelical women use popular works of Christian fiction by authors from Grace Livingston Hill to Janette Oke to Beverly Lewis. Focuses on images and motifs of particular importance to female readers.
Nord, David Paul. *Faith in Reading: Religious Publishing and the Birth of Mass Media in America.* Oxford, England: Oxford University Press, 2004. Contextualizes religious literature of the early nineteenth century against the growth of capitalistic enterprise and the beginnings of mass-produced culture. Discussion of Christian publishing houses, Bible distributors, and the birth of what would become an enormously profitable industry.
Pelikan, Jaroslav. *Credo: Historical and Theological Guide to Creeds and Confessions of Faith in the Christian Tradition.* New Haven, Conn.: Yale University Press, 2005. A comprehensive study of Christian creeds and their formation and transformation over time. Includes distinguishing features among creeds of various traditions and faiths and several line-by-line analyses of phrases or even words that are loaded with historical significance and conceal the sometimes bitter controversies that occurred in the "behind-the-scenes" composition.
Porterfield, Amanda, ed. *American Religious History.* Blackwell Readers in American Social and Cultural History series. New York: Blackwell, 2002. Collection of primary-source documents from American religious history, from John Winthrop's famous 1630 sermon "A Model of Christian Charity," which envisions America as God's "city on a hill," to an excerpt from the writings of contemporary evangelical Christian political activist Ralph Reed. Documents are arranged chronology and supplemented with brief introductory passages. Also included are a series of historical essays from contemporary religious studies scholars on key themes in American religious history such as gender and pluralism.
Robinson, James M., ed. *The Nag Hammadi Library in English.* 4th ed. New York: E. J. Brill, 1996. A compendium of translations of Gnostic writings such as the Gospel of Truth and the Apocalypse of Adam. Also includes the Gospel of Thomas, a much-studied extracanonical work. An updated version with translations and commentary by leading Bible scholars.
_____, et al. *The Sayings Gospel Q in Greek and English: With Parallels from*

the *Gospels of Mark and Thomas*. Leuven, Belgium: Fortress-Peeters, 2002. New Testament theologian Robinson provides an outline and translation of "Q," the hypothesized source (*quelle*, German for source) of the sayings of Jesus that appear in both Matthew and Luke in the same Greek translation.

Ryken, Leland, ed. *The Christian Imagination: The Practice of Faith in Literature and Writing*. Colorado Springs, Colo.: Shaw-Random House, 2002. A collection of essays from T. S. Eliot, C. S. Lewis, Annie Dillard, and others about the importance of Christian art and literature, the development of a Christian aesthetic, and the acts of reading and writing. Concludes with general critiques of Christian fiction, narrative, and poetry.

Spencer, Jon Michael. *Protest and Praise: Sacred Music of Black Religion*. Minneapolis, Minn.: Augsburg/Fortress, 1990. An examination of the oral tradition in African American churches with special attention to the interrelationships of gospel hymns and other musical forms such as blues, jazz, and even rock.

Strong, James, et al. *The Strongest Strong's Exhaustive Concordance of the Bible*. Grand Rapid, Mich.: Zondervan, 2001. The *Strong's Concordance* in its many editions lists the English translation of every word in the Hebrew Bible and New Testament and then indicates the chapters and verses that contain the word. Good for cross-textual analysis.

Vermes, Geza, trans. *The Complete Dead Sea Scrolls in English*. New York: Penguin, 2004. Translation of texts found during excavations in the 1940's and 1950's near Qumran (near the Dead Sea) and now believed to have been composed between the third century B.C.E. and the first century C.E., by Jewish outsiders with an apocalyptic worldview. The Dead Sea scrolls have long been of interest to both Jewish and Christian scholars. For the former, they give insight into changes in Judaism that were occurring in the years leading up to the Jewish Revolt against the Romans in 66 C.E. The Dead Sea scrolls are not Christian texts, but for scholars of early Christian literature, they provide an opportunity for comparative study between two marginalized communities within Second Temple-period Judaism with similar sets of concerns, particularly in the expectation of the coming apocalypse.

Walker, Barbara. *The Librarian's Guide to Developing Christian Fiction Collections for Adults*. New York: Neal-Schuman, 2005. Part subject analysis and part annotated bibliography, this work orients librarians and other interested readers to the growing field of Christian fiction, with all of its subgenres, related markets (such as music and DVDs), and controversies. An extensive introductory survey outlines the theological debates that surround the production of Christian fiction both historically and in the twenty-first century.

_____. *The Librarian's Guide to Developing Christian Fiction Collections for Children*. New York: Neal-Schuman, 2005. Similar to Walker's guide for adults, but focuses on the special problems that arise in children's writings.

_____. *The Librarian's Guide to Developing Christian Fiction Collections for Young Adults*. New York: Neal-Schuman, 2005. Another guide marketed to librarians, Walker's young-adult edition is of potential interest to general readers because of its attention to controversial subjects in Christian literature and to related censorship debates in public school libraries.

Warner, Michael, ed. *American Sermons: The Pilgrims to Martin Luther King, Jr.* New York: Library of America, 1999. Organized chronologically, this collection includes sermons that have now become part of classic American literature such as Cotton Mather's "The Wonders of the Invisible World," Dwight Moody's "On Being Born Again," Henry Emerson Fosdick's "Shall the Fundamentalists Win?" and Martin Luther King, Jr.'s "I've Been to the Mountaintop." Also included, however, are lesser known sermons that were significant in their times on topics ranging from swearing to slavery to the Holy Spirit.

White, James F. *Documents of Christian Worship: Descriptive and Interpretive Sources.* Louisville, Ky.: Westminster John Knox, 1992. Begins with small excerpts from church leaders and writers about the celebration of "the Sabbath" and proceeds to more extended treatment of the form of the Mass and Christian worship service. Discusses the structure of daily and yearly prayers and church and cathedral architecture. Also includes information about the symbols used in Christian rituals and what they signify.

Young, Frances, eds., et al. *The Cambridge History of Early Christian Literature.* Cambridge, England: Cambridge University Press, 2004. A collection of independently authored essays arranged thematically, beginning with New Testament writings and contemporaneous extracanonical works and proceeding through the early Christian apologists and teachers. Some essays on canon formation and conciliar literature. Concludes with hagiographies, monastic works, women's writings, and an essay about the early canon and the formation of a particular Christian identity.

Jennifer Heller

ELECTRONIC RESOURCES

The sites listed below were visited in 2006. Because URLs frequently change or are moved, the accuracy of these sites cannot be guaranteed; however, long-standing sites such as those of university departments, national organizations, and government agencies generally maintain links when sites move or upgrade their offerings, and care has been taken to include such stable sites. For more on Web resources, see Jeffrey K. Hadden and Douglas E. Cowan, eds., *Religion on the Internet: Research Prospects and Promises* (New York: JAI Press, 2000), a collection of scholarly articles focused on several areas studying and teaching religion in relation to the Internet; Elena Larsen, *CyberFaith: How Americans Pursue Religion Online* (Washington, D.C.: Pew Internet & American Life Project, 2001, available at http://www.pewtrusts.com), a report that profiles Web surfing for relgious content and common online activities, including useful statistics, charts, and a case study; Bruce B. Lawrence, *The Complete Idiot's Guide to Religions Online* (Indianapolis, Ind.: Alpha Books, 2000), which provides a useful introduction to finding religion on the Internet; John Mort, *Christian Fiction: A Guide to the Genre*, a valuable collection development tool arranged by subgenre, with a section on readers' advisory Web sites; and Mark Stover, *Theological Librarians and the Internet: Implications for Practice* (Binghamton, N.Y.: Haworth Information Press, 2001), which includes chapters about religious and theological journals online and selected Internet resources.

Archives

The Vatican
http://www.vatican.va

Abundant information resides on this beautiful site. Multiple areas within the site contain papal writings and speeches, along with the *Catechism of the Catholic Church*. The Library, Secret Archives, and Museum are essential for researchers and are complemented by virtual tours.

World Council of Churches Archives
http://library.wcc-coe.org/Archives.393.0.html

The Archives preserves the "institutional memory of the ecumenical movement." Includes a collection for photographs depicting religious activities from around the world.

Authors

Christian Authors Database
http://faith.propadeutic.com/authors/authors.html

Offers brief biographical and professional information on nearly seven hundred authors, complemented by pictures of the authors. Browse by author or subject. Clearly stated disclaimers, clarifications, and acknowledgments. Very comprehensive for a free Web site.

Awards and Best Sellers
Religious Best Sellers and Book Awards
http://web.nmsu.edu/~ebosman/church/bestsellers.shtml
   Maintained by a professional librarian since 1997, this site compiles, describes, and links to religious book awards and best-seller lists.

Book Clubs, Online Discussion Groups, Reading Guides
Book-Clubs-Resource
http://www.book-clubs-resource.com
   Focuses on all topics related to book clubs. Includes annotated links to numerous resources divided into sections about running a book club, reading group guides, lists of online book clubs, and discount book clubs.

BookClubDeals
http://www.bookclubdeals.com/christian-book-clubs.html
   Lists and profiles different Christian book clubs.

FaithfulReader
http://www.faithfulreader.com
   An attractive, nondenominational site with a limited supply of reading guides but abundant in other features, such as readers' reviews, author interviews, book excerpts, and a free newsletter.

Bookstores
Christianbook.com
http://www.christianbook.com
   A bookstore site whose format will be familiar to denizens of Amazon.com, dedicated to Christian literature. Offers access to books and other products by category, along with category lists and author profiles.

Indexes and Databases
ATLA Religion Database
http://www.atla.com/products/catalogs/catalogs_rdb.html
   Available via subscription, this product combines three publications of the American Theological Library Association, otherwise available by separate subscription. *Religion Index One* and *Religion Index Two* are essential to religious studies research, while *Index to Book Reviews in Religion* has provided reviews since 1949. Includes citations from *Methodist Reviews Index* (1818-1985).

Catholic Periodical and Literature Index
http://www.atla.com/products/catalogs/catalogs_cpli.html
   A subscription product produced by the Catholic Library Association and the American Theological Library Association since 1930. Issued annually.

Christian Periodical Index
http://www.acl.org/cpi.cfm

An index to subjects, authors, and book reviews established in 1957 and published semiannually by the Association of Christian Librarians. Available via subscription in CD-ROM or full text online.

Religious & Theological Abstracts
http://rtabst.org

Summarizes scholarly journal articles covering a variety of religious faiths. Free searching available, but results are limited to five citations. Affordable individual subscriptions. Available in a quarterly-updated, online format or issued annually in CD-ROM.

Journals

Books and Culture: A Christian Review
http://www.christianitytoday.com/books

Provides evangelical analysis of books through lengthy interdisciplinary essays mixing social commentary and reviewing. Essays are descriptive and critical, signed by credentialed and often eminent writers. Indexed. Contains back issues and a search mechanism. A refreshing approach.

Christian Library Journal
http://www.christianlibraryj.org

Subscription-based journal reviewing materials from a Christian point of view. Reviews, approximately 250 per issue, include works in nonprint formats. Short, descriptive reviews arranged by age and genre include recommended interest levels. Numeric quality and acceptability ratings are unique. Indexed. Highly recommended for its breadth of coverage.

Christianity and Literature
http://www.pepperdine.edu/sponsored/ccl/journal.html

A "scholarly exploration of how literature engages Christian thought, experience, and practice," this publication contains an extensive review section featuring authoritative, signed reviews. Each quarterly issue comprises approximately twenty reviews. Complete bibliographic citations complement the essays, which range in length between five hundred and one thousand words. Indexed.

Denver Journal
http://www.denverseminary.edu/dj

An online review of current biblical and theological thought. Arranged by subject, the signed scholarly commentaries average five hundred to eight hundred words each. Clearly stated purpose, scope, and audience level are reflected in the content.

Religion Bookline
http://www.publishersweekly.com/index.asp?layout=eletters&industry=Religion+BookLine
Offered via email, *Religion Bookline* delivers news, features, and expert commentary to those interested in religious books and publishing. Signed reviews average one hundred words and cover a variety of religious practices.

Review of Biblical Literature
http://www.bookreviews.org
The review sections of *Journal of Biblical Literature* and *Critical Review of Books in Religion* in electronic form, browsable by subject and searchable by all available years. Signed, critical reviews average one thousand words. Recommended for its scholarly nature and search capabilities.

Meta Sites

Beliefnet
http://www.beliefnet.com
A large, nondenominational site dedicated to helping people find and walk a spiritual path. Leading practitioners of each faith explain their beliefs. News, articles, discussion boards, quizzes, prayer circles, expert advice, dating services, and many other features are available. Useful for basic introductions to various beliefs.

Religious Resources
http://www.religiousresources.org
A comprehensive directory of Internet resources for all major religions organized into a hierarchical directory. An ttractive, well-organized, independently owned and operated clearinghouse. Advertising is nonintrusive. Search and browse capabilities.

Publishers and Book Sellers

Abingdon Press
http://www.abingdonpress.com
Originally the United Methodist Publishing House, in operation since 1789. Since the early 1920's Abingdon has published "academic, professional, and inspirational, and life-affirming religious literature to enrich church communities across the globe."

Bethany House
http://www.bethanyhouse.com
This Christian publisher's Web site includes links to author Web sites, reading group guides, and book series information.

Catholic University of America Press
http://cuapress.cua.edu
Site of the *New Catholic Encyclopedia*, the Library of Early Christianity series, and other books and journals devoted to the history and documents of the Roman Catholic Church.

Christian Bookstore Association
http://www.cbaonline.org

The trade association for the Christian retail channel, serving the interests and meeting the needs of nearly 2,300 member Christian stores. Includes best sellers by category, ISBN lists, and a "Book Core Inventory Report" that lists the top one thousand titles sold in Christian stores by dollar-value contribution (based on suggested retail price).

Crossroad Publishing Company
http://cpcbooks.com/default.asp

The Crossroad Publishing Company, a division the two-hundred-year-old international Catholic publishing house Herder & Herder, dedicated to publishing "engaging books of original thinking, pastoral sensitivity, and prophetic vision."

Eerdmans.com
http://www.eerdmans.com

Home of the Wm. B. Eerdmans publishing company, which specializes in Bibles, Bible study, and academic titles in the study of the Christian religion and social studies related to religion.

Evangelical Christian Publishers Association
http://www.ecpa.org

Site of the trade organization that is the sponsor of the Christian Book Awards. Lists award winners by category.

Good News & Crossway
http://www.gnpcb.org

Home to the evangelical Good News Publishers, with its Crossway Books, Good News Tracts, and the English Standard Version of the Bible. Good News Publishers describes itself as "a not-for-profit Christian ministry and exists solely for the purpose of proclaiming the gospel through publishing and all other means in order, by God's grace." Books and other products browsable by author, title, subject, and series.

Manuscript Editing's List of Religious Publishers
http://www.manuscriptediting.com/publishers-religious.htm

A large list linking to publishers specializing in religious materials.

Tyndale House Publishers
http://www.tyndale.com

Home of the publishers of the New Living Bible and other spiritual literature. Offers titles in all genres, with emphasis on church resources.

Zondervan
http://www.zondervan.com/cultures/en-us/home.htm

Home of the Bible and Christian literature publisher founded in 1931.

Readers' Advisories

BookBrowse
https://www.bookbrowse.com
   Recommends current titles. Conduct a search or browse by genre, country, time period, or theme. View cover art and reviews, read excerpts, check out reader's reviews, and see a brief author biography. A relatively inexpensive subscription service available to individuals or libraries.

FictionConnection
http://www.fictionconnection.com
   This subscription database, available to libraries, is searchable by author, title, ISBN, or keyword to recommended books based on readers' preferences. Searches are easily refined by genre, location, topic, setting, and many other criteria. Sortable by relevance, year, author, or title.

Fiction_L
http://www.webrary.org/rs/flmenu.html
   Sponsored by the Morton Grove Public Library, this exceptional site offers Fiction_L, a subscription service to electronic mailing lists devoted to readers' advisory topics such as book discussions, book talks, collection development issues, bibliographies, and a wide variety of other topics of interest to librarians.

Genreflecting.com
http://www.genreflecting.com
   The term "genreflecting" was coined by Betty Rosenberg and refers to classifying books according to types that align with reader preferences. Genres range from romance and mystery to Christian fiction; here, Christion fiction is defined as "stories that reflect the Christian world view" in which "the relationship between the protagonist and God plays a pivotal role." Lists such fiction in subgenres: romance, suspense, futuristic, historical, mystery, and others. Also offers a list of "must read" authors.

NoveList
http://www.epnet.com/thisTopic.php?marketID=6&topicID=16
   A subscription-based product found in many public and school libraries, NoveList assists readers by recommending books based on a variety of factors, including favorite author or plot. Includes book reviews, author information, and discussion guides. User can search, make a reading list, and customize results.

Reader's Advisor Online
http://rainfo.lu.com
   A subscription database sponsored by Libraries Unlimited. More than four hundred genres, including Christian fiction and nonfiction, are covered. Titles can be searched by reading interest, character, location, series title, and other characteristics. Based on the popular Genreflecting advisory series.

Sacred Texts
Christian Classics Ethereal Library
http://www.ccel.org
  Concentrates on post-Reformation works representing the Catholic, Orthodox, and Protestant views. Search or browse sacred texts, encyclopedias, classic Christian fiction, and the writings of church fathers. One of the oldest, most comprehensive sacred texts sites on the Internet, CCEL was founded in 1994 by Calvin College.

Internet Sacred Text Archive
http://www.sacred-texts.com
  Founded in 1999, this site contains approximately forty-five thousand unique files from many religious traditions. The Christianity section is subdivided into Scriptures, Gnosticism, Early Christian, Eastern Churches, Reformation and Renaissance, and Modern. Users may browse or search for creeds, prayers and prayer books, or catechisms. A convenient starting point for researchers.

Unbound Bible
http://www.unboundbible.com
  Search book, chapter, verse, or keywords in up to nine parallel versions in multiple languages, including Hebrew and Greek. View results by verse, with optional contextual entries and commentary from seventeenth century clergyman Matthew Henry. A product of Biola University.

Statistics
Adherents.com
http://www.adherents.com
  Culled from print resources, this site provides statistical, historical data concerning religious adherents. Arranged by religious group and geography, more than forty-two hundred religions are represented. Unusual topical trivia, including the religious affiliations for world leaders and comic-book characters. The unique content makes up for the clunky interface. Browse capability only.

Association of Religion Data Archives
http://www.thearda.com
  This archive, launched in 1998, collates statistical data. Predominantly American in perspective with selected data down to the county level, although some international data are provided. Users will find 350 files on an array of subjects, including denominational studies, and teachers might find the learning modules useful. May be searched or browsed.

World Christian Database
http://www.worldchristiandatabase.org/wcd
  A subscription-based archive of statistics based on *World Christian Encyclopedia and World Christian Trends* and maintained by the Center for the Study of Global

Christianity. Data cover nine thousand Christian denominations, thirteen thousand ethnolinguistic peoples, five thousand cities, three thousand provinces, and 238 countries. Search, browse, and customize results. Examples include data on the status of missions work and the availability of printed religious literature.

Ellen Bosman

CHRONOLOGICAL LIST OF TITLES

Below the titles covered in this publication are listed in rough chronological order on the basis of the earliest date of appearance: Although usually that date is a date of publication, in known cases where writing, transcription, or other appearance was significantly earlier than publication date, we have listed the earlier date. Date ranges are arranged by earliest date in the range.

Before Christ (Before Common Era)

c. 1030-c. 962 B.C.E.	Psalms (David)
c. tenth-c. second century B.C.E.	Hebrew Bible (Unknown)
c. mid-sixth century B.C.E.	Books of the Prophets (Isaiah/Jeremiah/Amos/Micah)

Ancient Times After Christ

c. 50-c. 65 C.E.	New Testament Letters (Paul)
60 C.E. or c. 80-150 C.E.	Acts of the Apostles (Unknown)
c. 95 C.E.	Book of Revelation (John)
c. 100 C.E.	Gospel of John (John, son of Zebedee)
c. 140 C.E.	Synoptic Gospels (Matthew/Mark/Luke)
147-157 C.E.	First and Second Apologies, The (Justin Martyr)
c. 180 C.E.	Against Heresies (Irenaeus)
c. 190-200 C.E.	Instructor, The (Clement of Alexandria)
c. 190-200 C.E.	Miscellanies (Clement of Alexandria)
197 C.E.	Apology (Tertullian)
220-230 C.E.	On First Principles (Origen)
c. 256-270 C.E.	Enneads, The (Plotinus)
Before 325 C.E.	On the Incarnation of the Word of God (Athanasius of Alexandria)
370-419 C.E.	Letters of Saint Jerome, The (Jerome)
Late fourth century	Lord's Prayer and the Beatitudes, The (Gregory of Nyssa)
388 C.E.	Baptismal Instruction (Chrysostom)
397-400 C.E.	Confessions (Augustine)
413-427 C.E.	City of God, The (Augustine)
c. 420-429 C.E.	Conferences (Cassian)
c. 500 C.E.	Mystical Theology (Pseudo-Dionysius)
c. 540 C.E.	Rule of St. Benedict (Benedict of Nursia)
c. 640 C.E.	Ladder of Divine Ascent, The (John Climacus)
Before c. 700 C.E.	"Dream of the Rood, The" (Unknown)
851 C.E.	Treatise on Divine Predestination (Erigena)

Chronological List of Titles

Middle Ages to 1500

c. 1000	Beowulf (Unknown)
1098	Cur Deus Homo (Anselm)
c. 1126-1141	On Loving God (Bernard of Clairvaux)
1148-1151	Four Books of Sentences (Peter Lombard)
1163-1173	Book of Divine Works (Hildegard von Bingen)
1259	Mind's Road to God, The (Bonaventure)
c. 1265-1273	Summa Theologica (Thomas Aquinas)
after 1300	On Divine Love (Duns Scotus)
c. 1300-1327	Sermons and Treatises, The (Eckhart)
c. 1320	Divine Comedy, The (Dante)
c. 1328	Little Flowers of St. Francis, The (Unknown)
c. 1362, c. 1377, c. 1393	Piers Plowman (Langland)
c. 1373	Showings (Julian of Norwich)
Late fourteenth century	Cloud of Unknowing, The (Unknown)
Late fourteenth century	Pearl (Pearl-Poet)
Late fourteenth century	Sir Gawain and the Green Knight (Pearl-Poet)
c. 1377	Dialogue, The (Catherine of Siena)
1377-1378	On the Truth of Holy Scripture (Wyclif)
1386-1390	Confessio Amantis (Gower)
1387-1400	Canterbury Tales, The (Chaucer)
1413	Church, The (Hus)
c. 1427	Imitation of Christ, The (Thomas à Kempis)
1440	Of Learned Ignorance (Nicholas of Cusa)
1498	Prison Meditations on Psalms 51 and 31 (Savonarola)

Sixteenth Century

1508	Everyman (Unknown)
1520	Freedom of a Christian, The (Luther)
1524	On the Freedom of the Will (Erasmus)
1527	Third Spiritual Alphabet, The (Osuna)
1530	Augsburg Confession of Faith, The (Melanchthon)
1530	On Providence (Zwingli)
1536	Institutes of the Christian Religion (Calvin)
1539	"New Birth, The" (Menno Simons)
1548	Spiritual Exercises, The (Ignatius of Loyola)
1549	Book of Common Prayer (Cranmer)
1554	"Confession" (Menno Simons)
1566	Catechism of the Catholic Church (Council of Trent)
1577	Interior Castle (Teresa of Ávila)
1578-1579	Ascent of Mount Carmel (John of the Cross)
c. 1585	Dark Night of the Soul (John of the Cross)
1588	Doctor Faustus (Marlowe)

1590-1609	Faerie Queene, The (Spenser)
c. 1596-1597	Merchant of Venice, The (Shakespeare)
1597	Metaphysical Demonstration of the Existence of God, The (Suárez)

Seventeenth Century

1608	Declaration of the Sentiments of Arminius, A (Arminius)
1623	Way to Christ, The (Böhme)
1624	Devotions upon Emergent Occasions (Donne)
1631	Labyrinth of the World and the Paradise of the Heart, The (Comenius)
1632	Country Parson, The (Herbert)
1633, 1635	"Holy Sonnets" (Donne)
1633	Temple, The (Herbert)
1635	Religio Medici (Browne)
1644	Bloudy Tenent of Persecution for Cause of Conscience, The (Williams, Roger)
1646	"In the Holy Nativity of Our Lord God" (Crashaw)
1649	Great Exemplar, The (Taylor)
1655	"They Are All Gone into the World of Light!" (Vaughan)
1657	Cherubinic Wanderer, The (Silesius)
1666	"Here Follows Some Verses upon the Burning of Our House July 10th, 1666" (Bradstreet)
1667-1674	Paradise Lost (Milton)
1670	Pensées (Pascal)
1671	Paradise Regained (Milton)
1678-1684	Pilgrim's Progress, The (Bunyan)
1694	Journal of George Fox, The (Fox, G.)
1695	Reasonableness of Christianity as Delivered in the Scriptures, The (Locke)

Eighteenth Century

1708	Argument Against Abolishing Christianity (Swift)
1709	Hymns and Spiritual Songs (Watts)
1710	Theodicy (Leibniz)
1726	Fifteen Sermons Preached at the Rolls Chapel (Butler, J.)
1728	Serious Call to a Devout and Holy Life, A (Law)
1746	Treatise Concerning Religious Affections, A (Edwards)
1759	Theory of Moral Sentiments, The (Smith, A.)
1766	Plain Account of Christian Perfection, A (Wesley)
1766	Vicar of Wakefield, The (Goldsmith)
1774	Journal of John Woolman, The (Woolman)
1789-1794	Songs of Innocence and of Experience (Blake)

1790	Marriage of Heaven and Hell, The (Blake)
1790-1833	Faust (Goethe)
1793	Religion Within the Bounds of Mere Reason (Kant)
c. 1793-1800	Early Theological Writings (Hegel)
1794	View of the Evidences of Christianity, A (Paley)
1798	Rime of the Ancient Mariner, The (Coleridge)
1800	Vocation of Man, The (Fichte)

Nineteenth Century

1807	"Ode: Intimations of Immortality" (Wordsworth)
1821-1822	Christian Faith, The (Schleiermacher)
1825	Aids to Reflection (Coleridge)
1830	Book of Mormon (Smith, J.)
1830	Red and the Black, The (Stendhal)
1834	Last Days of Pompeii, The (Bulwer-Lytton)
1835	Lectures on Revivals of Religion (Finney)
1835	Life of Jesus Critically Examined, The (Strauss)
1838	Divinity School Address, The (Emerson)
1841	Essence of Christianity, The (Feuerbach)
1843	"Christmas Carol, A" (Dickens)
1846	Hymns (Whittier)
1847	Purity of Heart Is to Will One Thing (Kierkegaard)
1850	In Memoriam (Tennyson)
1850	Scarlet Letter, The (Hawthorne)
1851-1852	Uncle Tom's Cabin (Stowe)
1855	"Epistle, An" (Browning)
1855	Leaves of Grass (Whitman)
1858	Phantastes (MacDonald)
1858	Scenes of Clerical Life (Eliot, G.)
1863	Life of Jesus, The (Renan)
1864	Apologia pro vita sua (Newman)
1875	Science and Health with Key to the Scriptures (Eddy)
1877	"Windhover, The" (Hopkins)
1879-1880	Brothers Karamazov, The (Dostoevski)
1880	Ben-Hur (Wallace)
1886	Death of Ivan Ilyich, The (Tolstoy)
1891	Rerum Novarum (Leo XIII)
1892	Face of the Deep, The (Rossetti)
1893	Kingdom of God Is Within You, The (Tolstoy)
1896	Quo Vadis (Sienkiewicz)
1897	In His Steps (Sheldon)

1900's

1902	Jefferson Bible, The (Jefferson)
1902	Varieties of Religious Experience, The (James)
1903	Souls of Black Folk, The (Du Bois)
1903	Way of All Flesh, The (Butler, S.)
1904-1905	Protestant Ethic and the Spirit of Capitalism, The (Weber)
1906	Divine and Human (Tolstoy)
1906	Double Search, The (Jones)
1907	Shepherd of the Hills, The (Wright, H. B.)
1908	Mystical Element of Religion, The (Hügel)
1908	Orthodoxy (Chesterton)

1910's

1911	Mysticism (Underhill)
1912	Social Teaching of the Christian Churches, The (Troeltsch)
1913	Problem of Christianity, The (Royce)
1915	Meaning of Prayer, The (Fosdick)
1917	Humani Generis Redemptionem (Benedict XV)
1917	Idea of the Holy, The (Otto)
1917	Theology for the Social Gospel, A (Rauschenbusch)
1919	Epistle to the Romans, The (Barth)

1920's

1920-1922	Kristin Lavransdatter (Undset)
1921	Essays and Addresses on the Philosophy of Religion (Hügel)
1923	Saint Joan (Shaw)
1924	Billy Budd, Foretopman (Melville)
1925	Man Nobody Knows, The (Barton)
1926	Religion in the Making (Whitehead)
1927	Death Comes for the Archbishop (Cather)
1927	Elmer Gantry (Lewis, S.)
1927	"Feet of Jesus" (Hughes)
1927	God's Trombones (Johnson, J. W.)
1927	Unutterable Beauty, The (Studdert Kennedy)
1929	Magnificent Obsession (Douglas)
1929	Man Who Died, The (Lawrence)
1929	Prodigal Girl, The (Hill, Grace Livingston)

1930's

1930	Agape and Eros (Nygren)
1930	Casti Connubii (Pius XI)
1930	War in Heaven (Williams, C.)
1931	Destiny of Man, The (Berdyaev)

1931	Out of My Life and Thought (Schweitzer)
1931	Place of the Lion, The (Williams, C.)
1931	Quadragesimo Anno (Pius XI)
1931	Saint Manuel Bueno, Martyr (Unamuno y Jugo)
1933	"Dialogue of Self and Soul, A" (Yeats)
1935	Last Puritan, The (Santayana)
1936	Bread and Wine (Silone)
1936	Diary of a Country Priest, The (Bernanos)
1936-1943	Four Quartets (Eliot, T. S.)
1937	Divini Redemptoris (Pius XI)
1937	Lord, The (Guardini)
1937	Mit brennender Sorge (Pius XI)
1937	Their Eyes Were Watching God (Hurston)
1938	Philosophy of Existence (Jaspers)
1939	Idea of a Christian Society, The (Eliot, T. S.)

1940's

1940	Power and the Glory, The (Greene)
1941	God and Philosophy (Gilson)
1941	Keys of the Kingdom, The (Cronin)
1941	Mind of the Maker, The (Sayers)
1941	Revelation and Reason (Brunner)
1941	Screwtape Letters, The (Lewis, C. S.)
1941	Woman of the Pharisees, The (Mauriac)
1941-1943	Nature and Destiny of Man, The (Niebuhr)
1942	Robe, The (Douglas)
1943	Christianity and Democracy (Maritain)
1943	"In Distrust of Merits" (Moore, M.)
1944	Drama of Atheist Humanism, The (Lubac)
1944	"Three Versions of Judas" (Borges)
1945	Brideshead Revisited (Waugh)
1945	Friendly Persuasion, The (West, J.)
1946	Great Divorce, The (Lewis, C. S.)
1946	Miracle of the Bells, The (Janney)
1946	Source of Human Good, The (Wieman)
1947	Age of Anxiety, The (Auden)
1947	Bishop's Mantle, The (Turnbull)
1947	Uneasy Conscience of Modern Fundamentalism, The (Henry)
1948	Divine Relativity, The (Hartshorne)
1948	God Was in Christ (Baillie, D. M.)
1948	Seven Storey Mountain, The (Merton)
1949	Ethics, 1949 (Bonhoeffer)
1949	Greatest Story Ever Told, The (Oursler)

1950's

1950	Barabbas (Lagerkvist)
1950	Waiting for God (Weil)
1951	Letters and Papers from Prison (Bonhoeffer)
1951-1956	Chronicles of Narnia, The (Lewis, C. S.)
1952	Courage to Be, The (Tillich)
1952	Mere Christianity (Lewis, C. S.)
1952	Power of Positive Thinking, The (Peale)
1952	Silver Chalice, The (Costain)
1952	Waiting for Godot (Beckett)
1952	Wise Blood (O'Connor)
1953	Go Tell It on the Mountain (Baldwin)
1953	Trip to Bountiful, The (Foote)
1953-1957	Life Is Worth Living (Sheen)
1954	Man for All Seasons, A (Bolt)
1954-1955	Lord of the Rings, The (Tolkien)
1955	Existentialist Theology, An (Macquarrie)
1955	Gift from the Sea (Lindbergh)
1955	Hinds' Feet on High Places (Hurnard)
1955	Last Temptation of Christ, The (Kazantzakis)
1955	Meaning of Persons, The (Tournier)
1955	On Listening to Another (Steere)
1955	"Word made Flesh is seldom, A" (Dickinson)
1956	Nun's Story, The (Hulme)
1956	Philosophy of Existentialism, The (Marcel)
1956	Prison Meditations of Father Alfred Delp (Delp)
1956	Seventh Seal, The (Bergman)
1957	Death in the Family, A (Agee)
1957	Divine Milieu, The (Teilhard de Chardin)
1957	Insight (Lonergan)
1958	Basic Christianity (Stott)
1958	Early Christian Doctrines (Kelly)
1958	J. B. (MacLeish)
1958	Jesus Christ and Mythology (Bultmann)
1959	"Advice to a Prophet" (Wilbur)
1959	Canticle for Leibowitz, A (Miller, W. M.)
1959	Dear and Glorious Physician (Caldwell)

1960's

1960	"For the Union Dead" (Lowell)
1960	To Kill a Mockingbird (Lee, H.)
1960	We Hold These Truths (Murray, J. C.)
1961	Mater et Magistra (John XXIII)

Chronological List of Titles

1961	Pontius Pilate (Caillois)
1962	Letters from the Earth (Twain)
1962	Lilies of the Field, The (Barrett)
1962	Memories, Dreams, Reflections (Jung)
1962	Morte d'Urban (Powers)
1962	Sense of the Presence of God, The (Baillie, J.)
1963	Loaves and Fishes (Day)
1963	Orthodox Church, The (Ware)
1963	Pacem in Terris (John XXIII)
1963	Shoes of the Fisherman, The (West, M.)
1963	Strength to Love (King, M. L.)
1964	Journal of a Soul (John XXIII)
1964	"Letter from Birmingham Jail" (King, M. L.)
1965	Gaudium et Spes (Vatican Council II)
1966	Evil and the God of Love (Hick)
1966	Gospel of Christian Atheism, The (Altizer)
1966	Silence (Endō)
1966-1967	Master and Margarita, The (Bulgakov)
1967	Christy (Marshall)
1967	Come Sweet Death (Napier)
1967	Confessions of Nat Turner, The (Styron)
1967	Populorum Progressio (Paul VI)
1967	Presence of the Word, The (Ong)
1968	Humanae Vitae (Paul VI)
1968	Introduction to Christianity (Ratzinger)
1969	Dream Songs, The (Berryman)
1969	In This House of Brede (Godden)

1970's

1970	Black Theology of Liberation, A (Cone)
1970	Jesus Christ Superstar (Rice, T., and Webber)
1970	Jesus in History (Kee)
1970	Late Great Planet Earth, The (Lindsey)
1971	Hiding Place, The (Ten Boom)
1971	Octogesima Adveniens (Paul VI)
1971	Theology of Liberation, A (Gutiérrez)
1972	Catholics (Moore, Brian)
1972	Crucified God, The (Moltmann)
1972	Politics of Jesus, The (Yoder)
1972	Three Essays (Ritschl)
1972	Two from Galilee (Holmes)
1972	Violence and the Sacred (Girard)
1973	Beyond God the Father (Daly)

1973	Life of Jesus, A (Endō)
1973	Suffering (Sölle)
1974	On Being a Christian (Küng)
1975	Christ in a Pluralistic Age (Cobb)
1975-1990	Singer Trilogy, The (Miller, C.)
1976	Foundations of Christian Faith (Rahner)
1976	Great Mysteries, The (Greeley)
1976	History of Christianity, A (Johnson, P.)
1976	How Should We Then Live? (Schaeffer)
1976	River Runs Through It, A (Maclean)
1976	Song of the Sparrow (Bodo)
1977	Apocalypse (Cardenal)
1977	Thorn Birds, The (McCullough)
1979	Moments of Grace (Jennings)
1979	With Head and Heart (Thurman)
1979-1989	Love Comes Softly Series (Oke)

1980's

1980	Godric (Buechner)
1980	Name of the Rose, The (Eco)
1980	Second Coming, The (Percy)
1980-1988	Theology of the Jewish Christian Reality, A (Van Buren)
1981	Aké (Soyinka)
1981	Midquest (Chappell)
1982	Color Purple, The (Walker)
1982	Prophesy Deliverance! (West, C.)
1982	Religion (Kołakowski)
1983	In Memory of Her (Schüssler Fiorenza)
1984	"Station Island" (Heaney)
1984	Subversion of Christianity, The (Ellul)
1984	Unattainable Earth (Miłosz)
1985	Arrival of the Future, The (Fairchild)
1985	Jesus Through the Centuries (Pelikan)
1985	Lake Wobegon Days (Keillor)
1985	Mary Magdalene (Traylor)
1986	Bible and Theology in African Christianity (Mbiti)
1986	First Coming, The (Sheehan)
1986	Rose (Lee, L.-Y.)
1986	This Present Darkness (Peretti)
1987	Abortion and Divorce in Western Law (Glendon)
1988	After the Lost War (Hudgins)
1988	Coming of the Cosmic Christ, The (Fox, M.)
1988	Ethics After Babel (Stout)

CHRONOLOGICAL LIST OF TITLES

1988	To Scorch or Freeze (Davie)
1989	African Heritage and Contemporary Christianity (Mugambi)
1989	All New People (Lamott)
1989	Prayer for Owen Meany, A (Irving)

1990's

1990	God Who Commands, The (Mouw)
1990	North of Hope (Hassler)
1990	What Are People For? (Berry)
1991	Apocrypha (Pankey)
1991	Burning Fields, The (Middleton)
1991	Centesimus Annus (John Paul II)
1991	Gospel According to Jesus Christ, The (Saramago)
1991	Redeeming Love (Rivers)
1991	Saint Maybe (Tyler)
1991-1993	Song of Albion Trilogy, The (Lawhead)
1992	Beasts of Bethlehem, The (Kennedy)
1992	Care of the Soul (Moore, T.)
1992	Christian Tradition, The (Kitagawa)
1992	Penitent Magdalene, The (Hopes)
1992	She Who Is (Johnson, E. A.)
1992	Virgin Time (Hampl)
1993	History of God, A (Armstrong)
1993	Knowledge and Faith (Stein)
1993	Veritatis Splendor (John Paul II)
1994	Angel of History, The (Forché)
1994	Creation, The (Beasley)
1994	Meeting Jesus Again for the First Time (Borg)
1994	Twilight of Courage, The (Thoene and Thoene)
1994	Wind in the Wheat, The (Arvin)
1995	Dawning of Deliverance, The (Pella)
1995	Evangelium Vitae (John Paul II)
1995	Figuring the Sacred (Ricœur)
1995	Jesus I Never Knew, The (Yancey)
1995	Sapphics and Uncertainties (Steele)
1995	Winter Garden, The (Verweerd)
1995-2007	Left Behind Series (LaHaye and Jenkins)
1996	Bioethics (Meilaender)
1996	Blood Ties (Brouwer)
1996	Book of God, The (Wangerin)
1996	Brightness That Made My Soul Tremble, A (Nesanovich)
1996	Even in Quiet Places (Stafford)
1996	Exclusion and Embrace (Volf)

1996	Good Book, The (Gomes)
1996	Great Wheel, The (Mariani)
1996	In the Beauty of the Lilies (Updike)
1996	Isaiah (Berrigan)
1996	Sparrow, The (Russell)
1997	Belief or Nonbelief? (Eco and Martini)
1997	Black Zodiac (Wright, C.)
1997	Bread for the Journey (Nouwen)
1997	Broken Lance (Sorensen)
1997	No Greater Love (Teresa)
1997	Questions for Ecclesiastes (Jarman)
1997	Secrets of Barneveld Calvary, The (Schaap)
1997	Shunning, The (Lewis, B.)
1997	Stream and the Sapphire, The (Levertov)
1997-2004	Christ Clone Trilogy (BeauSeigneur)
1998	Amazing Grace (Norris)
1998	Capital Offense, A (Parker)
1998	Color of Faith, The (Matsuoka)
1998	Crawl with God, Dance in the Spirit (Park)
1998	Divine Conspiracy, The (Willard)
1998	Eve's Striptease (Kasdorf)
1998	"Fall, The" (Bottum)
1998	Poisonwood Bible, The (Kingsolver)
1998	Seal of Gaia, The (Maddoux)
1998	Triumph of Love, The (Hill, Geoffrey)
1998-2003	Newpointe 911 (Blackstock)
1999	(Ado)ration (Glancy)
1999	Final Witness (Bell)
1999	For the Time Being (Dillard)
1999	New Song, A (Karon)
1999	Out of the Red Shadow (de Graaf)
1999	Resting in the Bosom of the Lamb (Trobaugh)
1999	Traveling Mercies (Lamott)
1999	Truth Teller, The (Hunt)

2000's

2000	Awakening Mercy (Benson)
2000	Death on a Friday Afternoon (Neuhaus)
2000	Edge of Honor (Morris, G.)
2000	Here I Stand (Spong)
2000	Home to Harmony (Gulley)
2000	Learning Human (Murray, L. A.)
2000	List, The (Whitlow)

CHRONOLOGICAL LIST OF TITLES

2000	Memoirs of Pontius Pilate (Mills)
2000	Mercy's Face (Craig)
2000	On Christian Theology (Williams, Rowan)
2000	Passing by Samaria (Foster)
2000	Paul (Wangerin)
2000	Praying God's Word (Moore, Beth)
2000	Transgression (Ingermanson)
2000	Velma Still Cooks in Leeway (Wright, V. H.)
2000	Warranted Christian Belief (Plantinga)
2000	What I Think I Did (Woiwode)
2001	Christ (Miles)
2001	Church Folk (Bowen)
2001	Constantine's Sword (Carroll)
2001	Dangerous Silence, A (Palmer)
2001	Drummer in the Dark (Bunn)
2001	Ezekiel's Shadow (Long)
2001	Holocaust Politics (Roth)
2001	Infidel, The (Musser)
2001	Interrogations at Noon (Gioia)
2001	Life Abundant (McFague)
2001	Long Trail Home, The (Bly)
2001	New Kind of Christian, A (McLaren)
2001	Oxygen (Ingermanson and Olson)
2001	While Mortals Sleep (Cavanaugh)
2001	With the Grain of the Universe (Hauerwas)
2002	Arena (Hancock)
2002	Directed Verdict (Singer)
2002	His Watchful Eye (Cavanaugh)
2002	Philokalia (Cairns)
2002	Place Called Wiregrass, A (Morris, M.)
2002	Purpose Driven Life, The (Warren)
2002	Reconciliation (de Gruchy)
2002	Time Lottery (Moser)
2002	True Honor (Henderson)
2003	Blue Like Jazz (Miller, D.)
2003	Da Vinci Code, The (Brown)
2003	Fire by Night (Austin)
2003	Flabbergasted (Blackston)
2003	Fools and Crows (Witek)
2003	Gospel of Mary of Magdala, The (King, K. L.)
2003	Music to Die For (Nehring)
2003	My God and I (Smedes)
2003	One Tuesday Morning (Kingsbury)

2003	Resurrection of God Incarnate, The (Swinburne)
2003	Songbird (Samson)
2003	Soon (Jenkins)
2003	Sutter's Cross (Cramer)
2003	Thr3e (Dekker)
2003	Walking by Faith (Grimké)
2004	Called to Question (Chittister)
2004	Circle Trilogy, The (Dekker)
2004	Complicated Kindness, A (Toews)
2004	Credo (Coffin)
2004	Gilead (Robinson)
2004	God Has a Dream (Tutu)
2004	Inscribing the Text (Brueggemann)
2004	King's Ransom (Beazely)
2004	Letters to a Young Catholic (Weigel)
2004	Tiger in the Shadows (Wilson)
2004	When Jesus Came to Harvard (Cox)
2004	Wonderful Words of Life (Mouw and Noll)
2005	"Amazing Peace" (Angelou)
2005	Bishop in the Old Neighborhood, The (Greeley)
2005	Christ the Lord (Rice, A.)
2005	Cure for the Common Life (Lucado)
2005	Don't Throw Away Tomorrow (Schuller)
2005	Economy of Grace (Tanner)
2005	Ghost Pain (Lea)
2005	Misquoting Jesus (Ehrman)
2005	Pearl (Gordon)
2005	Soul of Christianity, The (Smith, H.)
2005	Supplicating Voice, The (Johnson, S.)
2005	Unspeakable (Guinness)
2006	And I Alone Have Escaped to Tell You (McInerny)
2006	God's Silence (Wright, F.)
2006	Journey, The (Graham)
2006	Left to Tell (Ilibagiza)
2006	Secrets in the Dark (Buechner)
2006	Simply Christian (Wright, N. T.)
2006	Sinners Welcome (Karr)
2006	Tasks of Philosophy, The (MacIntyre)
2006	Three Hardest Words in the World to Get Right, The (Sweet)
2006	What Jesus Meant (Wills)

CORE ISSUES INDEX

LIST OF CORE ISSUES

Abortion 2009	Courage 2018
Acceptance. 2009	Creation 2018
Africa 2009	The Cross 2018
African Americans. 2009	Daily Living 2019
Agape 2009	Death. 2019
Alienation from God. 2010	The Deity 2020
Amish People 2010	Despair. 2020
Apocalypse. 2010	Devotional Life 2020
Arminianism. 2010	Discipleship 2020
Asceticism 2010	Discipline 2021
Asians or Asian Americans 2010	The Divine. 2021
Atheism 2011	Doubt 2021
Atonement 2011	The Eternal Now. 2022
Attachment and Detachment. 2011	Ethics 2022
Awakening. 2011	Eucharist. 2022
Baptism 2012	Evangelization. 2023
The Beatitudes. 2012	Expectancy. 2023
Beauty 2012	Faith 2023
The Bible. 2012	The Fall 2025
Bishops. 2012	Fasting 2025
Calvinism 2012	Fear 2025
Capitalism 2013	Forgiveness 2025
Catholics and Catholicism. 2013	Freedom and Free Will 2026
Cause Universal 2014	Friendship 2026
Celebration. 2014	Gnosticism. 2027
Charity. 2014	God. 2027
Chastity 2014	Good vs. Evil 2028
Children 2014	Gospels. 2029
Christmas 2014	Grace. 2029
Church 2014	Guidance. 2030
Clerical Life 2015	Guilt 2030
Coming of Age or Teen Life. 2015	Healing. 2030
Communion 2016	Heart. 2031
Communism 2016	Holiness 2031
Compassion 2016	Holy Spirit. 2031
Confession 2016	Homosexuality. 2031
Connectedness 2017	Hope 2031
Conscience. 2017	Humility 2032
Constancy 2017	Illumination 2032
Contemplation 2017	Imperialism 2032
Conversion. 2018	Incarnation. 2032

(continued)

List of Core Issues (continued)

Innocence 2033	Recollection 2046
Jesus Christ 2033	Reconciliation 2046
Judaism 2034	Redemption 2046
Justice 2034	Regeneration 2047
Knowledge 2035	Religion 2047
Latin Americans 2036	Repentance 2047
Life 2036	Resignation 2048
Listening 2036	Responsibility 2048
Loneliness 2036	Revelation 2048
Love 2036	The Sacraments 2048
Lutherans and Lutheranism 2037	Sacrifice 2048
Marriage 2037	Sainthood 2049
Martyrdom 2038	Salvation 2049
Memory 2038	Sanctification 2049
Mennonites 2038	Scriptures 2050
Methodists and Methodism 2038	Self-Abandonment 2050
Monasticism 2038	Self-Control 2050
Morality 2039	Selfishness 2050
Mormons and Mormonism 2039	Self-Knowledge 2050
Mysticism 2039	Service 2051
Myths 2040	Silence 2051
Native Americans 2040	Simplicity 2051
Nature 2040	Sin and Sinners 2051
Nonviolent Resistance 2040	Social Action 2052
Obedience and Disobedience 2040	Solitude 2053
Pastoral Role 2041	Soul 2053
Peace 2041	Spiritual Warfare 2053
Perfection 2041	Stoicism 2053
Persecution 2041	Submission 2053
Pilgrimage 2042	Suffering 2053
Poverty 2042	Surrender 2054
Prayer 2042	Theology 2054
Preaching 2043	Time 2054
Predestination 2043	The Trinity 2054
Priesthood 2043	Trust in God 2055
Problem of Evil 2043	Truth 2055
Protestants and Protestantism 2043	Union with God 2056
Psychology 2044	Virginity 2056
Purgation 2044	Virtue 2056
Puritans and Puritanism 2044	Wisdom 2056
Purity 2044	Women 2056
Quakers 2044	The Word 2057
Racism 2045	Works and Deeds 2057
Reason 2045	

CORE ISSUES INDEX

ABORTION
Abortion and Divorce in Western Law (Glendon), I-23
Bioethics (Meilaender), I-154
Casti Connubii (Pius XI), I-254
How Should We Then Live? (Schaeffer), II-806
Humanae Vitae (Paul VI), II-811

ACCEPTANCE
Age of Anxiety, The (Auden), I-50
All New People (Lamott), I-62
Care of the Soul (Moore, T.), I-251
Christ Clone Trilogy (BeauSeigneur), I-275
Courage to Be, The (Tillich), I-382
Death of Ivan Ilyich, The (Tolstoy), I-431
"Here Follows Some Verses upon the Burning of Our House July 10th, 1666" (Bradstreet), II-768
Long Trail Home, The (Bly), III-1066
Love Comes Softly series (Oke), III-1082
On Divine Love (Duns Scotus), III-1255
Philokalia (Cairns), III-1350
Resting in the Bosom of the Lamb (Trobaugh), III-1502
Sutter's Cross (Cramer), IV-1714
Trip to Bountiful, The (Foote), IV-1816
Truth Teller, The (Hunt), IV-1827

AFRICA
African Heritage and Contemporary Christianity (Mugambi), I-38
Aké (Soyinka), I-58
Bible and Theology in African Christianity (Mbiti), I-147
God Has a Dream (Tutu), II-694
Left to Tell (Ilibagiza), II-1010
Reconciliation (de Gruchy), III-1470

AFRICAN AMERICANS
All New People (Lamott), I-62
"Amazing Peace" (Angelou), I-69
Awakening Mercy (Benson), I-116
Bishop in the Old Neighborhood, The (Greeley), I-157

2009

Black Theology of Liberation, A (Cone), I-165
Church Folk (Bowen), I-316
Color of Faith, The (Matsuoka), I-334
Color Purple, The (Walker), I-338
Confessions of Nat Turner, The (Styron), I-370
"Feet of Jesus" (Hughes), II-614
Fire by Night (Austin), II-629
"For the Union Dead" (Lowell), II-650
Gilead (Robinson), II-683
Go Tell It on the Mountain (Baldwin), II-687
God's Trombones (Johnson, J. W.), II-716
Good Book, The (Gomes), II-720
"Letter from Birmingham Jail" (King, M. L.), II-1014
Lilies of the Field, The (Barrett), III-1050
New Song, A (Karon), III-1215
Passing by Samaria (Foster), III-1323
Place Called Wiregrass, A (Morris, M.), III-1371
Prophesy Deliverance! (West, C.), III-1434
Resting in the Bosom of the Lamb (Trobaugh), III-1502
Secrets of Barneveld Calvary, The (Schaap), III-1574
Songbird (Samson), IV-1651
Souls of Black Folk, The (Du Bois), IV-1668
Strength to Love (King, M. L.), IV-1693
Their Eyes Were Watching God (Hurston), IV-1730
Theology of the Jewish Christian Reality, A (Van Buren), IV-1746
Time Lottery (Moser), IV-1786
To Kill a Mockingbird (Lee, H.), IV-1790
Uncle Tom's Cabin (Stowe), IV-1841
With Head and Heart (Thurman), IV-1961

AGAPE
Agape and Eros (Nygren), I-47
God Has a Dream (Tutu), II-694
Life of Jesus, A (Endō), II-1040
On Divine Love (Duns Scotus), III-1255

On Loving God (Bernard of Clairvaux), III-1268
One Tuesday Morning (Kingsbury), III-1288
Spiritual Exercises, The (Ignatius of Loyola), IV-1680
Uncle Tom's Cabin (Stowe), IV-1841
Waiting for God (Weil), IV-1891

ALIENATION FROM GOD
Age of Anxiety, The (Auden), I-50
All New People (Lamott), I-62
Broken Lance (Sorensen), I-226
Catholics (Moore, Brian), I-261
Christian Faith, The (Schleiermacher), I-288
Come Sweet Death (Napier), I-342
Dear and Glorious Physician (Caldwell), I-420
Death in the Family, A (Agee), I-427
Divine and Human (Tolstoy), I-469
Divini Redemptoris (Pius XI), I-488
Doctor Faustus (Marlowe), I-496
Drama of Atheist Humanism, The (Lubac), I-508
Dream Songs, The (Berryman), I-515
Gospel of Christian Atheism, The (Altizer), II-728
How Should We Then Live? (Schaeffer), II-806
In the Beauty of the Lilies (Updike), II-855
J. B. (MacLeish), II-902
Letters and Papers from Prison (Bonhoeffer), II-1018
Long Trail Home, The (Bly), III-1066
Mit brennender Sorge (Pius XI), III-1172
New Song, A (Karon), III-1215
Passing by Samaria (Foster), III-1323
Power and the Glory, The (Greene), III-1401
Red and the Black, The (Stendhal), III-1474
Silence (Endō), IV-1616
Unutterable Beauty, The (Studdert Kennedy), IV-1853
Waiting for Godot (Beckett), IV-1897

AMISH PEOPLE
"Confession" (Menno Simons), I-361
"New Birth, The" (Menno Simons), I-361
Shunning, The (Lewis, B.), IV-1612

APOCALYPSE
Apocalypse (Cardenal), I-80
Book of Revelation (John), I-202
Canticle for Leibowitz, A (Miller, W. M.), I-245
Christ Clone Trilogy (BeauSeigneur), I-275
Circle Trilogy, The (Dekker), I-320
"For the Union Dead" (Lowell), II-650
Left Behind series (LaHaye and Jenkins), II-1005
Seal of Gaia, The (Maddoux), III-1564
Soon (Jenkins), IV-1660
This Present Darkness (Peretti), IV-1760

ARMINIANISM
Declaration of the Sentiments of Arminius, A (Arminius), I-439

ASCETICISM
Called to Question (Chittister), I-237
Conferences (Cassian), I-354
Divine Milieu, The (Teilhard de Chardin), I-480
Ladder of Divine Ascent, The (John Climacus), II-968
Last Days of Pompeii, The (Bulwer-Lytton), II-977
Lord's Prayer and the Beatitudes, The (Gregory of Nyssa), III-1078
Mystical Element of Religion, The (Hügel), III-1191
Sermons and Treatises, The (Eckhart), IV-1586

ASIANS OR ASIAN AMERICANS
Christian Tradition, The (Kitagawa), I-292
Crawl with God, Dance in the Spirit (Park), I-386
Life of Jesus, A (Endō), II-1040
Silence (Endō), IV-1616

Core Issues Index

ATHEISM
Confessions of Nat Turner, The (Styron), I-370
Divini Redemptoris (Pius XI), I-488
Drama of Atheist Humanism, The (Lubac), I-508
Gospel of Christian Atheism, The (Altizer), II-728
In the Beauty of the Lilies (Updike), II-855
Master and Margarita, The (Bulgakov), III-1110
Transgression (Ingermanson), IV-1798

ATONEMENT
Book of Mormon (Smith, J.), I-196
Crucified God, The (Moltmann), I-397
Cur Deus Homo (Anselm), I-401
Death on a Friday Afternoon (Neuhaus), I-435
Divine and Human (Tolstoy), I-469
Everyman (Unknown), II-574
Four Quartets (Eliot, T. S.), II-660
God Was in Christ (Baillie, D. M.), II-698
"Holy Sonnets" (Donne), II-799
On the Incarnation of the Word of God (Athanasius of Alexandria), III-1280
Resurrection of God Incarnate, The (Swinburne), III-1506
Rime of the Ancient Mariner, The (Coleridge), III-1514
Saint Maybe (Tyler), III-1541
Science and Health with Key to the Scriptures (Eddy), III-1557
Shepherd of the Hills, The (Wright, H. B.), IV-1602
"Station Island" (Heaney), IV-1685
Wise Blood (O'Connor), IV-1957

ATTACHMENT AND DETACHMENT
Burning Fields, The (Middleton), I-233
Come Sweet Death (Napier), I-342
Divine Milieu, The (Teilhard de Chardin), I-480
"Here Follows Some Verses upon the Burning of Our House July 10th, 1666" (Bradstreet), II-768
In This House of Brede (Godden), II-863
Ladder of Divine Ascent, The (John Climacus), II-968
Nun's Story, The (Hulme), III-1234
Phantastes (MacDonald), III-1346
Philokalia (Cairns), III-1350
Sermons and Treatises, The (Eckhart), IV-1586
Traveling Mercies (Lamott), IV-1802
True Honor (Henderson), IV-1823
Waiting for Godot (Beckett), IV-1897

AWAKENING
All New People (Lamott), I-62
Ben-Hur (Wallace), I-136
Christy (Marshall), I-303
Crawl with God, Dance in the Spirit (Park), I-386
Divine and Human (Tolstoy), I-469
Divine Milieu, The (Teilhard de Chardin), I-480
Ghost Pain (Lea), II-676
Here I Stand (Spong), II-772
Labyrinth of the World and the Paradise of the Heart, The (Comenius), II-964
Lectures on Revivals of Religion (Finney), II-1001
Long Trail Home, The (Bly), III-1066
Magnificent Obsession (Douglas), III-1087
Man Who Died, The (Lawrence), III-1098
Midquest (Chappell), III-1151
Miracle of the Bells, The (Janney), III-1164
Mysticism (Underhill), III-1200
New Song, A (Karon), III-1215
One Tuesday Morning (Kingsbury), III-1288
Place Called Wiregrass, A (Morris, M.), III-1371
Plain Account of Christian Perfection, A (Wesley), III-1378
Singer Trilogy, The (Miller, C.), IV-1627
Soon (Jenkins), IV-1660

Time Lottery (Moser), IV-1786
Treatise Concerning Religious Affections, A (Edwards), IV-1806

BAPTISM
Baptismal Instruction (Chrysostom), I-120
Book of Common Prayer (Cranmer), I-184
Book of Mormon (Smith, J.), I-196
"Confession" (Menno Simons), I-361
Country Parson, The (Herbert), I-378
Greatest Story Ever Told, The (Oursler), II-752
"New Birth, The" (Menno Simons), I-361
On Providence (Zwingli), III-1272
Waiting for God (Weil), IV-1891

THE BEATITUDES
Divine and Human (Tolstoy), I-469
Divine Conspiracy, The (Willard), I-477
Hiding Place, The (Ten Boom), II-775
Life of Jesus, A (Endō), II-1040
Loaves and Fishes (Day), III-1062
Lord's Prayer and the Beatitudes, The (Gregory of Nyssa), III-1078
Sapphics and Uncertainties (Steele), III-1545

BEAUTY
"Advice to a Prophet" (Wilbur), I-35
Brideshead Revisited (Waugh), I-218
Divinity School Address, The (Emerson), I-491
Fools and Crows (Witek), II-644
For the Time Being (Dillard), II-647
Interrogations at Noon (Gioia), II-891
Learning Human (Murray, L. A.), II-993
Letters to a Young Catholic (Weigel), II-1029
Midquest (Chappell), III-1151
"Ode: Intimations of Immortality" (Wordsworth), III-1241
River Runs Through It, A (Maclean), III-1518
Rose (Lee, L.-Y.), III-1525

Sapphics and Uncertainties (Steele), III-1545
Simply Christian (Wright, N. T.), IV-1624
Unattainable Earth (Miłosz), IV-1837
"Windhover, The" (Hopkins), IV-1949

THE BIBLE
Acts of the Apostles (Unknown), I-27
Bible in History, The, I-10
Book of Revelation (John), I-202
Books of the Prophets (Isaiah, Jeremiah, Amos, and Micah), I-206
Fools and Crows (Witek), II-644
Gospel of John (John, son of Zebedee), II-731
Hebrew Bible (Unknown), II-756
Letters of Saint Jerome, The (Jerome), II-1024
Lord's Prayer and the Beatitudes, The (Gregory of Nyssa), III-1078
Misquoting Jesus (Ehrman), III-1168
On First Principles (Origen), III-1259
Psalms (David), III-1442

BISHOPS
Death Comes for the Archbishop (Cather), I-423
Humani Generis Redemptionem (Benedict XV), II-815
Journal of a Soul (John XXIII), II-928
Orthodox Church, The (Ware), III-1291

CALVINISM
Declaration of the Sentiments of Arminius, A (Arminius), I-439
Gilead (Robinson), II-683
God Who Commands, The (Mouw), II-704
Gospel According to Jesus Christ, The (Saramago), II-724
Institutes of the Christian Religion (Calvin), II-877
My God and I (Smedes), III-1188
Protestant Ethic and the Spirit of Capitalism, The (Weber), III-1438
Three Essays (Ritschl), IV-1772

CAPITALISM

Apocalypse (Cardenal), I-80
Centesimus Annus (John Paul II), I-265
Economy of Grace (Tanner), II-531
Idea of a Christian Society, The (Eliot, T. S.), II-826
Life Abundant (McFague), II-1033
Loaves and Fishes (Day), III-1062
Man Nobody Knows, The (Barton), III-1094
Mater et Magistra (John XXIII), III-1114
Octogesima Adveniens (Paul VI), III-1238
Orthodoxy (Chesterton), III-1295
Populorum Progressio (Paul VI), III-1397
Prophesy Deliverance! (West, C.), III-1434
Protestant Ethic and the Spirit of Capitalism, The (Weber), III-1438
Quadragesimo Anno (Pius XI), III-1455
Theology for the Social Gospel, A (Rauschenbusch), IV-1738
What Are People For? (Berry), IV-1927

CATHOLICS AND CATHOLICISM

Against Heresies (Irenaeus), I-44
Agape and Eros (Nygren), I-47
And I Alone Have Escaped to Tell You (McInerny), I-73
Apocrypha (Pankey), I-84
Apologia pro vita sua (Newman), I-88
Apology (Tertullian), I-92
Belief or Nonbelief? (Eco and Martini), I-133
Bishop in the Old Neighborhood, The (Greeley), I-157
Book of Divine Works (Hildegard von Bingen), I-188
Bread and Wine (Silone), I-211
Called to Question (Chittister), I-237
Canticle for Leibowitz, A (Miller, W. M.), I-245
Casti Connubii (Pius XI), I-254
Catechism of the Catholic Church (Council of Trent), I-257
Catholics (Moore, Brian), I-261
Christ the Lord (Rice, A.), I-284
Christianity and Democracy (Maritain), I-296
Church, The (Hus), I-312
Constantine's Sword (Carroll), I-374
Da Vinci Code, The (Brown), I-408
Death Comes for the Archbishop (Cather), I-423
Diary of a Country Priest, The (Bernanos), I-462
Divine Comedy, The (Dante), I-473
Divini Redemptoris (Pius XI), I-488
Essays and Addresses on the Philosophy of Religion (Hügel), II-553
Four Books of Sentences (Peter Lombard), II-657
Gaudium et Spes (Vatican Council II), II-672
Great Mysteries, The (Greeley), II-746
History of Christianity, A (Johnson, P.), II-787
Humanae Vitae (Paul VI), II-811
In This House of Brede (Godden), II-863
Introduction to Christianity (Ratzinger), II-895
Journal of a Soul (John XXIII), II-928
Keys of the Kingdom, The (Cronin), II-945
Letters to a Young Catholic (Weigel), II-1029
Loaves and Fishes (Day), III-1062
Mit brennender Sorge (Pius XI), III-1172
Morte d'Urban (Powers), III-1180
No Greater Love (Teresa, Mother), III-1227
Pacem in Terris (John XXIII), III-1311
Power and the Glory, The (Greene), III-1401
Prison Meditations of Father Alfred Delp (Delp), III-1419
Protestant Ethic and the Spirit of Capitalism, The (Weber), III-1438
Saint Joan (Shaw), III-1533
Shoes of the Fisherman, The (West, M.), IV-1605

Silence (Endō), IV-1616
Song of the Sparrow (Bodo), IV-1648
Sparrow, The (Russell), IV-1676
Spiritual Exercises, The (Ignatius of Loyola), IV-1680
Stream and the Sapphire, The (Levertov), IV-1689
Thorn Birds, The (McCullough), IV-1764
Unattainable Earth (Miłosz), IV-1837
Virgin Time (Hampl), IV-1883
Wonderful Words of Life (Mouw and Noll), IV-1972

CAUSE UNIVERSAL
Mystical Theology (Pseudo-Dionysius), III-1197
Orthodox Church, The (Ware), III-1291
Pacem in Terris (John XXIII), III-1311
Singer Trilogy, The (Miller, C.), IV-1627

CELEBRATION
Hymns (Whittier), II-818
Hymns and Spiritual Songs (Watts), II-822
"In the Holy Nativity of Our Lord God" (Crashaw), II-859
Leaves of Grass (Whitman), II-997
"Word made Flesh is seldom, A" (Dickinson), IV-1976

CHARITY
Economy of Grace (Tanner), II-531
Fire by Night (Austin), II-629
Gaudium et Spes (Vatican Council II), II-672
Magnificent Obsession (Douglas), III-1087
Mater et Magistra (John XXIII), III-1114
Miracle of the Bells, The (Janney), III-1164
Mystical Element of Religion, The (Hügel), III-1191
Populorum Progressio (Paul VI), III-1397
Religio Medici (Browne), III-1482
Supplicating Voice, The (Johnson, S.), IV-1710

CHASTITY
Casti Connubii (Pius XI), I-254
Church Folk (Bowen), I-316
Faerie Queene, The (Spenser), II-601
Humanae Vitae (Paul VI), II-811
Last Temptation of Christ, The (Kazantzakis), II-985
Life of Jesus, The (Renan), III-1043
Woman of the Pharisees, The (Mauriac), IV-1968

CHILDREN
"Ode: Intimations of Immortality" (Wordsworth), III-1241
Out of the Red Shadow (de Graaf), III-1303
Pearl (Pearl-Poet), III-1335
Traveling Mercies (Lamott), IV-1802
Truth Teller, The (Hunt), IV-1827
While Mortals Sleep (Cavanaugh), IV-1941

CHRISTMAS
"Amazing Peace" (Angelou), I-69
Beasts of Bethlehem, The (Kennedy), I-130
"Christmas Carol, A" (Dickens), I-299
"In the Holy Nativity of Our Lord God" (Crashaw), II-859
Secrets in the Dark (Buechner), III-1571

CHURCH
Acts of the Apostles (Unknown), I-27
Against Heresies (Irenaeus), I-44
Amazing Grace (Norris), I-65
Argument Against Abolishing Christianity (Swift), I-99
Beyond God the Father (Daly), I-144
Bishop in the Old Neighborhood, The (Greeley), I-157
Bloudy Tenent of Persecution for Cause of Conscience, The (Williams, Roger), I-176
Called to Question (Chittister), I-237
Church, The (Hus), I-312
Church Folk (Bowen), I-316

City of God, The (Augustine), I-325
Da Vinci Code, The (Brown), I-408
Divine Milieu, The (Teilhard de Chardin), I-480
Early Theological Writings (Hegel), II-527
"Feet of Jesus" (Hughes), II-614
First Coming, The (Sheehan), II-636
Gaudium et Spes (Vatican Council II), II-672
Great Mysteries, The (Greeley), II-746
History of Christianity, A (Johnson, P.), II-787
Home to Harmony (Gulley), II-802
In Memory of Her (Schüssler Fiorenza), II-851
Introduction to Christianity (Ratzinger), II-895
Jesus in History (Kee), II-921
Lake Wobegon Days (Keillor), II-973
Letters and Papers from Prison (Bonhoeffer), II-1018
New Kind of Christian, A (McLaren), III-1211
No Greater Love (Teresa, Mother), III-1227
On Christian Theology (Williams, Rowan), III-1252
On the Truth of Holy Scripture (Wyclif), III-1284
Orthodox Church, The (Ware), III-1291
Problem of Christianity, The (Royce), III-1426
Purpose Driven Life, The (Warren), III-1452
Quadragesimo Anno (Pius XI), III-1455
Religion Within the Bounds of Mere Reason (Kant), III-1494
Rerum Novarum (Leo XIII), III-1498
Secrets in the Dark (Buechner), III-1571
Simply Christian (Wright, N. T.), IV-1624
Social Teaching of the Christian Churches, The (Troeltsch), IV-1639
Soul of Christianity, The (Smith, H.), IV-1664
Subversion of Christianity, The (Ellul), IV-1698

Temple, The (Herbert), IV-1726
Theology for the Social Gospel, A (Rauschenbusch), IV-1738
Uncle Tom's Cabin (Stowe), IV-1841
Waiting for God (Weil), IV-1891

CLERICAL LIFE
Bishop's Mantle, The (Turnbull), I-161
Book of Divine Works (Hildegard von Bingen), I-188
Called to Question (Chittister), I-237
Canterbury Tales, The (Chaucer), I-240
Catholics (Moore, Brian), I-261
Church Folk (Bowen), I-316
Death Comes for the Archbishop (Cather), I-423
Elmer Gantry (Lewis, S.), II-538
Home to Harmony (Gulley), II-802
Imitation of Christ, The (Thomas à Kempis), II-834
In the Beauty of the Lilies (Updike), II-855
Journal of a Soul (John XXIII), II-928
Journal of John Woolman, The (Woolman), II-936
Keys of the Kingdom, The (Cronin), II-945
Morte d'Urban (Powers), III-1180
Name of the Rose, The (Eco), III-1204
No Greater Love (Teresa, Mother), III-1227
Nun's Story, The (Hulme), III-1234
Scenes of Clerical Life (Eliot, G.), III-1553
Shoes of the Fisherman, The (West, M.), IV-1605
Sparrow, The (Russell), IV-1676
Vicar of Wakefield, The (Goldsmith), IV-1870
Way of All Flesh, The (Butler, S.), IV-1913
With Head and Heart (Thurman), IV-1961

COMING OF AGE OR TEEN LIFE
Complicated Kindness, A (Toews), I-350
Go Tell It on the Mountain (Baldwin), II-687

His Watchful Eye (Cavanaugh), II-783
In the Beauty of the Lilies (Updike),
    II-855
Kristin Lavransdatter (Undset), II-960
Prodigal Girl, The (Hill, Grace
    Livingston), III-1430
Shunning, The (Lewis, B.), IV-1612
Sinners Welcome (Karr), IV-1631
Their Eyes Were Watching God
    (Hurston), IV-1730
To Kill a Mockingbird (Lee, H.),
    IV-1790
Way of All Flesh, The (Butler, S.),
    IV-1913

COMMUNION
"Confession" (Menno Simons), I-361
Country Parson, The (Herbert), I-378
Divine Milieu, The (Teilhard de Chardin),
    I-480
Imitation of Christ, The (Thomas à
    Kempis), II-834
Interrogations at Noon (Gioia), II-891
"New Birth, The" (Menno Simons),
    I-361
Saint Maybe (Tyler), III-1541
Walking by Faith (Grimké), IV-1901

COMMUNISM
Bread and Wine (Silone), I-211
Divini Redemptoris (Pius XI), I-488
Life Is Worth Living (Sheen), II-1037
Out of the Red Shadow (de Graaf),
    III-1303
Quadragesimo Anno (Pius XI), III-1455
Tiger in the Shadows (Wilson), IV-1782
We Hold These Truths (Murray, J. C.),
    IV-1923

COMPASSION
Age of Anxiety, The (Auden), I-50
Apocalypse (Cardenal), I-80
Bread for the Journey (Nouwen), I-215
"Christmas Carol, A" (Dickens), I-299
Christy (Marshall), I-303
Color Purple, The (Walker), I-338

Dear and Glorious Physician (Caldwell),
    I-420
Edge of Honor (Morris, G.), II-534
Fifteen Sermons Preached at the Rolls
    Chapel (Butler, J.), II-618
Fire by Night (Austin), II-629
God's Silence (Wright, F.), II-712
History of God, A (Armstrong), II-791
Keys of the Kingdom, The (Cronin),
    II-945
King's Ransom (Beazely and Lemmons),
    II-952
Life of Jesus, A (Endō), II-1040
Meeting Jesus Again for the First Time
    (Borg), III-1125
One Tuesday Morning (Kingsbury),
    III-1288
River Runs Through It, A (Maclean),
    III-1518
Their Eyes Were Watching God
    (Hurston), IV-1730
Theory of Moral Sentiments (Smith, A.),
    IV-1749
To Kill a Mockingbird (Lee, H.), IV-1790
Trip to Bountiful, The (Foote), IV-1816
Twilight of Courage, The (Thoene and
    Thoene), IV-1830
Unutterable Beauty, The (Studdert
    Kennedy), IV-1853
Velma Still Cooks in Leeway (Wright,
    V. H.), IV-1862

CONFESSION
All New People (Lamott), I-62
Bishop in the Old Neighborhood, The
    (Greeley), I-157
Canterbury Tales, The (Chaucer), I-240
Confessio Amantis (Gower), I-357
Confessions (Augustine), I-365
Everyman (Unknown), II-574
Meaning of Persons, The (Tournier),
    III-1118
Purity of Heart Is to Will One Thing
    (Kierkegaard), III-1446
Reconciliation (de Gruchy), III-1470
"Station Island" (Heaney), IV-1685

CONNECTEDNESS
"Advice to a Prophet" (Wilbur), I-35
"Amazing Peace" (Angelou), I-69
Bishop's Mantle, The (Turnbull), I-161
Blue Like Jazz (Miller, D.), I-180
Broken Lance (Sorensen), I-226
Burning Fields, The (Middleton), I-233
Color Purple, The (Walker), I-338
Devotions upon Emergent Occasions (Donne), I-447
Double Search, The (Jones), I-503
Gaudium et Spes (Vatican Council II), II-672
God Has a Dream (Tutu), II-694
Here I Stand (Spong), II-772
History of God, A (Armstrong), II-791
Holocaust Politics (Roth), II-795
Learning Human (Murray, L. A.), II-993
"Letter from Birmingham Jail" (King, M. L.), II-1014
New Song, A (Karon), III-1215
No Greater Love (Teresa, Mother), III-1227
Passing by Samaria (Foster), III-1323
Populorum Progressio (Paul VI), III-1397
Soon (Jenkins), IV-1660
Soul of Christianity, The (Smith, H.), IV-1664
Strength to Love (King, M. L.), IV-1693
What Are People For? (Berry), IV-1927

CONSCIENCE
Apocalypse (Cardenal), I-80
Bloudy Tenent of Persecution for Cause of Conscience, The (Williams, Roger), I-176
Catholics (Moore, Brian), I-261
Existentialist Theology, An (Macquarrie), II-590
Here I Stand (Spong), II-772
Hiding Place, The (Ten Boom), II-775
Holocaust Politics (Roth), II-795
In His Steps (Sheldon), II-843
Isaiah (Berrigan), II-898
King's Ransom (Beazely and Lemmons), II-952

Lilies of the Field, The (Barrett), III-1050
Man for All Seasons, A (Bolt), III-1090
Out of My Life and Thought (Schweitzer), III-1299
Religion Within the Bounds of Mere Reason (Kant), III-1494
Sparrow, The (Russell), IV-1676
Veritatis Splendor (John Paul II), IV-1866
Vocation of Man, The (Fichte), IV-1887
Wind in the Wheat, The (Arvin), IV-1945

CONSTANCY
Book of Revelation (John), I-202
"Holy Sonnets" (Donne), II-799
Problem of Christianity, The (Royce), III-1426
True Honor (Henderson), IV-1823
Twilight of Courage, The (Thoene and Thoene), IV-1830

CONTEMPLATION
Cloud of Unknowing, The (Unknown), I-329
Conferences (Cassian), I-354
Confessio Amantis (Gower), I-357
Diary of a Country Priest, The (Bernanos), I-462
"Dream of the Rood, The" (Unknown), I-512
Face of the Deep, The (Rossetti), II-597
Gift from the Sea (Lindbergh), II-680
Great Wheel, The (Mariani), II-749
Interior Castle (Teresa of Ávila), II-887
Isaiah (Berrigan), II-898
Lord's Prayer and the Beatitudes, The (Gregory of Nyssa), III-1078
Mind's Road to God, The (Bonaventure), III-1159
Mysticism (Underhill), III-1200
Penitent Magdalene, The (Hopes), III-1339
Philosophy of Existence (Jaspers), III-1354
Religion in the Making (Whitehead), III-1490
Spiritual Exercises, The (Ignatius of Loyola), IV-1680

Time Lottery (Moser), IV-1786
Virgin Time (Hampl), IV-1883

CONVERSION
Amazing Grace (Norris), I-65
Apologia pro vita sua (Newman), I-88
Arena (Hancock), I-96
Brideshead Revisited (Waugh), I-218
"Confession" (Menno Simons), I-361
Confessions (Augustine), I-365
Dawning of Deliverance, The (Pella), I-416
Divine and Human (Tolstoy), I-469
Ezekiel's Shadow (Long), II-594
Flabbergasted (Blackston), II-640
Great Divorce, The (Lewis, C. S.), II-739
In This House of Brede (Godden), II-863
Infidel, The (Musser), II-866
Institutes of the Christian Religion (Calvin), II-877
Keys of the Kingdom, The (Cronin), II-945
Last Days of Pompeii, The (Bulwer-Lytton), II-977
Lectures on Revivals of Religion (Finney), II-1001
List, The (Whitlow), III-1054
Magnificent Obsession (Douglas), III-1087
Merchant of Venice, The (Shakespeare), III-1135
Mysticism (Underhill), III-1200
"New Birth, The" (Menno Simons), I-361
Pensées (Pascal), III-1342
Plain Account of Christian Perfection, A (Wesley), III-1378
Prayer for Owen Meany, A (Irving), III-1408
Quo Vadis (Sienkiewicz), III-1462
Robe, The (Douglas), III-1522
Screwtape Letters, The (Lewis, C. S.), III-1560
Seal of Gaia, The (Maddoux), III-1564
Seven Storey Mountain, The (Merton), IV-1591
Soon (Jenkins), IV-1660
Traveling Mercies (Lamott), IV-1802
Waiting for God (Weil), IV-1891
Way to Christ, The (Böhme), IV-1917

COURAGE
His Watchful Eye (Cavanaugh), II-783
Twilight of Courage, The (Thoene and Thoene), IV-1830
Two from Galilee (Holmes), IV-1834

CREATION
Book of Divine Works (Hildegard von Bingen), I-188
Christian Faith, The (Schleiermacher), I-288
Come Sweet Death (Napier), I-342
Creation, The (Beasley), I-390
Destiny of Man, The (Berdyaev), I-443
Four Books of Sentences (Peter Lombard), II-657
God and Philosophy (Gilson), II-691
God's Trombones (Johnson, J. W.), II-716
Hebrew Bible (Unknown), II-756
Mind of the Maker, The (Sayers), III-1155
On First Principles (Origen), III-1259
Sapphics and Uncertainties (Steele), III-1545
Showings (Julian of Norwich), IV-1609
Summa Theologica (Thomas Aquinas), IV-1706

THE CROSS
Basic Christianity (Stott), I-127
Ben-Hur (Wallace), I-136
Crucified God, The (Moltmann), I-397
Death on a Friday Afternoon (Neuhaus), I-435
"Dream of the Rood, The" (Unknown), I-512
Gospel of John (John, son of Zebedee), II-731
Greatest Story Ever Told, The (Oursler), II-752
Last Temptation of Christ, The (Kazantzakis), II-985

Memoirs of Pontius Pilate (Mills), III-1128
New Testament Letters (Paul), III-1219
Paul (Wangerin), III-1327
Synoptic Gospels (Matthew, Mark, and Luke), IV-1717
Unutterable Beauty, The (Studdert Kennedy), IV-1853

DAILY LIVING
Apology (Tertullian), I-92
Arrival of the Future, The (Fairchild), I-103
Bread for the Journey (Nouwen), I-215
Cure for the Common Life (Lucado), I-405
Diary of a Country Priest, The (Bernanos), I-462
Divine Conspiracy, The (Willard), I-477
Gift from the Sea (Lindbergh), II-680
Good Book, The (Gomes), II-720
Great Wheel, The (Mariani), II-749
Home to Harmony (Gulley), II-802
In His Steps (Sheldon), II-843
Journey, The (Graham), II-941
Lake Wobegon Days (Keillor), II-973
Learning Human (Murray, L. A.), II-993
Love Comes Softly series (Oke), III-1082
Meaning of Prayer, The (Fosdick), III-1121
On Being a Christian (Küng), III-1249
Power of Positive Thinking, The (Peale), III-1405
Praying God's Word (Moore, Beth), III-1412
Purpose Driven Life, The (Warren), III-1452
Rule of St. Benedict (Benedict of Nursia), III-1529
Screwtape Letters, The (Lewis, C. S.), III-1560
Serious Call to a Devout and Holy Life, A (Law), IV-1581
Spiritual Exercises, The (Ignatius of Loyola), IV-1680

Stream and the Sapphire, The (Levertov), IV-1689
Thr3e (Dekker), IV-1768
To Scorch or Freeze (Davie), IV-1794
When Jesus Came to Harvard (Cox), IV-1937

DEATH
"Advice to a Prophet" (Wilbur), I-35
After the Lost War (Hudgins), I-41
Beowulf (Unknown), I-140
Brideshead Revisited (Waugh), I-218
Cherubinic Wanderer, The (Silesius), I-268
Courage to Be, The (Tillich), I-382
Dangerous Silence, A (Palmer), I-412
Death in the Family, A (Agee), I-427
Death of Ivan Ilyich, The (Tolstoy), I-431
Death on a Friday Afternoon (Neuhaus), I-435
Devotions upon Emergent Occasions (Donne), I-447
Dream Songs, The (Berryman), I-515
Everyman (Unknown), II-574
"Fall, The" (Bottum), II-606
First and Second Apologies, The (Justin Martyr), II-633
For the Time Being (Dillard), II-647
Friendly Persuasion, The (West, J.), II-669
God's Trombones (Johnson, J. W.), II-716
Great Divorce, The (Lewis, C. S.), II-739
"Holy Sonnets" (Donne), II-799
"In Distrust of Merits" (Moore, M.), II-839
In Memoriam (Tennyson), II-847
Last Temptation of Christ, The (Kazantzakis), II-985
Leaves of Grass (Whitman), II-997
Moments of Grace (Jennings), III-1176
One Tuesday Morning (Kingsbury), III-1288
Pearl (Pearl-Poet), III-1335
Phantastes (MacDonald), III-1346
Prison Meditations of Father Alfred Delp (Delp), III-1419

Resurrection of God Incarnate, The (Swinburne), III-1506
Rose (Lee, L.-Y.), III-1525
Saint Manuel Bueno, Martyr (Unamuno y Jugo), III-1537
Second Coming, The (Percy), III-1568
Seventh Seal, The (Bergman), IV-1595
Supplicating Voice, The (Johnson, S.), IV-1710
"They Are All Gone into the World of Light!" (Vaughan), IV-1753

THE DEITY
Christ (Miles), I-272
Divine Relativity, The (Hartshorne), I-485
Epistle to the Romans, The (Barth), II-549
Idea of the Holy, The (Otto), II-830
"In the Holy Nativity of Our Lord God" (Crashaw), II-859
Metaphysical Demonstration of the Existence of God, The (Suárez), III-1147
On First Principles (Origen), III-1259
Religion (Kołakowski), III-1486
"Three Versions of Judas" (Borges), IV-1779

DESPAIR
Age of Anxiety, The (Auden), I-50
Angel of History, The (Forché), I-77
Capital Offense, A (Parker), I-248
Courage to Be, The (Tillich), I-382
Dear and Glorious Physician (Caldwell), I-420
Dream Songs, The (Berryman), I-515
Existentialist Theology, An (Macquarrie), II-590
Faust (Goethe), II-610
God's Silence (Wright, F.), II-712
How Should We Then Live? (Schaeffer), II-806
J. B. (MacLeish), II-902
Place Called Wiregrass, A (Morris, M.), III-1371
Prison Meditations on Psalms 51 and 31 (Savonarola), III-1423
Rime of the Ancient Mariner, The (Coleridge), III-1514
Suffering (Sölle), IV-1702
Waiting for Godot (Beckett), IV-1897

DEVOTIONAL LIFE
Bishop's Mantle, The (Turnbull), I-161
Bread for the Journey (Nouwen), I-215
Canticle for Leibowitz, A (Miller, W. M.), I-245
Christian Faith, The (Schleiermacher), I-288
First and Second Apologies, The (Justin Martyr), II-633
Imitation of Christ, The (Thomas à Kempis), II-834
Interior Castle (Teresa of Ávila), II-887
Lord's Prayer and the Beatitudes, The (Gregory of Nyssa), III-1078
Mercy's Face (Craig), III-1139
Mystical Element of Religion, The (Hügel), III-1191
Orthodox Church, The (Ware), III-1291
Out of My Life and Thought (Schweitzer), III-1299
Psalms (David), III-1442
Serious Call to a Devout and Holy Life, A (Law), IV-1581
Spiritual Exercises, The (Ignatius of Loyola), IV-1680

DISCIPLESHIP
Acts of the Apostles (Unknown), I-27
Blue Like Jazz (Miller, D.), I-180
Bread for the Journey (Nouwen), I-215
Divine Conspiracy, The (Willard), I-477
Fifteen Sermons Preached at the Rolls Chapel (Butler, J.), II-618
In His Steps (Sheldon), II-843
In Memory of Her (Schüssler Fiorenza), II-851
Journey, The (Graham), II-941
Life Abundant (McFague), II-1033
Loaves and Fishes (Day), III-1062
New Kind of Christian, A (McLaren), III-1211

Purpose Driven Life, The (Warren), III-1452
Robe, The (Douglas), III-1522
Synoptic Gospels (Matthew, Mark, and Luke), IV-1717
Three Hardest Words in the World to Get Right, The (Sweet), IV-1776

DISCIPLINE
Four Quartets (Eliot, T. S.), II-660
Nun's Story, The (Hulme), III-1234
Prodigal Girl, The (Hill, Grace Livingston), III-1430
Serious Call to a Devout and Holy Life, A (Law), IV-1581
Spiritual Exercises, The (Ignatius of Loyola), IV-1680

THE DIVINE
Barabbas (Lagerkvist), I-123
Black Theology of Liberation, A (Cone), I-165
Black Zodiac (Wright, C.), I-169
Christian Tradition, The (Kitagawa), I-292
Divine Comedy, The (Dante), I-473
Divine Milieu, The (Teilhard de Chardin), I-480
Divinity School Address, The (Emerson), I-491
Epistle to the Romans, The (Barth), II-549
For the Time Being (Dillard), II-647
Idea of the Holy, The (Otto), II-830
Jesus Christ Superstar (Rice, T., and Webber), II-913
Journal of George Fox, The (Fox, G.), II-931
Leaves of Grass (Whitman), II-997
Mere Christianity (Lewis, C. S.), III-1143
Metaphysical Demonstration of the Existence of God, The (Suárez), III-1147
Mind's Road to God, The (Bonaventure), III-1159

Place of the Lion, The (Williams, C.), III-1375
Varieties of Religious Experience, The (James), IV-1856

DOUBT
Angel of History, The (Forché), I-77
Apocrypha (Pankey), I-84
Arena (Hancock), I-96
Belief or Nonbelief? (Eco and Martini), I-133
Brothers Karamazov, The (Dostoevski), I-229
Capital Offense, A (Parker), I-248
Circle Trilogy, The (Dekker), I-320
Complicated Kindness, A (Toews), I-350
Courage to Be, The (Tillich), I-382
Dawning of Deliverance, The (Pella), I-416
Death in the Family, A (Agee), I-427
"Epistle Containing the Strange Medical Experience of Karshish, the Arab Physician, An" (Browning), II-545
Evil and the God of Love (Hick), II-582
Great Wheel, The (Mariani), II-749
In Memoriam (Tennyson), II-847
Infidel, The (Musser), II-866
J. B. (MacLeish), II-902
Jesus Christ Superstar (Rice, T., and Webber), II-913
Last Temptation of Christ, The (Kazantzakis), II-985
Letters from the Earth (Twain), II-1021
Mere Christianity (Lewis, C. S.), III-1143
Newpointe 911 (Blackstock), III-1223
Orthodoxy (Chesterton), III-1295
Oxygen (Ingermanson and Olson), III-1307
Power of Positive Thinking, The (Peale), III-1405
Purity of Heart Is to Will One Thing (Kierkegaard), III-1446
Second Coming, The (Percy), III-1568
Seventh Seal, The (Bergman), IV-1595
Stream and the Sapphire, The (Levertov), IV-1689

Transgression (Ingermanson), IV-1798
Unattainable Earth (Miłosz), IV-1837
Vocation of Man, The (Fichte), IV-1887
Warranted Christian Belief (Plantinga), IV-1909
With the Grain of the Universe (Hauerwas), IV-1965

THE ETERNAL NOW
On Divine Love (Duns Scotus), III-1255
Penitent Magdalene, The (Hopes), III-1339

ETHICS
Abortion and Divorce in Western Law (Glendon), I-23
Belief or Nonbelief? (Eco and Martini), I-133
Beyond God the Father (Daly), I-144
Bioethics (Meilaender), I-154
Black Theology of Liberation, A (Cone), I-165
Christianity and Democracy (Maritain), I-296
Credo (Coffin), I-393
Directed Verdict (Singer), I-465
Early Theological Writings (Hegel), II-527
Economy of Grace (Tanner), II-531
Ethics (Bonhoeffer), II-561
Ethics After Babel (Stout), II-565
Fifteen Sermons Preached at the Rolls Chapel (Butler, J.), II-618
God Who Commands, The (Mouw), II-704
Hiding Place, The (Ten Boom), II-775
Idea of a Christian Society, The (Eliot, T. S.), II-826
Insight (Lonergan), II-873
Jefferson Bible, The (Jefferson), II-906
Jesus Through the Centuries (Pelikan), II-925
Mere Christianity (Lewis, C. S.), III-1143
My God and I (Smedes), III-1188
New Testament Letters (Paul), III-1219
Orthodoxy (Chesterton), III-1295

Out of My Life and Thought (Schweitzer), III-1299
Oxygen (Ingermanson and Olson), III-1307
Pacem in Terris (John XXIII), III-1311
Philosophy of Existentialism, The (Marcel), III-1358
Politics of Jesus, The (Yoder), III-1389
Problem of Christianity, The (Royce), III-1426
Prophesy Deliverance! (West, C.), III-1434
Reasonableness of Christianity as Delivered in the Scriptures, The (Locke), III-1466
Religion Within the Bounds of Mere Reason (Kant), III-1494
Social Teaching of the Christian Churches, The (Troeltsch), IV-1639
Suffering (Sölle), IV-1702
Tasks of Philosophy, The (MacIntyre), IV-1722
Theology for the Social Gospel, A (Rauschenbusch), IV-1738
Theology of Liberation, A (Gutiérrez), IV-1742
Twilight of Courage, The (Thoene and Thoene), IV-1830
Uncle Tom's Cabin (Stowe), IV-1841
Uneasy Conscience of Modern Fundamentalism, The (Henry), IV-1845
Veritatis Splendor (John Paul II), IV-1866
When Jesus Came to Harvard (Cox), IV-1937
With the Grain of the Universe (Hauerwas), IV-1965

EUCHARIST
Book of Common Prayer (Cranmer), I-184
First and Second Apologies, The (Justin Martyr), II-633
On Christian Theology (Williams, Rowan), III-1252
On Providence (Zwingli), III-1272

EVANGELIZATION
Acts of the Apostles (Unknown), I-27
African Heritage and Contemporary Christianity (Mugambi), I-38
Augsburg Confession of Faith, The (Melanchthon), I-112
Crawl with God, Dance in the Spirit (Park), I-386
Death Comes for the Archbishop (Cather), I-423
Directed Verdict (Singer), I-465
"Dream of the Rood, The" (Unknown), I-512
History of Christianity, A (Johnson, P.), II-787
New Kind of Christian, A (McLaren), III-1211
Plain Account of Christian Perfection, A (Wesley), III-1378
This Present Darkness (Peretti), IV-1760
Tiger in the Shadows (Wilson), IV-1782
Wonderful Words of Life (Mouw and Noll), IV-1972

EXPECTANCY
For the Time Being (Dillard), II-647
Late Great Planet Earth, The (Lindsey), II-989
Questions for Ecclesiastes (Jarman), III-1459

FAITH
And I Alone Have Escaped to Tell You (McInerny), I-73
Apocrypha (Pankey), I-84
Apology (Tertullian), I-92
Augsburg Confession of Faith, The (Melanchthon), I-112
Awakening Mercy (Benson), I-116
Barabbas (Lagerkvist), I-123
Belief or Nonbelief? (Eco and Martini), I-133
Bible and Theology in African Christianity (Mbiti), I-147
Black Theology of Liberation, A (Cone), I-165

Bloudy Tenent of Persecution for Cause of Conscience, The (Williams, Roger), I-176
Book of Mormon (Smith, J.), I-196
Broken Lance (Sorensen), I-226
Brothers Karamazov, The (Dostoevski), I-229
Called to Question (Chittister), I-237
Capital Offense, A (Parker), I-248
Catholics (Moore, Brian), I-261
Christian Faith, The (Schleiermacher), I-288
Chronicles of Narnia, The (Lewis, C. S.), I-307
Church, The (Hus), I-312
Cloud of Unknowing, The (Unknown), I-329
Color Purple, The (Walker), I-338
"Confession" (Menno Simons), I-361
Confessions (Augustine), I-365
Courage to Be, The (Tillich), I-382
Credo (Coffin), I-393
Cure for the Common Life (Lucado), I-405
Dangerous Silence, A (Palmer), I-412
Dawning of Deliverance, The (Pella), I-416
Death Comes for the Archbishop (Cather), I-423
Death in the Family, A (Agee), I-427
Divine Conspiracy, The (Willard), I-477
Don't Throw Away Tomorrow (Schuller), I-500
"Epistle Containing the Strange Medical Experience of Karshish, the Arab Physician, An" (Browning), II-545
Epistle to the Romans, The (Barth), II-549
Essence of Christianity, The (Feuerbach), II-557
Eve's Striptease (Kasdorf), II-578
Existentialist Theology, An (Macquarrie), II-590
Ezekiel's Shadow (Long), II-594
Face of the Deep, The (Rossetti), II-597
Faerie Queene, The (Spenser), II-601
Figuring the Sacred (Ricœur), II-621

Final Witness (Bell), II-625
For the Time Being (Dillard), II-647
Freedom of a Christian, The (Luther), II-664
Gilead (Robinson), II-683
God's Silence (Wright, F.), II-712
Great Exemplar, The (Taylor), II-743
Great Mysteries, The (Greeley), II-746
Great Wheel, The (Mariani), II-749
Here I Stand (Spong), II-772
Hinds' Feet on High Places (Hurnard), II-779
His Watchful Eye (Cavanaugh), II-783
Hymns and Spiritual Songs (Watts), II-822
In Memoriam (Tennyson), II-847
In the Beauty of the Lilies (Updike), II-855
Insight (Lonergan), II-873
Instructor, The (Clement of Alexandria), II-881
Interior Castle (Teresa of Ávila), II-887
Introduction to Christianity (Ratzinger), II-895
Isaiah (Berrigan), II-898
J. B. (MacLeish), II-902
Jesus Christ and Mythology (Bultmann), II-909
Journey, The (Graham), II-941
Kingdom of God Is Within You, The (Tolstoy), II-948
Knowledge and Faith (Stein), II-956
Lake Wobegon Days (Keillor), II-973
Last Puritan, The (Santayana), II-981
Lectures on Revivals of Religion (Finney), II-1001
Lilies of the Field, The (Barrett), III-1050
Long Trail Home, The (Bly), III-1066
Magnificent Obsession (Douglas), III-1087
Master and Margarita, The (Bulgakov), III-1110
Memoirs of Pontius Pilate (Mills), III-1128
Mere Christianity (Lewis, C. S.), III-1143

Miracle of the Bells, The (Janney), III-1164
Miscellanies (Clement of Alexandria), II-881
Music to Die For (Nehring), III-1184
Nature and Destiny of Man, The (Niebuhr), III-1207
"New Birth, The" (Menno Simons), I-361
New Song, A (Karon), III-1215
New Testament Letters (Paul), III-1219
On Being a Christian (Küng), III-1249
On Providence (Zwingli), III-1272
On the Freedom of the Will (Erasmus), III-1276
On the Truth of Holy Scripture (Wyclif), III-1284
One Tuesday Morning (Kingsbury), III-1288
Orthodox Church, The (Ware), III-1291
Orthodoxy (Chesterton), III-1295
Oxygen (Ingermanson and Olson), III-1307
Paul (Wangerin), III-1327
Pensées (Pascal), III-1342
Philosophy of Existence (Jaspers), III-1354
Pilgrim's Progress, The (Bunyan), III-1366
Poisonwood Bible, The (Kingsolver), III-1384
Psalms (David), III-1442
Questions for Ecclesiastes (Jarman), III-1459
Quo Vadis (Sienkiewicz), III-1462
Religio Medici (Browne), III-1482
Saint Manuel Bueno, Martyr (Unamuno y Jugo), III-1537
Secrets in the Dark (Buechner), III-1571
Sense of the Presence of God, The (Baillie, J.), III-1578
Seven Storey Mountain, The (Merton), IV-1591
Seventh Seal, The (Bergman), IV-1595
Shoes of the Fisherman, The (West, M.), IV-1605
Songbird (Samson), IV-1651

Soon (Jenkins), IV-1660
Souls of Black Folk, The (Du Bois), IV-1668
Sparrow, The (Russell), IV-1676
Stream and the Sapphire, The (Levertov), IV-1689
Temple, The (Herbert), IV-1726
"They Are All Gone into the World of Light!" (Vaughan), IV-1753
This Present Darkness (Peretti), IV-1760
To Scorch or Freeze (Davie), IV-1794
Trip to Bountiful, The (Foote), IV-1816
Triumph of Love, The (Hill, Geoffrey), IV-1820
Two from Galilee (Holmes), IV-1834
Velma Still Cooks in Leeway (Wright, V. H.), IV-1862
Virgin Time (Hampl), IV-1883
Vocation of Man, The (Fichte), IV-1887
Waiting for God (Weil), IV-1891
Warranted Christian Belief (Plantinga), IV-1909
Way of All Flesh, The (Butler, S.), IV-1913
What Jesus Meant (Wills), IV-1934
With the Grain of the Universe (Hauerwas), IV-1965
Wonderful Words of Life (Mouw and Noll), IV-1972

THE FALL
Circle Trilogy, The (Dekker), I-320
Evil and the God of Love (Hick), II-582
"Fall, The" (Bottum), II-606
Paradise Lost (Milton), III-1315
Way to Christ, The (Böhme), IV-1917
Wise Blood (O'Connor), IV-1957

FASTING
Pearl (Gordon), III-1331
Spiritual Exercises, The (Ignatius of Loyola), IV-1680

FEAR
Devotions upon Emergent Occasions (Donne), I-447
Final Witness (Bell), II-625
Fire by Night (Austin), II-629
Idea of the Holy, The (Otto), II-830
Life Is Worth Living (Sheen), II-1037
Power and the Glory, The (Greene), III-1401
Power of Positive Thinking, The (Peale), III-1405
Prison Meditations on Psalms 51 and 31 (Savonarola), III-1423
Seventh Seal, The (Bergman), IV-1595
Sir Gawain and the Green Knight (Pearl-Poet), IV-1635
Their Eyes Were Watching God (Hurston), IV-1730
While Mortals Sleep (Cavanaugh), IV-1941

FORGIVENESS
All New People (Lamott), I-62
Awakening Mercy (Benson), I-116
Bishop in the Old Neighborhood, The (Greeley), I-157
Blue Like Jazz (Miller, D.), I-180
Books of the Prophets (Isaiah, Jeremiah, Amos, and Micah), I-206
Brightness That Made My Soul Tremble, A (Nesanovich), I-222
Dangerous Silence, A (Palmer), I-412
Death of Ivan Ilyich, The (Tolstoy), I-431
Gilead (Robinson), II-683
God Has a Dream (Tutu), II-694
God's Silence (Wright, F.), II-712
Hiding Place, The (Ten Boom), II-775
Holocaust Politics (Roth), II-795
Infidel, The (Musser), II-866
Left to Tell (Ilibagiza), II-1010
My God and I (Smedes), III-1188
Passing by Samaria (Foster), III-1323
Pearl (Gordon), III-1331
Problem of Christianity, The (Royce), III-1426
Quo Vadis (Sienkiewicz), III-1462
Reconciliation (de Gruchy), III-1470
Redeeming Love (Rivers), III-1478
Resting in the Bosom of the Lamb (Trobaugh), III-1502

Saint Maybe (Tyler), III-1541
Silence (Endō), IV-1616
Sir Gawain and the Green Knight (Pearl-Poet), IV-1635
Songbird (Samson), IV-1651
Triumph of Love, The (Hill, Geoffrey), IV-1820
Velma Still Cooks in Leeway (Wright, V. H.), IV-1862

FREEDOM AND FREE WILL
Beyond God the Father (Daly), I-144
Called to Question (Chittister), I-237
Centesimus Annus (John Paul II), I-265
Christianity and Democracy (Maritain), I-296
Complicated Kindness, A (Toews), I-350
Destiny of Man, The (Berdyaev), I-443
Eve's Striptease (Kasdorf), II-578
Evil and the God of Love (Hick), II-582
Existentialist Theology, An (Macquarrie), II-590
Foundations of Christian Faith (Rahner), II-654
Freedom of a Christian, The (Luther), II-664
God Has a Dream (Tutu), II-694
Great Mysteries, The (Greeley), II-746
His Watchful Eye (Cavanaugh), II-783
How Should We Then Live? (Schaeffer), II-806
Jesus Christ and Mythology (Bultmann), II-909
Lake Wobegon Days (Keillor), II-973
Letters to a Young Catholic (Weigel), II-1029
Mater et Magistra (John XXIII), III-1114
Meaning of Persons, The (Tournier), III-1118
New Testament Letters (Paul), III-1219
On First Principles (Origen), III-1259
On Providence (Zwingli), III-1272
On the Freedom of the Will (Erasmus), III-1276
Paul (Wangerin), III-1327

Philosophy of Existence (Jaspers), III-1354
Philosophy of Existentialism, The (Marcel), III-1358
Place Called Wiregrass, A (Morris, M.), III-1371
Shunning, The (Lewis, B.), IV-1612
Souls of Black Folk, The (Du Bois), IV-1668
Source of Human Good, The (Wieman), IV-1672
Strength to Love (King, M. L.), IV-1693
Theology of Liberation, A (Gutiérrez), IV-1742
Thr3e (Dekker), IV-1768
Uncle Tom's Cabin (Stowe), IV-1841
Veritatis Splendor (John Paul II), IV-1866
We Hold These Truths (Murray, J. C.), IV-1923
What Are People For? (Berry), IV-1927

FRIENDSHIP
"Amazing Peace" (Angelou), I-69
Beowulf (Unknown), I-140
Brideshead Revisited (Waugh), I-218
Christy (Marshall), I-303
Faerie Queene, The (Spenser), II-601
Flabbergasted (Blackston), II-640
Friendly Persuasion, The (West, J.), II-669
Home to Harmony (Gulley), II-802
In Memoriam (Tennyson), II-847
Last Puritan, The (Santayana), II-981
Music to Die For (Nehring), III-1184
My God and I (Smedes), III-1188
New Kind of Christian, A (McLaren), III-1211
Place Called Wiregrass, A (Morris, M.), III-1371
Place of the Lion, The (Williams, C.), III-1375
Prayer for Owen Meany, A (Irving), III-1408
Resting in the Bosom of the Lamb (Trobaugh), III-1502
She Who Is (Johnson, E. A.), IV-1598

Silver Chalice, The (Costain), IV-1620
Song of Albion Trilogy, The (Lawhead), IV-1643
Traveling Mercies (Lamott), IV-1802

GNOSTICISM
Against Heresies (Irenaeus), I-44
Agape and Eros (Nygren), I-47
Christ Clone Trilogy (BeauSeigneur), I-275
Da Vinci Code, The (Brown), I-408
Gospel of Mary of Magdala, The (King, K. L.), II-735
Instructor, The (Clement of Alexandria), II-881
Jesus in History (Kee), II-921
Marriage of Heaven and Hell, The (Blake), III-1102
Miscellanies (Clement of Alexandria), II-881
"Three Versions of Judas" (Borges), IV-1779

GOD
Acts of the Apostles (Unknown), I-27
Agape and Eros (Nygren), I-47
Aids to Reflection (Coleridge), I-54
Black Zodiac (Wright, C.), I-169
Book of God, The (Wangerin), I-192
Books of the Prophets (Isaiah, Jeremiah, Amos, and Micah), I-206
City of God, The (Augustine), I-325
Cloud of Unknowing, The (Unknown), I-329
Color Purple, The (Walker), I-338
Crucified God, The (Moltmann), I-397
Cur Deus Homo (Anselm), I-401
Dawning of Deliverance, The (Pella), I-416
Devotions upon Emergent Occasions (Donne), I-447
Divinity School Address, The (Emerson), I-491
Double Search, The (Jones), I-503
Drama of Atheist Humanism, The (Lubac), I-508

Epistle to the Romans, The (Barth), II-549
Essence of Christianity, The (Feuerbach), II-557
First and Second Apologies, The (Justin Martyr), II-633
Foundations of Christian Faith (Rahner), II-654
Four Books of Sentences (Peter Lombard), II-657
God and Philosophy (Gilson), II-691
God Has a Dream (Tutu), II-694
Gospel According to Jesus Christ, The (Saramago), II-724
Gospel of Christian Atheism, The (Altizer), II-728
Hebrew Bible (Unknown), II-756
History of God, A (Armstrong), II-791
Hymns and Spiritual Songs (Watts), II-822
Imitation of Christ, The (Thomas à Kempis), II-834
Jesus Christ and Mythology (Bultmann), II-909
Knowledge and Faith (Stein), II-956
Last Temptation of Christ, The (Kazantzakis), II-985
Letters and Papers from Prison (Bonhoeffer), II-1018
Life Abundant (McFague), II-1033
Master and Margarita, The (Bulgakov), III-1110
Meaning of Prayer, The (Fosdick), III-1121
Mere Christianity (Lewis, C. S.), III-1143
Metaphysical Demonstration of the Existence of God, The (Suárez), III-1147
Mind of the Maker, The (Sayers), III-1155
Mind's Road to God, The (Bonaventure), III-1159
Mystical Theology (Pseudo-Dionysius), III-1197
On Christian Theology (Williams, Rowan), III-1252
On First Principles (Origen), III-1259
On Listening to Another (Steere), III-1263

On Loving God (Bernard of Clairvaux), III-1268
Pensées (Pascal), III-1342
Prison Meditations of Father Alfred Delp (Delp), III-1419
Purity of Heart Is to Will One Thing (Kierkegaard), III-1446
Reasonableness of Christianity as Delivered in the Scriptures, The (Locke), III-1466
Religion (Kołakowski), III-1486
Religion in the Making (Whitehead), III-1490
Resurrection of God Incarnate, The (Swinburne), III-1506
Science and Health with Key to the Scriptures (Eddy), III-1557
Screwtape Letters, The (Lewis, C. S.), III-1560
Sense of the Presence of God, The (Baillie, J.), III-1578
Serious Call to a Devout and Holy Life, A (Law), IV-1581
Seven Storey Mountain, The (Merton), IV-1591
Seventh Seal, The (Bergman), IV-1595
She Who Is (Johnson, E. A.), IV-1598
Showings (Julian of Norwich), IV-1609
Simply Christian (Wright, N. T.), IV-1624
Source of Human Good, The (Wieman), IV-1672
Summa Theologica (Thomas Aquinas), IV-1706
Theodicy (Leibniz), IV-1734
Theology of the Jewish Christian Reality, A (Van Buren), IV-1746
"They Are All Gone into the World of Light!" (Vaughan), IV-1753
Waiting for God (Weil), IV-1891

GOOD VS. EVIL
Angel of History, The (Forché), I-77
Apocalypse (Cardenal), I-80
Beowulf (Unknown), I-140
Billy Budd, Foretopman (Melville), I-150
Blood Ties (Brouwer), I-173
Book of Revelation (John), I-202
Bread and Wine (Silone), I-211
Brothers Karamazov, The (Dostoevski), I-229
Christ Clone Trilogy (BeauSeigneur), I-275
Chronicles of Narnia, The (Lewis, C. S.), I-307
Circle Trilogy, The (Dekker), I-320
Color of Faith, The (Matsuoka), I-334
Death in the Family, A (Agee), I-427
Destiny of Man, The (Berdyaev), I-443
Divine Comedy, The (Dante), I-473
Doctor Faustus (Marlowe), I-496
Drama of Atheist Humanism, The (Lubac), I-508
Ethics (Bonhoeffer), II-561
Exclusion and Embrace (Volf), II-586
Faust (Goethe), II-610
Figuring the Sacred (Ricœur), II-621
Final Witness (Bell), II-625
Go Tell It on the Mountain (Baldwin), II-687
Gospel According to Jesus Christ, The (Saramago), II-724
Insight (Lonergan), II-873
Interrogations at Noon (Gioia), II-891
King's Ransom (Beazely and Lemmons), II-952
Last Temptation of Christ, The (Kazantzakis), II-985
Late Great Planet Earth, The (Lindsey), II-989
Left Behind series (LaHaye and Jenkins), II-1005
Left to Tell (Ilibagiza), II-1010
Letters from the Earth (Twain), II-1021
List, The (Whitlow), III-1054
Lord of the Rings, The (Tolkien), III-1073
Marriage of Heaven and Hell, The (Blake), III-1102
Master and Margarita, The (Bulgakov), III-1110
Mercy's Face (Craig), III-1139
Newpointe 911 (Blackstock), III-1223
Paradise Lost (Milton), III-1315

CORE ISSUES INDEX

Paradise Regained (Milton), III-1319
Place of the Lion, The (Williams, C.), III-1375
Prison Meditations of Father Alfred Delp (Delp), III-1419
Prophesy Deliverance! (West, C.), III-1434
Purity of Heart Is to Will One Thing (Kierkegaard), III-1446
Quo Vadis (Sienkiewicz), III-1462
Religion (Kołakowski), III-1486
Religion Within the Bounds of Mere Reason (Kant), III-1494
Seal of Gaia, The (Maddoux), III-1564
Singer Trilogy, The (Miller, C.), IV-1627
Song of Albion Trilogy, The (Lawhead), IV-1643
Songs of Innocence and of Experience (Blake), IV-1655
Source of Human Good, The (Wieman), IV-1672
Sparrow, The (Russell), IV-1676
Strength to Love (King, M. L.), IV-1693
This Present Darkness (Peretti), IV-1760
Thr3e (Dekker), IV-1768
Transgression (Ingermanson), IV-1798
Triumph of Love, The (Hill, Geoffrey), IV-1820
True Honor (Henderson), IV-1823
Twilight of Courage, The (Thoene and Thoene), IV-1830
Unattainable Earth (Miłosz), IV-1837
Unutterable Beauty, The (Studdert Kennedy), IV-1853
Veritatis Splendor (John Paul II), IV-1866
War in Heaven (Williams, C.), IV-1905
While Mortals Sleep (Cavanaugh), IV-1941

GOSPELS
Agape and Eros (Nygren), I-47
Bible and Theology in African Christianity (Mbiti), I-147
Bible in History, The, I-10
Book of God, The (Wangerin), I-192
Christ the Lord (Rice, A.), I-284

Divine and Human (Tolstoy), I-469
Drama of Atheist Humanism, The (Lubac), I-508
First Coming, The (Sheehan), II-636
Greatest Story Ever Told, The (Oursler), II-752
Jefferson Bible, The (Jefferson), II-906
Jesus I Never Knew, The (Yancey), II-917
Jesus in History (Kee), II-921
Life of Jesus, A (Endō), II-1040
Life of Jesus, The (Renan), III-1043
Life of Jesus Critically Examined, The (Strauss), III-1046
Lord, The (Guardini), III-1070
Meeting Jesus Again for the First Time (Borg), III-1125
Misquoting Jesus (Ehrman), III-1168
Paradise Regained (Milton), III-1319
Synoptic Gospels (Matthew, Mark, and Luke), IV-1717
Violence and the Sacred (Girard), IV-1879
What Jesus Meant (Wills), IV-1934

GRACE
Agape and Eros (Nygren), I-47
Amazing Grace (Norris), I-65
Blue Like Jazz (Miller, D.), I-180
Brideshead Revisited (Waugh), I-218
"Confession" (Menno Simons), I-361
Economy of Grace (Tanner), II-531
Epistle to the Romans, The (Barth), II-549
Faust (Goethe), II-610
Foundations of Christian Faith (Rahner), II-654
Holocaust Politics (Roth), II-795
Infidel, The (Musser), II-866
Lord of the Rings, The (Tolkien), III-1073
Meaning of Persons, The (Tournier), III-1118
Moments of Grace (Jennings), III-1176
"New Birth, The" (Menno Simons), I-361
New Testament Letters (Paul), III-1219
On Divine Love (Duns Scotus), III-1255
On the Freedom of the Will (Erasmus), III-1276

Paul (Wangerin), III-1327
Penitent Magdalene, The (Hopes), III-1339
Pilgrim's Progress, The (Bunyan), III-1366
Rime of the Ancient Mariner, The (Coleridge), III-1514
Scenes of Clerical Life (Eliot, G.), III-1553
Seven Storey Mountain, The (Merton), IV-1591
Shoes of the Fisherman, The (West, M.), IV-1605
Songbird (Samson), IV-1651
Treatise on Divine Predestination (Erigena), IV-1812
Winter Garden, The (Verweerd), IV-1953
Wise Blood (O'Connor), IV-1957

GUIDANCE
"Advice to a Prophet" (Wilbur), I-35
Arena (Hancock), I-96
Care of the Soul (Moore, T.), I-251
Catechism of the Catholic Church (Council of Trent), I-257
Chronicles of Narnia, The (Lewis, C. S.), I-307
Cure for the Common Life (Lucado), I-405
Great Exemplar, The (Taylor), II-743
Journey, The (Graham), II-941
List, The (Whitlow), III-1054
Power of Positive Thinking, The (Peale), III-1405
Praying God's Word (Moore, Beth), III-1412
Serious Call to a Devout and Holy Life, A (Law), IV-1581
Spiritual Exercises, The (Ignatius of Loyola), IV-1680
Treatise Concerning Religious Affections, A (Edwards), IV-1806
Two from Galilee (Holmes), IV-1834
When Jesus Came to Harvard (Cox), IV-1937

GUILT
Constantine's Sword (Carroll), I-374
Courage to Be, The (Tillich), I-382
Cur Deus Homo (Anselm), I-401
Godric (Buechner), II-708
Gospel According to Jesus Christ, The (Saramago), II-724
Out of the Red Shadow (de Graaf), III-1303
Pearl (Gordon), III-1331
Power and the Glory, The (Greene), III-1401
Redeeming Love (Rivers), III-1478
Scarlet Letter, The (Hawthorne), III-1549
Thorn Birds, The (McCullough), IV-1764
To Kill a Mockingbird (Lee, H.), IV-1790
Winter Garden, The (Verweerd), IV-1953

HEALING
After the Lost War (Hudgins), I-41
Awakening Mercy (Benson), I-116
Bible and Theology in African Christianity (Mbiti), I-147
Care of the Soul (Moore, T.), I-251
Creation, The (Beasley), I-390
Dear and Glorious Physician (Caldwell), I-420
Devotions upon Emergent Occasions (Donne), I-447
Edge of Honor (Morris, G.), II-534
"Epistle Containing the Strange Medical Experience of Karshish, the Arab Physician, An" (Browning), II-545
Hinds' Feet on High Places (Hurnard), II-779
Man Who Died, The (Lawrence), III-1098
Mary Magdalene (Traylor), III-1106
Meaning of Persons, The (Tournier), III-1118
Moments of Grace (Jennings), III-1176
One Tuesday Morning (Kingsbury), III-1288
Out of the Red Shadow (de Graaf), III-1303
Place Called Wiregrass, A (Morris, M.), III-1371

Robe, The (Douglas), III-1522
Science and Health with Key to the Scriptures (Eddy), III-1557
Songbird (Samson), IV-1651
Thorn Birds, The (McCullough), IV-1764
Velma Still Cooks in Leeway (Wright, V. H.), IV-1862
Winter Garden, The (Verweerd), IV-1953

HEART
"Dialogue of Self and Soul, A" (Yeats), I-458
Thr3e (Dekker), IV-1768
Treatise Concerning Religious Affections, A (Edwards), IV-1806

HOLINESS
Brightness That Made My Soul Tremble, A (Nesanovich), I-222
Christian Faith, The (Schleiermacher), I-288
Essays and Addresses on the Philosophy of Religion (Hügel), II-553
Hebrew Bible (Unknown), II-756
Kingdom of God Is Within You, The (Tolstoy), II-948
Purpose Driven Life, The (Warren), III-1452
Seventh Seal, The (Bergman), IV-1595
Spiritual Exercises, The (Ignatius of Loyola), IV-1680
Treatise Concerning Religious Affections, A (Edwards), IV-1806

HOLY SPIRIT
Acts of the Apostles (Unknown), I-27
Crawl with God, Dance in the Spirit (Park), I-386
Mind of the Maker, The (Sayers), III-1155
On First Principles (Origen), III-1259
Plain Account of Christian Perfection, A (Wesley), III-1378
She Who Is (Johnson, E. A.), IV-1598
Silver Chalice, The (Costain), IV-1620
Simply Christian (Wright, N. T.), IV-1624

Spiritual Exercises, The (Ignatius of Loyola), IV-1680
Subversion of Christianity, The (Ellul), IV-1698
This Present Darkness (Peretti), IV-1760
Treatise Concerning Religious Affections, A (Edwards), IV-1806

HOMOSEXUALITY
Beyond God the Father (Daly), I-144
Confessions of Nat Turner, The (Styron), I-370
Good Book, The (Gomes), II-720
Here I Stand (Spong), II-772

HOPE
After the Lost War (Hudgins), I-41
"Amazing Peace" (Angelou), I-69
Blue Like Jazz (Miller, D.), I-180
Book of Revelation (John), I-202
Color of Faith, The (Matsuoka), I-334
Death on a Friday Afternoon (Neuhaus), I-435
Don't Throw Away Tomorrow (Schuller), I-500
Figuring the Sacred (Ricœur), II-621
God Has a Dream (Tutu), II-694
"Here Follows Some Verses upon the Burning of Our House July 10th, 1666" (Bradstreet), II-768
In Memoriam (Tennyson), II-847
Isaiah (Berrigan), II-898
Lord of the Rings, The (Tolkien), III-1073
Miracle of the Bells, The (Janney), III-1164
My God and I (Smedes), III-1188
North of Hope (Hassler), III-1230
Phantastes (MacDonald), III-1346
Prison Meditations on Psalms 51 and 31 (Savonarola), III-1423
Second Coming, The (Percy), III-1568
Secrets in the Dark (Buechner), III-1571
Secrets of Barneveld Calvary, The (Schaap), III-1574
Strength to Love (King, M. L.), IV-1693
Tiger in the Shadows (Wilson), IV-1782

HUMILITY

Beasts of Bethlehem, The (Kennedy), I-130
Brightness That Made My Soul Tremble, A (Nesanovich), I-222
Cherubinic Wanderer, The (Silesius), I-268
Christian Faith, The (Schleiermacher), I-288
Elmer Gantry (Lewis, S.), II-538
Face of the Deep, The (Rossetti), II-597
Interrogations at Noon (Gioia), II-891
Keys of the Kingdom, The (Cronin), II-945
Ladder of Divine Ascent, The (John Climacus), II-968
Lilies of the Field, The (Barrett), III-1050
Little Flowers of St. Francis, The (Unknown), III-1058
Nun's Story, The (Hulme), III-1234
Rule of St. Benedict (Benedict of Nursia), III-1529
Sapphics and Uncertainties (Steele), III-1545
Sir Gawain and the Green Knight (Pearl-Poet), IV-1635
Spiritual Exercises, The (Ignatius of Loyola), IV-1680
Theory of Moral Sentiments, The (Smith, A.), IV-1749
Way to Christ, The (Böhme), IV-1917
Wind in the Wheat, The (Arvin), IV-1945

ILLUMINATION

All New People (Lamott), I-62
Ascent of Mount Carmel (John of the Cross), I-107
Dark Night of the Soul (John of the Cross), I-107
Enneads, The (Plotinus), II-542
Faust (Goethe), II-610
Ghost Pain (Lea), II-676
Here I Stand (Spong), II-772
"In the Holy Nativity of Our Lord God" (Crashaw), II-859
Ladder of Divine Ascent, The (John Climacus), II-968
Memories, Dreams, Reflections (Jung), III-1131
Mind's Road to God, The (Bonaventure), III-1159
Mysticism (Underhill), III-1200
Questions for Ecclesiastes (Jarman), III-1459
"Station Island" (Heaney), IV-1685
Two from Galilee (Holmes), IV-1834
Way to Christ, The (Böhme), IV-1917

IMPERIALISM

Christian Tradition, The (Kitagawa), I-292
Saint Joan (Shaw), III-1533
Seal of Gaia, The (Maddoux), III-1564

INCARNATION

Basic Christianity (Stott), I-127
Christ (Miles), I-272
Christ in a Pluralistic Age (Cobb), I-280
Cur Deus Homo (Anselm), I-401
Divinity School Address, The (Emerson), I-491
Four Quartets (Eliot, T. S.), II-660
God Was in Christ (Baillie, D. M.), II-698
God's Silence (Wright, F.), II-712
Gospel According to Jesus Christ, The (Saramago), II-724
Gospel of John (John, son of Zebedee), II-731
Greatest Story Ever Told, The (Oursler), II-752
"In the Holy Nativity of Our Lord God" (Crashaw), II-859
Jesus I Never Knew, The (Yancey), II-917
Last Temptation of Christ, The (Kazantzakis), II-985
Life Abundant (McFague), II-1033
Mind of the Maker, The (Sayers), III-1155
On Christian Theology (Williams, Rowan), III-1252
On First Principles (Origen), III-1259
On the Incarnation of the Word of God (Athanasius of Alexandria), III-1280

Philokalia (Cairns), III-1350
Place of the Lion, The (Williams, C.), III-1375
Reconciliation (de Gruchy), III-1470
Resurrection of God Incarnate, The (Swinburne), III-1506
Scenes of Clerical Life (Eliot, G.), III-1553
Summa Theologica (Thomas Aquinas), IV-1706
Two from Galilee (Holmes), IV-1834
Unutterable Beauty, The (Studdert Kennedy), IV-1853
"Word made Flesh is seldom, A" (Dickinson), IV-1976

INNOCENCE
Aké (Soyinka), I-58
Beasts of Bethlehem, The (Kennedy), I-130
Billy Budd, Foretopman (Melville), I-150
Capital Offense, A (Parker), I-248
Interrogations at Noon (Gioia), II-891
Passing by Samaria (Foster), III-1323
Thr3e (Dekker), IV-1768

JESUS CHRIST
Apocrypha (Pankey), I-84
Barabbas (Lagerkvist), I-123
Basic Christianity (Stott), I-127
Beasts of Bethlehem, The (Kennedy), I-130
Ben-Hur (Wallace), I-136
Black Theology of Liberation, A (Cone), I-165
Book of God, The (Wangerin), I-192
Book of Mormon (Smith, J.), I-196
Bread and Wine (Silone), I-211
Christ (Miles), I-272
Christ Clone Trilogy (BeauSeigneur), I-275
Christ in a Pluralistic Age (Cobb), I-280
Christ the Lord (Rice, A.), I-284
Coming of the Cosmic Christ, The (Fox, M.), I-346

Crucified God, The (Moltmann), I-397
Da Vinci Code, The (Brown), I-408
Death on a Friday Afternoon (Neuhaus), I-435
Dialogue, The (Catherine of Siena), I-453
Divine Conspiracy, The (Willard), I-477
Divine Milieu, The (Teilhard de Chardin), I-480
Divinity School Address, The (Emerson), I-491
Double Search, The (Jones), I-503
"Dream of the Rood, The" (Unknown), I-512
Early Christian Doctrines (Kelly), II-523
Early Theological Writings (Hegel), II-527
"Epistle Containing the Strange Medical Experience of Karshish, the Arab Physician, An" (Browning), II-545
Essays and Addresses on the Philosophy of Religion (Hügel), II-553
Ethics (Bonhoeffer), II-561
"Feet of Jesus" (Hughes), II-614
First and Second Apologies, The (Justin Martyr), II-633
First Coming, The (Sheehan), II-636
"For the Union Dead" (Lowell), II-650
Foundations of Christian Faith (Rahner), II-654
Four Books of Sentences (Peter Lombard), II-657
God Was in Christ (Baillie, D. M.), II-698
Gospel of Christian Atheism, The (Altizer), II-728
Gospel of John (John, son of Zebedee), II-731
Great Exemplar, The (Taylor), II-743
Greatest Story Ever Told, The (Oursler), II-752
Hiding Place, The (Ten Boom), II-775
History of Christianity, A (Johnson, P.), II-787
Hymns (Whittier), II-818
Imitation of Christ, The (Thomas à Kempis), II-834
In His Steps (Sheldon), II-843

Introduction to Christianity (Ratzinger), II-895
Jefferson Bible, The (Jefferson), II-906
Jesus Christ Superstar (Rice, T., and Webber), II-913
Jesus I Never Knew, The (Yancey), II-917
Jesus in History (Kee), II-921
Jesus Through the Centuries (Pelikan), II-925
Last Temptation of Christ, The (Kazantzakis), II-985
Life of Jesus, A (Endō), II-1040
Life of Jesus, The (Renan), III-1043
Life of Jesus Critically Examined, The (Strauss), III-1046
Little Flowers of St. Francis, The (Unknown), III-1058
Lord, The (Guardini), III-1070
Man Nobody Knows, The (Barton), III-1094
Man Who Died, The (Lawrence), III-1098
Master and Margarita, The (Bulgakov), III-1110
Meeting Jesus Again for the First Time (Borg), III-1125
Memoirs of Pontius Pilate (Mills), III-1128
Mercy's Face (Craig), III-1139
Mind of the Maker, The (Sayers), III-1155
New Testament Letters (Paul), III-1219
On Being a Christian (Küng), III-1249
On First Principles (Origen), III-1259
On the Incarnation of the Word of God (Athanasius of Alexandria), III-1280
Paradise Regained (Milton), III-1319
Paul (Wangerin), III-1327
Pontius Pilate (Caillois), III-1393
Reasonableness of Christianity as Delivered in the Scriptures, The (Locke), III-1466
Resurrection of God Incarnate, The (Swinburne), III-1506
Robe, The (Douglas), III-1522
Silver Chalice, The (Costain), IV-1620
Simply Christian (Wright, N. T.), IV-1624
Singer Trilogy, The (Miller, C.), IV-1627
Sinners Welcome (Karr), IV-1631
Social Teaching of the Christian Churches, The (Troeltsch), IV-1639
Songs of Innocence and of Experience (Blake), IV-1655
Spiritual Exercises, The (Ignatius of Loyola), IV-1680
Suffering (Sölle), IV-1702
Synoptic Gospels (Matthew, Mark, and Luke), IV-1717
Three Hardest Words in the World to Get Right, The (Sweet), IV-1776
"Three Versions of Judas" (Borges), IV-1779
Violence and the Sacred (Girard), IV-1879
Way to Christ, The (Böhme), IV-1917
What Jesus Meant (Wills), IV-1934
"Windhover, The" (Hopkins), IV-1949
"Word made Flesh is seldom, A" (Dickinson), IV-1976

JUDAISM
Constantine's Sword (Carroll), I-374
Dear and Glorious Physician (Caldwell), I-420
Good Book, The (Gomes), II-720
Hebrew Bible (Unknown), II-756
History of Christianity, A (Johnson, P.), II-787
Holocaust Politics (Roth), II-795
King's Ransom (Beazely and Lemmons), II-952
Merchant of Venice, The (Shakespeare), III-1135
Transgression (Ingermanson), IV-1798
Twilight of Courage, The (Thoene and Thoene), IV-1830
Two from Galilee (Holmes), IV-1834
When Jesus Came to Harvard (Cox), IV-1937

JUSTICE
Abortion and Divorce in Western Law (Glendon), I-23
Apocalypse (Cardenal), I-80

Apology (Tertullian), I-92
Billy Budd, Foretopman (Melville), I-150
Bishop in the Old Neighborhood, The (Greeley), I-157
Book of Divine Works (Hildegard von Bingen), I-188
Bread and Wine (Silone), I-211
Brightness That Made My Soul Tremble, A (Nesanovich), I-222
Brothers Karamazov, The (Dostoevski), I-229
Centesimus Annus (John Paul II), I-265
Christianity and Democracy (Maritain), I-296
Color of Faith, The (Matsuoka), I-334
Credo (Coffin), I-393
Directed Verdict (Singer), I-465
Even in Quiet Places (Stafford), II-571
Evil and the God of Love (Hick), II-582
Faerie Queene, The (Spenser), II-601
Gaudium et Spes (Vatican Council II), II-672
Gilead (Robinson), II-683
Hebrew Bible (Unknown), II-756
In Memory of Her (Schüssler Fiorenza), II-851
King's Ransom (Beazely and Lemmons), II-952
Learning Human (Murray, L. A.), II-993
Life Abundant (McFague), II-1033
Mater et Magistra (John XXIII), III-1114
Merchant of Venice, The (Shakespeare), III-1135
Name of the Rose, The (Eco), III-1204
Newpointe 911 (Blackstock), III-1223
Octogesima Adveniens (Paul VI), III-1238
Pacem in Terris (John XXIII), III-1311
Pontius Pilate (Caillois), III-1393
Prophesy Deliverance! (West, C.), III-1434
Quadragesimo Anno (Pius XI), III-1455
Reconciliation (de Gruchy), III-1470
Rerum Novarum (Leo XIII), III-1498
Saint Joan (Shaw), III-1533

Simply Christian (Wright, N. T.), IV-1624
Strength to Love (King, M. L.), IV-1693
Their Eyes Were Watching God (Hurston), IV-1730
Theology of Liberation, A (Gutiérrez), IV-1742
To Kill a Mockingbird (Lee, H.), IV-1790
We Hold These Truths (Murray, J. C.), IV-1923
What Are People For? (Berry), IV-1927

KNOWLEDGE
And I Alone Have Escaped to Tell You (McInerny), I-73
Angel of History, The (Forché), I-77
Bible and Theology in African Christianity (Mbiti), I-147
Canticle for Leibowitz, A (Miller, W. M.), I-245
Divine Relativity, The (Hartshorne), I-485
Enneads, The (Plotinus), II-542
Essence of Christianity, The (Feuerbach), II-557
Figuring the Sacred (Ricœur), II-621
God and Philosophy (Gilson), II-691
Insight (Lonergan), II-873
Jesus Through the Centuries (Pelikan), II-925
Knowledge and Faith (Stein), II-956
Memories, Dreams, Reflections (Jung), III-1131
Name of the Rose, The (Eco), III-1204
Of Learned Ignorance (Nicholas of Cusa), III-1245
Philosophy of Existence (Jaspers), III-1354
Philosophy of Existentialism, The (Marcel), III-1358
Questions for Ecclesiastes (Jarman), III-1459
Religion in the Making (Whitehead), III-1490
Revelation and Reason (Brunner), III-1510
Sense of the Presence of God, The (Baillie, J.), III-1578

Singer Trilogy, The (Miller, C.), IV-1627
Source of Human Good, The (Wieman), IV-1672
Tasks of Philosophy, The (MacIntyre), IV-1722
View of the Evidences of Christianity, A (Paley), IV-1875
Vocation of Man, The (Fichte), IV-1887

LATIN AMERICANS
Apocalypse (Cardenal), I-80
Power and the Glory, The (Greene), III-1401
Theology of Liberation, A (Gutiérrez), IV-1742
"Three Versions of Judas" (Borges), IV-1779

LIFE
Arrival of the Future, The (Fairchild), I-103
Bioethics (Meilaender), I-154
City of God, The (Augustine), I-325
"Dialogue of Self and Soul, A" (Yeats), I-458
Divinity School Address, The (Emerson), I-491
Don't Throw Away Tomorrow (Schuller), I-500
Gospel of John (John, son of Zebedee), II-731
Hebrew Bible (Unknown), II-756
Journey, The (Graham), II-941
Labyrinth of the World and the Paradise of the Heart, The (Comenius), II-964
Midquest (Chappell), III-1151
Out of My Life and Thought (Schweitzer), III-1299
Philosophy of Existentialism, The (Marcel), III-1358
Unattainable Earth (Miłosz), IV-1837

LISTENING
On Listening to Another (Steere), III-1263
Presence of the Word, The (Ong), III-1415

LONELINESS
Age of Anxiety, The (Auden), I-50
God's Silence (Wright, F.), II-712
Waiting for Godot (Beckett), IV-1897
Woman of the Pharisees, The (Mauriac), IV-1968

LOVE
Agape and Eros (Nygren), I-47
Awakening Mercy (Benson), I-116
Barabbas (Lagerkvist), I-123
Blue Like Jazz (Miller, D.), I-180
Brothers Karamazov, The (Dostoevski), I-229
Cherubinic Wanderer, The (Silesius), I-268
Christy (Marshall), I-303
Circle Trilogy, The (Dekker), I-320
City of God, The (Augustine), I-325
Cloud of Unknowing, The (Unknown), I-329
Complicated Kindness, A (Toews), I-350
Confessio Amantis (Gower), I-357
Creation, The (Beasley), I-390
Dangerous Silence, A (Palmer), I-412
Destiny of Man, The (Berdyaev), I-443
Dialogue, The (Catherine of Siena), I-453
Double Search, The (Jones), I-503
Edge of Honor (Morris, G.), II-534
"Epistle Containing the Strange Medical Experience of Karshish, the Arab Physician, An" (Browning), II-545
Essence of Christianity, The (Feuerbach), II-557
Figuring the Sacred (Ricœur), II-621
Final Witness (Bell), II-625
Flabbergasted (Blackston), II-640
Friendly Persuasion, The (West, J.), II-669
Great Wheel, The (Mariani), II-749
Hebrew Bible (Unknown), II-756
Hymns (Whittier), II-818
In Memoriam (Tennyson), II-847
"In the Holy Nativity of Our Lord God" (Crashaw), II-859

Jesus Christ Superstar (Rice, T., and Webber), II-913
Kristin Lavransdatter (Undset), II-960
Leaves of Grass (Whitman), II-997
Letters to a Young Catholic (Weigel), II-1029
Life Is Worth Living (Sheen), II-1037
Lord, The (Guardini), III-1070
Love Comes Softly series (Oke), III-1082
Mary Magdalene (Traylor), III-1106
Master and Margarita, The (Bulgakov), III-1110
Midquest (Chappell), III-1151
Miracle of the Bells, The (Janney), III-1164
Moments of Grace (Jennings), III-1176
No Greater Love (Teresa, Mother), III-1227
North of Hope (Hassler), III-1230
On Divine Love (Duns Scotus), III-1255
On Loving God (Bernard of Clairvaux), III-1268
One Tuesday Morning (Kingsbury), III-1288
Out of My Life and Thought (Schweitzer), III-1299
Oxygen (Ingermanson and Olson), III-1307
Pearl (Gordon), III-1331
Quo Vadis (Sienkiewicz), III-1462
Red and the Black, The (Stendhal), III-1474
Redeeming Love (Rivers), III-1478
Rime of the Ancient Mariner, The (Coleridge), III-1514
River Runs Through It, A (Maclean), III-1518
Rose (Lee, L.-Y.), III-1525
Scenes of Clerical Life (Eliot, G.), III-1553
Screwtape Letters, The (Lewis, C. S.), III-1560
Second Coming, The (Percy), III-1568
Shoes of the Fisherman, The (West, M.), IV-1605
Showings (Julian of Norwich), IV-1609

Sinners Welcome (Karr), IV-1631
Song of Albion Trilogy, The (Lawhead), IV-1643
Strength to Love (King, M. L.), IV-1693
Theology for the Social Gospel, A (Rauschenbusch), IV-1738
Three Hardest Words in the World to Get Right, The (Sweet), IV-1776
Triumph of Love, The (Hill, Geoffrey), IV-1820
True Honor (Henderson), IV-1823
Velma Still Cooks in Leeway (Wright, V. H.), IV-1862
Waiting for God (Weil), IV-1891
What Are People For? (Berry), IV-1927
Woman of the Pharisees, The (Mauriac), IV-1968

LUTHERANS AND LUTHERANISM
Augsburg Confession of Faith, The (Melanchthon), I-112
Death on a Friday Afternoon (Neuhaus), I-435
Jesus Christ and Mythology (Bultmann), II-909
Lake Wobegon Days (Keillor), II-973
On the Freedom of the Will (Erasmus), III-1276
Three Essays (Ritschl), IV-1772

MARRIAGE
Abortion and Divorce in Western Law (Glendon), I-23
Bishop in the Old Neighborhood, The (Greeley), I-157
Brideshead Revisited (Waugh), I-218
Canterbury Tales, The (Chaucer), I-240
Casti Connubii (Pius XI), I-254
Church Folk (Bowen), I-316
Ethics (Bonhoeffer), II-561
Flabbergasted (Blackston), II-640
Fools and Crows (Witek), II-644
Friendly Persuasion, The (West, J.), II-669
Gift from the Sea (Lindbergh), II-680
Go Tell It on the Mountain (Baldwin), II-687

Humanae Vitae (Paul VI), II-811
Kristin Lavransdatter (Undset), II-960
Midquest (Chappell), III-1151
Newpointe 911 (Blackstock), III-1223
Poisonwood Bible, The (Kingsolver), III-1384
Redeeming Love (Rivers), III-1478
Rose (Lee, L.-Y.), III-1525
Shunning, The (Lewis, B.), IV-1612
Songbird (Samson), IV-1651
Vicar of Wakefield, The (Goldsmith), IV-1870

MARTYRDOM
Book of Revelation (John), I-202
"For the Union Dead" (Lowell), II-650
His Watchful Eye (Cavanaugh), II-783
Jesus Christ Superstar (Rice, T., and Webber), II-913
Last Temptation of Christ, The (Kazantzakis), II-985
Prayer for Owen Meany, A (Irving), III-1408
Quo Vadis (Sienkiewicz), III-1462
Robe, The (Douglas), III-1522
Saint Joan (Shaw), III-1533
Silence (Endō), IV-1616
"Three Versions of Judas" (Borges), IV-1779
Uncle Tom's Cabin (Stowe), IV-1841

MEMORY
Aké (Soyinka), I-58
Brideshead Revisited (Waugh), I-218
Dream Songs, The (Berryman), I-515
Four Quartets (Eliot, T. S.), II-660
Godric (Buechner), II-708
Great Wheel, The (Mariani), II-749
Inscribing the Text (Brueggemann), II-870
Memories, Dreams, Reflections (Jung), III-1131
"Ode: Intimations of Immortality" (Wordsworth), III-1241
One Tuesday Morning (Kingsbury), III-1288

Presence of the Word, The (Ong), III-1415
Resting in the Bosom of the Lamb (Trobaugh), III-1502
River Runs Through It, A (Maclean), III-1518
Second Coming, The (Percy), III-1568
Secrets in the Dark (Buechner), III-1571
Time Lottery (Moser), IV-1786
Triumph of Love, The (Hill, Geoffrey), IV-1820
Unattainable Earth (Miłosz), IV-1837
What I Think I Did (Woiwode), IV-1931

MENNONITES
Complicated Kindness, A (Toews), I-350
"Confession" (Menno Simons), I-361
Eve's Striptease (Kasdorf), II-578
"New Birth, The" (Menno Simons), I-361

METHODISTS AND METHODISM
Declaration of the Sentiments of Arminius, A (Arminius), I-439
Place Called Wiregrass, A (Morris, M.), III-1371
Plain Account of Christian Perfection, A (Wesley), III-1378

MONASTICISM
Amazing Grace (Norris), I-65
Canticle for Leibowitz, A (Miller, W. M.), I-245
Catholics (Moore, Brian), I-261
Conferences (Cassian), I-354
Imitation of Christ, The (Thomas à Kempis), II-834
In This House of Brede (Godden), II-863
Ladder of Divine Ascent, The (John Climacus), II-968
Letters of Saint Jerome, The (Jerome), II-1024
Nun's Story, The (Hulme), III-1234
Rule of St. Benedict (Benedict of Nursia), III-1529
Seven Storey Mountain, The (Merton), IV-1591

Spiritual Exercises, The (Ignatius of Loyola), IV-1680

MORALITY
Aids to Reflection (Coleridge), I-54
Belief or Nonbelief? (Eco and Martini), I-133
Bioethics (Meilaender), I-154
Centesimus Annus (John Paul II), I-265
Confessio Amantis (Gower), I-357
"Dialogue of Self and Soul, A" (Yeats), I-458
Early Theological Writings (Hegel), II-527
Elmer Gantry (Lewis, S.), II-538
Ethics After Babel (Stout), II-565
Everyman (Unknown), II-574
"For the Union Dead" (Lowell), II-650
God Who Commands, The (Mouw), II-704
Idea of a Christian Society, The (Eliot, T. S.), II-826
Jesus Through the Centuries (Pelikan), II-925
Kingdom of God Is Within You, The (Tolstoy), II-948
Labyrinth of the World and the Paradise of the Heart, The (Comenius), II-964
Leaves of Grass (Whitman), II-997
Letters from the Earth (Twain), II-1021
Life Is Worth Living (Sheen), II-1037
Octogesima Adveniens (Paul VI), III-1238
Out of My Life and Thought (Schweitzer), III-1299
Problem of Christianity, The (Royce), III-1426
Religion (Kołakowski), III-1486
Religion Within the Bounds of Mere Reason (Kant), III-1494
Seal of Gaia, The (Maddoux), III-1564
Serious Call to a Devout and Holy Life, A (Law), IV-1581
Strength to Love (King, M. L.), IV-1693
Subversion of Christianity, The (Ellul), IV-1698

Theory of Moral Sentiments, The (Smith, A.), IV-1749
To Kill a Mockingbird (Lee, H.), IV-1790
Veritatis Splendor (John Paul II), IV-1866
Violence and the Sacred (Girard), IV-1879
Vocation of Man, The (Fichte), IV-1887
We Hold These Truths (Murray, J. C.), IV-1923
When Jesus Came to Harvard (Cox), IV-1937

MORMONS AND MORMONISM
Book of Mormon (Smith, J.), I-196
Broken Lance (Sorensen), I-226

MYSTICISM
Book of Divine Works (Hildegard von Bingen), I-188
Cherubinic Wanderer, The (Silesius), I-268
Coming of the Cosmic Christ, The (Fox, M.), I-346
Double Search, The (Jones), I-503
Godric (Buechner), II-708
Idea of the Holy, The (Otto), II-830
Knowledge and Faith (Stein), II-956
Labyrinth of the World and the Paradise of the Heart, The (Comenius), II-964
Last Days of Pompeii, The (Bulwer-Lytton), II-977
Mystical Element of Religion, The (Hügel), III-1191
Mystical Theology (Pseudo-Dionysius), III-1197
Mysticism (Underhill), III-1200
Of Learned Ignorance (Nicholas of Cusa), III-1245
Out of My Life and Thought (Schweitzer), III-1299
Plain Account of Christian Perfection, A (Wesley), III-1378
Rose (Lee, L.-Y.), III-1525
Spiritual Exercises, The (Ignatius of Loyola), IV-1680
"Station Island" (Heaney), IV-1685
Suffering (Sölle), IV-1702

"They Are All Gone into the World of
    Light!" (Vaughan), IV-1753
Third Spiritual Alphabet, The (Osuna),
    IV-1756
This Present Darkness (Peretti), IV-1760
Varieties of Religious Experience, The
    (James), IV-1856
Waiting for God (Weil), IV-1891
War in Heaven (Williams, C.), IV-1905
Way to Christ, The (Böhme), IV-1917
With Head and Heart (Thurman), IV-1961

MYTHS
    Jesus Christ and Mythology (Bultmann),
        II-909
    Life of Jesus Critically Examined, The
        (Strauss), III-1046
    Man Who Died, The (Lawrence), III-1098
    Memories, Dreams, Reflections (Jung),
        III-1131
    Song of Albion Trilogy, The (Lawhead),
        IV-1643
    War in Heaven (Williams, C.), IV-1905

NATIVE AMERICANS
    Blood Ties (Brouwer), I-173
    Broken Lance (Sorensen), I-226
    Dangerous Silence, A (Palmer), I-412
    Death Comes for the Archbishop (Cather),
        I-423

NATURE
    "Advice to a Prophet" (Wilbur), I-35
    After the Lost War (Hudgins), I-41
    Apocrypha (Pankey), I-84
    Arrival of the Future, The (Fairchild),
        I-103
    Black Zodiac (Wright, C.), I-169
    Book of Divine Works (Hildegard von
        Bingen), I-188
    Divinity School Address, The (Emerson),
        I-491
    Even in Quiet Places (Stafford), II-571
    "Fall, The" (Bottum), II-606
    Fools and Crows (Witek), II-644
    Gift from the Sea (Lindbergh), II-680

God and Philosophy (Gilson), II-691
In Memoriam (Tennyson), II-847
Learning Human (Murray, L. A.), II-993
Leaves of Grass (Whitman), II-997
Life Abundant (McFague), II-1033
Lord of the Rings, The (Tolkien), III-1073
Moments of Grace (Jennings), III-1176
"Ode: Intimations of Immortality"
    (Wordsworth), III-1241
Out of the Red Shadow (de Graaf),
    III-1303
Phantastes (MacDonald), III-1346
Religio Medici (Browne), III-1482
Rime of the Ancient Mariner, The
    (Coleridge), III-1514
River Runs Through It, A (Maclean),
    III-1518
Source of Human Good, The (Wieman),
    IV-1672
"They Are All Gone into the World of
    Light!" (Vaughan), IV-1753
What Are People For? (Berry), IV-1927
"Windhover, The" (Hopkins), IV-1949

NONVIOLENT RESISTANCE
    Credo (Coffin), I-393
    Even in Quiet Places (Stafford), II-571
    God Has a Dream (Tutu), II-694
    Isaiah (Berrigan), II-898
    Loaves and Fishes (Day), III-1062
    Politics of Jesus, The (Yoder), III-1389
    Strength to Love (King, M. L.), IV-1693

OBEDIENCE AND DISOBEDIENCE
    Acts of the Apostles (Unknown), I-27
    Apologia pro vita sua (Newman), I-88
    Bloudy Tenent of Persecution for Cause
        of Conscience, The (Williams, Roger),
        I-176
    Book of Mormon (Smith, J.), I-196
    Catholics (Moore, Brian), I-261
    Church, The (Hus), I-312
    City of God, The (Augustine), I-325
    Complicated Kindness, A (Toews), I-350
    Da Vinci Code, The (Brown), I-408
    Dialogue, The (Catherine of Siena), I-453

Doctor Faustus (Marlowe), I-496
Ethics (Bonhoeffer), II-561
Hinds' Feet on High Places (Hurnard), II-779
Journal of John Woolman, The (Woolman), II-936
Kristin Lavransdatter (Undset), II-960
Ladder of Divine Ascent, The (John Climacus), II-968
Nun's Story, The (Hulme), III-1234
On the Freedom of the Will (Erasmus), III-1276
Paradise Lost (Milton), III-1315
Rule of St. Benedict (Benedict of Nursia), III-1529
Shunning, The (Lewis, B.), IV-1612
Strength to Love (King, M. L.), IV-1693
Way of All Flesh, The (Butler, S.), IV-1913

PASTORAL ROLE
African Heritage and Contemporary Christianity (Mugambi), I-38
Bishop's Mantle, The (Turnbull), I-161
Canterbury Tales, The (Chaucer), I-240
Church Folk (Bowen), I-316
Death Comes for the Archbishop (Cather), I-423
Diary of a Country Priest, The (Bernanos), I-462
Humani Generis Redemptionem (Benedict XV), II-815
Inscribing the Text (Brueggemann), II-870
Morte d'Urban (Powers), III-1180
New Song, A (Karon), III-1215
On the Truth of Holy Scripture (Wyclif), III-1284
Pacem in Terris (John XXIII), III-1311
Poisonwood Bible, The (Kingsolver), III-1384
Souls of Black Folk, The (Du Bois), IV-1668
Temple, The (Herbert), IV-1726
While Mortals Sleep (Cavanaugh), IV-1941

PEACE
"Amazing Peace" (Angelou), I-69
City of God, The (Augustine), I-325
Credo (Coffin), I-393
Dialogue, The (Catherine of Siena), I-453
Gaudium et Spes (Vatican Council II), II-672
God Has a Dream (Tutu), II-694
Imitation of Christ, The (Thomas à Kempis), II-834
"In Distrust of Merits" (Moore, M.), II-839
Isaiah (Berrigan), II-898
Kingdom of God Is Within You, The (Tolstoy), II-948
Left to Tell (Ilibagiza), II-1010
Life Is Worth Living (Sheen), II-1037
Lord's Prayer and the Beatitudes, The (Gregory of Nyssa), III-1078
Pacem in Terris (John XXIII), III-1311
Populorum Progressio (Paul VI), III-1397

PERFECTION
Dialogue, The (Catherine of Siena), I-453
Enneads, The (Plotinus), II-542
Plain Account of Christian Perfection, A (Wesley), III-1378
Purity of Heart Is to Will One Thing (Kierkegaard), III-1446
Walking by Faith (Grimké), IV-1901

PERSECUTION
Bloudy Tenent of Persecution for Cause of Conscience, The (Williams, Roger), I-176
Book of Revelation (John), I-202
Church, The (Hus), I-312
Constantine's Sword (Carroll), I-374
Directed Verdict (Singer), I-465
Divini Redemptoris (Pius XI), I-488
First and Second Apologies, The (Justin Martyr), II-633
His Watchful Eye (Cavanaugh), II-783
Holocaust Politics (Roth), II-795
King's Ransom (Beazely and Lemmons), II-952

Merchant of Venice, The (Shakespeare), III-1135
Mit brennender Sorge (Pius XI), III-1172
Power and the Glory, The (Greene), III-1401
Prison Meditations of Father Alfred Delp (Delp), III-1419
Robe, The (Douglas), III-1522
Seal of Gaia, The (Maddoux), III-1564
Silence (Endō), IV-1616
Soon (Jenkins), IV-1660
Tiger in the Shadows (Wilson), IV-1782
While Mortals Sleep (Cavanaugh), IV-1941

PILGRIMAGE
Canterbury Tales, The (Chaucer), I-240
Chronicles of Narnia, The (Lewis, C. S.), I-307
City of God, The (Augustine), I-325
Dear and Glorious Physician (Caldwell), I-420
In This House of Brede (Godden), II-863
Phantastes (MacDonald), III-1346
Piers Plowman (Langland), III-1362
Pilgrim's Progress, The (Bunyan), III-1366
"Station Island" (Heaney), IV-1685
Virgin Time (Hampl), IV-1883

POVERTY
"Christmas Carol, A" (Dickens), I-299
Economy of Grace (Tanner), II-531
Gaudium et Spes (Vatican Council II), II-672
Little Flowers of St. Francis, The (Unknown), III-1058
Loaves and Fishes (Day), III-1062
Mater et Magistra (John XXIII), III-1114
No Greater Love (Teresa, Mother), III-1227
Populorum Progressio (Paul VI), III-1397
Quadragesimo Anno (Pius XI), III-1455
Rerum Novarum (Leo XIII), III-1498
Serious Call to a Devout and Holy Life, A (Law), IV-1581

Theology for the Social Gospel, A (Rauschenbusch), IV-1738
Uneasy Conscience of Modern Fundamentalism, The (Henry), IV-1845

PRAYER
Awakening Mercy (Benson), I-116
Bible and Theology in African Christianity (Mbiti), I-147
Book of Common Prayer (Cranmer), I-184
Capital Offense, A (Parker), I-248
Cloud of Unknowing, The (Unknown), I-329
Conferences (Cassian), I-354
Country Parson, The (Herbert), I-378
Creation, The (Beasley), I-390
Devotions upon Emergent Occasions (Donne), I-447
Face of the Deep, The (Rossetti), II-597
Final Witness (Bell), II-625
Friendly Persuasion, The (West, J.), II-669
Hebrew Bible (Unknown), II-756
Inscribing the Text (Brueggemann), II-870
Left to Tell (Ilibagiza), II-1010
Letters to a Young Catholic (Weigel), II-1029
Life Is Worth Living (Sheen), II-1037
List, The (Whitlow), III-1054
Lord's Prayer and the Beatitudes, The (Gregory of Nyssa), III-1078
Meaning of Prayer, The (Fosdick), III-1121
North of Hope (Hassler), III-1230
On Christian Theology (Williams, Rowan), III-1252
On Listening to Another (Steere), III-1263
Passing by Samaria (Foster), III-1323
Praying God's Word (Moore, Beth), III-1412
Prodigal Girl, The (Hill, Grace Livingston), III-1430
Psalms (David), III-1442

Science and Health with Key to the Scriptures (Eddy), III-1557
Serious Call to a Devout and Holy Life, A (Law), IV-1581
Showings (Julian of Norwich), IV-1609
Sinners Welcome (Karr), IV-1631
Song of the Sparrow (Bodo), IV-1648
Soul of Christianity, The (Smith, H.), IV-1664
Spiritual Exercises, The (Ignatius of Loyola), IV-1680
Supplicating Voice, The (Johnson, S.), IV-1710
Third Spiritual Alphabet, The (Osuna), IV-1756
This Present Darkness (Peretti), IV-1760
Virgin Time (Hampl), IV-1883

PREACHING
Country Parson, The (Herbert), I-378
Divinity School Address, The (Emerson), I-491
God's Trombones (Johnson, J. W.), II-716
Humani Generis Redemptionem (Benedict XV), II-815
Inscribing the Text (Brueggemann), II-870
Journal of George Fox, The (Fox, G.), II-931
Journal of John Woolman, The (Woolman), II-936
Morte d'Urban (Powers), III-1180
Poisonwood Bible, The (Kingsolver), III-1384
Songbird (Samson), IV-1651

PREDESTINATION
Bloudy Tenent of Persecution for Cause of Conscience, The (Williams, Roger), I-176
Church, The (Hus), I-312
Gilead (Robinson), II-683
On Providence (Zwingli), III-1272
Treatise on Divine Predestination (Erigena), IV-1812

PRIESTHOOD
Death Comes for the Archbishop (Cather), I-423
Diary of a Country Priest, The (Bernanos), I-462
Hebrew Bible (Unknown), II-756
Keys of the Kingdom, The (Cronin), II-945
Morte d'Urban (Powers), III-1180
North of Hope (Hassler), III-1230
Thorn Birds, The (McCullough), IV-1764

PROBLEM OF EVIL
Evil and the God of Love (Hick), II-582
God's Silence (Wright, F.), II-712
Insight (Lonergan), II-873
J. B. (MacLeish), II-902
Mystical Element of Religion, The (Hügel), III-1191
Newpointe 911 (Blackstock), III-1223
Problem of Christianity, The (Royce), III-1426
Religion (Kołakowski), III-1486
Religion in the Making (Whitehead), III-1490
Songs of Innocence and of Experience (Blake), IV-1655
Sparrow, The (Russell), IV-1676
Strength to Love (King, M. L.), IV-1693
Theodicy (Leibniz), IV-1734
Treatise on Divine Predestination (Erigena), IV-1812
Unspeakable (Guinness), IV-1849

PROTESTANTS AND PROTESTANTISM
Agape and Eros (Nygren), I-47
Aids to Reflection (Coleridge), I-54
Apologia pro vita sua (Newman), I-88
Argument Against Abolishing Christianity (Swift), I-99
Augsburg Confession of Faith, The (Melanchthon), I-112
Bishop's Mantle, The (Turnbull), I-161
Book of Common Prayer (Cranmer), I-184
Dangerous Silence, A (Palmer), I-412

Freedom of a Christian, The (Luther), II-664
God Who Commands, The (Mouw), II-704
Good Book, The (Gomes), II-720
History of Christianity, A (Johnson, P.), II-787
Institutes of the Christian Religion (Calvin), II-877
Lake Wobegon Days (Keillor), II-973
Nature and Destiny of Man, The (Niebuhr), III-1207
New Kind of Christian, A (McLaren), III-1211
On Providence (Zwingli), III-1272
Plain Account of Christian Perfection, A (Wesley), III-1378
Protestant Ethic and the Spirit of Capitalism, The (Weber), III-1438
Saint Joan (Shaw), III-1533
Serious Call to a Devout and Holy Life, A (Law), IV-1581
Three Essays (Ritschl), IV-1772
Wonderful Words of Life (Mouw and Noll), IV-1972

PSYCHOLOGY
All New People (Lamott), I-62
Arena (Hancock), I-96
Divine Milieu, The (Teilhard de Chardin), I-480
Double Search, The (Jones), I-503
Idea of the Holy, The (Otto), II-830
Meaning of Persons, The (Tournier), III-1118
Memories, Dreams, Reflections (Jung), III-1131
"Ode: Intimations of Immortality" (Wordsworth), III-1241
Power of Positive Thinking, The (Peale), III-1405
Presence of the Word, The (Ong), III-1415
Protestant Ethic and the Spirit of Capitalism, The (Weber), III-1438
Thr3e (Dekker), IV-1768

Time Lottery (Moser), IV-1786
Varieties of Religious Experience, The (James), IV-1856

PURGATION
Ascent of Mount Carmel (John of the Cross), I-107
Dark Night of the Soul (John of the Cross), I-107
Mysticism (Underhill), III-1200
Spiritual Exercises, The (Ignatius of Loyola), IV-1680
Third Spiritual Alphabet, The (Osuna), IV-1756

PURITANS AND PURITANISM
Bloudy Tenent of Persecution for Cause of Conscience, The (Williams, Roger), I-176
God Who Commands, The (Mouw), II-704
"Here Follows Some Verses upon the Burning of Our House July 10th, 1666" (Bradstreet), II-768
Paradise Lost (Milton), III-1315
Pilgrim's Progress, The (Bunyan), III-1366
Protestant Ethic and the Spirit of Capitalism, The (Weber), III-1438
Scarlet Letter, The (Hawthorne), III-1549

PURITY
Journal of John Woolman, The (Woolman), II-936
Pearl (Gordon), III-1331
Spiritual Exercises, The (Ignatius of Loyola), IV-1680

QUAKERS
Friendly Persuasion, The (West, J.), II-669
Home to Harmony (Gulley), II-802
Hymns (Whittier), II-818
Journal of George Fox, The (Fox, G.), II-931

Journal of John Woolman, The (Woolman), II-936
On Listening to Another (Steere), III-1263
Walking by Faith (Grimké), IV-1901

RACISM
Black Theology of Liberation, A (Cone), I-165
Church Folk (Bowen), I-316
Color of Faith, The (Matsuoka), I-334
Color Purple, The (Walker), I-338
Constantine's Sword (Carroll), I-374
"Feet of Jesus" (Hughes), II-614
"For the Union Dead" (Lowell), II-650
Gilead (Robinson), II-683
Go Tell It on the Mountain (Baldwin), II-687
Good Book, The (Gomes), II-720
Left to Tell (Ilibagiza), II-1010
"Letter from Birmingham Jail" (King, M. L.), II-1014
Lilies of the Field, The (Barrett), III-1050
Merchant of Venice, The (Shakespeare), III-1135
Passing by Samaria (Foster), III-1323
Prophesy Deliverance! (West, C.), III-1434
Rose (Lee, L.-Y.), III-1525
Souls of Black Folk, The (Du Bois), IV-1668
Strength to Love (King, M. L.), IV-1693
Uneasy Conscience of Modern Fundamentalism, The (Henry), IV-1845
Walking by Faith (Grimké), IV-1901
With Head and Heart (Thurman), IV-1961

REASON
Aids to Reflection (Coleridge), I-54
Apocrypha (Pankey), I-84
Apologia pro vita sua (Newman), I-88
Belief or Nonbelief? (Eco and Martini), I-133
Canticle for Leibowitz, A (Miller, W. M.), I-245

Christ Clone Trilogy (BeauSeigneur), I-275
Divine Relativity, The (Hartshorne), I-485
Early Theological Writings (Hegel), II-527
Essence of Christianity, The (Feuerbach), II-557
Ethics After Babel (Stout), II-565
Fifteen Sermons Preached at the Rolls Chapel (Butler, J.), II-618
Four Books of Sentences (Peter Lombard), II-657
God and Philosophy (Gilson), II-691
Here I Stand (Spong), II-772
History of God, A (Armstrong), II-791
How Should We Then Live? (Schaeffer), II-806
Jefferson Bible, The (Jefferson), II-906
Life of Jesus Critically Examined, The (Strauss), III-1046
Mere Christianity (Lewis, C. S.), III-1143
Mystical Theology (Pseudo-Dionysius), III-1197
Name of the Rose, The (Eco), III-1204
Nature and Destiny of Man, The (Niebuhr), III-1207
On First Principles (Origen), III-1259
Orthodoxy (Chesterton), III-1295
Pensées (Pascal), III-1342
Philosophy of Existence (Jaspers), III-1354
Philosophy of Existentialism, The (Marcel), III-1358
Religion in the Making (Whitehead), III-1490
Religion Within the Bounds of Mere Reason (Kant), III-1494
Resurrection of God Incarnate, The (Swinburne), III-1506
Revelation and Reason (Brunner), III-1510
Saint Joan (Shaw), III-1533
Source of Human Good, The (Wieman), IV-1672
Summa Theologica (Thomas Aquinas), IV-1706

Tasks of Philosophy, The (MacIntyre), IV-1722
Theodicy (Leibniz), IV-1734
View of the Evidences of Christianity, A (Paley), IV-1875
Vocation of Man, The (Fichte), IV-1887
Warranted Christian Belief (Plantinga), IV-1909
Way of All Flesh, The (Butler, S.), IV-1913
Way to Christ, The (Böhme), IV-1917
We Hold These Truths (Murray, J. C.), IV-1923

RECOLLECTION
Black Zodiac (Wright, C.), I-169
Mysticism (Underhill), III-1200
Third Spiritual Alphabet, The (Osuna), IV-1756

RECONCILIATION
Color of Faith, The (Matsuoka), I-334
Exclusion and Embrace (Volf), II-586
Gilead (Robinson), II-683
God Was in Christ (Baillie, D. M.), II-698
Reconciliation (de Gruchy), III-1470
Souls of Black Folk, The (Du Bois), IV-1668
Winter Garden, The (Verweerd), IV-1953

REDEMPTION
Basic Christianity (Stott), I-127
Ben-Hur (Wallace), I-136
Blood Ties (Brouwer), I-173
Blue Like Jazz (Miller, D.), I-180
Book of Mormon (Smith, J.), I-196
Care of the Soul (Moore, T.), I-251
"Christmas Carol, A" (Dickens), I-299
Color of Faith, The (Matsuoka), I-334
Come Sweet Death (Napier), I-342
Confessions of Nat Turner, The (Styron), I-370
Crucified God, The (Moltmann), I-397
Destiny of Man, The (Berdyaev), I-443
Drama of Atheist Humanism, The (Lubac), I-508

"Dream of the Rood, The" (Unknown), I-512
Everyman (Unknown), II-574
Final Witness (Bell), II-625
God's Silence (Wright, F.), II-712
Greatest Story Ever Told, The (Oursler), II-752
"Here Follows Some Verses upon the Burning of Our House July 10th, 1666" (Bradstreet), II-768
Hinds' Feet on High Places (Hurnard), II-779
"In Distrust of Merits" (Moore, M.), II-839
Infidel, The (Musser), II-866
Kristin Lavransdatter (Undset), II-960
Left Behind series (LaHaye and Jenkins), II-1005
Long Trail Home, The (Bly), III-1066
On the Incarnation of the Word of God (Athanasius of Alexandria), III-1280
Piers Plowman (Langland), III-1362
Pilgrim's Progress, The (Bunyan), III-1366
Prayer for Owen Meany, A (Irving), III-1408
Problem of Christianity, The (Royce), III-1426
Redeeming Love (Rivers), III-1478
Resting in the Bosom of the Lamb (Trobaugh), III-1502
Saint Maybe (Tyler), III-1541
Scarlet Letter, The (Hawthorne), III-1549
Scenes of Clerical Life (Eliot, G.), III-1553
Secrets of Barneveld Calvary, The (Schaap), III-1574
Shepherd of the Hills, The (Wright, H. B.), IV-1602
Shoes of the Fisherman, The (West, M.), IV-1605
Sinners Welcome (Karr), IV-1631
Soul of Christianity, The (Smith, H.), IV-1664
"Station Island" (Heaney), IV-1685
Sutter's Cross (Cramer), IV-1714

Triumph of Love, The (Hill, Geoffrey), IV-1820
Twilight of Courage, The (Thoene and Thoene), IV-1830
Velma Still Cooks in Leeway (Wright, V. H.), IV-1862
Wise Blood (O'Connor), IV-1957
Woman of the Pharisees, The (Mauriac), IV-1968
"Word made Flesh is seldom, A" (Dickinson), IV-1976

REGENERATION
Age of Anxiety, The (Auden), I-50
Ben-Hur (Wallace), I-136
Bioethics (Meilaender), I-154
Devotions upon Emergent Occasions (Donne), I-447
Ezekiel's Shadow (Long), II-594
Interrogations at Noon (Gioia), II-891
Man Who Died, The (Lawrence), III-1098
Redeeming Love (Rivers), III-1478

RELIGION
Agape and Eros (Nygren), I-47
Aké (Soyinka), I-58
Apology (Tertullian), I-92
Called to Question (Chittister), I-237
Christian Tradition, The (Kitagawa), I-292
Death in the Family, A (Agee), I-427
Directed Verdict (Singer), I-465
Divini Redemptoris (Pius XI), I-488
Divinity School Address, The (Emerson), I-491
Drama of Atheist Humanism, The (Lubac), I-508
Early Theological Writings (Hegel), II-527
Elmer Gantry (Lewis, S.), II-538
Essays and Addresses on the Philosophy of Religion (Hügel), II-553
Essence of Christianity, The (Feuerbach), II-557
God and Philosophy (Gilson), II-691
God Who Commands, The (Mouw), II-704

Great Mysteries, The (Greeley), II-746
In the Beauty of the Lilies (Updike), II-855
Jesus Through the Centuries (Pelikan), II-925
Mit brennender Sorge (Pius XI), III-1172
Nature and Destiny of Man, The (Niebuhr), III-1207
Orthodox Church, The (Ware), III-1291
Out of My Life and Thought (Schweitzer), III-1299
Philosophy of Existence (Jaspers), III-1354
Philosophy of Existentialism, The (Marcel), III-1358
Prison Meditations of Father Alfred Delp (Delp), III-1419
Reasonableness of Christianity as Delivered in the Scriptures, The (Locke), III-1466
Science and Health with Key to the Scriptures (Eddy), III-1557
Seal of Gaia, The (Maddoux), III-1564
Soul of Christianity, The (Smith, H.), IV-1664
Subversion of Christianity, The (Ellul), IV-1698
Varieties of Religious Experience, The (James), IV-1856
Warranted Christian Belief (Plantinga), IV-1909

REPENTANCE
Baptismal Instruction (Chrysostom), I-120
Book of Mormon (Smith, J.), I-196
Death of Ivan Ilyich, The (Tolstoy), I-431
Everyman (Unknown), II-574
Exclusion and Embrace (Volf), II-586
Hinds' Feet on High Places (Hurnard), II-779
"Holy Sonnets" (Donne), II-799
Lord's Prayer and the Beatitudes, The (Gregory of Nyssa), III-1078
Piers Plowman (Langland), III-1362
Prison Meditations on Psalms 51 and 31 (Savonarola), III-1423

Saint Maybe (Tyler), III-1541
Sir Gawain and the Green Knight
 (Pearl-Poet), IV-1635
Thorn Birds, The (McCullough),
 IV-1764

RESIGNATION
Fifteen Sermons Preached at the Rolls
 Chapel (Butler, J.), II-618
Penitent Magdalene, The (Hopes),
 III-1339
Serious Call to a Devout and Holy Life, A
 (Law), IV-1581
Trip to Bountiful, The (Foote), IV-1816
Waiting for Godot (Beckett), IV-1897

RESPONSIBILITY
Awakening Mercy (Benson), I-116
Beowulf (Unknown), I-140
Dangerous Silence, A (Palmer), I-412
Edge of Honor (Morris, G.), II-534
Existentialist Theology, An (Macquarrie),
 II-590
Here I Stand (Spong), II-772
His Watchful Eye (Cavanaugh), II-783
Jesus Christ and Mythology (Bultmann),
 II-909
Jesus Christ Superstar (Rice, T., and
 Webber), II-913
Magnificent Obsession (Douglas),
 III-1087
Man for All Seasons, A (Bolt), III-1090
Meaning of Persons, The (Tournier),
 III-1118
Music to Die For (Nehring), III-1184
New Song, A (Karon), III-1215
Saint Maybe (Tyler), III-1541
Serious Call to a Devout and Holy Life,
 A (Law), IV-1581
Song of Albion Trilogy, The (Lawhead),
 IV-1643
Theory of Moral Sentiments, The
 (Smith, A.), IV-1749
True Honor (Henderson), IV-1823
Winter Garden, The (Verweerd),
 IV-1953

REVELATION
Divinity School Address, The (Emerson),
 I-491
Face of the Deep, The (Rossetti), II-597
Gospel of John (John, son of Zebedee),
 II-731
Here I Stand (Spong), II-772
"In the Holy Nativity of Our Lord God"
 (Crashaw), II-859
Left Behind series (LaHaye and Jenkins),
 II-1005
Pearl (Pearl-Poet), III-1335
Revelation and Reason (Brunner),
 III-1510
Sense of the Presence of God, The
 (Baillie, J.), III-1578
Singer Trilogy, The (Miller, C.), IV-1627
Subversion of Christianity, The (Ellul),
 IV-1698
Theology of the Jewish Christian Reality,
 A (Van Buren), IV-1746
Two from Galilee (Holmes), IV-1834

THE SACRAMENTS
"Confession" (Menno Simons), I-361
Devotions upon Emergent Occasions
 (Donne), I-447
Early Christian Doctrines (Kelly), II-523
"New Birth, The" (Menno Simons), I-361

SACRIFICE
Billy Budd, Foretopman (Melville), I-150
Books of the Prophets (Isaiah, Jeremiah,
 Amos, and Micah), I-206
Cur Deus Homo (Anselm), I-401
Death on a Friday Afternoon (Neuhaus),
 I-435
Gospel According to Jesus Christ, The
 (Saramago), II-724
His Watchful Eye (Cavanaugh), II-783
"In Distrust of Merits" (Moore, M.),
 II-839
Kingdom of God Is Within You, The
 (Tolstoy), II-948
Last Days of Pompeii, The (Bulwer-
 Lytton), II-977

CORE ISSUES INDEX

Lord of the Rings, The (Tolkien), III-1073
On the Incarnation of the Word of God (Athanasius of Alexandria), III-1280
Oxygen (Ingermanson and Olson), III-1307
Pearl (Gordon), III-1331
Pontius Pilate (Caillois), III-1393
Power and the Glory, The (Greene), III-1401
Saint Manuel Bueno, Martyr (Unamuno y Jugo), III-1537
Silver Chalice, The (Costain), IV-1620
"Three Versions of Judas" (Borges), IV-1779
Twilight of Courage, The (Thoene and Thoene), IV-1830
Violence and the Sacred (Girard), IV-1879
While Mortals Sleep (Cavanaugh), IV-1941

SAINTHOOD
Canticle for Leibowitz, A (Miller, W. M.), I-245
Godric (Buechner), II-708
Mercy's Face (Craig), III-1139
Saint Maybe (Tyler), III-1541
Stream and the Sapphire, The (Levertov), IV-1689

SALVATION
Acts of the Apostles (Unknown), I-27
Against Heresies (Irenaeus), I-44
Chronicles of Narnia, The (Lewis, C. S.), I-307
City of God, The (Augustine), I-325
Death on a Friday Afternoon (Neuhaus), I-435
Declaration of the Sentiments of Arminius, A (Arminius), I-439
Dialogue, The (Catherine of Siena), I-453
Divine Comedy, The (Dante), I-473
Doctor Faustus (Marlowe), I-496
"Dream of the Rood, The" (Unknown), I-512
Early Christian Doctrines (Kelly), II-523
Faust (Goethe), II-610

Foundations of Christian Faith (Rahner), II-654
Four Books of Sentences (Peter Lombard), II-657
Go Tell It on the Mountain (Baldwin), II-687
Hinds' Feet on High Places (Hurnard), II-779
"In Distrust of Merits" (Moore, M.), II-839
Journey, The (Graham), II-941
Last Temptation of Christ, The (Kazantzakis), II-985
Left Behind series (LaHaye and Jenkins), II-1005
Left to Tell (Ilibagiza), II-1010
Lord, The (Guardini), III-1070
Love Comes Softly series (Oke), III-1082
New Testament Letters (Paul), III-1219
On Divine Love (Duns Scotus), III-1255
On First Principles (Origen), III-1259
On Providence (Zwingli), III-1272
On the Freedom of the Will (Erasmus), III-1276
Paradise Lost (Milton), III-1315
Paradise Regained (Milton), III-1319
Paul (Wangerin), III-1327
Pearl (Pearl-Poet), III-1335
Pilgrim's Progress, The (Bunyan), III-1366
Purpose Driven Life, The (Warren), III-1452
Religio Medici (Browne), III-1482
Saint Manuel Bueno, Martyr (Unamuno y Jugo), III-1537
Screwtape Letters, The (Lewis, C. S.), III-1560
Serious Call to a Devout and Holy Life, A (Law), IV-1581
Summa Theologica (Thomas Aquinas), IV-1706
What Jesus Meant (Wills), IV-1934

SANCTIFICATION
"Advice to a Prophet" (Wilbur), I-35
Divine Conspiracy, The (Willard), I-477

Plain Account of Christian Perfection, A (Wesley), III-1378

SCRIPTURES
Acts of the Apostles (Unknown), I-27
Book of God, The (Wangerin), I-192
Christ Clone Trilogy (BeauSeigneur), I-275
Confessions of Nat Turner, The (Styron), I-370
Early Christian Doctrines (Kelly), II-523
"Epistle Containing the Strange Medical Experience of Karshish, the Arab Physician, An" (Browning), II-545
Figuring the Sacred (Ricœur), II-621
Go Tell It on the Mountain (Baldwin), II-687
Good Book, The (Gomes), II-720
Gospel of Mary of Magdala, The (King, K. L.), II-735
In Memory of Her (Schüssler Fiorenza), II-851
Inscribing the Text (Brueggemann), II-870
Isaiah (Berrigan), II-898
Jesus in History (Kee), II-921
Lord, The (Guardini), III-1070
Meeting Jesus Again for the First Time (Borg), III-1125
Misquoting Jesus (Ehrman), III-1168
Nature and Destiny of Man, The (Niebuhr), III-1207
On the Freedom of the Will (Erasmus), III-1276
On the Truth of Holy Scripture (Wyclif), III-1284
Religio Medici (Browne), III-1482
Science and Health with Key to the Scriptures (Eddy), III-1557
Synoptic Gospels (Matthew, Mark, and Luke), IV-1717
Theology of the Jewish Christian Reality, A (Van Buren), IV-1746
View of the Evidences of Christianity, A (Paley), IV-1875

SELF-ABANDONMENT
His Watchful Eye (Cavanaugh), II-783
Mysticism (Underhill), III-1200
Seven Storey Mountain, The (Merton), IV-1591
Twilight of Courage, The (Thoene and Thoene), IV-1830

SELF-CONTROL
Fools and Crows (Witek), II-644
Interrogations at Noon (Gioia), II-891
Paradise Regained (Milton), III-1319
Praying God's Word (Moore, Beth), III-1412
Serious Call to a Devout and Holy Life, A (Law), IV-1581
Spiritual Exercises, The (Ignatius of Loyola), IV-1680
Theory of Moral Sentiments, The (Smith, A.), IV-1749

SELFISHNESS
"Christmas Carol, A" (Dickens), I-299
Fire by Night (Austin), II-629
Place of the Lion, The (Williams, C.), III-1375

SELF-KNOWLEDGE
Aids to Reflection (Coleridge), I-54
Amazing Grace (Norris), I-65
Arena (Hancock), I-96
Beyond God the Father (Daly), I-144
Bishop's Mantle, The (Turnbull), I-161
Care of the Soul (Moore, T.), I-251
Christ the Lord (Rice, A.), I-284
Color Purple, The (Walker), I-338
Cure for the Common Life (Lucado), I-405
Death of Ivan Ilyich, The (Tolstoy), I-431
Existentialist Theology, An (Macquarrie), II-590
Here I Stand (Spong), II-772
In the Beauty of the Lilies (Updike), II-855
Insight (Lonergan), II-873

CORE ISSUES INDEX 2051

Jesus Christ and Mythology (Bultmann), II-909
Labyrinth of the World and the Paradise of the Heart, The (Comenius), II-964
Letters from the Earth (Twain), II-1021
Man for All Seasons, A (Bolt), III-1090
Memories, Dreams, Reflections (Jung), III-1131
Paradise Regained (Milton), III-1319
Phantastes (MacDonald), III-1346
Power of Positive Thinking, The (Peale), III-1405
Religion in the Making (Whitehead), III-1490
Second Coming, The (Percy), III-1568
Secrets of Barneveld Calvary, The (Schaap), III-1574
Shunning, The (Lewis, B.), IV-1612
Sir Gawain and the Green Knight (Pearl-Poet), IV-1635
Time Lottery (Moser), IV-1786
Traveling Mercies (Lamott), IV-1802
Walking by Faith (Grimké), IV-1901
Winter Garden, The (Verweerd), IV-1953
Woman of the Pharisees, The (Mauriac), IV-1968

SERVICE
Christy (Marshall), I-303
Credo (Coffin), I-393
Cure for the Common Life (Lucado), I-405
Edge of Honor (Morris, G.), II-534
Fire by Night (Austin), II-629
First and Second Apologies, The (Justin Martyr), II-633
In His Steps (Sheldon), II-843
Magnificent Obsession (Douglas), III-1087
Out of My Life and Thought (Schweitzer), III-1299
Place Called Wiregrass, A (Morris, M.), III-1371
Saint Manuel Bueno, Martyr (Unamuno y Jugo), III-1537

Serious Call to a Devout and Holy Life, A (Law), IV-1581
Song of the Sparrow (Bodo), IV-1648
True Honor (Henderson), IV-1823
Wind in the Wheat, The (Arvin), IV-1945

SILENCE
Man for All Seasons, A (Bolt), III-1090
Mystical Theology (Pseudo-Dionysius), III-1197
Mysticism (Underhill), III-1200
On Listening to Another (Steere), III-1263
Presence of the Word, The (Ong), III-1415
Questions for Ecclesiastes (Jarman), III-1459
Rule of St. Benedict (Benedict of Nursia), III-1529
Sermons and Treatises, The (Eckhart), IV-1586
Silence (Endō), IV-1616
Virgin Time (Hampl), IV-1883
Walking by Faith (Grimké), IV-1901

SIMPLICITY
Beasts of Bethlehem, The (Kennedy), I-130
Gift from the Sea (Lindbergh), II-680
Journal of John Woolman, The (Woolman), II-936
Ladder of Divine Ascent, The (John Climacus), II-968
Little Flowers of St. Francis, The (Unknown), III-1058
Mysticism (Underhill), III-1200
Wind in the Wheat, The (Arvin), IV-1945

SIN AND SINNERS
Basic Christianity (Stott), I-127
Books of the Prophets (Isaiah, Jeremiah, Amos, and Micah), I-206
Canterbury Tales, The (Chaucer), I-240
Circle Trilogy, The (Dekker), I-320
City of God, The (Augustine), I-325
Confessio Amantis (Gower), I-357
Cur Deus Homo (Anselm), I-401

Death Comes for the Archbishop (Cather), I-423
Dialogue, The (Catherine of Siena), I-453
Doctor Faustus (Marlowe), I-496
Elmer Gantry (Lewis, S.), II-538
"Fall, The" (Bottum), II-606
Godric (Buechner), II-708
Gospel of Christian Atheism, The (Altizer), II-728
"Holy Sonnets" (Donne), II-799
Kristin Lavransdatter (Undset), II-960
Lord, The (Guardini), III-1070
Orthodoxy (Chesterton), III-1295
Paradise Lost (Milton), III-1315
Pilgrim's Progress, The (Bunyan), III-1366
Plain Account of Christian Perfection, A (Wesley), III-1378
Prison Meditations of Father Alfred Delp (Delp), III-1419
Prodigal Girl, The (Hill, Grace Livingston), III-1430
Religion (Kołakowski), III-1486
Scarlet Letter, The (Hawthorne), III-1549
Screwtape Letters, The (Lewis, C. S.), III-1560
Showings (Julian of Norwich), IV-1609
Sinners Welcome (Karr), IV-1631
Treatise on Divine Predestination (Erigena), IV-1812
Velma Still Cooks in Leeway (Wright, V. H.), IV-1862
What Jesus Meant (Wills), IV-1934

SOCIAL ACTION

Angel of History, The (Forché), I-77
Black Theology of Liberation, A (Cone), I-165
Books of the Prophets (Isaiah, Jeremiah, Amos, and Micah), I-206
Bread and Wine (Silone), I-211
Centesimus Annus (John Paul II), I-265
"Christmas Carol, A" (Dickens), I-299
Color of Faith, The (Matsuoka), I-334
Confessions of Nat Turner, The (Styron), I-370
Crawl with God, Dance in the Spirit (Park), I-386
Credo (Coffin), I-393
Divini Redemptoris (Pius XI), I-488
Economy of Grace (Tanner), II-531
Gaudium et Spes (Vatican Council II), II-672
Gilead (Robinson), II-683
God Has a Dream (Tutu), II-694
His Watchful Eye (Cavanaugh), II-783
How Should We Then Live? (Schaeffer), II-806
In His Steps (Sheldon), II-843
In Memory of Her (Schüssler Fiorenza), II-851
Infidel, The (Musser), II-866
Jesus Through the Centuries (Pelikan), II-925
Kingdom of God Is Within You, The (Tolstoy), II-948
"Letter from Birmingham Jail" (King, M. L.), II-1014
Mater et Magistra (John XXIII), III-1114
Miracle of the Bells, The (Janney), III-1164
Mit brennender Sorge (Pius XI), III-1172
Octogesima Adveniens (Paul VI), III-1238
On Christian Theology (Williams, Rowan), III-1252
Out of the Red Shadow (de Graaf), III-1303
Pacem in Terris (John XXIII), III-1311
Poisonwood Bible, The (Kingsolver), III-1384
Populorum Progressio (Paul VI), III-1397
Prison Meditations of Father Alfred Delp (Delp), III-1419
Quadragesimo Anno (Pius XI), III-1455
Reconciliation (de Gruchy), III-1470
Rerum Novarum (Leo XIII), III-1498
Strength to Love (King, M. L.), IV-1693
Suffering (Sölle), IV-1702
Theology for the Social Gospel, A (Rauschenbusch), IV-1738
Three Essays (Ritschl), IV-1772

CORE ISSUES INDEX

Tiger in the Shadows (Wilson), IV-1782
Uncle Tom's Cabin (Stowe), IV-1841
Uneasy Conscience of Modern Fundamentalism, The (Henry), IV-1845
We Hold These Truths (Murray, J. C.), IV-1923

SOLITUDE
Gift from the Sea (Lindbergh), II-680
Religion in the Making (Whitehead), III-1490
Scarlet Letter, The (Hawthorne), III-1549

SOUL
After the Lost War (Hudgins), I-41
Ascent of Mount Carmel (John of the Cross), I-107
Black Zodiac (Wright, C.), I-169
Dark Night of the Soul (John of the Cross), I-107
Devotions upon Emergent Occasions (Donne), I-447
"Dialogue of Self and Soul, A" (Yeats), I-458
Divine Milieu, The (Teilhard de Chardin), I-480
Divinity School Address, The (Emerson), I-491
Double Search, The (Jones), I-503
Essays and Addresses on the Philosophy of Religion (Hügel), II-553
Journal of a Soul (John XXIII), II-928
Mind's Road to God, The (Bonaventure), III-1159
Mysticism (Underhill), III-1200
"Ode: Intimations of Immortality" (Wordsworth), III-1241
On First Principles (Origen), III-1259
Sermons and Treatises, The (Eckhart), IV-1586
Souls of Black Folk, The (Du Bois), IV-1668
Summa Theologica (Thomas Aquinas), IV-1706

"They Are All Gone into the World of Light!" (Vaughan), IV-1753
Treatise Concerning Religious Affections, A (Edwards), IV-1806
Treatise on Divine Predestination (Erigena), IV-1812
Varieties of Religious Experience, The (James), IV-1856
Way to Christ, The (Böhme), IV-1917

SPIRITUAL WARFARE
"Dialogue of Self and Soul, A" (Yeats), I-458
Doctor Faustus (Marlowe), I-496
Last Temptation of Christ, The (Kazantzakis), II-985
Late Great Planet Earth, The (Lindsey), II-989
Paradise Lost (Milton), III-1315
Paradise Regained (Milton), III-1319
Praying God's Word (Moore, Beth), III-1412
Screwtape Letters, The (Lewis, C. S.), III-1560
Song of Albion Trilogy, The (Lawhead), IV-1643
This Present Darkness (Peretti), IV-1760
War in Heaven (Williams, C.), IV-1905

STOICISM
Beowulf (Unknown), I-140
Pontius Pilate (Caillois), III-1393

SUBMISSION
Ben-Hur (Wallace), I-136
Billy Budd, Foretopman (Melville), I-150
"Here Follows Some Verses upon the Burning of Our House July 10th, 1666" (Bradstreet), II-768

SUFFERING
Apocalypse (Cardenal), I-80
Brothers Karamazov, The (Dostoevski), I-229
Christian Tradition, The (Kitagawa), I-292
Come Sweet Death (Napier), I-342

Creation, The (Beasley), I-390
Death of Ivan Ilyich, The (Tolstoy), I-431
Devotions upon Emergent Occasions (Donne), I-447
Doctor Faustus (Marlowe), I-496
Evil and the God of Love (Hick), II-582
Exclusion and Embrace (Volf), II-586
Faust (Goethe), II-610
"Feet of Jesus" (Hughes), II-614
God's Silence (Wright, F.), II-712
"In Distrust of Merits" (Moore, M.), II-839
J. B. (MacLeish), II-902
Last Temptation of Christ, The (Kazantzakis), II-985
Life Is Worth Living (Sheen), II-1037
Mary Magdalene (Traylor), III-1106
Moments of Grace (Jennings), III-1176
Prison Meditations of Father Alfred Delp (Delp), III-1419
Purity of Heart Is to Will One Thing (Kierkegaard), III-1446
Scarlet Letter, The (Hawthorne), III-1549
Sermons and Treatises, The (Eckhart), IV-1586
She Who Is (Johnson, E. A.), IV-1598
Sinners Welcome (Karr), IV-1631
Sparrow, The (Russell), IV-1676
Suffering (Sölle), IV-1702
Supplicating Voice, The (Johnson, S.), IV-1710
Synoptic Gospels (Matthew, Mark, and Luke), IV-1717
Theodicy (Leibniz), IV-1734
Trip to Bountiful, The (Foote), IV-1816
Twilight of Courage, The (Thoene and Thoene), IV-1830
Unspeakable (Guinness), IV-1849
Unutterable Beauty, The (Studdert Kennedy), IV-1853
Waiting for God (Weil), IV-1891
Waiting for Godot (Beckett), IV-1897
Woman of the Pharisees, The (Mauriac), IV-1968

SURRENDER
Hinds' Feet on High Places (Hurnard), II-779
Prison Meditations of Father Alfred Delp (Delp), III-1419
Sutter's Cross (Cramer), IV-1714

THEOLOGY
Apology (Tertullian), I-92

TIME
Burning Fields, The (Middleton), I-233
Cherubinic Wanderer, The (Silesius), I-268
Chronicles of Narnia, The (Lewis, C. S.), I-307
Destiny of Man, The (Berdyaev), I-443
Don't Throw Away Tomorrow (Schuller), I-500
For the Time Being (Dillard), II-647
Four Quartets (Eliot, T. S.), II-660
Great Divorce, The (Lewis, C. S.), II-739
Presence of the Word, The (Ong), III-1415
Time Lottery (Moser), IV-1786
What I Think I Did (Woiwode), IV-1931

THE TRINITY
Crucified God, The (Moltmann), I-397
Early Christian Doctrines (Kelly), II-523
Four Books of Sentences (Peter Lombard), II-657
"Holy Sonnets" (Donne), II-799
Introduction to Christianity (Ratzinger), II-895
Meeting Jesus Again for the First Time (Borg), III-1125
Mind of the Maker, The (Sayers), III-1155
Mind's Road to God, The (Bonaventure), III-1159
Mystical Theology (Pseudo-Dionysius), III-1197
On First Principles (Origen), III-1259
She Who Is (Johnson, E. A.), IV-1598

Core Issues Index

TRUST IN GOD
Arena (Hancock), I-96
Capital Offense, A (Parker), I-248
Christy (Marshall), I-303
Diary of a Country Priest, The (Bernanos), I-462
Ethics (Bonhoeffer), II-561
God's Silence (Wright, F.), II-712
Hebrew Bible (Unknown), II-756
"Here Follows Some Verses upon the Burning of Our House July 10th, 1666" (Bradstreet), II-768
Hiding Place, The (Ten Boom), II-775
Hinds' Feet on High Places (Hurnard), II-779
His Watchful Eye (Cavanaugh), II-783
Left to Tell (Ilibagiza), II-1010
Lilies of the Field, The (Barrett), III-1050
Little Flowers of St. Francis, The (Unknown), III-1058
Love Comes Softly series (Oke), III-1082
Music to Die For (Nehring), III-1184
Newpointe 911 (Blackstock), III-1223
Praying God's Word (Moore, Beth), III-1412
Prison Meditations on Psalms 51 and 31 (Savonarola), III-1423
Psalms (David), III-1442
Purpose Driven Life, The (Warren), III-1452
Sense of the Presence of God, The (Baillie, J.), III-1578
Shepherd of the Hills, The (Wright, H. B.), IV-1602
Song of the Sparrow (Bodo), IV-1648
Stream and the Sapphire, The (Levertov), IV-1689
Supplicating Voice, The (Johnson, S.), IV-1710
Sutter's Cross (Cramer), IV-1714
Tiger in the Shadows (Wilson), IV-1782
Truth Teller, The (Hunt), IV-1827
Two from Galilee (Holmes), IV-1834

TRUTH
Against Heresies (Irenaeus), I-44
And I Alone Have Escaped to Tell You (McInerny), I-73
Brightness That Made My Soul Tremble, A (Nesanovich), I-222
Da Vinci Code, The (Brown), I-408
Dialogue, The (Catherine of Siena), I-453
Edge of Honor (Morris, G.), II-534
Even in Quiet Places (Stafford), II-571
Faerie Queene, The (Spenser), II-601
Gospel of Mary of Magdala, The (King, K. L.), II-735
Here I Stand (Spong), II-772
How Should We Then Live? (Schaeffer), II-806
Insight (Lonergan), II-873
Instructor, The (Clement of Alexandria), II-881
Knowledge and Faith (Stein), II-956
Master and Margarita, The (Bulgakov), III-1110
Miscellanies (Clement of Alexandria), II-881
On Being a Christian (Küng), III-1249
On the Truth of Holy Scripture (Wyclif), III-1284
Out of My Life and Thought (Schweitzer), III-1299
Philosophy of Existence (Jaspers), III-1354
Purity of Heart Is to Will One Thing (Kierkegaard), III-1446
Reconciliation (de Gruchy), III-1470
Religion (Kołakowski), III-1486
Revelation and Reason (Brunner), III-1510
Sir Gawain and the Green Knight (Pearl-Poet), IV-1635
Time Lottery (Moser), IV-1786
To Kill a Mockingbird (Lee, H.), IV-1790
Veritatis Splendor (John Paul II), IV-1866
Warranted Christian Belief (Plantinga), IV-1909
What Jesus Meant (Wills), IV-1934
Winter Garden, The (Verweerd), IV-1953

UNION WITH GOD
Ascent of Mount Carmel (John of the Cross), I-107
Cherubinic Wanderer, The (Silesius), I-268
Circle Trilogy, The (Dekker), I-320
Conferences (Cassian), I-354
Dark Night of the Soul (John of the Cross), I-107
Dialogue, The (Catherine of Siena), I-453
Divine Comedy, The (Dante), I-473
Divine Milieu, The (Teilhard de Chardin), I-480
Double Search, The (Jones), I-503
God's Silence (Wright, F.), II-712
Hinds' Feet on High Places (Hurnard), II-779
History of God, A (Armstrong), II-791
Interior Castle (Teresa of Ávila), II-887
Introduction to Christianity (Ratzinger), II-895
Last Temptation of Christ, The (Kazantzakis), II-985
Meaning of Prayer, The (Fosdick), III-1121
Mind's Road to God, The (Bonaventure), III-1159
Mysticism (Underhill), III-1200
On the Incarnation of the Word of God (Athanasius of Alexandria), III-1280
Sermons and Treatises, The (Eckhart), IV-1586
Showings (Julian of Norwich), IV-1609
Third Spiritual Alphabet, The (Osuna), IV-1756

VIRGINITY
Letters of Saint Jerome, The (Jerome), II-1024
Two from Galilee (Holmes), IV-1834

VIRTUE
Beowulf (Unknown), I-140
Bioethics (Meilaender), I-154
Ethics After Babel (Stout), II-565
Faerie Queene, The (Spenser), II-601

Fifteen Sermons Preached at the Rolls Chapel (Butler, J.), II-618
Ladder of Divine Ascent, The (John Climacus), II-968
Serious Call to a Devout and Holy Life, A (Law), IV-1581
Temple, The (Herbert), IV-1726
Treatise Concerning Religious Affections, A (Edwards), IV-1806
Vicar of Wakefield, The (Goldsmith), IV-1870

WISDOM
Bread for the Journey (Nouwen), I-215
Care of the Soul (Moore, T.), I-251
Coming of the Cosmic Christ, The (Fox, M.), I-346
Ethics After Babel (Stout), II-565
Even in Quiet Places (Stafford), II-571
Hebrew Bible (Unknown), II-756
Here I Stand (Spong), II-772
Labyrinth of the World and the Paradise of the Heart, The (Comenius), II-964
Of Learned Ignorance (Nicholas of Cusa), III-1245
On First Principles (Origen), III-1259
Rime of the Ancient Mariner, The (Coleridge), III-1514
Theory of Moral Sentiments, The (Smith, A.), IV-1749

WOMEN
Abortion and Divorce in Western Law (Glendon), I-23
Aké (Soyinka), I-58
Baptismal Instruction (Chrysostom), I-120
Belief or Nonbelief? (Eco and Martini), I-133
Beyond God the Father (Daly), I-144
Brightness That Made My Soul Tremble, A (Nesanovich), I-222
Called to Question (Chittister), I-237
Eve's Striptease (Kasdorf), II-578
Gift from the Sea (Lindbergh), II-680
Gospel of Mary of Magdala, The (King, K. L.), II-735

In Memory of Her (Schüssler Fiorenza), II-851
In This House of Brede (Godden), II-863
Kristin Lavransdatter (Undset), II-960
Mary Magdalene (Traylor), III-1106
Saint Joan (Shaw), III-1533
Scarlet Letter, The (Hawthorne), III-1549
She Who Is (Johnson, E. A.), IV-1598
Shunning, The (Lewis, B.), IV-1612
Walking by Faith (Grimké), IV-1901

THE WORD
Bible in History, The, I-10
Four Quartets (Eliot, T. S.), II-660
Gospel of John (John, son of Zebedee), II-731
Hebrew Bible (Unknown), II-756
Humani Generis Redemptionem (Benedict XV), II-815
Instructor, The (Clement of Alexandria), II-881
Jesus Christ and Mythology (Bultmann), II-909
Jesus in History (Kee), II-921
Marriage of Heaven and Hell, The (Blake), III-1102
Miscellanies (Clement of Alexandria), II-881
Misquoting Jesus (Ehrman), III-1168
On First Principles (Origen), III-1259
Praying God's Word (Moore, Beth), III-1412
Presence of the Word, The (Ong), III-1415
Theology of the Jewish Christian Reality, A (Van Buren), IV-1746
"Word made Flesh is seldom, A" (Dickinson), IV-1976

WORKS AND DEEDS
Book of Revelation (John), I-202
Don't Throw Away Tomorrow (Schuller), I-500
Everyman (Unknown), II-574
Freedom of a Christian, The (Luther), II-664
Life of Jesus, The (Renan), III-1043
Morte d'Urban (Powers), III-1180
Questions for Ecclesiastes (Jarman), III-1459
Serious Call to a Devout and Holy Life, A (Law), IV-1581

GENRE INDEX

List of Categories

Adventure 2059	Instructional Manuals 2068
Africa 2059	Journals or Diaries 2068
Allegory 2059	Legends 2068
Alternate Universes 2059	Letters 2068
Apocalyptic Fiction 2059	Literary Fiction 2069
Autobiographies 2059	Lyric Poetry 2069
Biblical Fiction 2060	Meditation and Contemplation 2070
Biblical Studies 2060	Morality Tales 2071
Biographies 2060	Mystery and Detective Fiction 2071
Catholic Fiction 2061	Mysticism 2072
Church Histories 2061	Narrative Poetry 2072
Comedy 2062	Novellas 2072
Creeds 2062	Novels 2073
Critical Analyses 2062	Opera 2075
Debate 2062	Parables and Fables 2075
Devotions 2063	Philosophy 2075
Dialogue 2063	Poetry 2075
Didactic Treatises 2063	Prayer Books 2076
Drama 2064	Problem Play 2076
Dramatic Monologue 2064	Proverbs 2076
Encyclicals 2064	Rock Opera 2076
Epic Literature 2064	Romances 2076
Epigrams 2064	Sagas 2077
Essays 2064	Saint's Meditations 2077
Evangelical Fiction 2065	Satires 2077
Exegeses 2065	Science Fiction 2077
Fantasy 2065	Screenplay 2077
Guidebooks 2066	Sermons 2077
Handbooks for Living 2066	Short Fiction 2077
Hermeneutics 2066	Spiritual Treatises 2078
Historical Fiction 2067	Stories 2078
History 2067	Theology 2079
Holy Writings 2067	Thrillers/Suspense 2081
Homilies 2068	Time Travel 2081
Humor 2068	Westerns 2081

GENRE INDEX

ADVENTURE
Ben-Hur (Wallace), I-136
Broken Lance (Sorensen), I-226
Chronicles of Narnia, The (Lewis, C. S.), I-307
Circle Trilogy, The (Dekker), I-320
Dawning of Deliverance, The (Pella), I-416
Lord of the Rings, The (Tolkien), III-1073
Sir Gawain and the Green Knight (Pearl-Poet), IV-1635
Time Lottery (Moser), IV-1786
True Honor (Henderson), IV-1823

AFRICA
God Has a Dream (Tutu), II-694

ALLEGORY
Age of Anxiety, The (Auden), I-50
Arena (Hancock), I-96
Billy Budd, Foretopman (Melville), I-150
Divine Comedy, The (Dante), I-473
Everyman (Unknown), II-574
Faerie Queene, The (Spenser), II-601
Great Divorce, The (Lewis, C. S.), II-739
Hinds' Feet on High Places (Hurnard), II-779
Labyrinth of the World and the Paradise of the Heart, The (Comenius), II-964
Mind's Road to God, The (Bonaventure), III-1159
Piers Plowman (Langland), III-1362
Pilgrim's Progress, The (Bunyan), III-1366
Singer Trilogy, The (Miller, C.), IV-1627
Songs of Innocence and of Experience (Blake), IV-1655
"Station Island" (Heaney), IV-1685

ALTERNATE UNIVERSES
Chronicles of Narnia, The (Lewis, C. S.), I-307
Song of Albion Trilogy, The (Lawhead), IV-1643

APOCALYPTIC FICTION
Canticle for Leibowitz, A (Miller, W. M.), I-245
Christ Clone Trilogy (BeauSeigneur), I-275
Circle Trilogy, The (Dekker), I-320
Left Behind series (LaHaye and Jenkins), II-1005
Seal of Gaia, The (Maddoux), III-1564
Soon (Jenkins), IV-1660
This Present Darkness (Peretti), IV-1760

AUTOBIOGRAPHIES
Aké (Soyinka), I-58
Amazing Grace (Norris), I-65
And I Alone Have Escaped to Tell You (McInerny), I-73
Apologia pro vita sua (Newman), I-88
Blue Like Jazz (Miller, D.), I-180
Called to Question (Chittister), I-237
Confessions (Augustine), I-365
Ghost Pain (Lea), II-676
Here I Stand (Spong), II-772
Hiding Place, The (Ten Boom), II-775
In Memoriam (Tennyson), II-847
Journal of George Fox, The (Fox, G.), II-931
Journal of John Woolman, The (Woolman), II-936
Labyrinth of the World and the Paradise of the Heart, The (Comenius), II-964
Last Temptation of Christ, The (Kazantzakis), II-985
Left to Tell (Ilibagiza), II-1010
Loaves and Fishes (Day), III-1062
Memories, Dreams, Reflections (Jung), III-1131
Midquest (Chappell), III-1151
My God and I (Smedes), III-1188
Orthodoxy (Chesterton), III-1295
Out of My Life and Thought (Schweitzer), III-1299
Philosophy of Existentialism, The (Marcel), III-1358
Seven Storey Mountain, The (Merton), IV-1591

Sinners Welcome (Karr), IV-1631
Souls of Black Folk, The (Du Bois), IV-1668
Traveling Mercies (Lamott), IV-1802
Walking by Faith (Grimké), IV-1901
What I Think I Did (Woiwode), IV-1931
With Head and Heart (Thurman), IV-1961

BIBLICAL FICTION
Barabbas (Lagerkvist), I-123
Ben-Hur (Wallace), I-136
Book of God, The (Wangerin), I-192
Christ the Lord (Rice, A.), I-284
Divine and Human (Tolstoy), I-469
Gospel According to Jesus Christ, The (Saramago), II-724
Greatest Story Ever Told, The (Oursler), II-752
J. B. (MacLeish), II-902
Jesus Christ Superstar (Rice, T., and Webber), II-913
Last Temptation of Christ, The (Kazantzakis), II-985
Letters from the Earth (Twain), II-1021
Master and Margarita, The (Bulgakov), III-1110
Memoirs of Pontius Pilate (Mills), III-1128
Paradise Regained (Milton), III-1319
Paul (Wangerin), III-1327
Pontius Pilate (Caillois), III-1393
Silver Chalice, The (Costain), IV-1620
Two from Galilee (Holmes), IV-1834

BIBLICAL STUDIES
Against Heresies (Irenaeus), I-44
Agape and Eros (Nygren), I-47
Christ (Miles), I-272
Crucified God, The (Moltmann), I-397
Death on a Friday Afternoon (Neuhaus), I-435
Divine Conspiracy, The (Willard), I-477
Existentialist Theology, An (Macquarrie), II-590
Face of the Deep, The (Rossetti), II-597
First Coming, The (Sheehan), II-636

Good Book, The (Gomes), II-720
Gospel of John (John, son of Zebedee), II-731
History of God, A (Armstrong), II-791
In Memory of Her (Schüssler Fiorenza), II-851
Inscribing the Text (Brueggemann), II-870
Isaiah (Berrigan), II-898
Jefferson Bible, The (Jefferson), II-906
Jesus Christ and Mythology (Bultmann), II-909
Jesus I Never Knew, The (Yancey), II-917
Jesus in History (Kee), II-921
Late Great Planet Earth, The (Lindsey), II-989
Life Is Worth Living (Sheen), II-1037
Life of Jesus, A (Endō), II-1040
Life of Jesus Critically Examined, The (Strauss), III-1046
Lord, The (Guardini), III-1070
Meeting Jesus Again for the First Time (Borg), III-1125
Politics of Jesus, The (Yoder), III-1389
Resurrection of God Incarnate, The (Swinburne), III-1506
Science and Health with Key to the Scriptures (Eddy), III-1557
Synoptic Gospels (Matthew, Mark, and Luke), IV-1717
View of the Evidences of Christianity, A (Paley), IV-1875
Violence and the Sacred (Girard), IV-1879
When Jesus Came to Harvard (Cox), IV-1937

BIOGRAPHIES
Books of the Prophets (Isaiah, Jeremiah, Amos, and Micah), I-206
Christ (Miles), I-272
Gospel of John (John, son of Zebedee), II-731
Great Exemplar, The (Taylor), II-743
Journal of a Soul (John XXIII), II-928

Life of Jesus, A (Endō), II-1040
Life of Jesus, The (Renan), III-1043
Man Nobody Knows, The (Barton), III-1094
Memoirs of Pontius Pilate (Mills), III-1128
Memories, Dreams, Reflections (Jung), III-1131
Mystical Element of Religion, The (Hügel), III-1191
Nun's Story, The (Hulme), III-1234
Saint Joan (Shaw), III-1533
"Station Island" (Heaney), IV-1685

CATHOLIC FICTION
Bishop in the Old Neighborhood, The (Greeley), I-157
Brideshead Revisited (Waugh), I-218
Canticle for Leibowitz, A (Miller, W. M.), I-245
Catholics (Moore, Brian), I-261
Da Vinci Code, The (Brown), I-408
Dear and Glorious Physician (Caldwell), I-420
In This House of Brede (Godden), II-863
Keys of the Kingdom, The (Cronin), II-945
Miracle of the Bells, The (Janney), III-1164
North of Hope (Hassler), III-1230
Nun's Story, The (Hulme), III-1234
Power and the Glory, The (Greene), III-1401
Quo Vadis (Sienkiewicz), III-1462
Saint Manuel Bueno, Martyr (Unamuno y Jugo), III-1537
Second Coming, The (Percy), III-1568
Shoes of the Fisherman, The (West, M.), IV-1605
Silence (Endō), IV-1616
Silver Chalice, The (Costain), IV-1620
Woman of the Pharisees, The (Mauriac), IV-1968

CHURCH HISTORIES
African Heritage and Contemporary Christianity (Mugambi), I-38
Agape and Eros (Nygren), I-47
And I Alone Have Escaped to Tell You (McInerny), I-73
Apologia pro vita sua (Newman), I-88
Apology (Tertullian), I-92
Bible and Theology in African Christianity (Mbiti), I-147
Conferences (Cassian), I-354
Constantine's Sword (Carroll), I-374
Crawl with God, Dance in the Spirit (Park), I-386
Essays and Addresses on the Philosophy of Religion (Hügel), II-553
First Coming, The (Sheehan), II-636
Gospel of Mary of Magdala, The (King, K. L.), II-735
History of Christianity, A (Johnson, P.), II-787
History of God, A (Armstrong), II-791
Jesus in History (Kee), II-921
Misquoting Jesus (Ehrman), III-1168
Nature and Destiny of Man, The (Niebuhr), III-1207
On Being a Christian (Küng), III-1249
Orthodox Church, The (Ware), III-1291
Problem of Christianity, The (Royce), III-1426
Protestant Ethic and the Spirit of Capitalism, The (Weber), III-1438
Robe, The (Douglas), III-1522
Social Teaching of the Christian Churches, The (Troeltsch), IV-1639
Soul of Christianity, The (Smith, H.), IV-1664
Subversion of Christianity, The (Ellul), IV-1698
Wonderful Words of Life (Mouw and Noll), IV-1972

COMEDY
  Merchant of Venice, The (Shakespeare),
    III-1135

CREEDS
  Early Christian Doctrines (Kelly), II-523

CRITICAL ANALYSES
  Belief or Nonbelief? (Eco and Martini),
    I-133
  Black Theology of Liberation, A (Cone),
    I-165
  Christian Tradition, The (Kitagawa),
    I-292
  Color of Faith, The (Matsuoka), I-334
  Crawl with God, Dance in the Spirit
    (Park), I-386
  Destiny of Man, The (Berdyaev), I-443
  Drama of Atheist Humanism, The
    (Lubac), I-508
  Economy of Grace (Tanner), II-531
  Essence of Christianity, The (Feuerbach),
    II-557
  Ethics (Bonhoeffer), II-561
  Evil and the God of Love (Hick), II-582
  Figuring the Sacred (Ricœur), II-621
  Foundations of Christian Faith (Rahner),
    II-654
  Gospel of Mary of Magdala, The (King,
    K. L.), II-735
  Holocaust Politics (Roth), II-795
  How Should We Then Live? (Schaeffer),
    II-806
  Idea of a Christian Society, The (Eliot,
    T. S.), II-826
  Idea of the Holy, The (Otto), II-830
  Insight (Lonergan), II-873
  Jesus in History (Kee), II-921
  Life of Jesus Critically Examined, The
    (Strauss), III-1046
  Lord, The (Guardini), III-1070
  Mind of the Maker, The (Sayers), III-1155
  Misquoting Jesus (Ehrman), III-1168
  Mit brennender Sorge (Pius XI), III-1172
  Mystical Element of Religion, The
    (Hügel), III-1191
  On Being a Christian (Küng), III-1249
  Philosophy of Existentialism, The
    (Marcel), III-1358
  Problem of Christianity, The (Royce),
    III-1426
  Protestant Ethic and the Spirit of
    Capitalism, The (Weber), III-1438
  Religion (Kołakowski), III-1486
  Religion Within the Bounds of Mere
    Reason (Kant), III-1494
  Resurrection of God Incarnate, The
    (Swinburne), III-1506
  Simply Christian (Wright, N. T.),
    IV-1624
  Social Teaching of the Christian
    Churches, The (Troeltsch), IV-1639
  Souls of Black Folk, The (Du Bois),
    IV-1668
  Source of Human Good, The (Wieman),
    IV-1672
  Subversion of Christianity, The (Ellul),
    IV-1698
  Theodicy (Leibniz), IV-1734
  Theory of Moral Sentiments, The (Smith,
    A.), IV-1749
  Three Hardest Words in the World to Get
    Right, The (Sweet), IV-1776
  Unspeakable (Guinness), IV-1849
  Violence and the Sacred (Girard),
    IV-1879
  Warranted Christian Belief (Plantinga),
    IV-1909
  We Hold These Truths (Murray, J. C.),
    IV-1923
  What Are People For? (Berry), IV-1927
  What Jesus Meant (Wills), IV-1934
  When Jesus Came to Harvard (Cox),
    IV-1937
  With the Grain of the Universe
    (Hauerwas), IV-1965
  Wonderful Words of Life (Mouw and
    Noll), IV-1972

DEBATE
  "Dialogue of Self and Soul, A" (Yeats),
    I-458

Genre Index

DEVOTIONS
Bread for the Journey (Nouwen), I-215
Devotions upon Emergent Occasions (Donne), I-447
Great Exemplar, The (Taylor), II-743
Hymns and Spiritual Songs (Watts), II-822
"In the Holy Nativity of Our Lord God" (Crashaw), II-859
On Listening to Another (Steere), III-1263
Philokalia (Cairns), III-1350
Prison Meditations on Psalms 51 and 31 (Savonarola), III-1423
Psalms (David), III-1442
Purpose Driven Life, The (Warren), III-1452
Supplicating Voice, The (Johnson, S.), IV-1710

DIALOGUE
Dialogue, The (Catherine of Siena), I-453
"Dialogue of Self and Soul, A" (Yeats), I-458

DIDACTIC TREATISES
Abortion and Divorce in Western Law (Glendon), I-23
Against Heresies (Irenaeus), I-44
Argument Against Abolishing Christianity (Swift), I-99
Bioethics (Meilaender), I-154
Bloudy Tenent of Persecution for Cause of Conscience, The (Williams, Roger), I-176
Catechism of the Catholic Church (Council of Trent), I-257
Church, The (Hus), I-312
Cloud of Unknowing, The (Unknown), I-329
Country Parson, The (Herbert), I-378
Divine Comedy, The (Dante), I-473
Drama of Atheist Humanism, The (Lubac), I-508
Enneads, The (Plotinus), II-542
Ethics (Bonhoeffer), II-561
First and Second Apologies, The (Justin Martyr), II-633
Four Books of Sentences (Peter Lombard), II-657
God Who Commands, The (Mouw), II-704
Humani Generis Redemptionem (Benedict XV), II-815
Idea of a Christian Society, The (Eliot, T. S.), II-826
Insight (Lonergan), II-873
Journal of George Fox, The (Fox, G.), II-931
Journal of John Woolman, The (Woolman), II-936
Kingdom of God Is Within You, The (Tolstoy), II-948
Knowledge and Faith (Stein), II-956
Ladder of Divine Ascent, The (John Climacus), II-968
Lectures on Revivals of Religion (Finney), II-1001
Meaning of Persons, The (Tournier), III-1118
Memories, Dreams, Reflections (Jung), III-1131
Mere Christianity (Lewis, C. S.), III-1143
On Providence (Zwingli), III-1272
On the Freedom of the Will (Erasmus), III-1276
On the Incarnation of the Word of God (Athanasius of Alexandria), III-1280
On the Truth of Holy Scripture (Wyclif), III-1284
Pacem in Terris (John XXIII), III-1311
Prophesy Deliverance! (West, C.), III-1434
Purity of Heart Is to Will One Thing (Kierkegaard), III-1446
Religion (Kołakowski), III-1486
Serious Call to a Devout and Holy Life, A (Law), IV-1581
Soul of Christianity, The (Smith, H.), IV-1664
Spiritual Exercises, The (Ignatius of Loyola), IV-1680

Summa Theologica (Thomas Aquinas), IV-1706
Theory of Moral Sentiments, The (Smith, A.), IV-1749
Treatise on Divine Predestination (Erigena), IV-1812
View of the Evidences of Christianity, A (Paley), IV-1875

DRAMA
Doctor Faustus (Marlowe), I-496
Everyman (Unknown), II-574
Faust (Goethe), II-610
J. B. (MacLeish), II-902
Jesus Christ Superstar (Rice, T., and Webber), II-913
Man for All Seasons, A (Bolt), III-1090
Merchant of Venice, The (Shakespeare), III-1135
Saint Joan (Shaw), III-1533
Seventh Seal, The (Bergman), IV-1595
Trip to Bountiful, The (Foote), IV-1816
Waiting for Godot (Beckett), IV-1897

DRAMATIC MONOLOGUE
"Epistle Containing the Strange Medical Experience of Karshish, the Arab Physician, An" (Browning), II-545

ENCYCLICALS
Casti Connubii (Pius XI), I-254
Centesimus Annus (John Paul II), I-265
Divini Redemptoris (Pius XI), I-488
Evangelium Vitae (John Paul II), II-568
Humanae Vitae (Paul VI), II-811
Humani Generis Redemptionem (Benedict XV), II-815
Mater et Magistra (John XXIII), III-1114
Mit brennender Sorge (Pius XI), III-1172
Octogesima Adveniens (Paul VI), III-1238
Pacem in Terris (John XXIII), III-1311
Populorum Progressio (Paul VI), III-1397
Quadragesimo Anno (Pius XI), III-1455
Rerum Novarum (Leo XIII), III-1498
Veritatis Splendor (John Paul II), IV-1866

EPIC LITERATURE
Beowulf (Unknown), I-140
Book of God, The (Wangerin), I-192
Faerie Queene, The (Spenser), II-601
Paradise Lost (Milton), III-1315
Paradise Regained (Milton), III-1319

EPIGRAMS
Apocalypse (Cardenal), I-80
Cherubinic Wanderer, The (Silesius), I-268
Sapphics and Uncertainties (Steele), III-1545

ESSAYS
Christian Tradition, The (Kitagawa), I-292
Divinity School Address, The (Emerson), I-491
Early Theological Writings (Hegel), II-527
Economy of Grace (Tanner), II-531
Figuring the Sacred (Ricœur), II-621
For the Time Being (Dillard), II-647
God Was in Christ (Baillie, D. M.), II-698
Good Book, The (Gomes), II-720
Idea of a Christian Society, The (Eliot, T. S.), II-826
Jesus Through the Centuries (Pelikan), II-925
Knowledge and Faith (Stein), II-956
Letters from the Earth (Twain), II-1021
Metaphysical Demonstration of the Existence of God, The (Suárez), III-1147
New Kind of Christian, A (McLaren), III-1211
Orthodoxy (Chesterton), III-1295
Philosophy of Existence (Jaspers), III-1354
Philosophy of Existentialism, The (Marcel), III-1358
Presence of the Word, The (Ong), III-1415
Problem of Christianity, The (Royce), III-1426
Sense of the Presence of God, The (Baillie, J.), III-1578

GENRE INDEX

Souls of Black Folk, The (Du Bois), IV-1668
Supplicating Voice, The (Johnson, S.), IV-1710
Tasks of Philosophy, The (MacIntyre), IV-1722
Theodicy (Leibniz), IV-1734
Three Essays (Ritschl), IV-1772
Traveling Mercies (Lamott), IV-1802
Uneasy Conscience of Modern Fundamentalism, The (Henry), IV-1845
Varieties of Religious Experience, The (James), IV-1856
Waiting for God (Weil), IV-1891
We Hold These Truths (Murray, J. C.), IV-1923
What Are People For? (Berry), IV-1927
With the Grain of the Universe (Hauerwas), IV-1965

EVANGELICAL FICTION
Bishop's Mantle, The (Turnbull), I-161
Blood Ties (Brouwer), I-173
Capital Offense, A (Parker), I-248
Circle Trilogy, The (Dekker), I-320
Dangerous Silence, A (Palmer), I-412
Directed Verdict (Singer), I-465
Divine and Human (Tolstoy), I-469
Final Witness (Bell), II-625
In His Steps (Sheldon), II-843
List, The (Whitlow), III-1054
Long Trail Home, The (Bly), III-1066
Love Comes Softly series (Oke), III-1082
Magnificent Obsession (Douglas), III-1087
Miracle of the Bells, The (Janney), III-1164
New Song, A (Karon), III-1215
One Tuesday Morning (Kingsbury), III-1288
Passing by Samaria (Foster), III-1323
Resting in the Bosom of the Lamb (Trobaugh), III-1502
Seal of Gaia, The (Maddoux), III-1564

Soon (Jenkins), IV-1660
This Present Darkness (Peretti), IV-1760
Thr3e (Dekker), IV-1768
Tiger in the Shadows (Wilson), IV-1782
Velma Still Cooks in Leeway (Wright, V. H.), IV-1862
While Mortals Sleep (Cavanaugh), IV-1941

EXEGESES
Baptismal Instruction (Chrysostom), I-120
Divine Conspiracy, The (Willard), I-477
Epistle to the Romans, The (Barth), II-549
Face of the Deep, The (Rossetti), II-597
In Memory of Her (Schüssler Fiorenza), II-851
Jesus I Never Knew, The (Yancey), II-917
Lord, The (Guardini), III-1070
Lord's Prayer and the Beatitudes, The (Gregory of Nyssa), III-1078
On Providence (Zwingli), III-1272
On the Freedom of the Will (Erasmus), III-1276
On the Incarnation of the Word of God (Athanasius of Alexandria), III-1280
Politics of Jesus, The (Yoder), III-1389
Reasonableness of Christianity as Delivered in the Scriptures, The (Locke), III-1466
Veritatis Splendor (John Paul II), IV-1866

FANTASY
Chronicles of Narnia, The (Lewis, C. S.), I-307
Great Divorce, The (Lewis, C. S.), II-739
Lord of the Rings, The (Tolkien), III-1073
Master and Margarita, The (Bulgakov), III-1110
Place of the Lion, The (Williams, C.), III-1375
Singer Trilogy, The (Miller, C.), IV-1627
Song of Albion Trilogy, The (Lawhead), IV-1643

GUIDEBOOKS
Bread for the Journey (Nouwen), I-215
Catechism of the Catholic Church
  (Council of Trent), I-257
Cure for the Common Life (Lucado),
  I-405
Don't Throw Away Tomorrow (Schuller),
  I-500
Imitation of Christ, The (Thomas à
  Kempis), II-834
In His Steps (Sheldon), II-843
Ladder of Divine Ascent, The (John
  Climacus), II-968
Mind's Road to God, The (Bonaventure),
  III-1159
Power of Positive Thinking, The (Peale),
  III-1405
Praying God's Word (Moore, Beth),
  III-1412
Rule of St. Benedict (Benedict of Nursia),
  III-1529
Spiritual Exercises, The (Ignatius of
  Loyola), IV-1680

HANDBOOKS FOR LIVING
Bioethics (Meilaender), I-154
Blue Like Jazz (Miller, D.), I-180
Books of the Prophets (Isaiah, Jeremiah,
  Amos, and Micah), I-206
Bread for the Journey (Nouwen), I-215
Called to Question (Chittister), I-237
Care of the Soul (Moore, T.), I-251
Country Parson, The (Herbert), I-378
Courage to Be, The (Tillich), I-382
Cure for the Common Life (Lucado),
  I-405
Divine Conspiracy, The (Willard),
  I-477
Don't Throw Away Tomorrow (Schuller),
  I-500
Great Mysteries, The (Greeley), II-746
In His Steps (Sheldon), II-843
Instructor, The (Clement of Alexandria),
  II-881
Journal of George Fox, The (Fox, G.),
  II-931

Journal of John Woolman, The
  (Woolman), II-936
Journey, The (Graham), II-941
Life Is Worth Living (Sheen), II-1037
Meaning of Persons, The (Tournier),
  III-1118
Miscellanies (Clement of Alexandria),
  II-881
No Greater Love (Teresa, Mother),
  III-1227
Power of Positive Thinking, The (Peale),
  III-1405
Praying God's Word (Moore, Beth),
  III-1412
Purpose Driven Life, The (Warren),
  III-1452
Rule of St. Benedict (Benedict of Nursia),
  III-1529
Science and Health with Key to the
  Scriptures (Eddy), III-1557
Unspeakable (Guinness), IV-1849
When Jesus Came to Harvard (Cox),
  IV-1937

HERMENEUTICS
Figuring the Sacred (Ricœur), II-621
First Coming, The (Sheehan), II-636
God's Silence (Wright, F.), II-712
Good Book, The (Gomes), II-720
In Memory of Her (Schüssler Fiorenza),
  II-851
Inscribing the Text (Brueggemann), II-870
Insight (Lonergan), II-873
Jesus Christ and Mythology (Bultmann),
  II-909
Life of Jesus Critically Examined, The
  (Strauss), III-1046
On Christian Theology (Williams,
  Rowan), III-1252
On the Truth of Holy Scripture (Wyclif),
  III-1284
Reasonableness of Christianity as
  Delivered in the Scriptures, The
  (Locke), III-1466
Warranted Christian Belief (Plantinga),
  IV-1909

GENRE INDEX

HISTORICAL FICTION
Ben-Hur (Wallace), I-136
Billy Budd, Foretopman (Melville), I-150
Broken Lance (Sorensen), I-226
Christ the Lord (Rice, A.), I-284
Christy (Marshall), I-303
Confessions of Nat Turner, The (Styron), I-370
Dawning of Deliverance, The (Pella), I-416
Dear and Glorious Physician (Caldwell), I-420
Death Comes for the Archbishop (Cather), I-423
Edge of Honor (Morris, G.), II-534
Fire by Night (Austin), II-629
Friendly Persuasion, The (West, J.), II-669
Gilead (Robinson), II-683
Godric (Buechner), II-708
His Watchful Eye (Cavanaugh), II-783
In the Beauty of the Lilies (Updike), II-855
Infidel, The (Musser), II-866
King's Ransom (Beazely and Lemmons), II-952
Kristin Lavransdatter (Undset), II-960
Last Days of Pompeii, The (Bulwer-Lytton), II-977
Love Comes Softly series (Oke), III-1082
Man for All Seasons, A (Bolt), III-1090
Mary Magdalene (Traylor), III-1106
Name of the Rose, The (Eco), III-1204
One Tuesday Morning (Kingsbury), III-1288
Out of the Red Shadow (de Graaf), III-1303
Paul (Wangerin), III-1327
Pontius Pilate (Caillois), III-1393
Quo Vadis (Sienkiewicz), III-1462
Robe, The (Douglas), III-1522
Saint Joan (Shaw), III-1533
Seventh Seal, The (Bergman), IV-1595
Silence (Endō), IV-1616
Silver Chalice, The (Costain), IV-1620

Transgression (Ingermanson), IV-1798
Twilight of Courage, The (Thoene and Thoene), IV-1830
Two from Galilee (Holmes), IV-1834
While Mortals Sleep (Cavanaugh), IV-1941

HISTORY
Acts of the Apostles (Unknown), I-27
Book of Mormon (Smith, J.), I-196
Christianity and Democracy (Maritain), I-296
City of God, The (Augustine), I-325
Constantine's Sword (Carroll), I-374
Courage to Be, The (Tillich), I-382
Drama of Atheist Humanism, The (Lubac), I-508
God Has a Dream (Tutu), II-694
Hebrew Bible (Unknown), II-756
Hiding Place, The (Ten Boom), II-775
History of Christianity, A (Johnson, P.), II-787
History of God, A (Armstrong), II-791
Holocaust Politics (Roth), II-795
How Should We Then Live? (Schaeffer), II-806
Jesus Through the Centuries (Pelikan), II-925
Life of Jesus, The (Renan), III-1043
Mysticism (Underhill), III-1200
Presence of the Word, The (Ong), III-1415
Protestant Ethic and the Spirit of Capitalism, The (Weber), III-1438
Reconciliation (de Gruchy), III-1470
Sense of the Presence of God, The (Baillie, J.), III-1578
Souls of Black Folk, The (Du Bois), IV-1668
Unspeakable (Guinness), IV-1849
View of the Evidences of Christianity, A (Paley), IV-1875

HOLY WRITINGS
Acts of the Apostles (Unknown), I-27
Bible in History, The, I-10

Book of Mormon (Smith, J.), I-196
Book of Revelation (John), I-202
Books of the Prophets (Isaiah, Jeremiah, Amos, and Micah), I-206
Gospel of John (John, son of Zebedee), II-731
Hebrew Bible (Unknown), II-756
Psalms (David), III-1442
Synoptic Gospels (Matthew, Mark, and Luke), IV-1717

HOMILIES
Lord's Prayer and the Beatitudes, The (Gregory of Nyssa), III-1078

HUMOR
Complicated Kindness, A (Toews), I-350
Flabbergasted (Blackston), II-640
Home to Harmony (Gulley), II-802
Lake Wobegon Days (Keillor), II-973
Letters from the Earth (Twain), II-1021
Orthodoxy (Chesterton), III-1295
Screwtape Letters, The (Lewis, C. S.), III-1560
Vicar of Wakefield, The (Goldsmith), IV-1870
Wise Blood (O'Connor), IV-1957

INSTRUCTIONAL MANUALS
Apology (Tertullian), I-92
Cloud of Unknowing, The (Unknown), I-329
Lectures on Revivals of Religion (Finney), II-1001
Lord's Prayer and the Beatitudes, The (Gregory of Nyssa), III-1078
Mind's Road to God, The (Bonaventure), III-1159
Purpose Driven Life, The (Warren), III-1452
Serious Call to a Devout and Holy Life, A (Law), IV-1581
Spiritual Exercises, The (Ignatius of Loyola), IV-1680

JOURNALS OR DIARIES
Called to Question (Chittister), I-237
Journal of George Fox, The (Fox, G.), II-931
Journal of John Woolman, The (Woolman), II-936
New Kind of Christian, A (McLaren), III-1211
Prison Meditations of Father Alfred Delp (Delp), III-1419
Virgin Time (Hampl), IV-1883
Walking by Faith (Grimké), IV-1901

LEGENDS
Doctor Faustus (Marlowe), I-496
Faust (Goethe), II-610
Lilies of the Field, The (Barrett), III-1050
Little Flowers of St. Francis, The (Unknown), III-1058
Rime of the Ancient Mariner, The (Coleridge), III-1514
Saint Joan (Shaw), III-1533

LETTERS
Belief or Nonbelief? (Eco and Martini), I-133
"Epistle Containing the Strange Medical Experience of Karshish, the Arab Physician, An" (Browning), II-545
"Letter from Birmingham Jail" (King, M. L.), II-1014
Letters and Papers from Prison (Bonhoeffer), II-1018
Letters of Saint Jerome, The (Jerome), II-1024
Letters to a Young Catholic (Weigel), II-1029
New Testament Letters (Paul), III-1219
Prison Meditations of Father Alfred Delp (Delp), III-1419
Screwtape Letters, The (Lewis, C. S.), III-1560
Waiting for God (Weil), IV-1891

Genre Index

LITERARY FICTION

All New People (Lamott), I-62
Bread and Wine (Silone), I-211
Brothers Karamazov, The (Dostoevski), I-229
"Christmas Carol, A" (Dickens), I-299
Color Purple, The (Walker), I-338
Complicated Kindness, A (Toews), I-350
Da Vinci Code, The (Brown), I-408
Death Comes for the Archbishop (Cather), I-423
Death in the Family, A (Agee), I-427
Death of Ivan Ilyich, The (Tolstoy), I-431
Diary of a Country Priest, The (Bernanos), I-462
Elmer Gantry (Lewis, S.), II-538
Friendly Persuasion, The (West, J.), II-669
Gilead (Robinson), II-683
Go Tell It on the Mountain (Baldwin), II-687
Infidel, The (Musser), II-866
Man Who Died, The (Lawrence), III-1098
Morte d'Urban (Powers), III-1180
Pearl (Gordon), III-1331
Poisonwood Bible, The (Kingsolver), III-1384
Pontius Pilate (Caillois), III-1393
Power and the Glory, The (Greene), III-1401
Prayer for Owen Meany, A (Irving), III-1408
Red and the Black, The (Stendhal), III-1474
River Runs Through It, A (Maclean), III-1518
Saint Maybe (Tyler), III-1541
Scenes of Clerical Life (Eliot, G.), III-1553
Second Coming, The (Percy), III-1568
Secrets of Barneveld Calvary, The (Schaap), III-1574
Shunning, The (Lewis, B.), IV-1612
Silence (Endō), IV-1616
Songbird (Samson), IV-1651
Sutter's Cross (Cramer), IV-1714
Their Eyes Were Watching God (Hurston), IV-1730
Thorn Birds, The (McCullough), IV-1764
"Three Versions of Judas" (Borges), IV-1779
To Kill a Mockingbird (Lee, H.), IV-1790
Trip to Bountiful, The (Foote), IV-1816
Velma Still Cooks in Leeway (Wright, V. H.), IV-1862
Waiting for Godot (Beckett), IV-1897
Way of All Flesh, The (Butler, S.), IV-1913
Wind in the Wheat, The (Arvin), IV-1945
Winter Garden, The (Verweerd), IV-1953
Wise Blood (O'Connor), IV-1957
Woman of the Pharisees, The (Mauriac), IV-1968

LONG FICTION. See NOVELS

LYRIC POETRY

(Ado)ration (Glancy), I-31
"Advice to a Prophet" (Wilbur), I-35
"Amazing Peace" (Angelou), I-69
Angel of History, The (Forché), I-77
Apocalypse (Cardenal), I-80
Arrival of the Future, The (Fairchild), I-103
Beasts of Bethlehem, The (Kennedy), I-130
Black Zodiac (Wright, C.), I-169
Brightness That Made My Soul Tremble, A (Nesanovich), I-222
Burning Fields, The (Middleton), I-233
Cherubinic Wanderer, The (Silesius), I-268
Creation, The (Beasley), I-390
"Dialogue of Self and Soul, A" (Yeats), I-458
Dream Songs, The (Berryman), I-515
Even in Quiet Places (Stafford), II-571
Eve's Striptease (Kasdorf), II-578
"Fall, The" (Bottum), II-606
"Feet of Jesus" (Hughes), II-614
Fools and Crows (Witek), II-644

"For the Union Dead" (Lowell), II-650
Ghost Pain (Lea), II-676
God's Silence (Wright, F.), II-712
God's Trombones (Johnson, J. W.), II-716
Hebrew Bible (Unknown), II-756
"Here Follows Some Verses upon the Burning of Our House July 10th, 1666" (Bradstreet), II-768
"Holy Sonnets" (Donne), II-799
Hymns (Whittier), II-818
"In Distrust of Merits" (Moore, M.), II-839
In Memoriam (Tennyson), II-847
"In the Holy Nativity of Our Lord God" (Crashaw), II-859
Isaiah (Berrigan), II-898
J. B. (MacLeish), II-902
Jesus Christ Superstar (Rice, T., and Webber), II-913
Learning Human (Murray, L. A.), II-993
Leaves of Grass (Whitman), II-997
Mercy's Face (Craig), III-1139
Midquest (Chappell), III-1151
Moments of Grace (Jennings), III-1176
"Ode: Intimations of Immortality" (Wordsworth), III-1241
Penitent Magdalene, The (Hopes), III-1339
Philokalia (Cairns), III-1350
Piers Plowman (Langland), III-1362
Psalms (David), III-1442
Questions for Ecclesiastes (Jarman), III-1459
Rose (Lee, L.-Y.), III-1525
Sapphics and Uncertainties (Steele), III-1545
Sinners Welcome (Karr), IV-1631
Song of the Sparrow (Bodo), IV-1648
Songs of Innocence and of Experience (Blake), IV-1655
"Station Island" (Heaney), IV-1685
Stream and the Sapphire, The (Levertov), IV-1689
Temple, The (Herbert), IV-1726
"They Are All Gone into the World of Light!" (Vaughan), IV-1753
To Scorch or Freeze (Davie), IV-1794
Triumph of Love, The (Hill, Geoffrey), IV-1820
Unattainable Earth (Miłosz), IV-1837
Unutterable Beauty, The (Studdert Kennedy), IV-1853
"Windhover, The" (Hopkins), IV-1949
"Word made Flesh is seldom, A" (Dickinson), IV-1976

MEDITATION AND CONTEMPLATION
Aids to Reflection (Coleridge), I-54
All New People (Lamott), I-62
Amazing Grace (Norris), I-65
Apocalypse (Cardenal), I-80
Apocrypha (Pankey), I-84
Ascent of Mount Carmel (John of the Cross), I-107
Black Zodiac (Wright, C.), I-169
Book of Divine Works (Hildegard von Bingen), I-188
Bread for the Journey (Nouwen), I-215
Brightness That Made My Soul Tremble, A (Nesanovich), I-222
Burning Fields, The (Middleton), I-233
Cherubinic Wanderer, The (Silesius), I-268
Christian Faith, The (Schleiermacher), I-288
Coming of the Cosmic Christ, The (Fox, M.), I-346
Dark Night of the Soul (John of the Cross), I-107
Death on a Friday Afternoon (Neuhaus), I-435
Devotions upon Emergent Occasions (Donne), I-447
Dialogue, The (Catherine of Siena), I-453
Divine Milieu, The (Teilhard de Chardin), I-480
Double Search, The (Jones), I-503
Even in Quiet Places (Stafford), II-571
Face of the Deep, The (Rossetti), II-597
Fools and Crows (Witek), II-644
For the Time Being (Dillard), II-647

Four Quartets (Eliot, T. S.), II-660
Freedom of a Christian, The (Luther), II-664
Gift from the Sea (Lindbergh), II-680
Gilead (Robinson), II-683
God's Silence (Wright, F.), II-712
Great Exemplar, The (Taylor), II-743
Here I Stand (Spong), II-772
Imitation of Christ, The (Thomas à Kempis), II-834
In Memoriam (Tennyson), II-847
"In the Holy Nativity of Our Lord God" (Crashaw), II-859
Interior Castle (Teresa of Ávila), II-887
Learning Human (Murray, L. A.), II-993
Letters and Papers from Prison (Bonhoeffer), II-1018
Lord, The (Guardini), III-1070
Lord's Prayer and the Beatitudes, The (Gregory of Nyssa), III-1078
Meaning of Prayer, The (Fosdick), III-1121
Moments of Grace (Jennings), III-1176
My God and I (Smedes), III-1188
No Greater Love (Teresa, Mother), III-1227
Of Learned Ignorance (Nicholas of Cusa), III-1245
On Loving God (Bernard of Clairvaux), III-1268
Orthodoxy (Chesterton), III-1295
Out of My Life and Thought (Schweitzer), III-1299
Pearl (Pearl-Poet), III-1335
Pensées (Pascal), III-1342
Philokalia (Cairns), III-1350
Prison Meditations of Father Alfred Delp (Delp), III-1419
Prison Meditations on Psalms 51 and 31 (Savonarola), III-1423
Purity of Heart Is to Will One Thing (Kierkegaard), III-1446
Religio Medici (Browne), III-1482
Religion in the Making (Whitehead), III-1490

Rose (Lee, L.-Y.), III-1525
Sermons and Treatises, The (Eckhart), IV-1586
Showings (Julian of Norwich), IV-1609
Song of the Sparrow (Bodo), IV-1648
Spiritual Exercises, The (Ignatius of Loyola), IV-1680
Suffering (Sölle), IV-1702
"They Are All Gone into the World of Light!" (Vaughan), IV-1753
Third Spiritual Alphabet, The (Osuna), IV-1756
To Scorch or Freeze (Davie), IV-1794
Traveling Mercies (Lamott), IV-1802
Triumph of Love, The (Hill, Geoffrey), IV-1820
Virgin Time (Hampl), IV-1883
Vocation of Man, The (Fichte), IV-1887
Way to Christ, The (Böhme), IV-1917

MORALITY TALES
Confessio Amantis (Gower), I-357
Divine and Human (Tolstoy), I-469
Doctor Faustus (Marlowe), I-496
Everyman (Unknown), II-574
Hebrew Bible (Unknown), II-756
Jesus Christ Superstar (Rice, T., and Webber), II-913
Little Flowers of St. Francis, The (Unknown), III-1058
Shepherd of the Hills, The (Wright, H. B.), IV-1602

MYSTERY AND DETECTIVE FICTION
Bishop in the Old Neighborhood, The (Greeley), I-157
Blood Ties (Brouwer), I-173
Capital Offense, A (Parker), I-248
Drummer in the Dark (Bunn), II-519
Music to Die For (Nehring), III-1184
Name of the Rose, The (Eco), III-1204
Newpointe 911 (Blackstock), III-1223
Place of the Lion, The (Williams, C.), III-1375
Thr3e (Dekker), IV-1768
War in Heaven (Williams, C.), IV-1905

MYSTICISM
Ascent of Mount Carmel (John of the Cross), I-107
Book of Divine Works (Hildegard von Bingen), I-188
Care of the Soul (Moore, T.), I-251
Cherubinic Wanderer, The (Silesius), I-268
Dark Night of the Soul (John of the Cross), I-107
Dialogue, The (Catherine of Siena), I-453
Interior Castle (Teresa of Ávila), II-887
Labyrinth of the World and the Paradise of the Heart, The (Comenius), II-964
Master and Margarita, The (Bulgakov), III-1110
Mind's Road to God, The (Bonaventure), III-1159
Mystical Element of Religion, The (Hügel), III-1191
Mystical Theology (Pseudo-Dionysius), III-1197
Mysticism (Underhill), III-1200
Rose (Lee, L.-Y.), III-1525
Sermons and Treatises, The (Eckhart), IV-1586
Showings (Julian of Norwich), IV-1609
Third Spiritual Alphabet, The (Osuna), IV-1756
Way to Christ, The (Böhme), IV-1917

NARRATIVE POETRY
After the Lost War (Hudgins), I-41
Age of Anxiety, The (Auden), I-50
Arrival of the Future, The (Fairchild), I-103
Beasts of Bethlehem, The (Kennedy), I-130
Beowulf (Unknown), I-140
Canterbury Tales, The (Chaucer), I-240
Come Sweet Death (Napier), I-342
Confessio Amantis (Gower), I-357
Divine Comedy, The (Dante), I-473
"Dream of the Rood, The" (Unknown), I-512
Dream Songs, The (Berryman), I-515

"Epistle Containing the Strange Medical Experience of Karshish, the Arab Physician, An" (Browning), II-545
Faerie Queene, The (Spenser), II-601
Ghost Pain (Lea), II-676
Great Wheel, The (Mariani), II-749
Hebrew Bible (Unknown), II-756
Interrogations at Noon (Gioia), II-891
Marriage of Heaven and Hell, The (Blake), III-1102
Midquest (Chappell), III-1151
Paradise Lost (Milton), III-1315
Paradise Regained (Milton), III-1319
Pearl (Pearl-Poet), III-1335
Piers Plowman (Langland), III-1362
Questions for Ecclesiastes (Jarman), III-1459
Rime of the Ancient Mariner, The (Coleridge), III-1514
Singer Trilogy, The (Miller, C.), IV-1627
Sinners Welcome (Karr), IV-1631
Sir Gawain and the Green Knight (Pearl-Poet), IV-1635
"Station Island" (Heaney), IV-1685
Unutterable Beauty, The (Studdert Kennedy), IV-1853

NONFICTION. See AUTOBIOGRAPHIES

NOVELLAS
All New People (Lamott), I-62
Billy Budd, Foretopman (Melville), I-150
Catholics (Moore, Brian), I-261
Death of Ivan Ilyich, The (Tolstoy), I-431
Great Divorce, The (Lewis, C. S.), II-739
Labyrinth of the World and the Paradise of the Heart, The (Comenius), II-964
Lilies of the Field, The (Barrett), III-1050
Man Who Died, The (Lawrence), III-1098
New Kind of Christian, A (McLaren), III-1211
River Runs Through It, A (Maclean), III-1518
Saint Manuel Bueno, Martyr (Unamuno y Jugo), III-1537
Wise Blood (O'Connor), IV-1957

GENRE INDEX

NOVELS
Arena (Hancock), I-96
Awakening Mercy (Benson), I-116
Barabbas (Lagerkvist), I-123
Ben-Hur (Wallace), I-136
Bishop in the Old Neighborhood, The (Greeley), I-157
Bishop's Mantle, The (Turnbull), I-161
Blood Ties (Brouwer), I-173
Book of God, The (Wangerin), I-192
Bread and Wine (Silone), I-211
Brideshead Revisited (Waugh), I-218
Broken Lance (Sorensen), I-226
Brothers Karamazov, The (Dostoevski), I-229
Canticle for Leibowitz, A (Miller, W. M.), I-245
Capital Offense, A (Parker), I-248
Christ Clone Trilogy (BeauSeigneur), I-275
Christ the Lord (Rice, A.), I-284
Christy (Marshall), I-303
Chronicles of Narnia, The (Lewis, C. S.), I-307
Church Folk (Bowen), I-316
Circle Trilogy, The (Dekker), I-320
Color Purple, The (Walker), I-338
Complicated Kindness, A (Toews), I-350
Confessions of Nat Turner, The (Styron), I-370
Da Vinci Code, The (Brown), I-408
Dangerous Silence, A (Palmer), I-412
Dawning of Deliverance, The (Pella), I-416
Dear and Glorious Physician (Caldwell), I-420
Death Comes for the Archbishop (Cather), I-423
Death in the Family, A (Agee), I-427
Diary of a Country Priest, The (Bernanos), I-462
Directed Verdict (Singer), I-465
Drummer in the Dark (Bunn), II-519
Edge of Honor (Morris, G.), II-534
Elmer Gantry (Lewis, S.), II-538

Ezekiel's Shadow (Long), II-594
Final Witness (Bell), II-625
Fire by Night (Austin), II-629
Flabbergasted (Blackston), II-640
Gilead (Robinson), II-683
Go Tell It on the Mountain (Baldwin), II-687
Godric (Buechner), II-708
Gospel According to Jesus Christ, The (Saramago), II-724
Greatest Story Ever Told, The (Oursler), II-752
Hinds' Feet on High Places (Hurnard), II-779
His Watchful Eye (Cavanaugh), II-783
Home to Harmony (Gulley), II-802
In His Steps (Sheldon), II-843
In the Beauty of the Lilies (Updike), II-855
In This House of Brede (Godden), II-863
Infidel, The (Musser), II-866
Keys of the Kingdom, The (Cronin), II-945
King's Ransom (Beazely and Lemmons), II-952
Kristin Lavransdatter (Undset), II-960
Lake Wobegon Days (Keillor), II-973
Last Days of Pompeii, The (Bulwer-Lytton), II-977
Last Puritan, The (Santayana), II-981
Last Temptation of Christ, The (Kazantzakis), II-985
Left Behind series (LaHaye and Jenkins), II-1005
List, The (Whitlow), III-1054
Long Trail Home, The (Bly), III-1066
Lord of the Rings, The (Tolkien), III-1073
Love Comes Softly series (Oke), III-1082
Magnificent Obsession (Douglas), III-1087
Mary Magdalene (Traylor), III-1106
Master and Margarita, The (Bulgakov), III-1110

Memoirs of Pontius Pilate (Mills), III-1128
Miracle of the Bells, The (Janney), III-1164
Morte d'Urban (Powers), III-1180
Music to Die For (Nehring), III-1184
Name of the Rose, The (Eco), III-1204
New Song, A (Karon), III-1215
Newpointe 911 (Blackstock), III-1223
North of Hope (Hassler), III-1230
Nun's Story, The (Hulme), III-1234
One Tuesday Morning (Kingsbury), III-1288
Out of the Red Shadow (de Graaf), III-1303
Oxygen (Ingermanson and Olson), III-1307
Passing by Samaria (Foster), III-1323
Paul (Wangerin), III-1327
Pearl (Gordon), III-1331
Phantastes (MacDonald), III-1346
Pilgrim's Progress, The (Bunyan), III-1366
Place Called Wiregrass, A (Morris, M.), III-1371
Place of the Lion, The (Williams, C.), III-1375
Poisonwood Bible, The (Kingsolver), III-1384
Pontius Pilate (Caillois), III-1393
Power and the Glory, The (Greene), III-1401
Prayer for Owen Meany, A (Irving), III-1408
Prodigal Girl, The (Hill, Grace Livingston), III-1430
Quo Vadis (Sienkiewicz), III-1462
Red and the Black, The (Stendhal), III-1474
Redeeming Love (Rivers), III-1478
Resting in the Bosom of the Lamb (Trobaugh), III-1502
Robe, The (Douglas), III-1522
Saint Maybe (Tyler), III-1541
Scarlet Letter, The (Hawthorne), III-1549
Screwtape Letters, The (Lewis, C. S.), III-1560
Seal of Gaia, The (Maddoux), III-1564
Second Coming, The (Percy), III-1568
Shepherd of the Hills, The (Wright, H. B.), IV-1602
Shoes of the Fisherman, The (West, M.), IV-1605
Shunning, The (Lewis, B.), IV-1612
Silence (Endō), IV-1616
Silver Chalice, The (Costain), IV-1620
Song of Albion Trilogy, The (Lawhead), IV-1643
Songbird (Samson), IV-1651
Soon (Jenkins), IV-1660
Sparrow, The (Russell), IV-1676
Sutter's Cross (Cramer), IV-1714
Their Eyes Were Watching God (Hurston), IV-1730
This Present Darkness (Peretti), IV-1760
Thorn Birds, The (McCullough), IV-1764
Thr3e (Dekker), IV-1768
Tiger in the Shadows (Wilson), IV-1782
Time Lottery (Moser), IV-1786
To Kill a Mockingbird (Lee, H.), IV-1790
Transgression (Ingermanson), IV-1798
True Honor (Henderson), IV-1823
Truth Teller, The (Hunt), IV-1827
Twilight of Courage, The (Thoene and Thoene), IV-1830
Two from Galilee (Holmes), IV-1834
Uncle Tom's Cabin (Stowe), IV-1841
Velma Still Cooks in Leeway (Wright, V. H.), IV-1862
Vicar of Wakefield, The (Goldsmith), IV-1870
War in Heaven (Williams, C.), IV-1905
Way of All Flesh, The (Butler, S.), IV-1913
While Mortals Sleep (Cavanaugh), IV-1941
Wind in the Wheat, The (Arvin), IV-1945
Winter Garden, The (Verweerd), IV-1953
Woman of the Pharisees, The (Mauriac), IV-1968

GENRE INDEX

OPERA
Jesus Christ Superstar (Rice, T., and Webber), II-913

PARABLES AND FABLES
Age of Anxiety, The (Auden), I-50
Gospel According to Jesus Christ, The (Saramago), II-724
Hinds' Feet on High Places (Hurnard), II-779
Marriage of Heaven and Hell, The (Blake), III-1102
Rime of the Ancient Mariner, The (Coleridge), III-1514
Waiting for Godot (Beckett), IV-1897

PHILOSOPHY
Christian Faith, The (Schleiermacher), I-288
Christianity and Democracy (Maritain), I-296
Divinity School Address, The (Emerson), I-491
God and Philosophy (Gilson), II-691
History of God, A (Armstrong), II-791
Insight (Lonergan), II-873
Instructor, The (Clement of Alexandria), II-881
Miscellanies (Clement of Alexandria), II-881
Pensées (Pascal), III-1342
Philosophy of Existence (Jaspers), III-1354
Philosophy of Existentialism, The (Marcel), III-1358
Religion in the Making (Whitehead), III-1490
Religion Within the Bounds of Mere Reason (Kant), III-1494
Three Essays (Ritschl), IV-1772
Three Hardest Words in the World to Get Right, The (Sweet), IV-1776
Unspeakable (Guinness), IV-1849
Varieties of Religious Experience, The (James), IV-1856

POETRY
(Ado)ration (Glancy), I-31
"Advice to a Prophet" (Wilbur), I-35
After the Lost War (Hudgins), I-41
Age of Anxiety, The (Auden), I-50
"Amazing Peace" (Angelou), I-69
Angel of History, The (Forché), I-77
Apocalypse (Cardenal), I-80
Apocrypha (Pankey), I-84
Arrival of the Future, The (Fairchild), I-103
Beasts of Bethlehem, The (Kennedy), I-130
Beowulf (Unknown), I-140
Black Zodiac (Wright, C.), I-169
Brightness That Made My Soul Tremble, A (Nesanovich), I-222
Burning Fields, The (Middleton), I-233
Canterbury Tales, The (Chaucer), I-240
Cherubinic Wanderer, The (Silesius), I-268
Come Sweet Death (Napier), I-342
Confessio Amantis (Gower), I-357
Creation, The (Beasley), I-390
"Dialogue of Self and Soul, A" (Yeats), I-458
Divine Comedy, The (Dante), I-473
"Dream of the Rood, The" (Unknown), I-512
Dream Songs, The (Berryman), I-515
"Epistle Containing the Strange Medical Experience of Karshish, the Arab Physician, An" (Browning), II-545
Even in Quiet Places (Stafford), II-571
Eve's Striptease (Kasdorf), II-578
Faerie Queene, The (Spenser), II-601
"Fall, The" (Bottum), II-606
"Feet of Jesus" (Hughes), II-614
Fools and Crows (Witek), II-644
"For the Union Dead" (Lowell), II-650
Four Quartets (Eliot, T. S.), II-660
Ghost Pain (Lea), II-676
God's Silence (Wright, F.), II-712
God's Trombones (Johnson, J. W.), II-716
Great Wheel, The (Mariani), II-749

"Here Follows Some Verses upon the Burning of Our House July 10th, 1666" (Bradstreet), II-768
"Holy Sonnets" (Donne), II-799
Hymns (Whittier), II-818
"In Distrust of Merits" (Moore, M.), II-839
In Memoriam (Tennyson), II-847
"In the Holy Nativity of Our Lord God" (Crashaw), II-859
Interrogations at Noon (Gioia), II-891
Isaiah (Berrigan), II-898
Learning Human (Murray, L. A.), II-993
Leaves of Grass (Whitman), II-997
Marriage of Heaven and Hell, The (Blake), III-1102
Mercy's Face (Craig), III-1139
Midquest (Chappell), III-1151
Moments of Grace (Jennings), III-1176
"Ode: Intimations of Immortality" (Wordsworth), III-1241
Paradise Lost (Milton), III-1315
Paradise Regained (Milton), III-1319
Pearl (Pearl-Poet), III-1335
Penitent Magdalene, The (Hopes), III-1339
Philokalia (Cairns), III-1350
Piers Plowman (Langland), III-1362
Psalms (David), III-1442
Questions for Ecclesiastes (Jarman), III-1459
Rime of the Ancient Mariner, The (Coleridge), III-1514
Rose (Lee, L.-Y.), III-1525
Sapphics and Uncertainties (Steele), III-1545
Singer Trilogy, The (Miller, C.), IV-1627
Sinners Welcome (Karr), IV-1631
Sir Gawain and the Green Knight (Pearl-Poet), IV-1635
Song of the Sparrow (Bodo), IV-1648
Songs of Innocence and of Experience (Blake), IV-1655
"Station Island" (Heaney), IV-1685

Stream and the Sapphire, The (Levertov), IV-1689
Temple, The (Herbert), IV-1726
"They Are All Gone into the World of Light!" (Vaughan), IV-1753
To Scorch or Freeze (Davie), IV-1794
Triumph of Love, The (Hill, Geoffrey), IV-1820
Unattainable Earth (Miłosz), IV-1837
Unutterable Beauty, The (Studdert Kennedy), IV-1853
"Windhover, The" (Hopkins), IV-1949
"Word made Flesh is seldom, A" (Dickinson), IV-1976

PRAYER BOOKS
Book of Common Prayer (Cranmer), I-184
Hymns and Spiritual Songs (Watts), II-822
Meaning of Prayer, The (Fosdick), III-1121

PROBLEM PLAY
Merchant of Venice, The (Shakespeare), III-1135

PROVERBS
Marriage of Heaven and Hell, The (Blake), III-1102

ROCK OPERA
Jesus Christ Superstar (Rice, T., and Webber), II-913

ROMANCES
Arena (Hancock), I-96
Awakening Mercy (Benson), I-116
Christy (Marshall), I-303
Church Folk (Bowen), I-316
Dangerous Silence, A (Palmer), I-412
Edge of Honor (Morris, G.), II-534
Faerie Queene, The (Spenser), II-601
Fire by Night (Austin), II-629
Flabbergasted (Blackston), II-640

GENRE INDEX

Love Comes Softly series (Oke),
  III-1082
New Song, A (Karon), III-1215
Passing by Samaria (Foster), III-1323
Phantastes (MacDonald), III-1346
Place Called Wiregrass, A (Morris, M.),
  III-1371
Prodigal Girl, The (Hill, Grace
  Livingston), III-1430
Quo Vadis (Sienkiewicz), III-1462
Redeeming Love (Rivers), III-1478
Scarlet Letter, The (Hawthorne), III-1549
Second Coming, The (Percy), III-1568
Sir Gawain and the Green Knight
  (Pearl-Poet), IV-1635
True Honor (Henderson), IV-1823
Uncle Tom's Cabin (Stowe), IV-1841
Vicar of Wakefield, The (Goldsmith),
  IV-1870

SAGAS
  Book of God, The (Wangerin), I-192
  Christy (Marshall), I-303
  Dawning of Deliverance, The (Pella),
    I-416
  Edge of Honor (Morris, G.), II-534
  In the Beauty of the Lilies (Updike),
    II-855
  Thorn Birds, The (McCullough),
    IV-1764

SAINT'S MEDITATIONS
  Godric (Buechner), II-708
  Interior Castle (Teresa of Ávila), II-887

SATIRES
  Elmer Gantry (Lewis, S.), II-538
  Flabbergasted (Blackston), II-640
  Letters from the Earth (Twain), II-1021
  Marriage of Heaven and Hell, The
    (Blake), III-1102
  Master and Margarita, The (Bulgakov),
    III-1110
  Morte d'Urban (Powers), III-1180
  Way of All Flesh, The (Butler, S.),
    IV-1913

SCIENCE FICTION
  Arena (Hancock), I-96
  Canticle for Leibowitz, A (Miller, W. M.),
    I-245
  Christ Clone Trilogy (BeauSeigneur),
    I-275
  Oxygen (Ingermanson and Olson),
    III-1307
  Seal of Gaia, The (Maddoux), III-1564
  Sparrow, The (Russell), IV-1676
  Time Lottery (Moser), IV-1786
  Transgression (Ingermanson), IV-1798
  Truth Teller, The (Hunt), IV-1827

SCREENPLAY
  Seventh Seal, The (Bergman), IV-1595

SERMONS
  Baptismal Instruction (Chrysostom), I-120
  Book of Mormon (Smith, J.), I-196
  Credo (Coffin), I-393
  Fifteen Sermons Preached at the Rolls
    Chapel (Butler, J.), II-618
  God's Trombones (Johnson, J. W.), II-716
  Inscribing the Text (Brueggemann),
    II-870
  Life Is Worth Living (Sheen), II-1037
  Plain Account of Christian Perfection, A
    (Wesley), III-1378
  Purity of Heart Is to Will One Thing
    (Kierkegaard), III-1446
  Science and Health with Key to the
    Scriptures (Eddy), III-1557
  Secrets in the Dark (Buechner), III-1571
  Sermons and Treatises, The (Eckhart),
    IV-1586
  Strength to Love (King, M. L.), IV-1693
  Supplicating Voice, The (Johnson, S.),
    IV-1710

SHORT FICTION
  "Christmas Carol, A" (Dickens), I-299
  Divine and Human (Tolstoy), I-469
  Friendly Persuasion, The (West, J.),
    II-669
  Letters from the Earth (Twain), II-1021

Scenes of Clerical Life (Eliot, G.),
III-1553
Secrets of Barneveld Calvary, The
(Schaap), III-1574
"Three Versions of Judas" (Borges),
IV-1779

SPIRITUAL TREATISES
Aids to Reflection (Coleridge), I-54
Ascent of Mount Carmel (John of the
Cross), I-107
Basic Christianity (Stott), I-127
Bloudy Tenent of Persecution for Cause
of Conscience, The (Williams, Roger),
I-176
Blue Like Jazz (Miller, D.), I-180
Book of Revelation (John), I-202
Care of the Soul (Moore, T.), I-251
Cloud of Unknowing, The (Unknown),
I-329
Come Sweet Death (Napier), I-342
Conferences (Cassian), I-354
Confessions (Augustine), I-365
Dark Night of the Soul (John of the
Cross), I-107
Destiny of Man, The (Berdyaev), I-443
Dialogue, The (Catherine of Siena), I-453
Double Search, The (Jones), I-503
Essays and Addresses on the Philosophy
of Religion (Hügel), II-553
Exclusion and Embrace (Volf), II-586
Existentialist Theology, An (Macquarrie),
II-590
Freedom of a Christian, The (Luther),
II-664
God Has a Dream (Tutu), II-694
God Who Commands, The (Mouw),
II-704
Instructor, The (Clement of Alexandria),
II-881
Journal of George Fox, The (Fox, G.),
II-931
Journal of John Woolman, The
(Woolman), II-936
Kingdom of God Is Within You, The
(Tolstoy), II-948

Ladder of Divine Ascent, The (John
Climacus), II-968
Meaning of Persons, The (Tournier),
III-1118
Mere Christianity (Lewis, C. S.), III-1143
Mind of the Maker, The (Sayers), III-1155
Mind's Road to God, The (Bonaventure),
III-1159
Miscellanies (Clement of Alexandria),
II-881
My God and I (Smedes), III-1188
Mystical Theology (Pseudo-Dionysius),
III-1197
Mysticism (Underhill), III-1200
Of Learned Ignorance (Nicholas of Cusa),
III-1245
On Loving God (Bernard of Clairvaux),
III-1268
Pacem in Terris (John XXIII), III-1311
Plain Account of Christian Perfection, A
(Wesley), III-1378
Prison Meditations on Psalms 51 and 31
(Savonarola), III-1423
Serious Call to a Devout and Holy Life, A
(Law), IV-1581
Sermons and Treatises, The (Eckhart),
IV-1586
Showings (Julian of Norwich), IV-1609
Simply Christian (Wright, N. T.), IV-1624
Synoptic Gospels (Matthew, Mark, and
Luke), IV-1717
Three Essays (Ritschl), IV-1772
Treatise Concerning Religious Affections,
A (Edwards), IV-1806
Unattainable Earth (Miłosz), IV-1837
Vocation of Man, The (Fichte), IV-1887
Way to Christ, The (Böhme), IV-1917

STORIES
Arrival of the Future, The (Fairchild),
I-103
Canterbury Tales, The (Chaucer), I-240
Flabbergasted (Blackston), II-640
Hebrew Bible (Unknown), II-756
Scenes of Clerical Life (Eliot, G.),
III-1553

GENRE INDEX

THEOLOGY

Acts of the Apostles (Unknown), I-27
Agape and Eros (Nygren), I-47
Aids to Reflection (Coleridge), I-54
Amazing Grace (Norris), I-65
Apologia pro vita sua (Newman), I-88
Apology (Tertullian), I-92
Augsburg Confession of Faith, The (Melanchthon), I-112
Beyond God the Father (Daly), I-144
Bible and Theology in African Christianity (Mbiti), I-147
Black Theology of Liberation, A (Cone), I-165
Bloudy Tenent of Persecution for Cause of Conscience, The (Williams, Roger), I-176
Book of Divine Works (Hildegard von Bingen), I-188
Book of Mormon (Smith, J.), I-196
Book of Revelation (John), I-202
Catechism of the Catholic Church (Council of Trent), I-257
Centesimus Annus (John Paul II), I-265
Christ in a Pluralistic Age (Cobb), I-280
Christian Faith, The (Schleiermacher), I-288
Christianity and Democracy (Maritain), I-296
City of God, The (Augustine), I-325
Come Sweet Death (Napier), I-342
Coming of the Cosmic Christ, The (Fox, M.), I-346
Conferences (Cassian), I-354
Constantine's Sword (Carroll), I-374
Courage to Be, The (Tillich), I-382
Crawl with God, Dance in the Spirit (Park), I-386
Credo (Coffin), I-393
Crucified God, The (Moltmann), I-397
Cur Deus Homo (Anselm), I-401
Death on a Friday Afternoon (Neuhaus), I-435
Declaration of the Sentiments of Arminius, A (Arminius), I-439
Destiny of Man, The (Berdyaev), I-443

Divine Conspiracy, The (Willard), I-477
Divine Relativity, The (Hartshorne), I-485
Early Christian Doctrines (Kelly), II-523
Early Theological Writings (Hegel), II-527
Economy of Grace (Tanner), II-531
Enneads, The (Plotinus), II-542
Epistle to the Romans, The (Barth), II-549
Essays and Addresses on the Philosophy of Religion (Hügel), II-553
Essence of Christianity, The (Feuerbach), II-557
Ethics (Bonhoeffer), II-561
Ethics After Babel (Stout), II-565
Evangelium Vitae (John Paul II), II-568
Evil and the God of Love (Hick), II-582
Exclusion and Embrace (Volf), II-586
Existentialist Theology, An (Macquarrie), II-590
Figuring the Sacred (Ricœur), II-621
First and Second Apologies, The (Justin Martyr), II-633
For the Time Being (Dillard), II-647
Foundations of Christian Faith (Rahner), II-654
Four Books of Sentences (Peter Lombard), II-657
Gaudium et Spes (Vatican Council II), II-672
God and Philosophy (Gilson), II-691
God Was in Christ (Baillie, D. M.), II-698
God Who Commands, The (Mouw), II-704
God's Silence (Wright, F.), II-712
Gospel of Christian Atheism, The (Altizer), II-728
Gospel of John (John, son of Zebedee), II-731
Great Mysteries, The (Greeley), II-746
Hebrew Bible (Unknown), II-756
Here I Stand (Spong), II-772
History of God, A (Armstrong), II-791
Holocaust Politics (Roth), II-795
How Should We Then Live? (Schaeffer), II-806

In Memory of Her (Schüssler Fiorenza), II-851
Institutes of the Christian Religion (Calvin), II-877
Introduction to Christianity (Ratzinger), II-895
Jesus Christ and Mythology (Bultmann), II-909
Jesus I Never Knew, The (Yancey), II-917
Kingdom of God Is Within You, The (Tolstoy), II-948
Knowledge and Faith (Stein), II-956
Last Puritan, The (Santayana), II-981
Life Abundant (McFague), II-1033
Lord, The (Guardini), III-1070
Meaning of Prayer, The (Fosdick), III-1121
Meeting Jesus Again for the First Time (Borg), III-1125
Mere Christianity (Lewis, C. S.), III-1143
Metaphysical Demonstration of the Existence of God, The (Suárez), III-1147
Mind of the Maker, The (Sayers), III-1155
Mystical Theology (Pseudo-Dionysius), III-1197
Nature and Destiny of Man, The (Niebuhr), III-1207
New Testament Letters (Paul), III-1219
Octogesima Adveniens (Paul VI), III-1238
On Being a Christian (Küng), III-1249
On Christian Theology (Williams, Rowan), III-1252
On Divine Love (Duns Scotus), III-1255
On First Principles (Origen), III-1259
On Providence (Zwingli), III-1272
On the Freedom of the Will (Erasmus), III-1276
On the Incarnation of the Word of God (Athanasius of Alexandria), III-1280
On the Truth of Holy Scripture (Wyclif), III-1284
Orthodox Church, The (Ware), III-1291
Paradise Lost (Milton), III-1315
Pensées (Pascal), III-1342
Philosophy of Existence (Jaspers), III-1354
Presence of the Word, The (Ong), III-1415
Psalms (David), III-1442
Reasonableness of Christianity as Delivered in the Scriptures, The (Locke), III-1466
Reconciliation (de Gruchy), III-1470
Religion in the Making (Whitehead), III-1490
Religion Within the Bounds of Mere Reason (Kant), III-1494
Resurrection of God Incarnate, The (Swinburne), III-1506
Revelation and Reason (Brunner), III-1510
Sense of the Presence of God, The (Baillie, J.), III-1578
She Who Is (Johnson, E. A.), IV-1598
Simply Christian (Wright, N. T.), IV-1624
Social Teaching of the Christian Churches, The (Troeltsch), IV-1639
Source of Human Good, The (Wieman), IV-1672
Subversion of Christianity, The (Ellul), IV-1698
Suffering (Sölle), IV-1702
Summa Theologica (Thomas Aquinas), IV-1706
Synoptic Gospels (Matthew, Mark, and Luke), IV-1717
Theodicy (Leibniz), IV-1734
Theology for the Social Gospel, A (Rauschenbusch), IV-1738
Theology of Liberation, A (Gutiérrez), IV-1742
Theology of the Jewish Christian Reality, A (Van Buren), IV-1746
Three Essays (Ritschl), IV-1772
Treatise on Divine Predestination (Erigena), IV-1812

Uneasy Conscience of Modern Fundamentalism, The (Henry), IV-1845
Warranted Christian Belief (Plantinga), IV-1909
What Jesus Meant (Wills), IV-1934
With the Grain of the Universe (Hauerwas), IV-1965
Wonderful Words of Life (Mouw and Noll), IV-1972

THRILLERS/SUSPENSE
Blood Ties (Brouwer), I-173
Christ Clone Trilogy (BeauSeigneur), I-275
Dangerous Silence, A (Palmer), I-412
Directed Verdict (Singer), I-465
Drummer in the Dark (Bunn), II-519
Ezekiel's Shadow (Long), II-594
Final Witness (Bell), II-625
His Watchful Eye (Cavanaugh), II-783

King's Ransom (Beazely and Lemmons), II-952
List, The (Whitlow), III-1054
Name of the Rose, The (Eco), III-1204
Newpointe 911 (Blackstock), III-1223
Oxygen (Ingermanson and Olson), III-1307
This Present Darkness (Peretti), IV-1760
Thr3e (Dekker), IV-1768
Tiger in the Shadows (Wilson), IV-1782
Truth Teller, The (Hunt), IV-1827
War in Heaven (Williams, C.), IV-1905

TIME TRAVEL
Time Lottery (Moser), IV-1786
Transgression (Ingermanson), IV-1798

WESTERNS
Broken Lance (Sorensen), I-226
Long Trail Home, The (Bly), III-1066

GEOGRAPHICAL INDEX

LIST OF CATEGORIES

Africa	2082	The Netherlands	2089
Algeria	2083	Nicaragua	2090
Argentina	2083	Nigeria	2090
Asia	2083	Northern Ireland	2090
Australia	2083	Norway	2090
Austria	2083	Peru	2090
Canada	2083	Poland	2090
Croatia	2083	Portugal	2090
Czech Republic	2083	Romania	2090
Denmark	2083	Russia	2090
Egypt	2083	Rwanda	2090
England	2084	Scotland	2090
France	2086	South Africa	2091
Germany	2086	South America	2091
Greece	2087	South Korea	2091
India	2087	Spain	2091
Ireland	2087	Sweden	2091
Israel	2088	Switzerland	2091
Italy	2088	Syria	2091
Japan	2089	Tunisia	2091
Kenya	2089	Turkey	2091
Lebanon	2089	United Kingdom	2092
Lithuania	2089	United States	2094
Macedonia	2089	Wales	2100
Middle East	2089		

AFRICA
Abrams, Douglas
  God Has a Dream, II-694
Athanasius of Alexandria, Saint
  On the Incarnation of the Word
  of God, III-1280
Augustine, Saint
  City of God, The, I-325
  Confessions, I-365
De Gruchy, John W.
  Reconciliation, III-1470
Erwin, Steve
  Left to Tell, II-1010

Ilibagiza, Immaculée
  Left to Tell, II-1010
Mbiti, John Samuel
  Bible and Theology in African
  Christianity, I-147
Mugambi, J. N. K.
  African Heritage and Contemporary
  Christianity, I-38
Origen
  On First Principles, III-1259
Plotinus
  Enneads, The, II-542
Soyinka, Wole
  Aké, I-58

GEOGRAPHICAL INDEX

Tertullian
  Apology, I-92
Tutu, Desmond
  God Has a Dream, II-694

ALGERIA
Augustine, Saint
  City of God, The, I-325
  Confessions, I-365

ARGENTINA
Borges, Jorge Luis
  "Three Versions of Judas,"
  IV-1779

ASIA
Endō, Shūsaku
  Life of Jesus, A, II-1040
  Silence, IV-1616
Kitagawa, Joseph Mitsuo
  Christian Tradition, The, I-292
Park, Jong Chun
  Crawl with God, Dance in the Spirit, I-386

AUSTRALIA
McCullough, Colleen
  Thorn Birds, The, IV-1764
Murray, Les A.
  Learning Human, II-993
West, Morris
  Shoes of the Fisherman, The, IV-1605

AUSTRIA
Hügel, Baron Friedrich von
  Essays and Addresses on the Philosophy of Religion, II-553
  Mystical Element of Religion, The, III-1191
Wright, Franz
  God's Silence, II-712

CANADA
Brouwer, Sigmund
  Blood Ties, I-173

Costain, Thomas B.
  Silver Chalice, The, IV-1620
Lonergan, Bernard J. F.
  Insight, II-873
Moore, Brian
  Catholics, I-261
Neuhaus, Richard John
  Death on a Friday Afternoon, I-435
Nouwen, Henri J. M.
  Bread for the Journey, I-215
Oke, Janette
  Love Comes Softly series, III-1082
Peretti, Frank E.
  This Present Darkness, IV-1760
Toews, Miriam
  Complicated Kindness, A, I-350

CROATIA
Jerome, Saint
  Letters of Saint Jerome, The, II-1024
Volf, Miroslav
  Exclusion and Embrace, II-586

CZECH REPUBLIC
Comenius, John Amos
  Labyrinth of the World and the Paradise of the Heart, The, II-964
Hus, Jan
  Church, The, I-312

DENMARK
Kierkegaard, Søren
  Purity of Heart Is to Will One Thing, III-1446

EGYPT
Athanasius of Alexandria, Saint
  On the Incarnation of the Word of God, III-1280
Origen
  On First Principles, III-1259
Plotinus
  Enneads, The, II-542

ENGLAND

Anselm, Saint
   Cur Deus Homo, I-401
Armstrong, Karen
   History of God, A, II-791
Auden, W. H.
   Age of Anxiety, The, I-50
Blake, William
   Marriage of Heaven and Hell, The, III-1102
   Songs of Innocence and of Experience, IV-1655
Bolt, Robert
   Man for All Seasons, A, III-1090
Browne, Sir Thomas
   Religio Medici, III-1482
Browning, Robert
   "Epistle Containing the Strange Medical Experience of Karshish, the Arab Physician, An," II-545
Bulwer-Lytton, Edward
   Last Days of Pompeii, The, II-977
Bunyan, John
   Pilgrim's Progress, The, III-1366
Butler, Joseph
   Fifteen Sermons Preached at the Rolls Chapel, II-618
Butler, Samuel
   Way of All Flesh, The, IV-1913
Chaucer, Geoffrey
   Canterbury Tales, The, I-240
Chesterton, G. K.
   Orthodoxy, III-1295
Coleridge, Samuel Taylor
   Aids to Reflection, I-54
   Rime of the Ancient Mariner, The, III-1514
Cranmer, Thomas
   Book of Common Prayer, I-184
Crashaw, Richard
   "In the Holy Nativity of Our Lord God," II-859
Cronin, A. J.
   Keys of the Kingdom, The, II-945
Davie, Donald
   To Scorch or Freeze, IV-1794

Dickens, Charles
   "Christmas Carol, A," I-299
Donne, John
   Devotions upon Emergent Occasions, I-447
   "Holy Sonnets," II-799
Eliot, George
   Scenes of Clerical Life, III-1553
Eliot, T. S.
   Four Quartets, II-660
   Idea of a Christian Society, The, II-826
Fox, George
   Journal of George Fox, The, II-931
Godden, Rumer
   In This House of Brede, II-863
Goldsmith, Oliver
   Vicar of Wakefield, The, IV-1870
Gower, John
   Confessio Amantis, I-357
Greene, Graham
   Power and the Glory, The, III-1401
Herbert, George
   Country Parson, The, I-378
   Temple, The, IV-1726
Hick, John
   Evil and the God of Love, II-582
Hill, Geoffrey
   Triumph of Love, The, IV-1820
Hopkins, Gerard Manley
   "Windhover, The," IV-1949
Hügel, Baron Friedrich von
   Essays and Addresses on the Philosophy of Religion, II-553
   Mystical Element of Religion, The, III-1191
Hurnard, Hannah
   Hinds' Feet on High Places, II-779
Jennings, Elizabeth
   Moments of Grace, III-1176
Johnson, Paul
   History of Christianity, A, II-787
Johnson, Samuel
   Supplicating Voice, The, IV-1710
Julian of Norwich
   Showings, IV-1609

GEOGRAPHICAL INDEX

Kelly, J. N. D.
    Early Christian Doctrines, II-523
Langland, William
    Piers Plowman, III-1362
Law, William
    Serious Call to a Devout and Holy Life,
      A, IV-1581
Lawrence, D. H.
    Man Who Died, The, III-1098
Levertov, Denise
    Stream and the Sapphire, The, IV-1689
Lewis, C. S.
    Chronicles of Narnia, The, I-307
    Great Divorce, The, II-739
    Mere Christianity, III-1143
    Screwtape Letters, The, III-1560
Locke, John
    Reasonableness of Christianity as
      Delivered in the Scriptures, The,
      III-1466
Macintyre, Alasdair
    Tasks of Philosophy, The, IV-1722
Macquarrie, John
    Existentialist Theology, An, II-590
Marlowe, Christopher
    Doctor Faustus, I-496
Milton, John
    Paradise Lost, III-1315
    Paradise Regained, III-1319
Newman, John Henry
    Apologia pro vita sua, I-88
Paley, William
    View of the Evidences of Christianity,
      A, IV-1875
Pearl-Poet
    Pearl, III-1335
    Sir Gawain and the Green Knight,
      IV-1635
Rice, Tim
    Jesus Christ Superstar, II-913
Rossetti, Christina
    Face of the Deep, The, II-597
Sayers, Dorothy L.
    Mind of the Maker, The, III-1155
Shakespeare, William
    Merchant of Venice, The, III-1135

Shaw, George Bernard
    Saint Joan, III-1533
Spenser, Edmund
    Faerie Queene, The, II-601
Stott, John R. W.
    Basic Christianity, I-127
Studdert Kennedy, G. A.
    Unutterable Beauty, The, IV-1853
Swift, Jonathan
    Argument Against Abolishing
      Christianity, I-99
Swinburne, Richard
    Resurrection of God Incarnate, The,
      III-1506
Taylor, Jeremy
    Great Exemplar, The, II-743
Tennyson, Alfred, Lord
    In Memoriam, II-847
Tolkien, J. R. R.
    Lord of the Rings, The, III-1073
Underhill, Evelyn
    Mysticism, III-1200
Unknown
    Beowulf, I-140
    Cloud of Unknowing, The, I-329
    "Dream of the Rood, The," I-512
    Everyman, II-574
Ware, Timothy
    Orthodox Church, The, III-1291
Watts, Isaac
    Hymns and Spiritual Songs, II-822
Waugh, Evelyn
    Brideshead Revisited, I-218
Webber, Andrew Lloyd
    Jesus Christ Superstar, II-913
Wesley, John
    Plain Account of Christian Perfection,
      A, III-1378
Whitehead, Alfred North
    Religion in the Making, III-1490
Williams, Charles
    Place of the Lion, The, III-1375
    War in Heaven, IV-1905
Williams, Roger
    Bloudy Tenent of Persecution for
      Cause of Conscience, The, I-176

Wordsworth, William
  "Ode: Intimations of Immortality,"
    III-1241
Wright, N. T.
  Simply Christian, IV-1624
Wyclif, John
  On the Truth of Holy Scripture,
    III-1284

FRANCE
Baldwin, James
  Go Tell It on the Mountain, II-687
Beckett, Samuel
  Waiting for Godot, IV-1897
Berdyaev, Nicolai
  Destiny of Man, The, I-443
Bernanos, Georges
  Diary of a Country Priest, The, I-462
Bernard of Clairvaux, Saint
  On Loving God, III-1268
Caillois, Roger
  Pontius Pilate, III-1393
Calvin, John
  Institutes of the Christian Religion,
    II-877
Cassian, John
  Conferences, I-354
Duns Scotus, John
  On Divine Love, III-1255
Ellul, Jacques
  Subversion of Christianity, The,
    IV-1698
Erasmus, Desiderius
  On the Freedom of the Will, III-1276
Erigena, John Scotus
  Treatise on Divine Predestination,
    IV-1812
Gilson, Étienne
  God and Philosophy, II-691
Girard, René
  Violence and the Sacred, IV-1879
Irenaeus, Saint
  Against Heresies, I-44
Lubac, Henri De
  Drama of Atheist Humanism, The,
    I-508

Marcel, Gabriel
  Philosophy of Existentialism, The,
    III-1358
Maritain, Jacques
  Christianity and Democracy, I-296
Mauriac, François
  Woman of the Pharisees, The,
    IV-1968
Pascal, Blaise
  Pensées, III-1342
Renan, Ernest
  Life of Jesus, The, III-1043
Ricœur, Paul
  Figuring the Sacred, II-621
Stendhal
  Red and the Black, The, III-1474
Teilhard De Chardin, Pierre
  Divine Milieu, The, I-480
Weil, Simone
  Waiting for God, IV-1891

GERMANY
Böhme, Jakob
  Way to Christ, The, IV-1917
Bonhoeffer, Dietrich
  Ethics, II-561
  Letters and Papers from Prison,
    II-1018
Bultmann, Rudolf
  Jesus Christ and Mythology, II-909
Delp, Alfred
  Prison Meditations of Father Alfred
    Delp, III-1419
Duns Scotus, John
  On Divine Love, III-1255
Eckhart, Johannes
  Sermons and Treatises, The,
    IV-1586
Feuerbach, Ludwig
  Essence of Christianity, The, II-557
Fichte, Johann Gottlieb
  Vocation of Man, The, IV-1887
Goethe, Johann Wolfgang von
  Faust, II-610
Guardini, Romano
  Lord, The, III-1070

Hegel, Georg Wilhelm Friedrich
   Early Theological Writings, II-527
Hildegard von Bingen
   Book of Divine Works, I-188
Hus, Jan
   Church, The, I-312
Jaspers, Karl
   Philosophy of Existence, III-1354
Kant, Immanuel
   Religion Within the Bounds of Mere Reason, III-1494
Küng, Hans
   On Being a Christian, III-1249
Leibniz, Gottfried Wilhelm
   Theodicy, IV-1734
Luther, Martin
   Freedom of a Christian, The, II-664
Melanchthon, Philipp
   Augsburg Confession of Faith, The, I-112
Menno Simons
   "Confession," I-361
   "New Birth, The," I-361
Moltmann, Jürgen
   Crucified God, The, I-397
Nicholas of Cusa
   Of Learned Ignorance, III-1245
Otto, Rudolf
   Idea of the Holy, The, II-830
Rahner, Karl
   Foundations of Christian Faith, II-654
Ratzinger, Joseph
   Introduction to Christianity, II-895
Ritschl, Albrecht
   Three Essays, IV-1772
Schleiermacher, Friedrich
   Christian Faith, The, I-288
Schüssler Fiorenza, Elizabeth
   In Memory of Her, II-851
Schweitzer, Albert
   Out of My Life and Thought, III-1299
Silesius, Angelus
   Cherubinic Wanderer, The, I-268
Sölle, Dorothee
   Suffering, IV-1702
Strauss, David Friedrich
   Life of Jesus Critically Examined, The, III-1046
Thomas À Kempis
   Imitation of Christ, The, II-834
Tillich, Paul
   Courage to Be, The, I-382
Troeltsch, Ernst
   Social Teaching of the Christian Churches, The, IV-1639
Weber, Max
   Protestant Ethic and the Spirit of Capitalism, The, III-1438

GREAT BRITAIN. *See* UNITED KINGDOM

GREECE
Chrysostom, Saint John
   Baptismal Instruction, I-120
Clement of Alexandria
   Instructor, The, II-881
   Miscellanies, II-881
Kazantzakis, Nikos
   Last Temptation of Christ, The, II-985
Origen
   On First Principles, III-1259
Plotinus
   Enneads, The, II-542

INDIA
Teresa, Mother
   No Greater Love, III-1227

IRELAND. *See also* NORTHERN IRELAND
Beckett, Samuel
   Waiting for Godot, IV-1897
De Graaf, Anne
   Out of the Red Shadow, III-1303
Erigena, John Scotus
   Treatise on Divine Predestination, IV-1812
Goldsmith, Oliver
   Vicar of Wakefield, The, IV-1870

Heaney, Seamus
  "Station Island," IV-1685
Lewis, C. S.
  Chronicles of Narnia, The, I-307
  Great Divorce, The, II-739
  Mere Christianity, III-1143
  Screwtape Letters, The, III-1560
Moore, Brian
  Catholics, I-261
Shaw, George Bernard
  Saint Joan, III-1533
Swift, Jonathan
  Argument Against Abolishing
    Christianity, I-99
Yeats, William Butler
  "Dialogue of Self and Soul, A,"
    I-458

ISRAEL
Hurnard, Hannah
  Hinds' Feet on High Places, II-779
Van Buren, Paul M.
  Theology of the Jewish Christian
    Reality, A, IV-1746

ITALY
Anselm, Saint
  Cur Deus Homo, I-401
Athanasius of Alexandria, Saint
  On the Incarnation of the Word of God,
    III-1280
Benedict XV
  Humani Generis Redemptionem,
    II-815
Benedict of Nursia
  Rule of St. Benedict, III-1529
Bonaventure, Saint
  Mind's Road to God, The, III-1159
Catherine of Siena, Saint
  Dialogue, The, I-453
Council of Trent
  Catechism of the Catholic Church,
    I-257
Dante
  Divine Comedy, The, I-473

Eco, Umberto
  Belief or Nonbelief?, I-133
  Name of the Rose, The, III-1204
Erasmus, Desiderius
  On the Freedom of the Will, III-1276
Guardini, Romano
  Lord, The, III-1070
Ignatius of Loyola, Saint
  Spiritual Exercises, The, IV-1680
John XXIII
  Journal of a Soul, II-928
  Mater et Magistra, III-1114
  Pacem in Terris, III-1311
Justin Martyr, Saint
  First and Second Apologies, The, II-633
Leo XIII
  Rerum Novarum, III-1498
Martini, Carlo Maria
  Belief or Nonbelief?, I-133
Nicholas of Cusa
  Of Learned Ignorance, III-1245
Paul VI
  Humanae Vitae, II-811
  Octogesima Adveniens, III-1238
  Populorum Progressio, III-1397
Peter Lombard
  Four Books of Sentences, II-657
Pius XI
  Casti Connubii, I-254
  Divini Redemptoris, I-488
  Mit brennender Sorge, III-1172
  Quadragesimo Anno, III-1455
Plotinus
  Enneads, The, II-542
Savonarola, Girolamo
  Prison Meditations on Psalms 51
    and 31, III-1423
Silone, Ignazio
  Bread and Wine, I-211
Thomas Aquinas, Saint
  Summa Theologica, IV-1706
Unknown
  Little Flowers of St. Francis, The,
    III-1058
Vatican Council II
  Gaudium et Spes, II-672

GEOGRAPHICAL INDEX

JAPAN
  Endō, Shūsaku
    Life of Jesus, A, II-1040
    Silence, IV-1616
  Kitagawa, Joseph Mitsuo
    Christian Tradition, The, I-292

KENYA
  Mbiti, John Samuel
    Bible and Theology in African Christianity, I-147
  Mugambi, J. N. K.
    African Heritage and Contemporary Christianity, I-38

KOREA. *See* SOUTH KOREA

LATIN AMERICA. *See* SOUTH AMERICA

LEBANON
  Origen
    On First Principles, III-1259

LITHUANIA
  Miłosz, Czesław
    Unattainable Earth, IV-1837

MACEDONIA
  Teresa, Mother
    No Greater Love, III-1227

MIDDLE EAST
  Amos
    Books of the Prophets, I-206
  David
    Psalms, III-1442
  Isaiah
    Books of the Prophets, I-206
  Jeremiah
    Books of the Prophets, I-206
  John
    Book of Revelation, I-202
  John Climacus
    Ladder of Divine Ascent, The, II-968
  John, son of Zebedee
    Gospel of John, II-731
  Luke
    Synoptic Gospels, IV-1717
  Mark
    Synoptic Gospels, IV-1717
  Matthew
    Synoptic Gospels, IV-1717
  Micah
    Books of the Prophets, I-206
  Origen
    On First Principles, III-1259
  Paul, Saint
    New Testament Letters, III-1219
  Pseudo-Dionysius the Areopagite
    Mystical Theology, III-1197
  Unknown
    Acts of the Apostles, I-27
    Hebrew Bible, II-756
  Van Buren, Paul M.
    Theology of the Jewish Christian Reality, A, IV-1746

THE NETHERLANDS
  Arminius, Jacobus
    Declaration of the Sentiments of Arminius, A, I-439
  De Graaf, Anne
    Out of the Red Shadow, III-1303
  Erasmus, Desiderius
    On the Freedom of the Will, III-1276
  Nouwen, Henri J. M.
    Bread for the Journey, I-215
  Sherrill, Elizabeth
    Hiding Place, The, II-775
  Sherrill, John
    Hiding Place, The, II-775
  Ten Boom, Corrie
    Hiding Place, The, II-775
  Thomas À Kempis
    Imitation of Christ, The, II-834
  Verweerd, Johanna
    Winter Garden, The, IV-1953

NICARAGUA
 Cardenal, Ernesto
  Apocalypse, I-80

NIGERIA
 Soyinka, Wole
  Aké, I-58

NORTHERN IRELAND. *See also*
 IRELAND
 Heaney, Seamus
  "Station Island," IV-1685
 Lewis, C. S.
  Chronicles of Narnia, The, I-307
  Great Divorce, The, II-739
  Mere Christianity, III-1143
  Screwtape Letters, The, III-1560
 Moore, Brian
  Catholics, I-261

NORWAY
 Undset, Sigrid
  Kristin Lavransdatter, II-960

PERU
 Gutiérrez, Gustavo
  Theology of Liberation, A,
   IV-1742

POLAND
 John Paul II
  Centesimus Annus, I-265
  Evangelium Vitae, II-568
  Veritatis Splendor, IV-1866
 Kołakowski, Leszek
  Religion, III-1486
 Miłosz, Czesław
  Unattainable Earth, IV-1837
 Schleiermacher, Friedrich
  Christian Faith, The, I-288
 Sienkiewicz, Henryk
  Quo Vadis, III-1462
 Stein, Edith
  Knowledge and Faith, II-956

PORTUGAL
 Saramago, José
  Gospel According to Jesus Christ, The,
   II-724

ROMANIA
 Cassian, John
  Conferences, I-354

RUSSIA
 Berdyaev, Nicolai
  Destiny of Man, The, I-443
 Bulgakov, Mikhail
  Master and Margarita, The, III-1110
 Dostoevski, Fyodor
  Brothers Karamazov, The, I-229
 Kant, Immanuel
  Religion Within the Bounds of Mere
   Reason, III-1494
 Tolstoy, Leo
  Death of Ivan Ilyich, The, I-431
  Divine and Human, I-469
  Kingdom of God Is Within You, The,
   II-948

RWANDA
 Erwin, Steve
  Left to Tell, II-1010
 Ilibagiza, Immaculée
  Left to Tell, II-1010

SCOTLAND
 Baillie, D. M.
  God Was in Christ, II-698
 Baillie, John
  Sense of the Presence of God, The,
   III-1578
 Cronin, A. J.
  Keys of the Kingdom, The, II-945
 Duns Scotus, John
  On Divine Love, III-1255
 Macdonald, George
  Phantastes, III-1346
 Macquarrie, John
  Existentialist Theology, An, II-590

Smith, Adam
   Theory of Moral Sentiments, The,
     IV-1749

SOUTH AFRICA
   Abrams, Douglas
     God Has a Dream, II-694
   De Gruchy, John W.
     Reconciliation, III-1470
   Tutu, Desmond
     God Has a Dream, II-694

SOUTH AMERICA
   Borges, Jorge Luis
     "Three Versions of Judas," IV-1779
   Cardenal, Ernesto
     Apocalypse, I-80
   Gutiérrez, Gustavo
     Theology of Liberation, A, IV-1742

SOUTH KOREA
   Park, Jong Chun
     Crawl with God, Dance in the Spirit,
     I-386

SOVIET UNION. *See* RUSSIA

SPAIN
   Ignatius of Loyola, Saint
     Spiritual Exercises, The, IV-1680
   John of the Cross, Saint
     Ascent of Mount Carmel, I-107
     Dark Night of the Soul, I-107
   Osuna, Francisco De
     Third Spiritual Alphabet, The,
     IV-1756
   Santayana, George
     Last Puritan, The, II-981
   Suárez, Francisco
     Metaphysical Demonstration of the
     Existence of God, The, III-1147
   Teresa of Ávila, Saint
     Interior Castle, II-887
   Unamuno y Jugo, Miguel De
     Saint Manuel Bueno, Martyr, III-1537

SWEDEN
   Bergman, Ingmar
     Seventh Seal, The, IV-1595
   Lagerkvist, Pär
     Barabbas, I-123
   Nygren, Anders
     Agape and Eros, I-47

SWITZERLAND
   Barth, Karl
     Epistle to the Romans, The, II-549
   Brunner, Emil
     Revelation and Reason, III-1510
   Calvin, John
     Institutes of the Christian Religion,
     II-877
   Jung, Carl Gustav
     Memories, Dreams, Reflections,
     III-1131
   Küng, Hans
     On Being a Christian, III-1249
   Tournier, Paul
     Meaning of Persons, The, III-1118
   Zwingli, Ulrich
     On Providence, III-1272

SYRIA
   John Climacus
     Ladder of Divine Ascent, The,
     II-968
   Pseudo-Dionysius the Areopagite
     Mystical Theology, III-1197

TUNISIA
   Tertullian
     Apology, I-92

TURKEY
   Chrysostom, Saint John
     Baptismal Instruction, I-120
   Gregory of Nyssa, Saint
     Lord's Prayer and the Beatitudes, The,
     III-1078
   Irenaeus, Saint
     Against Heresies, I-44

UNITED KINGDOM
Anselm, Saint
   Cur Deus Homo, I-401
Armstrong, Karen
   History of God, A, II-791
Auden, W. H.
   Age of Anxiety, The, I-50
Baillie, John
   Sense of the Presence of God, The,
      III-1578
Beckett, Samuel
   Waiting for Godot, IV-1897
Blake, William
   Marriage of Heaven and Hell, The,
      III-1102
   Songs of Innocence and of Experience,
      IV-1655
Bolt, Robert
   Man for All Seasons, A, III-1090
Browne, Sir Thomas
   Religio Medici, III-1482
Browning, Robert
   "Epistle, An," II-545
Bulwer-Lytton, Edward
   Last Days of Pompeii, The, II-977
Bunyan, John
   Pilgrim's Progress, The, III-1366
Butler, Joseph
   Fifteen Sermons Preached at the Rolls
      Chapel, II-618
Butler, Samuel
   Way of All Flesh, The, IV-1913
Chaucer, Geoffrey
   Canterbury Tales, The, I-240
Chesterton, G. K.
   Orthodoxy, III-1295
Coleridge, Samuel Taylor
   Aids to Reflection, I-54
   Rime of the Ancient Mariner, The,
      III-1514
Cranmer, Thomas
   Book of Common Prayer, I-184
Crashaw, Richard
   "In the Holy Nativity of Our Lord
      God," II-859

Cronin, A. J.
   Keys of the Kingdom, The, II-945
Davie, Donald
   To Scorch or Freeze, IV-1794
Dickens, Charles
   "Christmas Carol, A," I-299
Donne, John
   Devotions upon Emergent Occasions,
      I-447
   "Holy Sonnets," II-799
Duns Scotus, John
   On Divine Love, III-1255
Eliot, George
   Scenes of Clerical Life, III-1553
Eliot, T. S.
   Four Quartets, II-660
   Idea of a Christian Society, The, II-826
Erigena, John Scotus
   Treatise on Divine Predestination,
      IV-1812
Fox, George
   Journal of George Fox, The, II-931
Godden, Rumer
   In This House of Brede, II-863
Goldsmith, Oliver
   Vicar of Wakefield, The, IV-1870
Gower, John
   Confessio Amantis, I-357
Greene, Graham
   Power and the Glory, The, III-1401
Heaney, Seamus
   "Station Island," IV-1685
Herbert, George
   Country Parson, The, I-378
   Temple, The, IV-1726
Hill, Geoffrey
   Triumph of Love, The, IV-1820
Hopkins, Gerard Manley
   "Windhover, The," IV-1949
Hügel, Baron Friedrich von
   Essays and Addresses on the
      Philosophy of Religion, II-553
   Mystical Element of Religion, The,
      III-1191
Hurnard, Hannah
   Hinds' Feet on High Places, II-779

GEOGRAPHICAL INDEX

Jennings, Elizabeth
  Moments of Grace, III-1176
Johnson, Paul
  History of Christianity, A, II-787
Johnson, Samuel
  Supplicating Voice, The, IV-1710
Julian of Norwich
  Showings, IV-1609
Kelly, J. N. D.
  Early Christian Doctrines, II-523
Langland, William
  Piers Plowman, III-1362
Law, William
  Serious Call to a Devout and Holy Life,
    A, IV-1581
Lawrence, D. H.
  Man Who Died, The, III-1098
Levertov, Denise
  Stream and the Sapphire, The, IV-1689
Lewis, C. S.
  Chronicles of Narnia, The, I-307
  Great Divorce, The, II-739
  Mere Christianity, III-1143
  Screwtape Letters, The, III-1560
Locke, John
  Reasonableness of Christianity as
    Delivered in the Scriptures, The,
    III-1466
Macdonald, George
  Phantastes, III-1346
Macintyre, Alasdair
  Tasks of Philosophy, The, IV-1722
Macquarrie, John
  Existentialist Theology, An, II-590
Marlowe, Christopher
  Doctor Faustus, I-496
Milton, John
  Paradise Lost, III-1315
  Paradise Regained, III-1319
Newman, John Henry
  Apologia pro vita sua, I-88
Paley, William
  View of the Evidences of Christianity,
    A, IV-1875
Pearl-Poet
  Pearl, III-1335

Sir Gawain and the Green Knight,
  IV-1635
Rice, Tim
  Jesus Christ Superstar, II-913
Rossetti, Christina
  Face of the Deep, The, II-597
Sayers, Dorothy L.
  Mind of the Maker, The, III-1155
Shakespeare, William
  Merchant of Venice, The, III-1135
Shaw, George Bernard
  Saint Joan, III-1533
Smith, Adam
  Theory of Moral Sentiments, The,
    IV-1749
Spenser, Edmund
  Faerie Queene, The, II-601
Stott, John R. W.
  Basic Christianity, I-127
Studdert Kennedy, G. A.
  Unutterable Beauty, The,
    IV-1853
Swift, Jonathan
  Argument Against Abolishing
    Christianity, I-99
Swinburne, Richard
  Resurrection of God Incarnate, The,
    III-1506
Taylor, Jeremy
  Great Exemplar, The, II-743
Tennyson, Alfred, Lord
  In Memoriam, II-847
Tolkien, J. R. R.
  Lord of the Rings, The, III-1073
Underhill, Evelyn
  Mysticism, III-1200
Unknown
  Beowulf, I-140
  Cloud of Unknowing, The, I-329
  "Dream of the Rood, The," I-512
  Everyman, II-574
Vaughan, Henry
  "They Are All Gone into the World of
    Light!," IV-1753
Ware, Timothy
  Orthodox Church, The, III-1291

Watts, Isaac
   Hymns and Spiritual Songs, II-822
Waugh, Evelyn
   Brideshead Revisited, I-218
Webber, Andrew Lloyd
   Jesus Christ Superstar, II-913
Wesley, John
   Plain Account of Christian Perfection, A, III-1378
Whitehead, Alfred North
   Religion in the Making, III-1490
Williams, Charles
   Place of the Lion, The, III-1375
   War in Heaven, IV-1905
Williams, Roger
   Bloudy Tenent of Persecution for Cause of Conscience, The, I-176
Williams, Rowan
   On Christian Theology, III-1252
Wordsworth, William
   "Ode: Intimations of Immortality," III-1241
Wright, N. T.
   Simply Christian, IV-1624
Wyclif, John
   On the Truth of Holy Scripture, III-1284

UNITED STATES
Agee, James
   Death in the Family, A, I-427
Altizer, Thomas J. J.
   Gospel of Christian Atheism, The, II-728
Angelou, Maya
   "Amazing Peace," I-69
Arvin, Reed
   Wind in the Wheat, The, IV-1945
Auden, W. H.
   Age of Anxiety, The, I-50
Austin, Lynn N.
   Fire by Night, II-629
Baldwin, James
   Go Tell It on the Mountain, II-687
Barrett, William E.
   Lilies of the Field, The, III-1050

Barton, Bruce
   Man Nobody Knows, The, III-1094
Beasley, Bruce
   Creation, The, I-390
Beauseigneur, James
   Christ Clone Trilogy, I-275
Beazely, Jan
   King's Ransom, II-952
Bell, James Scott
   Final Witness, II-625
Benson, Angela
   Awakening Mercy, I-116
Berrigan, Daniel
   Isaiah, II-898
Berry, Wendell
   What Are People For?, IV-1927
Berryman, John
   Dream Songs, The, I-515
Blackstock, Terri
   Newpointe 911, III-1223
Blackston, Ray
   Flabbergasted, II-640
Bly, Stephen A.
   Long Trail Home, The, III-1066
Bodo, Murray
   Song of the Sparrow, IV-1648
Borg, Marcus J.
   Meeting Jesus Again for the First Time, III-1125
Bottum, Joseph
   "Fall, The," II-606
Bowen, Michele Andrea
   Church Folk, I-316
Bradstreet, Anne
   "Here Follows Some Verses upon the Burning of Our House July 10th, 1666," II-768
Brown, Dan
   Da Vinci Code, The, I-408
Brueggemann, Walter
   Inscribing the Text, II-870
Buechner, Frederick
   Godric, II-708
   Secrets in the Dark, III-1571
Bunn, T. Davis
   Drummer in the Dark, II-519

Cairns, Scott
   Philokalia, III-1350
Caldwell, Taylor
   Dear and Glorious Physician, I-420
Carlson, C. C.
   Late Great Planet Earth, The, II-989
Carroll, James
   Constantine's Sword, I-374
Cather, Willa
   Death Comes for the Archbishop, I-423
Cavanaugh, Jack
   His Watchful Eye, II-783
   While Mortals Sleep, IV-1941
Chappell, Fred
   Midquest, III-1151
Chittister, Joan D., O.S.B.
   Called to Question, I-237
Cobb, John B., Jr.
   Christ in a Pluralistic Age, I-280
Coffin, William Sloane
   Credo, I-393
Cone, James H.
   Black Theology of Liberation, A, I-165
Costain, Thomas B.
   Silver Chalice, The, IV-1620
Cox, Harvey
   When Jesus Came to Harvard, IV-1937
Craig, David
   Mercy's Face, III-1139
Cramer, W. Dale
   Sutter's Cross, IV-1714
Cronin, A. J.
   Keys of the Kingdom, The, II-945
Daly, Mary
   Beyond God the Father, I-144
Day, Dorothy
   Loaves and Fishes, III-1062
De Graaf, Anne
   Out of the Red Shadow, III-1303
Dekker, Ted
   Circle Trilogy, The, I-320
   Thr3e, IV-1768
Dickinson, Emily
   "Word made Flesh is seldom, A," IV-1976

Dillard, Annie
   For the Time Being, II-647
Douglas, Lloyd C.
   Magnificent Obsession, III-1087
   Robe, The, III-1522
Du Bois, W. E. B.
   Souls of Black Folk, The, IV-1668
Eddy, Mary Baker
   Science and Health with Key to the Scriptures, III-1557
Edwards, Jonathan
   Treatise Concerning Religious Affections, A, IV-1806
Ehrman, Bart D.
   Misquoting Jesus, III-1168
Eliot, T. S.
   Four Quartets, II-660
   Idea of a Christian Society, The, II-826
Emerson, Ralph Waldo
   Divinity School Address, The, I-491
Fairchild, B. H.
   Arrival of the Future, The, I-103
Finney, Charles Grandison
   Lectures on Revivals of Religion, II-1001
Foote, Horton
   Trip to Bountiful, The, IV-1816
Forché, Carolyn
   Angel of History, The, I-77
Fosdick, Harry Emerson
   Meaning of Prayer, The, III-1121
Foster, Sharon Ewell
   Passing by Samaria, III-1323
Fox, Matthew
   Coming of the Cosmic Christ, The, I-346
Gioia, Dana
   Interrogations at Noon, II-891
Girard, René
   Violence and the Sacred, IV-1879
Glancy, Diane
   (Ado)ration, I-31
Glendon, Mary Ann
   Abortion and Divorce in Western Law, I-23

Gomes, Peter J.
    Good Book, The, II-720
Gordon, Mary
    Pearl, III-1331
Graham, Billy
    Journey, The, II-941
Greeley, Andrew M.
    Bishop in the Old Neighborhood,
        The, I-157
    Great Mysteries, The, II-746
Grimké, Angelina Emily
    Walking by Faith, IV-1901
Guinness, Os
    Unspeakable, IV-1849
Gulley, Philip
    Home to Harmony, II-802
Hampl, Patricia
    Virgin Time, IV-1883
Hancock, Karen
    Arena, I-96
Hartshorne, Charles
    Divine Relativity, The, I-485
Hassler, Jon
    North of Hope, III-1230
Hauerwas, Stanley
    With the Grain of the Universe,
        IV-1965
Hawthorne, Nathaniel
    Scarlet Letter, The, III-1549
Henderson, Dee
    True Honor, IV-1823
Henry, Carl F. H.
    Uneasy Conscience of Modern
        Fundamentalism, The, IV-1845
Hill, Grace Livingston
    Prodigal Girl, The, III-1430
Holmes, Marjorie
    Two from Galilee, IV-1834
Hopes, David Brendan
    Penitent Magdalene, The, III-1339
Hudgins, Andrew
    After the Lost War, I-41
Hughes, Langston
    "Feet of Jesus," II-614
Hulme, Kathryn C.
    Nun's Story, The, III-1234

Hunt, Angela Elwell
    Truth Teller, The, IV-1827
Hurston, Zora Neale
    Their Eyes Were Watching God,
        IV-1730
Ingermanson, Randall Scott
    Oxygen, III-1307
    Transgression, IV-1798
Irving, John
    Prayer for Owen Meany, A, III-1408
James, William
    Varieties of Religious Experience, The,
        IV-1856
Janney, Russell
    Miracle of the Bells, The, III-1164
Jarman, Mark
    Questions for Ecclesiastes, III-1459
Jefferson, Thomas
    Jefferson Bible, The, II-906
Jenkins, Jerry B.
    Left Behind series, II-1005
    Soon, IV-1660
Johnson, Elizabeth A.
    She Who Is, IV-1598
Johnson, James Weldon
    God's Trombones, II-716
Jones, Rufus M.
    Double Search, The, I-503
Karon, Jan
    New Song, A, III-1215
Karr, Mary
    Sinners Welcome, IV-1631
Kasdorf, Julia
    Eve's Striptease, II-578
Kee, Howard Clark
    Jesus in History, II-921
Keillor, Garrison
    Lake Wobegon Days, II-973
Kennedy, X. J.
    Beasts of Bethlehem, The, I-130
King, Karen L.
    Gospel of Mary of Magdala, The,
        II-735
King, Martin Luther, Jr.
    "Letter from Birmingham Jail," II-1014
    Strength to Love, IV-1693

Kingsbury, Karen
  One Tuesday Morning, III-1288
Kingsolver, Barbara
  Poisonwood Bible, The, III-1384
Kitagawa, Joseph Mitsuo
  Christian Tradition, The, I-292
Lahaye, Tim
  Left Behind series, II-1005
Lamott, Anne
  All New People, I-62
  Traveling Mercies, IV-1802
Lawhead, Stephen R.
  Song of Albion Trilogy, The,
    IV-1643
Lea, Sydney
  Ghost Pain, II-676
Lee, Harper
  To Kill a Mockingbird, IV-1790
Lee, Li-Young
  Rose, III-1525
Lemmons, Thom
  King's Ransom, II-952
Levertov, Denise
  Stream and the Sapphire, The,
    IV-1689
Lewis, Beverly
  Shunning, The, IV-1612
Lewis, Sinclair
  Elmer Gantry, II-538
Lindbergh, Anne Morrow
  Gift from the Sea, II-680
Lindsey, Hal
  Late Great Planet Earth, The, II-989
Long, David Ryan
  Ezekiel's Shadow, II-594
Lowell, Robert
  "For the Union Dead," II-650
Lucado, Max
  Cure for the Common Life, I-405
McFague, Sallie
  Life Abundant, II-1033
McInerny, Ralph
  And I Alone Have Escaped to Tell
    You, I-73
McLaren, Brian D.
  New Kind of Christian, A, III-1211

Maclean, Norman
  River Runs Through It, A, III-1518
Macleish, Archibald
  J. B., II-902
Maddoux, Marlin
  Seal of Gaia, The, III-1564
Mariani, Paul
  Great Wheel, The, II-749
Marshall, Catherine
  Christy, I-303
Matsuoka, Fumitaka
  Color of Faith, The, I-334
Meilaender, Gilbert
  Bioethics, I-154
Melville, Herman
  Billy Budd, Foretopman, I-150
Merton, Thomas
  Seven Storey Mountain, The, IV-1591
Middleton, David
  Burning Fields, The, I-233
Miles, Jack
  Christ, I-272
Miller, Calvin
  Singer Trilogy, The, IV-1627
Miller, Donald
  Blue Like Jazz, I-180
Miller, Walter M., Jr.
  Canticle for Leibowitz, A, I-245
Mills, James R.
  Memoirs of Pontius Pilate, III-1128
Moore, Beth
  Praying God's Word, III-1412
Moore, Marianne
  "In Distrust of Merits," II-839
Moore, Thomas
  Care of the Soul, I-251
Morris, Gilbert
  Edge of Honor, II-534
Morris, Michael
  Place Called Wiregrass, A, III-1371
Moser, Nancy
  Time Lottery, IV-1786
Mouw, Richard J.
  God Who Commands, The, II-704
  Wonderful Words of Life,
    IV-1972

Murray, John Courtney, S.J.
    We Hold These Truths, IV-1923
Musser, Joe
    Infidel, The, II-866
Napier, Bunyan Davie
    Come Sweet Death, I-342
Nehring, Radine Trees
    Music to Die For, III-1184
Nesanovich, Stella Ann
    Brightness That Made My Soul
        Tremble, A, I-222
Neuhaus, Richard John
    Death on a Friday Afternoon, I-435
Niebuhr, Reinhold
    Nature and Destiny of Man, The,
        III-1207
Noll, Mark A.
    Wonderful Words of Life, IV-1972
Norris, Kathleen
    Amazing Grace, I-65
Nouwen, Henri J. M.
    Bread for the Journey, I-215
O'Connor, Flannery
    Wise Blood, IV-1957
Olson, John B.
    Oxygen, III-1307
Ong, Walter J.
    Presence of the Word, The, III-1415
Oursler, Fulton
    Greatest Story Ever Told, The,
        II-752
Palmer, Catherine
    Dangerous Silence, A, I-412
Pankey, Eric
    Apocrypha, I-84
Parker, Gary E.
    Capital Offense, A, I-248
Peale, Norman Vincent
    Power of Positive Thinking, The,
        III-1405
Pelikan, Jaroslav
    Jesus Through the Centuries, II-925
Pella, Judith
    Dawning of Deliverance, The, I-416
Percy, Walker
    Second Coming, The, III-1568

Plantinga, Alvin
    Warranted Christian Belief, IV-1909
Powers, J. F.
    Morte d'Urban, III-1180
Rauschenbusch, Walter
    Theology for the Social Gospel, A,
        IV-1738
Rice, Anne
    Christ the Lord, I-284
Rivers, Francine
    Redeeming Love, III-1478
Robinson, Marilynne
    Gilead, II-683
Roth, John K.
    Holocaust Politics, II-795
Royce, Josiah
    Problem of Christianity, The,
        III-1426
Russell, Mary Doria
    Sparrow, The, IV-1676
Samson, Lisa
    Songbird, IV-1651
Schaap, James C.
    Secrets of Barneveld Calvary, The,
        III-1574
Schaeffer, Francis A.
    How Should We Then Live?, II-806
Schuller, Robert H.
    Don't Throw Away Tomorrow,
        I-500
Schüssler Fiorenza, Elizabeth
    In Memory of Her, II-851
Sheehan, Thomas
    First Coming, The, II-636
Sheen, Fulton J.
    Life Is Worth Living, II-1037
Sheldon, Charles Monroe
    In His Steps, II-843
Sherrill, Elizabeth
    Hiding Place, The, II-775
Sherrill, John
    Hiding Place, The, II-775
Singer, Randy
    Directed Verdict, I-465
Smedes, Lewis B.
    My God and I, III-1188

Smith, Huston
    Soul of Christianity, The, IV-1664
Smith, Joseph
    Book of Mormon, I-196
Sorensen, Michele
    Broken Lance, I-226
Spong, John Shelby
    Here I Stand, II-772
Stafford, William
    Even in Quiet Places, II-571
Steele, Timothy
    Sapphics and Uncertainties, III-1545
Steere, Douglas V.
    On Listening to Another, III-1263
Stout, Jeffrey
    Ethics After Babel, II-565
Stowe, Harriet Beecher
    Uncle Tom's Cabin, IV-1841
Styron, William
    Confessions of Nat Turner, The, I-370
Sweet, Leonard
    Three Hardest Words in the World to Get Right, The, IV-1776
Tanner, Kathryn
    Economy of Grace, II-531
Ten Boom, Corrie
    Hiding Place, The, II-775
Thoene, Bodie
    Twilight of Courage, The, IV-1830
Thoene, Brock
    Twilight of Courage, The, IV-1830
Thurman, Howard
    With Head and Heart, IV-1961
Tillich, Paul
    Courage to Be, The, I-382
Traylor, Ellen Gunderson
    Mary Magdalene, III-1106
Trobaugh, Augusta
    Resting in the Bosom of the Lamb, III-1502
Turnbull, Agnes Sligh
    Bishop's Mantle, The, I-161
Twain, Mark
    Letters from the Earth, II-1021
Tyler, Anne
    Saint Maybe, III-1541

Updike, John
    In the Beauty of the Lilies, II-855
Van Buren, Paul M.
    Theology of the Jewish Christian Reality, A, IV-1746
Volf, Miroslav
    Exclusion and Embrace, II-586
Walker, Alice
    Color Purple, The, I-338
Wallace, Lew
    Ben-Hur, I-136
Wangerin, Walter, Jr.
    Book of God, The, I-192
    Paul, III-1327
Warren, Rick
    Purpose Driven Life, The, III-1452
Weigel, George
    Letters to a Young Catholic, II-1029
West, Cornel
    Prophesy Deliverance!, III-1434
West, Jessamyn
    Friendly Persuasion, The, II-669
Whitlow, Robert
    List, The, III-1054
Whitman, Walt
    Leaves of Grass, II-997
Whittier, John Greenleaf
    Hymns, II-818
Wieman, Henry Nelson
    Source of Human Good, The, IV-1672
Wilbur, Richard
    "Advice to a Prophet," I-35
Willard, Dallas
    Divine Conspiracy, The, I-477
Williams, Roger
    Bloudy Tenent of Persecution for Cause of Conscience, The, I-176
Wills, Garry
    What Jesus Meant, IV-1934
Wilson, Debbie
    Tiger in the Shadows, IV-1782
Witek, Terri
    Fools and Crows, II-644
Woiwode, Larry
    What I Think I Did, IV-1931

Woolman, John
   Journal of John Woolman, The, II-936
Wright, Charles
   Black Zodiac, I-169
Wright, Franz
   God's Silence, II-712
Wright, Harold Bell
   Shepherd of the Hills, The, IV-1602
Wright, Vinita Hampton
   Velma Still Cooks in Leeway, IV-1862
Yancey, Philip
   Jesus I Never Knew, The, II-917

Yoder, John H.
   Politics of Jesus, The, III-1389

WALES
Herbert, George
   Country Parson, The, I-378
   Temple, The, IV-1726
Vaughan, Henry
   "They Are All Gone into the World of Light!," IV-1753
Williams, Rowan
   On Christian Theology, III-1252

MASTERPLOTS II
CHRISTIAN LITERATURE

TITLE INDEX

Abortion and Divorce in Western Law (Glendon), I-23
Acts of the Apostles (Unknown), I-27
Ad illustrissimum Cattorum principem Philippum, sermonis de providentia Dei anamnema. *See* On Providence
(Ado)ration (Glancy), I-31
Adversus haereses. *See* Against Heresies
"Advice to a Prophet" (Wilbur), I-35
African Heritage and Contemporary Christianity (Mugambi), I-38
After the Lost War (Hudgins), I-41
Against Heresies (Irenaeus), I-44
Agape and Eros (Nygren), I-47
Age of Anxiety, The (Auden), I-50
Aids to Reflection (Coleridge), I-54
Aké (Soyinka), I-58
All New People (Lamott), I-62
Amazing Grace (Norris), I-65
"Amazing Peace" (Angelou), I-69
And I Alone Have Escaped to Tell You (McInerny), I-73
Angel of History, The (Forché), I-77
Apocalypse (Cardenal), I-80
Apocrypha (Pankey), I-84
Apokalypsis. *See* Book of Revelation
Apologeticus. *See* Apology
Apologia prima and Apologia secunda. *See* First and Second Apologies, The
Apologia pro vita sua (Newman), I-88
Apology (Tertullian), I-92
Arena (Hancock), I-96
Argument Against Abolishing Christianity (Swift), I-99
Arrival of the Future, The (Fairchild), I-103
Ascent of Mount Carmel (John of the Cross), I-107
Attente de Dieu. *See* Waiting for God
Augsburg Confession of Faith, The (Melanchthon), I-112
Aus meinem Leben und Denken. *See* Out of My Life and Thought
Awakening Mercy (Benson), I-116

Baptismal Instruction (Chrysostom), I-120
Barabbas (Lagerkvist), I-123
Basic Christianity (Stott), I-127
Beasts of Bethlehem, The (Kennedy), I-130
Belief or Nonbelief? (Eco and Martini), I-133
Ben-Hur (Wallace), I-136
Beowulf (Unknown), I-140
Bestimmung des Menschen, Die. *See* Vocation of Man, The
Beyond God the Father (Daly), I-144
Bible and Theology in African Christianity (Mbiti), I-147
Bible in History, The, I-10
Billy Budd, Foretopman (Melville), I-150
Bioethics (Meilaender), I-154
Bishop in the Old Neighborhood, The (Greeley), I-157
Bishop's Mantle, The (Turnbull), I-161
Black Theology of Liberation, A (Cone), I-165
Black Zodiac (Wright, C.), I-169
Blood Ties (Brouwer), I-173
Bloudy Tenent of Persecution for Cause of Conscience, The (Williams, Roger), I-176
Blue Like Jazz (Miller, D.), I-180
Book of Common Prayer (Cranmer), I-184
Book of Divine Works (Hildegard von Bingen), I-188
Book of God, The (Wangerin), I-192
Book of Mormon (Smith, J.), I-196
Book of Revelation (John), I-202
Books of the Prophets (Isaiah, Jeremiah, Amos, and Micah), I-206
"Bozheskoe I chelovecheskoe." *See* Divine and Human
Bread and Wine (Silone), I-211
Bread for the Journey (Nouwen), I-215
Brideshead Revisited (Waugh), I-218
Brightness That Made My Soul Tremble, A (Nesanovich), I-222
Broken Lance (Sorensen), I-226
Brot und Wein. *See* Bread and Wine

Brothers Karamazov, The (Dostoevski), I-229
Burning Fields, The (Middleton), I-233

Called to Question (Chittister), I-237
Canterbury Tales, The (Chaucer), I-240
Canticle for Leibowitz, A (Miller, W. M.), I-245
Capital Offense, A (Parker), I-248
Care of the Soul (Moore, T.), I-251
Casti Connubii (Pius XI), I-254
Castillo interior, El. *See* Interior Castle
Catecheses ad illuminandos. *See* Baptismal Instruction
Catechism of the Catholic Church (Council of Trent), I-257
Catechismus Catholicae Ecclesiae. *See* Catechism of the Catholic Church
Catholics (Moore, Brian), I-261
Centesimus Annus (John Paul II), I-265
Cherubinic Wanderer, The (Silesius), I-268
Chimmoku. *See* Silence
Christ (Miles), I-272
Christ Clone Trilogy (BeauSeigneur), I-275
Christ in a Pluralistic Age (Cobb), I-280
Christ sein. *See* On Being a Christian
Christ the Lord (Rice, A.), I-284
Christian Faith, The (Schleiermacher), I-288
Christian Marriage. *See* Casti Connubii
Christian Tradition, The (Kitagawa), I-292
Christianae religionis institutio. *See* Institutes of the Christian Religion
Christianisme et démocratie. *See* Christianity and Democracy
Christianity and Democracy (Maritain), I-296
Christliche Glaube, Der. *See* Christian Faith, The
"Christmas Carol, A" (Dickens), I-299
Christy (Marshall), I-303
Chronicles of Narnia, The (Lewis, C. S.), I-307
Church, The (Hus), I-312
Church Folk (Bowen), I-316
Circle Trilogy, The (Dekker), I-320
City of God, The (Augustine), I-325

Cloud of Unknowing, The (Unknown), I-329
Collationes. *See* Conferences
Color of Faith, The (Matsuoka), I-334
Color Purple, The (Walker), I-338
Come Sweet Death (Napier), I-342
Coming of the Cosmic Christ, The (Fox, M.), I-346
Complicated Kindness, A (Toews), I-350
Conferences (Cassian), I-354
Confessio Amantis (Gower), I-357
Confessio Augustana. *See* Augsburg Confession of Faith, The
"Confession" (Menno Simons), I-361
Confessions (Augustine), I-365
Confessions of Nat Turner, The (Styron), I-370
Constantine's Sword (Carroll), I-374
Corte ende grondighe verclaringhe uyt de Heylighe Schrift.... *See* Declaration of the Sentiments of Arminius, A
Country Parson, The (Herbert), I-378
Courage to Be, The (Tillich), I-382
Crawl with God, Dance in the Spirit (Park), I-386
Creation, The (Beasley), I-390
Credo (Coffin), I-393
Crucified God, The (Moltmann), I-397
Cur Deus Homo (Anselm), I-401
Cure for the Common Life (Lucado), I-405

Dangerous Silence, A (Palmer), I-412
Dark Night of the Soul (John of the Cross), I-107
Da Vinci Code, The (Brown), I-408
Dawning of Deliverance, The (Pella), I-416
De amore Dei. *See* On Loving God
De beatitudinibus. *See* Lord's Prayer and the Beatitudes, The
De civitate Dei. *See* City of God, The
De divina praedestinatione liber. *See* Treatise on Divine Predestination
De docta ignorantia. *See* Of Learned Ignorance
De ecclesia. *See* Church, The
De incarnatione Verbi Dei. *See* On the Incarnation of the Word of God

TITLE INDEX

De Libero Arbitrio. *See* On the Freedom of the Will
De operatione Dei. *See* Book of Divine Works
De oratione dominica. *See* Lord's Prayer and the Beatitudes, The
De veritate sacrae scripturae. *See* On the Truth of Holy Scripture
Dear and Glorious Physician (Caldwell), I-420
Death Comes for the Archbishop (Cather), I-423
Death in the Family, A (Agee), I-427
Death of Ivan Ilyich, The (Tolstoy), I-431
Death on a Friday Afternoon (Neuhaus), I-435
Declaration of the Sentiments of Arminius, A (Arminius), I-439
Den kristna kärlekstanken genom tiderna. *See* Agape and Eros
Destiny of Man, The (Berdyaev), I-443
Devotions upon Emergent Occasions (Donne), I-447
Dialogue, The (Catherine of Siena), I-453
"Dialogue of Self and Soul, A" (Yeats), I-458
Diary of a Country Priest, The (Bernanos), I-462
Directed Verdict (Singer), I-465
Disputationer Metaphysicae. *See* Metaphysical Demonstration of the Existence of God, The
Divine and Human (Tolstoy), I-469
Divine Comedy, The (Dante), I-473
Divine Conspiracy, The (Willard), I-477
Divine Milieu, The (Teilhard de Chardin), I-480
Divine Relativity, The (Hartshorne), I-485
Divini Redemptoris (Pius XI), I-488
Divinia commedia, La. *See* Divine Comedy, The
Divinity School Address, The (Emerson), I-491
Doctor Faustus (Marlowe), I-496
Don't Throw Away Tomorrow (Schuller), I-500

Double Search, The (Jones), I-503
Drama of Atheist Humanism, The (Lubac), I-508
Drame de l'humanisme athée, Le. *See* Drama of Atheist Humanism, The
"Dream of the Rood, The" (Unknown), I-512
Dream Songs, The (Berryman), I-515
Drummer in the Dark (Bunn), II-519

Early Christian Doctrines (Kelly), II-523
Early Theological Writings (Hegel), II-527
Economy of Grace (Tanner), II-531
Edge of Honor (Morris, G.), II-534
Einführung in das Christentum. *See* Introduction to Christianity
Ejercicios espirituales. *See* Spiritual Exercises, The
Elmer Gantry (Lewis, S.), II-538
En attendant Godot. *See* Waiting for Godot
Enneads, The (Plotinus), II-542
Enneas. *See* Enneads, The
"Epistle Containing the Strange Medical Experience of Karshish, the Arab Physician, An" (Browning), II-545
Epistle to the Romans, The (Barth), II-549
Erinnerungen, Träume, Gedanken. *See* Memories, Dreams, Reflections
Erkenntnis und Glaube. *See* Knowledge and Faith
Essais de théodicée sur la bonté de Dieu, la liberté de l'homme, et l'origine du mal. *See* Theodicy
Essays and Addresses on the Philosophy of Religion (Hügel), II-553
Essence of Christianity, The (Feuerbach), II-557
Ethics (Bonhoeffer), II-561
Ethics After Babel (Stout), II-565
Ethik. *See* Ethics
Euaggelion kata Matthaion, Markon, Lucan. *See* Synoptic Gospels
Evangelho segundo Jesus Cristo, O. *See* Gospel According to Jesus Christ, The
Evangelium Vitae (John Paul II), II-568
Even in Quiet Places (Stafford), II-571
Everyman (Unknown), II-574

Eve's Striptease (Kasdorf), II-578
Evil and the God of Love (Hick), II-582
Exclusion and Embrace (Volf), II-586
Existentialist Theology, An (Macquarrie), II-590
Existenzphilosophie. *See* Philosophy of Existence
Ezekiel's Shadow (Long), II-594

Face of the Deep, The (Rossetti), II-597
Facing Death. *See* Prison Meditations of Father Alfred Delp
Faerie Queene, The (Spenser), II-601
"Fall, The" (Bottum), II-606
Faust (Goethe), II-610
"Feet of Jesus" (Hughes), II-614
Fifteen Sermons Preached at the Rolls Chapel (Butler, J.), II-618
Figuring the Sacred (Ricœur), II-621
Final Witness (Bell), II-625
Fioretti di San Francesco d'Assissi. *See* Little Flowers of St. Francis, The
Fire by Night (Austin), II-629
First and Second Apologies, The (Justin Martyr), II-633
First Coming, The (Sheehan), II-636
Flabbergasted (Blackston), II-640
Fools and Crows (Witek), II-644
For the Time Being (Dillard), II-647
"For the Union Dead" (Lowell), II-650
Foundations of Christian Faith (Rahner), II-654
Four Books of Sentences (Peter Lombard), II-657
Four Quartets (Eliot, T. S.), II-660
Freedom of a Christian, The (Luther), II-664
Friendly Persuasion, The (West, J.), II-669

Gaudium et Spes (Vatican Council II), II-672
Geistreiche Sinn-und Schluss-reime. *See* Cherubinic Wanderer, The
Gekreuzigte Gott, Der. *See* Crucified God, The
Ghost Pain (Lea), II-676

Gift from the Sea (Lindbergh), II-680
Gilead (Robinson), II-683
Giornale dell'anima, Il. *See* Journal of a Soul
Go Tell It on the Mountain (Baldwin), II-687
God and Philosophy (Gilson), II-691
God Has a Dream (Tutu), II-694
God Was in Christ (Baillie, D. M.), II-698
God Who Commands, The (Mouw), II-704
Godric (Buechner), II-708
God's Silence (Wright, F.), II-712
God's Trombones (Johnson, J. W.), II-716
Good Book, The (Gomes), II-720
Gospel According to Jesus Christ, The (Saramago), II-724
Gospel of Christian Atheism, The (Altizer), II-728
Gospel of John (John, son of Zebedee), II-731
Gospel of Life, The. *See* Evangelium Vitae
Gospel of Mary of Magdala, The (King, K. L.), II-735
Great Divorce, The (Lewis, C. S.), II-739
Great Exemplar, The (Taylor), II-743
Great Mysteries, The (Greeley), II-746
Great Wheel, The (Mariani), II-749
Greatest Story Ever Told, The (Oursler), II-752
Grundkurs des Glaubens. *See* Foundations of Christian Faith

Hebrew Bible (Unknown), II-756
Hegels theologische Jugendschriften. *See* Early Theological Writings
Heilige, Das. *See* Idea of the Holy, The
"Here Follows Some Verses upon the Burning of Our House July 10th, 1666" (Bradstreet), II-768
Here I Stand (Spong), II-772
Herr, Der. *See* Lord, The
Hiding Place, The (Ten Boom), II-775
Hinds' Feet on High Places (Hurnard), II-779
His Watchful Eye (Cavanaugh), II-783
History of Christianity, A (Johnson, P.), II-787
History of God, A (Armstrong), II-791
Holocaust Politics (Roth), II-795
"Holy Sonnets" (Donne), II-799

TITLE INDEX

Home to Harmony (Gulley), II-802
How Should We Then Live? (Schaeffer), II-806
Human Dignity and the Common Good. *See* Centesimus Annus
Humanae Vitae (Paul VI), II-811
Humani Generis Redemptionem (Benedict XV), II-815
Hymns (Whittier), II-818
Hymns and Spiritual Songs (Watts), II-822

Idea of a Christian Society, The (Eliot, T. S.), II-826
Idea of the Holy, The (Otto), II-830
Iesu no shōgai. *See* Life of Jesus, A
Im Angesicht des Todes. *See* Prison Meditations of Father Alfred Delp
Imitatio Christi. *See* Imitation of Christ, The
Imitation of Christ, The (Thomas à Kempis), II-834
In cosa crede chi non crede? *See* Belief or Nonbelief?
"In Distrust of Merits" (Moore, M.), II-839
In His Steps (Sheldon), II-843
In Memoriam (Tennyson), II-847
In Memory of Her (Schüssler Fiorenza), II-851
In the Beauty of the Lilies (Updike), II-855
"In the Holy Nativity of Our Lord God" (Crashaw), II-859
In This House of Brede (Godden), II-863
Infelix ego. *See* Prison Meditations on Psalms 51 and 31
Infidel, The (Musser), II-866
Inscribing the Text (Brueggemann), II-870
Insight (Lonergan), II-873
Institutes of the Christian Religion (Calvin), II-877
Instructor, The (Clement of Alexandria), II-881
Interior Castle (Teresa of Ávila), II-887
Interrogations at Noon (Gioia), II-891
Introduction to Christianity (Ratzinger), II-895
Isaiah (Berrigan), II-898

J. B. (MacLeish), II-902
Jefferson Bible, The (Jefferson), II-906
Jesus Christ and Mythology (Bultmann), II-909
Jesus Christ Superstar (Rice, T., and Webber), II-913
Jesus I Never Knew, The (Yancey), II-917
Jesus in History (Kee), II-921
Jesus Through the Centuries (Pelikan), II-925
Journal d'un curé de campagne. *See* Diary of a Country Priest, The
Journal of a Soul (John XXIII), II-928
Journal of George Fox, The (Fox, G.), II-931
Journal of John Woolman, The (Woolman), II-936
Journey, The (Graham), II-941

Kata Ioannen. *See* Gospel of John
Keys of the Kingdom, The (Cronin), II-945
Kingdom of God Is Within You, The (Tolstoy), II-948
King's Ransom (Beazely and Lemmons), II-952
Klimax tou paradeisou. *See* Ladder of Divine Ascent, The
Knowledge and Faith (Stein), II-956
Kristin Lavransdatter (Undset), II-960

Labirynt světa a ráj srdce. *See* Labyrinth of the World and the Paradise of the Heart, The
Labyrinth of the World and the Paradise of the Heart, The (Comenius), II-964
Ladder of Divine Ascent, The (John Climacus), II-968
Lake Wobegon Days (Keillor), II-973
Last Days of Pompeii, The (Bulwer-Lytton), II-977
Last Puritan, The (Santayana), II-981
Last Temptation of Christ, The (Kazantzakis), II-985
Late Great Planet Earth, The (Lindsey), II-989
Learning Human (Murray, L. A.), II-993
Leaves of Grass (Whitman), II-997

MASTERPLOTS II

Leben Jesu, Das. *See* Life of Jesus Critically Examined, The
Lectures on Revivals of Religion (Finney), II-1001
Left Behind series (LaHaye and Jenkins), II-1005
Left to Tell (Ilibagiza), II-1010
Leiden. *See* Suffering
"Letter from Birmingham Jail" (King, M. L.), II-1014
Letters and Papers from Prison (Bonhoeffer), II-1018
Letters from the Earth (Twain), II-1021
Letters of Saint Jerome, The (Jerome), II-1024
Letters to a Young Catholic (Weigel), II-1029
Libro della divina dottrina. *See* Dialogue, The
Life Abundant (McFague), II-1033
Life Is Worth Living (Sheen), II-1037
Life of Jesus, A (Endō), II-1040
Life of Jesus, The (Renan), III-1043
Life of Jesus Critically Examined, The (Strauss), III-1046
Lilies of the Field, The (Barrett), III-1050
List, The (Whitlow), III-1054
Little Flowers of St. Francis, The (Unknown), III-1058
Loaves and Fishes (Day), III-1062
Long Trail Home, The (Bly), III-1066
Lord, The (Guardini), III-1070
Lord of the Rings, The (Tolkien), III-1073
Lord's Prayer and the Beatitudes, The (Gregory of Nyssa), III-1078
Love Comes Softly series (Oke), III-1082

Magnificent Obsession (Douglas), III-1087
Man for All Seasons, A (Bolt), III-1090
Man Nobody Knows, The (Barton), III-1094
Man Who Died, The (Lawrence), III-1098
Marriage of Heaven and Hell, The (Blake), III-1102
Mary Magdalene (Traylor), III-1106
Master and Margarita, The (Bulgakov), III-1110

Master i Margarita. *See* Master and Margarita, The
Mater et Magistra (John XXIII), III-1114
Meaning of Persons, The (Tournier), III-1118
Meaning of Prayer, The (Fosdick), III-1121
Meeting Jesus Again for the First Time (Borg), III-1125
Memoirs of Pontius Pilate (Mills), III-1128
Memories, Dreams, Reflections (Jung), III-1131
Merchant of Venice, The (Shakespeare), III-1135
Mercy's Face (Craig), III-1139
Mere Christianity (Lewis, C. S.), III-1143
Metaphysical Demonstration of the Existence of God, The (Suárez), III-1147
Midquest (Chappell), III-1151
Milieu divin, Le. *See* Divine Milieu, The
Mind of the Maker, The (Sayers), III-1155
Mind's Road to God, The (Bonaventure), III-1159
Miracle of the Bells, The (Janney), III-1164
Miscellanies (Clement of Alexandria), II-881
Misquoting Jesus (Ehrman), III-1168
Mit brennender Sorge (Pius XI), III-1172
Moments of Grace (Jennings), III-1176
Morte d'Urban (Powers), III-1180
Music to Die For (Nehring), III-1184
My God and I (Smedes), III-1188
Mystical Element of Religion, The (Hügel), III-1191
Mystical Theology (Pseudo-Dionysius), III-1197
Mysticism (Underhill), III-1200

Name of the Rose, The (Eco), III-1204
Nature and Destiny of Man, The (Niebuhr), III-1207
"New Birth, The" (Menno Simons), I-361
New Kind of Christian, A (McLaren), III-1211
New Song, A (Karon), III-1215
New Testament Letters (Paul), III-1219
Newpointe 911 (Blackstock), III-1223
Nieobjęta ziemia. *See* Unattainable Earth

TITLE INDEX

Nieuwe creatuere, Die. *See* "New Birth, The"
No Greater Love (Teresa), III-1227
Noche oscura del alma. *See* Dark Night of the Soul
Nome della rosa, Il. *See* Name of the Rose, The
North of Hope (Hassler), III-1230
Nun's Story, The (Hulme), III-1234

O Naznachenii cheloveka. *See* Destiny of Man, The
Octogesima Adveniens (Paul VI), III-1238
"Ode: Intimations of Mortality" (Wordsworth), III-1241
Of Learned Ignorance (Nicholas of Cusa), III-1245
Offenbarung und Vernunft. *See* Revelation and Reason
On Atheistic Communism. *See* Divini Redemptoris
On Being a Christian (Küng), III-1249
On Christian Theology (Williams, Rowan), III-1252
On Divine Love (Duns Scotus), III-1255
On First Principles (Origen), III-1259
On Listening to Another (Steere), III-1263
On Loving God (Bernard of Clairvaux), III-1268
On Providence (Zwingli), III-1272
On Reconstructing the Social Order. *See* Quadragesimo Anno
On the Freedom of the Will (Erasmus), III-1276
On the Incarnation of the Word of God (Athanasius of Alexandria), III-1280
On the Truth of Holy Scripture (Wyclif), III-1284
One Tuesday Morning (Kingsbury), III-1288
Orthodox Church, The (Ware), III-1291
Orthodoxy (Chesterton), III-1295
Out of My Life and Thought (Schweitzer), III-1299
Out of the Red Shadow (de Graaf), III-1303
Oxygen (Ingermanson and Olson), III-1307

Pacem in Terris (John XXIII), III-1311
Paidagogos. *See* Instructor, The
Pane e vino. *See* Bread and Wine
Paradise Lost (Milton), III-1315
Paradise Regained (Milton), III-1319
Passing by Samaria (Foster), III-1323
Paul (Wangerin), III-1327
Pauli Epistolas. *See* New Testament Letters
Pearl (Gordon), III-1331
Pearl (Pearl-Poet), III-1335
Penitent Magdalene, The (Hopes), III-1339
Pensées (Pascal), III-1342
Peri archōn. *See* On First Principles
Peri mustikes theologias. *See* Mystical Theology
Personnage et la personne, Le. *See* Meaning of Persons, The
Phantastes (MacDonald), III-1346
Pharisienne, La. *See* Woman of the Pharisees, The
Philokalia (Cairns), III-1350
Philosophy of Existence (Jaspers), III-1354
Philosophy of Existentialism, The (Marcel), III-1358
Piers Plowman (Langland), III-1362
Pilgrim's Progress, The (Bunyan), III-1366
Place Called Wiregrass, A (Morris, M.), III-1371
Place of the Lion, The (Williams, C.), III-1375
Plain Account of Christian Perfection, A (Wesley), III-1378
Poisonwood Bible, The (Kingsolver), III-1384
Politics of Jesus, The (Yoder), III-1389
Ponce Pilate. *See* Pontius Pilate
Pontius Pilate (Caillois), III-1393
Populorum Progressio (Paul VI), III-1397
Power and the Glory, The (Greene), III-1401
Power of Positive Thinking, The (Peale), III-1405
Praxeis Apostolon. *See* Acts of the Apostles
Prayer for Owen Meany, A (Irving), III-1408
Praying God's Word (Moore, Beth), III-1412
Presence of the Word, The (Ong), III-1415

Prison Meditations of Father Alfred Delp (Delp), III-1419
Prison Meditations on Psalms 51 and 31 (Savonarola), III-1423
Problem of Christianity, The (Royce), III-1426
Prodigal Girl, The (Hill, Grace Livingston), III-1430
Prophesy Deliverance! (West, C.), III-1434
Prophets, books of the. *See* Books of the Prophets
Protestant Ethic and the Spirit of Capitalism, The (Weber), III-1438
Protestantische Ethik und der Geist des Kapitalismus, Die. *See* Protestant Ethic and the Spirit of Capitalism, The
Psalmoi. *See* Psalms
Psalms (David), III-1442
Purity of Heart Is to Will One Thing (Kierkegaard), III-1446
Purpose Driven Life, The (Warren), III-1452

Quadragesimo Anno (Pius XI), III-1455
Questions for Ecclesiastes (Jarman), III-1459
Quo Vadis (Sienkiewicz), III-1462

Reasonableness of Christianity as Delivered in the Scriptures, The (Locke), III-1466
Reconciliation (de Gruchy), III-1470
Red and the Black, The (Stendhal), III-1474
Redeeming Love (Rivers), III-1478
Regula sancti Benedicti. *See* Rule of St. Benedict
Religio Medici (Browne), III-1482
Religion (Kołakowski), III-1486
Religion in the Making (Whitehead), III-1490
Religion innerhalb der Grenzen der blossen Vernunft, Die. *See* Religion Within the Bounds of Mere Reason
Religion Within the Bounds of Mere Reason (Kant), III-1494
Rerum Novarum (Leo XIII), III-1498
Resting in the Bosom of the Lamb (Trobaugh), III-1502

Resurrection of God Incarnate, The (Swinburne), III-1506
Revelation and Reason (Brunner), III-1510
Rime of the Ancient Mariner, The (Coleridge), III-1514
River Runs Through It, A (Maclean), III-1518
Robe, The (Douglas), III-1522
Römerbrief, Der. *See* Epistle to the Romans, The
Rose (Lee, L.-Y.), III-1525
Rouge et le noir, Le. *See* Red and the Black, The
Rule of St. Benedict (Benedict of Nursia), III-1529

Saint Joan (Shaw), III-1533
Saint Manuel Bueno, Martyr (Unamuno y Jugo), III-1537
Saint Maybe (Tyler), III-1541
San Manuel Bueno, Mártir. *See* Saint Manuel Bueno, Martyr
Sancti Eusebii Hieronymi Epistulae. *See* Letters of Saint Jerome, The
Sapphics and Uncertainties (Steele), III-1545
Scarlet Letter, The (Hawthorne), III-1549
Scenes of Clerical Life (Eliot, G.), III-1553
Science and Health with Key to the Scriptures (Eddy), III-1557
Screwtape Letters, The (Lewis, C. S.), III-1560
Seal of Gaia, The (Maddoux), III-1564
Second Coming, The (Percy), III-1568
Secrets in the Dark (Buechner), III-1571
Secrets of Barneveld Calvary, The (Schaap), III-1574
Sense of the Presence of God, The (Baillie, J.), III-1578
Sententiarum libri IV. *See* Four Books of Sentences
Serious Call to a Devout and Holy Life, A (Law), IV-1581
Sermons and Treatises, The (Eckhart), IV-1586
Seven Storey Mountain, The (Merton), IV-1591

TITLE INDEX

Seventh Seal, The (Bergman), IV-1595
She Who Is (Johnson, E. A.), IV-1598
Shepherd of the Hills, The (Wright, H. B.), IV-1602
Shoes of the Fisherman, The (West, M.), IV-1605
Showings (Julian of Norwich), IV-1609
Shunning, The (Lewis, B.), IV-1612
Silence (Endō), IV-1616
Silver Chalice, The (Costain), IV-1620
Simply Christian (Wright, N. T.), IV-1624
Singer Trilogy, The (Miller, C.), IV-1627
Sinners Welcome (Karr), IV-1631
Sir Gawain and the Green Knight (Pearl-Poet), IV-1635
Sjunde inseglet, Det. *See* Seventh Seal, The
Smert' Ivana Il'icha. *See* Death of Ivan Ilyich, The
Social Teaching of the Christian Churches, The (Troeltsch), IV-1639
Song of Albion Trilogy, The (Lawhead), IV-1643
Song of the Sparrow (Bodo), IV-1648
Songbird (Samson), IV-1651
Songs of Innocence and of Experience (Blake), IV-1655
Soon (Jenkins), IV-1660
Soul of Christianity, The (Smith, H.), IV-1664
Souls of Black Folk, The (Du Bois), IV-1668
Source of Human Good, The (Wieman), IV-1672
Soziallehren der christlichen Kirchen und Gruppen, Die. *See* Social Teaching of the Christian Churches, The
Sparrow, The (Russell), IV-1676
Spiritual Exercises, The (Ignatius of Loyola), IV-1680
Splendor of Truth, The. *See* Veritatis Splendor
"Station Island" (Heaney), IV-1685
Stream and the Sapphire, The (Levertov), IV-1689
Strength to Love (King, M. L.), IV-1693
Stromateis. *See* Miscellanies

Subida del monte Carmelo, La. *See* Ascent of Mount Carmel
Subversion du christianisme, La. *See* Subversion of Christianity, The
Subversion of Christianity, The (Ellul), IV-1698
Suffering (Sölle), IV-1702
Summa theologiae. *See* Summa Theologica
Summa Theologica (Thomas Aquinas), IV-1706
Supplicating Voice, The (Johnson, S.), IV-1710
Sutter's Cross (Cramer), IV-1714
Synoptic Gospels (Matthew, Mark, and Luke), IV-1717

Tasks of Philosophy, The (MacIntyre), IV-1722
Tehillim. *See* Psalms
Teleutaios peirasmos, Ho. *See* Last Temptation of Christ, The
Temple, The (Herbert), IV-1726
Teológia de la liberación. *See* Theology of Liberation, A
Tercer abecedario espiritual. *See* Third Spiritual Alphabet, The
Their Eyes Were Watching God (Hurston), IV-1730
Theodicy (Leibniz), IV-1734
Theology for the Social Gospel, A (Rauschenbusch), IV-1738
Theology of Liberation, A (Gutiérrez), IV-1742
Theology of the Jewish Christian Reality, A (Van Buren), IV-1746
Theory of Moral Sentiments, The (Smith, A.), IV-1749
"They Are All Gone into the World of Light!" (Vaughan), IV-1753
Third Spiritual Alphabet, The (Osuna), IV-1756
This Present Darkness (Peretti), IV-1760
Thorn Birds, The (McCullough), IV-1764
Thr3e (Dekker), IV-1768
Three Essays (Ritschl), IV-1772

Three Hardest Words in the World to Get Right, The (Sweet), IV-1776
"Three Versions of Judas" (Borges), IV-1779
Tiger in the Shadows (Wilson), IV-1782
Time Lottery (Moser), IV-1786
To Kill a Mockingbird (Lee, H.), IV-1790
To Scorch or Freeze (Davie), IV-1794
Transgression (Ingermanson), IV-1798
Traveling Mercies (Lamott), IV-1802
Treatise Concerning Religious Affections, A (Edwards), IV-1806
Treatise on Divine Predestination (Erigena), IV-1812
"Tres versiones de Judas." See "Three Versions of Judas"
Trip to Bountiful, The (Foote), IV-1816
Tristitia obsedit me. See Prison Meditations on Psalms 51 and 31
Triumph of Love, The (Hill, Geoffrey), IV-1820
True Honor (Henderson), IV-1823
Truth Teller, The (Hunt), IV-1827
Tsarstvo Bozhie vnutri vas. See Kingdom of God Is Within You, The
Twilight of Courage, The (Thoene and Thoene), IV-1830
Two from Galilee (Holmes), IV-1834

Unattainable Earth (Miłosz), IV-1837
Uncle Tom's Cabin (Stowe), IV-1841
Uneasy Conscience of Modern Fundamentalism, The (Henry), IV-1845
Unspeakable (Guinness), IV-1849
Unutterable Beauty, The (Studdert Kennedy), IV-1853

Varieties of Religious Experience, The (James), IV-1856
Velma Still Cooks in Leeway (Wright, V. H.), IV-1862
Veritatis Splendor (John Paul II), IV-1866
Vicar of Wakefield, The (Goldsmith), IV-1870
Vie de Jésus. See Life of Jesus, The
View of the Evidences of Christianity, A (Paley), IV-1875

Vino e pane. See Bread and Wine
Violence and the Sacred (Girard), IV-1879
Violence et la sacre, La. See Violence and the Sacred
Virgin Time (Hampl), IV-1883
Vocation of Man, The (Fichte), IV-1887
Von der Freiheit eines Christenmenschen. See Freedom of a Christian, The

Waiting for God (Weil), IV-1891
Waiting for Godot (Beckett), IV-1897
Walking by Faith (Grimké), IV-1901
War in Heaven (Williams, C.), IV-1905
Warranted Christian Belief (Plantinga), IV-1909
Way of All Flesh, The (Butler, S.), IV-1913
Way to Christ, The (Böhme), IV-1917
We Hold These Truths (Murray, J. C.), IV-1923
Weg zu Christo, Der. See Way to Christ, The
Wesen des Christentums, Das. See Essence of Christianity, The
What Are People For? (Berry), IV-1927
What I Think I Did (Woiwode), IV-1931
What Jesus Meant (Wills), IV-1934
When Jesus Came to Harvard (Cox), IV-1937
While Mortals Sleep (Cavanaugh), IV-1941
Widerstand und Ergebung. See Letters and Papers from Prison
Wind in the Wheat, The (Arvin), IV-1945
"Windhover, The" (Hopkins), IV-1949
Winter Garden, The (Verweerd), IV-1953
Wintertuin, De. See Winter Garden, The
Wise Blood (O'Connor), IV-1957
With Head and Heart (Thurman), IV-1961
With the Grain of the Universe (Hauerwas), IV-1965
Woman of the Pharisees, The (Mauriac), IV-1968
Wonderful Words of Life (Mouw and Noll), IV-1972
"Word made Flesh is seldom, A" (Dickinson), IV-1976

AUTHOR INDEX

ABRAMS, DOUGLAS
God Has a Dream, II-694
AGEE, JAMES
Death in the Family, A, I-427
ALTIZER, THOMAS J. J.
Gospel of Christian Atheism, The, II-728
AMOS
Books of the Prophets, I-206
ANGELOU, MAYA
"Amazing Peace," I-69
ANSELM, SAINT
Cur Deus Homo, I-401
ARMINIUS, JACOBUS
Declaration of the Sentiments of Arminius, A, I-439
ARMSTRONG, KAREN
History of God, A, II-791
ARVIN, REED
Wind in the Wheat, The, IV-1945
ATHANASIUS OF ALEXANDRIA, SAINT
On the Incarnation of the Word of God, III-1280
AUDEN, W. H.
Age of Anxiety, The, I-50
AUGUSTINE, SAINT
City of God, The, I-325
Confessions, I-365
AUSTIN, LYNN N.
Fire by Night, II-629

BAILLIE, D. M.
God Was in Christ, II-698
BAILLIE, JOHN
Sense of the Presence of God, The, III-1578
BALDWIN, JAMES
Go Tell It on the Mountain, II-687
BARRETT, WILLIAM E.
Lilies of the Field, The, III-1050
BARTH, KARL
Epistle to the Romans, The, II-549
BARTON, BRUCE
Man Nobody Knows, The, III-1094

BEASLEY, BRUCE
Creation, The, I-390
BEAUSEIGNEUR, JAMES
Christ Clone Trilogy, I-275
BEAZELY, JAN
King's Ransom, II-952
BECKETT, SAMUEL
Waiting for Godot, IV-1897
BELL, JAMES SCOTT
Final Witness, II-625
BENEDICT XV
Humani Generis Redemptionem, II-815
BENEDICT XVI. See RATZINGER, JOSEPH
BENEDICT OF NURSIA
Rule of St. Benedict, III-1529
BENSON, ANGELA
Awakening Mercy, I-116
BERDYAEV, NICOLAI
Destiny of Man, The, I-443
BERGMAN, INGMAR
Seventh Seal, The, IV-1595
BERNANOS, GEORGES
Diary of a Country Priest, The, I-462
BERNARD OF CLAIRVAUX, SAINT
On Loving God, III-1268
BERRIGAN, DANIEL
Isaiah, II-898
BERRY, WENDELL
What Are People For?, IV-1927
BERRYMAN, JOHN
Dream Songs, The, I-515
BEYLE, MARIE-HENRI. See STENDHAL
BLACKSTOCK, TERRI
Newpointe 911, III-1223
BLACKSTON, RAY
Flabbergasted, II-640
BLAKE, WILLIAM
Marriage of Heaven and Hell, The, III-1102
Songs of Innocence and of Experience, IV-1655
BLY, STEPHEN A.
Long Trail Home, The, III-1066

BODO, MURRAY
  Song of the Sparrow, IV-1648
BÖHME, JAKOB
  Way to Christ, The, IV-1917
BOLT, ROBERT
  Man for All Seasons, A, III-1090
BONAVENTURE, SAINT
  Mind's Road to God, The, III-1159
BONHOEFFER, DIETRICH
  Ethics, II-561
  Letters and Papers from Prison, II-1018
BORG, MARCUS J.
  Meeting Jesus Again for the First Time, III-1125
BORGES, JORGE LUIS
  "Three Versions of Judas," IV-1779
BOTTUM, JOSEPH
  "Fall, The," II-606
BOWEN, MICHELE ANDREA
  Church Folk, I-316
BRADSTREET, ANNE
  "Here Follows Some Verses upon the Burning of Our House July 10th, 1666," II-768
BROUWER, SIGMUND
  Blood Ties, I-173
BROWN, DAN
  Da Vinci Code, The, I-408
BROWNE, SIR THOMAS
  Religio Medici, III-1482
BROWNING, ROBERT
  "Epistle Containing the Strange Medical Experience of Karshish, the Arab Physician, An," II-545
BRUEGGEMANN, WALTER
  Inscribing the Text, II-870
BRUNNER, EMIL
  Revelation and Reason, III-1510
BUECHNER, FREDERICK
  Godric, II-708
  Secrets in the Dark, III-1571
BULGAKOV, MIKHAIL
  Master and Margarita, The, III-1110
BULTMANN, RUDOLF
  Jesus Christ and Mythology, II-909

BULWER-LYTTON, EDWARD
  Last Days of Pompeii, The, II-977
BUNN, T. DAVIS
  Drummer in the Dark, II-519
BUNYAN, JOHN
  Pilgrim's Progress, The, III-1366
BUTLER, JOSEPH
  Fifteen Sermons Preached at the Rolls Chapel, II-618
BUTLER, SAMUEL
  Way of All Flesh, The, IV-1913
CAILLOIS, ROGER
  Pontius Pilate, III-1393
CAIRNS, SCOTT
  Philokalia, III-1350
CALDWELL, TAYLOR
  Dear and Glorious Physician, I-420
CALVIN, JOHN
  Institutes of the Christian Religion, II-877
CARDENAL, ERNESTO
  Apocalypse, I-80
CARLSON, C. C.
  Late Great Planet Earth, The, II-989
CARROLL, JAMES
  Constantine's Sword, I-374
CASSIAN, JOHN
  Conferences, I-354
CATERINA DI GIACOMO DI BENINCASA. See CATHERINE OF SIENA, SAINT
CATHER, WILLA
  Death Comes for the Archbishop, I-423
CATHERINE OF SIENA, SAINT
  Dialogue, The, I-453
CAVANAUGH, JACK
  His Watchful Eye, II-783
  While Mortals Sleep, IV-1941
CHAPPELL, FRED
  Midquest, III-1151
CHAUCER, GEOFFREY
  Canterbury Tales, The, I-240
CHESTERTON, G. K.
  Orthodoxy, III-1295

AUTHOR INDEX

CHIESA, GIACOMO DELLA. *See*
  BENEDICT XV
CHITTISTER, JOAN D., O.S.B.
  Called to Question, I-237
CHRYSOSTOM, SAINT JOHN
  Baptismal Instruction, I-120
CLEMENS, SAMUEL LANGHORNE. *See*
  TWAIN, MARK
CLEMENT OF ALEXANDRIA
  Instructor, The, II-881
  Miscellanies, II-881
COBB, JOHN B., JR.
  Christ in a Pluralistic Age, I-280
COFFIN, WILLIAM SLOANE
  Credo, I-393
COLERIDGE, SAMUEL TAYLOR
  Aids to Reflection, I-54
  Rime of the Ancient Mariner, The, III-1514
COMENIUS, JOHN AMOS
  Labyrinth of the World and the Paradise of the Heart, The, II-964
CONE, JAMES H.
  Black Theology of Liberation, A, I-165
COSTAIN, THOMAS B.
  Silver Chalice, The, IV-1620
COUNCIL OF TRENT
  Catechism of the Catholic Church, I-257
COX, HARVEY
  When Jesus Came to Harvard, IV-1937
CRAIG, DAVID
  Mercy's Face, III-1139
CRAMER, W. DALE
  Sutter's Cross, IV-1714
CRANMER, THOMAS
  Book of Common Prayer, I-184
CRASHAW, RICHARD
  "In the Holy Nativity of Our Lord God," II-859
CRONIN, A. J.
  Keys of the Kingdom, The, II-945

DALY, MARY
  Beyond God the Father, I-144
DANTE
  Divine Comedy, The, I-473

DAVID
  Psalms, III-1442
DAVIE, DONALD
  To Scorch or Freeze, IV-1794
DAY, DOROTHY
  Loaves and Fishes, III-1062
DE GRAAF, ANNE
  Out of the Red Shadow, III-1303
DE GRUCHY, JOHN W.
  Reconciliation, III-1470
DEKKER, TED
  Circle Trilogy, The, I-320
  Thr3e, IV-1768
DELP, ALFRED
  Prison Meditations of Father Alfred Delp, III-1419
DICKENS, CHARLES
  "Christmas Carol, A," I-299
DICKINSON, EMILY
  "Word made Flesh is seldom, A," IV-1976
DILLARD, ANNIE
  For the Time Being, II-647
DONNE, JOHN
  Devotions upon Emergent Occasions, I-447
  "Holy Sonnets," II-799
DOSTOEVSKI, FYODOR
  Brothers Karamazov, The, I-229
DOUGLAS, LLOYD C.
  Magnificent Obsession, III-1087
  Robe, The, III-1522
DU BOIS, W. E. B.
  Souls of Black Folk, The, IV-1668
DUNS SCOTUS, JOHN
  On Divine Love, III-1255

ECKHART, JOHANNES
  Sermons and Treatises, The, IV-1586
ECO, UMBERTO
  Belief or Nonbelief?, I-133
  Name of the Rose, The, III-1204
EDDY, MARY BAKER
  Science and Health with Key to the Scriptures, III-1557

EDWARDS, JONATHAN
  Treatise Concerning Religious Affections,
    A, IV-1806
EHRMAN, BART D.
  Misquoting Jesus, III-1168
ELIOT, GEORGE
  Scenes of Clerical Life, III-1553
ELIOT, T. S.
  Four Quartets, II-660
  Idea of a Christian Society, The, II-826
ELLUL, JACQUES
  Subversion of Christianity, The, IV-1698
EMERSON, RALPH WALDO
  Divinity School Address, The, I-491
ENDŌ, SHŪSAKU
  Life of Jesus, A, II-1040
  Silence, IV-1616
ERASMUS, DESIDERIUS
  On the Freedom of the Will, III-1276
ERIGENA, JOHN SCOTUS
  Treatise on Divine Predestination,
    IV-1812
ERWIN, STEVE
  Left to Tell, II-1010
EUSEBIUS HIERONYMUS. *See* JEROME,
  SAINT

FAIRCHILD, B. H.
  Arrival of the Future, The, I-103
FEUERBACH, LUDWIG
  Essence of Christianity, The, II-557
FICHTE, JOHANN GOTTLIEB
  Vocation of Man, The, IV-1887
FIDANZA, GIOVANNI DI. *See*
  BONAVENTURE, SAINT
FINNEY, CHARLES GRANDISON
  Lectures on Revivals of Religion, II-1001
FOOTE, HORTON
  Trip to Bountiful, The, IV-1816
FORCHÉ, CAROLYN
  Angel of History, The, I-77
FOSDICK, HARRY EMERSON
  Meaning of Prayer, The, III-1121
FOSTER, SHARON EWELL
  Passing by Samaria, III-1323

FOX, GEORGE
  Journal of George Fox, The, II-931
FOX, MATTHEW
  Coming of the Cosmic Christ, The, I-346

GILSON, ÉTIENNE
  God and Philosophy, II-691
GIOIA, DANA
  Interrogations at Noon, II-891
GIRARD, RENÉ
  Violence and the Sacred, IV-1879
GLANCY, DIANE
  (Ado)ration, I-31
GLENDON, MARY ANN
  Abortion and Divorce in Western Law,
    I-23
GODDEN, RUMER
  In This House of Brede, II-863
GOETHE, JOHANN WOLFGANG VON
  Faust, II-610
GOLDSMITH, OLIVER
  Vicar of Wakefield, The, IV-1870
GOMES, PETER J.
  Good Book, The, II-720
GORDON, MARY
  Pearl, III-1331
GOWER, JOHN
  Confessio Amantis, I-357
GRAHAM, BILLY
  Journey, The, II-941
GREELEY, ANDREW M.
  Bishop in the Old Neighborhood, The,
    I-157
  Great Mysteries, The, II-746
GREENE, GRAHAM
  Power and the Glory, The, III-1401
GREGORY OF NYSSA, SAINT
  Lord's Prayer and the Beatitudes, The,
    III-1078
GRIMKÉ, ANGELINA EMILY
  Walking by Faith, IV-1901
GUARDINI, ROMANO
  Lord, The, III-1070
GUINNESS, OS
  Unspeakable, IV-1849

AUTHOR INDEX

GULLEY, PHILIP
  Home to Harmony, II-802
GUTIÉRREZ, GUSTAVO
  Theology of Liberation, A, IV-1742

HALL, HELEN DIANE. *See* GLANCY, DIANE
HAMMERKEN, THOMAS. *See* THOMAS À KEMPIS
HAMPL, PATRICIA
  Virgin Time, IV-1883
HANCOCK, KAREN
  Arena, I-96
HARTSHORNE, CHARLES
  Divine Relativity, The, I-485
HASSLER, JON
  North of Hope, III-1230
HAUERWAS, STANLEY
  With the Grain of the Universe, IV-1965
HAWTHORNE, NATHANIEL
  Scarlet Letter, The, III-1549
HEANEY, SEAMUS
  "Station Island," IV-1685
HEGEL, GEORG WILHELM FRIEDRICH
  Early Theological Writings, II-527
HENDERSON, DEE
  True Honor, IV-1823
HENRY, CARL F. H.
  Uneasy Conscience of Modern Fundamentalism, The, IV-1845
HERBERT, GEORGE
  Country Parson, The, I-378
  Temple, The, IV-1726
HICK, JOHN
  Evil and the God of Love, II-582
HILDEGARD VON BINGEN
  Book of Divine Works, I-188
HILL, GEOFFREY
  Triumph of Love, The, IV-1820
HILL, GRACE LIVINGSTON
  Prodigal Girl, The, III-1430
HOLMES, MARJORIE
  Two from Galilee, IV-1834
HOPES, DAVID BRENDAN
  Penitent Magdalene, The, III-1339

HOPKINS, GERARD MANLEY
  "Windhover, The," IV-1949
HUDGINS, ANDREW
  After the Lost War, I-41
HÜGEL, BARON FRIEDRICH VON
  Essays and Addresses on the Philosophy of Religion, II-553
  Mystical Element of Religion, The, III-1191
HUGHES, LANGSTON
  "Feet of Jesus," II-614
HULME, KATHRYN C.
  Nun's Story, The, III-1234
HUNT, ANGELA ELWELL
  Truth Teller, The, IV-1827
HURNARD, HANNAH
  Hinds' Feet on High Places, II-779
HURSTON, ZORA NEALE
  Their Eyes Were Watching God, IV-1730
HUS, JAN
  Church, The, I-312

IGNATIUS OF LOYOLA, SAINT
  Spiritual Exercises, The, IV-1680
ILIBAGIZA, IMMACULÉE
  Left to Tell, II-1010
INGERMANSON, RANDALL SCOTT
  Oxygen, III-1307
  Transgression, IV-1798
IRENAEUS, SAINT
  Against Heresies, I-44
IRVING, JOHN
  Prayer for Owen Meany, A, III-1408
ISAIAH
  Books of the Prophets, I-206

JAMES, WILLIAM
  Varieties of Religious Experience, The, IV-1856
JANNEY, RUSSELL
  Miracle of the Bells, The, III-1164
JARMAN, MARK
  Questions for Ecclesiastes, III-1459
JASPERS, KARL
  Philosophy of Existence, III-1354

JEFFERSON, THOMAS
   Jefferson Bible, The, II-906
JENKINS, JERRY B.
   Left Behind series, II-1005
   Soon, IV-1660
JENNINGS, ELIZABETH
   Moments of Grace, III-1176
JEREMIAH
   Books of the Prophets, I-206
JEROME, SAINT
   Letters of Saint Jerome, The, II-1024
JOHN
   Book of Revelation, I-202
JOHN XXIII
   Journal of a Soul, II-928
   Mater et Magistra, III-1114
   Pacem in Terris, III-1311
JOHN CLIMACUS
   Ladder of Divine Ascent, The, II-968
JOHN OF THE CROSS, SAINT
   Ascent of Mount Carmel, I-107
   Dark Night of the Soul, I-107
JOHN PAUL II
   Centesimus Annus, I-265
   Evangelium Vitae, II-568
   Veritatis Splendor, IV-1866
JOHN, SON OF ZEBEDEE
   Gospel of John, II-731
JOHNSON, ELIZABETH A.
   She Who Is, IV-1598
JOHNSON, JAMES WELDON
   God's Trombones, II-716
JOHNSON, MARGUERITE. *See*
   ANGELOU, MAYA
JOHNSON, PAUL
   History of Christianity, A, II-787
JOHNSON, SAMUEL
   Supplicating Voice, The, IV-1710
JONES, RUFUS M.
   Double Search, The, I-503
JULIAN OF NORWICH
   Showings, IV-1609
JUNG, CARL GUSTAV
   Memories, Dreams, Reflections, III-1131
JUSTIN MARTYR, SAINT
   First and Second Apologies, The, II-633

KANT, IMMANUEL
   Religion Within the Bounds of Mere Reason, III-1494
KARON, JAN
   New Song, A, III-1215
KARR, MARY
   Sinners Welcome, IV-1631
KASDORF, JULIA
   Eve's Striptease, II-578
KAZANTZAKIS, NIKOS
   Last Temptation of Christ, The, II-985
KEE, HOWARD CLARK
   Jesus in History, II-921
KEILLOR, GARRISON
   Lake Wobegon Days, II-973
KELLY, J. N. D.
   Early Christian Doctrines, II-523
KENNEDY, JOSEPH CHARLES. *See*
   KENNEDY, X. J.
KENNEDY, X. J.
   Beasts of Bethlehem, The, I-130
KIERKEGAARD, SØREN
   Purity of Heart Is to Will One Thing, III-1446
KING, KAREN L.
   Gospel of Mary of Magdala, The, II-735
KING, MARTIN LUTHER, JR.
   "Letter from Birmingham Jail," II-1014
   Strength to Love, IV-1693
KINGSBURY, KAREN
   One Tuesday Morning, III-1288
KINGSOLVER, BARBARA
   Poisonwood Bible, The, III-1384
KITAGAWA, JOSEPH MITSUO
   Christian Tradition, The, I-292
KOŁAKOWSKI, LESZEK
   Religion, III-1486
KRYFTS, NICHOLAS. *See* NICHOLAS OF CUSA
KÜNG, HANS
   On Being a Christian, III-1249

LAGERKVIST, PÄR
   Barabbas, I-123
LAHAYE, TIM
   Left Behind series, II-1005

AUTHOR INDEX

LAMOTT, ANNE
  All New People, I-62
  Traveling Mercies, IV-1802
LANGLAND, WILLIAM
  Piers Plowman, III-1362
LAW, WILLIAM
  Serious Call to a Devout and Holy Life, A, IV-1581
LAWHEAD, STEPHEN R.
  Song of Albion Trilogy, The, IV-1643
LAWRENCE, D. H.
  Man Who Died, The, III-1098
LEA, SYDNEY
  Ghost Pain, II-676
LEE, HARPER
  To Kill a Mockingbird, IV-1790
LEE, LI-YOUNG
  Rose, III-1525
LEIBNIZ, GOTTFRIED WILHELM
  Theodicy, IV-1734
LEMMONS, TOM
  King's Ransom, II-952
LEO XIII
  Rerum Novarum, III-1498
LEVERTOV, DENISE
  Stream and the Sapphire, The, IV-1689
LEWIS, BEVERLY
  Shunning, The, IV-1612
LEWIS, C. S.
  Chronicles of Narnia, The, I-307
  Great Divorce, The, II-739
  Mere Christianity, III-1143
  Screwtape Letters, The, III-1560
LEWIS, SINCLAIR
  Elmer Gantry, II-538
LINDBERGH, ANNE MORROW
  Gift from the Sea, II-680
LINDSEY, HAL
  Late Great Planet Earth, The, II-989
LOCKE, JOHN
  Reasonableness of Christianity as Delivered in the Scriptures, The, III-1466
LONERGAN, BERNARD J. F.
  Insight, II-873

LONG, DAVID RYAN
  Ezekiel's Shadow, II-594
LOWELL, ROBERT
  "For the Union Dead," II-650
LUBAC, HENRI DE
  Drama of Atheist Humanism, The, I-508
LUCADO, MAX
  Cure for the Common Life, I-405
LUKE
  Acts of the Apostles, I-27
  Synoptic Gospels, IV-1717
LUTHER, MARTIN
  Freedom of a Christian, The, II-664

McCULLOUGH, COLLEEN
  Thorn Birds, The, IV-1764
MacDONALD, GEORGE
  Phantastes, III-1346
McFAGUE, SALLIE
  Life Abundant, II-1033
McINERNY, RALPH
  And I Alone Have Escaped to Tell You, I-73
MacINTYRE, ALASDAIR
  Tasks of Philosophy, The, IV-1722
McLAREN, BRIAN D.
  New Kind of Christian, A, III-1211
MACLEAN, NORMAN
  River Runs Through It, A, III-1518
MacLEISH, ARCHIBALD
  J. B., II-902
MACQUARRIE, JOHN
  Existentialist Theology, An, II-590
MADDOUX, MARLIN
  Seal of Gaia, The, III-1564
MARCEL, GABRIEL
  Philosophy of Existentialism, The, III-1358
MARIANI, PAUL
  Great Wheel, The, II-749
MARITAIN, JACQUES
  Christianity and Democracy, I-296
MARK
  Synoptic Gospels, IV-1717
MARLOWE, CHRISTOPHER
  Doctor Faustus, I-496

MARSHALL, CATHERINE
  Christy, I-303
MARTINI, CARLO MARIA
  Belief or Nonbelief?, I-133
MATSUOKA, FUMITAKA
  Color of Faith, The, I-334
MATTHEW
  Synoptic Gospels, IV-1717
MAURIAC, FRANÇOIS
  Woman of the Pharisees, The, IV-1968
MBITI, JOHN SAMUEL
  Bible and Theology in African
    Christianity, I-147
MEILAENDER, GILBERT
  Bioethics, I-154
MELANCHTHON, PHILIPP
  Augsburg Confession of Faith, The, I-112
MELVILLE, HERMAN
  Billy Budd, Foretopman, I-150
MENNO SIMONS
  "Confession," I-361
  "New Birth, The," I-361
MERTON, THOMAS
  Seven Storey Mountain, The, IV-1591
MICAH
  Books of the Prophets, I-206
MIDDLETON, DAVID
  Burning Fields, The, I-233
MIGHELL, MARJORIE. *See* HOLMES,
  MARJORIE
MILES, JACK
  Christ, I-272
MILLER, CALVIN
  Singer Trilogy, The, IV-1627
MILLER, DONALD
  Blue Like Jazz, I-180
MILLER, WALTER M., JR.
  Canticle for Leibowitz, A, I-245
MILLS, JAMES R.
  Memoirs of Pontius Pilate, III-1128
MIŁOSZ, CZESŁAW
  Unattainable Earth, IV-1837
MILTON, JOHN
  Paradise Lost, III-1315
  Paradise Regained, III-1319

MOLTMANN, JÜRGEN
  Crucified God, The, I-397
MONTINI, GIOVANNI BATTISTA. *See*
  PAUL VI
MOORE, BETH
  Praying God's Word, III-1412
MOORE, BRIAN
  Catholics, I-261
MOORE, MARIANNE
  "In Distrust of Merits," II-839
MOORE, THOMAS
  Care of the Soul, I-251
MORRIS, GILBERT
  Edge of Honor, II-534
MORRIS, MICHAEL
  Place Called Wiregrass, A, III-1371
MOSER, NANCY
  Time Lottery, IV-1786
MOUW, RICHARD J.
  God Who Commands, The, II-704
MOUW, RICHARD J. (ed.)
  Wonderful Words of Life, IV-1972
MUGAMBI, J. N. K.
  African Heritage and Contemporary
    Christianity, I-38
MURRAY, JOHN COURTNEY, S.J.
  We Hold These Truths, IV-1923
MURRAY, LES A.
  Learning Human, II-993
MUSSER, JOE
  Infidel, The, II-866

NAPIER, BUNYAN DAVIE
  Come Sweet Death, I-342
NEHRING, RADINE TREES
  Music to Die For, III-1184
NESANOVICH, STELLA ANN
  Brightness That Made My Soul Tremble,
    A, I-222
NEUHAUS, RICHARD JOHN
  Death on a Friday Afternoon, I-435
NEWMAN, JOHN HENRY
  Apologia pro vita sua, I-88
NICHOLAS OF CUSA
  Of Learned Ignorance, III-1245

AUTHOR INDEX

NIEBUHR, REINHOLD
  Nature and Destiny of Man, The, III-1207
NOLL, MARK A. (ed.)
  Wonderful Words of Life, IV-1972
NORRIS, KATHLEEN
  Amazing Grace, I-65
NOUWEN, HENRI J. M.
  Bread for the Journey, I-215
NYGREN, ANDERS
  Agape and Eros, I-47

O'CONNOR, FLANNERY
  Wise Blood, IV-1957
OKE, JANETTE
  Love Comes Softly series, III-1082
OLSON, JOHN B.
  Oxygen, III-1307
ONG, WALTER J.
  Presence of the Word, The, III-1415
ORIGEN
  On First Principles, III-1259
OSUNA, FRANCISCO DE
  Third Spiritual Alphabet, The, IV-1756
OTTO, RUDOLF
  Idea of the Holy, The, II-830
OURSLER, FULTON
  Greatest Story Ever Told, The, II-752

PALEY, WILLIAM
  View of the Evidences of Christianity, A, IV-1875
PALMER, CATHERINE
  Dangerous Silence, A, I-412
PANKEY, ERIC
  Apocrypha, I-84
PARK, JONG CHUN
  Crawl with God, Dance in the Spirit, I-386
PARKER, GARY E.
  Capital Offense, A, I-248
PASCAL, BLAISE
  Pensées, III-1342
PAUL, SAINT
  New Testament Letters, III-1219
PAUL VI
  Humanae Vitae, II-811

Octogesima Adveniens, III-1238
Populorum Progressio, III-1397
PEALE, NORMAN VINCENT
  Power of Positive Thinking, The, III-1405
PEARL-POET
  Pearl, III-1335
  Sir Gawain and the Green Knight, IV-1635
PECCI, GIOACCHINO VINCENZO
  RAFFAELE LUIGI. See LEO XIII
PELIKAN, JAROSLAV
  Jesus Through the Centuries, II-925
PELLA, JUDITH
  Dawning of Deliverance, The, I-416
PERCY, WALKER
  Second Coming, The, III-1568
PERETTI, FRANK E.
  This Present Darkness, IV-1760
PETER LOMBARD
  Four Books of Sentences, II-657
PIUS XI
  Casti Connubii, I-254
  Divini Redemptoris, I-488
  Mit brennender Sorge, III-1172
  Quadragesimo Anno, III-1455
PLANTINGA, ALVIN
  Warranted Christian Belief, IV-1909
PLOTINUS
  Enneads, The, II-542
POWERS, J. F.
  Morte d'Urban, III-1180
PSEUDO-DIONYSIUS THE AREOPAGITE
  Mystical Theology, III-1197

RAHNER, KARL
  Foundations of Christian Faith, II-654
RATTI, AMBROGIO DAMIANO ACHILLE. See PIUS XI
RATZINGER, JOSEPH
  Introduction to Christianity, II-895
RAUSCHENBUSCH, WALTER
  Theology for the Social Gospel, A, IV-1738
RENAN, ERNEST
  Life of Jesus, The, III-1043

RICE, ANNE
  Christ the Lord, I-284
RICE, TIM
  Jesus Christ Superstar, II-913
RICŒUR, PAUL
  Figuring the Sacred, II-621
RITSCHL, ALBRECHT
  Three Essays, IV-1772
RIVERS, FRANCINE
  Redeeming Love, III-1478
ROBINSON, MARILYNNE
  Gilead, II-683
RONCALLI, ANGELO GIUSEPPE. *See* JOHN XXIII
ROSSETTI, CHRISTINA
  Face of the Deep, The, II-597
ROTH, JOHN K.
  Holocaust Politics, II-795
ROYCE, JOSIAH
  Problem of Christianity, The, III-1426
RUSSELL, MARY DORIA
  Sparrow, The, IV-1676

SAMSON, LISA
  Songbird, IV-1651
SANTAYANA, GEORGE
  Last Puritan, The, II-981
SARAMAGO, JOSÉ
  Gospel According to Jesus Christ, The, II-724
SAVONAROLA, GIROLAMO
  Prison Meditations on Psalms 51 and 31, III-1423
SAYERS, DOROTHY L.
  Mind of the Maker, The, III-1155
SCHAAP, JAMES C.
  Secrets of Barneveld Calvary, The, III-1574
SCHAEFFER, FRANCIS A.
  How Should We Then Live?, II-806
SCHLEIERMACHER, FRIEDRICH
  Christian Faith, The, I-288
SCHULLER, ROBERT H.
  Don't Throw Away Tomorrow, I-500
SCHÜSSLER FIORENZA, ELIZABETH
  In Memory of Her, II-851

SCHWEITZER, ALBERT
  Out of My Life and Thought, III-1299
SHAKESPEARE, WILLIAM
  Merchant of Venice, The, III-1135
SHAW, GEORGE BERNARD
  Saint Joan, III-1533
SHEEHAN, THOMAS
  First Coming, The, II-636
SHEEN, FULTON J.
  Life Is Worth Living, II-1037
SHELDON, CHARLES MONROE
  In His Steps, II-843
SHERRILL, ELIZABETH
  Hiding Place, The, II-775
SHERRILL, JOHN
  Hiding Place, The, II-775
SIENKIEWICZ, HENRYK
  Quo Vadis, III-1462
SILESIUS, ANGELUS
  Cherubinic Wanderer, The, I-268
SILONE, IGNAZIO
  Bread and Wine, I-211
SINGER, RANDY
  Directed Verdict, I-465
SMEDES, LEWIS B.
  My God and I, III-1188
SMITH, ADAM
  Theory of Moral Sentiments, The, IV-1749
SMITH, HUSTON
  Soul of Christianity, The, IV-1664
SMITH, JOHN ALLYN. *See* BERRYMAN, JOHN
SMITH, JOSEPH
  Book of Mormon, I-196
SÖLLE, DOROTHEE
  Suffering, IV-1702
SORENSEN, MICHELE
  Broken Lance, I-226
SOYINKA, WOLE
  Aké, I-58
SPENSER, EDMUND
  Faerie Queene, The, II-601
SPONG, JOHN SHELBY
  Here I Stand, II-772

AUTHOR INDEX

STAFFORD, WILLIAM
  Even in Quiet Places, II-571
STEELE, TIMOTHY
  Sapphics and Uncertainties, III-1545
STEERE, DOUGLAS V.
  On Listening to Another, III-1263
STEIN, EDITH
  Knowledge and Faith, II-956
STENDHAL
  Red and the Black, The, III-1474
STOTT, JOHN R. W.
  Basic Christianity, I-127
STOUT, JEFFREY
  Ethics After Babel, II-565
STOWE, HARRIET BEECHER
  Uncle Tom's Cabin, IV-1841
STRAUSS, DAVID FRIEDRICH
  Life of Jesus Critically Examined, The, III-1046
STUDDERT KENNEDY, G. A.
  Unutterable Beauty, The, IV-1853
STYRON, WILLIAM
  Confessions of Nat Turner, The, I-370
SUÁREZ, FRANCISCO
  Metaphysical Demonstration of the Existence of God, The, III-1147
SWEET, LEONARD
  Three Hardest Words in the World to Get Right, The, IV-1776
SWIFT, JONATHAN
  Argument Against Abolishing Christianity, I-99
SWINBURNE, RICHARD
  Resurrection of God Incarnate, The, III-1506

TANNER, KATHRYN
  Economy of Grace, II-531
TAYLOR, JEREMY
  Great Exemplar, The, II-743
TEILHARD DE CHARDIN, PIERRE
  Divine Milieu, The, I-480
TEN BOOM, CORRIE
  Hiding Place, The, II-775
TENNYSON, ALFRED, LORD
  In Memoriam, II-847

TERESA, MOTHER
  No Greater Love, III-1227
TERESA OF ÁVILA, SAINT
  Interior Castle, II-887
TERTULLIAN
  Apology, I-92
TERTULLIANUS, QUINTUS SEPTIMIUS FLORENS. *See* TERTULLIAN
THOENE, BODIE
  Twilight of Courage, The, IV-1830
THOENE, BROCK
  Twilight of Courage, The, IV-1830
THOMAS À KEMPIS
  Imitation of Christ, The, II-834
THOMAS AQUINAS, SAINT
  Summa Theologica, IV-1706
THURMAN, HOWARD
  With Head and Heart, IV-1961
TILLICH, PAUL
  Courage to Be, The, I-382
TOEWS, MIRIAM
  Complicated Kindness, A, I-350
TOLKIEN, J. R. R.
  Lord of the Rings, The, III-1073
TOLSTOY, LEO
  Death of Ivan Ilyich, The, I-431
  Divine and Human, I-469
  Kingdom of God Is Within You, The, II-948
TOURNIER, PAUL
  Meaning of Persons, The, III-1118
TRANQUILLI, SECONDO. *See* SILONE, IGNAZIO
TRAYLOR, ELLEN GUNDERSON
  Mary Magdalene, III-1106
TROBAUGH, AUGUSTA
  Resting in the Bosom of the Lamb, III-1502
TROELTSCH, ERNST
  Social Teaching of the Christian Churches, The, IV-1639
TURNBULL, AGNES SLIGH
  Bishop's Mantle, The, I-161
TUTU, DESMOND
  God Has a Dream, II-694

TWAIN, MARK
  Letters from the Earth, II-1021
TYLER, ANNE
  Saint Maybe, III-1541

UNAMUNO Y JUGO, MIGUEL DE
  Saint Manuel Bueno, Martyr, III-1537
UNDERHILL, EVELYN
  Mysticism, III-1200
UNDSET, SIGRID
  Kristin Lavransdatter, II-960
UNKNOWN
  Acts of the Apostles, I-27
  Beowulf, I-140
  Cloud of Unknowing, The, I-329
  "Dream of the Rood, The," I-512
  Everyman, II-574
  Hebrew Bible, II-756
  Little Flowers of St. Francis, The, III-1058
UPDIKE, JOHN
  In the Beauty of the Lilies, II-855

VAN BUREN, PAUL M.
  Theology of the Jewish Christian Reality, A, IV-1746
VATICAN COUNCIL II
  Gaudium et Spes, II-672
VAUGHAN, HENRY
  "They Are All Gone into the World of Light!," IV-1753
VERWEERD, JOHANNA
  Winter Garden, The, IV-1953
VERWEERD, JOKE. See VERWEERD, JOHANNA
VOLF, MIROSLAV
  Exclusion and Embrace, II-586

WALKER, ALICE
  Color Purple, The, I-338
WALLACE, LEW
  Ben-Hur, I-136
WANGERIN, WALTER, JR.
  Book of God, The, I-192
  Paul, III-1327

WARE, KALLISTOS. See WARE, TIMOTHY
WARE, TIMOTHY
  Orthodox Church, The, III-1291
WARREN, RICK
  Purpose Driven Life, The, III-1452
WATTS, ISAAC
  Hymns and Spiritual Songs, II-822
WAUGH, EVELYN
  Brideshead Revisited, I-218
WEBBER, ANDREW LLOYD
  Jesus Christ Superstar, II-913
WEBER, MAX
  Protestant Ethic and the Spirit of Capitalism, The, III-1438
WEIGEL, GEORGE
  Letters to a Young Catholic, II-1029
WEIL, SIMONE
  Waiting for God, IV-1891
WESLEY, JOHN
  Plain Account of Christian Perfection, A, III-1378
WEST, CORNEL
  Prophesy Deliverance!, III-1434
WEST, JESSAMYN
  Friendly Persuasion, The, II-669
WEST, MORRIS
  Shoes of the Fisherman, The, IV-1605
WHITEHEAD, ALFRED NORTH
  Religion in the Making, III-1490
WHITLOW, ROBERT
  List, The, III-1054
WHITMAN, WALT
  Leaves of Grass, II-997
WHITTIER, JOHN GREENLEAF
  Hymns, II-818
WIEMAN, HENRY NELSON
  Source of Human Good, The, IV-1672
WILBUR, RICHARD
  "Advice to a Prophet," I-35
WILLARD, DALLAS
  Divine Conspiracy, The, I-477
WILLIAMS, CHARLES
  Place of the Lion, The, III-1375
  War in Heaven, IV-1905

AUTHOR INDEX

WILLIAMS, ROGER
Bloudy Tenent of Persecution for Cause of Conscience, The, I-176
WILLIAMS, ROWAN
On Christian Theology, III-1252
WILLS, GARRY
What Jesus Meant, IV-1934
WILSON, DEBBIE
Tiger in the Shadows, IV-1782
WITEK, TERRI
Fools and Crows, II-644
WOIWODE, LARRY
What I Think I Did, IV-1931
WOJTYŁA, KAROL JOZEF. *See* JOHN PAUL II
WOOLMAN, JOHN
Journal of John Woolman, The, II-936
WORDSWORTH, WILLIAM
"Ode: Intimations of Immortality," III-1241
WRIGHT, CHARLES
Black Zodiac, I-169

WRIGHT, FRANZ
God's Silence, II-712
WRIGHT, HAROLD BELL
Shepherd of the Hills, The, IV-1602
WRIGHT, N. T.
Simply Christian, IV-1624
WRIGHT, VINITA HAMPTON
Velma Still Cooks in Leeway, IV-1862
WYCLIF, JOHN
On the Truth of Holy Scripture, III-1284

YANCEY, PHILIP
Jesus I Never Knew, The, II-917
YEATS, WILLIAM BUTLER
"Dialogue of Self and Soul, A," I-458
YODER, JOHN H.
Politics of Jesus, The, III-1389

ZWINGLI, ULRICH
On Providence, III-1272